OFFICIAL HISTORY OF THE INDIAN ARMED FORCES IN THE SECOND WORLD WAR 1939-45

CAMPAIGNS IN SOUTH-EAST ASIA
1941-42

COMBINED INTER-SERVICES HISTORICAL SECTION
INDIA & PAKISTAN
1960

The Naval & Military Press Ltd

Published by

The Naval & Military Press Ltd
Unit 5 Riverside, Brambleside
Bellbrook Industrial Estate
Uckfield, East Sussex
TN22 1QQ England

Tel: +44 (0)1825 749494

www.naval-military-press.com
www.nmarchive.com

In reprinting in facsimile from the original, any imperfections are inevitably reproduced and the quality may fall short of modern type and cartographic standards.

CAMPAIGNS IN SOUTH-EAST ASIA
1941-42

K. D. Bhargava, M.A.
K. N. V. Sastri, Ph.D.

TO ALL WHO SERVED

ADVISORY COMMITTEE

Chairman

SECRETARY, MINISTRY OF DEFENCE, INDIA

Members

DR. TARA CHAND

DR. S. N. SEN

PROF. K. A. NILAKANTA SASTRI

PROF. MOHAMMAD HABIB

DR. R. C. MAJUMDAR

GENERAL K. S. THIMAYYA

LIEUT.-GENERAL SIR DUDLEY RUSSELL

LIEUT.-GENERAL S. P. P. THORAT

MILITARY ADVISER TO THE HIGH COMMISSIONER FOR PAKISTAN IN INDIA

Secretary

DR. BISHESHWAR PRASAD

CAMPAIGNS IN THE EASTERN THEATRE

Campaigns in South-East Asia 1941-42

Retreat from Burma 1941-42

Arakan Operations 1942-45

Reconquest of Burma 1942-45, Two Volumes

Post-War Occupation Forces: Japan and South-East Asia

PREFACE

The tales of glory and military conquests have often been the theme of national histories, for they rouse the imagination of people and inspire the future generations to emulate the heroism of their ancestors. But when it comes to defeat and disaster, the historian's task becomes arduous, for not only has he to narrate the events without gloss but also to explain the reasons for the tragic results. The opening of the Second World War in eastern and south-eastern Asia was one such chapter of reverses sustained by the Allied Powers at the hands of Japan. The British possessions in Hong Kong, Malaya and Borneo were overrun by the Japanese armed forces and for a time the whole of Asia up to the frontiers of India in the east formed part of the Japanese Co-Prosperity Sphere. It is the story of this military misfortune of the British Empire that is narrated in this volume. Beginning with the short struggle for the possession of Hong Kong, the narrative proceeds to outline the rapid step-back of the Indian, British and Australian forces from the northern tip of Malaya down its spine to the island of Singapore where the last stand was made for the control of the eastern gates of the Indian Ocean. The odds were against the Allied forces which were compelled to surrender, leaving the vast land mass of Asia from the Netherlands East Indies to Burma to the Japanese. It is a tale of hasty retreats, encirclements and surrenders, the forests and swamps making the prospect of escape grim and frequently impossible. Yet the troops retained courage and showed a high degree of morale, which is lost sight of owing to the abject mass surrender in Singapore. Whoever may have been responsible for that decision, it is certain that the Indian army had not lost its appetite for fight and had acquitted itself well in every situation where it was placed. The ill-equipped army without prospect of any strong reinforcements, with the Japanese in command of the sea and air, was unable to combat the eastern Power for long; and this circumstance prevailed with the local Command to surrender in Singapore. The last portion of the volume deals with the disaster in Borneo, which completed the story of the effacement of the British and Dutch Empires in that region for the moment. The Japanese thrust and the consequent expulsion of the British Commonwealth military power from South-East Asia is the subject of the narrative in this volume.

This is the ninth volume to be published in the series 'Official History of the Indian Armed Forces in the Second World War' by the Combined Inter-Services Historical Section, an organisation which was set up by the Government of India before the partition and which was subsequently continued as a joint venture of the two Dominions of India and Pakistan with the object of producing an official history of the part played by the pre-partition India and its armed forces in the World War of 1939-45. This history was to be a truthful, objective, analysed record of military operations and organisational activities and was to cover every important phase of the activities of the armed forces of India then. The history has been divided into three series, one of which relates to the campaigns in the eastern theatre, comprising Burma, Malaya and other parts of South-East Asia. The present volume is the last of this series to be published. It is based on official records, war diaries, despatches and reports of the commanders in the fields, which are confined to the level of the army commanders, as we had little access to the documents relating to higher strategy and diplomatic developments for which I have depended on published works. Yet it is not a mere chronicle of events, for every endeavour has been made to view the action in the field in the background of strategy and the general forces which were operating at the moment. The story is thus more a study of the dynamism of strategy than a static account of the doings of the individual units at a particular position. This mode of treatment has made it inevitable to comprehend all the forces, Australian, British and Indian, which fought side by side in a theatre, and not merely single out the operations of the Indian units. In Hong Kong, the British Indian and Canadian units jointly strove to keep the island free from the Japanese onslaught. In Malaya, the Indian forces cooperated with the British and Australian units to stem the tide of Japanese advance; while in Borneo the Indian units fought almost unsupported.

The volume or parts of it have been vetted by the commanders in the field, viz., Lieutenant-General A. E. Percival, Major-General D. M. Murray-Lyon, Major-General B. W. Key, Colonel A. M. L. Harrison, Major-General C. W. Maltby, Brigadier C. Wallis, Lieutenant-Colonel J. Wilson and Colonel Kamta Prasad, to whom I express my gratefulness for the pains they have undertaken. Their comments have been extremely valuable and have thrown light on many events for which the documentary material was meagre. I am indebted to Mr. Gavin Long, Chief Editor of the Australian War History, and Mr. Lionel Wigmore, of the Australian

High Commission in India, who is the author of *The Japanese Thrust*, the story of the Australian part in Malaya war, for reading the script and making some very useful suggestions which have been incorporated. I am also grateful to Brigadier H. B. Latham of the Cabinet Historical Section, U.K., and Colonel C. P. Stacey, Director, Historical Section, Army Headquarters, Ottawa, Canada, who read the narratives on Malaya and Hong Kong, respectively. I am also grateful to the members of the Advisory Committee for reading the draft and according their approval for its publication. The volume has also been seen by the Historical Section of Pakistan.

The original draft of the narrative on Hong Kong and Borneo was produced by Mr. K. D. Bhargava and that on Malaya by Dr. K. N. V. Sastri, both of whom were Narrators in the C.I.S. Historical Section. This draft has undergone considerable alterations at the hands of the editors and vetters, which is inevitable in a team work of this nature. To the two authors I must express my gratitude as also to Lieutenant-Colonel N. N. Madan, Dr. S. N. Prasad, and Mr. P. N. Khera who have assisted me in editing this volume and seeing it through the press, without whose co-operation my task would have been difficult. I am also thankful to Mr. T. D. Sharma for preparing the maps etc. for the volume. I also acknowledge the encouragement and support which I have received from the Ministries of Defence of India and Pakistan.

The Government of India have placed the documents at our disposal, but for the statements and views expressed herein I accept full responsibility.

BISHESHWAR PRASAD.

New Delhi,
January 1960.

CONTENTS

		Page
INTRODUCTION		xix

Chapter		Page
I.	Powers and Politics in East Asia	1
II.	War Strikes Hong Kong	8
III.	Operations on the Mainland	23
IV.	The End in Hong Kong	37
V.	Malaya, the Land and the People	73
VI.	Defence Plans for Malaya	93
VII.	The War in Northern Malaya	119
VIII.	The Struggle for Central Malaya	193
IX.	The Stand in South Malaya	252
X.	The Last Week in South Malaya	275
XI.	The Battle of Singapore	301
XII.	Japanese Attack on Sarawak	361
XIII.	Operations in Dutch North-West Borneo	383
APPENDICES		401
BIBLIOGRAPHY		414
INDEX		417

APPENDICES

		Page
A.	Garrison in Hong Kong	401
B.	Copy of Propaganda Leaflets dropped by the Japanese over Hong Kong	403
C.	Malaya Command–Order of Battle–8 December 1941	405
D.	The Japanese 25th Army–Brief Order of Battle–8 December 1941	406
E.	Order of Battle–8 Ind. Inf. Bde.–7 December 1941	407
F.	Order of the Day Issued on the 8th December 1941	408
G.	Malaya Command Operation Instruction No. 40	409
H.	Japanese Units and their Commanders in South-East Asia	411

MAPS

	Facing Page
South-East Asia	1
Hong Kong and New Territory showing Japanese advance	9
The Mainland—South of Tide Cove showing original inner line position of Mainland Brigade	29
Panoramic Section of Devil's Peak	35
Hong Kong Island showing dispositions of Allied Troops	39
Malaya, showing progress of Japanese Operations	73
Kelantan Troop Dispositions	*Page* 124
Kota Bharu Area	127
Kota Bharu Beach Defences	128
Jitra Area	141
Malaya, Kedah State	150
Gurun Area	171
Malaya, Kampar to Kuala Lumpur	204
Kampar—Telok Anson Area	212
Action at Trolak	*Facing Page* 215
Positions on the Slim River	219
Kuantan and Surrounding Area	*Page* 221
Malaya, Tampin to Rengam	248
Muar Area	259
Malaya, Batu Pahat to Singapore	272
Singapore Island—Dispositions of Troops, 8 February 1942	*Facing Page* 307
Singapore Island (South-West Sector)	*Page* 341
Singapore—Fighting in MacRitchie Reservoir Area, 12-15 February 1942	*Facing Page* 347
Borneo	361
Kuching Area (Sarawak) showing Dispositions of Sarfor on 22nd December, 1941 and line of withdrawal of 2/15 Punjab Regt. into Dutch Borneo	379
Dutch N. W. Borneo (Bengkajang—Sanggau Area)	385
Kuching (Sarawak) and Dutch West Borneo showing withdrawal route of 2/15 Punjab, 23 December 1941—29 March 1942	393

ILLUSTRATIONS

	Facing Page
Hong Kong and Kowloon	18
Major-General C. M. Maltby	19
Kaitak Aerodrome	19
General Sir Archibald P. Wavell	104
Admiral Sir Geoffrey Layton	104
Lieut.-General Sir Henry Pownall	105
Lieut.-General Sir Lewis Heath	105
Lieut.-General A. E. Percival and Major-General H. Gordon Bennett	186
Smoke rising from stocks of rubber burned	187
Australian soldiers manhandling an anti-tank gun	326
A forward Australian patrol	326
The Parit Sulong bridge towards which survivors of the 45th Indian Brigade and other Allied soldiers fought their way	327
Smoke from the Naval Base overshadows Singapore	352
After the withdrawal of the defending air forces from Malaya to Sumatra, the Singapore Island was subjected to increasingly heavy air attacks	353
The Causeway to Singapore Island blown after the withdrawal of Indian and other Allied forces from the Mainland	353

ABBREVIATIONS

ADB	..	American, Dutch, British.
APC	..	Anglo Persian Company.
A & SH	..	Argyll and Sutherland Highlanders.
ARP	..	Air Raid Precautions.
CID	..	Criminal Investigation Department.
FMSVF	..	Federated Malaya States Volunteer Force.
GR	..	Gurkha Rifles.
HKSRA	..	Hong Kong and Singapore Royal Artillery.
HKVDC	..	Hong Kong Volunteer Defence Corps.
MTB	..	Motor Torpedo Boat.
MRC	..	Mixed Reinforcement Camp.
NAAFI	..	Navy, Army and Air Force Institute.
NEI	..	Netherlands East Indies.
RAOC	..	Royal Army Ordnance Corps.
RASC	..	Royal Army Service Corps.
SCMS	..	Sarawak Coastal Marine Service.
SAP	..	Sarawak Armed Police.
SR	..	Sarawak Rangers.
SVF	..	Sarawak Volunteer Force.

INTRODUCTION

In September 1937, Mr. W. H. Chamberlain began his book *Japan over Asia* with the statement: "A spectre is haunting East Asia; the spectre of Japan. From icy Komsomolsk, eastern terminus of Russia's new strategic railway in Eastern Siberia, to humidly tropical Singapore, where Great Britain has built up a Far Eastern Gibraltar in the shape of a powerful naval and air base, on what was formerly a jungle swamp, Japan is the primary object of political, military and naval apprehensions and calculations".[1] An explanation of this fear psychosis is to be found in the policy and actions of Japan in the interval between the two World Wars. The development of Japan as a modern state had begun in the last quarter of the nineteenth century and she had profitably employed the lessons learnt in the universities and factories of Europe and America to build a powerful army and navy based on the solid foundations of modern industry. Her easy victories over China and Russia had established her claim to be counted as a Great Power. The Great War of 1914-18 provided an opportunity for not only laying claim to the German possessions in the Far East, but also to exploit the weakness and anarchy in China to impose the Twenty-one Demands for obtaining economic and political concessions in northern China, particularly in Manchuria and Mongolia; almost amounting to a "veiled protectorate over China".

American policy was reluctant to reconcile itself to such brazen-faced denunciation of the "Open Door" doctrine, which was the sheet anchor of the United States policy in China. The Lansing-Ishii Agreement of November 1917, and the Washington Conference of 1922, were the steps progressively adopted by the United States to save the integrity of the Chinese Republic. Japan had gained little beyond some Pacific islands of strategic value by the Peace Settlements of 1919-20, and had been compelled to withdraw even from eastern Siberia. The Washington Conference further aggravated her humiliation by laying down the 5:5:3 ratio between the capital ships of the United States, Britain and Japan, a disparity galling to national vanity. The Anglo-Japanese Alliance, continuing since 1902, was also renounced by Great Britain under American influence, thus heightening the diplomatic isolation of Japan. Events in the next few years helped

[1] *Japan over Asia*, p. 1.

little to heal her injured vanity. The passing of the United States Immigration Act of 1924, in violation of the "Gentlemen's Agreement" of 1907, limiting Japanese immigration to the United States, grossly offended Japanese self-respect. The Five-Power Naval Conference in London, in 1930, imposed a limitation on the number of auxiliary craft to be constructed by Japan. And all Japanese hopes of exploiting Chinese weakness were being frustrated by the continuous flow of Anglo-American aid to the Chinese Nationalists, who had fortified their position in 1927-28.

Economic factors further enhanced the sense of injury. Japan's industry, in the absence of a large colonial empire, depended on free entry in the world markets. But the economic depression of 1929-33 led the other Powers to turn increasingly protectionist. And though the Japanese did not hesitate to employ the "tariff protection of her own markets", they had, in the words of Sir Frederick Whyte, " pinned their faith in the peaceful expansion of trade abroad as the best means of relieving pressure at home ". And when " they found foreign tariffs raised to new heights against them, especially by those countries that refused to admit Japanese immigrants, Japan's predicament was seized by the military party to clinch their argument that no good could come from "internationalism", the League or the Washington Treaties, and that Japan must rely on her own power to secure her "place in the sun ".[2] The Ottawa Agreements for Imperial Preference had practically closed the markets of India and other portions of the British Empire to Japanese goods. The silk market of America was denied. The Chinese market was barred by intense nationalism culminating in a wide-spread boycott. These restrictions heightened the depression. But more important for Japan was the supply of essential raw materials in which she was deficient. Steel, rubber, oils, cotton and soya bean had to be imported, and in an age of competing imperialisms, with the spectre of war constantly haunting, and tariff walls daily mounting, it was inevitable for Japan to seek her own sources of raw materials. The occupation of Manchuria, the war with China and, to an extent, her drive against South-East Asia were prompted by this economic motive. Designs of conquest in Asia or the increasing hostility to the United States and Great Britain were the consequences of the sense of economic frustration and the desire for *lebensraum*. Circumstances were helping the rise of aggressive militarism which swamped liberalism and was fed by the Anglo-American policy of preventing Japanese supremacy in the western Pacific.

[2] Whyte: *The Rise and Fall of Japan.*

As an illustration of the then Japanese aggressive militarism and imperial expansionism in eastern Asia, reference may be made to the Tanaka Memorial, which appears to have been presented to the Emperor by Baron Tanaka, the Prime Minister, on 25 July 1927. The memorial is an index of the views and passions then prevailing among the dominant political sections in Japan and might be interpreted as a clear indication of the land hunger of the Japanese Government which planned to dominate the whole of Asia, step by step, beginning with the annexation of Manchuria. The document, however, deals primarily with Manchuria and points a way out of the unsettled economic conditions resulting from the Great War and the national humiliation consequent on the Washington Conference. The object of this memorial and the Officers Conference preceding it, was to " lay plans for the colonization of the Far East and development of our new continental empire ". Mainly there is reference to Manchuria where Japanese rights were affected by the signing of the Nine-Power Treaty, which " reduced our special rights and privileges " so that " the very existence of our country is endangered ".[3]

The Tanaka Memorial gives the appearance of Japanese designs of world empire, but it will be evident from a close study of this document, whose authenticity is not unquestioned, that the entire document deals only with the particular and limited design on the Three Eastern Provinces or Manchuria and Mongolia. It will be difficult to support the view that world domination or even the domination of the whole of Asia was a cardinal principle of Japanese policy in the twenties. But Manchuria was the immediate objective and in 1931, when the danger of its falling completely to the Chinese Nationalists became imminent, measures were taken to extend military and political control over that region. This step provoked the opposition of Great Britain and the United States who sought to invoke international sanctions. But Manchuria remained a part of the Japanese empire.

The occupation of Manchuria launched Japan into a further enterprise in China. The monopoly over Manchurian economic resources and a Japanese " Economic Monroe Doctrine " in contravention of the " Open Door ", were bound to affect prejudicially the Anglo-American interests and to lead to their opposition which was manifested in the form of aid to China. The Japanese policy " was almost a challenge to foreign Powers with interests in China to combine against her...... The meticulous crippling of non-Japanese enterprises would doubtless follow wherever the

[3] *Japan's Dream of World Empire*, pp. 20-23.

lengthening shadow of Japan should fall. A 'Stop Japan' movement on the part of foreign Powers was therefore a matter of enlightened self-interest if nothing else. It would complement China's own anti-Japanese front, and it might take practical form in financial and other material aids".[4] Both the United States and Britain, therefore, "moved to underpin the shaky finances of the Chinese Nationalist Government".[5] Large credits were opened by both the United States and Great Britain, and the collapse of Chinese currency was averted. This aid was disagreeable to Japan whose prospects of peaceful domination of China were thereby weakened. The fear of Anglo-American control over China with its consequent danger to Japanese hold over Manchuria, together with the internal difficulties and the uncertainty about the attitude of Soviet Russia led the militarist Government of Japan under Prince Konoye to expand the scope of their activity on the mainland of China. The penetration of north China was followed by the "China Incident" in 1937. Japan had taken this step after aligning herself with the Nazi Germany as a counterpoise against Soviet Russia, and had signed the Anti-Comintern Pact in 1936, which brought her into the camp of the totalitarian Central European Powers.

The Sino-Japanese War reacted on Anglo-American policy. The two Western Powers were opposed to China becoming a satellite state of Japan. "The maintenance of an independent sovereign China became the prime Far Eastern object of British and American policy".[6] Hence, the League of Nations denounced Japanese action as being contrary to the plea of self-defence but sanctions were not invoked owing to the fast developing crisis in Europe. However, effective aid in money and material to China was afforded by the two Powers. Great Britain used her hold on Hong Kong to transfuse supplies into China, and, later, when this route was blocked, the Burma Road was developed to rush military supplies into China to bolster up her resistance. American policy was not definite in the beginning, but soon after in December 1938, the Export-Import Bank opened a credit of 25 million dollars, and the American-Japanese Commercial Treaty of 1911 was denounced. To add to the difficulties of Japan, " a midget Soviet-Japanese War" had broken out in July 1938, but it was short-lived. It was also clear that Soviet Russia was not " disposed to allow Japan to persevere undisturbed in her prodigious attempt to

[4] *This Age of Conflict*, p. 435.
[5] *Ibid.* p. 436.
[6] Whyte, p. 15.

swallow the Chinese dragon".[7] All these expressions of the sympathy of the Western Powers for China lent themselves to the interpretation in Japan that these Powers were determined to maintain their hold over China and continue their imperial domination of Asia. Japan felt the sense of strangulation, and read in the effort to save the freedom of China an attempt to deny her the means of strengthening herself, and ultimately crushing her freedom. The spirit of self-preservation was thereby aroused and took the form of Co-Prosperity Sphere and the slogan of 'Asia for Asiatics'. Japan slowly began to adopt the role of the defender of the liberties of Asian peoples, and her aggressive moves were robed in the garb of championship of the cause of Asians against the western Imperial Powers.

When war began in Europe in 1939, Japan had been unable to crush Chinese resistance and was resenting the Western aid to her victim. She was eager to liquidate the 'Chinese Incident' early, and saw in the involvement of Great Britain and France in conflict with the Axis Powers an opportunity for realising her ambitions in the mainland of China. But the attitude of Soviet Russia was uncertain, and that of the United States definitely hostile. It was clear that without eliminating the fear of their active interference on behalf of China the prospect of her success was remote. Diplomacy and military preparedness were the means to that end. With Russia she ulitmately succeeded in signing a Non-Aggression Pact in April 1941, which secured her vulnerable right flank against attack. But vigilance was not to be relaxed and Japan maintained a strong force in the north in Manchuria to protect her boundaries. Later the German invasion of Russia insured the latter's adherence to the Non-Aggression Pact, and enabled Japan to contemplate aggressive moves in the south. However, the United States was not expected to forego her interest entirely in China and the Western Pacific; and with every obstacle in the rapid advance of the Japanese in China, their bitterness against the United States grew. The turn of the war also opened out a vast vision of conquest before Japan as the Axis victories in the west gave the appearance of knocking out the erstwhile imperialistic powers in the Far East, Britain, France and the Netherlands, and leaving open their vast colonial possessions for seizure by a powerful state. The Japanese schemes of a southern drive and the conquest of South-East Asia developed in these circumstances. Considerations of the defence of Japanese interests in China, the certainty of American hostility to her existence as the prime state in the Western Pacific, and the easy prospect of replacing European imperialism in southern Asia,

[7] *This Age of Conflict*, p. 445.

all these factors prompted her to plunge in war, and the occasion was propitious for her. The China Incident, in these circumstances, took on the aspect of a showdown between Japan and the Western Powers for control of the Far East.

The United States had started her career of overseas trade in the Far East, particularly in China, whose integrity she had come to regard as essential for her interests. Her insistence on the policy of "Open Door" was actuated by this motive. Hence she opposed every attempt, from whatever quarter, to dismember China or absorb her, and did not shirk from affording aid to any Chinese Government which might exhibit signs of preventing the rot. The United States had also patronised Japan in her early attempts at modernisation and was not sorry when the latter dismantled the fabric of Russian imperialism in the Far East. But with every progress in Japanese hegemony in eastern Asia, when the spectre of domination over China began to haunt, American jealousy and hostility grew against the rising Empire of the East. The Great War stiffened this attitude, and in 1922, the United States convened the Washington Conference to impose a limit to her rival's aggressiveness. The bar on Japanese immigration into California had estranged feelings in Japan. Observers, at the time, did not fail to notice the signs of impending and inevitable clash between the two.

With the passage of time this antagonism became more pronounced and the United States considered Japan as an obstacle to her supremacy of the Pacific. Japan's growing might was considered to be dangerous to the security of the American western coast. The Manchurian crisis and the threat to American economic interests in those regions heightened the tension. The United States retaliated by extending credit and doubling the sale of aeroplanes to the Chinese Government. The Far Eastern developments had also contributed to the belated recognition of the Soviet Union by the United States in November 1933, and " was regarded in Tokyo as a preliminary move by Washington to establish counterpoises to Japan in the Pacific ".[8] Later the Neutrality Act was not invoked as it might have affected shipping of war supplies to China. And when Japan propounded the " New Order ", the United States refused to recognise it, thus causing a diplomatic deadlock. Japan obtained a very large proportion of her scrap iron, steel, oil and metal-working machinery from the United States. On 26 July 1939, the United States Government gave notice of the abrogation of the old commercial treaty of 1911, so

---

[8] *This Age of Conflict*, p. 604.

as to impose an economic embargo on Japan which might bring her to her knees. In 1940 the United States passed the Compulsory Military Service Act, and appropriated funds for a large navy. Exports to Japan were placed on " a day to day basis ". All these developments were a clear indication of the opposition of the United States to Japanese position in eastern Asia and of her fear of Japanese supremacy in the Western Pacific.

British policy in relation to Japan, however, was not so markedly antagonistic, though in the inter-war years it was considerably influenced by American interests and wishes. The United Kingdom had been led to renounce the Anglo-Japanese Alliance which acted as an insurance against aggression on British interests in the Far East, because firstly its original objects had ceased to exist and secondly it had " become a source of offence to the United States ". But while abrogating it, the British statesmen ignored " the fact that its abolition would remove from Japan the obligation to respect Great Britain's Eastern colonies or to consult any interests but her own in whatever she chose to do in their furtherance in China or elsewhere ".[9] The Far Eastern developments, after that, were not convenient to the United Kingdom, and every move of Japan to acquire a further foothold on the Chinese mainland affected prejudicially British interests there. But owing to her peculiar situation, Britain was unable to adopt a determined attitude. Manchurian affair evoked only half-hearted measures and resort to sanctions was not made. Beyond giving financial aid to China and employing Hong Kong or Burma routes, until closed, to send her supplies, the United Kingdom did not adopt any positive measures to restrict Japanese action there. And even when humiliations were hurled at her nationals in Tientsin, the British Government did not make a strong diplomatic stand but tried a policy of appeasement. In July 1939 was signed the Craigie-Arita Agreement which recognised that " the Japanese forces in China have special requirements for the purpose of safeguarding their own security and maintaining public order in regions under their control. His Majesty's Government have no intention of countenancing any act prejudicial to the attainment of the aforesaid objects by the Japanese forces ".[10]

Great Britain had vital interests in the Far East, and the loss of Chinese freedom would have considerably prejudiced them. Hence British policy was opposed to any encroachments by Japan on the Chinese mainland. Moreover, British possessions of Hong Kong and Malaya, and to some extent Burma and India, were

[9] Longford, p. 243.
[10] *This Age of Conflict*. p. 443.

threatened by the preponderance of Japanese navy in the eastern waters, or Japanese army in China. Yet British strength, either on sea or land, was incapable of maintaining these far flung possessions in the east in face of Japanese hostility. The fast growing tension in Europe and the rapidly increasing power of the Axis countries made it impossible for the United Kingdom to station a strong fleet in the Far East or to effectively reinforce the garrisons there. All these factors necessitated a temporising policy which has been termed as one of appeasement. Yet there can be no doubt that, after 1932, the hostility of Japan was presupposed and the danger to British possessions of Malaya and Hong Kong from her aggressiveness was taken into consideration in all calculations and plans for defence.

Despite the 'New Order' for China and the unconcealed opposition of the United States to her expansion in that country, as also her alignment with the Axis Powers, Japan did not immediately plunge the Far East into war when Europe was involved in the armageddon. This may be explained by the fear of the United States and the purely selfish policy of the Japanese who do not appear to have subordinated their freedom of action to Germany. All that Japan desired at the moment was liberty to pursue the Chinese incident to the finish without intervention by England or America. But this assurance was not forthcoming. The war situation, however, was fast changing, opening out new vistas before Japanese militarists. About the middle of 1940, German arms had made rapid advance in Western Europe leading to the fall of Holland and France. The United Kingdom was also exposed to the full blight of German *blitzkrieg*. This development had its natural reaction in the Far East. The combination of Great Britain, France and Netherlands, a guarantee for the security of their possessions in Malaya, Hong Kong, Indo-China and the Netherlands East Indies, had practically disappeared. The integrity of the Dutch and French possessions was in jeopardy. The situation aroused the cupidity of Japan, for in the existing attitude of the United States, imposing practically an embargo on essential supplies to Japan, the oil and iron resources of the Netherlands East Indies would alone ensure her self-sufficiency and enable her to carry to completion her Chinese adventure. Similarly, Japan was intimately concerned with Indo-China, a sea-board for the southern China and a route for the flow of American supplies for the forces of Chiang Kai-shek. Japan feared that, unless immediate action was taken, Indo-China would pass under the control of the United Kingdom. Thus was added a new element in the Far Eastern situation, the fear of Japanese aggression against the

Netherlands East Indies and Indo-China. Her success in these lands would react on the security of Burma and Malaya and remotely affect the defences of Australia and India. The United States too did not remain unaffected by this new menace, for not only was there danger to China but also to the Philippines, leading to the upsetting of the balance in the Pacific.

To counteract this threat, Anglo-American policy was re-oriented and planning assumed the character of providing against the attack by Japan. On 2 July 1940, the Secretary of State for India informed the Viceroy that, " Developments in Japan indicate that in spite of restraining influence of present United States policy, advocates of intervention are rapidly gaining ground and represent serious threat to our own and French position in the Far East. We have therefore been obliged to consider change of policy and since any attack upon us is matter of common interest to United States of America, we have suggested to the United States Government that with a view to preventing such an attack U.S. Government should either increase pressure on Japan to the extent of full embargo or despatch ships to Singapore in full realisation that this may result in war with Japan, or with ourselves seek to wean Japan from aggression by a concrete offer on the following lines: (a) Great Britain and U.S. to assist Japan in reaching settlement with Chinese Government; (b) Japan formally to undertake to remain neutral in European war and to respect status quo of British, French, American and Dutch possessions in Pacific; (c) United States and members of British Commonwealth to give Japan financial and economic assistance; (d) Allied governments to receive full guarantees against re-exports to enemy countries; (e) question of future status of settlements and concessions in China to be left in abeyance until restoration of peace in Europe and China ".[11]

The United States was prepared " to restrain Japan by diplomatic pressure and economic threat and maintaining fleet in Pacific ", but could not take any action which might involve her in war. The American Government had no hopes of Japan agreeing to any peaceful settlement which might safeguard the interests of other powers, for her leaders were seeking this opportunity to advance political claims wherever they were not confronted with opposition. Hence, there was no prospect of weaning Japan " from aggression by policy of conciliation ". The policy suggested was that of " acquiescence in retreating under *force majeure* " and at the same time of " exploring possibility of

---

[11] Telegram No. 863, dated 2 July 1940.

settlement with Japan on terms acceptable to China and consistent with principles for which U.S. stand ".

Germs of future war were hidden in this attitude of the Powers. Japan was keen to exploit the war situation and gain territories held by France or Netherlands, ostensibly for reasons of self-preservation. The United States, though not engulfed in war for reasons of domestic policy, was keenly watching the developments and was ready to take measures to restrain Japanese expansionism. The United Kingdom was convinced of her weakness in the Far East but was not prepared to let Japan oust her from her possessions. And to this end diplomacy and preparedness were employed to ward off the evil day. Anglo-Dutch-United States cooperation was presupposed in any measures that might be adopted, and gradually the United States was drifting into the war. Japan was also not keen to take action immediately. Hence for more than a year diplomacy was active to prevent the Far East from being converted into a theatre of operations. However, there was an unreality in the negotiations, and the mailed fist, though concealed, was being strengthened to settle the issue by war.

Besides China, there was the problem of the security of the Netherlands East Indies and Indo-China. The British Government was vitally interested in the integrity of these areas, for their subjugation by the Japanese would affect the defence of Malaya, Burma and even the Indian Ocean and Australia, Hence, immediately after the fall of France, an appreciation was made of the defence position in the Far East and the possibility of Japanese action against the Dutch possessions. An assessment was made of the different factors which were likely to influence Japanese policy. Among these the most important were the China war, the state of Anglo-Dutch defences, the attitude of the United States, and the strain on Japan's economic resources. One of the hypotheses was that Japan could not take for granted the non-intervention of the United States who might send their fleet to the Philippines. Also it was felt that an important factor would be the " knowledge that further aggression may lead to a rupture of trade relations with the United States and Great Britain ". The United States had "warned Japan of her interest in the maintenance of the status quo in the Netherlands East Indies ". Japan's economic structure also was unlikely to bear the strain of a breach with the United States and Great Britain on whom she depended for some of her essential raw materials, unless she could exploit the resources of Netherlands East Indies, especially oil, rubber and tin. On a review of these factors, the conclusion of the British Chiefs of Staffs was that " until the issue of the war in Europe becomes clearer, it is probable that Japan will confine her action to the elimination of British influence from China and Hong Kong to the greatest possible extent without incurring a rupture with the United States and the British Empire ".[12]

In 1940, no fear was entertained of any immediate action by Japan, though it was believed that the war situation offered an opportunity to extend her interests. A sudden attack on the Netherlands East Indies or Singapore was feared, but there was greater probability that the first Japanese move would be into Indo-China or Thailand, followed later by an attack on the Dutch possessions. Yet, it was hoped that Japan would not "risk an open breach with the British Empire and the United States until the situation in Europe is clearer". The British Empire was also in no position to entertain the idea of going to war with Japan. Examining the possible courses of Japanese action, the Chiefs of Staff pointed out the risks to Thailand, Indo-China, and the Netherlands East Indies, and then considered the stage when it might be necessary to declare war on Japan owing to the vital interests being affected which primarily were the maintenance of sea communications. The Japanese penetration into Thailand or Indo-China was believed to threaten Singapore and make the defence of Burma and Malaya extremely difficult. But, it was held that "under present world conditions", Japanese action in either of these regions would not justify Britain " going to war with Japan " with the existing available resources, as sea communications would not be threatened. Japanese attack on the Dutch possessions was in a different category as it was likely to compromise gravely the security of vital sea communications and the base at Singapore. But even in this contingency, though the security of the Netherlands East Indies was regarded as essential to British interests, resort to war was not thought of as that purpose might be served by rendering full military and economic aid to the Dutch. The British authorities, therefore, did not want war in the Far East at this stage, though as an insurance against Japanese aggression, they were keen for collaboration with the Dutch and the United States without whose active support the security of the Far East was in danger. At the same time there was confidence that Japan, "unless driven to extreme measures by her extremity or tempted by our weakness, would also try to avoid war with the British Empire and the United States and endeavour to achieve her aims by stages which she might hope would not involve her

---

[12] Appreciation in the Far East; C. O. S. (40) 592. 15 August 1940. Also Tel No. 2461-S, Secretary of State to Viceroy, 14 August 1940.

openly in war ". British policy at this date was, therefore, to avoid open clash with Japan, and aimed at " a wide settlement in the Far East, including economic concessions to Japan ". But failing a settlement on satisfactory terms the momentary object was " to play for time, cede nothing until we must and build up our defences as soon as we can ".

The year 1940 also found the British military authorities drawing up appreciations and plans of defence which were based on the presumption of intervention by the United States and the Dutch, though no definite understandings had been arrived at with these Powers. Being unable to station the fleet in the Far East, the British Government did not want war in the east unless the United States got involved in it. Similarly Japan too does not appear to have been drawn towards war, though the temptation was there. An important factor in her attitude was the United States whose hostility could not be easily overlooked, particularly as it would vitally affect Japanese economy. Yet Japan was keen to conclude the Chinese war even by means of a reasonable peace; and was determined to eliminate all obstacles to it. It was clear to her war leaders that as long as China was able to get economic aid and supplies of military equipment from the United States and Great Britain, an early end of the Chinese incident was not in sight. Hence she desired to close the avenue of Indo-China and the Burma Road. The United Kingdom had closed the latter for three months, but under American pressure had reopened it for a constant flow of supplies. To Japan the closing of these routes was vital; hence she was keen to take necessary measures for preventing Indo-China being made any longer the base for assistance to China. She was also afraid that the French possessions might be occupied by Great Britain. Japan was therefore anxious to close that passage even by controlling or occupying Indo-China, if need be. This step was bound to cause misgivings in British circles and a sense of hostility in the United States. Important developments occurred in 1941 in this direction which culminated in war.

Even in 1940, under German pressure, Japan had been able to impose an agreement on Vichy France providing for the movement of Japanese troops through Indo-China and the use of air ports, and on 22 September, Japanese troops had landed at Saigon to begin the occupation of Hanoi and six other ports. This led further to economic and mutual defence agreements between Japan and Vichy France, in May and July 1941, respectively. The latter was aimed at giving to Japan eight air and two naval bases in Indo-China and freedom of movement and manoeuvres for 40,000 Japanese troops who would begin disembarking on

30 July 1941. This agreement superseded the earlier one of 22 September 1940, and was accepted by Marshal Petain. There was a guarantee for the integrity of Indo-China. The Japanese Government had tried to show that this action of mutual defence agreement, involving control over air and naval bases and stationing of troops in south Indo-China, was necessary " for ensuring an uninterrupted source of supply of rice and other foodstuffs as well as raw materials, the flow of which might be obstructed by Chinese forces and De Gaullist activities in southern Indo-China ".[13] Another justification advanced was that the step was taken " as a safeguard against the encirclement of Japan by the A.B.C.D. powers (American, British, Chinese and Dutch Governments) ".[14] The unseemly haste in occupying bases in Indo-China was ascribed by the British Ambassador in Tokyo to the feeling that " time is working against them and that if they intend to seize bases there they should act quickly to forestall possible counter-action on our part. They would then be able to develop these bases so that when they have achieved their object in North they will be ready for any further southward advance which may then seem expedient ".[15] It is not possible to know to what extent any preparations had been made by the British to occupy Indo-China, but these seem to be unlikely. All that was contemplated was to make an offer of support to M. Decuox, the Governor General there, and anti-Vichy elements to fortify their resistance to Japanese aggression. The Western Allies were interested in the fate of Indo-China and, given time, would be prepared to adopt measures to counteract Japanese aggression there.

It has been mentioned above that Japan took two steps in 1940, viz., the signing of the Tripartite Pact with Germany and Italy and the pressure on Indo-China leading to its military occupation, which pointed to a significant step in her anti-Anglo-American policy and had serious reactions on the other side. It may be pertinent here to examine first the motives of Japan in launching on that course and then to analyse the corresponding attitude and policy of the Western Powers. We get a glimpse of Japanese policy from the British report of their Ambassador's talk with the Japanese Minister for Foreign Affairs on 8 October 1940. Matsuoko discussed the Tripartite Pact and gave the following as reasons for Japan's participation in it:—

(i) the increasingly unfriendly attitude of the United States

---
[13] *This Age of Conflict*, p. 595.
[14] *Ibid.*
[15] Tel No. 245 Craigie to Foreign Office, 23 July 1941.

    which necessitated defensive measures on the part of Japan,

  (ii) intention to localise the war and bring to an end the tragic struggle then going on in Europe and China.

The Minister repudiated any suggestion of " aggressive intention " and emphasised that though some sections in Japan " favoured more aggressive policy " the Prime Minister was opposed to such a course. He also explained that the Pact had not deprived Japan of her freedom to decide about peace or war for herself, and in this connection made a very important declaration of policy " that Japan would not enter the war if for instance the United States were to take action as a result of provocation from the Axis ".[16] The same sentiments were reiterated in a subsequent interview between the two. The Foreign Minister said, " It would be a great mistake to regard the Three Power Pact as implying either that Japan wanted trouble with Britain or that she wished to see Britain lose the war. His impelling motive in concluding this pact had been his conviction that the United States' entry into the war would inevitably involve other States including Japan. Thus in due course the war would become world-wide and this in turn would mean Armageddon ". He emphasised " his fervent desire to avoid war with Great Britain or the United States ", and did not hesitate to remark that " Nothing would provoke the Japanese Government except America's entry into the European war or some serious provocation such as the visit of a powerful American squadron to Singapore ".[17]

  Yet by the end of 1940, Japan's drift into the Axis camp had become definite, and schemes of a " New Order in Greater East Asia " were vaguely entertained. The direction of her aggressive advance had also been indicated and Indo-China was the first objective southwards. Whether the move was a safeguard against the apprehended Anglo-American aggression and as a means of strengthening the defences of Japan and her occupied territories in China or a preliminary step to the conquest of the whole of South Asia in the event of war developments being propitious, it is difficult to be dogmatic about. But one point is clear that Japan was committed to her Axis allies to keep the United States outside the war in Europe. She was also afraid of her American rival, and desired to possess positions of vantage in case the United States entered the war, which would be the signal for the Pacific War also to begin.

---

[16] Secretary of State to Viceroy, 1 December 1940.
[17] *Ibid.*

Until Indo-China had been lost to Japan, the A.B.C.D. powers had not applied any sanctions and were content merely to resent Japan's policy. Her admission into the Tripartite Pact caused misgivings and hostile comments in the Anglo-American countries. Japan may have been " alarmed at firm front shown " by them. But this led the British Government to conclude " that she is not prepared at the moment to face war against both of us. While therefore she has in no way abandoned her aims, she has decided to moderate tempo of her advance in the hope, if not the conviction, that circumstances of war in Europe will presently turn to her advantage and afford her a more favourable opportunity of gaining her ends, at comparatively small cost ". This estimate led to the view that " a firmer front " should be built with the United States. The natural conclusion was that " until both we and the United States can convince Japan that we have the will and power to resist her by force if need be, our position in Far East and in Pacific is likely to remain insecure ".[18] The British Government was keen to keep out of the war in the Far East unless the United States was actively involved in it, and was also aware of the temper of the Government across the Atlantic. The United States Government was conscious of the danger to American interests in the victory of the Axis Powers, and appeared to be keen to prevent it. But owing to domestic reasons, the United States was in no position to enter the war immediately. But she was also averse to the expansion of Japan's political or economic influence in Asia. Hence, an anti-Japanese wave was prevailing there, and hopes were entertained that the United States would enter the war in the east to protect Anglo-Dutch interests. On this hope British policy thrived. But the occasion for this development was lacking. It was, however, provided by the final occupation of Indo-China by Japan with the corresponding imposition of economic sanctions by the Western Allies, a step which hastened war.

The danger of Japanese southward movement was realised quite early, and measures were taken by the British Government to arrange for collective action with the Netherlands and the United States. The Singapore Defence Conference convened in October 1940 had stressed the importance of mutual support in the defence of South-East Asia and had emphasised the necessity of securing definite agreements with the United States for joint naval and military action in that area. In Washington, Staff conversations were held between 29 January and the end of March 1941,

[18] Secretary of State to Viceroy, 1 December 1940.

and certain general principles of collaboration were outlined. These emphasised the prime importance of concentrating effort on the defeat of Germany in the Atlantic and European theatres; hence in case Japan entered the war, the only strategy possible was to be on the defensive. To achieve this object, it was agreed that though the United States would not increase her military strength in the Far East area, her " Pacific Fleet will operate from Hawaii against Japanese Pacific communications in defence of United States and British Commonwealth trade and with the object of diverting Japanese strength away from Malaya area ". A joint plan agreed between the Staffs of the two nations was now there, and though at governmental level no pact or agreement of mutual defence or joint action was contemplated, yet at the Chiefs of Staff level the mode of joint action had been evolved.[19] This was followed by the American-Dutch-British conversations which were held in April 1941 to " prepare plan for conduct of military operations in Far East on basis of report of Washington conversations ".[20]

It may not be necessary here to discuss in detail the plan evolved at Singapore, but it will be pertinent to refer to the agreement relating to the Japanese actions which would call for measures of collective military counteraction, as otherwise the Associated Powers would be at great " military disadvantage, should Japan subsequently attack ". These were:

"(a) A direct act of war by Japanese armed forces against the Territory or Mandated Territory of any of the Associated Powers.

(b) The movement of the Japanese forces into any part of Thailand to the West of 100° East or to the South of 10° North.

(c) The movement of a large number of Japanese warships or of a convoy of merchant ships escorted by Japanese warships, which from its position and course was clearly directed upon the Philippine Islands, the East Coast of the Isthmus of Kra or the East coast of Malaya, or had crossed the parallel of 6° North between Malaya and the Philippines, a line from the Gulf of Daras to Waigeo Island or the Equator East of Waigeo ".

In these talks also emphasis was laid on a defensive strategy, but offensive air operations were discussed.

Indo-China was outside the zone of special interests for defence, hence any Japanese action against the integrity of that

[19] Secretary of State to Viceroy-8 June 1941.
[20] A. D. B. Conversations, Report, para 2.

French colony did not automatically involve the application of the plans of defence discussed at Singapore. Yet Japanese action against that strategic country which, on the one side, commanded communications into China and, on the other, was a base for operations against Malaya, were not altogether ignored, and called for retaliatory measures. These were to be economic as Japan was believed to be essentially susceptible to an economic embargo. Hence, when the danger to Indo-China was imminent, the Anglo-American Governments decided on a joint course of " drastic economic action against Japan ". which " may force Japanese to choose between reversing their pro-Axis policy, or proceeding with their southward move to point of war with Netherlands East Indies and ourselves in an endeavour to obtain control of sources of raw material ".[21]

Economic sanctions being decided upon by the United States Government, His Majesty's Government in the United Kingdom readily fell into line with that repressive action. Their policy, at the moment, was enunciated as follows by the Secretary of State for India:—

"(i) that we must on no account discourage any action which U.S.A. may wish to take in pressure on Japan and that we must as far as possible match our action with theirs.

(ii) that although we see no objection to our own point of view that best moment to force the issue might be when (and if) Japan became involved with Russia we must in paramount interests of Anglo-United States cooperation be prepared to follow a United States lead in forcing issue over Indo-China bases and

(iii) that if we are called upon to go to lengths which involve a risk of war between ourselves and Japan we should make every effort to obtain clearest possible indication from United States that if war between British Empire and Japan follows consequent upon an attack by Japan either on ourselves or on Dutch we can count without reservation on active armed support of U.S.A."[22]

The United States Government had decided to freeze Japanese assets and similar action was demanded of other Governments. India was also called upon to issue freezing orders simultaneously.

A drastic application of economic sanctions had a serious effect on Japanese economy and, in the words of Churchill,

---

[21] Secretary of State to Governor General E. A. dated No. 8588, 23 July 1941, para 1.
[22] *Ibid*, para 2.

"brought to a head the internal crisis in Japanese politics...... It was evident that this was a stranglehold, and that the choice before them was either for Japan to reach an agreement with the United States or go to war. The American requirements involved Japanese withdrawal not only from these new aggressions in Indo-China, but from China itself, where they had already been fighting at heavy expenses for so long".[23]

The economic embargo and freezing of the assets intensified the tension. "The cessation of shipments of aviation gasoline and lubricating oil from the United States to Japan, the licensing of Japanese trade with the United States, the appointment of Owen Lattimore as special political adviser to Chiang Kai-shek, the extension of the 50,000,000 dollar stabilization credit to China for another year, delays imposed upon Japanese vessels seeking to traverse the Panama Canal, the "general freezing policy" whereby the Japanese assets were frozen not only in the United States but throughout the British Empire and the Dutch East Indies, the closing of British coaling stations to Japanese ships, and the appointment of General Douglas MacArthur as Commander-in-Chief of all the United States forces in the Far East—all during the summer of 1941—combined to indicate the growing tensions which boded ill for the Pacific area".[24] Japan was now face to face with "the greatest emergency in history" and the alternative before her was to defy the Anglo-American opposition or to surrender all schemes of realising her "divine mission". The choice was hard and the Japanese Government, in spite of the growing bellicosity of the people, decided upon the method of negotiations with the United States. "The conservative politicians and the Imperial Court hoped to obtain terms which would enable them to control their war party at home".[25] To this end, conversations were held in Washington which continued till the very eve of Pearl Harbour. Prince Konoye, the Japanese Prime Minister, had proposed a personal meeting with President Roosevelt to settle the issues, but his proposal did not find favour with the President. This refusal cost him his position and the Government was formed by General Tojo, who had the confidence of the army. He renewed diplomatic efforts to solve the tangle and the Emperor persisted in the hope of peaceful solution. But he was willing to let preparations for war proceed, if negotiations did not bear fruit.

It is clear from Mr. Churchill's account that, in November 1941, a stage had been reached when peaceful settlement appeared

[23] Churchill, Vol. III, pp. 521-2.
[24] Godshal, *Origins and Consequence of World War II*, p. 520.
[25] Churchill, Vol. III, p. 522.

to be in sight. On 20 November, Japan had forwarded her final proposals to Washington. These related to the evacuation of Southern Indo-China by her, pending a general settlement with China, when she would withdraw completely from the whole of Indo-China. " In return, the United States was to supply Japan with petroleum, to refrain from interfering with Japan's efforts to restore peace in China, to help Japan to obtain the products of the Netherlands East Indies, and to place commercial relations between Japan and the United States on a normal basis. Both sides were to agree to make no " armed advancement " in North-East Asia and the Southern Pacific ".[26] The American Government appears to have been agreeable to these terms with certain specific conditions being attached to the withdrawal from South Indo-China, and by modifying the extent of the removal of the economic embargo. These were to be for a period of three months within which a general settlement covering the whole of the Pacific area was to be discussed. Mr. Churchill has opened a window on the course of diplomacy which prevented this " modus vivendi " from being operative. China was naturally alarmed and it appears that Great Britain was also not happy with this development, for if the United States would not break with Japan, all prospects of her being a party to the war, on which alone depended the chances of British victory over the Nazi forces, would be over. The fate of Chiang Kai-shek was the deciding factor; and the British Prime Minister's appeal to the President " that the regard of the United States for the Chinese cause will govern your action " had the effect of diverting the trend of negotiations in Washington. The United States Government presented the " Ten-Point Note " to the Japanese envoys, and this included a demand for the withdrawal of all Japanese forces from China and Indo-China and the recognition of National Government alone in China.[27] This was the end of all prospects of peace. The die was cast and the United States and Japan both had now to tread the path of war.

It will be futile to throw the blame on one party or the other; as the conditions for peace perhaps militated against the national honour and interest of either of them. In Japan a large section was keen to exploit the war situation to fulfil the expansionist aims in eastern Asia, and this they wanted to achieve before Germany had completed her conquest of Europe and the West. The ' East Asia Co-prosperity Sphere ' was a reality for these people and they were not prepared to brook any hostile opposition to their objects. Particularly at a time when South-East Asia seemed to be within

[26] Churchill, Vol. III, p. 530.
[27] Churchill, Vol. III, pp. 530-1.

their grasp, they were furious when they found the United States thwarting their ambitions. In the absence of any honourable settlement which would have eased the economic situation without seriously humbling their pride, the Japanese Government decided to take up arms.

It is difficult to probe into the motives of the United States. Perhaps it was the climax of the fear of Japanese predominance in the Far East, which had influenced American policy since 1905, and which now sought an occasion to make the Pacific pre-eminently a zone of United States interests. There is no doubt that the United States had been impelled by the considerations of the integrity of Nationalist China with whose existence as an independent state were closely associated the Far Eastern interests of the American Republic. It may also be surmised that the United States Government was influenced by the war situation in Europe and the Atlantic, and found in the Japanese attitude a means of influencing American public opinion for their entry into the war on the side of Great Britain. The British Government had been building their hopes of defending the eastern empire on the close collaboration and active support of the United States. All plans for the defence of Malaya, Netherlands East Indies or Australia were based on the participation of the United States Fleet in the Pacific to counteract Japanese naval superiority. It was, therefore, in the interest of the British Empire that tension, leading ultimately to the United States entry into the war, should continue.

While negotiations were proceeding in Washington, and when hopes of peaceful settlement had receded, Japan had been preparing for a sudden stroke to herald her coming into the war. On 23 November 1941, the United States Government had begun to suspect the warlike preparations of Japan and the President had warned the High Commissioner of the Philippines of the impending danger to the Burma Road, Thailand, Malaya, Netherlands East Indies or the Philippines. He also expressed the belief " that this next Japanese aggression might cause an outbreak of hostilities between the U.S. and Japan ".[28] A week later the British Ambassador at Washington was also informed that diplomacy had yielded place to the war machine and the matter was in the hands of the officials of the Army and Navy. The probability of a sudden Japanese move was expressed. In Japan also the imminence of war was discussed and their carrier fleet with a considerable naval air force had sailed to attack Pearl Harbour on 25 November. On 1 December, the Imperial Conference at Tokyo decided on

[28] Quoted by Churchill, Vol. III, p. 532.

war with the United States. At the same time fleets had sailed for the Gulf of Siam, and forces had moved in other directions on particular assignments. The British Government feared that possibly the attack might be aimed against the Kra Isthmus or the Netherlands East Indies in which case the United States might not be involved in war, owing to the Congressional opposition. Hence for the United States to be in the war it was necessary that Japan should appear to be aggressive and actually strike a blow against American territory. These expectations were fulfilled by Japan attacking the Pearl Harbour on 7 December and strafing the American fleet there. This stroke provided the opportunity for the United States Government to set the war machine in motion and thereby throw in the American resources in the scale against the Central European Powers. To Japan, the crippling of the Pacific Fleet was essential to prevent immediate American intervention in her aggressive designs in South-East Asia. The Pearl Harbour made the conquest of Hong Kong, Malaya, Borneo, Netherlands East Indies and Burma possible for Japan, as the United States had no Fleet left in the Pacific to intercept Japanese moves in the southern seas, or to render active support to the British and Dutch forces in the South West Pacific regions. Thus the war came in the east and Japan was in a position to win the first round, at a moment when the British forces were weak in the east and the United States had not been able to mobilize her full strength to strike simultaneously both in the west and the east.

The immediate effect of war was felt in Hong Kong, Malaya and Borneo. The story of the Anglo-Japanese conflict in these regions, in which the Indian armed forces along with those of the Commonwealth countries, Great Britain, Canada and Australia participated, is described in the pages below. It is a tale of defeats and disasters, which were the inevitable consequence of imperfect planning and inadequate preparations.

Bisheshwar Prasad

Hong Kong

CHAPTER I

Powers and Politics in East Asia

THE INTERNATIONAL SCENE

The security of the British possessions in East Asia was gradually affected by the rise of modern Japan. When Commodore Perry of the United States Navy first visited the Japanese islands in 1853, he found a feudal society and an agricultural economy, a people no different from any of the other 'backward', peaceful, communities in Asia. So the next year he returned with a bigger force and compelled the Japanese to accord 'trade facilities'. Within ten years, other Western Powers came in; an unfortunate incident took place and the British Navy bombarded the port of Kagoshima. It seemed inevitable that events would run true to the usual nineteenth century pattern of an industrially advanced European Power coming into contact with a backward community. But the Japanese quickly realised the peril of their situation and decided to become modernised. Within a few decades, feudalism gave way to a modern monarchy, efficient armed forces were set up, the country was industrialised and a militant nationalism emerged. In 1894 Japan proved her equality to the West by fighting and defeating the Chinese, and in 1902 she took her place in the comity of nations by means of an alliance of friendship with Great Britain. There followed the brilliant Japanese victory over Imperial Russia in 1905, and the Japanese participation in the First Great War, as an ally of the British Empire. As agreed beforehand, the Japanese occupied during the war all the German islands in the Mariana, Caroline and Marshall groups, and this occupation was confirmed by a 'Mandate' from the League of Nations after the war.

These acquisitions, however, merely served to whet her appetite. At the time the fundamental problem for Japan was to feed and give employment to about eighty million of her people crowded in a few small islands, not particularly rich in minerals and other raw materials. The approved solution of such a problem was before her eyes in the British, Dutch, Belgian and even Portuguese empires in Asia and Africa. It is no wonder, then, that imperialism, political or economic, became Japan's goal. Conflict between Japan and the Western Powers thereafter became inevitable.

Even in 1915, Japan's 'Twenty-one Demands' on China evoked opposition in the United States which successfully upheld her 'Open Door' policy. The Washington Naval Treaty of 1922 limited the naval armament race, but the British abrogation of the long standing Anglo-Japanese Alliance revealed the new diplomatic grouping in the Pacific region. Still, for nearly a decade after that, the climate of peace continued. In April 1930, Japan agreed to the London Naval Treaty. But the situation deteriorated soon after by the Japanese occupation of Manchuria in 1931 and her withdrawal from the League of Nations in 1933. In December 1934, Japan denounced the Washington Treaty, and two years later signed the Anti-Comintern Pact with Nazi Germany. The notorious 'China Incident' began on 7 July 1937, and the Rome-Berlin-Tokyo Axis appeared soon after.

Henceforth, Japan's over-all strategy became apparent. She was determined to expand her territories in the south, and she claimed a sort of 'Monroe Doctrine' for South-East Asia by insisting on establishing a 'Co-prosperity' zone there. This claim was emphasised in Prince Konoye's public statements of 3 November and 22 December 1938.

Japan was not content merely with the theoretical declaration of a 'Co-prosperity' zone, but took practical steps to realise her ambitions. In spite of the protests of Great Britain, the United States and France, Japanese forces occupied the island of Hainan in June 1939, justifying the step on military grounds. Soon after, the Japanese Government announced the occupation of Spratley Island, situated halfway between Borneo and French Indo-China, over which France claimed jurisdiction. Further evidence of Japan's aggressive designs came in the form of the virtual blockade of Hong Kong's leased territory from the landward side.

The collapse of Holland and France during the first half of 1940 opened up fresh avenues of conquest for the militarists in Japan. Having effectively stopped supplies to China through French Indo-China, Japan turned her attention to the Burma Road, and demanded that it should be closed to China. The United Kingdom, at this juncture, was not in a position to refuse the demand. Her position was desperate. The British Expeditionary Force in France had lost almost all its equipment, casualties in its ranks had been heavy, and the Battle of Britain was about to start. Under the circumstances the British Government agreed to close the Burma Road for three months with effect from 18 July 1940, to specified categories of war material. This step was adversely commented upon, specially in the United States, where it was considered as smacking of appeasement similar to that in Europe with regard to Germany and Italy.

After the closing of the Burma Road, two events occurred which hardened feelings in the United Kingdom and the United States against Japan. The first was Japan's adherence to the Axis, and the second the pressure put on Indo-China for stationing Japanese troops in Tong-king. The latter was a step in the direction of assuming ultimate control of Indo-China. As a reaction against these two events, and because British position had greatly improved since July, Mr. Winston Churchill announced the reopening of the Burma Road on 17 October 1940.

In July 1941, the British Government denounced the Anglo-Japanese treaties and froze Japanese assets. This belated action, far from deterring Japan, helped to strengthen her militarists. In order to prove really effective, these economic sanctions ought to have been matched by the necessary naval and military dispositions, but this was never done. Siam (Thailand) was the next victim of Japanese aggression. In October 1941, the Japanese occupied Indo-China, and threw down the gauntlet to Great Britain.

A new Japanese cabinet was formed on 16 October 1941, headed by General Tojo. This was followed by bellicose speeches to the effect that Japan was determined to settle the 'China Incident' and to establish a 'Greater East-Asia Co-prosperity sphere'. In a speech on national policy on 17 November 1941, Tojo hoped that Third Powers would refrain from obstructing the successful conclusion of the China War, and concluded that Japan was " at the cross-roads of her 2,600 years of history ". The effect of these speeches was to further the bonds of amity and goodwill between the United Kingdom and the United States and to strengthen their united determination to put a stop to Japanese aggression. In his Mansion House speech on 10 November, Mr. Churchill said :

" They (the United States) are doing their utmost to find ways of preserving peace in the Pacific. We do not know whether their efforts will be successful, but, should they fail, I take this occasion to say, and it is my duty to say, that should the United States become involved in war with Japan, British declaration will follow within the hour ".

The real source of friction in East Asia may be found in " economic nationalism and imperialism " which characterised the years after 1930, when " the world tended to split up into economic blocs, and international trade was being diverted into certain well defined areas for the attainment of political objectives;

Japan was intent on establishing a yen bloc, embracing China, Manchukuo and herself. Nazi Germany was attempting the economic consolidation of Central and South-Eastern Europe.... Great Britain inaugurated an era of bloc economy at Ottawa with a system of Empire preference. Even the Netherlands Indies turned protectionist in 1933. Economic liberalism abdicated in favour of economic nationalism and the tendency was for each nation to isolate itself from world markets".[1] British commerical policy was designed to restrict Japanese competition, and the Ottawa Agreements of 1932 marked the beginning of " an economico-political offensive against Japanese goods ".[2] The Indo-Japanese Trade Treaty was abrogated in 1933 at the behest of Lancashire interests. In 1934 the British Government had imposed restrictions on Japanese imports into British colonies. These economic measures were bound to affect the national prosperity of Japan. On the other hand, Japanese measures in China could not fail to injure British interests there, particularly in the Yangtze Valley. Yanaga has remarked that " the Amau Statement of April 17, 1934, and other pronouncements did not serve to relieve Anglo-Japanese tension. Trade controversies in India, Australia, and elsewhere further aggravated the rapidly deteriorating relationship between the two countries that once had been close allies ".[3] Developments in 1935 and 1936 made the relations worse still, and in December 1935 the United Kingdom became the target of Japanese press tirade. The 'China Incident' increased the tension and "in the summer of 1939 a serious clash had occurred in Tientsin between the British and the Japanese ", leading to a Japanese blockade of British and French concessions. 1940 saw *Asama Maru* and *Tatsuta Maru* incidents which were a clear indication of deteriorating Anglo-Japanese relations.

Relations between Japan and the United States were equally strained. The Manchurian crisis had brought the United States out of her self-imposed isolation when she agreed to participate in the League of Nations' enquiry which declared Japan an aggressor. Japanese action in China was directly prejudicial to the whole course of American policy there and, if successful, would have effectively blocked her economic interests in the West Pacific. The growing military might of the island empire, her control over the mandatory German islands in the Pacific Ocean and their rapid transformation into naval bases, her repudiation of the naval strength formula of 1922 and her overt designs of the conquest of

---

[1] Yanaga, *Japan Since Perry*, p. 579
[2] *Ibid* p. 579.
[3] *Ibid* p. 580.

China, all helped to alienate American opinion. The Amau Statement of 1934 was "a reflection of Japan's restiveness at the cumulative effects of foreign activities in China ".[4] The United States adopted the Neutrality Act in 1935, prohibiting the carrying of arms to belligerent States, which was aimed against Japan's capacity to fight China. The Sino-Japanese War brought America more openly in the field as the main prop of the Kuomintang. Every turn in the progress of this war made the relations between Japan and the United States more difficult of accommodation.

It will be evident from the above review of the diplomatic developments in the Far East, that while the waters of the Pacific had remained outwardly calm, clouds were gathering on the horizon and storms were brewing. The United States could not afford to ignore the developments in China or let Japan fortify her position so as to challenge American interests in the West Pacific. The United Kingdom, too, was affected by the policy and position of Japan, whose hostility to the British Empire was easily discernible. The Far East could no longer be considered safe; the security of the British Empire was directly threatened by the rise of Japan into a powerful imperialistic state in East Asia. Circumstances had changed and there could be no more of the old complacence about the absence of danger to Hong Kong, Malaya, Sarawak, Burma or India.

DEFENCE PLANS

When, after the First Great War, Japan emerged as the naval rival of Great Britain in East Asia, British statesmen and soldiers began to look to the defences of Imperial possessions in that region. These possessions included Hong Kong, British Borneo and Malaya, with Australia, New Zealand, Burma, Ceylon and India behind them. Hong Kong was nearest to Japan and had no defensive depth and no space for manoeuvring. Hong Kong was, therefore, judged impossible to hold indefinitely against a full-scale Japanese attack. Only a tactical defensive for a limited period was considered practicable there, for which it would be sufficient to leave a small force on the island. British Borneo and Sarawak were more important, both strategically and economically. There were valuable oil-wells in Borneo, many small harbours such as Kuching, Victoria and Sandakan, and several aerodromes and landing grounds. It flanked the sea routes to Singapore and the Sunda Straits, and bombers and

---

[4] *Ibid*, p. 567.

submarines based there could seriously interfere with Japanese convoys moving against Malaya as well as Java. But, unfortunately, neither the British nor the Dutch had sufficient resources to hold Borneo in strength. For Malaya was far more valuable than Borneo, and Singapore at its southern tip controlled the entrance to the Indian Ocean. Singapore, therefore, was to be the main bastion of defence for the British possessions in that region. Together with the American fortress of Corregidor, it was to support a wide defensive arc blocking Japanese advance southwards.

British appreciation was that Japan would be able to attack Malaya only by sea and her main objective would be Singapore, where it was decided to build a strong naval base. The protection of the naval base and of the air bases built in support of it became the main concern of the defence plans. If the chief danger to Malaya was a sea-borne invasion by the Japanese, the naval base was obviously of the greatest importance. Its security, of course, " depended ultimately on the ability of the British fleet to control sea communications in the approaches to Singapore ".[5] This was possible only when the fleet was concentrated there. The then appreciation was that the Japanese would have to launch a direct attack on the Island of Singapore. Owing to the limited range of aircraft, which could at best operate from the east coast of Johore only in the vicinity of Mersing, the Japanese would have to attack by sea. A long sea voyage would necessarily limit the size of the expedition. The strength of the British fleet and the belief in its ability to concentrate within 70 days in Singapore waters gave confidence, and for many years " the problem of defence was one mainly of the defence of that island and the adjoining waters " till the fleet arrived. For this limited commitment a very small garrison was considered sufficient.

But soon the rapid development of air power complicated the problem of defence. Singapore was " exposed to attack by carrier-borne and shore-based aircraft operating from much greater distances ".[6] The defence plans had therefore to be modified, though not till the very eve of the Second World War was the danger to the whole of Malaya fully realised, or the probability of a land attack properly appreciated. Singapore Naval Base continued to be the chief object of defence preparations. Hence in May 1932, the Sub-Committee of the Committee of Imperial Defence laid down the following points :

[5] Percival's Despatch in supplement to the London Gazette of Friday, the 20th February 1948, para 19.
[6] *Ibid*, para 20.

"(a) Coast defence should be organised on the basis of co-operation between the three Defence Services, the gun retaining its place as the main deterrent against naval attack.

"(b) The first stage of the plan of defence for the Naval Base at Singapore, modified in the light of the latest developments in coast artillery, should be proceeded with.

"(c) The Royal Air Force should continue to co-operate in the defence of Singapore with such forces as might from time to time be considered desirable. Such co-operation should extend to all branches of the defence, including A.A. Defence (Fighters) and offensive operations against aircraft carriers, capital ships, and other forms of attack by sea, land and air".

In 1933, when Japan withdrew from the League of Nations, the British Government decided to take immediate steps for increasing the defences of the Island of Singapore. Earlier the defence of Singapore had primarily been a naval commitment with the aid of the Royal Air Force. But it was gradually realised that it might not be practicable for the Royal Navy to concentrate more than a small fleet in the Far East owing to the British Empire being involved in war elsewhere. In these circumstances, the defence of Malaya and Singapore was to devolve largely on the air force whose role was to destroy or sufficiently weaken the attacking Japanese force on the sea before it reached the coast of Malaya. Hence arose the necessity of constructing air fields which, against all canons of safety, were to be built on the eastern coast. However, progress was not immediate and only two aerodromes were made on the Island of Singapore till nearly the eve of the Second World War.

The changing plans for the defence of Singapore will be reviewed later. Enough has probably been said to indicate the fundamental causes of the conflict and the basic problems of defence in East Asia. The danger was clear, and the British authorities had taken certain measures to meet it. But the Empire was too vast for the United Kingdom to maintain sufficient defensive strength in each part. When war came, her defensive preparations were found inadequate and resulted in the loss not only of Hong Kong and Borneo but also of Malaya and Singapore,

CHAPTER II

War Strikes Hong Kong

THE CROWN COLONY OF HONG KONG

The British Crown Colony of Hong Kong originally consisted of a number of islands off the south-east coast of China, which together commanded the entrance to the Canton river. These islands had a bad reputation due to the prevalence of piracy in the neighbouring waters. In addition, the Colony included the peninsula of Kowloon on the mainland opposite, and a large strip of territory known as New Territory leased by China on a 99 years' tenure in 1898. The estimated area of the entire colony was 391 square miles. Together with Singapore and Corregidor in Manila Bay, it stood as "the third leg in a tripod of Anglo-Saxon power and influence in the Far East."

Hong Kong island, with an area of only 32 square miles, lies close to the Chinese mainland being separated from it at Kowloon Point by some 1300 to 1400 yards of sea, and at Lei U Mun by only 500 yards. The channel, which separates the island from the mainland, provides good anchorage throughout its length except in the Lei U Mun Gap where the water is deep. Extremely irregular in outline, the island is about 11 miles long from east to west, the breadth varying from 2 to 5 miles. It has the shape of "a rough and broken ellipse with two long promontories running out to the south and south-east". The island consists of a chain of hilly ridges which extend throughout its length, the highest point being the Victoria Peak which rises to over 1800 feet and served as a signalling station for approaching vessels in the harbour. The hills consist of low granite ridges broken at intervals by tortuous valleys. The central Wong Nei Chong Gap divides the island clearly into two sectors, east and west, and is of vital strategic importance.

The coast-line is deeply indented, specially in the south where Tytam Bay runs inland for about $2\frac{1}{2}$ miles. In the northwest sector of the island, lies the city of Victoria which stretches for about 4 miles, and between the town and the mainland is situated the harbour, one of the most picturesque and spacious harbours in the world, with a water area of more than 10 miles. But this harbour had to be cleared of shipping in the first week of December 1941 when war with Japan appeared imminent, and Aberdeen in the south-western part of the island became the principal harbour.

Victoria was the chief and only city on the island with a population of about half a million.[1] There were a number of villages, the most important of which were Sau-Ki-Wan in the north-east and Aberdeen in the south-west.

Of the small neighbouring islands forming part of the Colony, the Stonecutter's Island lies to the north-west of Hong Kong. About a mile in length and a quarter of a mile in breadth, this island, which contained the main naval communication depot and wireless transmission station, was fully fortified. The largest of the surrounding islands, Lamma, has the famous peak, Mount Stenhouse, which rises to a height of 1140 feet.

Directly opposite Victoria lies the peninsula of Kowloon, mostly inhabited by Chinese, which was ceded to Great Britain under the Treaty of Peking of 1860. To the north-east of the city of Kowloon lay Kai Tak aerodrome, the only one in the Colony, which prior to 1941, was being used for both commercial and military purposes. The main roads cut across the peninsula and a railway from the southern tip went north as far as Canton, passing through Beacon Hill and crossing the frontier south of Sham Chun Hu.

The New Territory lay to the north of Kowloon on the Mainland and was of value to Hong Kong because of the protection it afforded to Kowloon from an attack from the landside. The Mainland, with the exception of a broad strip of swamp and irrigated land running south-west from the frontier, was for the most part mountainous and uncultivated, a series of steep, grassy ridges strewn with granite boulders and intersected by many inlets and scrub covered valleys. The whole territory was washed on the west by Deep Bay and on the east by Mirs Bay.

A 50-mile road encircled the main portion of the New Territory and its eastern arc ran close to the Kowloon-Canton Railway. Two good roads—the Castle Peak Road on the west and Taipo Road on the east—ran from Fanling and linked up to the south-east of Golden Hill. It was along these roads that the Japanese advance on the mainland took place. A number of mule tracks ran through the narrow passes giving access to the south.

All the approaches from the north were dominated by the Golden Hill—Smuggler's Ridge region which was itself completely overlooked by Tai Mo Shan and Needle Hill. From a tactical point of view, the most important was the Devil's Peak Peninsula overlooking Lei U Mun strait.

---

[1] In 1940 the population was 416, 955.

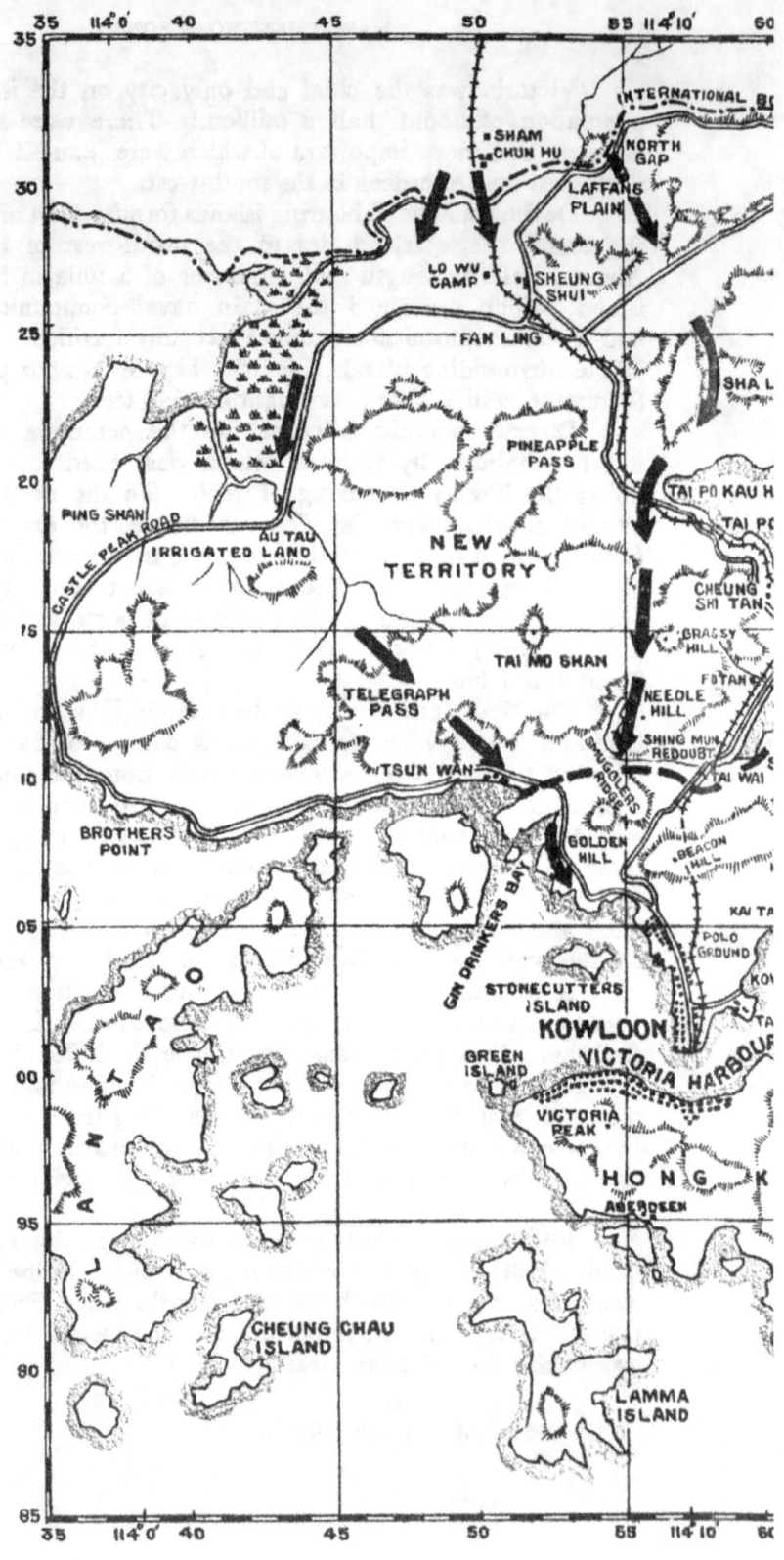

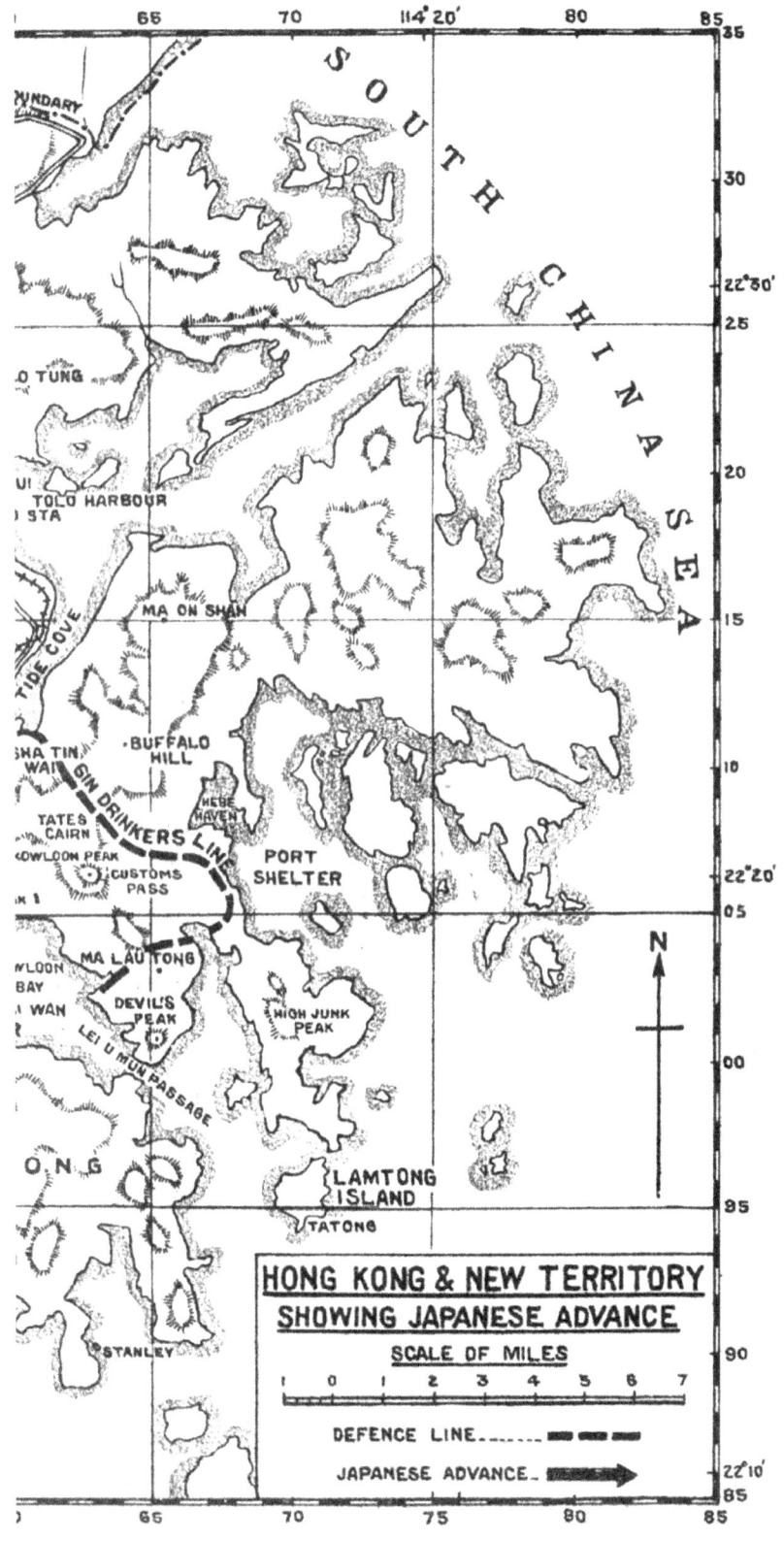

The Colony of Hong Kong lies within the tropics. Its temperature ranges between 90° and 40° F. During the winter months, from October to February, the climate is delightful. There is very little rain, and the air is cool and bracing. The temperature begins to rise during March and April and a few showers fall. The rainy season begins in May and lasts upto early August. This period is marked by intermittent rainfall and extreme heat. The mean annual rainfall is 85 inches. Hong Kong is subject to typhoons about the autumn equinox, which occasionally cause great damage to shipping in the harbour.

The population of the Colony increased remarkably during the last fifty years. In 1891 the total population was only 221,441 but the census taken in April 1941 showed that it had risen to 1,500,000, an increase of about 700 per cent. According to the despatch submitted by Sir Robert Brooke-Popham, Commander-in-Chief Far East, to the British Chiefs of Staff on 28 May 1942,[2] the population exclusive of that of the New Territory on the Mainland in April 1941 was:—

Hong Kong	709,000
Kowloon	581,000
Floating Population	154,000
Total	1,444,000

At the outbreak of hostilities it amounted to nearly 1,750,000 and included a large proportion of Chinese, whose number had doubled during the three years between 1938 and 1941, owing to the large influx of refugees from China since the Japanese capture of Canton. This great increase led to serious food and water difficulties when war broke out, and made it easy for the Japanese to launch fifth column activities on a large scale. In mid-December 1941, a War Office appreciation contained the remark, " the most serious weakness of the situation was the presence of 750,000 Chinese in the city of Victoria ". Prior to December 1941, on the advice of military authorities, a large number of European women and children had been evacuated.

The administration of the Colony was vested in a Governor who was assisted by an Executive and a Legislative Council. Sir Geoffrey Northcote handed over charge as Governor to Sir Mark Young on 10 September 1941, who continued to hold this office during the critical days of December 1941. The Executive Council consisted of six officers, including the General

---

[2] Sir Robert Brooke-Popham's Despatch, in Supplement to the London Gazette dated Tuesday, 20 January 1948, p. 542.

Officer Commanding, besides the Governor. The Legislative Council was composed of eight non-official members and nine officials, presided over by the Governor. Of the eight non-official members, six were nominated by the Crown, three of whom were Chinese, one by the Chamber of Commerce and one by the Justices of the Peace from their body. The people had therefore practically no say in their own governance and little enthusiasm for the cause of their rulers.

HISTORY

Great Britain was at the pinnacle of her power and glory in the 19th century. The Industrial Revolution had made her 'the workshop of the world' and the battle of Trafalgar had left her without a rival on the seas. The old colonial policy of the 18th century had given way to a policy of free trade and the principle of the 'Open Door'. Britain's command of the seas enabled her to open up new markets everywhere for her goods, and it was in pursuance of her trade and commercial interests that she came into conflict with China. China figured prominently as a commercial El Dorado in British eyes offering magnificent prospects for her trade; and British diplomacy was actively interested in opening the China market progressively, irrespective of whether it meant war or peace. The Chinese reacted violently to this attempt to force foreign goods on them, which led to open hostilities in 1839.

The first of the Anglo-Chinese Wars arose over the notorious opium trade. The importation of opium into China had been banned by an Imperial edict of 1800, but the trade flourished at Canton because of the activities of the British traders and Chinese smugglers who found it extremely profitable. In the course of the war in 1841, Great Britain occupied Hong Kong which was subsequently ceded by the Treaty of Nanking, August 1842. Hong Kong thus came into British possession. The island was then inhabited by nearly 7,500 Chinese fishermen, and was considered one of the most unhealthy places in the world. From the very beginning no restrictions were placed on other nations trading with China through Hong Kong and it has remained an open port ever since. No special privileges were reserved either for British traders or British vessels. In 1843 it was constituted a Crown Colony.

The next stage in the growth of the colony of Hong Kong commenced in 1856 when war broke out again between Great Britain and China. The immediate cause of the war was the capture by the Chinese of a trading ship, the *Arrow*, sailing under British colours. The Treaty of Tientsin was signed in June 1858 after a series of warlike operations, but trouble arose later when the British envoy was obstructed on his way to Peking to get the treaty ratified. Then re-commenced the hostilities; a joint Anglo-French expedition invested the Taku forts and occupied them, marched on Peking and forced the Chinese to sue for peace. By the convention of Peking signed in October 1860, Kowloon, on the mainland opposite the island of Hong Kong, was handed over to the British. The occupation of Kowloon peninsula greatly strengthened the defensive position of Hong Kong.

A further addition to British territories of Hong Kong was made in 1898 by the acquisition of a considerable area of land to the north of Kowloon on the Mainland, and of a number of islands situated near Hong Kong. These territories were leased for 99 years on the ground that it would help in the proper defence and protection of the Colony from hostile attacks. Possession of the New Territory was taken over a year later, but its inhabitants did not like this change-over. They revolted against the British occupation authority, but were soon crushed on 18 April 1899. The convention of 1860 had originally provided for the continuance of Chinese jurisdiction in the city of Kowloon, "except as far as may be inconsistent with the military requirements for the defence of Hong Kong", but the disturbances of 1899 were made an excuse by the British for the definite inclusion of the city under full British control.

DEFENCE SCHEMES

In the years that followed, Hong Kong enjoyed complete immunity from danger due to the Anglo-Japanese Alliance. Even after the First World War the Washington Treaty maintained a certain stability in the region. But with Japan's repudiation of that treaty in 1936 and her attack on China in 1937, Hong Kong lost her sense of security. The Japanese capture of Canton, only 90 miles away in 1938, was obviously a grave threat to Hong Kong.

In the event of war, it became apparent that Japan would attack through New Territory and Kowloon. On 27 June 1940, news came that Japanese troops had taken up stations on the land-frontier of Hong Kong thereby blockading the Colony from the Mainland. Subsequent border incidents recurring with monotonous regularity had " created an attitude bordering on philosophical resignation, fostered by the belief that hostilities must sooner or later break out ".³

The defences of Hong Kong were on a very limited scale as it was considered officially as " an undesirable military commitment, or else as an outpost to be held as long as possible ". At one time even the demilitarisation of Hong Kong was seriously considered, but it was ruled out by the Chiefs of Staff Committee in October 1940. The Defence Plan, prepared as far back as 1937, did not contemplate a prolonged defence of the Mainland, but, in view of the limited strength of the armed forces, confined its purview to a defence of the Island only. The main object of the plan was to deny the use of the harbour to the Japanese rather than to retain it for use as an advanced base of operations for the British fleet. On the Mainland, the Defence Plan envisaged only a delaying action while necessary demolitions were being carried out and evacuation completed. This plan must be considered as a part of the general defence policy in the Far East. After the collapse of France in June 1940, it was considered advisable to withdraw British troops from Peking, Shanghai and Tientsin, but troops could not be withdrawn from Hong Kong because of its strategic importance to China. The Island was extremely valuable to the Chinese as a port of access. It has been estimated that 60% of China's arms were imported through this port; Chinese interests therefore demanded the retention of the Island as long as possible, and with the increase in China's difficulties as the war against Japan developed, their anxiety for the safety of Hong Kong also increased. General Chiang Kai-shek actually offered to send ten divisions of trained soldiers to help in the defence of the Mainland if the British could provide the necessary arms. But due to a woeful shortage of arms and munitions the proposal could not materialise If the Chinese had anticipated that Britain did not consider the defence of Hong Kong a practical proposition for any length of time, the effect on their morale might have been bad. As it was, Britain's determination to fight to the last in spite of meagre resources strengthened General Chiang Kai-shek's hands and " in all probability played an important part at a critical period in China's War effort. "⁴

There were two phases of the Defence Plan. The first related to defence on the Mainland, and the second, and the more important, to the defence of the Island. It was not considered feasible to fight for an indefinite period on the Mainland with the

³ The War in Hong Kong—2/14 Punjab, p. 2.
⁴ Sir Robert Brooke-Popham's Despatch op. cit., p. 541.

forces then available; hence the fighting there was intended to be a delaying action only, which would provide the defenders in the Island valuable breathing time. According to Major G. E. Gray of 2nd Battalion, the 14th Punjab Regiment, there were three plans for the defence of the Mainland which may be conveniently referred to as 'A', 'B' and 'C'. 'A' was the original defence plan which envisaged fighting on the Mainland to be conducted by one battalion only. This plan was never brought into action, because the arrival of the two Canadian battalions on 16 November 1941 considerably reinforced the Hong Kong garrison. 'B' was the actual plan adopted which provided for the defence of the Mainland by three battalions. It was anticipated that casualties in their ranks would not adversely affect the subsequent defence of the Island. Plan 'C' would have been put into operation if another battalion from Canada had arrived in time to participate in the fighting.

It was not intended to hold the frontier posts on the Mainland and in the event of an attack forward troops were to withdraw after carrying out successive demolitions. The main line of defence on the Mainland was the Gindrinkers Line or 'Inner Line'. This line had been constructed several years before the war when the Maginot Line mentality dominated military strategy, and the intention was to hold it by a force larger than a brigade. Besides pill-boxes, there were "dug-in positions, later surrounded by mines and barbed wire". Sir Robert Brooke-Popham estimated that a proper defence of this line would have required two divisions or more.

The Island had been, however, carefully prepared for defence and "much originality and initiative", had been displayed in the construction and concealment of pill-boxes and other obstacles. But the civil authorities did not take all the necessary measures. Major-General Maltby attributes it to three factors:

"(a) The general doubt that Japan would declare war against the Allied Powers.
(b) The weakness of our intelligence system.
(c) The belief that Japan was bluffing and would continue to bluff to the last. The true gravity of the state of affairs was not reflected in the embassy despatches from Tokyo".[5]

Since full Civil Defence Plans were not put into operation, the Japanese exploited transport and supplies to their own use, as for example when they crossed over from the Mainland to the

---

[5] Maltby's Desptach in Supplement to the London Gazette, 27 January 1948, p. 699.

Island, small craft and sampans were utilised by them and they also found large supplies in Kowloon.

The normal garrison in the Colony consisted of one British and one Indian unit. After the fall of Canton at the end of 1938, its strength was doubled. In October-November 1940, with the arrival of 5/7 Rajput and 2/14 Punjab from India, there were two British and two Indian battalions in Hong Kong. Two Canadian battalions also arrived in November 1941, but unfortunately without their mechanised transport which had been despatched separately. The first load on board the *Don Jose* reached Manila in the Philippines on 19 December 1941, but was held up there, and there being no prospect of its reaching Hong Kong, it was made available for use by the American forces. The other consignment on board the S. S. *Fernplant* could not proceed beyond Los Angeles from where it was returned to Canada owing to the impossibility of its ever reaching the destination. How far did this deficiency affect the value and usefulness of the force is difficult to assess, for otherwise these troops were reputed to be " well-trained and well provided with equipment ".[6] The Canadian force had been sent in response to an urgent request by the British Government in September 1941 and was the best which could be provided in the circumstances.[7] By this addition the strength of the garrison was raised to six battalions besides auxiliary troops whose details are given later. It is difficult to be sanguine about the fighting value of every one of the component units and the competence of this small garrison to hold Hong Kong for long against a major attack is doubtful.[8]

There was practically no air power available for the defence of the Colony. Among the limitations of the force under his command, Major-General Maltby put the absence of modern air power first. The garrison's air force consisted of six planes—two Walrus amphibians and four Vildebeestes, which were located at Kai Tak, the only aerodrome in the Colony.[9] On 24 November 1941, a signal

---

[6] Report No. 163, Historical Section, Canadian Military Headquarters, Canadian Participation in the Defence of Hong Kong, December 1941 paras, 39-44.

[7] *The Canadian Army* 1939-45. pp. 273-4.

[8] The Indian Infantry battalions were not fully equipped and did not have mortars or ammunition till immediately before the outbreak of hostilities and had, according to Brigadier Wallis, their first practice with this weapon during the battle on the Mainland. The morale of the Royal Scots was alleged to be low. The Canadian units have been reported by Brigadier Wallis to lack training, though they contained a sprinkling of veterans. They had little of small arms or signal training when they landed, and every effort was made to make good these deficiencies, but the time available was too short.

[9] Canadian reports speak of only 3 Vildebeeste aircraft. The figure of 4 has been accepted on the authority of the War Office. See Report 163, Para 61, File 601/7809/H.

was sent to the Chiefs of Staff for stationing a fighter squadron at Kai Tak, but this was not agreed to. These planes were not expected to last long in case of war because the aerodrome was an open target without adequate anti-aircraft protection. The aeroplanes being antiquated were no match for the Japanese fighters. They were all virtually put out of action by the first Japanese raid on the aerodrome. The garrison also suffered a great deal from lack of air reconnaissance. There was also no radar equipment available. The few AA guns did often engage the Japanese aircraft but that had no effect on their activities. Royal Air Force personnel in Hong Kong consisted of 8 officers and about 80 other ranks. No outside air support could be expected by the defenders as the nearest British aerodrome at Kota Bharu was nearly 1500 miles away.[10]

Neither were the naval defences of the Colony in a satisfactory condition. The cruiser squadron and the powerful submarine flotilla usually stationed at Hong Kong had been withdrawn. Simultaneously a number of naval units had been transferred to Singapore. "It was a matter of general knowledge that Singapore, in view of the perilous situation of Hong Kong vis-a-vis Japan, was being set up and fortified as the main Far Eastern base".[11] At the time of the Japanese attack, the naval units available in Hong Kong were: one destroyer, the *Thracian*, four gunboats, eight motor torpedo boats, seven auxiliary patrol vessels, and an auxiliary craft used for minefield duty (not a fighting unit).[12] Naval personnel numbered about 1300 British and 300 Indian and Chinese. Since the Victoria Dockyard was vulnerable to attack from the Mainland, it was decided to transfer the navy to Aberdeen. Defence measures consisted of patrolling the approaches to Hong Kong and laying mines.[13]

---

[10] Maltby (p. 700) writes:—
" The lack of reconnaissance both landwards and seawards was naturally a serious handicap. Study of the past history of Japanese operations had led me to believe that they were past masters in combined operations, and throughout the period of the siege I always anticipated a landing on the southern shores of the Island, and lack of distant seaward reconnaissance was for me a distinct handicap. Similarly I knew that the lack of opposition to the incessant enemy air raids had a somewhat depressing effect towards the end on the troops, and definitely increased the accuracy of the enemy bombing and the material damage done. For similar reasons the enemy's counter battery tasks were very much simplified ".

[11] " C " Force Report, p. 19 cited in Canadian Participation in the Defence of Hong Kong December 1941.

[12] Interview with Commodore A.G. Collinson, C.B.E., R.N. (Retd.) at C.M. H.Q., 27 June 1946 cited in note on Canadian Participation.

[13] Major-General Maltby wrote appreciatively of the work done by the naval personnel; " the forces available carried out their duties in very difficult circumstances with the utmost gallantry and in the true tradition of the Royal Navy. I have nothing but praise for their gallant conduct...... Maltby's Despatch, p. 700. op. cit.

DIFFICULTIES ENCOUNTERED IN DEFENCE

The presence of a population of about a million and three quarters in the Colony was a serious handicap to the defence plan. The normal population was swollen by the large influx or refugees from China after Japan's capture of Canton in 1938. It is not surprising, therefore, to find references to the difficulties of rice distribution in the short official communiques. Most of the rice needed for Hong Kong was imported from Siam and Burma, and it was found difficult to keep up even the normal rice imports because of shortage of vessels. Moreover, since fish might not be available in case of war, and storage of alternatives over a period of months was difficult, the problem of providing rice supplement was serious. Food difficulties apart, the tremendous increase in population had led to medical, police control and water supply difficulties. It was almost impossible to keep a careful watch on the floating Chinese population moving constantly to and fro between the Mainland and the Island, and this enabled the Japanese fifth column to get fairly detailed and accurate information regarding the disposition of troops, nature of terrain etc. One of the great factors contributing to Japanese victory was the splendid work done by Japanese spies, whose task was greatly facilitated by the constant movements of the population.

A number of good reservoirs on Hong Kong Island and the Mainland gave a plentiful supply of water. The main reservoirs on the Island were situated east of Wong-Nei-Chong Gap in the Tytam region. They were partly filled by rain-water and partly by supply from the Mainland. Normally in a year of good or even average rainfall, no difficulties were experienced regarding the supply of water, which was however seriously affected when the supply from the Mainland was cut off. The early capture of these reservoirs by the Japanese proved later to be one of the factors in the ultimate surrender of the garrison.

The Air Raid Precautions Organisation consisted of about 12,000 personnel of all categories before the war. Near the town of Victoria, air raid shelters had been dug out of granite hills, which were considered bomb-proof. The tunnels and strengthened houses could accommodate nearly 300,000 persons at one time, and the rest of the population could be lodged in hutments outside the town in case of emergency.

A very large number of European women and children had been evacuated from Hong Kong by July 1941. Those remaining in the Island consisted of 918 women who were employed as nurses and clerks or were engaged in Air Raid Precaution duties.

A 'stand by' order was issued on 1 December and in the evening an official announcement stated :—

"The Government considers it desirable that persons not required for duty in the Colony in the event of an outbreak of hostilities, and who are able to remove themselves and their families from the Colony should take any existing opportunity to do so".

A special ship was chartered to evacuate people, but the response was so poor that the proposed sailing was cancelled. It was so particularly because the European and Chinese business men could not believe that the war was so near. Passages were booked in other steamers for the few who had registered.

During the first week of December 1941, the situation became critical and war was expected any moment. At To Kat, only 8 miles from the frontier, three Japanese divisions were reported to have been mobilised and on 7 December Japanese troop concentrations were definitely seen in the frontier villages. It will thus be clear that the Allied forces had to face a very difficult situation. Without any substantial air or naval support, and with no hope of receiving reinforcements from elsewhere, Hong Kong was doomed from the outset if the Japanese were to attack with vastly superior numbers, which they actually did.

BRITISH TROOP DISPOSITIONS

The land forces in Hong Kong consisted of Headquarters China Command and two infantry brigades (each consisting of three battalions), one employed on the Mainland and the other in the Island. The two brigades with supporting arms and ancillary troops were under the over-all command of Major-General Maltby.

Mainland Infantry Brigade

The Mainland Infantry Brigade was under the command of Brigadier C. Wallis with brigade headquarters at Sham Sui Po and tactical headquarters at the north end of Waterloo Road, Kowloon.[14] The forward troops led by Major G. E. Gray consisted of one company (C) of 2/14 Punjab, four carriers, two armoured cars and other ancillary units. Their headquarters were at Fanling, the junction of Taipo and Castle Peak Roads. The object of the force was to ensure that all prepared demolitions were carried out and to delay the advance of the Japanese towards the Gindrinkers or Inner Line. Three Infantry battalions manned the

---

[14] See Map facing page 28.

PLATE I

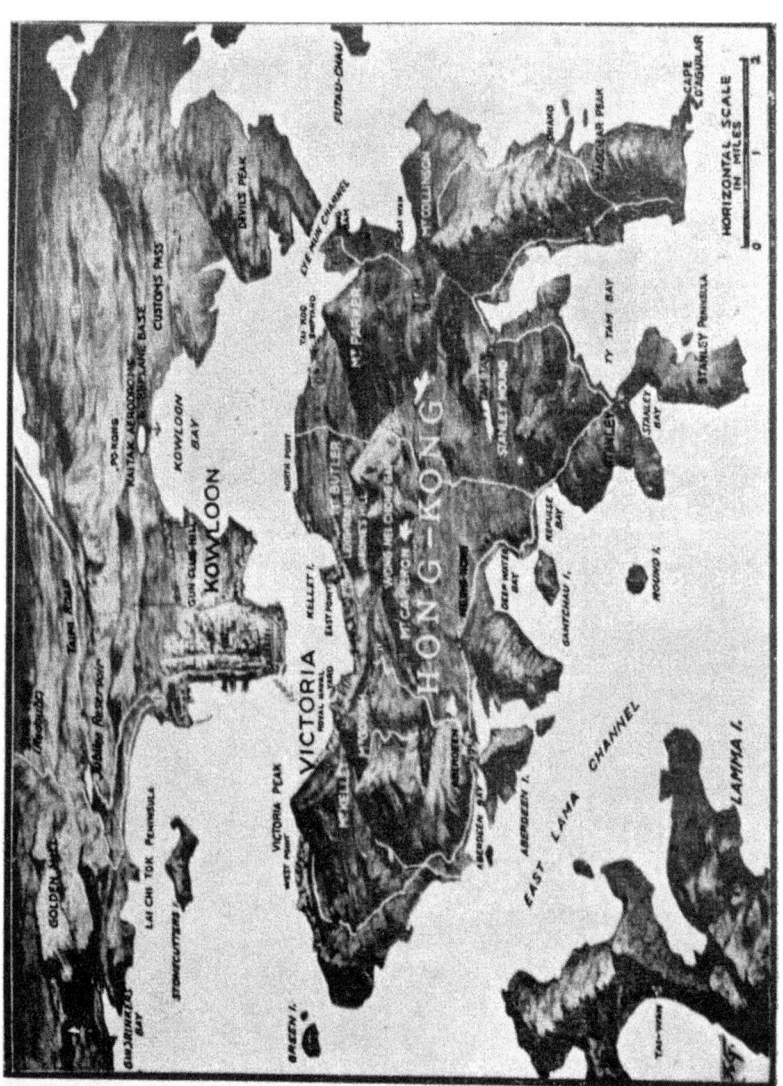

Hong Kong and Kowloon

PLATE II

Major-General C. M. Maltby, G. O. C., Hong Kong

Kaitak Aerodrome

Gindrinkers Line; the right flank was defended by 5/7 Rajput, the centre by 2/14 Punjab and the left by 2 Royal Scots.[15]

There was a gap of about 1500 yards between 2 Royal Scots and 2/14 Punjab along the Shingmun Nulla. The Reserve Company (D) of 5/7 Rajput was brought up from the rear to fill up this gap on 9 December, while C Company, 2/14 Punjab, forming the bulk of forward troops, did not take up its position in the Gindrinkers Line till the evening of 9 December after withdrawal from Fanling. The three infantry battalions occupied a front of approximately $10\frac{1}{4}$ miles " on very commanding country but with certain inherent weaknesses. It had necessarily little depth, which in two localities was particularly dangerous, viz. Customs Pass and the Pass between Golden Hill and Laichikok Peninsula ".[16] Each battalion's lay-out consisted of a line of platoon localities, the intervening gaps being covered by fire by day, and at night by patrolling. There were very few troops available as reserve, and it was not found possible to employ more than one company of each battalion for this purpose. These reserve companies were located in prepared positions and covered the most dangerous lines of Japanese approach.

Of the two Indian battalions manning Mainland defences, 2/14 Punjab, which had been assigned the original role as a Mainland battalion, made little alteration in its former dispositions.[17] The 5/7 Rajput commenced wiring beaches at Port Shelter only on 14 November 1941 and started work on defences in its area as late as 22 November 1941. Both the Indian battalions had been weakened by repeated "milkings" for new units, and the reinforcements which they received consisted of only "partially trained recruits".[18] There were serious gaps in their equipment also, particularly in mortar, and in training in its use as platoon weapon.

In addition to the three infantry battalions, No. 1 Company of Hong Kong Volunteer Defence Corps (HKVDC) was stationed at Kai Tak aerodrome to prevent any attempt by Japanese paratroops to land in force. There were also four troops of the 1st Hong Kong Singapore Regiment (HKSRA), deployed as follows:—

Filter Beds (4·5 in. Howitzer)

---

[15] The Company lay-out of the three battalions has been indicated on Map facing p. 28. The 2 Royal Scots were in a highly malarial area and had many cases. Out of a total strength of 771, they had only 600 effectives. (Maltby's Despatch, f. n., op. cit. 702).
[16] Maltby's Despatch, op. cit. p. 702.
[17] War Diary and Narrative "Mainland Infantry Brigade and Attached Troops," p. 4.
[18] Ibid. p. 5.

Tai Wai	(3·7 in. Howitzer)
Customs Pass and	(3·7 in. Howitzer)
Kowloon Polo Ground	(6 in. Howitzer).

Island Brigade

Brigadier J. K. Lawson was in-charge of the forces on the Island, which consisted of the two Canadian battalions (Royal Rifles of Canada and Winnipeg Grenadiers) and 1 Middlesex Regiment. The last battalion had been in Hong Kong since August 1937, and being a machine-gun battalion, occupied pill-boxes on the perimeter of the Island. The brigade headquarters was at Wong Nei Chong Gap in the centre of the Island. The Royal Rifles of Canada and the Winnipeg Grenadiers had their headquarters in Tytam Gap and Wanchai Gap, respectively.

All the anti-aircraft artillery in the colony, consisting of 20 guns of different types, was sited in the Island, at various points, inland and around the coast. 3 and 4 Medium Batterys of the 1st Hong Kong Regiment were deployed on coastal defence and other vulnerable points.

The Hong Kong Volunteer Defence Corps supplemented the regular forces of the Colony and numbered approximately 2,000. Colonel H. B. Rose commanded the force which represented many nationalities. They gave valuable support to regular troops in the defence of the Island.[19]

Strength of the Forces

The total strength of the garrison,[20] and of all personnel mobilised at the outbreak of war with Japan, was 14,554, details of which are as follows:—

British	3,652
Canadian	1,972
Indian	2,254
Local Colonial	2,428
Hong Kong Volunteer Defence Corps	2,000
Auxiliary Defence Units	2,112
Nursing Detachment	136
Total	14,554

[19] Major-General Maltby, the G.O.C., later paid a magnificent tribute to their work.

" They proved themselves to be a very valuable portion of the garrison. In peace they had surrendered a great deal of their leisure to training, their mobilisation was completed smoothly and quickly, and in action they proved themselves stubborn and gallant soldiers ". (Maltby's Despatch, *op. cit.* p. 702).

[20] Brooke-Popham's Despatch, op. cit Appendix ' H '. Local Colonial and Auxiliary Defence Units included Hong Kong and Singapur RA, Hong Kong Signal Company and Hong Kong Mule Corps.

JAPANESE FORCES

Estimates of the strength of the forces which the Japanese would throw into the battle differed widely, and the cardinal error which the Far East Command made was that of underestimating it. It has been recorded by the Winnipeg Grenadiers that at a lecture delivered to the Canadian officers soon after their arrival in the Colony, they were given to understand that the Japanese had only about 5,000 troops with very little artillery support opposing the Allies from the north; that their troops were ill-equipped and not used to night fighting; that their aircraft were very mediocre; and their pilots were incapable of dive bombing owing to poor eyesight.

The General Officer Commanding Hong Kong had also arrived at the following conclusions from the information made available to him:— " That the

(a) Japanese night work was poor.
(b) Japanese preferred stereotyped methods and fixed plan.
(c) Japanese light automatics were not as numerous as ours nor so up to date.
(d) Japanese " Combined Operations " were thorough and that they had excellent boats and equipment, but their successes against the Chinese were flattering as there had never been real opposition.
(e) Japanese Air Force was not up to first class European standards, that their bombing was poor, and that they would not go in for night bombing.
(f) Japanese fifth column activities would be encountered, though no actual proof of such organisations existed. The proximity of Formosa, with its mixed population of Japanese and Chinese Formosans, and, Canton, furnished the enemy with admirable intelligence bases".[21]

However, three or four weeks before the outbreak of war with Japan, there was unusual activity in Canton. The Japanese garrison there was considerably reinforced, and their defence lines " had been drawn in so as to encircle the city more closely".[22] The Allied commander obtained a good deal of useful information from a Japanese deserter who came across the frontier on 1 November 1941. His information showed heavy concentrations of Japanese troops across the frontier of New Territory, and Major-General Maltby estimated that the Japanese had a corps of large

---

[21] Maltby's Despatch, *op. cit.* pp. 703-4.
[22] *Ibid*, p. 703.

calibre artillery. According to Chinese reports three Japanese divisions were concentrated for attack on 5 December at To Kat, about 8 miles from the frontier. The Far East Combined Bureau, Singapore, considered that the attack on the Mainland would be launched by only one division, another being held in reserve.

According to reports appearing in the Japanese press soon after the invasion, the attack on Hong Kong was carried out by the *9th Division* and the *103rd Division*, with a third division held in reserve.[23] Early intelligence reports in the War Office mentioned the Japanese *18th Division* and *104th Division* as taking part in the Hong Kong operation, although it is now known that the former was landed in Malaya.[24] The latest information on the subject has led the British official historians to believe that only the Japanese *38th Division* (Lieut.-General T. Sano), with certain additional units under command, was involved in the invasion of Hong Kong. The *66th Infantry Regiment* of the *38th Division* was detailed to check any Chinese attack to link up with the Hong Kong garrison, so only three Japanese infantry regiments are now said to have been available for the invasion of Hong Kong.[25] These regiments were supported by heavy artillery and aircraft in large numbers. Careful and exhaustive preparations for the campaign had been made by the Japanese Army. There are said to have been three companies of infantry composed of expert swimmers, " who swam across the narrowest part of the channel dividing the island from the mainland and gained a footing on the shore ".

[23] Japanese Land Operations, File 8117.
[24] Canadian Participation, Footnote 2, para 202.
[25] Kirby S. Woodburn: *The War Against Japan*, Vol. I, Appendix 6; Her Majesty's Stationery Office, London, 1957.

CHAPTER III

Operations On The Mainland

THE INITIAL ATTACK

On 8 December 1941, Japan attacked the American naval base at Pearl Harbour at 0125 hours, Hong Kong time.[1] At 0445 hours intelligence sources of the General Staff intercepted a Tokyo broadcast message warning the Japanese that war with Great Britain and the United States of America was imminent. This information was immediately passed on to the Governor and was at the same time conveyed to all units. Major G. E. Gray, commanding forward troops, consisting of C Company of 2/14 Punjab, and four carriers, two armoured cars of HKVDC and detachments of Royal Engineers and Signals, was ordered to blow the frontier belt of demolitions east and north of Fanling. Two hours later the whole garrison had been told that they were at war with Japan.

The Japanese struck soon after. At 0800 hours their bombers which had taken off from an aerodrome on the outskirts of Canton, launched a heavy attack on Kai Tak aerodrome. Some of these bombers attacked from a height of not more than 60 feet, inflicting heavy damage on the parked aircraft. The Royal Air Force Hong Kong detachment lost three planes, in addition to one seriously damaged and one slightly damaged. The entire commercial fleet of China National Aviation Corporation, consisting of one clipper and seven other planes, was either destroyed or seriously damaged, and one of the huge oil tanks of the Standard Oil Company was directly hit. The Japanese did not lose a single plane in the course of this action. " Cruising leisurely over the field, the Japanese airmen bombed these targets with no more difficulty than if they had been on bombing practice on a range in peacetime ".[2] They also strafed the areas held by B and D Companies of 2/14 Punjab but without causing any casualty. According to a report from 2 Royal Scots the number of Japanese bombers participating in the attack was twenty-seven,[3] but the figure of thirty-six mentioned by Major-General Maltby

---

[1] The Hawaiian time was 0755 hours on 7 December. The timings mentioned here are all Hong Kong time.
[2] Japanese Land Operations, p. 3.
[3] War Diary and Narrative, Mainland Infantry Brigade, p. 6.

appears to be more reliable.[4] The Japanese bombers had fighter escort.

At about the same time, twelve Japanese planes bombed brigade headquarters at Shamsuipo which received four or five direct hits, but fortunately the number of casualties was very small. The heaviest bombs dropped weighed 250 lbs., but a large number were of lesser weight, and most of them fell into the sea.[5] There were further raids in the course of the day on Kai Tak aerodrome and the Stanley Peninsula, but these were on a smaller scale and did not cause any appreciable damage. Japanese planes also dropped propaganda leaflets addressed mainly to the Indian troops and Chinese auxiliaries, but these do not seem to have had any effect on them. As Major-General Maltby puts it, "They were poorly drawn up and carried no weight either with British or Indian troops".[6]

At 0820 hours 5/7 Rajput was asked to send an officer to Kai Tak to take all necessary defence measures, and to keep a sharp look-out for Japanese paratroops. As the first bombs were dropping on Kai Tak aerodrome, the leading units of the Japanese army were crossing the border of the New Territory. At 0730 hours on 8 December, the Allied frontier observation posts reported Japanese bridging parties south and south-west of Sham Chun Hu, and within half an hour a large number of troops estimated to be a battalion began advancing through the North Gap into Laffans Plain. Another battalion of Japanese troops advanced a little later straight down the Taipo Road. The tactics adopted by the Japanese "were almost invariably to push a strong body up the nearest hill and round a flank directly any line of approach was found to be blocked".[7]

ACTION OF FORWARD TROOPS ON THE TAIPO ROAD

Immediately on the declaration of war with Japan, orders had been given to blow the frontier belt of demolitions in accordance with the plan of defence prepared by the General Officer Commanding. The most important of these "blows" was at Lo Wu Railway Bridge, which was successfully carried out at about 0900 hours on 8 December after a hectic three and a half hours' work of charging.[8] In the meantime the threat of a battalion moving round

[4] Lt. Col. Kamta Prasad (2/14 Punjab) confirmed the number as 36 in his Notes. He was in the area over which the aircraft flew when proceeding towards Kai Tak.
[5] War Diary, Mainland Infantry Brigade.
[6] Maltby's Despatch, *op. cit.* p. 704.
[7] *Ibid.*
[8] The War in Hong Kong—2/14 Punjab, p. 4.

their right flank was becoming serious for Major Gray's troops. He, therefore, decided to withdraw his troops south in accordance with the pre-arranged plans on the Fanling—Taipo Road after making sure of the big demolitions, one mile north of Taipo in the narrow Pineapple Pass. These demolitions blocked the road for about thirty yards and the railway also for some distance. But the advancing Japanese troops by-passed the railway and the Taipo Road and made their way towards Taipo down the Shalo Tung track. They were, however, engaged by Allied machine-gun fire at a range of eleven hundred yards and a few casualties were inflicted.

By 1500 hours, a large number of Japanese troops were concentrated in the Taipo area, but their initial attack was beaten off by heavy fire. Soon after, the Japanese abandoned the idea of a frontal attack on the Allied postitions, but carried out outflanking movements which necessitated a further withdrawal of Allied troops to the south of the Taipo Causeway.[9]

The Japanese continued their advance and infiltrated on the left flank of 2/14 Punjab at about 1730 hours which forced the latter to withdraw as far as the high ground to the southeast, where Major Gray hoped to remain for the night. A Japanese platoon was ambushed to the north-west of Taipo, and heavy casualties were inflicted on it by machine-gun and light automatic fire from a range of one hundred yards. But in the bright moonlight, the Japanese, aided by local guides, never relaxed their pressure. Late in the evening, about 150 Japanese troops landed in sampans behind Allied troops near Cheung Shui Tan, again forcing them to withdraw. The Allied troops took up fresh positions along the line of the Fotan Valley an hour after midnight due to Japanese infiltration behind the dispositions of the forward troops. Meanwhile, by 0330 hours on 9 December all demolitions had been successfully completed except one at Taipo where the Japanese forestalled Allied plans by an extremely quick action of their forward patrols. Later at dawn the whole Allied force had reached Monastery Ridge, where it maintained the positions all day denying reconnaissance of the Gindrinkers Line to the Japanese. The force was subsequently ordered at dusk to withdraw into Gindrinkers Line, which it did under mortar and small arms fire. Throughout the rapid withdrawal of the forward troops, communications were well maintained. The approximate number of casualties inflicted on the Japanese was one hundred. " The enemy forces opposing the forward troops were estimated at three

---

[9] Maltby's Despatch *op. cit.* p. 704.

battalions of infantry, one eight-gun medium battery, tractor drawn, and three light batteries on pack ".[10] The Forward Troops, in the words of Major-General Maltby, " had fulfilled their role admirably ",[11] and had successfully carried out sixteen major demolitions on the road and railway.

OPERATIONS ALONG THE CASTLE PEAK ROAD

While the troops of 2/14 Punjab were falling back along the Taipo Road, the Japanese were advancing along the Castle Peak Road, the other main line of approach, running west of the Mainland. In accordance with the pre-arranged plans, the Au Tau bridge was blown up in the morning of 8 December, and late in the evening Japanese transport was seen banking up there, which testified to the thoroughness of the demolition. 5·9-inch guns were drawn by tractors up to the bridge and then manhandled by the Japanese into a village to the east. This battery fired at intervals on Hong Kong Island during the next thirty-six hours, and several shells fell near Aberdeen Reservoir.

The Carrier Platoon of 2 Royal Scots on the left was in contact with the Japanese at Ping Shan about halfway up the road. In the course of the day after successfully blowing the prepared demolition on the road, except the one at the Dairy Farm, Allied patrols withdrew at first to Brothers Point along the Castle Peak Road and subsequently to Tsun Wan Wai, north-west of Gindrinkers Bay, where they stayed for the night. Meanwhile the Japanese column had pushed south through Telegraph Pass, and their pressure forced the Allied troops to withdraw into the Gindrinkers Line by first light of 9 December. 2 Royal Scots took up positions on the left of the Gindrinkers Line covering the entire area from Gindrinkers Bay north to Golden Hill and Shingmun Redoubt.[12]

During the course of their advance along the two main roads, the Japanese had shown considerable knowledge of the cross-country tracks and, led by the local guides, developed their attack over difficult country very quickly. The Japanese also displayed " a high standard of night training ".

THE GINDRINKERS LINE

By the evening of 8 December, two battalions, 2 Royal Scots and 2/14 Punjab, were in their positions inside the Gindrinkers

---

[10] The War in Hong Kong—2/14 Punjab, p. 5.
[11] Maltby's Despatch, *op. cit.* p. 705.
[12] *Ibid.* p. 704.

Line, and the third 5/7 Rajput defended the right end of the Line. Owing to the shortage of troops, there existed a gap south-east of the Shingmun Redoubt between 2 Royal Scots, who held a sector from Gindrinkers Bay to Shingmun Redoubt, and 2/14 Punjab who defended the line from the Shingmun Nulla to Wong Uk. The Shingmun Redoubt, itself a strong-point of defence, was held by only one platoon of 2 Royal Scots, a very meagre garrison to man the defences. Hence, early in the morning of 9 December, 5/7 Rajput was ordered to move its reserve company (D) to man the gap until the direction of the main Japanese thrust was disclosed. Along the remainder of the front, however, only minor adjustments were made during the day and activity was largely confined to patrol work and sporadic shelling of troop movements. 2 Royal Scots sent strong patrols on the tracks leading south-east from the Kam Tin area, which confirmed the news that the Japanese troops were making use of Chinese guides drawn mostly from the village of Tsun Wan Wai. Small bodies of Japanese troops were also reported to be crossing Tide Cove towards Buffalo Hill. A precautionary day and night standing patrol on Heather Hill was, therefore, organised. No serious attack, however, developed from this direction until the evening of 11 December.

By the evening of Tuesday, 9 December, the entire Mainland Infantry Brigade commanded by Brigadier Wallis was in position behind the general line, Tsun Wan Wai-Wong Uk-Heather Hill—Punjab Hill.[13] The brigade commander hoped to hold this line for at least a week, but during the night the surprise capture by the Japanese of Shingmun Redoubt held by 2 Royal Scots, forced the Allied troops to withdraw further south to a line along Golden Hill Ridge. It was clear that A Company of 2 Royal Scots had been surprised in the Redoubt, having failed to maintain active patrolling as ordered by the brigade commander. The loss of this key position which dominated the left flank was a grievous blow and had serious consequences on the subsequent defence arrangements. The possession of this strong-point by the Japanese gave them a covered route into the British area and they were now in a position to exert pressure on the defence line from the flanks and rear. The possibility of an immediate counter-attack in this area was discussed by Major-General Maltby with Brigadier Wallis, but it was not considered practicable because " the nearest troops were a mile away, the gound precipitous and broken, and the exact situation round the Redoubt very obscure ".[14] The Japanese

[13] See Map facing page 28
[14] Maltby's Despatch, *op. cit.* p. 705.

worked feverishly throughout the night to reorganise the captured position to meet the counter-attack which never materialised.

At midnight on 9/10 December the reserve company of the Winnipeg Grenadiers, which was in position at Wong Nei Chong Gap, was moved from the Island to reinforce the garrison on the Mainland. The company reached the Mainland Headquarters at 0400 hours, and was placed in brigade reserve at the Kowloon Polo Ground, ready to give all possible support. Moreover, in an effort to stem the Japanese advance south-east of Smuggler's Ridge, an artillery concentration was directed against the Redoubt which took heavy toll of the moving Japanese columns. Confused fighting took place in this area for some time, but further Japanese advance was stopped by the vigorous action taken by the Officer Commanding D Company of 5/7 Rajput, supported by artillery. The Japanese were compelled to retreat into Shingmun Redoubt which was then shelled by 6-inch howitzers. Severe casualties were inflicted on them in this action.

At 0930 hours the next day, Brigadier Wallis asked the Officer Commanding, 2 Royal Scots, for his plans regarding counter-attack, but the latter felt that this task was beyond the capacity of his battalion because the Japanese were strongly entrenched in Shingmun, and the ground was both difficult and exposed. Moreover, the battalion had been weakened by sickness and casualties in its ranks and the morale was not high. It was, therefore, decided to relinquish all thought of a counter-attack and to establish a new line between Golden Hill and Lai Chi Kok to the south-west at dusk. The withdrawal was carried out without any incident by 1930 hours on 10 December, the Japanese making no attempt to intercept the retreating troops. Some necessary adjustments in the position of 2 Royal Scots were also carried out before dawn.

In the sector between Shingmun Redoubt and Wong Uk occupied by 2/14 Punjab the situation developed rapidly after the withdrawal of the troops inside the Inner Line. The Japanese advanced along the line of the hill-tracks north of Needle Hill, and troop movements were also noticed in the valleys running up from Tide Cove. Throughout the day, the positions occupied by 2/14 Punjab were heavily shelled from gun-positions along the Taipo Road, out of effective machine-gun range. Many forward pill-boxes at Wong Uk received direct hits and some of these were totally destroyed. A Company of 2/14 Punjab suffered heavy casualties during the shelling of the pill-boxes. It is apparent that spies had given information to the Japanese which made their fire so accurate.

During the afternoon on 10 December small Japanese parties reached Monastery Ridge and the lower slopes of Needle Hill. D Company of 2/14 Punjab brought its mortars to bear on these troops, but the effect could not be observed. At about 1630 hours two sampans appeared in Tide Cove, moving in the direction of the beach to the east of Wong Uk. They contained Japanese troops disguised in Chinese dress. The sampans were sunk by a 2/14 Punjab pill-box at Wong Uk, flinging their occupants into the water, where most of them were drowned. A few survivors were observed to reach the shore who finally escaped into the dense country near Buffalo Hill. A Japanese patrol under cover of darkness also came out in the vicinity of Shatin level-crossing, contact with which caused one casualty.

The Dome Hill sector occupied by C Company of 5/7 Rajput was also shelled in the course of the day, and some of their pill-boxes were either damaged or destroyed. The troops occupying them were immediately moved to their alternative positions, but these were also found to be untenable sometime later and the troops had therefore to withdraw at dusk further south. A medium machine-gun section was moved up at about the same time to one Rise More, south-east of Dome Hill, to reinforce the right flank of the Rajput company.

On 10 December the Royal Air Force evacuated Kai Tak aerodrome after destroying machines and equipment. According to Major-General Maltby, at this time there was left only one machine fit to operate. Obstructions were placed on the aerodrome by using " concrete sections of drains, railings from the surrounds and derelict M.T. ".

Throughout the night of 10/11 December there was intermittent shelling on the Mainland and the Island by the Japanese. The shelling on the Mainland was directed against the area Tai-Wai—Wong Uk. Before dawn four hits had been scored on Bowen Road Hospital.[15]

On the Mainland at dawn of 11 December, the Japanese launched an attack on the left flank of 2 Royal Scots, preceded by heavy mortar fire. In face of this pressure, the Royal Scots retreated in disorder as far back as the Pencil Factory, thereby exposing the junction of the Castle Peak and Taipo Roads, and jeopardising the position of the troops based on the Taipo Road (2/14 Punjab, one company 5/7 Rajput and troops 4·5-inch and 3·7-inch howitzers). Hence one company of Winnipeg Grenadiers and the Bren Carriers

---

[15] *Ibid.* p. 706.

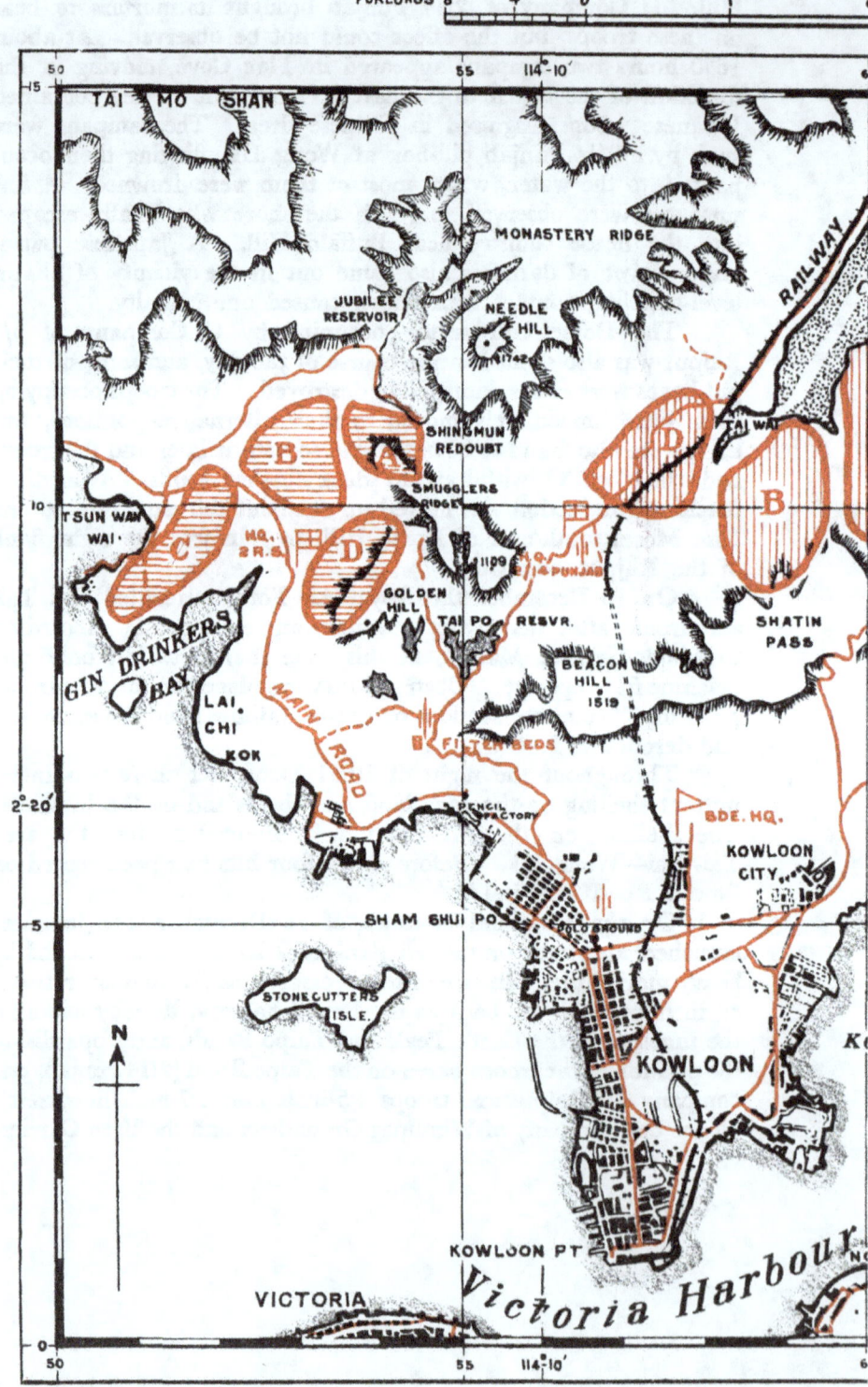

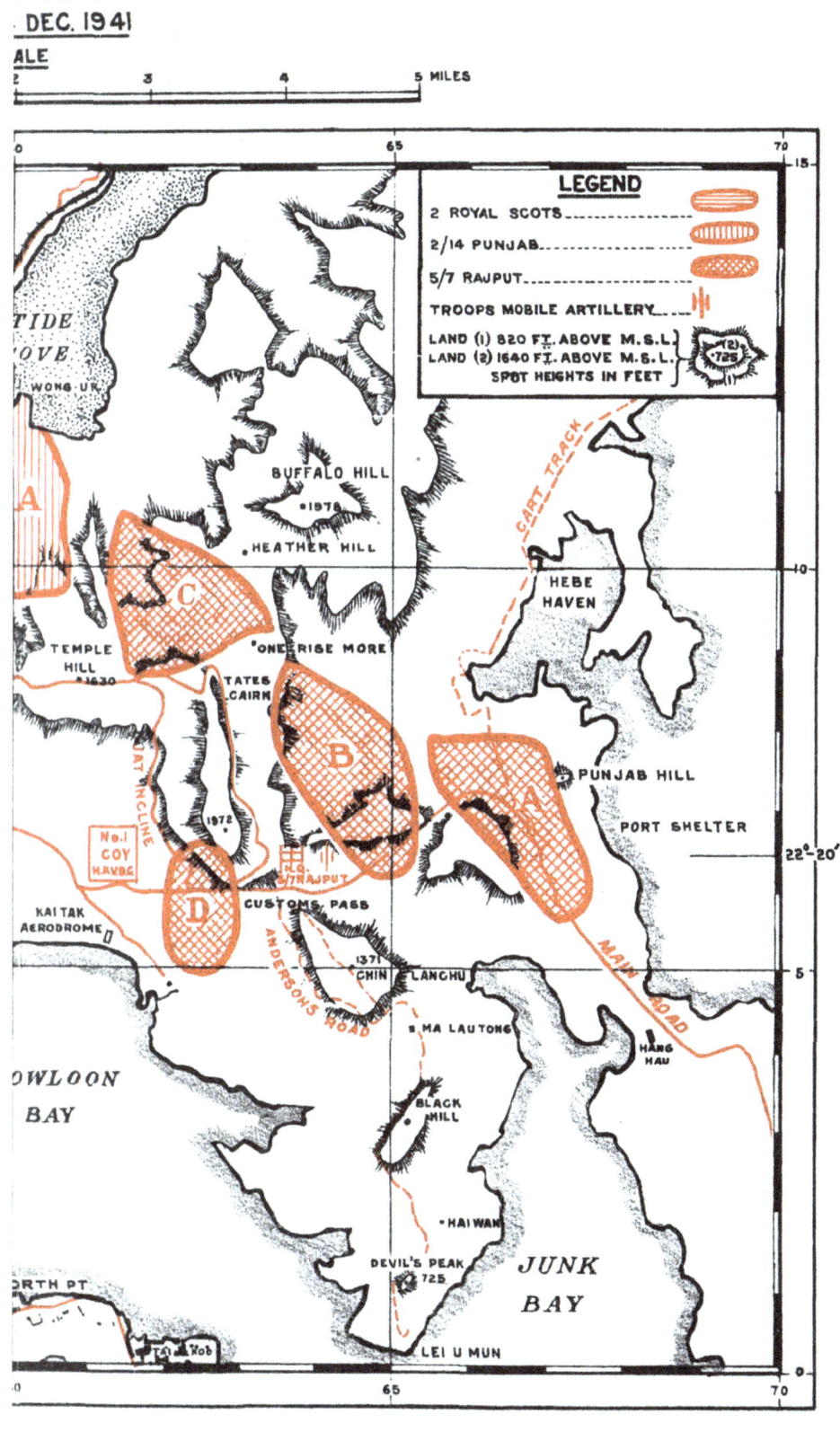

from Kai Tak aerodrome were moved into position to cover the gap. B Company of 2/14 Punjab which was in the process of withdrawing, however, engaged the Japanese trucks with small arms fire and 3 inch mortars and knocked out one of them. That stopped further Japanese advance temporarily.

At 0800 hours on 11 December, at a routine conference held by Brigadier Wallis, plans were explained for a general withdrawal to the Island, if this should become necessary. Up to this time there was no thought of immediate withdrawal and the General Officer Commanding was hoping to keep the Japanese troops at bay for a week or ten days. This conference laid down careful plans for successive "laybacks". Within two hours, however, the alarming news of the hasty retreat of the two forward companies of 2 Royal Scots on the left flanks was received, which entirely changed the situation. The reasons for the withdrawal of the Royal Scots will never be fully known, since the two company commanders were both killed in the action. According to Brigadier Wallis, the probable reason was that "the two left companies were again surprised by a strong enemy patrol near the main road when some light mortar fire was in progress. One platoon panicked and retired and then others in turn also withdrew and refused to remain, thinking they were being heavily attacked".[16] Major-General Maltby felt that the position of Allied troops had become exceedingly precarious because of the presence of a Japanese force south of Golden Hill and the obvious threat to Kowloon. In order to avoid a large portion of the brigade from being cut off, he decided on immediate withdrawal. All Mainland troops (less 5/7 Rajput and troops of 1 Mountain Battery, RA) were ordered to start evacuation at dusk that day. 5/7 Rajput had been detailed under the scheme of withdrawal for the occupation of Devil's Peak Peninsula. The withdrawal of 2/14 Punjab over hills and difficult tracks in broad daylight was fully exposed to Japanese fire, which was directed against its B Company in full measure. The situation was made worse by observation by Japanese aircraft. Nevertheless, the battalion continued its move, manhandling anti-tank rifles, 3-inch mortars and machine-guns over the steep hills to the Devil's Peak. Men had no food either, and the first meal which they had was tea in the Island at about 0300 hours on 12 December. The route had not been reconnoitred earlier, but luckily there was no follow up by the Japanese.

---

[16] War Diary and Narrative—Mainland Infantry Brigade pp. 23-24.
This diary was compiled by Brigadier C. Wallis in Shamshuipo and Argyle Street Prisoners of War Camps between 16 April and 30 May 1942.

At 1000 hours on 11 December the Japanese began landing on Lamma Island, and they were fired at by guns of Aberdeen and Jubilee batteries. A Japanese attempt to land on Aberdeen in Chinese sampans at 1300 hours was foiled by machine-gun fire. During the afternoon a concentration of about one hundred Japanese junks off Lamma was engaged by artillery fire. Meanwhile, Japanese bombardment of Stonecutters Island continued throughout the day. Much damage was caused to buildings and telephone communications. British troops were withdrawn from the Island in the afternoon, after successfully carrying out the destruction of guns and immovable stores, plans for which had been prepared well in advance.

While the situation on the front held by Allied troops was rapidly deteriorating, fifth columnists in dark grey uniform and armed with rifles were active in Kowloon. Also rioting and looting occurred in the streets. To add to the embarrassment of the defence personnel, a large number of lorry and car drivers, and a number of launch crew—almost all of them local residents—deserted, dislocating plans of evacuation.

Hong Kong was repeatedly bombed throughout the day. Although casualties were few, much damage was caused to the Royal Navy Dockyard, RASC and RAOC Depots.[17] The morale of the civil population did not go down appreciably, but the news of the early evacuation of the Mainland had a rather depressing effect on them.

WITHDRAWAL OF TROOPS FROM THE MAINLAND

The withdrawal from the Mainland was "well carried out" according to Major-General Maltby.[18] 2/14 Punjab, along with D Company 5/7 Rajput, was to retire through the passes along Anderson Road to the Devil's Peak, an isolated and commanding position. The covering troops consisted of the main body of 5/7 Rajput and one battery of 3·7-inch howitzers. This was a very difficult operation since it involved a move by night across the whole front through Kowloon Pass, Shatin Pass and Grasscutters Pass, but the Indian troops performed it successfully and acquitted themselves well. The Mule Corps assisted in this evacuation since mechanical transport was of little use over such a difficult terrain, the roads being quite impassable at several places. Brigade Headquarters, 2 Royal Scots and various administrative

---

[17] Maltby's Despatch, *op. cit.* pp. 706-7.
[18] *Ibid*, p. 707

units and sections were to cross over from embarkation points on the east side of Kowloon Peninsula. Civilians and food stores were evacuated from the west side. The whole operation had to be carried out at very short notice, but it was unavoidable owing to the sudden and rapid deterioration in the military situation. An illustration is afforded by the signals about whom Major-General Maltby has written, "In spite of the short notice the Royal Signals personnel successfully evacuated 49 miles of D 8 cable and 20 tons of buried type cable."[19]

The 2/14 Punjab front between Wong Uk and Tai Wai had been subjected to heavy shelling and aerial reconnaissance since dawn of 11 December and maintenance of communications had become extremely difficult owing to the frequent breakdown of signal cables and lines. Due to the disruption of communications, the order for withdrawal had to be conveyed to A Company of 2/14 Punjab by a runner and the order reached the last section of the forces at Shatin Pass not before 1330 hours. D Company took up fresh positions in the Beacon Hill area before withdrawing south. Soon after the receipt by B Company of the order to withdraw, 30 Japanese troops mounted on two trucks attacked the Tai Wai level crossing. The attack was beaten off. The withdrawal by 2/14 Punjab then commenced at 1900 hours on 11 December. A and B Companies reached Devil's Peak via Customs Pass and subsequently crossed over to the Island in launches at about 0100 hours on 12 December without incident. It was originally planned to withdraw the remainder of the Punjab Regiment along the Taipo Road and via Kowloon, but this was found to be impracticable because of congestion on the road caused by the retirement of the Royal Scots on the left. It was therefore decided that Headquarters and C and D Companies of 2/14 Punjab should take the line of the water catchment and proceed to Devil's Peak via Upper Shatin. The retreating force numbered about 300 and had with it ten sections of machine-guns and two sections of mortars. The troops set out from Taipo Reservoir Headquarters at about 1845 hours on 11 December on a pitch dark night when no stars could be seen owing to low clouds. Since no mule transport was available, all equipment had to be manhandled. The troops had to leave behind their rations and blankets, because they wanted to salvage as much of arms and ammunition as possible. The last meal had been taken early in the morning of the 11th and no iron rations were available.

[19] *Ibid*, p. 706.

During the first part of the march along the catchment path to Shatin Pass, the going was good and maintenance of direction easy. The troops arrived at Customs Pass safely soon after midnight. As Tate's Cairn had been occupied by the Japanese moving from Tide Cove and Buffalo Hill, 2/14 Punjab had to move over Temple Hill down Jat Incline to Customs Pass. They were, therefore, unable to keep the time schedule. The long trek down the Devil's Peak Peninsula was more difficult. Slowly the weight of the equipment carried by the soldiers began to tell upon them, and they showed signs of exhaustion. At Ma Lau Tong the force was divided into two columns; and from this place onwards, the most difficult part of the withdrawal operation began. The two columns reached the Devil's Peak Jetty at 0715 hours (12 December) after a march of about twenty-five miles lasting more than twelve hours. The loss in equipment was two anti-tank rifles, jettisoned by order, while of the personnel, only one was missing.[20] " The whole march was a tribute to the determination of the men and in particular those of the machine-gun and mortar sections ". They stayed the whole of that day dispersed in the foothills at the southern end.[21]

Meanwhile Lieut.-Colonel Rawlinson (5/7 Rajput) had been expecting the Punjabis to arrive at about 2000 hours on 11 December at Customs Pass which was his headquarters, but there was no trace of the Punjabis even till 2130. Half an hour later Major-General Maltby ordered the Rajputs to commence withdrawal to the Ma Lau Tong line. About this time rapid small-arms fire was heard from the direction of Tates Cairn, but C Company of the Rajputs was able to extricate itself without heavy casualties and retired to Kowloon through Customs Pass. Just before midnight Tactical Headquarters finally left Customs Pass.

Lieut.-Colonel Rawlinson met the 2/14 Punjab party led by Lieut.-Colonel Kidd on Anderson Road. D Company of the Rajputs followed behind this party and reached Hai Wan soon after 0400 hours on 12 December, from where they went into reserve. A and B Rajput Companies occupied their new positions in Ma Lau Tong line at about 0200 hours, and by first light MMG and 3″ mortar sections were ready for action in the area. C Company and Battalion Headquarters were stationed at Hai Wan. A nucleus brigade headquarters was established west of Devil's Peak to act as a link between the Rajputs and Fortress Headquarters and to provide moral support.

[20] The War in Hong Kong—2/14 Punjab, p. 9.
[21] Maltby's Despatch, *op. cit.* p. 707.

The morale and standard of discipline of the personnel of the two Indian battalions was high, although they were exhausted after "four days of continuous day and night vigilance and long night carries, over rough tracks and coolie paths, of many machine-guns, light automatics and mortars."[22] Great difficulty was experienced by the troops in the course of their withdrawal due to acute shortage of mule transport. Even during peace exercises, the shortage of mules was clear, but the situation had become worse with the arrival of the two Canadian battalions, whose mechanical transport had not been received when war broke out. Great credit is due to all concerned with the withdrawal operations. The whole operation was carried out successfully except for one solitary incident. In the darkness Headquarters details of 2/14 Punjab and some other troops came down to Kai Tak aerodrome by mistake and became involved in street fighting with fifth columnists in the outskirts of the city of Kowloon.[23]

2 Royal Scots withdrew through the line held by D Company Winnipeg Grenadiers and down the Kowloon Peninsula, and finally embarked from one of the Kowloon docks. A situation report described this withdrawal as "a difficult operation in view of constant pressure by superior numbers, who were very good at turning the flanks which were necessarily often offered owing to the smallness of units".[24] The Winnipeg Grenadiers company covered the withdrawal of 2 Royal Scots and overcame the slight opposition offered by the fifth columnists in Kowloon. By 2230 hours on 11 December, the Royal Scots had reached Victoria, and three hours later D Company Winnipeg Grenadiers crossed over to the Island. All armoured cars, some mechanical transport and nearly all Bren carriers were evacuated. At dawn the Royal Scots took over the north-east sector of the Island defences as a precautionary measure. It had previously been occupied by some Headquarters personnel of 1 Middlesex plus a platoon of No. 3 Company HKVDC.

FIGHTING IN THE DEVIL'S PEAK PENINSULA

The Hong Kong Defence Plan had envisaged that in the event of failure to hold the Gindrinkers Line, the Mainland Brigade would retire to the Island, leaving 5/7 Rajput to continue the fight around Devil's Peak. This plan was now given effect to.

[22] *Ibid*,
[23] *Ibid*.
[24] Cited in Canadian Participation, p. 26.

At dawn A and B Companies of 5/7 Rajput occupied forward position south-west and east of Ma Lau Tong with Battalion Headquarters and C Company at Hai Wan in the rear. Last minute improvements were made during the course of the day in this line, which had been specially prepared, and fresh rations and ammunition were brought forward. Owing to shortness of time, communications in the Devil's Peak area were still incomplete. At about 1000 hours the Japanese made a heavy dive-bombing attack on the administrative area, but no casualties were suffered by the personnel or animals.

Late in the afternoon of 12 December it became clear that the Japanese had occupied Chin Lan Chu and from there at about 1745 hours they launched an attack on the two forward Rajput companies. The Japanese attacking force was estimated at one battalion. By 1815 hours, the attack was beaten off by heavy machine-gun and artillery fire. The Japanese withdrew in disorder having failed to penetrate the frontal belt of wire and after suffering heavy casualties.[25] 6-inch howitzers opened an accurate and devastating fire on the retreating force until darkness obscured the targets. By 2100 hours all was quiet again along the line, but the Japanese were in close contact with B Company. An hour later Major-General Maltby decided to evacuate one Rifle Company and No. 1 Battery RA to the Island, and ordered the Rajputs to withdraw to the shorter Hai Wan line because their flanks were exposed to water-borne attacks. This withdrawal was also considered necessary in view of the pressure by the Japanese, " the rapid development of their heavy mortar fire, the constricted passage across the Lei U Mun Strait, (and) the shortage of launch crews ".[26]

About this time 2/14 Punjab Battalion Headquarters and C and D Companies began embarking for the Island. Their withdrawal was followed by the evacuation of the 3·7-inch howitzers which had given valuable support to the defenders throughout the day. It was proposed to hold the short Hai Wan line by 5/7 Rajput with Headquarters and two companies, which were to be the last to withdraw from the Mainland. The rest of that battalion was to withdraw from the Mainland, after 3·7-inch howitzer troops had moved. By midnight A and B Rajput Companies had withdrawn from their Ma Lau Tong positions, the withdrawal having been covered by a D Company platoon on Black Rock Hill. An hour later B and C Companies occupied their new positions on Hai

[25] This was the only occasion when the Japanese attack was not made under cover of heavy initial artillery and mortar bombardment.
[26] Maltby's Despatch, *op. cit.* pp. 707-8.

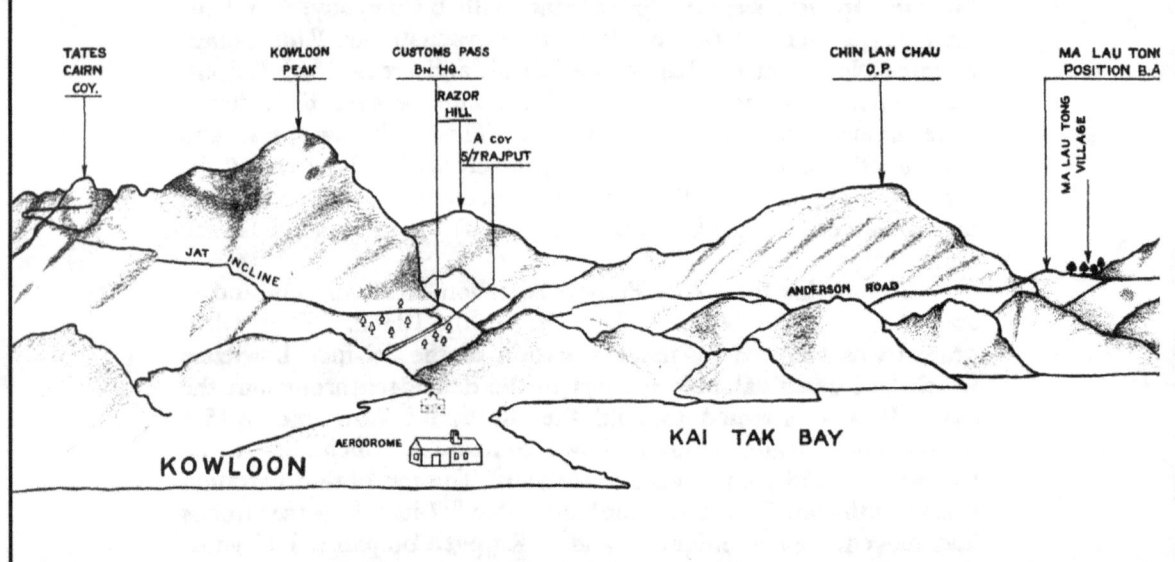

ON OF DEVIL'S PEAK

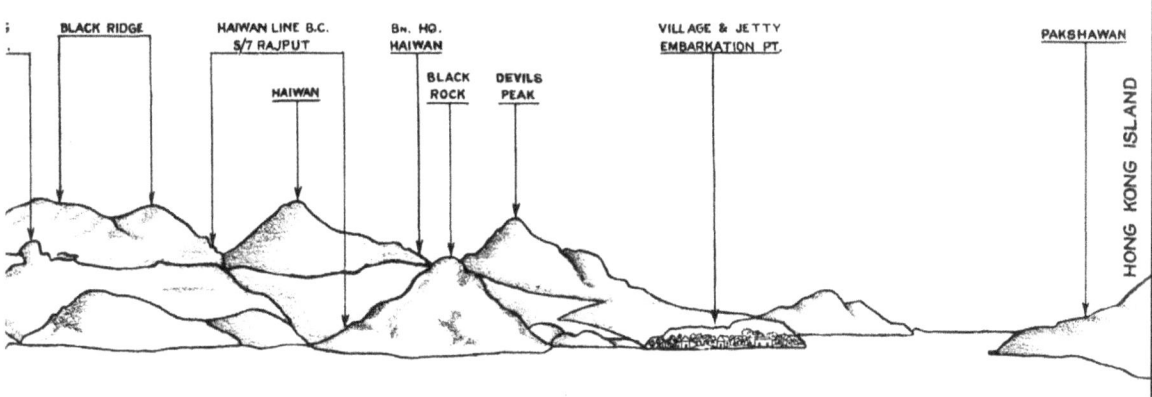

Wan Line, the former occupying the right sector and the latter the left.

During the final withdrawal to the Island, the water-transport position became extremely precarious because of the desertion of the Chinese crew and the bad condition of the launches. This involved serious delay in the time schedule, and it was not till 0130 hours on 13 December that 2/14 Punjab was across.

At 0400 hours on 13 December the bulk of the first troop RA and one company of Rajputs had safely embarked, but the Mule Corps had not arrived. After a discussion with Brigadier Wallis, Major-General Maltby decided to withdraw all the troops to the Island immediately to avoid the danger of daylight crossings.[27] One Rajput company was ordered to cover the withdrawal of the rest, and then itself to embark in the last ferries. Brigadier Wallis was at first reluctant to withdraw from the Devil's Peak, thus leaving to the Japanese a feature which completely overlooked the eastern extremity of the Island, but the necessity of saving the small Rajput force from eventual destruction by a superior Japanese force led him to decide upon immediate withdrawal to the Island. To assist in the evacuation, three motor torpedo boats came from Aberdeen and an additional MTB was recalled from patrol in Junk Bay. The destroyer *Thracian* also assisted in evacuating personnel and equipment which was being done slowly and steadily by the *Victoria*.

By 0730 hours on 13 December, Battalion Headquarters 5/7 Rajput and the last covering troops were withdrawing in broad daylight, and they reached Aberdeen at 0920 hours. Fortunately there was no Japanese air activity. The evacuation was completed without casualties, covered by artillery fire from several island positions. Almost the entire 5/7 Rajput Battalion assembled in the Tytam Gap area by noon and was given twenty-four hours to rest and refit before taking over the north-east sector of the Island from 2 Royal Scots. At the same time, 2/14 Punjab occupied the north-west sector of the Island.

The invasion of Hong Kong Island was now considered imminent. The Japanese could attack either through the narrow strait of Lei U Mun or through the water passage of Victoria. The rapid withdrawal from the Mainland came as a great shock to the civilians, who had anticipated a much longer resistance from the Allied troops in view of the proclaimed strength of the defences.

[27] In the plan for Mainland defence, no withdrawal was contemplated from the Devil's Peak.

CHAPTER IV

The End in Hong Kong

THE INTERIM PERIOD

The withdrawal of Allied troops from the Mainland marked the end of one phase of the Hong Kong campaign and the beginning of another, during which the Island was subjected to a heavy attack and intense fire by the Japanese. This was preceded, however, by a Japanese offer of peace, induced, perhaps, by the disorder and chaos in Kowloon after the retreat of the Allied forces. At 0900 hours on 13 December a ship flying the flag of truce arrived at Victoria Pier. A staff officer of General Officer Commanding Japanese forces, delivered a letter to Sir Mark Young, the Governor of Hong Kong, in which the Japanese demanded an unconditional surrender of the Colony, threatening severe aerial bombardment and artillery fire in case of refusal of the demand. But the Japanese ultimatum which was due to expire at 1500 hours on 13 December was summarily rejected by the Governor. There could be no question of laying down arms so long as the garrison could obtain food, water and ammunition. The Governor's refusal to surrender had the full approval of Mr. Winston Churchill, the British Prime Minister. In a message to the Governor and defenders of the Island, on 14 December, he said:

"We are watching day by day and hour by hour your stubborn defence of the port and fortress of Hong Kong. You guard a vital link long famous in world civilization between the Far East and Europe. All our hearts are with you in your ordeal. Every day of your resistance brings nearer our certain victory".

With the withdrawal to the Island, the Allied forces were faced with the possibility of a stronger attack from the Japanese when their own strength was reduced by the casualties they had suffered. In view of the fact that British attention was divided over many theatres of war, the beleaguered garrison had little hope of receiving any reinforcements or outside support. However, they stuck to their task manfully until the inevitable happened. The first centenary of British occupation of Hong Kong coincided with its tragic fall to the invaders.

Dispositions

In the reorganisation of dispositions of troops, the positions at midday of 13 December were as follows:—

2 Royal Scots had taken over temporarily the north-eastern sector of the Island from 1 Middlesex.

2/14 Punjab occupied the western sector facing Victoria water-front from Green Isle to Causeway Bay and also the high ground to the rear with battalion headquarters in Garden Road.

5/7 Rajput was resting in the Tytam area before taking up its allotted place on the north-east sector.

Royal Rifles of Canada and Winnipeg Grenadiers occupied the south-east and south-west portions of the Island. Anti-paratroop posts were established in the area held by Royal Rifles of Canada to prevent possible parachute landings.

1 Middlesex had its headquarters at Leighton Hill and manned the pill-boxes along the perimeter of the Island.

On the evening of 15 December, the Rajputs occupied the north-eastern sector between Causeway Bay and Pak Sha Wan with headquarters at Taikoo relieving 2 Royal Scots who in turn moved at about 1830 hours to the Stubbs Road area, east of Wanchai Gap. A small area between 1 Middlesex and 2/14 Punjab, north of Mount Parish, was taken over by a company of the Royal Scots.

The garrison was now divided into two brigades—East and West Infantry Brigades—under command of Brigadiers Wallis and Lawson, respectively. The inter-brigade boundary, inclusive to East Brigade, was Pill-Box 52—the north-east corner of Causeway—Tai Hang village—Jardine's Lookout—(exclusive) Wong Nei Chong Reservoir—Voilet Hill—(inclusive) Stanley Mound—Chung Ham Kok.[1] All troops east of this line came under Brigadier Wallis with headquarters at Tytam Gap. They consisted of 5/7 Rajput, Royal Rifles of Canada with attached troops (1 and 2 Companies HKVDC), two companies of 1 Middlesex—in the pill-boxes of the beach defences from Sai Wan Bay to West Bay. The troops to the west of the line formed the West Infantry Brigade and comprised 2/14 Punjab, 2 Royal Scots and Winnipeg Grenadiers. Besides there were the troops under the command of the Fortress Headquarters consisting of the headquarters and two companies of 1 Middlesex, one of which was in the pill-boxes while the other was in reserve.

" This eased the situation for Brigadier Wallis who had the larger half of the Island to command and for Brigadier Lawson who was unfamiliar with the ground ".[2] In support of each

---

[1] Brigadier C. Wallis, War Diary and Narrative of East Infantry Brigade and Attached troops, page 4. This War Diary and Narrative was compiled in Argyle Street, Kowloon, Prisoners of War Camp, between 1 June and 15 August. 1942

[2] Maltby's Despatch, *op. cit.* p. 710.

brigade were mobile batteries of the 1st Hong Kong Regiment, HKSRA and coastal defence guns ranging in calibre from 4 to 9·2 inches.

Major-General Maltby apprehended that an attack on the Island from the Mainland might well be in combination with landings on the south shore at a number of points simultaneously—a danger emphasised by several Japanese landings on Lamma Island during 11 and 12 December. He therefore considered that a dispersal of the forces under this command was essential, in order to cover the entire perimeter of the Island.

All pill-boxes around the Island were effectively manned with the purpose of inflicting maximum casualties on the Japanese attacking force. Behind these pill-boxes were stationed on high ground the five infantry battalions with their own reserves ready to counter-attack in case of Japanese infiltration at any point. In the north-east sector where the Japanese were expected to launch their initial attack, B and C Companies of 5/7 Rajput were held in reserve near Tai Hang village and south of Taikoo Headquarters. B Company was expected to cover the North Point area, while C Company was ordered to counter-attack near Quarry Point or Braemar. In the north-west sector B Company of 2/14 Punjab was held in reserve at Tai Ping Shan because the sector was partly covered by an anti-boat boom laid off shore between Green Isle and Sheung Wan (547005). The continuation of this boom towards Kellet Island was, however, prevented by the desertion of Chinese crew.

All available mechanical transport in the Island was concentrated at the Happy Valley Race Track to the east of Victoria. From this Vehicle Control Centre, trucks were lent to units by the Officer-in-Charge and were to be returned to him on completion of their allotted task.[3]

Preliminary Operations

During the period between the evacuation of the Mainland and the first Japanese landings on the Island (December 13-18), the Japanese were busy restoring order in Kowloon, collecting all available boats for transporting their forces mainly at Bailey's Shipyard, bringing up their heavy artillery and dropping leaflets on the Island. But there was no respite for the besieged garrison from Japanese shelling and bombing. Soon after the rejection of the unconditional surrender ultimatum, Japanese artillery fire from Kowloon and various other places on the Mainland

---
[3] Canadian Participation, p. 29.

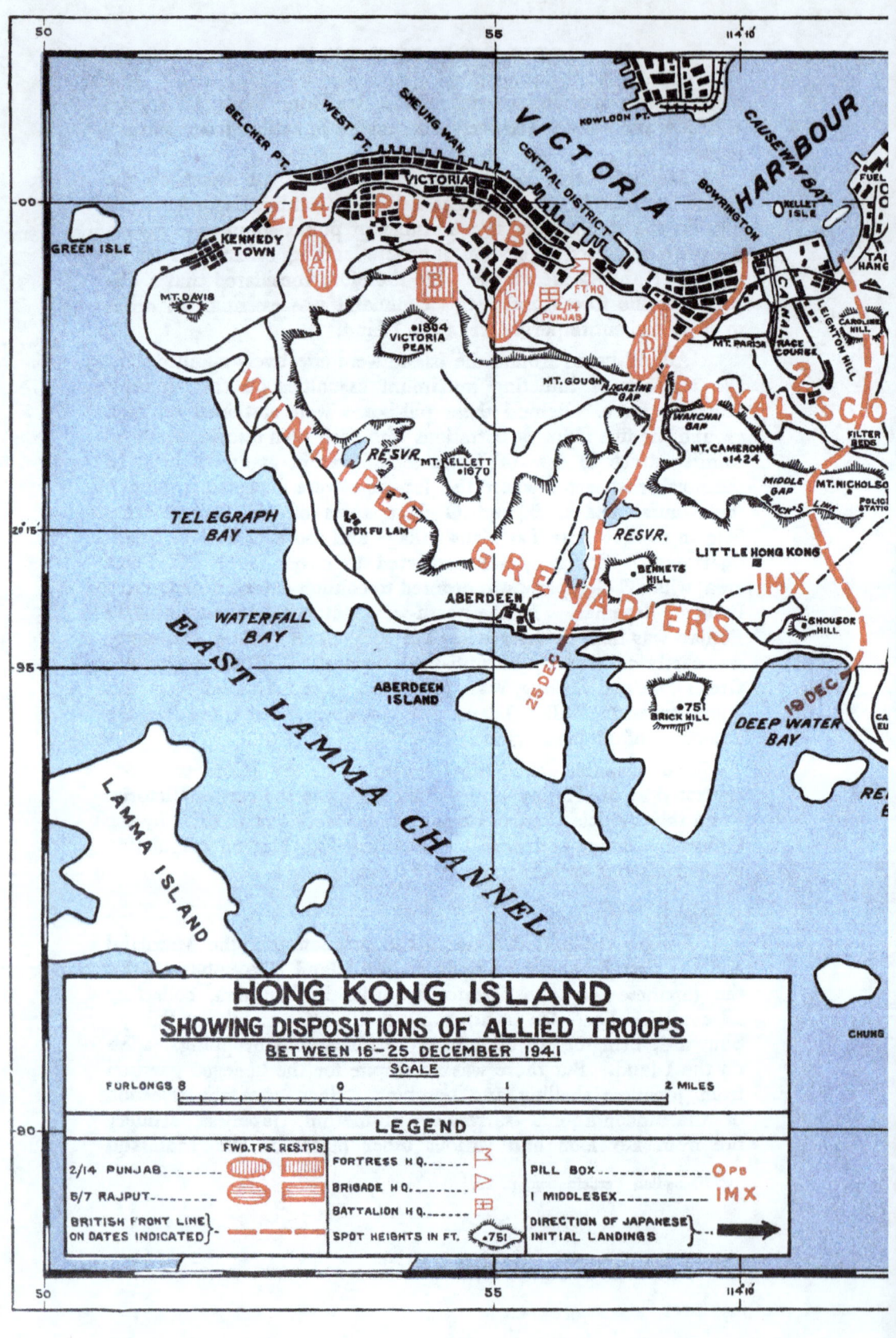

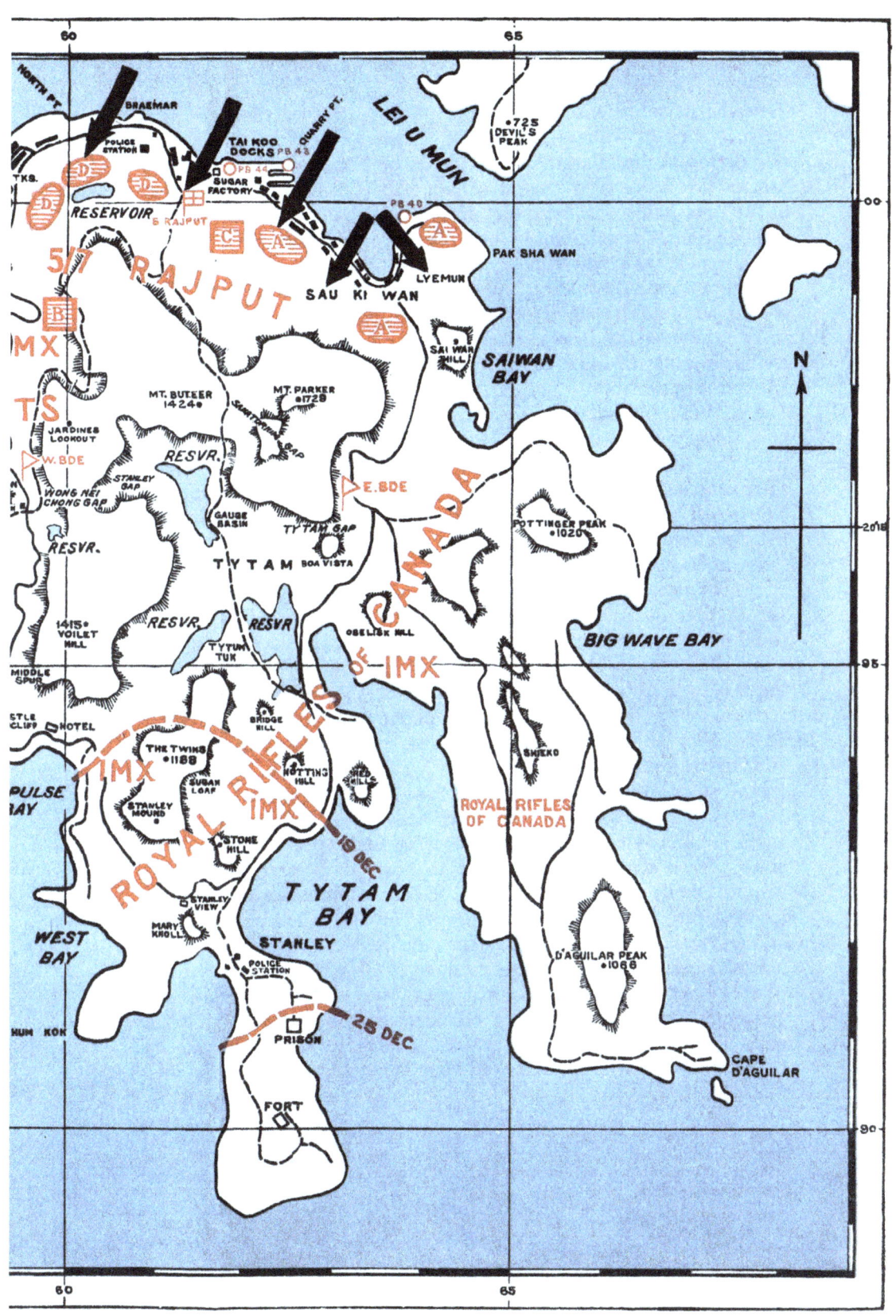

increased in intensity and accuracy. A direct hit knocked out one 9·2-inch gun at Mount Davis, and Belcher Point in the north-west sector of the Island was set aflame by heavy shelling at dusk. Serious fires were also started at Kennedy Town and West Point in the area held by a company of 2/14 Punjab. Coastal defence and HKSRA Batteries could not offer any effective opposition to the Japanese concentration of fire as they were far out-numbered and their targets were too numerous and well-concealed.[4] The official communique described the day as "difficult", and difficult it certainly was. Japanese shelling and bombardment shook civilian morale to some extent. Japanese fifth columnists exploited this opportunity. The anti-aircraft search-light position at Sau Ki Wan was attacked at night by fifth columnists who helped in sniping and spreading false alarm. A large number of army transport drivers also deserted, and some even took away their vehicles with them. This created serious transport difficulties. The police however took some action in the matter which prevented the situation from worsening. They were also able to maintain order in Victoria except in the ARP tunnels.

The next day (14 December) was one of great anxiety. The serious fires at Belcher Point and Kennedy Town at 0200 hours could not be put out by civilian fire-brigades, and military assistance was called for. Their combined efforts, did, however, control the fire by midday. There was chaos in the whole area due to fifth column activities and each telephone call had to be checked up carefully before action could be taken. Police found it extremely difficult to keep law and order with the limited resources, and several vulnerable points had perforce to be left unguarded.

Throughout the day, the north-west sector of the Island was again subjected to intense and accurate shelling from the Mainland. Some damage was caused to guns at Belcher Point and Mount Davis, and the latter place had its communications cut off for a couple of hours. A direct hit on one 3-inch anti-aircraft gun at Mount Davis caused 30 per cent casualties to the personnel and led to the desertion of a large number of Chinese gunners. Telephone wires were constantly being cut and a particularly heavy concentration of artillery fire on Magazine Gap damaged eight main cables involving 195 circuits. All these were repaired by the Royal Corps of Signals, but such incidents undoubtedly laid

---

[4] According to Japanese accounts, the British troops were "inactive". "Little if any attempt was made to interdict the passes over the hills north of Kowloon, and the invaders poured troops down into the plain, in full view of the observation posts on Victoria Peak, with very little interference and with a minimum of casualties". (Japanese Operations, pp. 5-6).

a heavy burden on the detachments working on line-repairs and impaired the garrison's communications.

While the defenders in the north-west sector were having a hard time, there was no respite from Japanese shelling for British troops in the north-east sector also. It has been estimated that by 16 December more than half the pill-boxes between Lei U Mun and Bowrington had been put out of action, testifying to the remarkable accuracy of the Japanese shell and mortar fire. One pill-box had "forty holes drilled right through by a high velocity gun of small calibre located on Kowloon peninsula". Many instances were reported of lights being flashed from crude lamps across the sea to the Mainland to direct artillery fire on to concealed gun positions and mechanical transport. Whenever such signallers were intercepted, they were shot.

There was inadequate provision of alternative pill-box emplacements. Less than a dozen positions had been completed before war broke out. These should have been completed in peace-time, but in the words of Major-General Maltby "it would have meant requisitioning valuable 'Godown' and office properties", and requisitioning had not been sanctioned until the proposed "Precautionary Period".[5] In any case the alternative positions which were rapidly prepared in basements and godowns were also shelled and hit. By nightfall, all civil and military telephone communications were severely interrupted in the north-east sector, including those to pill-boxes Nos. 40 to 53. But repair work was at once taken in hand and communications were partially restored before daybreak.

On 15 December, there was heavy shelling of Sai Wan anti-aircraft redoubt at 1004 hours. At noon mortar fire from specially prepared positions fell near the Royal Navy Dockyard, Command Headquarters and Lower Peak Tramway terminus. The Japanese boldly attempted a surprise night landing which was reported by Pak Sha Wan Battery. The invaders, with small rubber boats and petrol tin rafts as their equipment, tried to swim across in fair strength, but they were all shot in the water.[6] Estimates of their strength varied from one to three companies.

During the day, final adjustments to dispositions of troops were carried out and Indian troops occupied the whole north face of the Island and manned the pill-boxes. A War Office appreciation of the situation in Hong Kong at this time took a gloomy view of "an undoubtedly serious situation".[7] The strength of the

[5] Maltby's Despatch, *op. cit.* p. 710.
[6] *Ibid.*
[7] Canadian Participation, Appendix 'F'.

garrison was considered sufficient to hold only the Island and to offer "prolonged resistance". The possibility of early relief was ruled out altogether in view of the grave situation in Malaya which was "expected to deteriorate seriously".[8]

Aberdeen was heavily bombed, eight times in all on 16 December, which caused damage to the dock, some casualties to naval personnel, and the loss of one Motor Torpedo Boat. Japanese parties landed on Lamma Island. A column of Japanese motor and mule transport near Customs Pass on the Mainland was effectively dispersed by artillery fire and a troop concentration was scattered in Waterloo Road. Japanese troop movements were also noticed towards High Junk and Clear Water Bay areas.

Aerial bombing and artillery shelling of military objectives by the Japanese were on an increased scale throughout the day and showed a higher standard of accuracy. The first air-raid lasting for 23 minutes occurred at 0900 hours. Seventeen Japanese planes bombed Mount Davis in the afternoon and an unexploded 9-inch shell entered the Fortress Plotting Room, damaging instruments. Several men of 2/14 Punjab were wounded when B Company received a "near miss" which however had killed many Chinese civilians, for whose removal no arrangement existed. That caused serious demoralisation among the Chinese. Heavy civilian casualties were also caused by a bomb explosion in Sau Ki Wan, while Shiek O and Lei U Mun were also bombed. Maintenance of communications became extremely difficult in the north-east sector occupied by 5/7 Rajput on account of "repeated breaks from hostile fire". Throughout these heavy dive-bombing attacks the Japanese lost only two planes. One crashed into the sea near Tatong, and the other was hit by the Brick Hill 3·7-inch gun.

In the meantime, both the reserve Rajput companies spent the day planning their counter-attack roles. B Company's role was to prevent Japanese penetration between Tai Hang village and Braemar and C Company was to perform a similar role between Braemar and Sau Ki Wan. Their commander stressed upon them the necessity of making themselves thoroughly acquainted with the nature of the terrain and being able to move quickly by night.

The next day (17 December) Japanese light bombers made two separate attacks on Sau Ki Wan and the city area, which were followed by a short but severe artillery and mortar bombardment of Central District (Victoria) and the coastal road between Braemar and Sau Ki Wan. Shortly afterwards, a second demand for the

---

[8] *Ibid.*

garrison's surrender was made by the Japanese, who crossed over to the harbour in two launches flying a white flag. The proposals were signed by the Japanese Commander, Lieut.-General Sakai and the Naval Commander-in-Chief, Vice-Admiral Niimi. The proposal to surrender was accompanied by a threat of indiscriminate bombing in case of refusal. Sir Mark Young the Governor, again summarily rejected the proposal in the following words:—

" The Governor and Commander-in-Chief of Hong Kong declines most absolutely to enter into any negotiations for the surrender of Hong Kong and he takes this opportunity of notifying Lieut.-General Takaishi Sakai and Vice-Admiral Masaichi Niimi that he is not prepared to receive any further communication from them on the subject ".

This message won the whole-hearted approval of His Majesty's Government in Great Britain. The Secretary of State for the Colonies added: " Your resolute leadership and the stirring conduct of all defenders of the fortress are being watched with admiration and confidence by the whole Empire and by our Allies throughout the world. Hold on ". The envoys who brought the proposals " appeared genuinely surprised and disconcerted " at this rejection. Major-General Maltby thought that the second demand for surrender suggested that either they disliked the prospect of attacking across the water, or that the Chinese threat in their rear was taking effect, or that it was an attempt to undermine Allied morale by thoughts of peace and quiet.[9] The first two suggestions cannot hold water, because subsequent events on the Island belied them. The Japanese probably thought that the Allied commander would not unnecessarily sacrifice men and material in view of the apparently hopeless position of the defenders.

These proposals meant a welcome lull for the defenders until 1600 hours which was utilised to repair communications etc. Considerable Japanese activity was observed seawards about this time; a 2000-ton freighter was noticed to the west of Lamma Island and other vessels—launches, barges, ferry boats, one steam tug and a motor boat—were noticed near Kai Tak and Kowloon shipyard on the Mainland.

Shelling commenced soon after the truce period was over and continued throughout the evening. Surprisingly enough, for the first time in several days British artillery suffered neither casualties nor damage. On the other hand, a number of Japanese batteries on Devil's Peak, and Gun Club Hill and also three mortars

---

[9] Maltby's Despatch, *op. cit.* p. 711.

on the Kowloon water-front were effectively silenced by counter-battery action during the day. At about 2100 hours on 17 December, the large paint works at Braemar were set aflame by the Japanese artillery. This necessitated the removal to an alternative position of two 18-pounder Beach Defence guns which were nearby. The shelling of the north-east sector was very heavy and due to breakage of wires and cables many pill-boxes were out of touch. Brigadier Wallis informed the General Officer Commanding-in-Chief, that the situation on north face was "not very bright".

Between midnight and one in the morning of 18 December, Aberdeen came again under shell-fire from the sea. One shell struck the Industrial School, but fortunately failed to explode. Heavy shelling also commenced almost at first light along the entire 5/7 Rajput front. Owing to terrific fire, C Company was forced to change its "lying up area", but this was done without any casualty. At 0930 hours, the Battalion Headquarters at Tytam received a direct hit which cut off the main telegraph lines. Half an hour later, Japanese fire was concentrated on the Sugar Factory and Taikoo Dock areas. Some necessary relief was given after dark to the Pak Sha Wan platoon which had suffered heavy casualties from incessant Japanese fire. Petrol and oil storage tanks at North Point were set ablaze and were subjected to shelling at intervals throughout the day. The North Point fixed beam across to Kowloon Point could not function owing to the intensity of the heat and the dense smoke arising from the burning of oil installations. This fire, continuing for several days, proved a serious handicap to observation. The two 18-pounder Beach Defence guns, in their new position at Braemar Police Station were blown up by direct hits. The crew fortunately managed somehow to clear out. By early afternoon the road between Sau Ki Wan and Causeway Bay was studded with large bomb craters at several places, and the fallen tramwires and standards had made the road well-nigh impassable for mechanical transport and despatch riders.

At 1000 hours an air raid of considerable intensity took place on the Central District and Victoria. Further raids occurred from 1500 hours onwards and the Sai Wan artillery observation post was divebombed and also shelled. Major-General Maltby and Brigadier Wallis were certain that the Japanese would make an attempt at landing after dusk in view of the extremely heavy bombardment by artillery and mortars on Lei U Mun Peninsula. Numerous collections of small crafts and troop movements between the south end of the Devil's Peak and Kai Tak were noticed.

It will not be out of place here to mention the effect of bombing and shelling on civilian morale. As Japanese bombardment of the Central District and Victoria increased in intensity, there was an exodus of people to the southern parts of the Hong Kong Island. This considerably increased the strain on the authorities. On 15 December Sir Mark Young, the Governor, had felt that the most serious problem was the control of the Chinese population. A large number of Chinese workers had deserted, and in most cases it became increasingly difficult to depend on their steadfastness. Desertions from duty were particularly conspicuous in the case of army transport drivers. Thereby the distribution of supplies and ammunition was seriously affected. Japanese propaganda was carried on side by side. A number of leaflets were dropped to wean away the sympathies of people from the Allied cause. To counteract this, authorities in the Island took some action, but its effect cannot be correctly assessed in view of the slender evidence available. Major-General Maltby has categorically stated that civilian morale improved on 16 and 17 December and that rice distribution was easier. The arrest of a prominent Chinese merchant for " defeatist talk " on 16 December is reported to have produced good results.

During the period 13-18 December the Japanese made a serious attempt to soften up Allied defences in the north-east and north-west sectors of the Island and they were fairly successful in achieving their object. By the evening of 18 December, it was clear that the Japanese would make an attempt to land on the Island during the night in the north-east sector taking advantage of the fact that the area was obscured by smoke drifting across the water. By 2100 hours the Japanese were successful in affecting landings at serveral places, and thus began the last phase of the campaign.

THE LANDINGS ON HONG KONG ISLAND

The North-East Sector

On the night of 18 December, the final and most desperate phase of the campaign began. The Japanese crossed the narrow Lei U Mun channel at about 2030 hours and landed simultaneously on North Point and Lyemun under cover of darkness and of the heavy pall of smoke from the burning oil and petrol tanks at North Point. The confusion caused by smoke perhaps prevented the defenders from realising what was happening, and two companies of the Japanese leading battalion were already ashore before they could be brought under fire. 5/7 Rajput Pill-Boxes 43 and 44 at Taikoo Docks, observed Japanese troops approaching the shore in small boats towed by ferry steamers and immediately opened fire on them. In spite of this, the invaders were able to land on Taikoo Docks, Aldrich Bay and the Sugar Refinery Wharves. Japanese landings were greatly assisted by the successful reconnoitring work done the previous evening by a Japanese officer, Lieut. Zempei Masu Shima, who swam ashore at Taikoo to find "weak spots" in the Allied defences, and discovered suitable landing sites both at Taikoo and North Point for subsequent Japanese landings.[10]

The defence wire in the Taikoo Dock and the Sau Ki Wan areas had been cut, evidently by fifth columnists[11] before the invaders landed there. Within an hour of the landings, the invaders surrounded Pill-Box 44 and knocked it out. This success enabled them to infiltrate across the main road to the high ground between Taikoo and Braemar. C Company (less two platoons), one of the two 5/7 Rajput reserve companies, was ordered to prevent the invaders from moving south. Soon after, an excellent 6" artillery concentration was put on sugar Factory and Dock area of Taikoo which inflicted considerable damage on the invaders and temporarily delayed their advance. As Lieut.-Colonel Cadogan Rawlinson puts it: "It came down actually 100 yards too short causing some casualties to my men, but was invaluable for its speed, morale effect and delaying action on the enemy".[12] The crew of Pill-Box 43 fought bravely and continued to inflict heavy losses on the Japanese till about midnight when most of them were wiped out.[13]

Withdrawal by Battalion Headquarters:

By 2200 hours confused fighting was in progress in the streets and on the high ground, east and west of Taikoo Headquarters. Due to pressure by the invaders, 5/7 Rajput Headquarters was temporarily forced to withdraw to a position south on the road to Sanatorium Gap. It returned to its old Battalion Headquarters temporarily by dislodging the Japanese, but was finally forced to withdraw again by midnight. By this time situation in the north-

---

[10] This information appeared for the first time in the *Japan Times Weekly* of 17 September 1942 (Vol. XIII No. 3) in a citation for bravery. (War Diary 5/7 Rajput, p. 20).
[11] War Diary, p. 11 (Appendix B. 1, of Maltby's Despatch *op. cit.*).
[12] War Diary, 5/7 Rajput, p. 18.
[13] Mr. Winston Churchill sent the following message to the Governor of Hong Kong: "We were greatly concerned to hear of landings on Hong Kong Island which have been effected by Japanese. There must however be no thought of surrender. Every part of the Island must be fought and enemy resisted with utmost stubbornness". (General Headquarters Far East War Diary, Vol. IV, Appendix No. 303).

east coastal sector was out of control. An hour later, however, the survivors of battalion headquarters were occupying new positions on the south-west slopes of Sanatorium re-entrant. This site was chosen firstly to give depth to A Company and secondly because it permitted withdrawal towards Tai Hang and North Point localities in case A Company positions were forced.

About 0200 hours on 19 December, 5/7 Rajput Battalion Headquarters was attacked from the left, which necessitated withdrawal to a position on the slopes of Mount Butler, which in turn was attacked about 0330 hours. Heavy casualties were inflicted on a strong Japanese patrol moving in close formation along the road, but in spite of this set-back, the Japanese continued to press the defenders hard. Ultimately, the Rajputs were forced to quit this position also. Their commander moved with a nucleus battle headquarters over Mount Butler with the object of joining B Company at Tai Hang village via Jardines Lookout. The remaining personnel were sent to Tytam at first light. When the party reached Jardines Lookout half an hour later, heavy fire was opened on them from a distance of 400 yards. Under cover of this fire, the Japanese advanced up the north-west slopes and prevented these men from slipping to Tai Hang. They were, therefore, forced to go through the Japanese positions via Gauge Basin to Tytam Tuk after suffering some casualties. The commander explained the whole position to Brigadier Wallis and expressed his opinion that the line of the high ground would not hold for more than two hours. In the meantime, Brigadier Wallis had received orders to withdraw to the Stone Hill—Stanley area and asked the Battalion Commander to defend the cross-roads at Tytam Tuk to ensure that the brigade's withdrawal was not interfered with by the invaders.[14]

Operations East and West of Taikoo

While C Company of 5/7 Rajput was unsuccessfully trying to prevent Japanese infiltration between Taikoo and Braemar, the invaders secured a foothold in the North Point area held by D Company and rapidly began their advance towards Jardines Lookout. 5/7 Rajput Reserve Company B at Tai Hang had lost touch with battalion headquarters and was, therefore, unable to carry out its counter-attack role. The Japanese, consequently, easily broke through D Company's defences between Braemar and Tai Hang and were able to advance as far as Jardines Lookout, one of the highest peaks on the Island, without further opposition.

[14] War Diary and Narrative of East Infantry Brigade, Appendix B, pp. 89-92.

The last mentioned place, only lightly held by a platoon of the HKVDC, was occupied by the Japanese at midnight (18-19 December).

A Company's positions south of Aldrich Bay also were for the most part by-passed by the Japanese who rapidly occupied the north and north-eastern slopes of Mount Parker. This resulted in a Canadian (RRC) company on the eastern slopes being forced to fall back towards Tytam Gap. The fixed beam at Lyemun was twice attacked by a Japanese patrol with hand grenades and the Officer-in-Charge left the light exposed, locked the doors and withdrew his six men through the Japanese lines to join the Royal Rifles detachment near the Saiwan 6" gun positions in Lyemun Gap. " When he left, the Japanese were shooting straight down the beam with an " Infantry gun ", 50 per cent of the shots hitting the concrete surround of the light ".[15] In the meantime Saiwan anti-aircraft gun positions had been captured by the invaders. A counter-attack by two platoons of Canadians to regain this position was launched at 0100 hours, but it did not succeed. By midnight 18-19 December the situation in the whole north-east sector was fast deteriorating. B Company of 5/7 Rajput was now moving to the area of Pill-Box 43 to the west of North Point, a machine-gun platoon of 1 Middlesex Regiment was stationed near Pill-Box 50 and one platoon of B Company 5/7 Rajput was still holding out in North Point area.

The premises of the Hong Kong Electric Light Company in the same area were defended by a small group of elderly HKVDC volunteers known locally as the Hughesliers.[16] Some time after midnight, the Japanese increased their pressure on the Hughes group, and there was some talk of withdrawing the whole force, but in view of the importance of holding on to the position, it was decided to fight to the last. A withdrawal at this juncture would have saved many precious lives, but there can be no questioning the wisdom of the decision taken because it gave valuable time to the rest of the defenders. As Major-General Maltby himself writes, " The delay the force imposed was very valuable to me ".[17] The Hughesliers fought gallantly against heavy odds throughout the night but by 1000 hours on 19 December the Japanese were

[15] Maltby's Despatch, *op. cit.* p. 712.
[16] This force was formed soon after the outbreak of war in 1939 and consisted of Europeans over 55 years of age, many of them being men of considerable standing and influence in the Colony. This force worked under the Hon. Major J.J. Paterson and its role was the prevention of sabotage to the electric plant. The force was reinforced on 16 December by a number of volunteers which included two officers with military experience, Captains Egal and Jacosta.
[17] Maltby's Despatch, *op. cit.* p. 712.

in great force on the high ground above the Power Station and to the east and south of it. It had by then become obvious that no help could get through and the position being complicated by the presence of a number of women and civilians, a withdrawal was decided on, but a way of escape was denied to them. Scattered Japanese parties were in the coalyard and on either side of Electric Road; the pill-box in Causeway Bay had been overrun; and coming under cross-fire from machine-guns, the Hughes force was forced to seek shelter in the houses opposite the main gate of the King's Slipway. Late in the afternoon, the Japanese offered terms of surrender and threatened to burn the houses in case of refusal. The surrender terms were accepted by the force, only a few managing to escape.

D Company 5/7 Rajput was pressed hard but continued to fight in the same area until the afternoon. The Rajput B Company and 1 Middlesex platoon who were reconnoitring the area north of Tai Hang village were able to provide little assistance to this hard-pressed force. The Company Commander lost his life in action and only a few stragglers from his company managed to join 1 Middlesex positions south of Causeway Bay. Others surrendered along with the Hughesliers after a gallant resistance.

While the Hughesliers were putting up a stiff resistance, heavy fighting was taking place in the Mount Parker area and the sector occupied by A and C Companies of 5/7 Rajput. These two companies held their ground to the last, but their positions were mostly overrun in the early hours of the morning of 19 December. Pill-Box 40 continued to fire till 0330 hours and other isolated units in the area temporarily kept the invaders at bay until shortly before dawn when they were forced to surrender.

In unsuccessful counter-attacks which the Royal Rifles of Canada delivered in the Mount Parker and Sai Wan areas, it both suffered and inflicted heavy casualties. Between 0400 and 0600 hours, reinforcing platoons of the Royal Rifles of Canada were sent forward on to the Mount Parker high ground, but they failed in their efforts to evict the Japanese from the summit of the hill.

At daybreak on 19 December, the Japanese were securely in possession of Jardine's Lookout, Mount Bulter and the northern slopes of Mount Parker. With these places in their hands, the Japanese could fan out to the east and west and could easily advance up the valleys leading to the high ground in the centre of the Island, A signal sent from Hong Kong to General Headquarters Far East at this time described the situation as " very grave ",[18] because of

---

[18] War Diary, General Headquarters Far East, Vol. II, Sheet No. 308.

deep Japanese penetration. The small force at North Point was still holding out against heavy odds, but effective resistance was at an end in the whole north-east sector. The Royal Rifles of Canada found it increasingly difficult to maintain their positions on Mount Parker and since they were obviously not adequate to act as a serious 'stop' to the invaders, Major-General Maltby decided to withdraw them to Tytam Gap. 5/7 Rajput, who had borne the brunt of the initial Japanese push, was now completely disorganised. B Company and a few survivors at Tai Hang and a small number at Tytam were all that remained of that battalion and it was placed under command of 1 Middlesex at Leighton Hill.

In the early morning of 19 December, the Japanese sent heavy reinforcements to their Island force. A number of barges, motor launches and ferries loaded with troops crossed over to North Point; six Motor Torpedo Boats were detailed to attack these from Green Isle. The first attack by two Motor Torpedo Boats (07 to 09) was successful and led to the sinking of one Japanese landing craft; another was set on fire and a third was forced to go back. Each of these barges contained about 40 troops. One of the Allied Motor Torpedo Boats was damaged during the course of this action. The second attack however failed. Without causing any trouble to the invaders one Motor Torpedo Boat was badly damaged. In the course of the third attack by two Motor Torpedo Boats, one sank with all hands. The Japanese aircraft covered the landings by attacking Allied positions with light bombs and machine-gun fire. Allied casualties in this counter-attack, according to Major-General Maltby "amounted to 50 per cent".[19]

TYTAM GAP

The Japanese occupation of Mount Parker was a serious threat to the position of East Brigade Headquarters in Tytam Gap. At 0900 hours on 19 December small arms fire was directed on Tytam from Mount Parker. In the meantime No. 6 Platoon of No. 2 Company HKVDC at Pottinger engaged Japanese troops moving from Lyemun towards Tytam and one Japanese Platoon was observed moving down from Jardine's Lookout towards Wong Nei Chong, the headquarters of West Infantry Brigade. The fighting thereafter was chiefly concentrated around the Gaps (Tytam and Wong Nei Chong).

Half an hour later, Brigadier Wallis gave to the General Officer Commanding his appreciation of the situation, the main

---

[19] Maltby's Despatch, *op. cit.* p. 714.

object of which was to create a mobile reserve to operate effectively against the Japanese, whose estimated strength on the Island was two battalions which was being steadily reinforced. The Allied troops were widely scattered from Stanley View (613924) to Shiek O and were useless against an invader operating from high ground. Brigadier Wallis therefore suggested that all available infantry should be concentrated. His plan envisaged stationing of Royal Rifles of Canada, D Company 1 Middlesex and part of B Company 1 Middlesex and 2 Company HKVDC in Stone Hill—Stanley village area south of the Twins—Notting Hill line. All mobile artillery at the same time was to be withdrawn from Gauge Basin—Tytam Fork and Red Hill to Stanley peninsula. This force after concentration was to operate either through Gauge Basin or by the Repulse Bay route in order to recapture Mount Butler and Jardine's Lookout. The brigade headquarters was to move to Stone Hill where an exchange existed.

This plan was approved by Major-General Maltby and given effect to in the course of the day. In authorising the withdrawal Major-General Maltby felt that the position at Tytam Gap was extremely precarious and that in the event of a serious attack in that area there existed the grave danger of not only losing the Headquarters but the cutting off of all the troops in the area Collinson Battery—D'Aguilar Peninsula—Obelisk Hill. At the time the above appreciation was being conveyed to the General Officer Commanding, Tytam Gap had come under small arms fire directed from Saiwan Hill, and Brigadier Wallis expected shelling any moment from Mount Parker. The situation at Gauge Basin was uncertain and the Officer Commanding No.1 Company of HKVDC was ordered to hold the defile at all costs. The small Rajput Battalion Headquarters at Tytam Tuk Reservoir was detailed to hold the Tytam cross-roads and ensure adequate co-ordination of local defences until the last troops had passed through at about 1330 hours; it was then to be relieved by a platoon of the Royal Rifles of Canada.

During the withdrawal of the troops to their new positions, several mobile batteries were destroyed. By an unfortunate mistake the officer-in-charge Red Hill Battery (4·5"H) destroyed his guns. Similarly the battery commander at Gauge Basin by remaining in action too long, could not withdraw his guns. The loss of these mobile batteries was a great handicap in subsequent counterattacks by the Allied forces and " went a long way towards preventing East Brigade from again joining hands with West Brigade as the Infantry always found themselves confronted by enemy in commanding positions and were without the necessary covering fire to support any assault".[20]

No loss was suffered by the Allied troops during the course of this withdrawal because low clouds hampered Japanese bombers, but road discipline was bad. All attempts to prevent the bunching of men at the cross-roads proved futile. The withdrawal of the whole brigade, including some 40-50 of the Rajputs, was however completed soon after dusk. By 2200 hours on 19 December, the whole brigade was in its new positions. The remnants of 5/7 Rajput, consisting of some 40 or 50 other ranks along with their battalion commander, occupied positions in Stanley.[21] Royal Rifles of Canada held the line Stanley View—Stanley Mount—Sugar Loaf Hill—the north-east slopes of Stone Hill—Palm Villa. B and D Companies of 1 Middlesex occupied Pill-Boxes 23 to 28; one platoon covered the approaches to the Police Station, and two Platoons were located at Mary Knoll. No. 1 Company HKVDC was held in reserve at Stanley Fort to cover the northern approaches to it.

WONG NEI CHONG GAP

We may now turn to the activities of the West Infantry Brigade with Headquarters in Wong Nei Chong Gap. The retention of this strategically important Gap was a vital factor in the Island defence scheme. Situated in the centre of the Island. the main lines of communication between the East and West Brigades ran through it. Major-General Maltby took steps to reinforce this area in the early hours of the morning of 19 December and arranged with Chief Engineer to send a Royal Engineer party for an infantry fighting role. This party was composed of seventy British and Chinese personnel.[22] When it reached near Wong Nei Chong Gap, it found the West Brigade Headquarters under heavy machine-gun and mortar fire. In the face of this heavy fire, any access to brigade headquarters was out of the question and the Royal Engineers had perforce to take up a position nearby.

The Royal Navy also actively participated in land fighting. They were scheduled to take over Infantry posts in the area of Aberdeen—Little Hong Kong, thereby releasing A Company, Winnipeg Grenadiers, who were to move towards the Gap at about 0500 hours. Nothing is definitely known regarding the fate of this company. It appears that at first light it reached Wong Nei Chong Gap but was ambushed by superior Japanese forces. Some of the troops were killed and the rest were taken prisoner.

[20] War Diary and Narrative of East Infantry Brigade, p 23.
[21] War Diary—5/7 Rajput, p.13.
[22] Account to another report, the party consisted of 70 British and 70 Chinese.

Shortly after first light on 19 December, the Japanese advanced towards the Gap from Jardine's Lookout and occupied the Police Station situated on a prominent knoll within the Gap itself. The Allied forces made several attempts to dislodge the Japanese from this key position during the next two days, but their efforts were of no avail, although they partly reoccupied the Gap in one of their counter-attacks.

Accounts of the fighting in the Jardine's Lookout—Wong Nei Chong Gap area are extremely confused in character. This was perhaps inevitable, because no less than seven units were involved which had separate commanders, and some of the troops, like the Royal Navy, Royal Artillery and Royal Engineers, were fighting in an unaccustomed role over unfamiliar terrain. The rapid and unexpected advance of the Japanese during the course of the night had enabled them to concentrate troops in large numbers on the hill-sides surrounding important tactical points. At the same time the disruption of the Allied communications prevented a true appreciation of the situation.

At 0650 hours on 19 December, the Japanese attacked the 3·7-inch anti-aircraft positions at Stanley Gap from west and southwest. Two small reinforcing parties were wiped out by the Japanese. By 0830 hours the Allied troops had to be withdrawn on account of Japanese pressure. No. 3 Company HKVDC fought with great tenacity and bravery in this area suffering 85 casualties out of a total strength of 115. Major-General Maltby tried to create a diversion by means of a counter-attack on Jardine's Lookout. A Company of 2 Royal Scots was withdrawn from reserve in the defence sector of 2/14 Punjab. At 0730 hours this company left Wanchai Gap and proceeded along Stubbs Road up to the road-junction. Japanese automatic fire caused heavy casualties to this force, and fire from Jardine's Lookout was too heavy to permit an attack to be launched. By 1400 hours the force managed to force its way to within a few yards of West Brigade Headquarters but heavy machine-gun fire reduced the company to only 20 effectives or so.

Brigadier Lawson phoned Fortress Headquarters at 1000 hours on 19 December to say that he and his staff were about to go into action outside his Headquarters as his shelters were surrounded and firing was taking place at point-blank range inside them. He did so and was killed just outside. Fighting here was severe and practically continuous. Various shelters changed hands several times, but in spite of the best efforts of the Allies, the Japanese secured " a definite lodgment ". The Allies both inflicted and suffered heavy casualties. Major-General Maltby was informed by a Japanese Staff Officer after the capitulation that his side also had suffered very heavy casualties in this area.[23] The fighting here was of a "most confused" nature, and claims have been made that in the course of counter-attacks Wong Nei Chong Gap was regained by the Allies. The Allied troops certainly got within close proximity of the Gap and for most of the time, it was a hotly contested "no man's land".

A party of 2/14 Punjab was sent to Stubbs Road at 1000 hours on 19 December from Wanchai Gap with three Bren-carriers to cover the evacuation of West Brigade Headquarters, but it arrived at the place too late to be of any assistance. On its return journey the party was attacked and its officer was killed in a moment of exposure, although the three carriers were brought back safely.[24]

Meanwhile B Company 2/14 Punjab was moved out from the Police Station area in Victoria at 0330 hours with the object of capturing two small features north and north-west of Jardine's Lookout. The Japanese were contacted at about 0545 hours in the area of Petrol Pump and Filter Beds east of Jardine's Lookout, and were attacked with hand grenades and small arms. Shooting continued for nearly four hours causing heavy casualties on each side. But the hill features were occupied by 1000 hours and the Japanese were driven away from the neighbourhood of the Gap. This enabled 2/14 Punjab to man the gap between 1 Middlesex on Caroline Hill and 2 Royal Scots to their south. The battalion under its commander stuck to the posts against heavy mortar and shell fire in spite of the withdrawal of the flanking units. But after a gallant defence it was finally forced to retire during the afternoon of 21 December.

At 1100 hours on 19 December, the Commander 2/14 Punjab received orders to counter-attack with two companies, A and D, in an easterly direction from Leighton Hill with the object of linking up with D Company 5/7 Rajput in the North Point area. This attack, it was assumed, would cut in at the Japanese rear and also obstruct further landings and movements in the North Point area. 2/14 Punjab made a preliminary reconnaissance at about 1200 hours but little information about Japanese movements could be obtained. Liaison with the Middlesex Regiment produced no better results and owing to a break in communications between Fortress Headquarters and 1 Middlesex Headquarters no further information was obtained. The Punjabis reached their first objective, Caroline Hill, without incident, form where they

---

[23] Maltby's Despatch, *op. cit.* p. 714 foot note.
[24] The War in Hong Kong—2/14 Punjab, p. 14.

wanted to attack up the slope of a high hill from which Causeway Bay Reservoir was clearly visible. The country was extremely difficult, consisting of deep ravines and steep ridges. Covering troops of 1 Middlesex came forward to support the Punjabi companies, and the combined force advanced to its final objective, a high-ridge overlooking Caroline Hill, nearly 1000 yards to the north-east. When the Allied troops were only a few feet from the top, contact was made with the Japanese. Then followed fierce fighting in the course of which one or two men managed to get a glimpse of the country beyond, but there was no sign of D Company 5/7 Rajput. Consequently the Allied troops, unable to force the Japanese position, withdrew to Caroline Hill and thence to the Race Course, where transport was waiting to take them back to their city positions. During this action, the Allies suffered casualties amounting to 30 killed and wounded. It was later learnt that while fighting was in progress, the few 5/7 Rajput survivors had slipped through Japanese lines and rejoined their battalion.[25]

Fully realising the necessity of the recapture of Wong Nei Chong Gap, Major-General Maltby ordered a general advance eastwards to begin at 1500 hours. The first objective to be reached was the line Middle Spur —Wong Nei Chong Reservoir—Clements Ride, after which they were to join up with the men of A and D Companies 2/14 Punjab who were carrying out an attack in the Tai Hang village area. Troops on the flank based on Mount Cameron were to attack the objectives Middle Gap—Wong Nei Chong Reservoir—Gauge Basin. The Royal Scots was detailed to counter-attack Jardine's Lookout, supported by only eight field-guns.

Two companies of 2 Royal Scots and one company of Winnipeg Grenadiers left Mount Cameron and proceeded along Black's Link with the intention of joining up with the other Allied troops at Wong Nei Chong Gap. By 1745 hours the entire force reached a point just short of Wong Nei Chong Gap. Subsequently, they could not make any headway due to heavy Japanese fire, and were forced to withdraw. They eventually reached Wanchai at 0200 hours on 20 December.[26] At dawn the same day the Winnipeg Grenadiers held the line Middle Gap—Cable Hill with 2 Royal Scots on the north-east slopes of Mount Nicholson.

In the meantime the general counter-attack by Major-General Maltby to recapture the Gap had failed, because the Japanese were found to be in greater strength than had been originally believed. On the other hand at about 1630 hours the

[25] *Ibid.* p. 16.
[26] Canadian Participation, p. 48.

invaders heavily shelled Leighton Hill area which was occupied by Headquarters 1 Middlesex, B Rajput Company and B Company of 2/14 Punjab.

During the night of 19/20 December West Brigade, reinforced by about 100 Indian gunners and 2 armoured cars, was sent from Repulse Bay by Brigadier Wallis, and temporarily reoccupied Wong Nei Chong Gap, which seems to have been deserted by the Japanese. An hour later an attack on the Police Station was launched by B Company of 2 Royal Scots under covering fire from Bren Guns. These troops forced their way up to the Police Station but there met with heavy grenade fire. This prevented them from making further headway and they had to withdraw to the east end of Black's Link. Another attack on the Police Station at about 0300 hours had a similar fate. Meanwhile C Company of 2 Royal Scots attacked towards Jardine's Lookout, but the attempt was a failure. Just before dawn 2 Royal Scots took up defensive positions for the day; D Company just west of the Gap and B Company echeloned behind. By that time the Gap was a "no man's land", invested by the Japanese on three sides (north, south and east). One company of Winnipeg Grenadiers which had a protective role for West Brigade Headquarters, continued to hold its position to the north of the Police Station until 0700 hours of 22 December.

The Allied troops had now been fighting continuously for eleven days, and were undoubtedly suffering badly from lack of sleep. Signs of strain were beginning to appear. To encourage the tired forces the Governor sent the following message at 2030 hours—" The time has come to advance against the enemy. The eyes of the Empire are upon you. Be strong, be resolute and do your duty ".

FIGHTING IN THE EASTERN HALF OF THE ISLAND

The withdrawal of the East Brigade from Tytam Gap to its new positions had not only enabled the Japanese to consolidate their gains in the eastern half of the Island, but also to erect a double wedge between Stanley Peninsula and the western portion of the Island. Brick Hill in the south-west, and Violet Hill to the south of Stanley Gap had been occupied by them during the night and a small party had found lodgment in the buildings south-west of Repulse Bay Hotel by 0740 hours on 20 December. Japanese troops had also occupied Middle Spur thereby hindering any Allied advance from the south towards Wong Nei Chong Gap.

The Royal Rifles of Canada detailed for the counter-attack along the shore of Repulse Bay was not in good condition. Because of lack of proper nourishment and continuous fighting for several days, even in the earliest stage of the Island fighting, it is recorded: " some would fall down in the roadway and go to sleep, and it took several shakings to get them going again ". A counter-attack by an exhausted and depleted battalion without adequate fire support in a mountainous terrain was a task of great difficulty. Nevertheless, during the next three days the East Brigade at Stanley made a series of gallant attempts to drive northwards and join hands with the main body of troops by piercing through the Japanese lines. The first attempt took the form of a leftward thrust by the Repulse Bay route, as the unexpected withdrawal of Headquarters No. 1 Company HKVDC from Gauge Basin had rendered an advance by that line almost impossible. A Company Royal Rifles of Canada followed by B, and D Companies began the advance at 0800 hours and, after overcoming Japanese resistance, occupied Repulse Bay Hotel garage by 1100 hours. The Canadians then took up defensive positions in the Hotel and in a large private building just beyond Castle Eucliff since they were unable to advance further in the face of fierce machine-gun fire from hill positions. All attempts to capture Middle Spur or reach the road-junction failed. It was therefore decided to withdraw some of the troops to their original positions about noon.

A Company Royal Rifles of Canada was ordered to defend the Hotel at all costs, but it ran the risk of being surrounded during the night by the Japanese who were holding all the dominating features. D Company made an effort to reach Wong Nei Chong Gap across country by the east side of Violet Hill. ' An exceedingly stiff climb was followed by moves of some 2800 yards through two water catchments which ran generally in a north-westerly direction '. The troops came under heavy fire from artillery estimated to be 75-mm from Violet Hill, so their commander decided to give up the idea of reaching the West Brigade. The company returned to Stanley View at 2100 hours under heavy rain and took up positions at the Chung Ham Kok for the night.

After the failure of this effort, Brigadier Wallis decided upon a new plan of attack, confirmation of which was received from Fortress Headquarters late in the evening. The new plan envisaged an attack through Tytam Tuk and Gauge Basin and it was hoped that this would relieve pressure on West Brigade and Repulse Bay area and enable East Brigade to maintain contact with West Brigade. The plan was given effect to the next day. From intermittent rifle and LMG fire during the night of 20/21 December, it appeared that the Japanese were in contact with the Allied forces from the Twins feature.

FIGHTING IN THE WESTERN SECTOR

On the western side of the Japanese 'wedge', A Company 2/14 Punjab had been ordered to clear the road from Aberdeen to Shouson Hill to the south-east of Little Hong Kong and ultimately link up with East Brigade in the Middle Spur area. The company had little information concerning Japanese dispositions, but it was known that they held a position astride the main road between Aberdeen and Deep Water Bay. The company numbering only twenty-five reached Aberdeen via Pok Fulam. They came into contact with the Japanese at the road-junction Cookhouse Lane—Island Road, where the latter had a strong machine-gun post in a culvert under the road. All efforts to dislodge the Japanese failed in spite of several casualties suffered by this small force, which had to spend the night on the road. Two carriers sent from Rear Headquarters proved to be of little use with the road most effectively blocked by two 15-cwt. trucks disabled earlier in the day. The night passed off without incident, but the troops, without waterproofs and great-coats, had to undergo a severe ordeal on account of rain which fell throughout this period. Only in the morning (20 December) did the party receive some welcome food and ammunition.

The West Brigade had been without a commander after Brigadier Lawson's death till the morning of 20 December when Colonel H.B. Rose (HKVDC) took over command. Its role as before was to clear the Japanese from Wong Nei Chong Gap and to establish itself on Stanley Gap high ground. To achieve these objects a counter-attack was launched from Wanchai Gap via Black's Link at 1930 hours on 20 December by a company of Winnipeg Grenadiers. This company was given adequate artillery support, but nothing was achieved nor could it succeed in the preliminary clearing of Mount Nicholson owing to the strength of the Japanese there.

In the meantime, the Japanese had launched a counterattack at 1700 hours, and drove out a company of 2 Royal Scot and some Winnipeg Grenadiers from Wong Nei Chong Gap. From there, Japanese troops moved to the high ground, Mount Nicholson. Just before the last light they also succeeded in dislodging British and Canadian troops from their positions on the eastern slopes of Mount Nicholson, and by dawn of 21 December the Japanese had succeeded in advancing as far as the middle Gap after inflicting heavy casualties on the Canadian troops in that area.

During the afternoon the Japanese ferried considerable troops from the Mainland and landed them in the North Point area and Taikoo Docks. Landing areas were shelled by West Brigade artillery guns, but its results could not be observed. About this time, a report was received that Chinese planes had bombed Kowloon, and the Chinese had concentrated 60,000 troops at Sham Chun on the frontier ready to launch an attack. The following message was therefore issued to all units:—

"There are indications that Chinese forces are advancing towards the frontier to our aid. All ranks must therefore hold their positions at all costs and look forward to only a few more days of strain".

The night of 20/21 December caused severe strain to the tired forward troops in the different parts of the Island because of heavy rain and bad visibility. Few had great coats and many had to go without meals for about 24 hours. By midnight it was arranged to post two 3·7-inch howitzers near Stanley Prison and the East Brigade had at its disposal only one 18-pounder from a Beach Defence Unit. Lack of adequate artillery was one of the main reasons for the failure of the counter-attack launched by East-Brigade on 21 December. To encourage the garrison the Secretary of State for War sent another message which was received at 0445 hours on 21 December.

"We send you and troops under your command," said the message, "our congratulations on the splendid defence you are making. Your continued resistance plays an important part in our struggle with Japan by extending the enemy and denying to him facilities of great value. Your tenacity is worthy of the highest traditions of the Armies of the Empire. Secretary of State for the Colonies associates himself personally with this message and sends his own congratulations and good wishes to the Governor and his officers."

Brigadier Wallis, after the failure of the attempt to reach Wong Nei Chong Gap by the Repulse Bay route the previous day, decided to send his troops via Tytam. The attack was scheduled to be launched at 0900 hours on 21 December at the earliest, but delay was caused by lack of transport and the virtual breakdown of unit communications. The failure to move early cost the brigade dear. The carriers were slow in moving off and in the meantime the Japanese forestalled the column by occupying Red Hill—Tytam Tuk cross-roads and Bridge Hill. At 0915 hours the advance guard consisting of No. 1 Company HKVDC moved off from Palm Villa and soon after encountered strong opposition at the cross-roads south of Tytam Tuk Reservoir. The troops came under rifle and machine-gun fire from Notting Hill on the left and Red Hill on the right. The force was reinforced by D Company of Royal Rifles of Canada. An attack on the Japanese positions on Brigade Hill was pressed with great vigour and this hill feature along with Notting Hill came into Allied hands by 1300 hours. A Japanese party holding the cross-roads was almost wiped out, but the going was very slow.[27]

The advance was resumed, but it came to a halt in face of machine-gun fire from Tytam cross-roads and considerable resistance by Japanese troops. The road on the west of the Reservoir was clear of Japanese troops, but the Royal Rifles of Canada could not advance further because of the wide dispersal of the various companies. At 1700 hours the Japanese launched a counter-attack with three light tanks, but were forced to withdraw after a brisk exchange of fire. As darkness fell, it was realised that further advance was impossible and the footing gained on part of Brigade Hill was precarious. The Japanese were in strength in Gauge Basin and on the Twins and were in occupation of Red Hill and Tytam Tuk cross-roads. Thus there was a grave danger of the Japanese capturing Stone Hill Headquarters. It was therefore decided to withdraw all the troops to their former positions at 1800 hours. This was the last serious effort made by either East or West Brigade to recapture the Gap, and from then onwards both brigades worked independently.

During the day the gun-boat *Cicala* was ordered to assist land operations in the Deep Water Bay area. It shelled Japanese mortar and artillery positions, scoring several hits. Unfortunately due to repeated air attacks she was badly holed and sank later in the Lamma channel.

In the sector Aberdeen—Shouson Hill, the Japanese abandoned their previous positions and were now in occupation of Shouson Hill, which in normal times was a popular residential site. The Japanese had to be evicted by a very small 2/14 Punjab force with no machine-gun or mobile artillery support. The advance started at about 0800 hours on 21 December and all went well in the beginning. The party got within 20 yards of the summit, but scarcely had the final assault started when the company was caught by a withering fire from the summit of the hill and from a nearby house. There was no cover whatsoever and the steep ascent made

[27] War Diary and Narrative of East Infantry Brigade, p. 50.

a foothold difficult to maintain. In a close and extremely fierce fight, only eight men survived out of a total of 20.[28] The remnants of the party withdrew to Headquarters C Company 1 Middlesex at Little Hong Kong.

WANCHAI GAP AND THE STANLEY PENINSULA

In the north-west sector on 21 December, a fresh attack was launched by the Winnipeg Grenadiers from Middle Gap to recapture Wong Nei Chong Gap, but the attack was a failure and the Canadians withdrew after suffering some casualties. The position deteriorated in this area during the course of the day. At 1025 hours a report was received by the General Officer Commanding that the Allied troops were being pushed back north of Black Link and Mount Cameron. The Winnipeg Grenadiers holding the latter place were ordered to stick to their positions at all costs and they did hold it under heavy mortar fire and dive-bombing attacks throughout the day. In the meantime Major-General Maltby, in anticipation of a Japanese break-through from the Mount Cameron area, had reinforced Wanchai Gap (the headquarters West Infantry Brigade and the Winnipeg Grenadiers) with a section of machine-guns. All 2/14 Punjab garrisons from pill-boxes on the north shore were asked to withdraw to Battalion Headquarters. D Company 2/14 Punjab was rearranged facing south-east, linking up with the forces on its right at Wanchai Gap so as to cover a possible break-through by the Japanese from that direction. There was some mortar shelling and sniping of their area, but by nightfall all was fairly quiet.

The isolated B Company of 2/14 Punjab, with a total strength of only thirty-five, at the foot of Jardine's Lookout was attacked from three different sides in the afternoon of 21 December and compelled to withdraw to Headquarters 2 Royal Scots in Stubbs Road. At about midnight, while this company was with 2 Royal Scots, it had been also subjected on two occasions to very heavy and accurate mortar fire causing casualties. All movement in the area was under observation by the Japanese. During the night, two casualties were caused to B Company 2/14 Punjab by Japanese snipers, after which the company was recalled to Rear Battalion Headquarters and placed in reserve. In the south-west sector, by midday the Allied line of defence ran from Little Hong Kong area to the southern slopes of Mount Cameron. In the former area two parties were holding out and fought very

---

[28] The War in Hong Kong—2/14 Punjab, p. 17.

gallantly, repelling all Japanese attacks from 20 December to the afternoon of 25 December.

On 21 December no further Japanese advance occurred in the western half of the Island after midday. The Allied forces by nightfall held Wanchai Gap, the southern part of Mount Cameron, Little Hong Kong (with its RAOC magazine) and Bennets Hill. Japanese reinforcements continued to cross over to North Point in large numbers. Some troops were also landed near Causeway Bay and the housetops in that area were reported "crowded with them". During the afternoon pill-boxes on the north shore were subjected to accurate high velocity shell fire, Pill-Box 59 receiving as many as thirty direct hits.

At 1600 hours on 21 December, a telegram was received from Chungking that the main Chinese attack could not start before 1 January 1942, but they promised to bomb the aerodromes under Japanese possession.

The night 21/22 December passed quietly on all fronts and there were no attempted Japanese landings. On the 22nd the Japanese increased pressure in Stanley area where Brigadier Wallis had been placed in independent command. The idea of advancing north was given up in view of the Japanese attacks. About this time the Japanese succeeded in cutting off the water supply in Stanley by capturing the machinery in Tytam Reservoir area. There was only two days' supply of water and food for the Repulse Bay area. At 1400 hours the Japanese advanced in the area and the Hotel had to be evacuated by A Company Royal Rifles of Canada during the night. Small parties of women and children had to be left behind. The Japanese also began infiltrating south from the high ground, the Twins and Notting Hill, and by evening they had succeeded in occupying Stanley Mound. The position on Stone Hill was equally precarious. At midday Sugar Loaf Hill was occupied by the Japanese, but they were driven back from this feature by a spirited attack at nightfall. Japanese sniping and light machine-gun fire continued in the forward area throughout the night (22/23 December) but there was little artillery activity.

In the western sector, the Japanese began determined attacks on Mount Cameron during the course of the day (22 December). The area was heavily dive-bombed and mortared at 1030 hours and in the afternoon the Japanese began concentrating troops between Mount Cameron and Little Hong Kong, obviously with a view to attacking Wanchai Gap from that side. The Allied forces gallantly stuck to their posts throughout the day although they had no mortar support and no cover. They could do nothing except stick it out with small arms fire from behind the rocks. Fighting under those handicaps, it is no wonder that the morale of the troops came down perceptibly. In the words of Major-General Maltby, " Morale now had been seriously affected by the feeling that it was futile to continue resistance with insufficient equipment, with insufficient mobile artillery support, and without both air support and air observation ".[29]

On the northern slopes of Mount Nicholson, the Japanese consolidated their position in the early afternoon and began digging in within one hundred yards of the 2 Royal Scots' forward defence positions. This necessitated a readjustment of the Allied line in the area of the Filter Beds north of Mount Nicholson. There existed a gap between the right flank of the 2/14 Punjab and the left of 2 Royal Scots which gave the Japanese " a line of attack towards the Race Course ".[30] It was clear that an attack through this gap would envelop the whole Leighton Hill area, and cut straight in to Wanchai. Major-General Maltby felt that he had insufficient troops to meet such a contingency.[31] However, D Company of 2/14 Punjab was moved to the area south-east of the Race Course, thus establishing a link with the Royal Scots west of Mount Nicholson Camp.

At 1600 hours the Japanese opened a very heavy mortar fire in the Leighton Hill area, necessitating the withdrawal of Headquarters 1 Middlesex Regiment to Hennessey Road, Wanchai —the densely populated area—west of Mount Parish. The small Rajput group was ordered to face south-east as a precautionary measure against Japanese penetration in the area. The Japanese attacked the company's positions, but it held its ground successfully, although the company was of a composite nature of only two platoons formed from the remnants of B and D Companies of 5/7 Rajput.

After midnight the position in the whole of the Wanchai Gap area developed adversely for the defence. Mount Cameron was captured by the Japanese at about 0130 hours and the Allied troops withdrew in disorder between Magazine Gap and Mount Gough where an effort was made to rally them. The vital area between Magazine and Wanchai Gaps was lightly held at daybreak by Royal Engineer personnel and two companies of HKVDC. A party of marines was rushed up to this area, while considerable Japanese movements were noticed on Mounts Cameron and Nicholson.

[29] Maltby's Despatch, *op. cit.* p. 719.
[30] *Ibid.* p. 720.
[31] *Ibid.*

Between 0800 and 1100 hours on 23 December, the General Officer Commanding received conflicting reports regarding the situation in Mount Cameron area, but it was clear that the Japanese held "the crest of this commanding and important feature".[32] Their local headquarters and organising centre was located in Wong Nei Chong Gap but due to the configuration of the ground it was not possible to shell it effectively.

Meanwhile the situation at Leighton Hill gave some cause for anxiety. There was increasing artillery fire in this area during the morning and afternoon and the remnants of the composite company of 5/7 Rajput, sadly reduced in numbers and being short of food and ammunition, were forced to withdraw at about 0800 hours. This withdrawal exposed the right flank of the Middlesex position on Leighton Hill. At 0922 hours the Japanese infiltrated there in large numbers, occupying houses and streets, and at 1000 hours the Middlesex positions were attacked strongly.

By 1400 hours the Japanese had succeeded in forcing some of the Allied troops back from Leighton Hill after a severe artillery bombardment. At the same time Magazine and Wanchai Gaps were subjected to heavy bombing from the air. According to Major-General Maltby the position at these gaps was "unenviable" and provided "an excellent target for the enemy airforce, which did not fail to take due advantage of the opportunity".[33]

At 1430 hours on 23 December the new Allied line in the western sector ran from Wanchai Gap to Bennets Hill in the south, with the Royal Scots holding the west slopes of Mount Cameron and patrolling forward. Bennets Hill was successfully defended in the afternoon and a Japanese attack was beaten off. No further attacks took place in the evening and the night was comparatively quiet, except for a minor skirmish on the northern slopes of Mount Cameron in which a Japanese patrol suffered casualties.

The 2/14 Punjab positions in Victoria City underwent only slight change during 23-25 December. A Company personnel totalling only six went back to battalion headquarters from Little Hong Kong since they were serving no useful purpose there. This occurred on the morning of the 23rd. At that time B Company was in reserve while C and D Companies remained in their original positions near Fortress Headquarters in order to provide a "last ditch" resistance if it became necessary.

At the same time, in the Stanley Peninsula, the Allied forces did not fare any better. The counter-attack against Stanley Mound started at about 0730 hours on 23 December, but by 1040

[32] *Ibid.* p. 720.
[33] *Ibid.* p. 721.

hours it was clear that the attack had failed. The Royal Rifles of Canada had suffered heavy casualties, its losses since the outbreak of hostilities being 18 officers killed or wounded. The Japanese started infiltrating in this area soon after and the Canadians were forced to withdraw by 1900 hours, since they felt that they could put up a better resistance on flatter ground and on a narrower front. At last light the whole East Brigade was reorganised along the line across Stanley Peninsula from near Pill-Box 27, to Tytam Bay through St. Stephens College buildings to West Bay, with Brigade Headquarters at Stanley prison. The 1 Middlesex crew had withdrawn from the Repulse Bay area with all their equipment intact. Shelling of the whole of Stanley Peninsula area was severe on 23 and 24 December but there was enough food, water and ammunition for the garrison.

In the morning of 24 December dispositions of West Brigade were as follows:—Brigade Headquarters was at Magazine Gap; the Royal Scots and Winnipeg Grenadiers were holding Wanchai Gap; the Royal Scots still occupied west slopes of Mount Cameron; 1 Middlesex held Race Course and part of Leighton Hill and two companies (4 and 7) HKVDC manned the area from Mount Kellet to Mount Gough. The Japanese mainly concentrated on the Race Course—Leighton Hill sector in the north, and advanced to a point near the Cemetry south of the Race Course. One reserve platoon of Rajput was put on Mount Parish to strengthen that weakly held area. At the same time 30 marines arrived to patrol the higher ground on the right of this area, upto Wanchai Gap. At about 1500 hours after a severe artillery and mortar bombardment in addition to dive-bombing, the Japanese attacked Leighton Hill. The garrison, being pressed from three sides, was rapidly surrounded. The Hill feature was occupied by the Japanese at 1530 hours. At 1645 hours, troops were authorised to escape through the streets leading north-west to Canal Road. During the withdrawal, 1 Middlesex suffered 25 per cent casualties after a determined and valuable resistance. After withdrawal the troops took up defensive positions in the area between Lee Theatre and Canal Road. With the capture of Leighton Hill, the Rajput post to the south-east of Race Course was withdrawn, but there was no change in the other occupied positions. An attack on Mount Parish by the Japanese, shortly before midnight, was successfully repulsed by the Rajput platoon with casualties on both sides.

At about 2200 hours on 24 December there was a general move by the Japanese from Mount Nicholson—Mount Cameron area, northwards towards the Race Course. Between 2200 and

2300 hours the Central District of Victoria came under 3-inch mortar bombardment.

About this time Christmas greetings were sent to all units by the Governor and the Prime Minister. The former read:—

"In pride and admiration I send my greetings this Xmas Day to all who are fighting and to all who are working so nobly and so well to sustain Hong Kong against the assault of the enemy.

Fight on. Hold fast for King and Empire.

God bless you all in this your finest hour".

The message from the Prime Minister was as under:—

"Xmas greetings to you all. Let this day be historical in the proud annals of our Empire.

The order of the day is hold fast".

But Christmas Day was not destined to give any respite to the beleaguered garrison, which was utterly worn out in continuous "back to the wall" fighting.

The Royal Rifles of Canada was withdrawn to Stanley Fort well down the Peninsula away from contact with the Japanese. But this respite was of a very short duration. About 1800 hours on 24 December the Japanese, after a severe artillery and mortar bombardment of East Brigade positions, launched a strong offensive in the Stanley Peninsula area. They were able to move south by the eastern and western beaches and from house to house down the centre of the Peninsula. Very heavy fighting took place at Stanley Police Station until 2330 hours. Mary Knoll defenders continued to resist until 0500 hours on 25 December, and only a few survivors managed to escape. The position was captured by the Japanese at 0630 hours. The Japanese succeeded in infiltrating south-east from Stanley View about midnight on 24-25 December. The Royal Rifles had to be brought back in the early hours of Christmas Day because of increasing pressure. Brigadier Wallis ordered a counter-attack near Stanley Prison in the afternoon to recover the ground lost during the night. But it did not succeed although the attacking company suffered heavily. From about 1600 hours the Japanese intensified their artillery fire on Stanley Fort and destroyed much equipment. In the late evening another company of the Royal Rifles was moving forward in face of Japanese fire when a car, flying a white flag came down the road with the news that the Colony had surrendered to the invaders. Brigadier Wallis was not prepared to believe the news and continued the fight till he had confirmation for which he sent his Brigade Major to the headquarters. The latter returned in the early hours of 26 December with written orders to surrender and then Brigadier

Wallis ordered the hoisting of the white flag and the cease fire for Stanley Force at 0230 hours on 26 December.

In the western half of the Island, around midnight, a Japanese attack in the area to the south of Wanchai Gap was successful and they effected a slight penetration. They also succeeded in occupying the northern slopes of Bennets Hill where they " dug in " during the night of 24/25 December but the Allied troops continued to hold the eastern slopes till daylight.

At dawn on 25 December, the position in the Wanchai Gap area became serious for the defenders. Although anti-tank mines had been laid in the main approaches to Wanchai from the east, yet the invaders succeeded in infiltrating from house to house. At about 0700 hours the Japanese put up a heavy concentration of artillery and mortar fire on Wanchai Gap and an hour later they occupied a line from the south end of Canal Road to the west arm of Causeway Bay.

THE SURRENDER

The defenders of Hong Kong found themselves in desperate straits on the morning of 25 December. Shortly after 0900 hours two Englishmen, well-known in the Colony, came across the Japanese lines under a white flag. They were sent to Fortress Headquarters by the Japanese and described to the General Officer Commanding the " incredible " amount of Japanese guns and troops they had seen during their journey across the Island from Repulse Bay and emphasised the hopelessness of continuing further resistance. They also stated that the Japanese would observe a truce for three hours while the garrison debated the question of surrender. This impromptu " truce " was difficult to stage, for Japanese planes, operating from Canton, did not conform to this and kept bombing Stanley, Aberdeen and Mount Gough.

An emergency meeting of the Defence Council which met at 1000 hours on 25 December considered the proposal for surrender, and decided to continue the fight. After the expiry of the truce period at midday Japanese artillery opened up on a large-scale. The Japanese rapidly resumed their offensive and within half an hour a platoon 5/7 Rajput on Mount Parish reported fierce hand-to-hand fighting against an overwhelming number of Japanese troops. By 1300 hours the platoon was forced to withdraw to the north-west, and Mount Parish fell into the invaders' hands. With its fall, the Japanese advanced along Kennedy Road putting Fortress Headquarters area, which was garrisoned by only one platoon of 2/14 Punjab, in jeopardy. Communications were difficult to maintain and between 1100 and 1200 hours there was no contact by Fortress Headquarters with Stanley area, and Wanchai and Magazine Gaps. In many parts the North Face Road was quite impassable to all except runners due to damage caused by shell-fire.

Between 1300 and 1430 hours, the Allied troops consisting of 5/7 Rajput, some 60 to 70 men of 1 Middlesex Regiment and small parties of Royal Navy and Royal Engineers held the Canal area north of the Race Course when the Japanese increased their pressure. At 1430 hours B Company 2/14 Punjab was sent to reinforce them, but in spite of this a withdrawal to second line (O'Brien Street Line) 500 yards to the west, was considered advisable. Headquarters 1 Middlesex withdrew to Murray Barracks.

The situation then deteriorated rapidly. Wanchai Gap was captured by the Japanese shortly after 1430 hours after a heavy dive-bombing attack lasting for half an hour. Magazine Gap was similarly attacked and incendiaries were dropped which set the hill-side on fire and burnt the field cables. The Commander West Infantry Brigade reported to Fortress Headquarters that the area could not be held for more than 24 hours at the most against a determined attack. At 1450 hours the new 1 Middlesex—5/7 Rajput line less than a mile from Fortress Headquarters was reported to be breaking and could not hold out for more than half an hour. Bennets Hill had been forced to surrender. There had been no touch with Little Hong Kong and East Brigade Headquarters at Stanley since midday, and their resistance could not in any way influence the position in the western half of the Island. Two 2/14 Punjab companies (C and D) and a mere handful of tired troops stood between the invader and the thickly populated central district of Victoria.

Consequently, taking into consideration these and other factors like the strength of the Japanese, the exhaustion of the Allied troops by their strenuous struggle against enormous odds, the lack of ammunition and the serious water famine, Major-General Maltby decided that further fighting was no longer justified. Continuance of the fight would have meant useless slaughter of the remaining troops and considerable hardship to the civil population without affecting the final outcome of the struggle. At 1515 hours, therefore, he advised the Governor, Sir Mark Young, to cease fighting, and all commanding officers were ordered to break off fighting and surrender to the nearest Japanese commander as opportunity offered.

The formal surrender of the garrison took place at the Japanese Headquarters in Tai Hang at 1800 hours, but as mentioned earlier, the capitulation of the force at Stanley was delayed till the early hours of 26 December.

After the surrender, Lord Moyne, Secretary of State for the Colonies sent the following message to the Governor:—

"It is a good fight you have fought........The defence of Hong Kong will live in the story of the Empire, to which it adds yet another chapter of courage and endurance".

Thus Hong Kong became the first British possession in the Far East to fall into Japanese hands after a heroic struggle of eighteen days. The Colony fell to the Japanese assault more rapidly than had been expected, but Japan's control of the seas had sealed the fate of this isolated outpost long before the garrison actually surrendered. The defence of the Colony, short-lived though it was, was considered to be of great value to the Allied over-all strategy in the Pacific. In the words of Major-General Maltby:—

"I submit that although I and my forces may have been a hostage to fortune, we were a detachment that deflected from more important objectives, such as the Philippines, Singapore, or perhaps even Australia, an enemy force that consisted of two first line divisions, one reserve division, corps artillery, about eighty aircraft and a considerable naval blockade force. Strategically we gambled and lost, but it was a worthwhile gamble".[34]

[34] *Ibid.* p. 700

Malaya

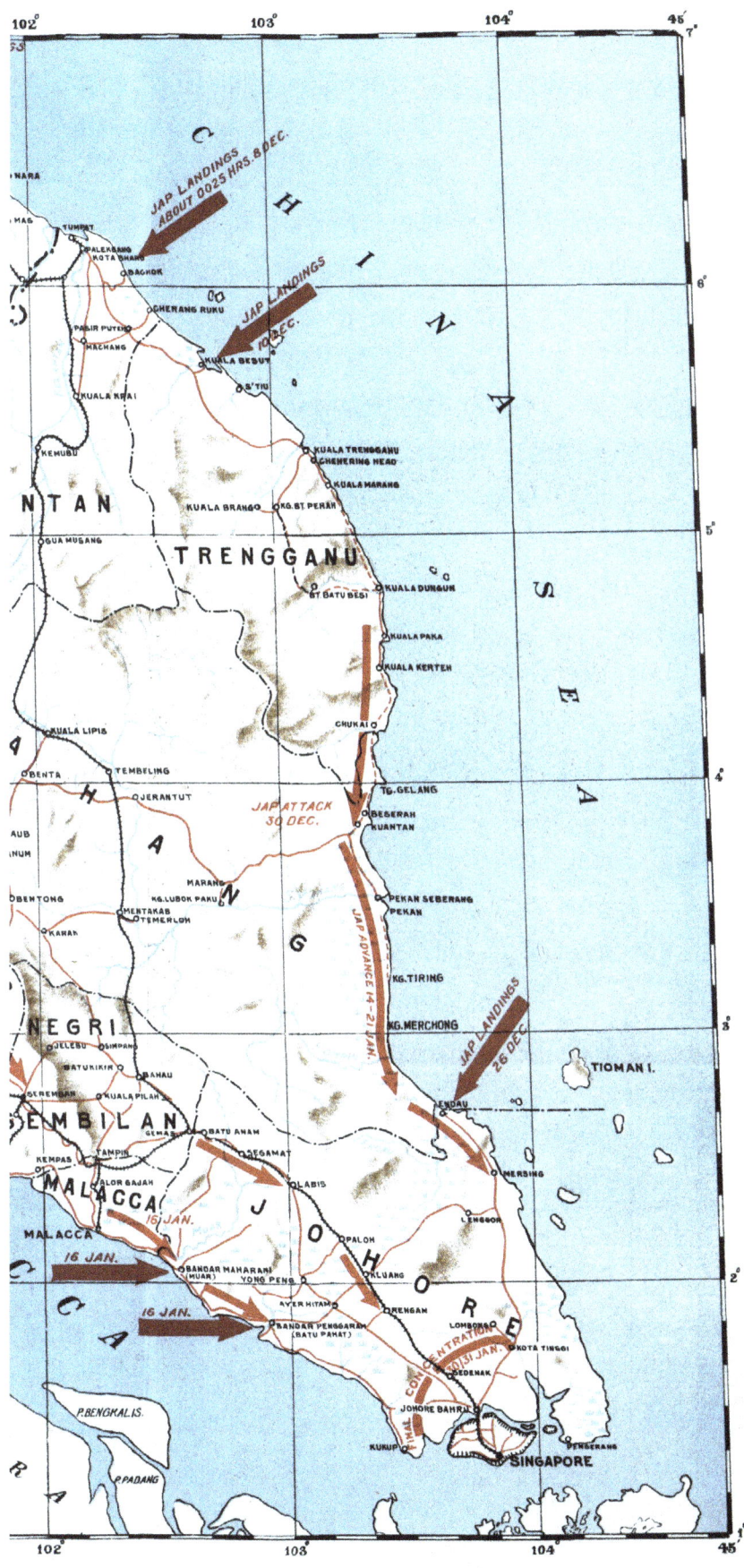

CHAPTER V

Malaya, the Land and the People

The sacrifice of the defenders of Hong Kong was meant primarily to give indirect help to the British forces in Malaya, which was of tremendous strategic importance for the control of South-East Asia. As such, the campaign in Malaya deserves to be studied in considerable detail.

GEOGRAPHY

Malaya is situated approximately between 1° and 7° North and 100° and 104° East. Geographically, the peninsula begins at the isthmus of Kra and ends at Tanjong Bulus, and is bounded by Thailand, China Sea, the Singapore Straits and the Strait of of Malacca. At the beginning of the Second World War, however, the territory of Malaya did not extend beyond Perlis in the north or Singapore in the south. Its length then was about six hundred miles and its breadth not more than two hundred.

A range of granite mountains runs like a spine north and south and divides the peninsula into two portions, the larger of which lies to the east. This is known as the Great Central Range. Smaller ranges run parallel to it in many places, and there are isolated spurs from almost all of them. The descent from the summits of the Central Range is gradual on the western side and full of alluvial deposits of tin, while on the eastern side it is extremely steep and covered by granite, quartz and limestone formations. The highest mountain is believed to be Gunong Tahan on the northern frontier of Pahang, with its tallest peak 7,160 feet high. On the west, the coast is bordered by mangrove-swamps many miles in width. The east coast is served by the north-east monsoon which occurs from November to February and has sandy beaches extending over several miles. Islands abound on either side of the peninsula with adjacent shore features.

The whole peninsula is one vast forest intersected in every direction by countless rivers and streams which together constitute one of the most lavish water-systems in the world. Only an insignificant fraction of these forests has ever been traversed by human beings, and those who travel rarely leave the banks of streams except to pass from one river system to another.

The principal rivers on the west coast are the Perak, the Bernam and the Muar. The first is navigable for steamers up to forty miles and for country craft upto two hundred and fifty miles. The Bernam is deeper and navigable for about one hundred miles, while the Muar irrigates a very fertile valley and is navigable for local craft to a hundred and fifty miles. On the east coast the rivers are the chief means of communication and the important ones among them are the Kuantan, Rompin, Kelantan, Pahang and Trengganu.

The soil of the peninsula is remarkably fertile both in the plains and on the mountain slopes. This is so partly owing to the decay of vegetable matter for ages, and partly to geological changes. The richness of soil has resulted in dense growth of huge trees, shrubs, bushes, underwood, creepers, climbing plants and trailing vines, all hung by ferns, mosses and parasitic growths and bound together by rattans and rope-like trailers. In most places the jungle is so thick that it is impossible to go through it without the aid of a wood-knife, and even the wild beasts are known to use well-worn game-tracks to move about. In the interior, brakes of bamboos are found, many of which spread for miles along the river-banks.

The fauna of Malaya is as varied as, and no less profuse and crowded than, its vegetable life. From the elephant to the cocoa-nut-monkey, the tiger to the jungle cat, the wild boar to the flying fox, the python to the hamadryad, the alligator to the squirrel and from a lemon-sized wasp to red ant, diverse varieties of beasts and insects abound. Birds, insects, scorpions and centipedes swarm the land, and though they open a splendid field for scientific research, are nevertheless pests for the ordinary man and the occasional visitor.

The climate is more like that of Burma than that of west Africa. But neither an Indian nor a European can be too fond of it. It is not only extremely humid but also invariably hot. On the whole it is enervating, and foreigners must leave Malaya every now and then for restoring their health elsewhere. Rain also is oppressive; out of 365 days, 160 to 200 days are rainy. On the west coast the quantity varies from 75 to 120 inches per annum, while on the east coast it is about 155 inches for the same period. But a few abnormalities of climate and rainfall have also been noted. On 27 December 1926, Kemmaman in Trengganu had $15\frac{1}{2}$ inches of rain. In the same month Trengganu received 76·54 inches of rain, the Perak river rose $38\frac{1}{2}$ feet at Kuala Kangsar and the Pahang over 60 feet at Temerloh. The 'Sumatras' or violent gusts of wind accompanied by heavy downpour of short duration are another characteristic of the climate of the peninsula.

Malaya falls broadly into two natural regions—Eastern and Western. The former has nine and the latter fourteen sub-regions, all of which have some common features.

The Eastern Region

The Eastern Region consists of the three states of Pahang, Trengganu and Kelantan and is featured by the series of parallel, generally north-south, ranges culminating in the water-shed of the Main Range which is the western boundary of this region. In its northern portion the East Coast Range peters out and overlooks the wide flat coastal plain of northern Kelantan. Throughout Trengganu this Range chokes out the coastal plain, but when it comes to Pahang it decreases in elevation and size and the coastal plain again attains some importance. The Range effectively prevents intercourse between the east and the west as there are few passes in it leading to the western coast. Only the Pahang river provides any means of communication below Temerloh.

The Kelantan and the Pahang are the two great rivers of this region. They draw their head-waters from the eastern slopes of the Main Range and flow north and south respectively through an important north-south valley along the eastern edge of the granite upland. Rapids interrupt the course of the rivers in the upland area and they frequently flow in deep gorges. Drawing to themselves the waters of many tributaries, these two rivers are subject to considerable rise in their level during the north-east monsoon (November-January). A rise of 20 feet is normal, but only for a few days.

The main lines of drainage are west to east in the coastal areas and north to south in the western part of the East Coast Range. To the west of this range lie also the largest areas of fresh water swamp, though there appear to be considerable areas of lopak in the Tasek Bera area lying south of the great bend of the Pahang and west of the lower remnants of the East Coast Range. Forest covers practically the whole region, and the cultivated areas are limited to the coastal area, banks of rivers and the north-south corridor along the eastern edge of the granitic upland.

Natural routes of this region are of three types:—
  (i) the intermittent sandy beaches of the east coast,
  (ii) the main rivers, the Kelantan and the Pahang, and
  (iii) the north-south corridor at the eastern boundary of the Main Range.

Only two major passes cross the Main Range and connect the eastern region with the west coast of Malaya. They are:—

(i) Gap and Fraser's Hill, with the road from Raub to Kuala Kubu Bahru.
(ii) Ginting Sempak, with the road from Bentong to Kuala Lumpur.

The Western Region

The Western Region lies west of the main divide and also includes the whole of the two states of Negri Sembilan and Johore. Its prominent topographical feature is a series of ridges running roughly north and south and more or less arranged in echelons. Far to the north-west runs the Nakawn Range, then comes the Kedah-Singgora Range, and lastly lies the Bintang Range extending from Bukit Bubus to the Dindings. The Main Range which extends along the whole eastern boundary of this region from the northern frontier to Tampin in north Malacca lies immediately behind the Bintang Range. In the remainder of the region the isolated peaks of Mt. Ophir and Ma'Okil and the low granite hills of eastern Johore mark the configuration of the upland areas.

Lapping the edges of these ranges are low-lying flat areas of alluvial deposits which form the bases of the western coastal plains. A considerable portion of the lowlands is swampy and there is usually a sharp line of division between the uplands and the plains which affect the drainage of the country and the course of the rivers.

The most important feature of its vegetation is the almost continuous tree cover. Only in southern Perlis, western Kedah and north-western Province Wellesley are there large open areas under paddy cultivation.

The Coast-line

The west coast from the Thailand border to Tanjong Prai (west of Singapore) is approximately 390 miles long. There are a number of islands off the coast, the Langkawi group, Penang and Pangkor, and the unnamed and uninhabited group of mangrove islands provide different grades of sheltered anchorages. Generally speaking the coast is fringed with mud, and there are only three stretches of coast where there are sandy beaches suitable for landing. These are to the north of Prai, in the Dindlings and from Port Swettenham to Malacca. There are, however, numerous places up the rivers where landings can be made, and there are sandy beaches also on the Langkawi Islands, Pulau Penang and Oulau Pangkor.

The coast is highly susceptible to ebbs and tides, the average being about two to three knots. There is a constant current in the Malacca Strait both in the north and the south, with an irregular one in the centre. The rise of tide above datum of soundings for the whole coast averages nine feet at springs and five to six feet at neaps. The exception to this phenomenon is at Port Swettenham where it is above thirteen and nine feet, respectively. At Penang (Georgetown) the spring rise is slightly less than the average, being seven and three-fourths feet.

Climatic Conditions

In Malaya there is little temperature variation throughout the year, winds are generally light, and rainfall is often heavy. The diurnal variation of weather is the predominant feature; it produces strong contrasts of rain and cloud between day and night, though the weather of one day does not necessarily repeat that of the day before. The average temperature range is from a maximum of 85° F during the day to a minimum of 73° F at night.

Four seasons can be distinguished :—

North-east monsoon season: late October to the end of March. North-easterly winds blow strongly over the sea and the east coast, but lightly elsewhere. Much heavy rain and low cloud occur over the east side of mountains.

South-west monsoon season: end of May or beginning of June to September. Winds are light, southerly near Singapore and variable. Rainfall is very heavy, with much cloud.

Two transitional seasons: April to May and October. Winds are generally light and variable. Rainfall is again heavy, with much cloud.

These are very broad generalizations; the seasons vary much in different parts of the peninsula. The nights are usually clear and quiet, and reasonably cool; towards morning mists may form in valleys and sheets of cloud mantle the slopes of the mountains, though the summits are usually cloudless. Soon after sunrise, however, the contours of distant mountains become less distinct and after an hour or two shimmer blurs their outline, the sun's heat increases so that it is uncomfortable to be without headgear, the sheets of cloud dissolve and for a short time the sky becomes cloudless, but by noon cumulus clouds frequently begin to form and the heat grows intense. During the late afternoon the cumulus clouds often increase to large drifting thunder-clouds, and thunderstorms occur. These may last only for about fifteen or thirty minutes, but they are very heavy and the rain may even overflow the road drains. During the early part of the night the thunder clouds tend to flatten out and by morning the sheets of stratocumulus cover the mountain slopes and the mists over the valleys return.

POLITICAL SYSTEM AND ECONOMIC RESOURCES

British Malaya was organised into three separate governmental units according to the manner in which areas were brought under British control.
1. The Straits Settlements, consisting of Singapore, Malacca, Penang and Province Wellesley, with Christmas Island and the Cocos-Keeling group in the Indian Ocean;
2. The Federated Malay States, which lie across the central area of the country and consist of Perak, Selangor, Negri Sembilan and Pahang;
3. The Unfederated Malay States, consisting of Johore in the extreme south and west, Kedah and Perlis in the north and Kelantan and Trengganu in the east.

The Straits Settlements were British territory administered as a Crown Colony; the Federated and Unfederated Malay States were British Protected States, under the rule of Sultans who were juridically independent, though politically dependent on the British Crown.

The Straits Settlements

The British Parliament was the final legislative authority as well as the final executive authority for the Crown Colonies, but it legislated for them only in matters unsuitable for local legislation. The Act of 1867 under which the Straits Settlements were constituted as a Crown Colony made provision for the establishment of a Legislative Council. In its latest form the Council was composed of the Governor as President, with thirteen official and thirteen non-official members, all of whom, under the Statute, had to be British subjects. Of the non-official members, eleven were nominated by the Governor and the remaining two, since 1924, had been elected, one by British members of the Chamber of Commerce at Singapore, and the other by those of the Penang Chamber of Commerce. The Governor had both an original and casting vote, so that there was, in effect, an official majority. The difficulties arising out of a constitutional system such as this were, however, in a great measure obviated by the relations which the Executive Government had established with the representatives of the different communities and the non-official members of the Legislative Council. There was a well-established convention by which difficult issues were made the subject of informal discussion and agreement outside the legislature, and where difference of opinion arose within the Legislative Council, the Executive showed itself increasingly responsive to the views of the non-official members.

The Federated Malay States

This area was not in the technical sense British territory, and its inhabitants did not rank as British subjects. British connection with these States orginated in the desire to protect Chinese residents in the Straits Settlements from piracy on the coastal waters of these States and from robbery and oppression when trading in them. There is much contemporary evidence to show that the prevailing condition in many parts of them was one of lawlessness and anarchy. In 1895 the growing need for joint action in matters of communication and the provision of economic and social services led to a more definite measure of co-ordination. By agreements made with the States in that year, they were federated under a Resident-General. The Act of Federation provided that the joint resources of the States might be used to assist any State which might require financial aid, and it is of interest to note that it also included a provision that if Her Majesty's Government were engaged in war with any other power, each State would provide a body of 'Indian' troops to serve in the Straits Settlements.

A further change was made in 1909 when a Federal Council was established, under a President who was styled High Commissioner and who was also the Governor of the adjacent Colony. The members were the Resident-General, whose designation was now altered to that of the Chief Secretary, the four Malay rulers, the four Residents and the four nominated non-officials British and Chinese. The Malay rulers showed themselves unwilling, on the ground of prestige, to take a personal part in the debates of the Federal Council, hence in 1927 they were relieved of membership, their places being taken by four Malay chiefs free to speak on their behalf. There were also added an Indian non-official member and the heads of the Medical, Public Works, Railway, Education, Labour, agriculture and Chinese Affairs departments, who were thus placed in a position to reply to the criticisms of the European and other non-official members. It became apparent, however, that the authority which the Federal Council had drawn to itself tended to deprive the four States of all power, not only over their own legislation but over their annual budgets. The rulers for their part regarded with some envy the greater liberty of action still enjoyed by the rulers of the Unfederated States.

Shortly before 1939 the post of Chief Secretary was abolished, and his place as a co-ordinating authority was taken by a Federal Secretary, junior to all the Residents. The powers of the Federal Council were also reduced. But it still safeguarded the financial credit of the Federation by keeping control of the collection and appropriation of its revenues as a whole, and instead of scrutinizing and fixing every detail of each State's expenditure, it made to each of them an annual block grant to meet the cost of the services which were now transferred to their control. These services comprised agriculture, co-operation, education, public-works, forests, public health, mines, prisons and the veterinary service. The power to legislate for education, forests, and some phases of health and agriculture was transferred back to the State Councils. Uniformity in legislation was secured by making the Federal Treasurer and the Federal Legal Adviser members of the four State Councils as well as of the Federal Council.

The Unfederated Malay States

The most important of these five States was Johore, with a population of nearly three-quarters of a million. It had been closely associated with the British ever since the foundation of Singapore in 1819. For many years it had a British Consular Agent, but in 1914 it asked for a British General Adviser. The British control over the northern States dates back to 1909, when suzerainty over them was formally ceded by Siam. Advisers were then appointed to them. There was, however, some difference in the extent of the authority possessed by the Advisers in the various States. In Trengganu, for example, the Adviser had only consular powers till 1919, and difficulty of communication tended to isolate Kelantan till 1931. The treaty relations with these States are best illustrated by the agreement concluded with Perlis in 1930. The State was declared to be under British protection and the rights of suzerainty were reserved to the Crown. There were to be no dealings with other Powers except through the Crown respresentative. The Resident would advise in all matters except those connected with Malay custom or the Islamic religion. The State would be governed by the Raja, with the assistance of a State Council, the composition of which was prescribed in the agreement. The Government of Perlis was to be conducted by Perlis Malay or pure natives except where there was any work which the State Council considered them incapable of performing. The successor of the Raja was to be a descendant of the existing Ruler or of his ancestors.

The General Status of the Malay States

There were in the Malay States no local laws of nationality, but in practice the Sultans regarded as their subjects only those who were of the Malay race and Mohammedan religion. Indian immigrants were normally British subjects but Chinese immigrants had in law only Chinese nationality. In practice, for travelling abroad, many inhabitants of the Malay States, whether recognized as subjects of those States or not, were granted a certificate of nationality as 'British protected persons', if not qualified as British subjects. Whether a man was a British subject or a British protected person made little difference to him in relation to foreign Powers.

While there were obvious differences between the juridical or constitutional position of the Malay States and that of the Straits Settlements, it was less easy to draw a marked line of distinction between the extent of the control exercised in practice by the British authorities in the States and the Colony, respectively. As far as circumstances permitted, it was the policy of the British Government to respect the position of the Sultans. Declarations made in 1925 by the Parliamentary Under Secretary of State for the Colonies, and again in 1932 by the Permanent Under Secretary, emphasised the fact that Britain's position in the Malay States rested on treaty obligations and that the maintenance of the authority and prestige of the rulers must always be a cardinal point in British policy. These declarations also called attention to the need for safeguarding the Malays from political submergence by the immigrant elements in the population. It is clear, however, that while the system of 'indirect' rule protected to some extent the prestige of the Sultan with his own subjects, there was in all essential matters a close measure of official control, which was not materially affected by the fact that it was expressed in terms of advice rather than of order. This may have been less marked in the Unfederated than in the Federated States, and the position no doubt tended to vary with the personality of the ruler and his council; but this was a difference mainly of degree. Although the administration of a number of economic and social services was declared to be under the control of the State Councils in the Federated States, these services were really controlled by the Governor, under the departmental direction of heads some of whose headquarters were in the Straits Settlements. The Chinese and Indian immigrants in the States tended to look primarily to the British administrator and not to the ruler and his council as the source of authority, and it was of particular significance to them that the ultimate guarantee for the maintenance of order and of an impartial judicial system lay with the British administration and not with the States' authorities.

Population

The total area of the three component parts of British Malaya was about 51,880 square miles, and in 1931, the last date for which detailed census figures are available, the total population was 4,385,346:—

	Approximate Area (sq. Miles)	Population 1931
Foreign		31,631
Straits Settlements ...	2,260	1,114,015
Federated Malay States	27,540	1,713,096
Unfederated Malay States	22,080	1,526,604
	51,880	4,385,346

At the end of 1938 the estimated population according to the land of origin was:—

Race	Straits Settlements	Federated Malay States	Unfederated Malay States	Total
Europeans	17,816	8,624	1,771	28,211
Eurasians	12,762	4,970	578	18,310
Chinese	861,940	921,701	436,603	2,220,244
Malayans	303,421	687,495	1,219,951	2,210,867
Indians	149,636	463,874	130,045	743,555
Others	12,279	17,065	28,335	57,679
Total	1,357,854	2,103,729	1,817,283	5,278,866

As compared with some of her neighbours, Malaya had a markedly low density of population. It was estimated in 1938 that only two-fifths of the total area was inhabited. There were large areas still under primeval evergreen forests, within which lived only a few jungle tribes known as Sakais.

The greater part of the indigenous population was to be found in the rural areas; there were only eleven towns which in

1931 had a population over 1,000 persons. The Malays were primarily agriculturists and fishermen. For the greater part they were peasant proprietors working their own land and did not provide any considerable amount of labour for the rubber plantations or mines. Their distribution and the proportions they bore to other elements in the total population depended mainly on the amount of good rice-land available, the suitability of the coast for fishing, and the remoteness of an area from large towns from which they tended to retreat.

The descendants of the Chinese who settled in Malacca as far back as three centuries ago are still to be found in Malaya, but the overwhelming majority of the Chinese population represents the result of immigration which has taken place in the twentieth century. The Chinese had formed a high proportion of the mining population, and were also engaged in planting. In contrast to the Malays, the Chinese appreciate the varied life of the town with its greater amenities and its greater opportunities for material advancement. Nearly all the shops in the towns were owned by them and, even in villages which were almost entirely peopled by Malays, Chinese shops predominated. In Singapore, where the total population was roughly half a million, nearly eighty per cent were Chinese. The contribution which they have made to the economic development of the country has been one of great importance, for they have exhibited not only the traditional Chinese qualities of industry and thrift but also a marked spirit of enterprise. They were pioneers in tin industry and later took full advantage of the developments which followed the wide-scale introduction of European capital at the beginning of this century. Not only have they occupied an important position in trade and commerce, but it was estimated in 1937 that they held sixteen per cent of the total area occupied by the rubber estates, and thirty-four per cent of the tin mining areas.

The Indian immigrant community, though less numerous than either the Malays or the Chinese, represented more varied types and was less easy to characterize as a whole. The Indian immigrants had arrived only recently, and their chief activity had been as labourers on the rubber estates. A certain proportion had taken part in commerce and industry; Indians had, for instance, in 1935, some four per cent of the rubber estates and there were about 40,000 employed as labourers or as subordinates in the different departments of government.

The Siamese numbered about 24,000 and were mainly to be found in the Malay States bordering Siamese territory or Thailand. Ceylon Tamils, about 18,000 to 19,000, formed a large proportion of the government clerical staff. There were a number of Arabs, of whom many were practically Malays with only an Arab strain. There were, lastly, some 6,500 Japanese, of whom over half were in Singapore and other towns. A considerable number were, however, interested in rubber planting. The Japanese owned important iron and manganese mines, and there was a considerable Japanese fishing community.

The Europeans in Malaya, the great majority of whom were British, numbered in 1931 under 18,000 or only 0·4 per cent of the total population. The largest proportion, over 10,000, were in the three ports of the Straits Settlements, the majority being in Singapore. Nearly 2,000 were soldiers, who were transferred every few years; some 400 were tin miners; there were 1,000 or so in the government services, and outside these services there were professional and business men. A large part of the European population was made up of women, most of whom had no employment. Moreover, although the majority of the male Europeans were employees, very few owned landed property or had any permanent stake in Malaya beyond owning shares in the various government loans and public companies.

Economic Resources

The excitement produced during the last one hundred and fifty years by Malaya in the west (including the United States) on account of her rubber and tin is very similar to that produced by India with her spices in the days of Elizabeth, and is still the cause of international misunderstandings. Malayan economy depends on two factors: the tropical climate and the mineral wealth. The first of these makes life one of ease and plenty, involving little enterprise. The second makes Malaya much more dependent on foreigners for her prosperity. The chief item of tropical produce which has attracted foreign capital and enterprise is rubber. It was introduced from Brazil over half a century ago and became the ' staple product of Malaya, accounting for one-half of the world's output. Its export value vastly exceeded that of any other commodity. In 1937 this stood at over £.56·5 millions, respresenting half of Malaya's total trade. But in 1938 it was less than £.32 millions. The Government had also restricted production for a few years by international agreement.

The following table relating to 1940 gives the figures of area under rubber cultivation and the population engaged in it according to the three categories of political units and the nationality of the people involved.

Territory	European		Chinese		Indian		Others		Total	
	No.	Acres	No.	Acres	No.	Acres	No.	Acres	No.	Acres
Federated Malay States	653	879·309	427	137·603	231	50·226	33	12·196	1·344	1,079·334
Straits Settlements	82	132·505	171	61·537	48	10·940	5	1·528	306	206·510
Unfederated Malay States (Including Brunei).	253	566·227	453	152·797	117	32·653	49	82·340	872	834·017
Total for Malaya	988	1,578·041	1051	351·937	396	93·819	87	96·064	2·522	2·119·861

A similar position was occupied by tin; over a third of the world output was mined in Malaya and it was the second in value of Malayan exports. The demand for this mineral had increased owing to the world's development of canning and motor-car industries, and as the Chinese could not produce adequately the Europeans entered the field and installed western machinery for quick and efficient production. In spite of this, however, the Chinese owned one-third of the mines in 1941. Practically all the ore was hitherto smelted by two British companies at Penang and Singapore, and an attempt by the United States to undertake this was thwarted by imposing a prohibitive export duty on the unsmelted ore.

The following figures represent production in various States:—

	1934	1935	1936	1937	1938	
Negri Sembilan	980	1·279	1·769	2·517	1·691	Long tons.
Pahang	1·443	1·771	2·760	3·158	1·924	,,
Perak	20·203	25·048	33·038	44·874	24·958	,,
Selangor	9·941	12·689	21·115	24·576	12·633	,,
All other States	1·352	1·532	2·021	2·074	2·054	,,
Total for Malaya	33·919	42·319	60·703	77·199	43·260	

Malaya's output estimated potentially as 10,000 tons in 1939 was limited by the International Tin Control scheme to keep up prices.

TRANSPORT AND COMMUNICATIONS

Foreign capital and enterprise were responsible also for the development of important communications, electric power and protected water-supply.

There were at least four types of means of communication. These were railways, roads, water-ways, and electrical communications.

Railways

The Federated Malay States Railway was the only line serving the peninsula. Trengganu was not served by this or any other railway. The total length was 1,068 miles of which seventeen and a half on the main line was double-tracked. It was connected with Bangkok without change of gauge, and trains ran through to that place from Singapore. This was known as the Main Line.

There was an alternative line from south to north from Gemas. This passed through a most difficult country and was comparatively unimportant. For about two hundred miles from Gemas it was at least sixty miles from the coast, and it touched the east coast only at its northern terminus. A causeway carried a single-track line and motor-road across the Johore Strait. Apart from the Taiping Pass Section and a number of major bridges, the country presented no problem in construction to the engineers. The average speed of trains was permitted up to forty-five miles per hour on certain sections of the Main Line, but it was not less than twenty-five elsewhere.

Besides the Main Line there were nine branch lines in the Main Section and one in the East Coast Section. Throughout most of its length the Main Line passed through the rubber-growing country. Rice-growing districts were traversed in Province Wellesley, Perak and Negri Sembilan, and the tin area was covered around Taiping, Ipoh and Kuala Lumpur. Similarly the branch lines served the most well-developed parts of the peninsula.

Before 1942 the railway was owned and administered by the Federated Malay States Government, except the portion in Johore State which was held in lease from that State. The total number employed in 1939 was about 12,600 but the Europeans were only 90 while the Indians and Ceylonese were about 9,300. Track maintenance was done with Tamil labour, ports were served by the Chinese and the Indian labour, and administration was in the hands of Europeans and Eurasians.

The standard of maintenance of the permanent way before the war was not uniform. That of the Main Line was generally good, while the line between Gemas and Johore Bahru was poor, the rails being of inferior quality and in poor condition. Swamp was troublesome in Port Swettenham branch, cotton soil gave a bad foundation in the Kedah region, and the East Coast Line was generally neglected. Second hand rails, mostly crippled, had been used on this line all through, and ballasting too was indifferent.

Railway telegraphs, telephones, block and electric-train-tablet system and certain other electrical equipment were maintained by the Federated Malay States Posts and Telegraphs Department under an agreement.

No part of the railway was electrified. The number of locomotives before the war was 185 and there were 12 steam railcars. Obviously these were inadequate to deal with the civil and military requirements, and locomotives were running a high average mileage of 102 per day.

Coal fuel was obtained from Batu Arang. But reserve stocks of hard coal were imported from India, and there was no dearth of coal at any time.

In January 1942 the stock of carriages and wagons was considerable. There were 515 carriages and 480 bogies and 5,150 four-wheeled wagons. All of them were in good condition but were fast becoming inadequate in view of the civil and military requirements.

The capacity of the line was between ten and twenty trains each day each way according to local circumstances, the East Coast Line from Prai to Singapore being capable of the maximum.

In the matter of vulnerability, there were four tunnels on the Main Line and nine tunnels on the East Coast Line and fifty underbridges on the Main Line and seventy-three on the East Coast Line. All were of first class workmanship.

There was a Central Workshop at Sentul. The railway owned ferries and wharves at all important places. Ferries plied between Prai and Penang and between Palekbang and Kota Bharu. Wharves were maintained at Prai, Port Weld, Telok Anson, Port Swettenham, Port Dickson, Palekbang and Tumpat. Sidings were numerous all over the railway.

In addition to the Federated Malay States Railway there were a number of isolated light railways and tramways, serving various mines, quarries, estates, etc. In the island of Tekon Besar and Elbin there were short lengths of line, and on Penang Island, about four miles west of Georgetown, there was an electrically-operated cable railway with two sections of 1400 and 900 yards each. The steepest gradient was 1: 1·95; near the top was a tunnel, 285 feet long, on a gradient of 1: 2·04. The upper station on Strawberry Hill was 2400 feet above the sea-level. There were metre and broad guage lines on the Singapore island administered by different authorities. On some plantations in the west of the island there were probably tramways.

Roads

These were mostly constructed by the State governments and fell into two systems, the east coast and the west coast, the division being made by the mountain range in the centre. There were two cross roads, Kuala Kubu to Rabu and Kuala Lumpur to Bentong, leading to Kuantan, and a third one between Batu Pahat and Mersing. The west coast road was the main trunk road. It ran from Thailand border to Singapore and for much of the distance, south of Kedah boundary, there was an alternative coast road. These two were inter-connected by an extensive network of metalled roads. The main network of the east coast was located in Kelantan which was connected southwards to Kuala Trengganu. South of this point as far as Endau various isolated stretches of road were known to exist along the coast. There was no continuous road from Kota Bharu to Singapore. The low mileage in Kelantan or Trengganu was highly significant.

The main trunk road and the principal branches and alternatives were well sign-posted prior to the Japanese occupation. These sign-posts were similar to those used in England, the rule of the road also being 'keep to the left'.

In general the roads were very narrow and, except in towns were suitable for single-line traffic only. But there were parts where turn-round had been made possible and most of these were at the entrance to estates. Bridges and culverts were of wood. Masonry or brick was confined to piers and abutments. But on all important roads timber bridges were being replaced by steel or reinforced concrete structures. This meant that there were three types of bridges before the war in Malaya, timber, steel and reinforced-concrete. The most difficult aspect of bridge-building was in relation to depth of soft mud in paddy-growing areas where concrete piles to a depth of sixty or more feet had to be driven before obtaining a set. Recently constructed bridges had been designed to carry two-thirds of the British Ministry of Transport standard train. For the older bridges no standard specification existed, and a list was kept according to the weight of traffic known to have crossed the bridges. There were no fords on the principal roads. On the coastal road in Johore there were important ferries at Muar and Batu Pahat. The Pahang Trunk Road crossed two ferries, east of Jerantut and west of Kuantan, and on the east coast generally there was a considerable number of smaller ferries over the river mouths used for local traffic on the rough coastal tracks. In general the gradients were very easy, not often exceeding 1 in 30. The steepest climbs occurred on the two main roads crossing the mountain range into Pahang over the Gap and Ginting Sempah. The gradients lay between 1 in 20 and 1 in 8. Those on the roads leading to Taiping—K. Kangsar Pass were between 1 in 30 and 1 in 20.

Many sections of the original roads were very winding, but improvements through the years had changed these into well-engineered curves, with moderate banks and good visibility. There were still a number of sharp turns on the secondary roads and in approaches to towns and bridges. Defiles were not many. The important ones among them were the mountain stretches of the two roads crossing the main range, where one-way traffic control was introduced in 1941 for the Royal Air Force vehicles crossing the Pahang Trunk Road. Many sections of the main and secondary roads were liable to flooding after heavy rains in the mountains where most of the rivers have their sources. Before the war considerable work was carried out to mitigate the effects of flood by raising the level of certain stretches of road and by re-aligning the course of rivers. Heavy rains could also cause slips to occur on the mountain sections of the two roads crossing the Main Range. Efforts were being made in 1941 to reconstruct these roads by widening the parts of the Pahang Trunk Road, but this work was not completed and both the mountain roads were still liable to blocking. The unmetalled roads became slippery in wet weather, and the laterite surface became sticky at the same time. Under heavy mechanical transport these roads would be quickly rutted and destroyed to the extent of becoming almost impassable for heavier vehicles.

In general the roads were not vulnerable apart from the bridges. The chief exceptions were the Muar and Batu Pahat ferries, the destruction of which would stop traffic on the coastal road in Johore unless suitable boats as an alternative could be brought into use. The mountain sections of the Pahang Trunk Road and Temerloh Road were also very vulnerable to blasting which could produce slips similar to those caused by heavy rains. There were some places in the hills, on the side of cliffs and through paddy fields, where the road could be effectively destroyed.

Waterways

There are not less than one hundred and thirteen waterways on the west coast and not more than twenty-five on the east coast and half a dozen in Singapore island. All these are so evenly distributed that if one is missed the other is not too far, especially on the west coast. The rivers in general are of no great length and are navigable only for comparatively short distances from their mouths, the Perak being a notable exception. Considerably more use was made of the rivers on the west coast than on the east coast partly for economic reasons and partly owing to the blocking of entrances by sand bars on the east coast. The more important rivers had ports at or within about five miles of the entrance, and a fair trade of coastal steamers was carried on between all ports. In the interior of the country where thick jungle predominates, river navigation by country boats was often the only means of communication. Apart from this limited use of the rivers there was one noteworthy cross-country route from the Muar to the Pahang. But it was usable only by small craft and involved a portage of about four hundred and fifty yards from one river to another.

Canals were intended almost exclusively for irrigation and drainage purposes. They were comparatively of small capacity and navigable only by boats for local traffic. All down the west coast there was a vast number of canals running down to the sea, which could be used for infiltration followed by scramble landings.

Malayan craft may be divided into two main categories, fishing and trading. The fishing craft were all small vessels of less than fifty feet in length, and with the exception of Chinese and Japanese power boats at Pangkor and Singapore respectively, all were country boats relying on sail, oar and paddle for propulsion. The trading craft may be subdivided into three groups: coastal trading, lighter and harbour, and miscellaneous. In 1938 there were about 10,500 fishing craft in the Straits Settlements and the Federated Malay States, and those in Singapore were Chinese-built and hence of sounder construction than many Penang lighters. There were construction and repair facilities all over the west coast. The Public Works Department had workshops at every conceivable port and important coastal town, but private engineering firms too had their own near the port areas.

Signals

As usual, these were by telephone, telegraph and wireless. Telephone and telegraph ran together on the same pole route, but there were minor places where one connected the other by a special arrangement. For instance, telephone wires running into rubber estates and of considerable lengths were connected with telegraph on the main routes, and post offices with telephone connection communicated messages by telegraph into areas not served by telephone. There were a number of zonal and internal exchanges, and underground cables were used in important places. The main trunk route of Malaya ran mainly in the railway reserve, on the east side of the track, from Singapore to Bukit Mertajam, the latter being the zone-centre trunk-exchange for Penang and north Malaya generally. This route had short sections of trunk-type underground cable with 100-lb. conductors at Kuala Lumpur and Ipoh.

The two authorities maintaining the telegraph and the telephone were the post offices and the railways, the two working in co-operation everywhere and supplementing each other's work. The whole system had access to the international telegraph service through the Singapore and Penang offices of the Eastern Extension Australia and China Telegraph Company Limited. There was also an international Air Line Circuit connecting Penang and Bangkok in Siam. In 1938, there were 3566 miles of pole lines and 296 miles of underground cables in the postal branch, there were 147 post offices with telegraph facilities and 81 railway stations with telegraph offices attached to them.

For the purpose of telephone communication, Malaya was divided into six zones with a zone-centre trunk-exchange for each. A seventh was planned for Kota Bharu, the intention being to provide direct connection between all zone centres. Each zone was divided into areas served by group-centre exchanges and each such exchange had, or would ultimately have had, direct connection to one or more zone-centre exchanges. Each of the remaining smaller exchanges, known as Department Exchanges, normally had direct connection either to a group or zone-centre exchange. The exceptions were some of the smallest exchanges, usually those with rural automatic exchange equipment, which were connected to a dependent exchange.

There were about twenty-seven wireless stations in Malaya when Singapore fell. Most of them were government-administered, the Penang and Singapore Broadcasting stations being administered semi-officially by a society or corporation. Apart from twelve broadcasting stations in the Straits Settlements, there were four in Pahang, three in Kelantan, two each in Kedah and Selangor and one each in Trengganu and Perak. The largest station was the one at Seletar in Singapore, owned and used by the Royal Navy.

Electricity Supply

During the last fifteen years before the war, the electrification of Malaya had developed considerably, and excluding the private supplies of power for tin mines, dredges and rubber factories, there were more than a hundred towns and villages in the peninsula with a public supply of electric power. Much of the development centred round the Perak river and tin-bearing valleys of the Kinta and the Selangor rivers. But the development of remote towns and villages by means of small oil stations continued satisfactorily, and connection to high voltage distribution systems would soon have become possible in many places. There was no grid system, and no inter-connection between the principal undertakings existed except between the two Singapore Power Stations. The pylons were generally steel lattice towers, but another type which was probably less common was the steel tubular 'Key' pylon.

Protected Water-supply

As stated before, there is plenty of water in Malaya. The rainfall is high, and rivers, streams and springs are always full of water. The only dry areas are coastal plains. All the larger and most of the smaller towns obtained an adequate supply of good water from impounding reservoirs. Another ready-made source of supply in tin-dredging areas was the 'paddock' or pool in which the dredge followed. This covered an area several acres in extent and contained an enormous volume of easily accessible potable water.

Malaya was a profitable Colony for the British which had lulled them into a life of ease and comfort. An administrative system with divided responsibility and a colonial economy, with undeveloped means of communication, prevented the concentration of its resources, both in men and material, for the purpose of defence. Moreover, the inhabitants of Malaya felt no bonds of loyalty to their government, which was foreign in its origin or control, and had no obligations for the defence of their homeland. This psychological factor was an element of weakness in the defence of Malaya which had been greatly complicated by the lack of adequate equipment and inability of the British Government to maintain a steady flow of men and material for military operations in Malaya.

CHAPTER VI
Defence Plans for Malaya

In June 1937, the British defence policy in the Far East was exhaustively reviewed by the Chiefs of Staff in the United Kingdom. The assessment of requirements was based on two assumptions, namely:—
> "(a) That any threat to our interests would be sea-borne,
> (b) that we should be able to send to the Far East within three months a fleet of sufficient strength to protect the Dominions and India and give cover to our communications in the Indian Ocean ".[1]

These assumptions gave weight to the ability of the British Fleet to ensure the safety of Singapore; and as the Fleet could arrive in the Far East within a maximum period of 90 days, the defence plans for Malaya had to provide only against such operations as might be completed by the Japanese within that period. The role of the garrison there was to hold on till the arrival of the Fleet.

General Percival has stated in his despatch that in November 1937 he made a careful study of the problem of defence of Singapore and prepared an appreciation of the plan of attack by the Japanese. In his deductions based on that appreciation, he, probably for the first time, took cognizance of the danger from the north and, though even now a naval attack on Singapore figured prominently, the threat to northern Malaya was nevertheless recognized. His appreciation was that southern Thailand would be used by the Japanese for invasion of Malaya, and that its northern area and Johore would then acquire increased importance from the point of view of defence. These areas were garrisoned by the volunteer forces raised in Malaya which were not deemed adequate for protection ; hence General Percival suggested reinforcement by some regular battalions. But even in this early prognostication of landward menace to Malaya, more emphasis was laid on the protection of Singapore for which a larger air force and stronger infantry units were demanded, as landing attacks were feared.

The local military authorities thenceforward became conscious of the danger from the north and from time to time gave expression to their fears. There was General Dobbie's appreciation of May 1938 in which he specifically drew attention to this aspect of defence.

---
[1] C.O.S. (40) 592, dated 15 August 1940.

He wrote: "It is an attack from the northward that I regard as the greatest potential danger to the fortress. Such attack could be carried out during the period of the north-east monsoon. The jungle is not in most places impassable for infantry".[2] The line of defence suggested by him was Johore River, Kota Tinggi, Kula Pulai River. But it was not till 1940 that the old assumption of the availability and efficacy of the British Fleet in the defence of Malaya made room for the conviction that, in the altered circumstances, overland threat had become a major menace and that land and air forces had an important role to play. Hence, just before the war started in Europe and when the political situation had grown tense, the 12th Indian Infantry Brigade group was sent to Malaya as reinforcement.

APPRECIATIONS OF 1940

The year 1940 is important for the development of defence plans and the gradual unfoldment of the danger which faced Malaya. It is also remarkable for the changes which were then being made in the organisation of commands. In April 1940, Lieut.-General Sir Lionel Bond, the General Officer Commanding Malaya Command, prepared a new appreciation on the ground of the possibility of a Japanese base being established in southern Thailand, and the northern borders of Malaya being " held against a considerable force for several months".[3] His estimate of the forces required was four divisions with three machine-gun battalions and two tank regiments. However, the strength of the army might admit of reduction if the Royal Air Force would undertake to prevent a Japanese base being established and the line of communication being operated. As General Percival has remarked, the problem now emerging prominently was "the defence of the whole of Malaya" and not merely of Singapore and its immediate neighbourhood.

With the collapse of France in June 1940 the risk to Malaya became greater still. It was in these fast developing new circumstances that the Chiefs of Staff prepared their Far East Appreciation, in August 1940, and officially recognised that the fundamental bases on which 1937 Appreciation was built were no longer tenable. It was now realised that the British Fleet might not be concentrated in the Far East, and that a Japanese threat to Malaya was a reality, which implied that it was not "sufficient to concentrate upon the

---

[2] Percival's Despatch, p. 9.
[3] *Ibid.* p. 10, para 23.

defence of Singapore Island ", but it was " necessary to hold the whole of Malaya ".

This Appreciation exhaustively reviewed the situation in the Far East and outlined the British policy for defence. It was held that Japan's aim was to exclude western influence from the Far East in order to be able to control the resources of raw materials in that region. To achieve this object, it would be necessary for Japan to capture Singapore, without which there would be a potential threat to her southward advance. Japan, it was believed, would take advantage of the war situation in Europe and risk an open breach with the British Empire. In the eventuality, with large commitments in Europe, the British Empire might not be in a position to measure swords with Japan in the East. Hence the British policy was to "avoid open clash with Japan". It was stated, " a general settlement, including economic concessions to Japan, is desirable. But the prospects are not favourable. Failing this settlement, our general policy must be to play for time, cede nothing until we must, and build up our defences as soon as we can. At the same time we should aim at securing the full military co-operation of the Dutch ".[4] The fundamental concept of British policy was to avoid war with Japan, and all defence measures in Malaya or other areas of the Far East were conditioned by it. Defence plans were also governed by the consideration that security of the region from India to Australia was related to the ability of the British to control sea communications leading to these lands; and therefore strategy in the Far East must have for its foundation the " basing of an adequate fleet on Singapore". But this fleet was not available at the moment, hence all efforts had to be directed to maintain a foothold from which in case of necessity, position might be retrieved in the future. Such a foothold was Singapore and its protection now depended on the defence of the whole of Malaya.

In the fall of 1940 two new dangers had been appreciated, one was the penetration by the Japanese forces of Indo-China and/or Thailand, and the other, the occupation of Borneo and the Netherlands East Indies. In case of Japanese action against Indo-China or Thailand, it was clearly realised that the British Government would be unable to prevent it or render assistance to the victims of aggression. The penetration of Thailand would enable the Japanese to "threaten Singapore and unquestionably make the defence of Burma and Malaya far more difficult ", by establishing " shore-based aircraft within range of Singapore, Penang, the

[4] C.O.S. (40) 592, dated 15 August 1940.

Malacca Straits and the Rangoon oil refineries ", as well as organising land advance against Malaya from the north. Moreover, there was danger to communications in the Indian Ocean with its effect on the security of Malaya, based as it was on direct help from the United Kingdom. This was a new likelihood which had developed owing to the collapse of France and the absence of the British Fleet from the Far Eastern waters. The danger to Indo-China and Thailand had developed, for it was easy for Japan to establish her bases there, whether by force or by persuasion. And with such bases being formed there it was practicable for Japan " to attempt a landing upcountry in Malaya and then operate southwards under cover of shore-based aircraft ". This was more feasible than a direct assault on Singapore Island, and would be preferred by the Japanese. Hence the whole aspect of defence planning had to alter, and, instead of the emphasis on sea-borne assault on Singapore which alone was apprehended earlier, an overland attack on Singapore was now to be provided against. The Chiefs of Staff referred " to the necessity for holding the whole of Malaya rather than concentrating on the defence of Singapore Island ". This involved larger land and air forces which were estimated as follows:—

Air Force
   Northern Malaya: Bombers: 4 squadrons (64 aircraft)
                            Fighters: 2 squadrons (32 aircraft)
   Singapore: Torpedo Bombers: 2 squadrons (32 aircraft)
                            Fighters: 2 squadrons (32 aircraft)
   East Malaya: G. R. Landplanes: 2 squadrons (42 aircraft)
                            G. R. Flying Boats: 1 squadrons (6 aircraft).

Besides this, provision was made for the protection of sea communications and the defence of Borneo. The total requirement was calculated at 336 first-line aircraft and the programme was to be completed by the end of 1941.

Land Forces
The army was required for holding the whole of Malaya and affording protection to the aerodromes. For this purpose, a force equivalent to six brigades with ancillary troops was estimated. At this stage primary reliance for defence was placed on the air force. Role of the army was the close defence of naval and air bases, internal security and dealing with such hostile troops as might gain a footing on the Malayan soil. For this purpose immediately three divisions were required. But the force available

in Malaya was far below this figure; and neither the United Kingdom nor India was in a position to spare the requisite reinforcements. Australia had trained troops available, and on that basis was now built up the plan of Commonwealth co-operation for the defence of Malaya. Dutch co-operation, too, was necessary. Hence the idea of joint defence plans by Australia, Britain and the Dutch (ABD) developed and many conferences were held to implement joint action.

Subsequent to the Appreciation by the Chiefs of Staff, a Tactical Appreciation was prepared by the Commanders in Singapore. Meanwhile in September 1940, the Japanese had occupied the northern portion of Indo-China which aggravated the threat to Singapore. This event considerably altered the basis of defence planning, for the Japanese invading force could now concentrate within close striking distance of Malaya instead of being transported all the way from Japan. The whole problem of the security of the Far East was examined by the Singapore Defence Conference which met in October 1940 and was attended by the representatives of Australia, Burma, India, New Zealand, Dutch East Indies and Malaya. An American observer was also present. The discussions at the Conference revolved round the Tactical Appreciation which was built up on the assumption that a strong fleet based on Singapore was essential for the protection of communications and Allied possessions in the Far East. But until such a fleet was available, the burden of defence must fall on the Royal Air Force backed by such land forces as might be necessary for garrison purposes in Malaya. The holding of the whole of Malaya was recognised as the basic principle of defence, for the appreciation was that Japan, despite the war with China and by maintaining peace with Russia, would have ample sea, land and air forces to attack Malaya from Indo-China and Thailand. In this contingency, the course open to the British was to be on the defensive with a strong army on the northern frontier, and if necessary to occupy southern Thailand. The Tactical Appreciation had also allocated the role of the three services, the Royal Air Force was to defeat all attacks, the army to defend all bases and defeat all forces intruding on land while the Royal Navy was to co-operate with the other two and protect trade. For this purpose the requirement was estimated at 566 aircraft of the first line, four brigade groups in addition to the static formations in garrisons.

The Singapore Defence Conference reviewed the entire situation in the Far East. It proceeded on the assumption of American and Dutch neutrality though their intervention was not completely ruled out; it was possible in the case of the former and probable in the latter. It was also assumed that in case of a Japanese invasion of Australia or New Zealand their naval forces would not be available, and that a battle cruiser and aircraft-carrier would operate in the Indian Ocean as desired by Mr. Winston Churchill. The Conference considered the various lines of action by the Japanese, namely, the invasion of Australia or New Zealand seizure of Islands in the Pacific Ocean, attack on Hong Kong, invasion of Malaya with the object of seizing Singapore, seizure of bases in British Borneo, overland attack on Burma from Indo-China and Thailand, and raids on shipping in the Pacific and Indian Oceans. Of these the invasion of Malaya was most probable. British policy, in the absence of sufficient naval forces for offensive action, was merely one of defence and concentration " on the protection of vital points and vital trade and convoys ".[5]

For the security of Malaya, which was the " first and immediate consideration ", the Conference endorsed the Tactical Appreciation and recommended the immediate remedying of deficiencies in the army and air force, by seeking the co-operation of India, Australia and New Zealand. The plan was outlined as follows; " what air forces are available we must use to prevent or at least to deter the Japanese from establishing naval and air bases within striking distances of our vital interests in Malaya, Burma, the Dutch East Indies, Australia and New Zealand. By using advanced operational bases throughout the area, we should aim at being able to concentrate aircraft at any point from our collective air resources in the Far East, Australia and New Zealand ".[6] For this purpose it was necessary to prepare facilities and ground organisation for the air force to operate.

Besides laying down the general principles for the defence of the Far East, the Conference also utilised the presence of American and Dutch representatives to discuss plans for co-ordinating the employment of British, Dutch and American forces in the event of war with Japan. It was fully realised by this time that in the Far East the interests of these powers were closely related and that, in case of war with Japan, combined action by them was inevitable. Hence staff conversations were suggested to afford the best employment of their respective forces and formulate common plans of defence. The Singapore Defence Conference paved the way for such discussion and, in the next few months, conversations made considerable progress. In November 1940, staff conversations were held with the officers from the Dutch

---

[5] Report of Singapore Defence Conference, October 1940, para 4.
[6] *Ibid*, para 6.

East Indies, and in February and April conferences were held with Australian, Dutch and American representatives.

DISCUSSION IN 1941

Between February and April 1941, three conferences were held in which the British, United States, Dutch and the Dominion representatives participated. The first conference met from 22 to 25 February 1941, and arrived at tentative conclusions relating to the extent and direction of the threat of Japanese attack, the attitude of the United States and the character of Japanese reaction, the need for co-operation in the Far East and the method of combined action. The report of the Anglo-Dutch-Australian Conversations (ADA) formed the basis of further conversations in which the co-operation of the United States was made more explicit. Meanwhile, staff talks had been held in Washington, wherein it was decided " to convene a conference at Singapore to prepare plans for conduct of military operations in Far East on basis of Anglo-U.S.-Dutch co-operation in conformity with report on Washington conversation but without political conversations ".[7] Consequently two sets of conversations were held, first between the American, Dutch and British representatives (called ADB conversations) and the second between the British, and Dutch representatives (called BD conversations). The value of these talks lay in the assessment of the danger and the resources which were available to counteract it. Plans then contemplated were based on two alternative assumptions, the United States entering the war on the side of the Associated Powers or remaining neutral. Anglo-Dutch co-operation for mutual defence was pre-supposed. The plans were also to be divided into two phases, one before the arrival of the Far East Fleet, which was contemplated by the Washington conversations, and the other after it. The plans envisaged employment and disposition of forces in the whole area of the Indian and Pacific Oceans and Australian and New Zealand waters.

At the outset it was made clear that priority would be accorded to the war in Europe and the first object was the defeat of Germany and her allies. This naturally limited the scope of activities in East Asia, where the object was defined to be the maintenance of " the position of the Associated Powers against Japanese attack, in order to sustain a long term economic pressure against Japan until we are in a position to take the offensive [8]"

---
[7] War Office to C-in-C Far East No. 580, 7 April 1941. (Appendix 38, General Headquarter War Diary, Far-East).
[8] War Diary of General Headquarters Far East, Appendix 45, para 4.

At the same time important Allied interests in East Asia were specified as "(a) the security of sea communications and (b) the security of Singapore". A subsidiary interest was also the security of Luzon in the Philippine Islands. In appraising the situation in east Asia it was realised that while Japan's object was "to obtain complete political and economic domination of South-East Asia and the islands in the Far East Area in order to secure control for herself of the sources of vital war supplies", her action would be governed by the knowledge that aggression against one of the Associated Powers would involve united resistance, by her lack of trust in Russia and the intensity of Chinese resistance which might gain momentum by the entry of the Associated Powers in the war against Japan. The direction of Japanese attack was also forecast with its relative intensity against several objectives. The Philippines, Hong Kong, Malaya, Burma, Borneo and sea communications were considered to be threatened. In the case of Malaya, it was stated that the attack would be through Thailand and would be made in two stages:

"(a) Political domination which would give some indication of intention,

(b) Military occupation which would take time and would provide an opportunity of forestalling action in the Kra Isthmus".[9]

Direct attack by landing on the east coast of Malaya was also not overlooked, as it could be "without preliminary warning", but this required on the part of Japan "a greater degree of control of the seas and air communications". The arrival of some reinforcements in Malaya made the task of invader not so easy and it was felt that until Hong Kong and Manila had been reduced, either line of attack would be "a formidable proposition" as "a long and precarious line of communications" was involved. Hence, until the air forces and submarines maintained in the Philippines had been eliminated, Japan would take a great risk in launching an attack towards the west on Malaya or the Netherlands East Indies or in the east against Austarlia and New Zealand.

This appreciation of the danger naturally led to the emphasis on collective action by the Associated Powers, and actions were enumerated the occurrence of which should be the signal for collective counteraction. Among these, movements of Japanese troops into any part of south Thailand and of a large number of their warships or a convoy of merchant ships, escorted by war ships, directed towards the Isthmus of Kra, or the east coast of Malaya,

---

[9] *Ibid*, para 14.

were considered to constitute a real danger against which measures of counteraction were to be initiated immediately. But the strategy in the Far East, as long as Germany and Italy had not been defeated, was to be mainly defensive.

These conversations also determined the employment of their respective naval and air forces and the divisions of command. We are not here concerned with the details about the dispositions of the naval and air forces which extended over the entire Far East Area. It may suffice to mention that the responsibility for the eastern portion of the Area was that of the United States Asiatic Fleet, and the British and Dutch naval units had as their charge the protection of their bases and the maintenance of sea communications in their zones. Also Singapore was to be the base from which in Phase II the British Eastern Fleet would operate. The employment of land and air forces to hold an attack was limited by the comparative smallness of the land frontiers which had to be guarded. These were only in Burma and Malaya. The northern frontier of the latter was strategically weak and attack could proceed from south Thailand or after a landing. Except, therefore, for these frontiers of Burma and Malaya, the hostile land forces attacking any part would necessarily be sea-borne, and their objective would be " the sea and air bases on which the defence mainly rests ". Consequently, the policy, as outlined, was " to organise the defence system to give the greatest possible security to these bases. This together with the denial of potential air and naval bases to enemy occupation, will be the primary task of the land forces. We can thus fully employ the mobility of air forces both independently and in co-operation with naval submarine and surface forces, to effect concentrations against any naval forces or sea-borne expeditions during their approach and landing, to discover and destroy enemy air forces and to operate dispersed for the protection of sea communications ".[10]

The ADB conversations were comprehensive and related to general strategy. Simultaneously with these, and in elucidation of the points agreed to at the ADA Conference in February 1941, conversations were held between the British and the Dutch, which made specific reference to the Anglo-Dutch co-operation in the western zone. About Malaya and the Netherlands East Indies including British North Borneo, it was agreed that simultaneous attacks might be launched against these, but owing to Japanese commitments in China a major attack would develop only in one

---

[10] American-Dutch-British Conversations. Singapore, April, 1941, Report p. 23, para 69. (General Headquarter Far-East War-Diary Appendix 45).

of these while against the other the attack would be on a smaller scale and "mainly of a subsidiary and diversionary nature". It was further assumed that Japan would develop her hold on Indo-China and Thailand and thereafter deliver her main attack on Malaya "with the object of securing Singapore". Hence the plan of action was directed towards the security of Singapore which depended largely on the defence of Malaya. In these conversations, as in the others, greater stress was laid on the effectiveness of air defence, the role of the land forces being largely "the defence of the naval and air bases and the denial of potential naval and air base to the enemy". It was further stated that "there is little possibility of strategic offensive action by land forces and a localised strategic policy is therefore already established for the land forces".[11] No co-ordination of command was therefore necessary in the case of land forces, which was however inevitable in the instance of naval and air forces.

It will appear from the preceding account that the basis for defence preparations in Malaya was the Chief of Staff Appreciation of 16 August 1940, which led to the framing of the Tactical Appreciation by the authorities in Malaya and the convening of Anglo-Dutch-American-Australian conversations for mutual co-operation in the defence of South-East Asia. British policy till about the end of 1941 continued to be one of avoiding war with Japan as long as the struggle in Europe absorbed her resources and prevented her from stationing a strong fleet in East Asia. Attitude of the United States, though apparently one of co-operation and collaboration against the Axis Powers, was not yet quite definite and could hardly permit of the defence plans being prepared on the basis of specific American military aid. The Dutch were presumed to be the victims of Japanese aggression equally with the British and their co-operation was assumed, but at this stage the British did not have enough resources to render military support to the Dutch, and unless the Netherlands East Indies were attacked simultaneously with Malaya or British Borneo, the British Chiefs of Staff were not confident of depending upon effective Dutch co-operation in the defence of Malaya. The situation in Europe made the prospects of releasing the fleet for action in East Asia quite remote, and without that, full security of British vital interests in that region was difficult of achievement. Hence in the "absence of capital ship fleet", reliance had to be placed primarily on air power "in conjunction with such naval forces as can be made available"; and land forces were to be employed against the landings.

[11] *Ibid*, para 36.

The estimate of forces, both air and land, was based on the threat to North Malaya from Indo-China or Thailand and sea-borne invasion on the eastern coast of Malaya or attack on Singapore Island itself. To contain this danger, a force of 336 first-line aircraft and six brigades with ancillary troops was originally estimated. These figures were added to subsequently, so that by the middle of 1941, the requirement mounted to 566 first-line aircraft and 26 battalions with supporting arms, ancillary services etc. But it was realised that the target of air forces might not be attained; Air Chief Marshal Sir Robert Brooke-Popham, Commander-in-Chief, Far East, did not hope that its strength by December 1941 would be higher than 186, a figure far below even the lowest appreciation. In the situation, General Percival, General Officer Commanding, Malaya Command, in August 1941, pitched his estimate of land forces required at:—[12]

48 infantry battalions.
4 Indian reconnaissance units.
9 Forward artillery regiments.
4 Light A.A. regiments.
2 Tank regiments.
3 Anti-tank regiments.
2 Mountain artillery regiments.
12 Field companies.

As the strength of the Royal Air Force could not materially increase, either in numbers or the quality of aircraft, this estimate of land forces was considered reasonable, and met with acceptance by the Chiefs of Staff, who, however, feared that "this target cannot be fulfilled in foreseeable future."

Tactical planning proceeded on these assumptions. In October 1940, an appreciation was prepared by the local Commanders of the three services in accordance with the Chief of Staff Strategical Appreciation, and in many particulars it continued to be the nucleus of subsequent planning. Its main object was to "make the best dispositions possible to secure most important of our (Far East) interests without the cover which capital ship fleet would provide".[13] Japanese occupation of Indo-China and South Thailand was an important assumption, as also that Japan had ample sea, land and air forces to launch land-based attack from Thailand, sea-borne attack on Malaya and to threaten sea communications with the latter concurrently. Kam Ranh Bay was the base from where Japanese fleet could operate, and Singapore was within

---

[12] Despatch by Major-General Percival *op. cit.* para 47.
[13] Singapore Defence Conference October 1940, Report para 2. (General Headquarter Far East War-Diary Appendix 26).

the range of heavy bombers. The whole of northern Malaya was within the range of even light bombers and fighters. Nor were the Japanese presumed to have any difficulty about reinforcements which they might easily get by virtue of their control over Indo-China and Thailand and the command of the China Sea. Hence a sudden Japanese attack, "fully prepared and in great strength" might be faced, and this Tactical Appreciation was framed to meet that contingency.

The role of the three services in this plan was defined. The air force was assigned the function of defeating Japanese attack, if sea-borne, at sea and during landing; and if land-based, by attacks on the advancing troops, landing grounds, lines of communication and military objectives. The role of the army was that of close defence of naval and air bases, internal security and defeat of Japanese forces gaining a foothold on British territory. The navy, whatever it was, was allotted the task of local defence, trade protection and reconnaissance of and attack on Japanese shipping. Primary emphasis at this stage was on the air force, and for that reason a force of 566 aircraft, distributed as below, was considered an essential minimum:

(a) Reconnaissance and attack on Japanese sea-borne forces .. 186 aircraft
(b) Bombers for striking land-based Japanese forces 192 ,,
(c) Fighters to oppose Japanese fighters and protect vital areas 144 ,,
(d) Army co-operation 44 ,,

566 ,,

But until the Royal Air Force had attained this strength, the deficiencies in it were to be made good by additional land forces, and " the available land and air forces were to be so distributed as to offer the maximum resistance and to provide the maximum deterrent to attack ". The disposition of land forces was related to the protection of existing aerodromes and maintaining intact their operational facilities. Aerodromes in Malaya had been sited at Seletar, Sembawang, Kallang, Tengah, Kluang, Alor Star, Kota Bharu, Sungei Patani, Penang, and Kuantan. Hence the land forces had to be organised for the defence of Kelantan, Pahang, Trenggannu, Perlis, Kedah, Penang, Singapore and Johore approaches, and the north-south communications on the west coast. On this calculation a force of four brigade groups besides the fixed garrisons of Singapore, Penang, Kota Bharu, and Kuantan was recommended for Malaya.

PLATE III

General Sir Archibald P. Wavell,
Supreme Commander ABDACOM

Admiral Sir Geoffrey Layton,
Commander Eastern Fleet

PLATE IV

Lieut.-General Sir Henry Pownall,
C-in-C Far East.

Lieut.-General Sir Lewis Heath,
Commander III Indian Corps.

In this Appreciation, defensive in its character, there is the first indication of the necessity of anticipating the Japanese troops in south Thailand or the Kra Isthmus. At the outset the local commanders recommended " that serious consideration should be given to the question whether, if Japan advances into Thailand, we should not in self-defence seize at least part of South Thailand ". The object in doing this was to " (1) deny to the Japanese the use of air and sea bases close to the Malayan Frontier, (2) improve the frontier we must hold and provide alternative communication with Kota Bharu, and (3) give some measure of protection to the chain of aerodromes between Burma and Malaya through which our air reinforcements must pass ".[14] But for political reasons this step was not considered feasible, though without it the weaknesses of the defence plan were glaring, and of which the authors of the Tactical Appreciation were fully conscious. Hence they stressed the importance of more reinforcements both for land and air forces. The problem was a difficult one as the forces were weak numerically and lacked essential equipment like artillery, tanks, anti-tank weapons, mortars, and Army Co-operation aircraft. There were also no reserves for the replacement of " tired " units. At every stage, taking into account the probable reinforcements, the deficiencies were serious and the force quite inadqeuate to cope with the danger.

From the middle of 1940, reinforcements had begun to arrive in Malaya and, by the middle of 1941, the elements of the 9th and 11th Indian Infantry Divisions, the 8th Australian Division and the nucleus of the III Indian Corps had gathered in Malaya. The air force had also expanded though not proportionately to the estimates under the plans, and the old obsolete types like Vildbeestes were still in operation. A number of aerodromes were constructed on the east coast and in the north, and the land force whose primary role was that of the defence of air bases was dispersed for this purpose.[15]

The then disposition was governed by the necessity of defending aerodromes and denying them to the Japanese. Sir Robert Brooke-Popham admits that the disposition might have been different if " the policy had been to defend Malaya by means of Army forces " and not " by means of air power " which was an essential feature of the then strategy.[16] Owing to the need for the defence of aerodromes, which were sited largely on the east coast " to provide reconnaissance over the South China Sea, from which

---

[14] Tactical Appreciation, October 1940, p. 3 para 17.
[15] See Percival's Despatch *op. cit.* for details.
[16] Brooke-Popham's Despatch *op. cit.* para 11.

direction the threat to Malaya by sea was greatest",[17] there was considerable dispersal of the land forces. There was great difference of view regarding the advisability of, and the best method for, defending the important sectors of the east coast. The length of the beach and the inadequacy of troops would, it was argued, make it difficult to prevent landings at every place, and would enable the Japanese to outflank the defenders. It was feared that an attempt to hold the beaches " would result in a purely linear defence, with insufficient troops in hand for counter-attack"; hence the best course would be " to fight on a prepared position in rear where the road leading into the interior could be defended ".[18] This view did not, however, find favour with the General Headquarters, Far East, who regarded the holding of the beaches essential during the period of landing, even if it might give the appearance of linear defence. All round perimeter defence was an alternative, but that failed to be practicable with the limited forces, and lack of reserves. Hence Sir Robert Brooke-Popham decided on the Plan that the first line of defence should be the beaches, and ordered preparation of obstacles and defence posts at Mersing, Kuantan and Kota Bharu. The Commander-in-Chief, Far East, also envisaged the possibility of a break-through in the Mersing area which would have isolated the southern and northern Malaya from Singapore. To provide against this danger depots were so sited as to enable the forces to be based on the Kuala Lumpur-Penang line of communication and thus be independent of Singapore.[19]

The whole scheme of defence thus was essentially defensive in character, and was based on the earlier appreciations of seaborne invasion and the reliance on air power to resist the attack. But when the realisation of land-based invasion arising from south Thailand grew, the strategic value of the Kra Isthmus for meeting the threat was fully appreciated. Sir Robert Brooke-Popham writes that " the possibility of an advance into this Isthmus, in order to hold a position North of Haad Yai Junction, was considered soon after the formation of General Headquarters, Far East ".[20] General Percival also mentions that before he left London to take over the Malaya Command, he had discussed on broad lines a proposal of this nature, and on his arrival in Malaya, he was commissioned by the Commander-in-Chief, Far East, to examine this matter in detail. These discussions led to the formulation of

[17] Maltby's Despatch *op. cit.* para 17.
[18] Brooke-Popham's Despatch *op. cit.* para. 48.
[19] *Ibid.*, para 49.
[20] *Ibid.*, para 50.

the Operation Matador which owing to its political implications could not be implemented without prior reference to London.

Matador

The object of this operation for forward defence was to meet the invader beyond the northern frontiers of Malaya on the soil of south Thailand or in the Kra Isthmus, which contained the main lines of communications leading into Malaya. The plan was to move the 11th Indian Division across the border to hold the Singora area and to fight defensively on the Patani-Kroh route. This step would enable the defenders to block the main road from Singora via Haad Yai junction into Kedah and the secondary road from Patani via Yala to Kroh in north Perak. The successful operation of this plan would have led to the " forestalling of the Japanese on a position near Singora ".[21] But its execution depended on being able to take action before the Japanese, which in the state of Thai neutrality and the policy of the British Government not to provoke hostilities with Japan, was not easily practicable. London did not permit any action without its prior sanction being obtained 24 hours before, and yielded to 72 hours notice only on 5 December 1941. Nevertheless the planning of the Operation Matador proceeded rapidly.

During July 1941, a staff conference was held at the headquarters of Malaya Command, which was attended by the representatives of the General Headquarters, Headquarters Malaya Command, III Indian Corps, 11th Indian Division, Royal Navy, and the Royal Air Force. The points for its consideration were two: one, how far the project for the occupation of the Kra Isthmus by a joint Army/RAF force from Malaya, which could deny to the Japanese the port and aerodrome facilities in that area, was feasible, and the other, whether this denial could be effected with the existing forces in Malaya. The conference recommended that Matador, holding Singora area and the ' Ledge ' was practicable if (a) two divisions were provided, a preliminary secret reconnaissance could be made, adequate warning was given and Patani-Kroh route was also held, and (b) a minimum of twenty-four hours start of the Japanese was granted and the whole plan was carried out during the north-east monsoon when the Japanese would not be able to use their tanks off the roads. The scheme was so attractive as an alternative to the most unsuitable Jitra position that it was readily approved by the Chiefs of Staff in London, and reconnaissance was made. Careful and comprehensive plans were drawn up to move troops by road and rail into

[21] *Ibid*, para 50.

Thailand with the co-operation of air force in northern Malaya, and the units were trained and trimmed for the jump at any moment.

Sandwich

The impracticability of Matador had also led to the formulation of an attenuated plan, called Operation Sandwich. This plan consisted of a move forward by road transport of the 6th Indian Infantry Brigade and 1/14 Punjab to Singora with the object of destroying its port facilities, opposing the Japanese landing and then falling back to Jitra carrying out demolitions on the route. This operation found greater favour with the Chiefs of Staff who had sanctioned it as a substitute for Matador, though in the later stages the Commander-in-Chief, Far East, was authorised to carry out Matador without reference to London in the event of either of the two contingencies: that information was available of the advance of the Japanese expedition into the Kra Isthmus or the Japanese had violated any other part of Thailand.

DEFENCE PLANS

The adoption of an offensive plan of operation to forestall the Japanese invasion was conditional upon many factors and was difficult of achievement, in view of the limited resources in Malaya. Hence the main emphasis was on the defence of the northern and eastern portions of the country, and the disposition of land and air forces was made on that basis. Initially stress was laid on air defence, and aerodromes were built or extended to make use of the mobility of aircraft for concentrating a large force in any area and also to cover a maximum distance both for reconnaissance and offensive operations. The number of aerodromes was related to the estimate of requirements of force, but as this target was never reached, many aerodromes were surplus to the needs and became a serious liability. The siting of these aerodromes was in reference to their suitability for flying operations or facility in movement of labour and material and did not bear any relation to their suitability for defence. But their location determined the disposition of the land forces, for the primary role of the army was to protect the aerodromes. The other commitment for the army, particularly after the danger of over-land invasion from the north was fully realised, was to deny to the Japanese the use of the railway and roads leading from the Thai border towards Singapore, whose Naval Base was the main object of defence. But as the direction of hostile approach might be either from the north from across the Thai border or from the north-east by way of sea, the defence preparations were directed towards preventing landward penetration from the north and landing on the beaches of the eastern coast of Malaya.

The Northern Frontier

The Malaya-Thailand frontier was crossed by only two roads and one railway, though there were a number of bush tracks also which might be used by stray parties. The main road from Alor Star in Kedah to Haad Yai in south Thailand and thence to Singora crossed the frontier a few miles north of Changlun. The other road crossed the frontier at Kroh and then ran to Patani in south Thailand. The railway, passing through Alor Star, crossed the frontier in the State of Perlis on its way to Haad Yai Junction and thence to Singora or Bangkok. These main approaches from the north were ordered by the Commander-in-Chief, Far East, to be put in a state of defence. In this area the main aerodromes were situated at Alor Star, and in Kedah and Province Wellesley, which had to be covered and protected. This involved the siting of the defences sufficiently north of Alor Star, and the position selected for this purpose was the village of Jitra, which lay at the junction of the main road with the branch road to Perlis, about 18 miles south of the frontier. "This position", according to General Percival, "had obvious disadvantages, chief of which was the weakness of the left flank in dry weather, for between it and the sea was a stretch of some 12 miles of open or semi-open country, intersected by small canals and ditches. The main defences were, therefore, concentrated astride the two roads, reliance being placed on a skeleton pill-box defence combined with a maximum use of natural obstacles for the protection of the left flank. Plans were made to flood an area astride the railway, which seemed to be a probable line of enemy advance. On the main front anti-tank ditches were dug where there were no natural obstacles and defended localities were constructed".[22] The Jitra line was 17 miles in extent, the east flank resting on the jungle.

On the other road on the Kroh-Patani road the most suitable defensive position was found to be "The Ledge", about 35 to 40 miles on the Thailand side of the frontier. Here the road had been cut out of a steep hillside, and could be easily blocked by demolitions. But no prior preparations were contemplated in peacetime. Hence another site known as Kedah position was being prepared just west of Kroh astride the Baling road, in order to protect the right flank of the Jitra position.

[22] Percival's Despatch *op. cit.* paras 30-31.

The main object of these northern defences was to guard the Alor Star aerodrome and delay the hostile advance for as long as possible. The northern defences were the responsibility of the 11th Indian Division, but from the very beginning it was realised that the force then available was wholly inadequate for the task. Moreover, the Jitra position excited no enthusiasm in the officers who preferred to meet the Japanese advance at Singora.

East Coast

The other threatened area was the east coast of Malaya which abounded in beaches suitable for landing, not only in the dry season but during the monsoon months as well. The east coast was an undeveloped area and lacked communications. But influenced by the needs of air defence, aerodromes had been constructed in that region, and the army was called upon to render protection to the aerodromes and deal with the hostile forces landing on the east coast. Three areas were primarily selected for the purpose; these were the Kelantan area, the Kuantan area and the East Johore area. According to General Percival, " the primary role of the Army in the first two of these, both of which were situated at the end of very long and vulnerable communications, was the defence of aerodromes which had been constructed there. In both cases, the forces which could be made available were inadequate for the task ".[23] There were three aerodromes in Kelantan, at Kota Bharu, Gong Kedah, and Machang, all east of the Kelantan river. The force resopnsible for the Kelantan area was the 8th Indian Infantry Brigade which had an extensive front comprising six beaches, each approximately 5 miles in length, and a river front about 10 miles, besides the local defence of the three aerodromes.

The Kuantan area was assigned to the 22nd Indian Infantry Brigade which had the liability to watch two long beaches besides an aerodrome, 9 miles west of Kuantan. Its task also included the guarding of approaches from the north through Trenggannu or from the south through Pekan at the mouth of the Pahang river. In the Kelantan area, beach defence pill-boxes were to be built and anti-tank obstructions constructed. So also material defences were to be constructed in the Kuantan area.

In east Johore, there were two small towns of strategic importance, Mersing and Endau. Mersing was connected with Singapore by a motor road and had good landing beaches, both north and south of it. It was also connected with Kluang in the centre of Johore and thence to Batu Pahat on the west coast by a

---

[23] Percival's Despatch. *op. cit.* para.33.

lateral road, which branched from the Mersing-Singapore road at Jemaluang. This Jemaluang road junction was vital to the defence of this area. In the Johore area, therefore, " there were three contingencies to be provided for: (a) an attempt by the enemy to land in the Endau area with the object of either moving on Mersing or via the Bukit Langkap iron ore mine to the Kluang road and the Kluang aerodrome situated close to it; (b) a landing in force in the Mersing area; (c) landing of small forces further south with a view to cutting communications with Singapore ". This task was allotted originally to the 12th Indian Infantry Brigade. " The general plan was to hold in force the Mersing area and the beaches to the south with a detachment at Endau and a reserve in a prepared position north of the Jemaluang road junction; other detachments watched the communications to Singapore ".[24] Beach defences were also prepared.

In addition to these defences, the Singapore Island defence was organised as fortress defence with its own aerodromes and fixed naval defences.

The defences as planned, irrespective of Matador or Sandwich, which had an offensive appearance about them, had as their object the watching of a long coast line with its beaches suitable for landing, and the northern frontier which allowed easy access, because of its roads and railway, to the invading forces. Prepared defences were to be sited in the north to cover the main approaches and to deny the aerodromes. On the coast line also three areas were to be defended which held the aerodromes and contained some important beaches from where road communication to Singapore was possible. These defences, though local, were linear in their character and were thin in disposition. Defences had not been prepared in depth, and owing to the paucity of troops, reserves were not adequate to deal with the invader when he succeeded in demolishing the first line of resistance or in outflanking it. This weakness of defence was evident to the Commanding Officers, but in the absence of sufficient aircraft or land forces, no other alternative was practicable.

REINFORCEMENTS

The gradual modification of the defence policy from a close defence of the Naval Base in Singapore Island to that of the whole of Malaya, involved an increase in the forces stationed in that country. It may be recalled that initially greater stress was laid

---

[24] *Ibid*, para 36.

on the effectiveness of the Royal Navy, but when in the early stages of the war in Europe it was found necessary to concentrate the British fleet nearer home, the burden shifted to the Royal Air Force on which was placed the primary responsibility for the protection of Malaya and the East Asian region. The first appreciation estimated a minimum force of 336 aircraft for the task. This was soon raised to 582; but this target was unattainable and at best the number did not rise above 180. Hence the army was to fill up the gap and compensate for the deficiency in aircraft and the absence of the navy. But here too the estimated strength for adequately guarding the peninsula could not be gathered. However, reinforcements flowed in during 1941 which we may now review.

Air Force

At the time when the estimate of requirements was fixed at 336 aircraft, the total strength of the air force in Malaya was 88 first line aircraft made up as follows:—

Bombers	2 squadrons Blenheim—	24 aircraft
Reconnaissance	2 squadrons Hudsons (RAAF)—	24
Torpedo Bombers	2 squadrons Vildebeestes—	24
General Purpose	1 squadron Wirraways (RAAF)—	12
Flying Boats	1 squadron Singapores—4 aircraft	4
	Total	88

Of this number, only Blenheims and Hudsons totalling 48 aircraft might be counted as modern. Vildebeestes were an obsolete type and were to be replaced by Beauforts which were to be manufactured in Australia. But circumstances prevented this replacement and this type continued to be there in Malaya when the Japanese invasion came. The other types were also needing overhaul. Yet the greatest weakness of the air force consisted in the utter absence of fighters. The deficiencies were too glaring and the Commander-in-Chief, Far East, was making fervent appeals from time to time for the inflow of necessary reinforcements, which failed to materialise except in driblets. There was no lack of proper understanding of the situation and the Chiefs of Staff cannot be blamed of neglecting the requirements of a theatre which was fast drifting into the whirl of war. But, as Mr. Winston Churchill has explained, the competing claims of other zones made Malaya to starve. He writes in his book, " as regards air reinforcements for Malaya, the Conference at Singapore recommended the urgent dispatch of considerable numbers of aircraft. With the ever-changing situation it is difficult to commit ourselves to the precise number of aircraft which we can make available for Singapore, and we certainly could not spare the flying-boats to lie about idle there on the remote chance of a Japanese attack when they ought to be playing their part in the deadly struggle on the North-Western Approaches. Broadly speaking, our policy is to build up as large as possible a Fleet, Army, and Air Force in the Middle East, and keep this in a fluid condition, either to prosecute war in Libya, Greece, and presently Thrace, or reinforce Singapore should the Japanese attitude change for the worse. In this way dispersion of forces will be avoided and victory will give its own far-reaching protections in many directions ".[25]

There appears to have been no support for this policy by the Chiefs of Staff, but the Prime Minister had his way. Consequently the air branch of Malaya or Far East defence remained unprovided and even neglected, and the position on 22 November 1941, has been so described by Sir Paul Maltby; " The R.A.F. Far East Command was not yet in a position to fulfil its responsibility of being the primary means of resisting Japanese aggression. The calls of the war in Europe had allowed it to develop only a fraction of the necessary strength (namely, 336 aircraft). Re-equipment of squadrons had not taken place and was not likely to do so in the near future; Vickers Vildebeestes were still our main striking strength. Buffalo fighters had arrived, it is true, but their performance and armament were disappointing, and inexperienced pilots were still being trained to man them. The aerodromes in Northern Malaya on which so much was to depend, especially during the early stages of the war, had none of the pre-requisites of secure air bases for occupation in the face of the enemy. The number of fighters available was very inadequate for providing effective fighter cover. Both heavy and light A.A. guns were quite insufficient. Dispersal arrangements for aircraft and their protection from blast were not as complete as was planned. And, in the absence of an adequate air raid warning system, the aerodromes were open to surprise attack. But the role of the command remained constant. It was not practicable to alter it. It was (a) to find the enemy at sea as far away from Malaya as possible; then (b) to strike hard and often, (c) to continue attacks during the landing operations: and (d) in co-operation with the

[25] Churchill, *The Second World War*, Vol. II, Appendix A, p. 629.

Army to delay his advance. While real progress had been made in fitting the Command for its allotted tasks, deficiencies were still apparent in almost every aspect of its functions.[26] As a matter of fact the position of the air force at the outbreak of war on 8 December 1941, was analogous to a bridge which gave way at the passing of the very first vehicle over it. The Commander-in-Chief, Far East, promised to do his best even after the outbreak of war with Japan to defend Malaya successfully if he could get more aircraft immediately, especially long-range bombers. But the British Cabinet closed the conversations with general remarks on the principle of air superiority in war, and with a promise of many things to come.[27] The strength of the air force, as on 7 December 1941, in Malaya was 157 serviceable aircraft, as against the lowest requirement of 336. Sir Robert Brooke-Popham has summarised the deficiencies in his despatch as follows:—

"Our most serious deficiency at that time was in reserves, partly of pilots, but principally aircraft. It was not only a stock of reserve aeroplanes was wanted, but also a continuous flow of new aircraft to replace wastage, for aeroplanes must be regarded as expendable material, and there must be a regular, continuous channel of supply. Without these it was impossible to keep the squadrons up to their first-line establishment. Apart from the material weakness, failure to keep up what is commonly known as "full breakfast table" always has an adverse effect on squadrons' morale".[28]

Navy

The position of the navy was no better. There was not a fleet worth the name in East Asia after the outbreak of war in Europe;[29] only the United States had anything which was good enough against Japan, as the table (on reverse) will show:[30]

In Australian waters there were 3 Australian cruisers, 3 destroyers, 1 Free French destroyer and 2 New Zealand cruisers.

As against this on 7 December 1941, Japan's operational strength was more probably 11 battleships, 8 carriers, 2 converted merchant-ship carriers, 8 seaplane carriers, 18 heavy cruisers, 20 light cruisers, 113 destroyers and 62 submarines. All these were comparatively far less scattered than the Allied fleet.

[26] Sir Paul Maltby's Despatch in supplement to the London Gazette, 26 February, 1948 p. 1361, paras 132 to 135.
[27] Cables Nos. 431/6, 487/6 and 56/7, dated 8, 11 and 17 December respectively, Easfar to Troopers. Most Secret Cables Nos. 56,829, and 58,683 Troopers to Easfar, 9 and 18 December 1941.
[28] Brooke-Popham's Despatch *op. cit.*
[29] Percival, Lt. Gen. A.E., *The War in Malaya*, p. 30, para 3.
[30] C.B. 3,081(8) Battle Summary No. 14, Loss of H.M.S. *Prince of Wales* and *Repulse*, p.8.

Nationality	Capital ships	Aircraft Carriers	Sea Plane Carrier	Heavy Cruisers	Light Cruisers	Destroyers	Submarines
British Empire	2	..		1	7	13	..
U.S.A.	8	3		13	11	90	60
Netherlands					3	7	13
Free France		..	..		1	..	..
Total	10	3		14	22	110	73
Japan	10	9	6	12	23	127	86

The British plan in August 1941 was to form a fleet of 7 capital ships, 1 aircraft carrier, 10 cruisers and 24 destroyers. But it was not carried out and various alternatives were considered. Meanwhile, the political situation in East Asia steadily deteriorated, and Mr. Winston Churchill and the Defence Committee considered it of some importance, at least psychologically, to send two capital ships, the *Prince of Wales* and the *Repulse*, to the Asian waters. It was thought that the presence of a strong United States fleet based on Hawaii would be sufficient to restrain Japan from undertaking any major venture involving the close support of their main fleet in the Gulf of Siam. The two capital ships with four destroyers (*Electra*, *Express*, *Encounter* and *Jupiter*) arrived at Singapore on 2 December 1941.

There was much regret at the very difficult position of this ' unbalanced force '. On 1 December 1941, the Admiralty suggested to Admiral Phillips to send the ships away from Singapore to disconcert the Japanese and increase the security of the force at one stroke. On 3 December 1941, the co-operation of the United States fleet was suggested. Admiral Phillips accepted the latter suggestion. But four days later the Japanese struck at Pearl Harbour and thereby completely altered the strategical situation. The basis on which the British ships had been sent to the east was thereby destroyed. A week later the British fleet was attacked and a vacuum was created in the defences of the British in the Far East. Thereafter, the duties of the British navy were performed only by submarines, minesweepers and destroyers aided by the air force, while all the battleships were warned not to come beyond Colombo without cruisers, destroyers and aeroplanes accompanying them.[31]

Army

In 1936 and 1937 there were only a few troops in Malaya, the bulk of them being in the island of Singapore. These were

---

[31] Secret Cable No. 782 C-in-C, Eastern Fleet to Admiralty, 11 December 1941.

three British battalions, viz. 2 Loyals, 2 Gordons and 1 Manchester in Singapore, one Indian Battalion viz. 2/17 Dogra at Taiping, and one Malaya Regiment at Port Dickson. In addition there were various volunteer units at Malacca and Penang, anti-aircraft defence units of the Royal Artillery and troops of several ancillary units in Singapore. By 1939 the volunteers had been organised into compact and trained battalions; and as the situation in Europe was deteriorating, the British Government ordered in August of that year reinforcements in the form of Force EMU to Malaya. This consisted of the 12th Indian Infantry Brigade, comprising 2 Argyll and Sutherland Highlanders, 4/19 Hyderabad Regiment and 5/14 Punjab Regiment, and was commanded by Brigadier Paris. 5/14 Punjab was sent to Penang, but the rest were stationed at Singapore.

General Dobbie, who was the General Officer Commanding-in-Chief, Malaya, placed requirements on the basis of his plan for the defence of Malaya at three divisions and two tank regiments. Nothing was done to bring the forces in Malaya to this level owing to the Battle of Britain being at its height. At the same time Japanese occupation of Northern Indo-China and her Tripartite Pact with Germany and Italy made the reinforcement question much more important than ever before. Consequently, one finds greater attention being paid to the strengthening of the Malaya army by some means or other.[32] In August 1940, when Shanghai was evacuated, the two British battalions, namely the Seaforth Highlanders and 2 East Surrey, were shifted to Malaya, the former to Penang, where 5/14 Punjab had been placed, and the latter being attached to the 6th Indian Infantry Brigade in February 1941. The 6th Infantry Brigade had come along with the 8th Indian Infantry Brigade in the course of October and November 1940. Of the three battalions of the 8th Indian Infantry Brigade, 2/10 Baluch Regiment, 3/17 Dogra Regiment and 2/18 Royal Garhwal Rifles, the first two were stationed at Kota Bharu and the third was disposed at Kuantan. In this same period the Headquarters of the 11th Indian Division also arrived and was stationed at Kuala Lumpur, where the division took over the command of the Northern Area from the Headquarters of Federated Malay States Volunteer Force. Major-General Murray-Lyon took charge of this command. In the beginning there were no artillery and signal units; but soon 22nd Mountain Regiment and a detachment of signal operators belonging to Federated Malaya States Volunteer Force was assigned to the division.

[32] Churchill: *The Second World War*, Vol. II, p. 442.

In February 1941, 1 Leicester arrived from India and relieved the Seaforth Highlanders at Penang, the latter going out of Malaya, and at the same time the 8th Australian Imperial Force Division under Major-General H. Gordon Bennett arrived; but it contained only the 22nd Australian Brigade and various divisional troops. At the moment the Australian Imperial Force acted as Command Reserve, and therefore the 22nd Australian Imperial Force Brigade was stationed in Port Dickson-Seremban area and the divisional headquarters was located at Kuala Lumpur.

During March next, the 15th Indian Infantry Brigade arrived, as also the Headquarters and two companies of the 11th Indian Division Signals from England. Of the three battalions of this Indian brigade, namely 2/9 Jat Regiment, 1/14 Punjab Regiment and 3/16 Punjab Regiment, the last was kept at Taiping while the other two were stationed in Ipoh area. Other arrivals in this month were a few Indian States Force battalions; all these were put down for aerodrome defence, Hyderabad to Kelantan, Mysore to Johore, and Jind and Kapurthala to Singapore.

In April 1941, the 22nd Indian Infantry Brigade arrived from India. At the same time 'Northern Area' was abolished, and the 11th Indian Division took its place in the west, and the 9th Indian Division, which had come just then from India, assumed responsibility of command in the east as far as and including Pahang. The headquarters of these divisions were Sungei Patani and Kuala Lumpur, respectively. The infantry of Bahawalpur State also arrived during this month. 3/16 Punjab Regiment moved to Kroh in the latter part of the month, and a line of communication area was created in the land comprised by Prai, Bukit Mertajam and Gemas.

General Percival assumed the command of Malaya on 16 May 1941. As it was his duty to review the strength required for the defence of Malaya, he gave it as his opinion that the III Indian Corps, which was then forming, should have full three divisions, the 8th Australian Imperial Force Division should contain both the brigades attached to it, a full division each would be needed for the General Headquarters reserve and the Fortress of Singapore, and one Tank Regiment of 14-ton tanks was the minimum force for the successful defence of Malaya.[33] It seems that the Commander-in-Chief, Far East, and the Chiefs of Staff, London, approved and accepted this estimate " but it was recognised that the target could not in the existing circumstances be fulfilled in the foreseeable future ".[34]

---

[33] The Malayan Campaign: Precis of a lecture by Lieutenant-General Sir Lewis Heath. 601/9849/H. p. 3.
[34] *The War in Malaya*, op. cit. p. 65, para 1.

In the month of June 1941, the III Indian Corps was finally established at Kuala Lumpur, the 22nd Indian Infantry Brigade Headquarters and 5/11 Sikh Regiment moved from Ipoh to Kuantan, 2/12 Frontier Force Regiment which was in Taiping shifted to the 8th Indian Infantry Brigade in Kelantan, and 1/13 Frontier Force Rifles remained at Mantin in the III Indian Corps reserve.

In August, the 8th A.I.F. Division received its second brigade, the 27th A.I.F. under Brigadier Maxwell; the 22nd A.I.F. Brigade then moved to Mersing area, while the 27th A.I.F. Brigade remained temporarily in Singapore. The 11th Indian Division was strengthened by the addition of 155 Field Regiment. At the beginning of September 1941, the 28th Indian Infantry Brigade with 2/1 and 2/2 Gurkha Rifles arrived and was stationed at Ipoh; its third battalion 2/9 Gurkha Rifles was stationed at Taiping. It was considered as a III Indian Corps reserve and meant to set 1/13 Frontier Force Rifles free to join the 8th Indian Infantry Brigade in Kelantan. But at the same time it became almost certain that the new brigade would join the 11th Indian Division if Japan attacked Malaya from Singora.

In October no fresh troops arrived in Malaya. The 27th A.I.F. Brigade was transferred from Singapore to west Johore; Brigade Headquarters and 29 Battalion went to Segamat, 26 Battalion to Jasin and 30 Battalion to Batu Pahat. Arrivals in November, most of which came from the United Kingdom, included 588 and 137 Field Regiments and 80 Anti-Tank Regiment, but India sent one reconnaissance regiment, 3rd Cavalry, which was yet in the process of mechanisation. This was attached to the 11th Indian Division.

Reinforcements of miscellaneous types also came to Malaya before the outbreak of war in December. These included technical and administrative units and personnel and weapons, ammunition, motor transport, supplies and other war material from the United Kingdom, India, Australia, and South Africa.

CHAPTER VII

The War in Northern Malaya

JAPANESE CONVOYS SIGHTED

At about 1300 hours on 6 December 1941, when the north-east monsoon was blowing and rains were pouring in torrents, the morning air reconnaissance which was watching the approaches to the Gulf of Thailand reported having sighted two Japanese convoys steaming due west. These convoys consisted of warships and transports and, when sighted, were approximately one hundred miles east-south-east of Pulau Obi, an island off the southern-most point of Indo-China. The first convoy, sighted at 1246 hours, at approximately 8 degrees north 106 degrees east, consisted of twenty five merchant ships escorted by one battleship, five cruisers and seven destroyers. The second convoy was sighted at 1300 hours in a position 7 degrees 35 minutes north 106 degrees 20 minutes east and comprised ten (later amended as twenty-one) merchant ships escorted by two cruisers and ten destroyers.[1] Earlier, at 1212 hours, one motor vessel and one mine-sweeper had been sighted nearly forty miles south-south-east of Pulau Obi steering northwest.[2] These sightings were all obtained in conditions of very poor visibility, and later evidence indicated that there was in fact only one major convoy which was sighted twice in different positions.

The same day, two hours later, General Percival ordered the commander of the III Indian Corps, Lieutenant-General Sir Lewis M. Heath, to assume the first degree of readiness, and, in anticipation of operation 'Matador' to instruct the commander of the 11th Indian Division, Major-General D.M. Murray-Lyon, to be ready to move at short notice.[3]

The Commander-in-Chief, Far East, Air Chief Marshal Sir Robert Brooke-Popham, in consultation with Admiral Sir Geoffrey Layton and Admiral Palliser, Admiral Sir Tom Phillips, Chief of Staff, concluded that the probability was that the convoys would not continue their course due west, which would have brought them on to the Kra Isthmus, but that they would follow the mine-layer and mine-sweeper and round Cambodia Point with a view to demonstrating against and bringing pressure to bear on Thailand. With this appreciation and bearing in mind the

---

[1] War Diary, General Headquarters Far East, 6 December 1941.
[2] See also, *Supplement to the London Gazette*, 26 February 1948, p. 1363, para 150(b) *Idem.* Serial No. 5.
[3] Percival's Despatch, *op. cit.* Section XVII, para 120.

policy of avoiding war with Japan, if possible, a principle which had been re-affirmed by the Chiefs of Staff as recently as 29 November, as well as in view of the situation in the United States where the Kurusu talks were still going on in Washington, the Commander-in-chief, Far East, decided not to order operation Matador at this stage and informed the General Officer Commanding, Malaya, accordingly.[4]

In spite of attempts by the British aircraft to watch the movement of these convoys, contact was lost and no definite information was available of the whereabouts of the Japanese ships. The presence of these convoys in the Thailand waters appeared ominous. Orders were, therefore, issued to fire on any aircraft not established to be friendly.

At 0900 hours on 7 December information was received from the Deputy Director of Military Intelligence that the United States Consul at Tsingtao had reported, on 1 December, that three loaded transports had been leaving Tsingtao daily since 21 November. It was presumed that their movement was in the direction of south-west as the Japanese troops were wearing summer uniform. The truth of this report was confirmed by the fact that a number of Japanese vessels were sighted by Hudson reconnaissances on this date. At 1345 hours one merchant vessel of 6,000 to 8,000 tons was sighted in the Gulf of Thailand steaming west and another was seen at 1545 hours, one hundred and twenty miles north of the Anambas Islands, steering south[5] with a large complement of men in Khaki on the deck. Later at 1750 hours one merchant vessel and one cruiser, steaming on a bearing of 340°, were sighted about a hundred and twelve miles north of Kota Bharu. Again at 1848 hours, under conditions of very bad visibility, four Japanese naval vessels, perhaps destroyers, were spotted sixty miles north of Patani steaming due south.[6]

It may be noted that owing to bad weather, for a period of nearly thirty hours after the first vessels had been sighted, the air reconnaissance had failed to make contact with the main Japanese invasion force. Meanwhile, the 11th Indian Division was still standing by for operation Matador with ammunition, rations and equipment already loaded, but there was no undue alarm owing to the view held by the General Headquarters that the Japanese expedition was directed against Thailand. It was propos-

---

[4] *The War in Malaya, op. cit.* p. 108.
[5] War Diary G.H.Q. Far East 7 December 1941.
[6] Sir Paul Maltby's Despatch *op. cit.* p. 1364, para 165. It is not possible to verify these reports regarding the exact positions of the ships owing to the subsequent destruction of records.

ed to verify this in the morning of 8 December by sending a coastal reconnaissance to the Lakon Roads.

INVASION BEGINS

At about 2345 hours on 7 December the beach defence troops near the Kota Bharu airfield reported ships anchoring off the coast. Shortly afterwards, at 0100 hours, the beach defence artillery opened fire and the Japanese ships replied by shelling the beaches.[7] At 0115 hours the Japanese started landing from the three or five ships lying three miles off shore. Thus began the invasion of Malaya.

Singapore woke up to the horrors of war soon after. Shortly after 0400 hours on 8 December, seventeen Japanese aeroplanes raided the Singapore area twice. They had probably come from Indo-China, a distance of about seven hundred miles. The air raid alarm was sounded, but the city was not blacked out when the aircraft arrived. Bombs were dropped on the Seletar and Tengah airfields and on the town itself. Damage to military installations including the aerodrome and a few aircraft at Tengah, was slight but there were considerable casualties amongst the civilian population. This was the first indication the citizens of Singapore had that war had broken out in East Asia.[8]

Simultaneously with the attack on Kota Bharu and Singapore, the Japanese had invaded Thailand and made landings at Singora and Patani. Communications between Thailand and Malaya were cut. The Thai resistance was insignificant and lasted only two hours. This token resistance confirmed the impression that it was a mere show and that the Japanese invasion had the countenance of the Thailand authorities.

Meanwhile the General Officer Commanding, Malaya, and the Air Officer Commanding, Far East, decided that the task of the air striking force was to co-operate with the army in repelling the attack on Kota Bharu. Accordingly, the squadrons based on the Kedah, Kuantan and Tengah airfields were ordered to attack the Japanese ships lying off Kota Bharu at dawn on 8 December. Upon arrival at Kota Bharu these aircraft were unable to find the Japanese transports, which had by then withdrawn behind the Perhentian Islands, nearly fifteen miles off the Kelantan coast. One squadron went on to Patani, where other Japanese transports were seen and attacked, but owing to fighter opposition

---

[7] Percival's Despatch *op. cit.*, Section XVII.
[8] *Idem.*, para 126. See also *The War in Malaya, op. cit.*, pp. 111 and 113.

it is doubtful if they succeeded in scoring any hits. Henceforth lack of modern escort fighters was keenly felt, particularly when Allied bombers were chased by Japanese fighters. The Alor Star airfield was attacked when the returning aircraft were landing. Of the ten aircraft, only two were left serviceable; the petrol dump exploded and the Operations Room was hit. The airfields at Sungei Patani, Butterworth, Penang, Kota Bharu, Gong Kedah and Machang were also attacked the same morning. Sungei Patani airfield was attacked at 0715 hours and again at 0915 hours. On the first occasion the petrol tanks were set on fire and three planes on the ground were destroyed. On the second occasion the Station Wireless and Operations rooms were hit, as well as four more planes on the ground. The performance of the Japanese aircraft of all types, and the accuracy of their high level bombing in regular formations of 27 to 60 aircraft had come as an unpleasant surprise. The Royal Air Force had been gravely weakened by the end of the day and the support to the army in the north-western part where the main Japanese advance was expected to develop was becoming progressively doubtful.

At 0800 hours, General Headquarters, Far East, received instructions from the Chiefs of Staff at London to go ahead with operation Matador. These instructions were passed on to the Malaya Command but with the addition of the words " Do not act ".[9] The principal reason for this decision was that the air reconnaissance sent to Singora and Patani at dawn reported at 0915 hours that the Japanese forces had landed at these places, that there were a number of ships lying off the coast and that the Singora aerodrome was being used by the Japanese. It was clearly too late then to adopt the offensive Operation Matador. General Percival was thereupon authorised at about 1100 hours to tell the Commander III Indian Corps to carry out the defensive plan already prepared. Consequently orders were issued to the Commander III Indian Corps to occupy the defensive positions on both the Singora and Kroh-Patani roads, and to send a mobile covering force across the frontier towards Singora to make contact with and to harass and delay the Japanese.[10] This order which implied that Matador was cancelled, arrived at 1330 hours in the Advanced Headquarters of the 11th Indian Division, in the Jitra position, after the British and the Japanese had been at war for over thirteen hours.[11]

[9] Percival's Despatch, *op. cit.*, Section XVII, para 128.
[10] *Ibid.*
[11] History of 11th Indian Division in Malaya, Colonel A.M.J. Harrison, Volume I Chapter III, p. 29.

The rest of the day on 8 December was eventful only in Kelantan. Various reports of the landing of more Japanese troops, of suspicious vessels lying off the east coast and of damages by raids were coming in and creating confusion. Fortunately, all of them were discovered to be false. But one fact was found to be true, that the Japanese were penetrating into the area and the situation on land was becoming serious. Towards 1600 hours the position at Kota Bharu aerodrome was dangerous. The Air Headquarters thereupon ordered the total evacuation of that aerodrome and the withdrawal of all aircraft from there to Kuantan to which they flew at 1620 hours. This rendered Gong Kedah aerodrome virtually undefended and exposed to the Japanese attacks from the coast.

By the evening of 8 December, the situation so developed that the Japanese expedition to capture the Kota Bharu aerodrome area was succeeding, and the use of aerodromes in this area was denied to the Royal Air Force. The troops of the III Indian Corps were thus without close air support. The Japanese main force was landing unimpeded in the Singora-Patani area, covered by air operations against the British aerodromes in north Malaya. Their advance towards the north-west frontier of Malaya had already begun, and the troops of the 11th Indian Division in the forward area had made contact. The Japanese ships at Singora had not been attacked, partly because the aircraft at Kota Bharu were busy locally and partly because the undefended aerodromes in north-western Malaya having been attacked, the squadrons based on them were rendered unfit for sustained operations. The Japanese air force was operating in strength from Singora aerodrome, and the invading troops were making good progress.

The Japanese thrust was in two directions, south-east in Kelantan and south-west towards Kedah. The story of their early advance and the resistance offered by the III Indian Corps may now be studied in the two sectors separately.

THE WAR IN NORTH-EAST OR KELANTAN

In December 1941, there were three modern airfields in Kelantan, one five miles north-east of Kota Bharu at Pengkalan Chepa, another at Gong Kedah, about thirty miles down the coast, and the third at Machang on the Krai—Kota Bharu road. All these lay east of the Kelantan river. When the 8th Indian Infantry Brigade moved into the area at the end of 1940, the commander was instructed that his primary task was to secure the aerodromes for use by the air force and to deny them to the

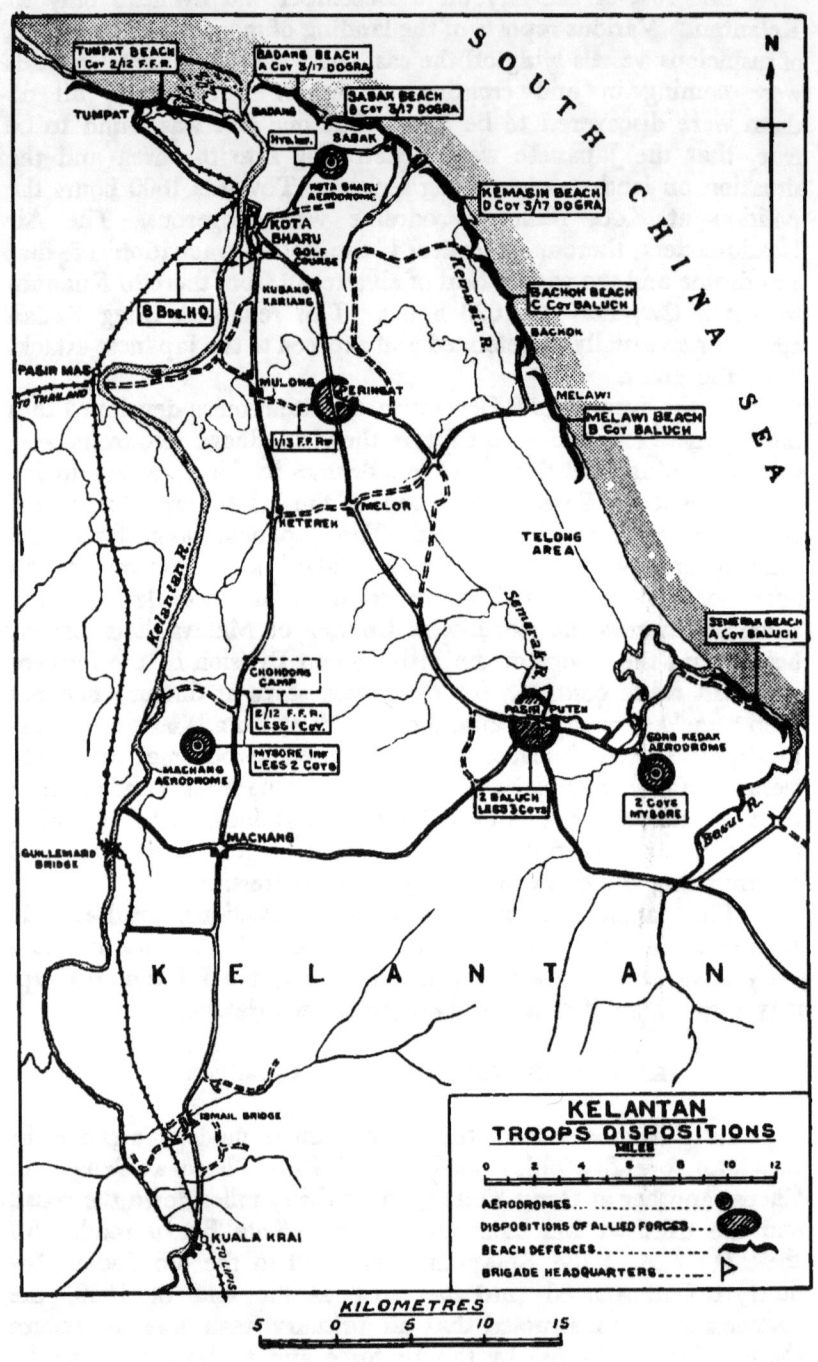

Japanese. He was also instructed that in order to carry out this task, he was to endeavour to prevent a hostile landing and that, for this purpose, pill-boxes were to be built and beach defences, both anti-personnel and anti-tank, were to be constructed as far as resources would permit. The commander decided to keep his force east of the Kelantan river, with the exception of small mobile detachments whose task was to watch the frontier and, in face of a Japanese advance in force, to fall back across the Kelantan river. Arrangements were also made to destroy the railway bridges near the frontier. The bulk of the force was therefore concentrated about the aerodromes at Kota Bharu and Gong Kedah with beach defence troops on the most likely landing areas. Reserves were held at Chongdong and Peringat. Headquarters was located in the Kota Bharu area, in touch with the Sultan and his British Adviser. Railhead was at Kuala Krai where the main reserves of supplies, stores etc. were held.[12]

On 7 December the order of battle of the 8th Indian Infantry Brigade was as shown in Appendix E.[13] The brigade dispositions were as follows:—

A. COMMAND

In Kota Bharu Town
    Headquarters 8th Indian Infantry Brigade.
    19 Indian Field Company R.B S & M.
    15 Indian Field Ambulance.
    The Kelantan Volunteers.

B. BEACH DEFENCES

1. *Right Sector*
    A frontage of approximately eighteen miles from exclusive Sungei Besut to exclusive Kuala Kemasin.
    2/10 Baluch with headquarters and reserve rifle company at Pasir Puteh. Under Command: Gong Kedah airfield with Air Force and Royal Australian Air Force ground staff; two companies Mysore Infantry; one machine-gun platoon, 4 Pahang Volunteers. Also, on the outbreak of war, 272 Anti-Tank Battery, situated at Gong Kedah came under command.
    The sector was divided into three company areas:
    (i) Semerak Beach.
        From exclusive S. Besut to inclusive S. Semerak.

[12] Percival's Despatch *op. cit.*, Section VI, para 34.
[13] See Appendix E.

Approximately 5,500 yards.

(ii) Melawi Beach

From inclusive Kuala Rekam to approximately 2,000 yards south of Bachok village. Approximately 6,000 yards.

(iii) Bachok Beach

From approximately 2,000 yards south of Bachok village to exclusive K. Kemasin. Approximately 9,000 yards.

The gap between the S. Semerak and Kuala Rekam, approximately 15,000 yards, was not held. Dummy defences, however, comprising dummy pill-boxes and one belt of wire, were constructed. It was felt that 18 miles was too great a frontage for one battalion to hold every point. It was therefore decided that the Telong Forest Reserve, a wooded, swampy area which presented a considerable obstacle to any hostile force attempting to penetrate inland, should be left unguarded.

2. *Central Sector*

Frontage of approximately ten miles from inclusive Kuala Kemasin to exclusive the Kelantan river.

3/17 Dogras with headquarters and reserve rifle company at the $3\frac{1}{2}$ M.S. Camp ($3\frac{1}{2}$ miles from Kota Bharu). Under command: one machine-gun platoon 4 Pahang Volunteers. In support: 21 Indian Mountain Battery, the guns being located at Kota Bharu airfield.

This sector was divided into three company areas:

(i) Kemasin Beach: From K. Kemasin to Sungei Pengkalan Datu.

(ii) Sabak Beach: From S. Pengkalan Datu to Kuala Pa'amat.

(iii) Badang Beach: From K. Pa'amat to the Kelantan river.

3. *Left Sector*

(The area west of the Kelantan river)

(a) Gual Periok

One company less two platoons 2/12 Frontier Force Regiment patrolling railway to the Siamese frontier.

(b) Tumpat

One platoon 2/12 Frontier Force Regiment on beach defence.

(c) Kampong Lubok Kawah.

One platoon 2/12 Frontier Force Regiment patrolling tracks leading from the Siamese frontier.

(d) Repek

Base for patrols from 1/13 Frontier Force Rifles.

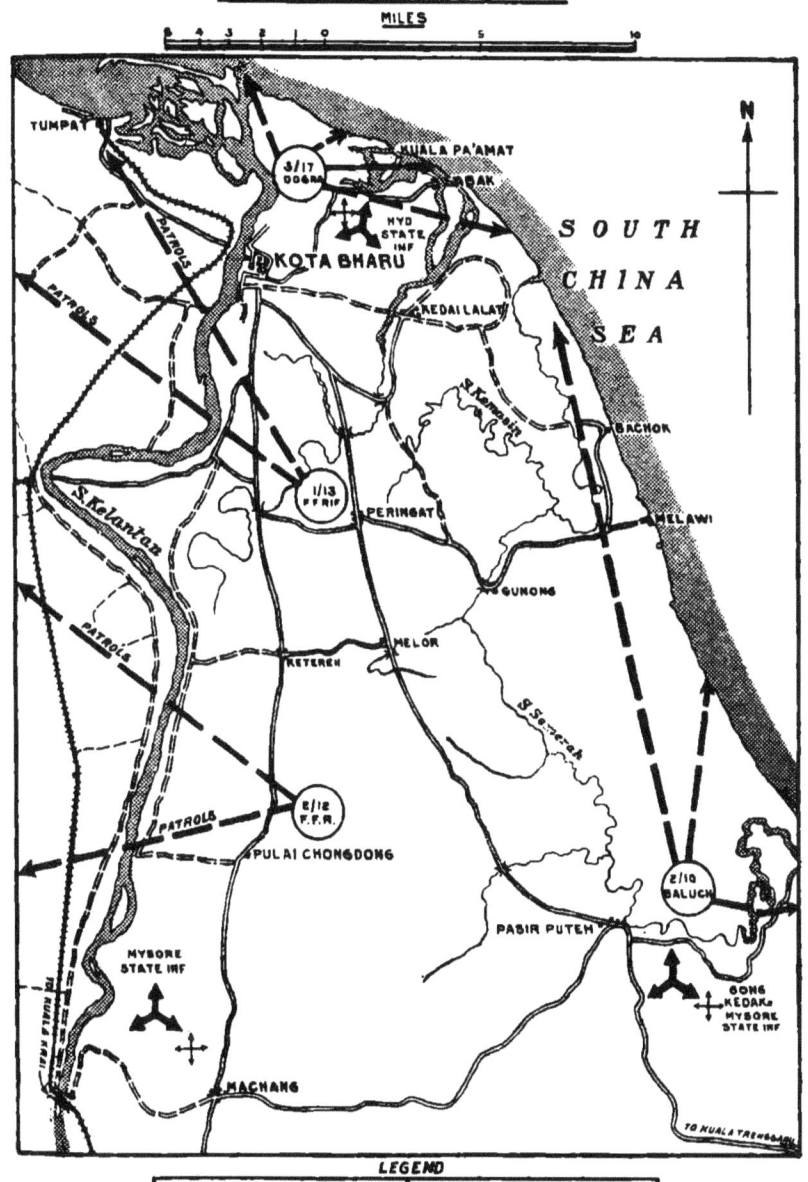

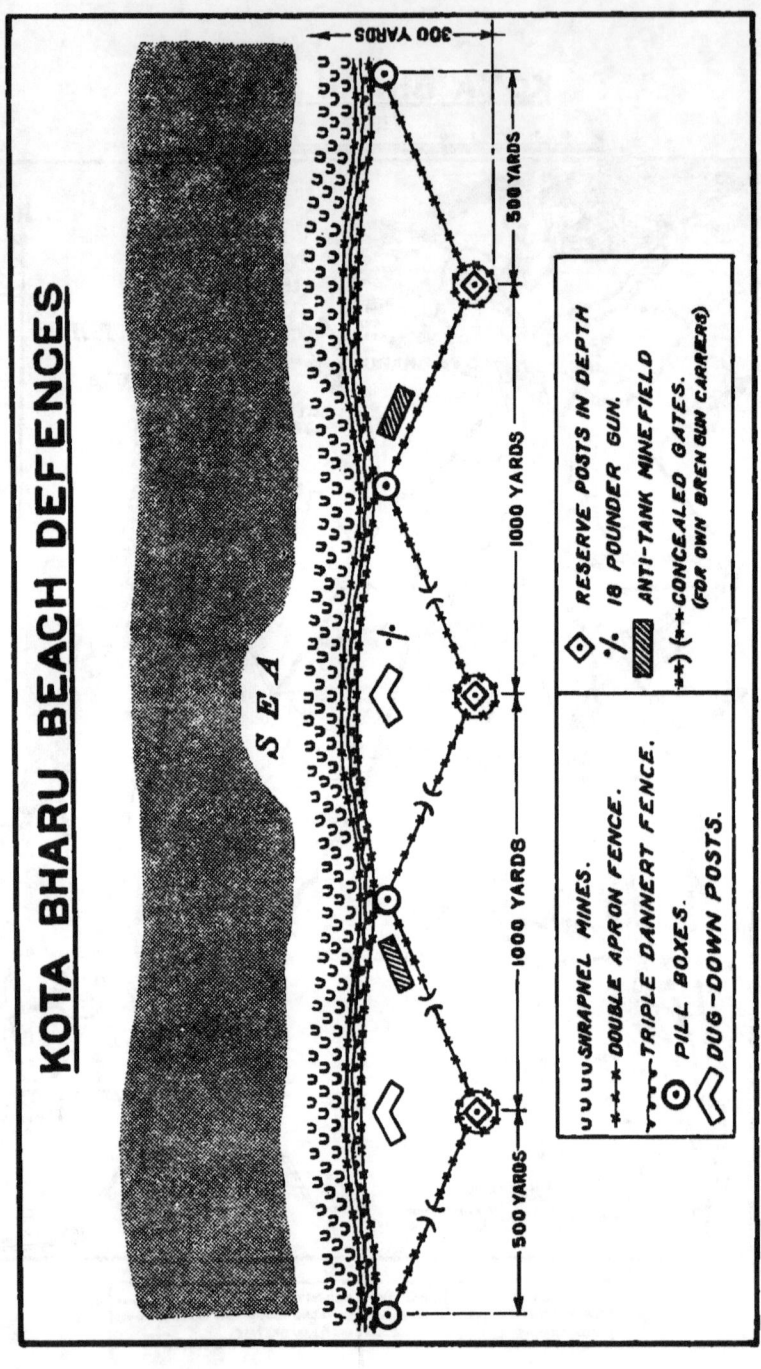

C. AIRFIELD DEFENCE
   Kota Bharu Airfield
      1 Hyderabad Infantry
      9 Battery (Heavy Anti-Aircraft) H.K.S.R.A.
   Gong Kedah Airfield
      Two companies 1 Mysore Infantry
      One platoon 1 Hyderabad Infantry—manning two Naval Anti-Aircraft guns.
   Machang Airfield
      1 Mysore Infantry—less two companies.

D. LINE OF COMMUNICATION DEFENCE
   Kuala Krai
      One company (less two platoons) the Malaya Regiment.
      Detachment Hyderabad Infantry.
   Dabong
      4 Pahang Volunteers (less two platoons) on the railway between Dabong and Kuala Lipis.
   Kuala Seli
      One platoon Perak Volunteers (Malaya Frontier Patrol) watching the approach to Dabong by the S. Pergau.

E. BRIGADE RESERVE
   2/12 Frontier Force Regiment (less one company) at Chongdong.
   1/13 Frontier Force Rifles at Peringat with patrols west of the river based on Repek.
   73 Field Battery (5 Field Regiment) at Chongdong.
   272 Anti-Tank Battery (80 Anti-Tank Regiment) at Gong Kedah.

F. AIR SUPPORT
   Kota Bharu Airfield
      One squadron of eleven Lockhead Hudsons and three Brewster Buffaloes.
   Gong Kedah
      One squadron of nine Vildebeeste Torpedo Bombers.

G. ANCILLARY AND ADMINISTRATION UNITS
   Based on Kuala Krai.

It may be noted that 2 Baluch and 3 Dogra each had two reconditioned 18-pounder guns manned by the battalion personnel. The total defences available for each beach were:—

Troops	Arms	Extra Armament
One Rifle coy	9 Bren guns 3 2" Mortars 2 A/Tk rifles 2 Tommy guns	2 18-pdr. guns 1 Northover Projector 1 or 2 Lyon Lights 275 A/Tk mines
One Sec (3) Carriers	3 Bren guns 1 A/Tk rifle	250 Shrapnel mines 96 No. 36 hand grenades
One Sec. 3" Mortars Four signallers	2 3" Mortars	2 Vickers M.M.Gs. Molotov Cocktails Verey pistols.

As will be seen, the beach defences covered a very wide stretch of the coast, and the estuaries of the Kelantan and several smaller rivers had to be watched. Of all the rivers in the area, only the mouth of the Kelantan river was protected by a boom. Many tracks coming from Thailand west of the river had also to be patrolled. The protection of such a large area by our brigade involved dispersal. The force was quite inadequate to provide for any defence in depth.

The beaches had multiple wire fences and a line of concrete pill-boxes about 1,000-1,200 yards apart. Though well constructed, these pill-boxes were too far apart for mutual support. Each pill-box was held by one non-commissioned officer and six men. Shrapnel and anti-tank mines were also laid near the pill-boxes, while dug-down posts were held between them. Concealed openings were provided in the wire fence for the defending carriers to move in for counter-attacks. The forward positions were connected to the Company Headquarters by telephone. Behind the line of pill-boxes were resreve posts similarly spaced, but even more lightly manned. In the case of the Dogra, each beach company had a front of three miles and this left a company reserve of approximately twenty-five men. The company frontage in the case of the Baluch was even greater. The Baluch reserve rifle company was at Pasir Puteh which was seven, twenty-two and twenty-six miles from the Semerak, Melawi and Bachok beaches, respectively.

Considering the distances and depths involved, it is at once obvious that all beaches were grossly under-manned and undergunned, and that unless brigade reserves and artillery support could reach the penetrated areas quickly, a break-through would be achieved at any point.

At about 2345 hours on 7 December, the beach defence troops on the Sabak and Badang beaches reported ships anchoring about 1½ miles from the coast. Shortly afterwards the beach defence artillery, consisting of one 18-pounder manned by the personnel of 3/17 Dogra and 21 Indian Mountain Battery opened fire. The Japanese replied with naval gunfire, particularly in the vicinity of numbers 13 and 14 pill-boxes, which were on either side of the Kuala Pa'amat (the mouth of the Sungei Pengkalan Chepa).[14]

At 0030 hours on 8 December, the Japanese attempted to land in the vicinity of numbers 13 and 14 pill-boxes. Small arms fire was found to be quite ineffective against the armour planting of the landing craft. Hence some of the landing craft entered the Kuala Pa'amat, and landings were effected behind the beach defences as well as in front of them, possibly led by some fifth columnists. By 0100 hours, the Japanese had succeeded in capturing the pill-boxes numbers 13 and 14, and had established defensive footholds on either side of the Kuala Pa'amat on the Sabak and Badang beaches. The garrisons of the two pill-boxes inflicted very heavy casualties on the invaders before being wiped out themselves almost to a man.

Thereafter the Japanese immediately began to fan out along and in the rear of the beaches which they had successfully breached once for all. Brigadier Key also was alert on his side. As soon as the first landing had taken place, 2/12 Frontier Force Regiment (less one company west of the Kelantan river) and 73 Field Battery were ordered up to Kota Bharu from Chongdong, and 1/13 Frontier Force Rifles, still in reserve, was warned to be ready to move at first light. Meanwhile, the reserve company of 3/17 Dogra had also moved to the south bank of the Sabak creek opposite to No. 13 pill-box to counter any penetration towards the air-field, and for the same reason the reserve company of the Hyderabad infantry was moved to the north corner of the Kota Bharu airfield opposite the Sausage Island, which lies in the delta of the river between Sabak and Badang beaches.

As soon as 2/12 Frontier Force Regiment began to arrive, Brigadier Key ordered one company to Sabak and another to Badang to be used in those areas to hold and counter-attack the Japanese who had already landed. The battalion, less these

[14] This river mouth is at the point of junction of the Sabak and Badang beaches and is about 1½ miles from the Kota Bharu airfield.

two companies and the company west of the river, was held in reserve immediately south of the aerodrome.

The 73rd Field Battery (less one troop) was sent to Montgomery Camp (south of the Kota Bharu airfield), and one troop moved to the main road junction immediately south of Kota Bharu.

Mention has already been made of the futile attacks of the British aircraft on the Japanese shipping at dawn of 8 December and also of the Japanese chase of these British planes to their base in Kedah and Kelantan. This was not all. In Kelantan, three aerodromes were attacked by the Japanese aircraft during that day. At Machang one company of the Mysore Infantry was caught at 0630 hours on the move from one position to another. The first Japanese planes dropped smoke bombs which caused panic due to the belief that gas was used. The remaining planes dropped high explosive bombs which caused thirty-five casualties.

About this time information was received from the police and customs posts that the Japanese were detraining at Sungei Kolok railway station which lay one mile inside the Siamese frontier. The Royal Australian Air Force was asked to destroy the Sungei Kolok railway bridge.[15] This task was successfully accomplished. In addition, one company of 1/13 Frontier Force Rifles was despatched to Pasir Mas (west of the Kelantan river) to contact the various patrols and the platoon of 2/12 Frontier Force Regiment on the railway, and to delay the Japanese advance.

Moreover, the dawn air reconnaissance reported, as stated already, that there were no ships off the coast further south. This enabled the brigade commander to move his only remaining reserve, 1/13 Frontier Force Rifles less one company watching the land frontier, from Peringat to assist in the operations on the Kota Bharu beaches. A co-ordinated counter-attack was planned to destroy the Japanese who had landed and to restore the situation.

Meanwhile, heavy fighting had continued on both the Sabak and Badang beaches. On the Sabak beach, in addition to No. 13 pill-box which was in Japanese hands, No. 12 pill-box had also been isolated. The situation had been restored by the company of 2/12 Frontier Force Regiment which had been originally sent to this beach. This company then continued down the beach to No. 13 pill-box but was held up nearly two hundred and fifty yards short of its objective.

On the Badang beach, No. 15 pill-box which had been temporarily lost had been retaken by the reserve of the company

---

[15] The Sungei Kolok was the frontier between Malaya and Siam.

of 3 Dogra which then moved down the beach towards No. 14 pill-box, captured by the Japanese half an hour after the initial landing. The reinforcing company of 2/12 Frontier Force Regiment also moved across country to co-ordinate its attack with the company reserve of 3 Dogra on No. 14 pill-box. This attack also failed. A Japanese counter-attack regained No. 15 pill-box, and the reinforcing company of 2/12 Frontier Force Regiment was held up by swampy ground near Sausage Island, where the company commander got killed.

Orders for the counter-attack by 2/12 Frontier Force Regiment from the south and 1/13 Frontier Force Rifles from the north were issued at 1030 hours. 2/12 Frontier Force Regiment (less three companies, two already committed and one west of the Kelantan river) was to cross the S. Pengkalan Chepa from the direction of the airfield, clear up Sausage Island from the south and prevent hostile infiltration from that direction towards the airfield. 1/13 Frontier Force Rifles (less one company sent to Pasir Mas and one company retained in the brigade reserve) was to counter-attack on Badang beach, restore the situation there and drive south to Sausage Island in order to link up with 2/12 Frontier Force Regiment. This move was directed by Brigadier Key as he realised the importance of closing the gap at the Kuala Pa'amat before dusk, when the Japanese were likely to commence landing fresh troops with a view to infiltrating into the airfield during the night.

But the counter-attack was doomed to failure. Both battalions were held up by the thick water-logged country and the deep creeks lying behind the beaches. At dusk both the battalions were at a standstill, 2/12 Frontier Force Regiment on the mainland south of Sausage Island and 1/13 Frontier Force Rifles at a point four hundred yards from No. 14 pill-box but separated from it by a deep creek.

At about 1700 hours, Royal Australian Air Force Station Commander received a report that the aerodrome was under small-arms fire from the Japanese ground troops. A similar report had earlier been received by Air Headquarters at Singapore, who had believed this, and ordered a withdrawal[16]. Brigadier Key immediately went to the aerodrome which was in a state of some confusion. The Japanese aircraft were machine-gunning and bombing it, while some of the British planes were taking off and a few of the huts were on fire. A reconnaissance however showed that the Japanese ground forces had not reached the aerodrome wire and no change had taken place in the dispositions of the troops defending it. However, by

---

[16] Lionel Wigmore : *The Japanese Thrust*, p. 138.

this time the Allied aircraft had gone, and an hour later the Australian ground staff was *en route* for Kuala Krai, leaving the petrol and bomb dumps and the air-field runways intact. Thus, one of the three aerodromes had been lost prematurely.

Shortly after 1800 hours, Brigadier Key was informed on the telephone by Major General Barstow, commanding the 9th Indian Division, that the holding of Kota Bharu was left to his discretion but that he was not to risk annihilation.

At 1900 hours, more hostile ships were reported off the Sabak beach. The general situation may be summed up from the reports received at the brigade headquarters between 1900 and 2000 hours of that day. Increased Japanese activity was reported across the S. Pengkalan Chepa and to the north-east of the airfield. This resulted in some desertions from 1 Hyderabad State Infantry which necessitated the use of Singnallers to cover artillery gun positions. Also headquarters company and the company of 1/13 Frontier Force Rifles which had returned from Badang and the company which had returned from Pasir Mas were sent to reinforce the Hyderabad State Infantry in the airfield area. Moreover 21 Indian Mountain Battery was ordered to rejoin 73 Field Battery in Montgomery Camp, south of the aerodrome.

At the Badang beach Japanese were infiltrating between the beach posts and it was doubtful if the company sited there could hold out until dawn. No reports were obtained from Sabak beach owing to the disruption of telephone lines.

On 2/10 Baluch front there was no activity except the bombing of Gong Kedah air-fields.

In view of these reports and the likelihood that the Japanese might land strong reinforcements from behind the Perhentian Islands during the night and because the air-field in Kota Bharu had been abandoned, the commander of the 8th Indian Infantry Brigade issued orders for a withdrawal to the general line Kedai Lalat—Sungei Raja Gali, a position covering Kota Bharu town, with the left based on the Kelantan river. This line was to be held as follows:—

> On the right: from exclusive Kedai Lalat to the cross-roads one mile east of M.S. 2 on the air-field—Kota Bharu road: Two companies of 2/12 Frontier force Regiment and two companies of 3/17 Dogra (from Sabak beach and creek area).
>
> In the centre: up to the Sungei Pengkalen Chepa: 1 Hyderabad State Infantry, 1/13 Frontier Force Rifles less one company; Headquarters Company 2/12 Frontier Force Regiment and 3/17 Dogra.

On the left: up to and inclusive of the Sungei Raja Gali beach: one company of 1/13 Frontier Force Rifles, one of 2/12 Frontier Force Regiment, one of 3/17 Dogra (all from Badang).

The withdrawal began at 2100 hours. The dark night, the swampy nature of the ground, heavy rain and hostile action, all these combined to make the operation extremely hazardous, difficult and confused. Also shortly after 2100 hours, the petrol dump at the Kota Bharu air-field was set on fire by 73 Field Battery. This lit up the whole area, and the Japanese, who had by now penetrated the aerodrome, opened heavy fire. The commanding officer and the adjutant of 1 Hyderabad State Infantry were killed and the battalion disintegrated. The companies of 2/12 Frontier Force Regiment and 1/13 Frontier Force Rifles had some difficulty in extricating themselves, but eventually they fell back to their allotted positions near M.S. $2\frac{1}{2}$. Moreover, the brigade across the creek at Sabak had been destroyed, and the Japanese were infiltrating down both the banks. These factors made the task of withdrawal in this area a formidable one, the troops experiencing the greatest difficulty in crossing the creek. Consequently the withdrawal could not be completed until after dawn on the 9th. Even so, many men were swept away in the current and others lost touch with the main body.

On the Badang beach the company commander of 3/17 Dogra was out of touch with the commanding officer of 1/13 Frontier Force Rifles and the company of 1/13 Frontier Force Rifles which had penetrated to the creek south of No. 14 pill-box. He was also not in telephonic communication with his own company posts. However, this company succeeded in withdrawing to the Sungei Raja Gali bridge by 0500 hours on 9 December along with part of the company of 2/12 Frontier Force Regiment originally sent as reinforcements. The officer commanding and the company of 1/13 Frontier Force Rifles could not be located and were, therefore, unaware of the withdrawal.

On the Kemasin beach (south of Sabak beach) the company of 3/17 Dogra which had not been attacked, withdrew during the night via Kedai Lalat and Peringat.

The situation of the 8th Indian Infantry Brigade on the morning of 9 December was extremly precarious. On the right there was no news of the troops from Sabak. In the centre the Hyderabad State Infantry had faded away. On the left there was still no news of the company of 1/13 Frontier Force Rifles. A thin line did exist, however, and was held on the right at the road junction immediately west of Kedai Lalat by a company of 3/17

Dogra. Along the lateral road to the road junction at M.S. 2½ were elements of 2/12 Frontier Force Regiment. At the Sungei Raja Gali bridge was the company of 3/17 Dogra and part of the company of 2/12 Frontier Force Regiment from Badang. Patrolling between the centre and the left was one section of carriers of 3/17 Dogra.

By 0730 hours the Japanese were advancing down the road from the aerodrome and also along the south bank of the Sungei Pengkalen Chepa. The centre of the brigade position came under considerable fire. The Japanese troops were also infiltrating between the M.S. 2½ road junction and the right flank. It was evident that they were on the point of launching an attack astride the air-field road. Thereupon, Brigadier Key authorised a withdrawal to the general line Kubang Krian—the northern exits from Kota Bharu. At the same time orders were issued to the troops west of the river Kelantan to complete demolitions and withdraw. The situation was fast growing desperate. The situation report at 0900 hours on 9 December 1941 made mention of further Japanese landings on 8 December and their ships were believed to be lying behind Perhentian Islands from which they were landing troops and stores by lighters. Considerable infiltration was also proceeding and well armed Japanese parties were working round the flanks of the British positions. The defenders on their side had evacuated Kota Bharu aerodrome and demolished it and the 8th Indian Infantry Brigade had retreated to the north of Kota Bharu.[17] This line was untenable for defence, and a further withdrawal was ordered to the road junction immediately south of Kota Bharu.

But the Japanese followed closely on the heels of the Indian troops into Kota Bharu and there was considerable confusion. A rumour spread that the brigadier and the brigade staff had been overrun. This rumour was actually passed on to Kuala Lumpur where the Commander, III Indian Corps, was in conference with the Commander, 9th Indian Infantry Division.

In view of the rapid advance of the Japanese forces a further withdrawal down the Krai road to Kota Bharu was ordered at 1030 hours. This withdrawal was covered by the reserve company of 2/10 Baluch brought up from Pasir Puteh, and a position just south of Kota was established by parts of 1/13 Frontier Force Rifles and 2/12 Frontier Force Regiment.

The company of 3/17 Dogra and part of the company of 2/12 Frontier Force Regiment, which had been at Badang, were

[17] War Diary General Headquarters, Far East, Appendix No. 141, para 1.

sent to Chongdong to reorganise. The company of 3/17 Dogra which had been at the road junction immediately west of Kedai Lalat and one company of 1/13 Frontier Force Rifles adjacent to it, withdrew via Kubang Krian. The remaining troops from Sabak also arrived in Kubang Krian about this time. But the Japanese were still close on the heels of the withdrawing troops, and confused fighting took place in Kubang Krian, the Indian troops falling back to Peringat where the company of 3/17 Dogra from Kemasin beach had arrived late in the morning.

Meanwhile, the 4/19 Hyderabad Regiment of the 12th Indian Infantry Brigade, Malaya Command Reserve, had arrived in Kuala Krai from Mantin and also been ordered into a position immediately north of Ketereh (M.S. 12).

At about 1200 hours the Japanese were reported on the road running west from Kota through Salor to the Kelantan river immediately east of Pasir Mas. This necessitated a withdrawal to a position near M.S. 6 which was effected. During the afternoon the companies of 2/10 Baluch were withdrawn from the Melawi and Bachok beaches, those from the latter going to Peringat and those from the former to Melor, south of Peringat. At the same time such troops of 3/17 Dogra and 2/12 Frontier Force Regiment as had been engaged during the morning near Kubang Krian were sent back to Chongdong to rest and reorganise.

By dusk 4/19 Hyderabad was in position north of Ketereh and orders were given to the troops at M.S. 6 to withdraw to Chongdong. During the night of 9/10 December some wild firing was indulged in by 4/19 Hyderabad at what was probably a hostile patrol. At Peringat the companies of 2/10 Baluch and 3/17 Dogra maintained their position without any Japanese interference. Throughout the night, stragglers from the beaches and the Kota Bharu air-field, or from the skirmishes round Kota Bharu and Kubang Krian, found their way back to their own unit lines and were sent to Chongdong. The commanding officer and the company of 1/13 Frontier Force Rifles arrived early in the morning of 10 December having worked their way round the outskirts of Kota Bharu after the Japanese had occupied it.

On 10 December 1941, 2/10 Baluch was ordered to come nearer the main road between Kota Bharu and Kuala Krai, where the bulk of the Imperial army had been gathered on a line of general withdrawal. It occupied a position at M.S. 8 on the Machang—Pasir Puteh road. But the aerodrome runway could not be demolished and the diarist of this regiment bemoans that the whole sector was eventually surrendered without firing a single shot.[18] On the next day the aerodrome at Machang was similarly evacuated, with the runway again left intact. By now, the defenders had come as far back as M.S. 26½, which was about a mile from Machang, and Lieutenant-General Percival adds that 'the demolition of the great Guillemard bridge over the Kelantan river, the longest railway bridge in Malaya and an engineering showpiece, was ordered' on this day.[19]

From the standpoint of the Japanese, Kelantan was as good as conquered by 12 December 1941. When Kuantan was being threatened on one side and north-western Malaya was being overrun, the defence of Kelantan was no easy matter. There was no road between Kuala Krai and Kuala Lipis; the railway between these two towns was not dependable, for even if a single bridge was damaged, it would render the whole line worthless. Moreover there was no object in fighting for Kelantan when the aerodromes had been evacuated. Hence, it only remained to withdraw without much loss of men, material and morale. The movement of the Imperial army hereafter was anologous to that of a man walking back step by step while still facing the tiger with a sword in hand.

12 and 13 December 1941 were field days for the Baluch Regiment, which with 2/12 Frontier Force Regiment acted as the rearguard in contact with the Japanese patrols. The Baluch companies fought hard and inflicted severe losses on the Japanese while themselves suffering some losses. The ground was appallingly bad after the rains and with a waist-deep canal to cross besides. The Japanese were also using armour piercing ammunition in their rifles and light automatics, against which the thin walls of the Bren Gun Carriers afforded no protection. At the end of the day on 13 December, the Baluch withdrew to M.S. 34½ and very soon after was joined by 2/12 Frontier Force Regiment on the right of the road, while 3/17 Dogra and 1/13 Frontier Force Rifles went in reserve behind the brigade headquarters, with enough artillery for the forward battalions.

The brigade continued its withdrawal which ended on 22 December 1941 when it reached Kuala Lipis—Jerantut area (except for 2/12 Frontier Force Regiment, which went to Kuantan to rejoin the 22nd Indian Infantry Brigade). While these discouraging operations were taking place in North-East Malaya, the Japanese had attacked in the north-west corner also, and bitter fighting was in progress in Perlis.

[18] Narrative of 2/10 Baluch by Lieutenant-Colonel J. F. Frith., 10 December 1941. 601/574/H.
[19] *The War in Malaya*, op. cit. pp. 137-138.

THE WAR IN THE NORTH-WEST

On 29 November 1941, the 11th Indian Division had been put on six hours' notice to launch operation Matador. When the III Indian Corps assumed the first degree of readiness at 1515 hours on 6 December, the 11th Indian Division was placed at half an hour's notice for operation Matador, and all troops were moved to their posts for immediate action. The dispositions of the troops for this operation were as shown below:—

6th Indian Infantry Brigade

Padang Besar
: One Company 2/16 Punjab
One Section 7 Indian Mountain Battery
One Section 45 Army troops company S and M

Arau
: 2/16 Punjab (less one company) ⎫ Waiting
7 Indian Mountain Battery (less one Sector) ⎬ to entrain
One company 2 Jat ⎭

Tanjong Pau
: 2 Surreys ⎫ Waiting to
1/8 Punjab ⎬ embus
22 Indian Mountain Regiment (less 7 and 21 Batteries).

15th Indian Infantry Brigade

Bukit Kayu Hitam
: One Company 2 Jat
One platoon 1/8 Punjab

Arau
: One company 2 Jat

Tanjong Pau
: 2 Jat (less two companies)

Anak Bukit
: 1 Leicester ⎫
1/14 Punjab ⎬ Entrained

11th Indian Division

Sungei Patani
: Divisional Headquarters
155 Field Regiment
273 Battery of 80 Anti-tank Regiment.

At 1330 hours on 8 December orders arrived at the Tactical Headquarters of the 11th Indian Division at Tanjong Pau to the effect that Matador was cancelled and the Jitra position was to be occupied immediately. Also a small column was to be sent into Thailand to delay the Japanese advance from Singora and Krohcol was to advance and hold the 'Ledge'. The effect of the delay in communicating this decision was considerable. A whole day's work on the Jitra defences was lost; work on this position had of course been in abeyance since 29 November. It resulted in rushed moves which caused the troops avoidable fatigue. Worst of all, it lowered morale because it was a sudden, last-minute change from an offensive to a defensive role on the eve of the battle. The delay gave the Japanese at Patani a flying start in the race for the 'Ledge'.

Heavy work was required to complete the so-called Jitra position and the defences required considerable attention after the tropical rains which had started on 6 December and which continued, almost without break but with varying intensity, for a week. Wire had to be erected, mines laid and telephone cable run out. In addition, strong parties were required to carry wire, reserve ammunition, mines etc. to company locations because the weather had made the tracks impassable for mechanical transport.

The main position named after Jitra town stretched from the track between Bt. Penia and Bt. Tunggal Kechil through M.S. $13\frac{1}{2}$ on the Singora road and M.S. $13\frac{3}{4}$ on the Kodiang road along the Alor Changlun canal to the coast at the mouth of the Jerlung river. The right sector which was allotted to the 15th Indian Infantry Brigade had a frontage of approximately $3\frac{1}{2}$ miles from Bt. Tunggal Kechil to nearly M.S. 14 on the Kodiang road. The left sector was allotted to the 6th Indian Infantry Brigade and had a frontage of 15 miles, 8 miles of which lay south of a large impassable swamp and north of a wide expanse of paddy and were undefended. To make this position more secure, a scheme for flooding had been worked out but had been turned down owing to expense. The dividing line between the two sectors was the Kodiang road, which was included in the sector of the 15th Indian Infantry Brigade which had two forward battalions, 2/9 Jat on the right and 1 Leicester on the left, with their dividing line parallel to and three hundred yards east of the Singora road. 2/9 Jat covered a front of two thousand eight hundred yards and a depth of a thousand yards. The east side was flanked by jungle clad hills at the foot of which was a narrow expanse of rubber. West of this, paddy fields, thirteen hundred yards in width and a thousand yards in depth, filled the area between the rubber and the S. Bata, which was thirty feet wide. The paddy in December of 1941 was well-grown and the fields were knee-deep in mud and slush. Running through the centre of this paddy from north to south was the Palong, a stream with steep banks which, like the Bata, was at that season in full flood and unfordable. It had been bridged for foot traffic in two places. Both the Palong and the Bata

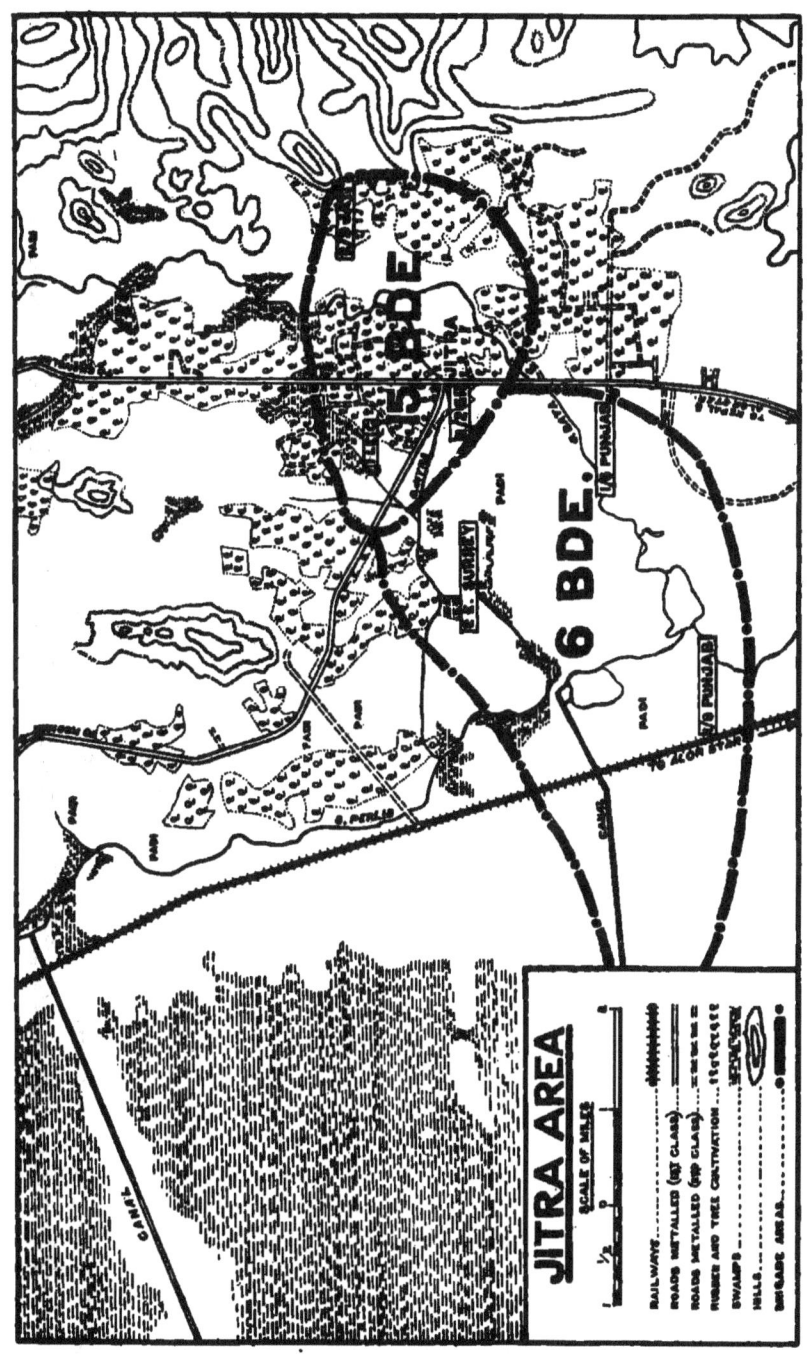

were fringed with trees and jungle to a depth of about fifty yards. The Palong stream not only cut across the field of fire of the localities flanking the paddy fields but also offered a covered line of approach to the Japanese. The remaining nine hundred yards of battalion front, west of the Bata, were covered with rubber trees, in the eastern half of which there was a strip of jungle.

The forward companies held the extremities of this extensive front and were separated by a tactical gap of thirteen hundred yards covered by paddy. On the right, B Company had a good field of fire over paddy fields, northwards to the pipeline five hundred yards ahead, and westwards to the Palong. Two machine-guns, a 3-inch mortar and a Breda gun were included in B Company's armament. On the left, D Company was in a well-wooded jungle and robber country; much of the jungle had been cleared, but the field of fire was short except eastwards towards the Palong. The southern edge of the tactical gap was held by C Company, one thousand yards south of B Company, and by A Company, six hundred yards south-east of D Company. The covered approach along the bank of the Palong was guarded by a fighting patrol from A Company.

The tactical gap had one great defect; the field of fire across it was interrupted by the wooded banks of the Palong. Moreover, the destruction of any Japanese troops who might advance into it demanded a strong mobile reserve specifically earmarked for this role, but the troops to form this reserve were not available. The anti-tank pitch was complete only from the battalions' left flank to the Palong. On the whole the position occupied by 2/9 Jat was a difficult sub-sector.

The other battalion, 1 Leicester, covered a front of three thousand two hundred yards which included both the Singora and Kodiang roads. There was a gap of some 200 yards of swampy ground which included a copse about seventy yards square on the right of this sub-sector. This copse had been left uncleared in order to conceal an anti-tank gun detachment lodged in it. Between the roads the forward positions lay just inside the rubber plantations which faced on to the paddy fields having width varying from four hundred to eight hundred yards. The paddy fields offered an excellent field of fire; moreover, the S. Kamunting, which crossed it from north-east to south-west was an effective obstacle.

The left position was Kg. Rimba where two pill-boxes armed with machine-guns had been constructed. The reserve battalion of the 15th Indian Infanry brigade was to be 1/14 Punjab after its withdrawal from the covering role at Asun. Its alternative positions about "Forward 50" or south of the Bata, astride the main road, were far from complete.

The Brigade Headquarters was located east of the main road just inside the north edge of Tanjong Pau Camp. There were no huts in this area. During the battle this headquarters worked in a sea of mud and under a sheet of rain, using its truck as an office.

The dispositions of the 6th Indian Infantry Brigade do not call for any detailed account. The right sub-sector of the brigade was held by 2 Surreys from Pisang to Budi (near the railway), a frontage of three thousand yards. The left sub-sector which included the undefended eight miles along the Alor Changilih canal was allotted to 2/16 Punjab. This battalion had its right company positioned astride the railway and its left company was at the junction of the canal and the Jerlun river. The other two companies were to be responsible for patrolling the canal when they returned from their forward role in the Padang Besar area.

The reserve battalion 1/8 Punjab, had a defensive position prepared one mile south of the railway bridge, but only one company was to be placed initially in this area. The rest of the battalion was to be held in the Tanjong Pau camp, west of the main road, ready to fulfil counter-attack roles.

The headquarters 6th Indian Infantry Brigade was located three thousand yards west of the 15th Indian Infantry Brigade headquarters and, like the latter, it was dependent on its office truck for cover.

The 28th Indian Infantry Brigade did not come under the command of the 11th Indian Division until 9 December. This brigade, (less 2/9 Gurkha Rifles which was placed at Bt. Besar 12 miles South of Alor Star with the task of defending the air-fields of Alor Star and Sungei Patani), on its arrival was disposed with 2/2 Gurkha Rifles east of the road on the south edge of Tanjong Pau camp, and 2/1 Gurkha Rifles one mile east of the Alor Star air-field at Kepala Batas. The role of the brigade was either to counter-attack in the Jat's sector or towards Rimba or to occupy a position astride the road on the south bank of the S. Besar at Kepla Batas.

The independent company was to guard the Japanese approach to Alor Star via Kuala Nerang and was at Pokok Sema, thirteen miles east of Alor Star. Of the Bahawalpur State Infantry one company was on the Alor Star air-field and its satellite air-strip at Jabi, one company was at Lubok Kiab air-field (twelve miles south-east of Sungei Patani) and its satellite air-strip, three miles to the north-east, near Batu Pekaka bridge over the Sungei Muda. The rest of the battalion was at Sungei Patani acting as an anti-paratroop mobile column. The Kedah Volunteer Force was at

Sungei Patani air-field with a detachment at Kulim. One squadron of the 3rd Cavalry was at Butterworth air-field and another squadron was in reserve at Sungei Patani.

Of the two batteries of the 155th Field Regiment, one was in support of the 15th Indian Infantry Brigade and the other in support of the 6th Indian Infantry Brigade. Of the 22 Indian Mountain Regiment (less 21 Battery, which was with the 9th Indian Division) 4 Battery was to be with the 15th Indian Infantry Brigade on the Singora Road, 7 Indian Mountain Battery with the 6th Indian Infantry Brigade on the Kodiang Road, and 10 Indian Mountain Battery in reserve in Tanjong Pau. The last was sent to Kroh on 9 December. Besides, there was 80 Anti-Tank Regiment (less 272 Battery with the 9th Indian Division). All these units were at Tanjong Pau camp.

The demolition scheme in, and north of, the Jitra position included six demolitions on the main Singora road of which the most important were the bridge at Asun, the bridge over the Kamunting and the bridge in Jitra itself. On the Kodiang road the most important of three demolitions was the one at Manggoi (0675). A section of 45 Army Troops Company was responsible for the demolitions on the railway, including that of the bridge over the Alor Changlun canal. Important demolitions in the rear belts were the Iron Bridge over the S. Bata, two bridges over the S. Besar north of Alor Star airfield, and the road and railway bridges at Alor Star.

17 Indian Field Company was responsible for the maintenance of tracks and for water supply. But the truth was that track maintenance, in the weather then prevailing, was far beyond the capability of a single Field Company. Cable layout was complete only in the right sector. Inter-communication was, however, adversely affected in this sector by the location of the 15th Indian Infantry Brigade Headquarters, which precluded it from using the other brigade's peace-time exchange in Tanjong Pau camp. In the 6th Indian Infantry Brigade area, signal communications were far from complete owing to the cable being reserved for operation Matador.

The Jitra plan included delaying action from the frontier. This was to be carried out by one battalion or its equivalent on each of the two roads, the Singora road which was the responsibility of the 15th Indian Infantry Brigade, and the railway and Kodiang road for which the 6th Indian Infantry Brigade was to be responsible. In the area assigned to the former an outpost position was to be occupied at Asun, $2\frac{1}{2}$ miles north of the main position. This position was to be manned by 1/14 Punjab, 4 Mountain Battery, one

Section 2 Anti-Tank Battery and 23 Indian Field Company.

The outpost position at Asun was covered by a marsh, the bridge over which had been, as stated earlier, prepared for demolition. This outpost garrison was to push forward to Bt. Kayu Hitam, almost on the frontier, a detachment consisting of two companies and a carrier platoon of 1/14 Punjab, 4 Mountain Battery, one section 2 A/Tk Battery and demolition parties from 23 Indian Field company. The main task of this forward contingent was to delay the Japanese advance from the frontier.

In the area assigned to the 6th Indian Infantry Brigade the forward role had been divided between two battalions. One detachment consisting of two companies of 2/16 Punjab, 7 Indian Mountain Battery and one section of 45 Army Troops Company was responsible for delaying the Japanese advance right from Padang Besar down to the outpost position by carrying out demolitions on the railway, to the left, and by delaying action on the main road. The outpost position was at Kg. Imam (0382), five miles north of the main Jitra position, and was to be manned by two companies of 1/8 Punjab, 7 Indian Mountain Battery, one Section 273 Anti-Tank Battery and 3 Indian Field Company.

Whilst the Jitra position, together with its outpost and covering positions, was being occupied, a mechanised column consisting of

    two companies 1/8 Punjab
    the carrier Platoon 1/8 Punjab
    one section 272 A/Tk Battery
    two sections 17 Ind Fd Coy

was ordered to " cross the frontier and gain contact with the enemy to impose maximum delay by harassing tactics and not to become inextricably involved ".[20] The column crossed the frontier on 8 December 1941 at 1730 hours and arrived at Ban Sadao, about ten miles inside Thailand, at 1815 hours. Here the telephone wires were cut and the troops disposed forward of the village, the left flank resting on the road which led to Padang Besar. Forward of this position the carriers were placed in depth off the road covering the anti-tank guns, which were sited to shoot down the road.

At about 2115 hours on 8 December the headlights of a Japanese mechanised column were seen approaching slowly. As their lights topped each rise of the undulating road they could be counted. Thirty-five vehicles were counted and, as they drew nearer, the noise of track indicated that the column was headed by tanks. Fire was held until the landing tank was within one

---

[20] History of 11th Indian Division in Malaya, Volume I, p. 29. (original.)

hundred yards. The three leading tanks were knocked out whilst those in the rear blazed away indiscriminately with their cannon and machine-guns. The close-grouped lorries, jerked to a halt by their surprised drivers, were sprayed by the Indian carriers' light automatics. This greeting, which was apparently unexpected by the Japanese, might well have shaken even seasoned troops. But the Japanese had evidently been trained to deal with such an emergency. The infantry rapidly debussed and started an enveloping movement supported by mortars which promptly came into action from the positions off the road. Two of the carriers were hit and destroyed by this mortar fire.[21] Faced by the strong opposition the Indian cloumn decided to withdraw, which it succeeded in doing under cover of the anti-tank guns and the carriers. On its way back into Malaya it demolished two bridges and a third one partially, and crossed the frontier at 0130 hours, passing through the forward covering position at Bt. Kayu Hitam. It is necessary to add here that concurrently with this column on the Singora road, an armoured train manned by one platoon of 2/16 Punjab and a detachment of 3 Indian Field Company advanced into Siam from Padang Besar. The train moved north as far as the 200-foot girder bridge immediately south of Klong Ngeh. But after this bridge was successfully destroyed the train pulled back and arrived at Padang Besar at 0200 hours on 9 December, where the forward covering detachment comprising two companies of 2/16 Punjab, 7 Indian Mountain Battery and one section 45 Army Troops Company was in position.[22]

9 December was utilised by the Japanese for establishing aerodromes in northern Malaya and at the same time in testing the strength of the British Imperial defence on the entire Thailand front. Consequently there was, to begin with, an intense raid on all aerodromes as far as Perak and Johore—at Alor Star, Sungei Patani, Butterworth and Kuantan. At the second of these four places five of the Japanese aeroplanes were shot down, but the aerodrome at Kuantan was evacuated owing to the virtual

---

[21] Basing their calculations on the reports received from Major Andrew's column, the Divisional Headquarters had estimated the Japanese column as consisting of twelve tanks and a battalion of infantry in lorries. But according to an account of the action which appeared in the "Nippon Times", Tokyo, the mechanised column had been the Saeki Unit under the command of Major Saeki, a former instructor at the Cavalry School, and the strength of the column was ten medium tanks, two guns and the "Honda Company." of four hundred "fighting engineers".

According to the British Official War History the Japanese force was the advanced guard of their 5th Division and consisted of 5th Reconnaissance Regiment, one battery of mountain artillery, one company of tanks, one platoon of engineers, and 11/41st Battalion.

[22] War Diary. General Headquarters, Far East, Cable No. 441/6, Easfar to Troopers, 9 December 1941, Appendix No. 141.

impossibility of defending it. Per contra, the Royal Air Force Blenheims, eleven in number, bombed the Singora aerodrome where forty Japanese bombers and forty fighters were located. But five of the Blenheims were lost.[23] What depressed most was the air reconnaissance report that the Japanese had brought one battleship, two cruisers and seven destroyers to Kota Bharu, one transport to Kuantan and a powerful force at Singora too. The Japanese did not make any demonstrations on land, hence the Indian troops, in their turn, spent the day in strengthening the Jitra positions without any interruption. So far as these were concerned, the day saw no change, although seven Japanese light tanks were claimed to have been destroyed in minor operations and the Krohcol reached Betong by 1800 hours, while the Kuantan troops drove off the Japanese who tried to land north of Beserah.

Now that the destruction of the Klong Ngeh bridge had effectively interrupted the running of trains from Singora, it was clear that nothing would be gained by retaining the detachment at Padang Besar. Accordingly, at 0300 hours on 9 December, this detachment received orders to withdraw to Bt. Ketri as soon as the installations at the station had been destroyed, and to demolish three railway bridges as it came back. The withdrawal, which was by train, was effected without incident.

At dawn on 9 December, the 28th Indian Infantry Brigade (Brigadier W. St. J. Carpendale) began to arrive and was ordered to the locations assigned to it. 2/9 Gurkha Rifles detrained at Kobah railway station and marched to Bt. Besar (about twelve miles south of Alor Star by road). 2/1 and 2/2 Gurkha Rifles detrained at Anak Bukit (about five miles north of Alor Star) marching thence to their allotted areas east of the Alor Star airfield at Kepala Batas and in Tanjong Pau Camp, respectively. All the three battalions were busy with reconnaissances throughout the day. The two forward battalions were warned that on 10 Decembr they would be asked to work in the reserve areas of the Jitra position.

At dusk on 9 December, the demolitions on the Singora road at M.S. $29\frac{1}{2}$ and 28 were blown. About midnight, the Japanese made contact with the forward troops, a platoon covering the demolished causeway at M.S. $29\frac{1}{2}$. Two hours later the position was outflanked and then the platoon had to be withdrawn.

Throughout the whole of 10 December the Indian troops were in contact with the Japanese forward elements, but at the same time

---

[23] One of the pilots shot down in this attack was Squadron Leader A.S.K. Scarf, who was subsequently awarded the Victoria Cross for his gallantry, this being the first Victoria Cross won in Malaya.

the detachment from Bt. Kayu Hitam withdrew. It was a fighting withdrawal over six miles of enclosed country carried out methodically and skilfully. It was dusk when the Changlun position behind the S. Laka at M.S. 23½ was reached. The detachment suffered only ten casualties.

Meanwhile there had been a slight change of plan. The divisional commander had informed Brigadier Garrett, the commander of the 15th Indian Infantry Brigade, that he wished the Japanese to be delayed north of the outpost position at Asun until at least the dawn of 11 December so that the troops in the main position could complete the essential work and also get some rest. The brigade commander represented that this would require the whole of 1/14 Punjab forward of Asun. His plea was accepted by the divisional commander, who, accordingly, ordered Brigadier Carpendale of the 28th Indian Infantry Brigade to place 2/1 Gurkha Rifles (less one company which was the airfield reserve at Alor Star) under the command of the 15th Indian Infantry Brigade to hold the Asun position so as to enable the employment of the whole of 1/14 Punjab forward. 2/1 Gurkha Rifles spent the day contructing reserve localities in the Jitra position and then marched at 1930 hours. The men were ferried in trucks to Asun where they all arrived at 2130 hours.

Elsewhere in the divisional area the day had been uneventful except in the State of Perlis, on the aerodromes of northern Malaya and on the Patani road. The detachment of 2/16 Punjab at Kodiang had withdrawn its platoon from Kuala Perlis and had blown the bridge at Kangar, the capital of Perlis, on orders from the divisional commander, thus leaving the area to the Japanese. Another unfortunate development was that during the morning of 10 December, Alor Star aerodrome was evacuated by the Royal Air Force.[24] This was done without any warning or subsequent report to the Divisional Headquarters, where some perturbation naturally arose when a huge pall of smoke was seen hanging over the aerodrome and the sound of explosion also was heard. The hangars had been fired and a few insignificant holes had been blown on the runway.

A third depressing incident was, as will be told in detail later, on the Patani Road where 3/16 Punjab was involved in trouble. This regiment had left Betong at 0400 hours, and, when 3½ miles short of the "Ledge", had met the Japanese who had put in a tank attack as a result of which two companies were found

---

[24] According to Royal Air Force sources the aerodrome was not evacuated till the afternoon of 10 December.

missing. In the evening of the same day the terrible news reached the division that H.M. battleship *Prince of Wales* and H.M. battle cruiser *Repulse* had been sunk by Japanese aircraft at midday, not far from Kuantan on the east coast of Malaya.

The Japanese had shown remarkable abilities of rapid infiltration and outflanking, even on the most difficult ground like that to the east of Changlun—Jitra road. Their planes gave splendid support to the ground troops, especially in the matter of directing the fire towards their enemy. Their artillery was lighter and their mortars more accurate than those of the British. All Japanese soldiers were supplied with tommy guns.

When the day dawned on 11 December the whole of 1/14 Punjab had been holding the Changlun position in Kedah. At about 0800 hours a mortar bombardment preceded Japanese attack on its right flank. This was driven back after a local counter-attack. At 1130 hours, the position was again heavily mortared. The demolition of the Changlun bridge was later effected as the Japanese were pressing forward, and a tank too had appeared. By midday, however, the Japanese attacking from the right flank had penetrated into the middle of the Changlun position and the commander of this " covering force " decided to withdraw behind the Asun outpost position, calculating that he would be able to reach it before the attacking tanks could negotiate the damaged bridges. Accordingly, 1/14 Punjab disengaged and withdrew to a position about $2\frac{1}{2}$ miles in the rear from where it was intended to withdraw later through the outpost troops at Asun, as its prime role was to delay but not to become involved. At 1430 hours, however, the commander of this " covering force " was ordered by the divisional commander to occupy a position $1\frac{1}{2}$ to 2 miles north of Asun with a view to imposing further delay on the Japanese. At about 1630 hours, as the 'covering force' was moving back, there occurred the first of many incidents which demonstrated the effectiveness of the tank especially against inexperienced troops. Screened by a deluge of rain, twelve Japanese medium tanks followed by infantry in lorries and by light tanks charged through the Punjab rear-guard into the rear of the withdrawing battalion. Few of the Indian troops in this area had seen a tank before. The tanks broke through the rear of the column, then through a company of 2/1 Gurkha Rifles which was in position at M.S. $18\frac{1}{2}$ to cover the withdrawal of 1/14 Punjab. Continuing down the road the Japanese flying column caught the bulk of 1/14 Punjab on the sides of the road waiting to go into position. Scattering these startled troops, the tanks continued on their way, and there was at the moment nothing to stop them

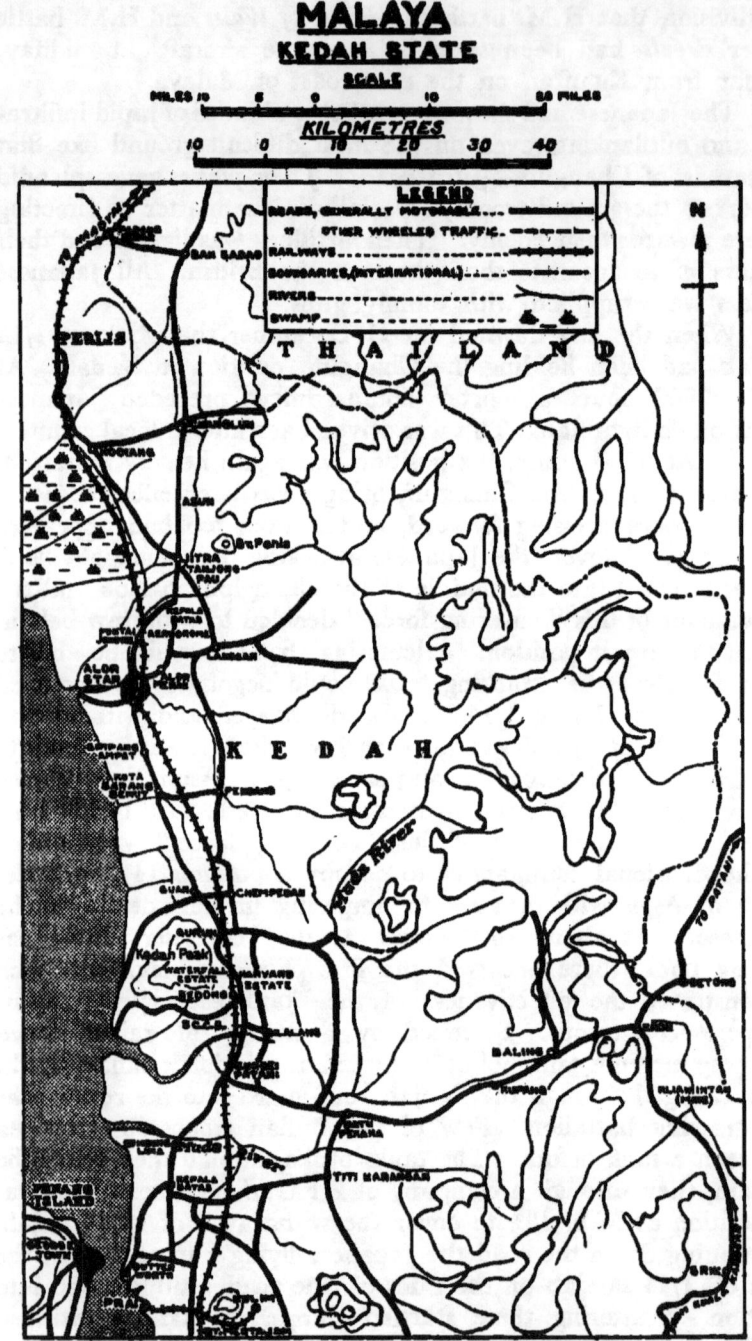

until they came to the Jitra position, except the Asun marsh, and that too only if the road-bridge across the Asun had been previously demolished. But such demolition had not been possible and the tanks attacked the bridge, blazing shells and bullets from their quick-firing cannon and machine-guns. The Viceroy's Commissioned Sapper Officer in-charge of demolition was hit. A Japanese shell cut the wires from the plunger to the demolition, and the Commander 23 Indian Field Company was wounded by Japanese machine-gun fire as he was attempting to mend the wires. The demolition did not materialise. But, providentially, the Company Havildar of 2/1 Gurkha Rifles aligned a Boyes anti-tank rifle and fired. The leading tank slued round and stopped. The second tank in attempting to pass the first was also hit. Two more tanks arrived, one was disabled and the other withdrew, whereupon the Company Havildar dashed foward and carried back the wounded Sapper officer. This anti-tank rifle was one of the two received by the battalion on the previous day and these were also the only two in the battalion. The Japanese advance had been halted by these stray weapons, but only temporarily and at heavy cost.

Many men and much material and equipment had been lost. Some two hundred men of 1/14 Punjab, with Brigadier Garrett who was visiting the battalion at the time, were cut off and rejoined the following day. But the battalion was overrun and temporarily rendered ineffective.

The Japanese infantry soon began infiltrating into the Asun position. Parties were dispersed by Gurkha bayonet and Kukri charges, but the Japanese kept coming on from the front and flank, wading chest-deep through the "impassable" marsh and screened by the gathering darkness of the late evening. Not long after, the two forward companies of 2/1 Gurkha Rifles were practically surrounded. At 1845 hours the tanks followed by infantry broke into the position, and seven tanks passed through the battalion headquarters. By 1930 hours, the line of communication with the two forward companies had ceased to function. Patrols were sent out but failed to return. The firing in both the forward company areas dwindled and died away. The commanding officer believed that these companies had either withdrawn or had been destroyed and therefore he withdrew with his headquarters; for the time being even this battalion was as good as useless.

Certain posts in the battalion headquarters area remained in position all night, repulsing every hostile attack. Some of these men were reported to have been killed when the Japanese closed in the next morning, the rest, however, escaped. Few survivors of the two forward companies and of the company which had been covering the withdrawal of 1/14 Punjab ever rejoined the battalion.

On the Kodiang road, the withdrawal of the detachment of 2/16 Punjab from Kodiang had conformed with that of 1/14 Punjab from Changlun.[25] At 1800 hours it had passed through the outpost position at Kg. Imam. The armoured train also had withdrawn down the railway and had crossed the railway bridge over the Alor—Changlun canal at about dusk when the bridge was also blown. Then occurred an unfortunate incident. As is understandable with inexperienced troops, a demolition was prematurely blown. This was the Manggoi demolition at M.S. 13¾ on the Kodiang road behind the outpost position at Kg. Imam. For various reasons it was not repaired in time, although there was fortunately no contact on this front, and all transport guns and carriers of the covering and outpost troops and seven anti-tank guns, which had been sited with the East Surrey's right company in the Pisang—Manggoi area, had their lines of withdrawal blocked, and were lost.

The disasters on the Singora and Kodiang road up till now had a profound influence on the battle of Jitra.[26] which was soon to follow. The Japanese position was strong not only in this part of Kedah but also on the Grik—Kroh road. The British official report of the operations on this road stated that "attacks by unexpectedly strong enemy forces which included tanks and light artillery forced our troops back towards the frontier. Situation confused but gives cause for some anxiety as, if this enemy force breaks through, whole of N. Kedah position will be threatened."[27] It was appreciated that the Japanese would certainly make a thrust down the road leading from Patani with a view to cutting the 11th Indian Division's lines of communications at Sungei Patani or Kuala Kangsar. If this were achieved whilst the division was fighting north of Sungei Patani or even in north Perak, it would be threatened with annihilation.

KROHCOL OPERATIONS

It was originally intended that the column operating on the Kroh-Patani, road known as Krohcol, should consist of 5/14

---

[25] War Diary General Headquarters, Far East, Cable No. 0161, General Singapore to Troopers, 12 December, 1941, 1430 hours G.M.T. Appendix No. 170.
[26] *The War in Malaya, op. cit.*, p. 127.
[27] W.D. General Headquarters, Far East, 12 December 1941, Appendix 170.

Punjab, 3/16 Punjab, and one battery FMSVF[28] besides the field company and field ambulance. The FMSVF battery had, however, been unable to mobilise in time, and was replaced later by 10 Indian Mountain Battery from the North Kedah front. 5/14 Punjab was moved up to Kroh on 8 December, leaving one company in Penang. The battalion (less one company) had not arrived when operations started. Responsibility for operations on the Kroh front was, on 8 December, therefore, delegated by the Commander III Indian Corps to the Commander 11th Indian Division.

The role of Krohcol was to stop the Japanese advancing down the Patani-Kroh road. It was understood that this might be achieved only if Krohcol gained possession of the " Ledge " in good time to carry out comprehensive demolitions on the stretch of this precipitous road-cut before the Japanese arrived. The " Ledge" was a six-mile stretch of the road cut out of the mountain side overlooking the Patani river. Its northern end lay thirty-five miles from the frontier and sixty-nine miles from Patani. The terrain at the " Ledge " was extremely difficult for infantry, and the repair of long stretches of road, the debris of which when demolished would literally fall down the hill-side, would be a lengthy and tedious business; it was estimated that comprehensive demolitions would delay the passage of lorries and tanks for at least two months.

The timely anticipation of the Japanese arrival at the "Ledge" was therefore a pre-requisite for holding up their advance. It was also hoped that they might be forestalled at Banangsta where a single ferry, whose capacity was only one lorry, crossed the Patani river. This village lay half way between Patani and the frontier.

In all the pre-war British High Command appreciations it had been considered that opposition by the Thais would be most unlikely; in fact it was expected that they would welcome British troops and give them every assistance. Krohcol commander, however, was taking no risks. The road between the frontier and

---

[28] It was commanded by Lt.-Colonel Moorhead of 3/16 Punjab and its final composition was:—
    5/14 Punjab (less one company retained in Penang).
    3/16 Punjab.
    10 Indian Mountain Battery.
    One troop 273 Anti-tank Battery.
    46 Army Troops Companies Sappers and Miners (less one section at Padang Besar).
    A detachment Div. Signals.
    A detachment 2/3 Australian Reserve Mechanical Transport Company.
    A detachment 36 Field Ambulance.
    2/3 Australian Motor Ambulance Convoy.

Betong passed a defile flanked on either side by high hills covered with thick jungle. In the unlikely event of the Thai opposition it would be fatal to be caught in lorries on this stretch of road. He, therefore, planned to march to Betong, and on arrival there to call up his troop-carrying lorries, embus his troops and occupy the " Ledge ".

The intitial occupation of the "Ledge" devolved on 3/16 Punjab. Because it was only after 1330 hours on 8 December, more than 12 hours after the Japanese began landing at Patani, that the order " Operate Ledge " was received by the Commander of Krohcol, and as 5/14 Punjab had not yet arrived, he had to move immediately in personal command of 3/16 Punjab which was his own battalion. At 1400 hours the leading scouts arrived at the frontier barrier gate. It had been closed and padlocked. So the scouts smashed it with axes and resumed their advance. Immediately the leading scout had set foot across the frontier he was greeted by a fusillade of fire and fell dead. This unexpectedly hostile reception required some readjustment of ideas, but for lack of time the advance was resumed within a few minutes. The carrier platoon moved ahead as advanced guard, while two companies cut their way through the jungle on either side of the road.

The locals, possibly assisted by the Japanese (who on 8 December had landed a strong force at Patani) employed guerilla tactics to obstruct their advance, and consequently the progress continued but slowly until dusk. Blocks were found at every bend of the winding road. The flank companies either hacked a laborious way or made quick advances, as jungle and rubber alternated. Thus, by dusk, 3/16 Punjab had covered only three miles in four and a half hours, at the cost of fifteen lives. Six dead Thais had been left on the ground, and five Japanese rifles and one Japanese light automatic had been captured. It was estimated that the battalion had been opposed by one hundred and fifty Thai gendarmes whose casualties were estimated at twenty-four.

The battalion went into perimeter camp for the night, when it was subjected to constant sniping. 5/14 Punjab (less one company) arrived at Kroh at 0400 hours on 9 December, but it was stopped there by the order of the commander of Krohcol as, in his opinion, the country did not allow the use of more than one battalion.

At first light on 9 December, 3/16 Punjab resumed its advance. It was now opposed by approximately three hundred and fifty Thai gendarmes who exhibited the same tactics as on the previous afternoon. Sappers of the 46th Company (Army Troops) did gallant work clearing several blocks. In the afternoon all opposition ceased as suddenly as it had begun, but the battalion had suffered fifteen more casualties. About thrity men of the hostile force had been killed in close fighting and six wounded Thais were captured.

At 1600 hours the battalion arrived at Betong which was decked with white flags. It was welcomed by a minor official of the Thai Government, who also apologised for the opposition which was due to, as he described it, a " mistake " and also the absence of the regular district officer.[29]

At 0600 hours on 10 December, 3/16 Punjab embussed in lorries of 2/3 Australian Reserve M.T. company and moved off, headed by the carrier platoon and one company. It debussed at 1330 hours at a point only six miles south of the " Ledge ", as there was no turning point for lorries further north. The move had not been without opposition from the air but no change occurred. No opposition was met with on the land until the advanced guard, comprising the carrier platoon and one company, had moved two thousand yards when they encountered slight opposition. This, however, caused little delay and they were able to continue their march for another mile before any stronger opposition was met. On this occasion the opposing force consisted of the Japanese who had covered seventy-eight miles from Patani within a little over thirty hours and on roads which were in very poor condition. They had presumably supplemented the single ferry at Banangsta. As against this the Krohcol had covered only thirty-two miles. The force was still three and a half miles south of the " Ledge ". The Japanese had won the race.

3/16 Punjab immediately began an outflanking movement west of the road. The first company (B) was held up after progressing a few hundred yards. A second company (D) advanced through the first company and occupied a hill, known as Jungle Hill, in the rear of the Japanese right flank. This caused the latter to withdraw and permitted a third company (A) to push ahead along the road. But suddenly a Japanese motorised column headed by tanks appeared. The company let the tanks pass and then attacked the lorries. However, another group of tanks was found to be following in the rear of the first, as a result of which A Company had to battle against overwhelming odds for thirty minutes by the end of which practically the whole of it had suffered casualties. It was indeed a gallant fight, which inspired the remainder and also gave to them a valuable respite during which they were able to occupy a defensive position behind the Kampong To stream, and also partially to wreck the wooden

---

[29] This District Officer's car was found ditched next day facing north. Apparently he had been up to warn the Japanese.

bridge across that rivulet. After dealing with the company on the road the Japanese tanks continued southwards but were stopped by the partially demolished bridge over the Kampong To stream and were forced to withdraw in the face of accurate anti-tank fire.

Meanwhile, the Japanese were also working round the west slopes of Jungle Hill and were threatening to cut off D Company from the rest of the battalion. The company commander decided to withdraw following a wide detour through the jungle. Thus, at nightfall, 3/16 Punjab was short by two companies. The battalion (less two companies) was then disposed south of the Kampong To stream. The unfordable S. Patani flowed one and a half miles east of the right flank, and both flanks of the position lay against steep hill-sides covered with thick jungle which was then classified as "impenetrable". Meanwhile 5/14 Punjab (less one company) with Indian Mountain Battery under command, had been ordered to occupy a position about nine miles north of Betong. It had been decided not to bring the battery forward in support of 3/16 Punjab as there were no suitable gun positions in the area.

The commander of Krohcol also sent a message to the divisional headquarters reporting the situation and stating that withdrawal was likely. The divisional commander, who was one hundred and thirteen miles from the scene of battle, was in no position to investigate the situation or to influence Krohcol operations. However, to reinforce the column, one troop of 273 Anti-tank Battery was sent from Jitra.

The night of 10/11 December was for 3/16 Punjab one of active patrolling. The sappers, though continuously sniped, completely demolished the wooden bridge over the Kampong To stream making it impassable even for infantry. By dawn of 11 December, the battalion less the two missing companies (A and D) was fairly well consolidated and an early morning bombardment by Japanese mortars had done little damage. At 1000 hours, D Company, the company from Jungle Hill, had also arrived back.

During the afternoon the Japanese launched three separate attacks. The first two, at 1500 hours and 1600 hours respectively, were beaten off with heavy losses. Later, at 1730 hours, a co-ordinated battalion attack was launched by the Japanese against the whole front. It was supported by infantry guns which concentrated on the British carriers which had been "dug in" near the road and camouflaged. Many of these carriers were literally blown out of the ground. The attack was, however, held and eventually the three-inch mortars silenced the Japanese guns.

In consequence of this fight the battalion had suffered thirty casualties, bringing the total to two hundred casualties since it had crossed the frontier, but it had held the Japanese and inflicted severe losses on them. The battalion however had now been on the move or in action for four days and had not slept for two nights. The mounting casualties and complete absence of sleep could not go on indefinitely. The commander of Krohcol, therefore, decided that it was essential to withdraw and join up with 5/14 Punjab before his unit became too shattered and worn-out to fight, and telephoned to the divisional commander who sent orders by the hand of an officer, giving discretion to the local commander to withdraw if necessary but reminding him of the vital importance of preventing the Japanese from reaching Sungei Patani. The Krohcol was also told that the prepared Kroh position must be the limit of their withdrawal.

At 0400 hours on 12 December, a strong attack against the centre of the position was repulsed after hand-to-hand fighting, but dawn revealed that the Japanese were by-passing the position along the banks of the Sungei Patani on the east flank. At 0700 hours again the Japanese launched the strongest attack yet made on the Indian battalion. Their outflanking troops used light automatic fire from the tree tops, and soon they were well round the east flank and threatening to cut the route of the Indian withdrawal.

By 0900 hours all carriers except four had been knocked out, and the derelicts were dragged on to the road as obstacles. By this time the west flank of the position had also been outflanked, but one company was sent back to occupy a " lay-back " position about a mile to the south. The other two companies were then withdrawn, covered by the four remaining carriers. Two more carriers were knocked out before the battle commander, who was himself personally in charge of the rear party, was satisfied that his forward troops were clear and could give the order to retire. The Japanese apparently felt that they had had enough, as they did not follow up the withdrawal. 3/16 Punjab was thereby enabled to move back in lorries of 2/3 Australian Reserve Mechanical Transport Company to the Kroh position, and at 1500 hours three hundred and fifty men of the battalion passed through 5/14 Punjab. On the night of 12/13 December, Krohcol ceased to be under the command of the 11th Indian Division and came under the direct control of the Corps Commander.

It is necessary to observe that the men of 3/16 Punjab had indeed put up a magnificent fight and added a glorious page to the history of their Regiment. This was due to the " psychological advantage"[30] which it enjoyed from its splendid initial advance into the "Ledge" area. This battalion, besides, alone of all the battalions in the 11th Indian Division, was spared the demoralising effect of that twelfth hour change of role from "Matador" to "Jitra", from offence to defence.

The Japanese attack on the Jitra position and Krohcol had considerably endangered the position of the army in the first three days of the war. It was further affected by the policy of withdrawal of the Royal Air Force. There was difference of opinion regarding the effective employment of the air force. The Air Officer Commanding believed that "the correct employment of air forces was in the attack of the shipping and concentrations in the Singora area",[31] while the General Officer Commanding wanted the British planes to attack the Japanese aerodromes and give immediate relief to his troops in northern Malaya. The question was of course decided according to the General's wish. But in the meantime the Royal Air Force had evacuated the aerodromes in the north, and taken shelter in more peaceful places like Ipoh, Kuala Lumpur and Singapore, and in a few places had failed to clear equipment and stores. In some places they had even left the runways intact, which enabled the Japanese to mount air attacks from these airfields without delay.

The situation at this stage of hostilities has been summarised by General Percival in the following terms: "In the air the situation was not much better (than on the sea). The Japanese Air Force was already well established on the aerodromes in South Thailand....There was also, of course, the long-range aircraft operating from the aerodromes in South Indo-China. The Japanese probably had at least 300 modern aircraft available at this time. Constant attacks were kept up on our small air force and its bases in North Malaya, in which we suffered heavy losses. The situation was made worse by our lack of fighter protection and of proper anti-aircraft ground defence".[32]

Meanwhile a War Council had started functioning at Singapore from 10 December, with the object of directing the war in the East. It asked Royal Air Force to afford air cover to the ground troops and maintain control over air primarily for the defence of Singapore and also to provide protection to the convoys bringing land and air reinforcements to Malaya. Next, it decided to withdraw the troops from Kelantan. Above all, the responsibility

---

[30] History of 11th Indian Division in Malaya, *op. cit.*, Vol. I. p. 120 (original).
[31] Sir Paul Maltby's Despatch., *op. cit.*, p. 1370, para 235.
[32] *The War in Malaya. op. cit.* p. 131.

for the Kroh front was transferred from the 11th Indian Division from the midnight of 12/13 December.

RETREAT FROM JITRA

In the battle of Jitra, by 1800 hours on 11 December, C Company of 2 Jat and a platoon of B Company in Kg. Malau had already engaged with the Japanese snipers who must have by-passed 1/14 Punjab during the encounter at Chunglun in the morning. At 1930 hours, when news reached the 11th Indian Division that Brigadier Garrett had been cut off on the Changlun road, Brigadier Carpendale of the 28th Indian Brigade was placed in command of the 15th Indian Brigade as well as his own.[33] By 2030 hours Japanese tanks, with headlights on, reached the demolition at M.S. 13½. This was covered by 1 Leicester and a section of 215 Anti-tank Battery. The demolition failed but two tanks were knocked out by the anti-tank section. The tanks which closed up behind and shelled the position were effectively engaged and silenced by an artillery concentration from 155 Field Regiment.

In the rear areas there had been a parachute scare. At 1322 hours a report that fifty parachutists had been seen landing between Gurun and Silk was received by 2/9 Gurkha Rifles at Bt. Besar.[34] Seven minutes later B Company moved off in mechanical transport accompanied by one section of the carrier platoon to deal with them. But the report proved to be baseless.

Shortly after midnight of 11/12 December, the Japanese infantry was in contact with the left forward company of Jat, east of the Singora Road. Two hours later the frontage had been extended to involve the right forward companies of 2 Jat and 1 Leicester. Firing was continuous but no attack developed. By 0400 hours on 12 December, the right rear company of 2 Jat was also being sniped.

In view of the persistent reports of considerable Japanese activity on the right flank, Brigadier Carpendale asked for reinforcements from the 6th Indian Infantry Brigade. The two companies of 2/16 Punjab, which had been forward at Padang Besar, were sent across to come under his orders. These two companies were put into position on the edge of the rubber plantation between Kg. Kelubi and "Rear 50" (1173) to deal with any hostile move round the right flank from the directions of Bt. Alur, and were in

---
[33] Percival's Despatch, *op. cit.* p. 58, para 105.
[34] War Diary, General Headquarters Far East, 11 December 1941, Serial No. 24.

position by dawn on 12 December.[35] Meanwhile 2/2 Gurkha Rifles had been ordered to occupy a reserve position on the south bank of the S. Bata with its left flank covering the Iron Bridge on the main road. Later 1/8 Punjab with its two companies (A and B) also arrived as reinforcement.

At M.S. 13½, when the demolition had failed to stop the Japanese, 1 Leicester had immediately erected a road-block just east of C Company's forward line. At 0300 hours, this road-block was also rushed by the Japanese and some Public Works Department huts west of the road and behind the company position were occupied by them. On the other hand, the night was a busy one also for the British gunners. 155 Field Regiment and the 4 Indian Mountain Battery had many calls for fire. 137 Field Regiment was moving up from Sungei Patani to occupy gun positions to cover the infantry in a battle which had already begun.

On 12 December the Japanese carried out three major attacks against the left company of 2 Jat and the right company of 1 Leicester, astride the main road. The road itself was still successfully blocked by the disabled Japanese tanks. The first attack came shortly after first light. It was barely dawn in a downpour of rain when the Japanese opened heavy fire from the Copse. Simultaneously the tanks on the road opened fire and with sustained screams of "Bansai" their infantry charged the left platoon of D Company of 2 Jat, from the front and flank. The charge was driven back except in the extreme left where the section protecting the concrete pill-box observation post was overrun. An immediate counter-attack by two sections from the reserve platoon was unsuccessful. The Gunner Field Observation Officer had been killed and throughout the day a small Japanese flag waved defiantly from the pill-box. The loss of this observation post seriously hampered the subsequent defence of this sector. The Japanese did not, however, seriously exploit their success except by infiltration which led to early sniping of the battalion headquarters of 2 Jat, five hundred yards in the rear.

The 6th Indian Infantry Brigade had not been engaged but, as a result of sending reinforcements to the 15th Indian Infantry Brigade, it was now reduced to 2 Surreys, flanking the approach by the Kodiang Road, 2/16 Punjab (less two companies with the 15th Indian Infantry Brigade) guarding the railway bridge and Jerlun, and 1/8 Punjab (less two companies also with the 15th Indian Infantry Brigade) serving as Brigadier Lay's only reserve. At the time the appreciation was that the Kodiang road

---

[35] History of 11th Indian Division in Malaya, *op. cit.* Vol. I. p. 51 (original).
"Rear 50" and "Forward 50" were hills in 1173 and 1174 respectively.

was not likely to be neglected by the Japanese; it led to Jitra directly behind the 15th Indian Infantry Brigade. The railway, too, easily reached from M.S. 16 on the Kodiang Road, led to the lines of communication of Anak Bukit.

The divisional commander considered the situation at 0800 hours on 12 December.[36] On the Patani Road the Japanese had won the race for the Ledge and had battered 3/16 Punjab, then in a situation from which it was difficult to extricate it. If 3/16 Punjab did not get back, for the defence of the Kroh position only 5/14 Punjab would be available. In any case it was then just a question of time before the Japanese might force their way through Kroh, and then move either down the road leading to Sungei Patani or to Kuala Kangsar.

The situation at Jitra did not compel withdrawal. But signs of deterioration were visible and the loss of two battalions at Asun and Changlun had reduced the divisional reserve to the negligible proportion of one company of 2/1 Gurkha Rifles in the Kepala Batas area. There were also strong indications of the not unexpected eastern out-flanking movement in the Jitra position. There were as yet few symptoms of Japanese advance down the Kodiang road, but this was unlikely to be deferred much longer.

If the layout for a night withdrawal was initiated at once while the two brigades were in control and not hotly engaged, an orderly withdrawal might be possible; but if the initial moves were deferred until the situation at Jitra had considerably deteriorated, such withdrawal might be extremely difficult. The plan of the divisional commander was therefore to pull back the 15th Indian Infantry Brigade to the line of the S. Bata and the 6th Indian Infantry Brigade to the S. Besar at once, and to withdraw behind the S. Kedah at Alor Star overnight. The request to permit withdrawal was sent to the III Indian Corps at 0830 hours. As the Corps Commander was on his way to Singapore, the message was referred direct to the General Officer Commanding Malaya who replied that pending further orders the battle was to be fought on the Jitra position.[37]

We may now revert to the fighting on the position near milestone 13½. It may be recalled that in the first attack on D Company of 2 Jat, C Company of 1 Leicester had also got involved in the fighting. A counter-attack by the remaining force of 1 Leicester drove out the Japanese from their foothold in the Public Works Department huts in C Company's area. But despite the

---

[36] History of 11th Indian Division in Malaya, *op. cit.* Vol. I, p. 53 (original).
[37] Percival's Despatch, *op. cit.*, Section XXII para 167. See also, *The War in Malaya, op. cit.* page 133.

success of the counter-attack by the reserve force of 1 Leicester, C Company was still in an unhappy situation. The tanks on the road and the Japanese snipers in the Market Garden Copse area were making conditions not too pleasant. A section of 215 Anti-Tank Battery was not well situated to deal with the Japanese tanks and orders were issued for the guns to move into a better position. Whilst moving, the guns and their crew were badly shot up and suffered heavy casualties before the survivors could run for cover. The guns continued to draw heavy fire from the Japanese tanks; shells and bullets were splashing around them and one gun was overturned by a direct hit. Nothing daunted, the leader of the anti-tank company rushed forward and sighted one of the guns. Thereafter, accurate fire from this gun silenced the Japanese tanks whose crew bolted away.

Although the tanks had been silenced, the Japanese in the Market Garden Copse area were still making things extremely unpleasant for both the Leicesters and the Jats. As the Leicesters apparently were unable to deal with the situation, Brigadier Carpendale asked Brigadier Lay for more reinforcements to enable him to stage a counter-attack in the area between the two battalions. Brigadier Lay agreed to send the remainder of 1/8 Punjab and, as time appeared to be of paramount importance, suggested that he himself should issue the orders for the counter-attack direct to the commanding officer of 1/8 Punjab. Brigadier Carpendale agreed to this and in the orders gave the Market Garden as the objective. He also agreed with Brigadier Lay's suggestion that the "starting point" for the counter-attack should be the Iron Bridge and the time 0930 hours.

Meanwhile a counter-attack was launched by a platoon of the reserve company of 2 Jat to recapture the pill-box behind their sector. The 1/8 Punjab counter-attack had an unhappy start. As the companies were advancing in open order through the close rubber plantation and jungle to the rear of the Jat headquarters, heavy fire was opened on them at very close range from the east. This unexpected appearance of the "enemy" behind the Jat sector caused panic among the tired troops. It took some minutes to restore control. It was soon found that the so-called "enemy" was no other than the reserve platoon of 2 Jat moving forward to the headquarters for a counter-attack on the pill-box. Both 1/8 Punjab and 2 Jat had mistaken each other for the Japanese.

The Market Garden Copse area was strongly held by the Japanese. The carriers of 2 Jat which were accompanying 1/8 Punjab to take part in the counter-attack could advance no further because they were getting bogged. There was no field Observation Officer and, therefore, there was no artillery support. Moreover the force had suffered casualties owing to the unfortunate mistake and had dwindled to about two platoons. This force was not adequate for the task but orders were received for the counter-attack to proceed. Despite the determination of the men to reach their objective, the mortar fire and the hail of bullets which greeted their advance reduced the ranks of the attackers. Those who reached the Copse were quickly liquidated in close combat with greatly superior numbers.

The next Japanese attack developed at 1230 hours. Between this and the last attacks there had of course been continuous firing by both the sides; under cover of heavy mortar fire there were repeated attempts at penetration on the part of the Japanese, who at points effected lodgements in the Jat area. The Japanese were also reported to be east of Kg. Penia. This second attack, unlike the first one at dawn, was fully co-ordinated, and it was also initiated by one battalion. The Japanese were met by intense artillery fire and they suffered heavy casualties. An hour and a half after the start of that attack, the British and Indian guns were running short of ammunition. Many of the rifles and light machine-guns of D Company of 2 Jat, the target of attack, were also getting too hot to hold, while some others were unworkable owing to being clogged with wet mud. Meanwhile, the Japanese were massing in the anti-tank ditch immediately in front of the company defences. The last conversation down the telephone between the company commander and his commanding officer was:—

"The men cannot fire, Sir".

"I can't give you permission to withdraw".

"O.K. Sir. We will fight it out with grenades and bayonets. The men are splendid. I reckon we have got about five minutes left".

"Good luck to you".[38]

When the Japanese charged, D Company faced them with fixed bayonets. At the end, only a few survivors emerged from that gallant stand of the Jats.

It was expected that the Japanese would soon reach the area of the Jat battalion headquarters and the Brigade Commander gave permission for the headquarters and A Company to move to the area behind C Company in the Kelubi Estate and link up with the detachment of 2/16 Punjab which was in position south of the Kelubi Estate between "Rear 50" and Kg. Kelubi. The Japanese, however, did not immediately exploit the success they

[38] History of 11th Indian Division in Malaya, *op. cit.*, vol. I, page 58 (Original).

had gained, and this move of the Jat battalion was carried out without interference.

The third Japanese attack was made immediately following the attack on the Jat left company. This new thrust was directed against B Company of 1 Leicester. The Japanese gained an early success by the capture of a locality on the right flank, but the situation was restored by a counter-attack by the carriers of East Survey.

By 1500 hours all the attacks had petered out. But with the capture of the area held by Jat D Company, the right flank of the Leicesters was completely exposed and there was a gap of one and a half miles between the positions held by the Leicesters and the Gurkhas behind the S. Bata. Into this gap the Japanese started to infiltrate, but were stopped on the S. Jitra by a company of 1/8 Punjab, sent forward by Brigadier Carpendale, and by a crossfire from the Leicesters.

Because of this gap the position needed immediate readjustment. The divisional commander agreed to Brigadier Carpendale's plan to hold the general line " Rear 50 "—S. Bata—Iron Bridge—Rimba with, from right to left, two companies of 2/16 Punjab; 2 Jat; A Company 1/8 Punjab; 2/2 G.R. and 1 Leicester. On the right all units were in position except 2 Jat. The holding of this line would entail pulling back B and C Companies of 2 Jat, the whole of 1 Leicester, already dangerously exposed to the Japanese attack on the east flank, and the East Surrey and the company of 2/16 Punjab at the Alor Changlun Canal railway bridge. The plan also included a counter-attack eastwards on the following day from the Leicester area between the Iron Bridge and Rimba. The objective was the area of the S. Bata between its junction with the S. Jitra and the S. Palong.

At about 1600 hours the withdrawal orders were issued. 1 Leicester strongly protested on being moved from prepared positions in which the men were quite happy, to an unprepared line two and half miles long. But their protest was overruled. All units were back on the line soon after dark, except the right forward company of 2 Jat which never received its withdrawal orders and its D Company which had been wiped out earlier. The line was now from Kelubi—exclusive Hill 50—Hill 50 area—the line of the S. Bata to inclusive the Iron Bridge—exclusive Iron Bridge—Rimba. 2/9 G.R. less two companies were astride the road at M.S. $10\frac{3}{4}$, about six hundred yards south of the Iron Bridge. But the situation was not too wholesome. 2/2 G.R. was being heavily mortared. The Japanese were massing on this front, and their tanks were moving down the road. Infiltration into the

Tanjong Pau camp area was also taking place between Rear 50 and the S. Bata. The Leicesters were in a bad plight and had sustained losses owing to the difficulty of communicating the withdrawal orders to all their sub-units. The men had no option but to stand in mud and paddy to obtain a field of fire, and there was the greatest difficulty in communications.

The Divisional Commander, therefore, decided that his force must withdraw that night. He applied again to the III Indian Corps for permission which was accorded at 2030 hours. The orders for the withdrawal from the Jitra position were issued to the brigades at 2200 hours on 12 December but it was not to commence before midnight. These orders required immediate withdrawal of the whole division to the south of Alor Star, as a step preparatory to the occupation of the Gurun position, which was to begin when the Japanese exerted heavy pressure on the Kedah line. As a result of the withdrawal the 6th Indian Infantry Brigade was to move first to the Kepala Batas area and later, when the other two brigades had withdrawn, it (less 2 Surrey) was to hold a rear intermediate position at Simpang Empat (seven miles south of Alor Star). The other brigade, the 28th Indian Infantry Brigade, was to withdraw to the S. Kedah. Out of its battalions, 2/2 G.R. was to move to Langgar, and 2/9 G.R. (less two companies), in position at the Tanjong Pau cross-roads, was to cover the retreat of all troops away from Jitra and was to withdraw eventually, through 2 Surrey, to Alor Star, where it was to hold a position south of the S. Kedah and east of the main road. 2 Surrey, holding the bridges over the S. Padang Terap and the S. Besar after covering the withdrawal of 2/9 G.R., was to withdraw to Alor Star and hold a position south of the S. Kedah and west of the main road linking with 2/9 G.R. The third brigade, the 15th Indian Infantry Brigade, was to be withdrawn into the divisional reserve.

The plan of withdrawal of the combined 15th and 28th Indian Infantry Brigades was for 1 Leicester to withdraw first through 2/2 G.R. and then for units south of the S. Bata to withdraw via the main road; the last unit, 2/2 G.R., to cover 2/9 G.R. which was acting as the rearguard at 0300 hours on 13 December, when 2/9 G.R. would also withdraw. The combined headquarters of these two brigades was opened at milestone 10, in the rear of 2/9 G.R.

The divisional artillery, except 501 Field Battery in support of the 28th Indian Infantry Brigade, was to move back and harbour clear of the paddy areas (which offered neither cover nor, except on the road, gun positions) and to make preparation to cover the Gurun position. It was further decided that the British officials of the Kedah Government at Alor Star were to evacuate immediately, but the movement of refugees was to be strictly forbidden.

However, the withdrawal did not go according to plan. The approach to the Iron Bridge was in Japanese hands and the wooden bridge further downstream had been swept away by the flood. When their time of withdrawal came the Leicesters attempted to cross the S. Bata by swimming and by sampans. By 0500 hours on 13 December only fifty men had managed to cross the flooded river. The commanding officer, therefore, decided to move the rest of the battalion (less two companies which did not receive the order to withdraw) across the country to the railway line and then along it to Alor Star. The fifty men who had managed to cross the S. Bata set off towards Tanjong Pau camp which they found to be occupied by the Japanese. The party turned westwards where it came to the paddy and swamp area south of the Alor Changlun canal. With the assistance of a Chinaman they reached Jerlun at 1830 hours and there found D Company of 2/16 Punjab who knew nothing about the Jitra engagement and had received no orders for withdrawal.

The next morning on 14 December the Leicester party and company of 2/16 Punjab set off for Kuala Kedah where they learnt that Alor Star was in Japanese hands. The whole party set sail in three junks for Penang where they arrived on 15 and 16 December. The entire Leicester party was there, and one hundred and twenty men had rejoined 2/16 Punjab.

The withdrawal of other units on the night of 12/13 December would have been difficult even under the most favourable circumstances. But with units all mixed up as a result of the day's fighting, a pitch dark night and communications broken, it was inevitable that orders would be delayed in communication. Some units and sub-units withdrew without incident; others, finding themselves unable to use the only road available, had to make their way as best as they could across country. Others again never received the withdrawal orders and were still in position the following day. 2 Jat (less B Company) and the detachment of 2/16 Punjab were heavily attacked on their withdrawal when they were about four hundred yards from the main road. In the ensuing melee the battalion disintegrated. The commanding officer, the second-in-command and the officer commanding 2/16 Punjab detachment endeavoured to collect as many men as possible and made their way southwards independently.

But the whole of the Jitra garrison had not withdrawn. To the east, covering Bt. Penia, B Company of 2 Jat was still in its original position. Three miles to the west were two companies of 1 Leicester standing knee-deep in the paddy, wondering why everything was so silent. On the eastern outskirts of Tanjong Pau camp ninety Gurkha survivors and their commander from Asun lay north of the track to Kelubi. Realisation slowly dawned and the sounds of battle far to the south convinced the forgotten men that the engagement at Jitra had been over and that they were left behind.

The remnants of 2/1 G.R. were the first to realise that the division had withdrawn, and they moved off at 0700 hours. When they arrived at Langgar at 1830 hours they had not eaten for forty-seven hours. One company of 1 Leicester was surprised to find a Japanese staff car coming up the Kodiang road from Jitra. Both the Leicester companies moved thereafter to the coast and thence southwards by sea and by land. Very few men from these two companies ever rejoined their parent unit.

It was not until 1830 hours on 13 December, that B Company of 2 Jat and about one hundred stragglers from Asun and Changlun started off. They had not gone far when the men, whose nerves were stretched to breaking point, began "seeing things" and the cry "Dushman"[39] caused the disintegration of the party. The company commander found himself alone with one British officer, seven Gurkhas and one Jat. This small party struck across country westwards reaching the coast on 15 December. Eventually they arrived in Sumatra by country craft on 23 December.

The artillery got away without difficulty, except for one battery of the 155th Field Regiment which became mixed up in a "battle" with some crackers. Heavy firing started at dusk to the left of 2/9 G.R. position and behind their left forward company. Every "weapon" in the area, including those of the stragglers who were passing through at the time, took up the fight. The "heavy firing" was caused by crackers which gave a very creditable imitation of light automatic and rifle fire. These crackers were apparently fired from a gun some miles away. After dark, when order had been restored, it was found that in the general rush on the part of the stragglers to get away from the firing the right forward company of 2/9 G.R. had been swept away, except its headquarters. The divisional withdrawal from Jitra was to be covered by battalion headquarters, the carrier platoon less two sections and one rifle company, B Company. This company

---

[39] Enemy.

was therefore moved to a position astride the road and when the withdrawal orders were received a road-block was constructed.

All units were supposed to pass through 2/9 G.R. But owing to the Japanese infiltration and the difficulty of movement in the dark, units bypassed the position and only one company of 2/2 G.R. passed through, and that too at 0300 hours. As 2/9 G.R. had seen nothing of 2 Jat, 2/16 Punjab, 2/1 G.R. or of 1 Leicester, the officiating commanding officer decided to wait in the hope that the others would soon appear. But hard on the heels of the company of 2/2 G.R. came the Japanese. An extremely fierce engagement thereupon ensued. The night was black and it was raining hard. The darkness and the patter of the rain on the rubber trees afforded all the cover which the Japanese needed. The first rush was silent and unseen. The company commander who was assisting in building the road-block was suddenly caught in the centre of a swirling mass of humanity on whom he used his fists, knees, feet and the butt of his revolver. The company commander's orderly was seized round the waist as he was fixing his bayonet. All he could do was to jab upwards, and this most effectively transfixed the Japanese. The anti-tank rifleman covering the block used his anti-tank rifle as a club.

Almost simultaneously with this rush on the road-block came the attack on battalion headquarters from the east. This attack was anything but silent. The Japanese came in screaming "Banzai" and blazing the way with their automatic weapons. The company fought its way back to protect the battalion headquarters where all Japanese attacks were successfully resisted, and they were also counter-charged three times. At 0430 hours on 13 December it was decided to withdraw. The battalion headquarters and B Company had to fight their way out. The unit had suffered thirty casualties during the course of the engagement.

The main delaying position from where it was possible to cover the withdrawal to Gurun was astride the two roads leading southwards at Langgar and Alor Star. At the Langgar position was 2/2 G.R., the company of 2/9 G.R. from the K. Nerang road junction, and one troop of 273 Anti-tank Battery. This position was under the command of Brigadier Carpendale. At Alor Star immediately south of the S. Kedah was to be 2/9 G.R. (less one company at Langgar) with one company of 2/1 G.R. from the Alor Star air-field under command, 2 East Surrey and No. 2 Anti-tank Battery.[40] Seven miles further south at Simpang Empat and Tokai were 1/8 and 2/16 Punjab Regiments respectively.

[40] This position was under the command of Lieut-Colonel Selby.

We may now review the circumstances in which this withdrawal was effected. The Indian Division had to face tremendous difficulties which made the task of retreat a formidable one. The Japanese had infiltrated into the gaps between the brigade headquarters and the outlying troops, owing to the length of the line covered. Moreover, the troops, specially 2 Jat, 1 Leicester and 1/8 Punjab had passed through a period of twenty-four hours of intense fighting in heavy rain; and 1 Leicester was dispersed over a wide area and the wooden bridge which carried its withdrawal was broken. The route leading to the fall-back area, a distance of 12 to 18 miles, was not free from Japanese infiltration, hence the withdrawal was made in close contact with them. The motor transport was fully employed in evacuating stores and supplies. The troops had therefore no alternative but to cover the distance on foot. The movement of stores-vehicles itself was no easy task. But despite these odds, the withdrawal was pushed through and except for the losses mentioned earlier, the three brigades had been able to extricate themselves and return to Gurun position.

Though 13 December was uneventful at Langgar, it was certainly not without incident at Alor Star. The line of the river was thinly held. On the right, exclusive of the main road, 2/9 G.R. front extended some two thousand five hundred yards and included the railway bridge. On the left was 2 Surrey. There was no artillery support as no gun positions were found in the extensive paddy areas to the south. At 0930 hours three Japanese motor cyclists came down the road and over the bridge. This was a complete surprise. The Divisional Commander, the Commander Royal Engineers and Commander 2/9 G.R. were standing a little south of the bridge at the time. They all drew their revolvers and fired. The leading Japanese cyclist got away but the second and third were killed. Suspecting that these cyclists were an advanced guard of their tanks and motorised troops the Divisional Commander ordered the road bridge to be blown at once. The road bridge was successfully demolished but the demolition of the railway bridge failed, and 2/9 G.R. fought the whole day to retain possession of the bridge and prevent its use by the Japanese tanks and motorised vehicles. The railway bridge was attacked several times and once a party of Japanese troops managed to cross the river. These were immediately killed.

Further withdrawal to Gurun position was now necessary, and it began at 1800 hours from Alor Star and two and half hours later from Langgar. The troops from Alor Star did not reach the Gurun position until the dawn of 14 December. However, the troops from Langgar fared worse, for they did not reach their sector of the Gurun position until 1900 hours on 14 December, having marched all the way via Padang.

THE BATTLE AT GURUN

The Japanese objective was to drive a wedge between Krohcol and the 11th Indian Division. Their weight was therefore directed against the area on the left flank of Krohcol and the right flank of the division. On 13 December, they were in contact with the right flank and had got tanks south of the demolitions at Alor Star.[41] This hostile penetration had led to some fighting, the losses in which had lowered the morale of the Indian force. It was to avert this new danger that the position in Gurun was organised, making the right flank immeasurably strong and the left flank comparatively less so.

Whilst the battle of Jitra was in progress on 11 and 12 December, Lieut-Colonel Selby (commanding 2/9 G.R.) was reconnoitring a position north-east of the jungle-clad Kedah Peak, known as Gunong Jerai. This thickly wooded precipitous mountain, 3,992 feet in height, filled the whole country west of the village of Gurun between the main road and the coast. The new position was known as the Gurun Position, across the main trunk road and railway, about three miles north of the village of Gurun. His recommendation was that the position should run along the East Road from milestone 25 on the Jeniang road to Guar Chempedak. This would leave the rubber estates with their roads to the south, while to the west of Guar Chempedak the forward localities would be aligned north of the road to Yen, so that the several hutted "islands" in the paddy would act as strong points. Not only would this ensure an excellent all-round field of fire but the marshy paddy fields would greatly hamper the attackers.

The Divisional Commander adopted these recommendations only partially, for, to him, the existence of paddy fields with their hutted islands was not an unmixed advantage. The paddy fields would restrict communications, and the islands were conspicuous and vulnerable to air and artillery action. There was also extreme difficulty in obtaining covered lines of withdrawal, and artillery support could only be given at extreme range owing to the lack of suitable gun positions. Hence he decided to align the central and left sectors south of the Yen road. This resulted in a number of concealed forming-up positions in the rubber plantations being

[41] War Diary, G.H.Q., Far East, Appendix No. 194. See also, Sir Paul Maltby's Despatch, 1941, para 252.

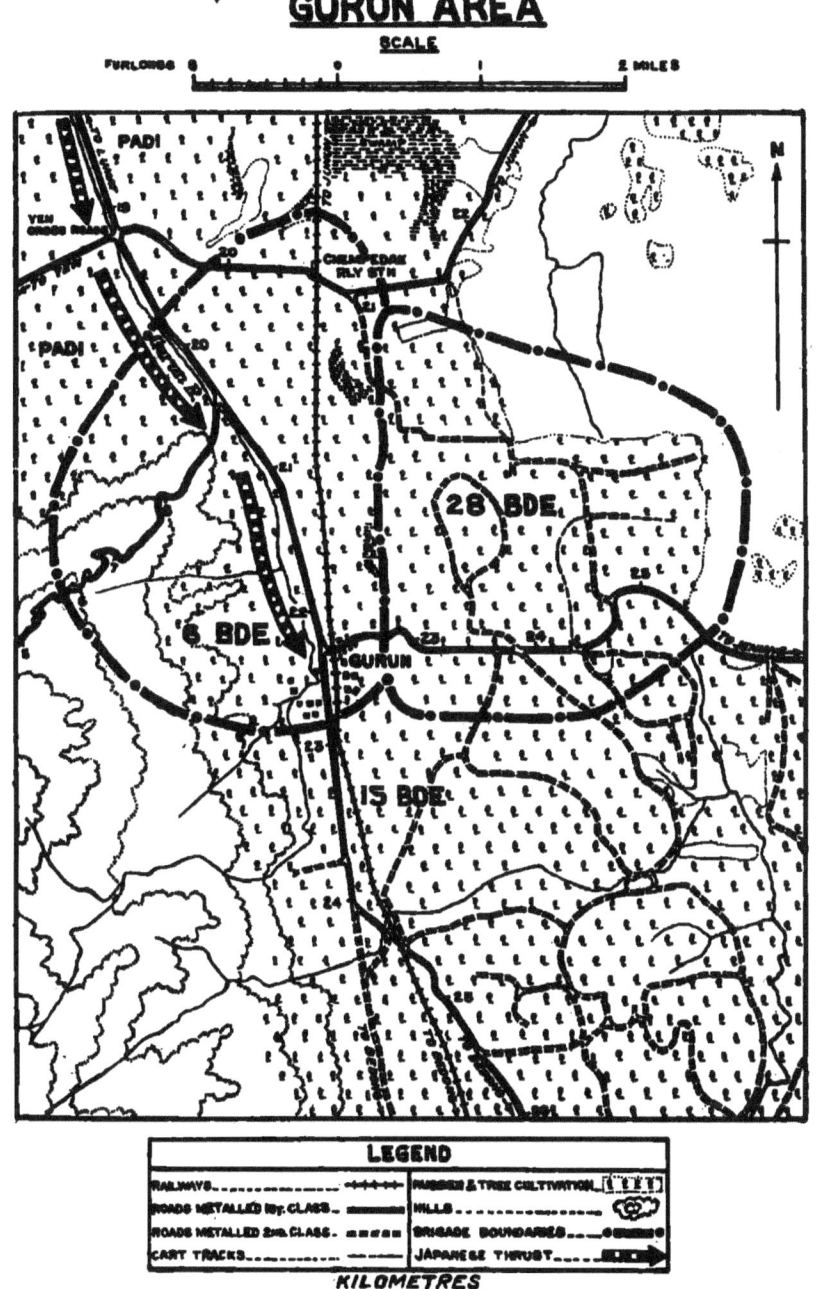

left for the Japanese, north of the selected line of the forward defended localities.

The forward localities of the Gurun position, occupied on 14 December, ran along the East Road to Guar Chempedak railway station and thence through milestone 20 on the main road to the village of Titi Teras. The 28th Indian Infantry Brigade was on the right and the 6th Indian Infantry Brigade on the left, their dividing line being the railway which was included in the sector of the latter. The 28th Indian Infantry Brigade was placed between milestone $24\frac{1}{2}$ and milestone 28 on the Jeniang road. All infantry was in the vicinity of milestone 25 and to the south of the road, while artillery positions were on hill-tops and in the valleys between the hills. None of the position was, however, complete for action though nature afforded excellent positions in this area.

The 6th Indian Infantry Brigade had been greatly depleted. However at Guar Chempedak railway station was located 2/16 Punjab, comprising only the battalion headquarters and B Company. Between the railway and the main road were two companies of 2 Surrey. A Company and headquarters of Surrey were at milestone 22. D Company had been detached from the battalion and was placed under the command of 1/8 Punjab. On the left, astride the main road and up to the village of Titi Teras, was 1/8 Punjab. This battalion was probably the most tired battalion of a weary brigade.

One gun of 215 Anti-tank Battery was in action about three quarters of a mile ahead of the forward infantry on the trunk road covering a demolished culvert immediately north of the Yen crossroads. It had an escort of one section of Surrey. The headquarters of the 6th Indian Infantry Brigade was situated in a small Malay hut on the southern outskirts of the village of Gurun. The only brigade reserve was the carrier platoon of 2/16 Punjab which had only one of its sections. The 88th Field Regiment and C Battery of the 155th Field Regiment were in support of the two forward brigades and the 215th Anti-tank Battery was under their command, one troop being allotted to the 28th Indian Infantry Brigade. The 501st Field Battery (137th Field Regiment) was under divisional control with the particular role of harassing the trunk road north of the Yen crossroads. Depth in anti-tank defence was provided by the 2nd and 273rd Anti-tank Battery.

The 15th Indian Infantry Brigade totalling barely six hundred men, was in divisional reserve in the area of milestone 23. One platoon of the Leicesters was detached to guard against an advance down the coastal road via Yen and Tg. Jaga.

The Gurun position would have been a formidable one if it had been fully prepared and occupied by a complete and fresh division with adequate reserves in hand. As regards preparations, arrangements had been made for two thousand coolies to start work on 13 December, but as a result of the news of the Japanese advance on Jitra and the bombing of Sungei Patani, the coolies had failed to appear. And the weary troops coming back from Jitra had little time to carry out the preparations.

As early as the noon of 14 December, Japanese patrols were in contact with the Surrey section at the Yen crossroads. Two hours later eleven lorries full of troops came down the road led by three tanks. These were held up by the demolition and were also immediately engaged by the forward anti-tank guns and 501 and 352 Field Batteries. At 1500 hours an enveloping attack forced the anti-tank gun and its escorting section to withdraw, and one hour later 1/8 Punjab was under heavy small-arms and mortar fire from the rubber plantation ahead of it.

There had been a certain amount of retrograde movement and Brigadier Lay (6th Indian Infantry Brigade) ordered one squadron of 3 Cavalry to push through 1/8 Punjab and attack the Japanese. These cavalrymen were mounted on trucks; they had no armoured cars and no carriers. Moving up the road in their vehicles this squadron was attacked by the Japanese infiltrators some considerable way south of milestone 20. Brigadier Lay who quickly learnt of the situation decided that it required his personal intervention. A counter-attack under his personal command was carried out by the carriers of 2/16 Punjab and by a mixed bag of fifty men from the Surreys, Brigade Headquarters, the 80th Anti-tank Regiment and 1/8 Punjab. This counter-attack was successful in clearing the whole area astride the main road up to milestone 20 of all infiltrators.

Immediately after his counter-attack, Brigadier Lay informed the Divisional Commander that it was imperative to occupy the Yen crossroads which he planned to do before dawn on 15 December, using the Surreys for the purpose. Meanwhile at 2000 hours on 14 December, heavy fire was opened on 1/8 Punjab. At 2230 hours the Surreys received Brigadier Lay's orders for the occupation of the Yen crossroads. Zero hours was fixed for 0515 hours on 15 December, following half an hour's preliminary artillery bombardment. As there were then only fifteen men left with A Company which was the battalion's only reserve, a runner was despatched to 1/8 Punjab asking for one platoon of D Company. But at 0100 hours on 15 December this platoon had not reached the Surrey battalion headquarters and the Adjutant was despatched to bring it back. At about the same time very intense fire was opened on the right flank of 1/8 Punjab. One hour later it was reported that the right flank of 1/8 Punjab was being pressed heavily and heavy casualties had ensued, and that in consequence it would be unable to hold out much longer. Line of communication between the headquarters of 1/8 Punjab and the Brigade Headquarters had meanwhile been cut. Ultimately, by 0300 hours the right flank of 1/8 Punjab was overrun. At 0400 hours the Adjutant of 2 Surrey arrived at the headquarters of 1/8 Punjab, having run into parties of Japanese troops who were south of the position and were by that time moving down the main road in considerable numbers. At about 0455 hours the Surrey headquarters at milestone 22 began to be heavily mortared. This continued for three quarters of an hour with steadily increasing intensity. By 0520 hours the much depleted A Company of 2 Surrey, which was four hundred yards north of the battalion headquarters, was overrun and the position was in Japanese hands. By 0530 hours the headquarters had also been overrun.

At 0500 hours shells from British guns began to fall into 1/8 Punjab's reserve position. They caused no casualties but they misled the Commanding Officer into making a faulty decision. He considered this to be an indication that the brigade commander had assumed that the battalion had either withdrawn or had been overwhelmed. He therefore decided to withdraw westwards and move down the Yen road to rejoin the division. Consequently 1/8 Punjab with C Company of 2 East Surrey left the main position at about 0600 hours. The main line of advance lay open to the Japanese. The subsequent fate of most of 1/8 Punjab and C Company of 2 East Surrey was the capture in Penang.

Meanwhile, further south, a composite company of 1 Leicester had been sent from the 15th Indian Infantry Brigade to the assistance of the 6th Indian Infantry Brigade to help restore the situation in the area round milestone 22. But before this company could arrive the Japanese had broken into the Brigade Headquarters and the Brigade Major, Staff Captain, Brigade Intelligence Officer and several others were killed. Brigadier Lay escaped as he had just left on a visit to the headquarters of the 28th Indian Infantry Brigade.

Things were obviously not going too well for the 6th Indian Infantry Brigade. The main road and the country to the west of it lay wide open. Of the brigade staff only the Brigade Commander was alive, both internal and external communications had broken down, and Brigadier Lay had known nothing of what had gone on in this brigade. However, the 28th Indian Infantry

Brigade was not yet in contact with the Japanese and the much depleted 15th Indian Infantry Brigade (numbering as stated already only about six hundred men) was still in the reserve position. 352nd Field Battery had one section in action at the road junction and one section at the level crossing. One section of 273rd Anti-tank Battery was also in action at these two places. Available as infantry in this area were about a dozen men of 80 Anti-tank Regiment and the whole of the 28th Indian Infantry Brigade's employment platoon and its signal section. This "infantry" was disposed about the level crossing and road junction and was ordered to construct a road-block on the Jeniang road.

Brigadier Carpendale, (15th Indian Infantry Brigade) on hearing of the disaster, immediately ordered the carrier platoon and two companies of 2/2 G.R. to move to his headquarters. 2/1 G.R., now little more than two companies in strength, was moved west to cover the railway. Meanwhile, Brigadier Lay had contacted the composite company from 1 Leicester near the road junction. He ordered one platoon to drive off the Japanese who were west of the south-end of Gurun. But this platoon was forced to break action and withdraw in a south-westerly direction owing to the overwhelming numerical superiority of the hostile force. The second platoon was then ordered to drive the Japanese from the former headquarters area of the 6th Indian Infantry Brigade, but it was also immediately pinned down by fire. The third platoon, meanwhile, was placed astride the main road, north of the road junction.

At 0800 hours on 15 December, considerable Japanese mortar fire began to be directed on the village, the road junction and the railway, north of the level-crossing. The road junction was also under small-arms and light automatic fire. As against this, only one section of the 352nd Field Battery at the road junction was in action.

As soon as the carriers of 2/2 G.R. arrived, Brigadier Carpendale sent them to Brigadier Lay who was at the road junction. The carriers, which were five in number, were ordered to clear the village. They reported that the village was clear of the Japanese up to six hundred yards north of Gurun. The carriers were then ordered to carry on up the main road with a view to gaining contact with such forward troops of the 6th Indian Infantry Brigade as might still be left. When they had hardly proceeded two hundred yards, the carriers encountered the Japanese tanks, one of which was compelled to turn tail, but soon the carriers were themselves driven back by the remaining tanks. All communications to the forward elements of the 6th Indian Infantry Brigade had ceased; even runners could not get forward owing to the large number of Japanese in the area.

The Japanese infantry was also converging on the road junction and the guns had to pull out. The engagement had also extended to the area of the 28th Indian Infantry Brigade Headquarters, two hundred yards east of the level crossing. But the Japanese main attack was launched against the headquarters of the 6th Indian Infantry Brigade which was forced to move further east, giving the appearance as if the whole brigade had been overrun or had disintegrated. Brigadier Lay, as he had apparently nothing left to command, moved away from the area to acquaint the Divisional Commander of the situation. At the same time Brigadier Carpendale sent orders for 2/9 G.R. to withdraw to his headquarters and for 2/1 G.R. to move to the level crossing. This order puzzled the Officer Commanding 2/9 G.R. because he knew that the whole of the 28th Indian Infantry Brigade was intact and had not even been engaged. He knew also that B Company of 2/16 Punjab was in position south of Guar Chempedak railway station. He, therefore, reported in person to the Brigade Headquarters, where he arrived at the same time as the Divisional Commander.

The situation, as explained to the Divisional Commander by Brigadier Carpendale, was as follows:—

(a) As far as could be surmised 2 East Surrey and 1/8 Punjab had been overrun.

(b) The 6th Indian Infantry Brigade Headquarters position had been captured and most of the staff either killed or wounded.

(c) The Japanese were in possession of the area of the headquarters previously occupied by the 28th Indian Infantry Brigade.

The force which the Divisional Commander then had in hand was:—

28th Indian Infantry Brigade (with 2/1 G.R. very weak), one company of 2/16 Punjab,

15th Indian Infantry Brigade, which numbered about six hundred men who were not in a fighting condition.

The position was very well represented in the official stuation report which, after describing the weight of Japanese attack, mentioned:—

"Touch not yet restored in spite of counter-attack by two battalions of 28 Indian Brigade. Command reserve consisting of 12 Indian Brigade group less one battalion has been sent to this front. Trouble arises from impossibility of relieving exhausted troops who have now been fighting continuously for over a week owing to lack of adequate reserves in Malaya and danger of uncovering Fortress area in view of our naval and air weakness. Doubtful if it will be possible to hold Penang which has no adequate garrison for increased scale of attack. In Kedah enemy attacks pressed home with fanatical courage in spite of very heavy losses, and Kedah is his main effort ".[42]

In view of these circumstances, the Divisional Commander decided to break action and withdraw behind the river Muda. Consequently he issued the following orders:—

(a) 15th Indian Infantry Brigade was to withdraw to the Sungei Lalang where the independent company which had arrived from Penang the previous evening was already in position.

(b) Under Brigadier Carpendale's command
 (i) 2/2 G.R. to withdraw to a position covering the Sungei Tok Pawang (two and a half miles north of Bedong);
 (ii) The rear elements of 2/16 Punjab and 2 East Surrey and all stragglers to withdraw behind the Sungei Lalang.

(c) Under command of the Officer Commanding 2/9 G.R.
 (i) 2/9 G.R., 2/1 G.R. and any troops of the 6th Indian Infantry Brigade still on the ground were to cover the withdrawal and then withdraw through Sungei Lalang;
 (ii) The withdrawal was not to start before 1200 hours on 15 December.

The withdrawal of the 15th Indian Infantry Brigade, covered by the carrier platoon of 2/2 G.R. and the detachment of the 80th Anti-tank Regiment, began at once. By 1300 hours, the brigade was back at Sungei Lalang and had found the independent company holding the south bank of the Sungei Getah.

The Divisional Commander issued other orders which were as follows:—

(a) 15th Indian Infantry Brigade to hold the Sungei Lalang.
(b) Independent company, under its command to hold the Sungei Bangkok south of Bedong.
(c) 28th Indian Infantry Brigade to continue its withdrawal through Bedong and Sungei Lalang and to occupy a position on the Sungei Patani.

---

[42] War Diary, General Headquarter Far-East, Appendices Nos. 203 and 208.

(d) All troops of the 6th Indian Infantry Brigade to come under the command of the 15th Indian Infantry Brigade.

(e) 137th Field Regiment and 80th Anti-tank Regiment to support the 15th Brigade and subsequently the 28th Brigade (the platoon of the Leicesters at Tg. Jaga was withdrawn without incident).

Meanwhile the rearguard under 2/9 G.R. had contacted both the companies of 2 East Surrey and collected one. The other moved back independently to join 2/2 G.R. behind the Sungei Tok Pawang. 2/16 Punjab from Guar Chempedak railway station was also collected. The withdrawal south, which was to pass two miles east of Gurun through the Harvard Rubber Estate and across the Sungei Bangkok immediately south of this estate, began at 1300 hours. The withdrawal went without hitch until the Harvard Estate bridge across the Sungei Bangkok was found to be demolished and the river so flooded as to be impassable. This meant that the withdrawal route of the rearguard of the 28th Indian Infantry Brigade via the East Road was blocked. This rearguard then made for the main road which was free from the Japanese, but it was found that the bridge across the Sungei Bangkok immediately south of Bedong had also been demolished. The force slowly and with considerable difficulty clambered over the wreckage of the bridge, and it was not until after mid-night that all men were south of the Sungei Bangkok. All transport with this rearguard had to be destroyed.

Meanwhile the 11th Indian Division had been withdrawn back from the Sungei Lalang. It was not until 0200 hours on 16 December that the rearguard made contact with the division in Sungei Patani and motor transport was sent to pick up this extremely weary force three miles north of the town.

On 16 December the situation in Kedah was reported officially at dawn to be as follows:—

"Heavy fighting continues. 11 Indian Division is now on line of R. Muda with 12 Indian Infantry Brigade protecting its right flank. Losses in men and equipment have been heavy. This coupled with exhaustion of troops has necessitated a further withdrawal behind line of R. Krian where it is hoped to be able to reorganise force. In consequence it will no longer be possible to hold Penang from which some troops have already been drawn to join Kedah battle. 6 Indian Infantry Brigade cut off yesterday and strength reduced to a few hundreds. 15 Indian Infantry Brigade also very weak. Intention henceforth is to cover Perak tin mining area which mostly lies round Ipoh which was bombed morning

15/12 by 20 aircraft, part of aerodrome petrol dump being hit."⁴³

The report sent later on that date added that further withdrawal behind R. Krian was in progress. At the same time the prospects of stabilising the situation even at that point were not at all good. The brigade, which was the sole command reserve, had been committed in the north-west, and only reinforcements from outisde Malaya could help strengthen the force in that corner.

WITHDRAWAL SOUTH OF THE KRIAN RIVER

By the morning of 16 December, the 11th Indian Division was south of the river Muda and had passed into Province Wellesley. It settled down to rest behind the flimsy screen guarding the approaches to the river Muda which, on the left, were held by a composite force known as Holmes Force. It comprised:—

One squadron 3 Cavalry at Kota Ferry,

The Independent Company and one company 1 Leicester, covering the two bridges at Bumbong Lima,

The armoured train guarding the Bt. Pinang Tunggal railway bridge and

137 Field Regiment with the Mountain Battery under command.

On the right, 3 Cavalry (less one squadron) guarded the crossings at Batu Pekaka and Kuala Ketil.

During the early hours of 16 December, 5/2 Punjab from the 12th Indian Infantry Brigade, relieved 3 Cavalry (less one squadron) at Batu Pekka and Kuala Ketil. The latter then moved to the Padang Serai area. At Batu Pekka the bridge had been partially demolished before the arrival of 5/2 Punjab and was unfit for vehicles, although it could be used by the infantry.

In four days the 11th Indian Division had retreated seventy miles and lost much of its strength. Of the 6th Indian Infantry Brigade (whose commander was admitted to hospital on 16 December) 1/8 Punjab had been completely lost, 2 East Surrey mustered only ten officers and two hundred and sixty men and 2/16 Punjab which had done practically no fighting had only about five hundred men. The three battalions of the 15th Indian Infantry Brigade totalled less than the war establishment for one battalion. The 28th Indian Infantry Brigade had only one battalion intact,

---

⁴³ War Diary, General Headquarter, Far-East, Appendices No. 213 and 224 (read with Appendix No. 208). See also Sir Paul Maltby's Despatch *Op. cit.* p. 1371, para 253.

namely, 2/2 Gurkha Rifles. 2/9 Gurkha Rifles apart from battle casualties had one company cut off by the Japanese during the withdrawal from Gurun, and 2/1 Gurkha Rifles which had till then been cut off three times mustered only three hundred men. Apart from the numerical losses there had been grave losses in arms, equipment, carriers and vehicles. The survivors in the battalions were badly short of food and desperately short of sleep. The sick were numerous, many had fever or were suffering from suppurating sores caused by leeches. The 11th Indian Division was therefore in no fit state for further operations. Fresh troops, as stated already, were not available. The only solution was to put a considerable distance between the Japanese and the weary Indian and British troops, and hope to delay the hostile advance by demolitions.

At 1030 hours on 16 December, as the last battalion of the 28th Indian Infantry Brigade (namely 2/9 Gurkha Rifles) was arriving in its rest area at Jarak (seven miles north of Bt. Mertajam), the Corps Commander visited the Divisional Headquarters at Tasek Glugor. After discussing the situation with the latter the former issued his orders, that the 11th Indian Division should move back behind the Krian river, which was to be held from Mahang to the coast. The move was to be completed by the morning of 18 December and was to be co-ordinated with the withdrawal of the 12th Indian Infantry Brigade which was moving to Taiping, where 5/14 Punjab would come under its command. The 11th Indian Division was also to take Krohcol under its command. The 6th and 15th Indian Infantry Brigades were to move direct to Taiping and the 28th Indian Infantry Brigade was to occupy the south bank of the Krian river. Penang was to be evacuated by 17 December.

The withdrawal was made none too easy owing to traffic control on 16 December having completely broken down. The 28th Indian Infantry Brigade, after crossing the river Muda, had taken four hours to travel as many miles. Fortunately no Japanese air-craft appeared and the 11th Indian Division was able to settle down for a short rest in comparative peace. Meanwhile, the Japanese on reaching Sungei Patani, directed their main thrust down the Sungei Patani—Batu Pekaka road, instead of pressing down the main road towards Bumbong Lima. This road was covered by 5/2 Punjab which had one company at Kuala Ketil (3694) and another at the Batu Pekaka bridge (3293); the remainder of the battalion being in reserve at the road junction (3490) one mile north of Merbau Pulas. On 16 December, at about 1500 hours, one European and about twelve Asians in

Khaki uniforms approached the Batu Pekaka bridge from the direction of Sungei Patani. They waved white handkerchiefs, and the European, who appeared to be a British planter, spoke in indifferent Hindustani to the bridge guard. He was told to leave his companions on the bank and to advance alone to the bridge. This he did and approaching a Havildar on the bridge grappled with him. This was the signal for the " planter's " party to open fire. The European, who in all probability was a German, was killed and the party of Japanese driven off. Shortly after this incident the Japanese made determined efforts to cross the river and at 1800 hours they succeeded in establishing themselves on the south bank; but an immediate counter-attack by one company of 5/2 Punjab led by the commanding officer restored the situation.

It was deduced from the absence of Japanese activity on the main road and from their determined action at Batu Pekaka that their intention was to by-pass the 11th Indian Division in Province Wellesley. To counteract this move, 2 Argyll and Sutherland Highlanders (less one company which had been ordered by III Corps to Grik on 13 December) belonging to the 12th Indian Infantry Brigade, who had a quiet day in the Baling area, were ordered back during the evening and ensuing night through 5/2 Punjab to line Titi Karangan (3384) which they were ordered to deny to the Japanese until 1200 hours on 17 December. 5/2 Punjab had also been ordered to deny Merbau Pulas, three miles north of Titi Karangan and three miles south of the river Muda, until 0630 hours on that day.

At 0200 hours on 17 December, after the rear party of 2 A and SH had passed through, 5/2 Punjab commenced withdrawal from the Kuala Ketil—Batu Pekaka position and by 0530 hours its rear party had reached Merbau Pulas. The Japanese followed up quickly and rushed the Merbau Pulas bridge, but the attack was repulsed and the bridge was successfully blown at 0600 hours.

The position on 17 December was not very hopeful, as the detachment defending Grik area had been attacked by the Japanese in some strength. Reinforcements locally available had been sent to repulse the attack but these were neither considerable, nor very effective. In this situation, the British appreciation was that " if this attack develops it will constitute serious threat against communications of our forces north of Kuala Kangsar ". To prevent an ugly situation from developing, withdrawal was the only alternative. Hence the 11th Indian Division was to withdraw in the night of 17/18 December from the line of Muda river to the south of Krian river. This withdrawal was proceeding according to plan. The III Indian Corps was also authorised to withdraw behind the Perak river. The 12th Indian Infantry Brigade continued to cover the right flank of the 11th Indian Division, while the 28th Indian Infantry Brigade was on Sungei Krian. The 6th and 15th Brigades arrived in Taiping, having suffered some casualties.[44]

In the course of withdrawal on 17 December at 0930 hours, 5/2 Punjab passed through 2 A and SH and moved to Lunas. Half an hour later the forward company of 2 A and SH was attacked. A brief but successful action was fought in which the Japanese suffered no less than two hundred casualties compared with the eleven sustained by the Argylls. At 1200 hours, 2 A and SH withdrew and moved to the Terap—K. Selama area. 3 Cavalry (less the squadron with Holmes Force) which had acted as the west flank-guard during the early stages of the withdrawal and had been harassed by the Japanese outflanking parties, withdrew in conjunction with 2 A and SH from the Padang Serai area to Terap. 5/2 Punjab, then at Lunas, further withdrew in the late afternoon through Terap to Selama, where it came under the command of Krohcol and moved to take up its position covering the crossings over the S. Krian in the Mahang area.

During the night of 16/17 December and the morning of 17 December the remnants of the 6th and the 15th Indian Infantry Brigades moved from the Kapala Batas—Bt. Mertajam area by road and rail to Taiping. On the same morning, the Japanese reconnaissance parties also began to appear on the north bank of the river Muda in front of Holmes Force. Apart from this and a dive-bombing attack on 1 Battery of 137 Field Regiment, there was no excitment in the Holmes Force area. Shortly before noon, however, the appointed hour for withdrawal, a large party of stragglers arrived on the north bank of the river Muda, opposite Kota. The time for withdrawal was put back, sunken sampans were salvaged on both banks and the stragglers were ferried across. These numbered about two hundred and comprised a large body of 1/8 Punjab from Gurun and a number of stragglers from other battalions including forty of 1/14 Punjab who had escaped at Asun. Holmes Force withdrew at 1500 hours, the squadron of 3 Cavalry moving to Bandar Bahru on the Krian river close to Parit Buntar and coming under the command of the 28th Indian Infantry Brigade. The remainder of Holmes Force moved back to Taiping.

By the night of 17 December the whole of the 11th Indian Division and the 12th Indian Infantry Brigade, with the exception of 2A and SH (then acting as rearguard eight miles north of the

---

[44] War Diary, General Headquarter, Far-East, Appendices Nos. 228 and 242 (read together).

Terah until 0800 hours on 18 December) and 3 Cavalry (less one squadron) then at Terap, were behind the Krian river. Meanwhile, the evàcuation of Penang was being hastily carried out. The removal of ammunition and ordnance stores from the ordnance depot had started some days previously and the bulk of these were got away. The cable station was put out of action, the aerodrome which was on reclaimed ground was flooded; the rail and dock facilities were damaged as much as possible. Although the rapid evacuation of the island was on the whole well carried out there were two serious omissions; one was the failure to dispose of a number of motor propelled craft, which were later used by the Japanese as a means of outflanking Indian positions on the west coast, and the other was that the Penang Broadcasting Station was left intact, which was consequently taken into immediate use by the Japanese when they occupied the island on 19 December.

Some of the Penang troops were evacuated by sea to Singapore, others were used temporarily to hold the Bogah Ferry—Nibong Tebal bridge sector of the Krian river, whilst the 28th Indian Infantry Brigade was resting. The troops carrying out this task were 3 Mixed Reinforcement Camp and the European elements of the Penang and Province Wellesley Volunteer Force (the indigenous portion of this unit having been disbanded). In addition a company of 2 Malaya Regiment which had been employed in protecting the ordnance field park and ammunition dumps at Val Do'r (south of Bt. Mertajam) was placed under the command of 3 M.R.C., as was a part of the Bahawalpur State Infantry when the latter moved back from Bt. Mertajam.

The Krian position which was occupied by the division on the night of 17/18 December covered thirty miles of front from Mahang to the coast. On this front the Japanese had two main lines of approach, the road from Kulim to Selama and the main road which crossed the river by the Nibong Tebal bridge. The distance between Selama and Nibong Tebal was fifteen miles, along which many tracks from the north led to the river. The separation of the two localities was accentuated by the floods which had extended across the lateral road from Selama via Briah to Bagan Serai; thus communications between the two localities by road entailed a fifty-mile detour via Semangol. Nibong Tebal was defended by the 28th Brigade while the 3/16 Punjab held Selama. Krohcol was disbanded.

On the evening of 17 December the Corps Commander reviewed the situation. Owing to the threat down the Grik road and the possibility of a threat from the coast once the Japanese occupied Penang, it was evident that any protracted defence of the Krian river line was impossible. The question at the moment was: Where was the Japanese advance to be stopped ? The next possible stop line was the line of the S. Perak. This was little better than the Krian river line. The Perak river line was also greatly extended and would require to be held in two widely separated sectors, one in the Iskandar and Enggor bridges area near Kuala Kangsar, and the other in the Blanja Pontoon bridge area near Siputeh. The latter sector was considerably south of the former and by road, via Ipoh, the distance was about fifty-five miles. Moreover, west of the river the Japanese would have two roads on which to advance towards the Blanja Pontoon bridge. Furthermore, the Iskandar and Enggor bridges sector could be outflanked from the north by means of a track leading from the upper part of the Chenderoh lake to Kampong Chadek, whence there was a road to Sungei Siput on the main road south of Kuala Kangsar. The Corps Commander, therefore, planned to stop the Japanese at some place south of Ipoh. The exact position had yet to be selected, but he had in mind the position about Kampar, twenty-four miles south of Ipoh.

The immediate role of the 11th Indian Division was however to hold the line of the Krian river. The next bound would be no doubt to the Perak river.

WITHDRAWAL EAST OF THE PERAK RIVER

The Main Road Contingent

On the morning of 18 December, 2 A and SH (less one company on the Grik road) covered by 3 Cavalry (less one squadron), withdrew across the Selama bridge held by 3/16 Punjab and moved to Kuala Kangsar in readiness to move up the Grik road. After 2 A and SH had crossed the Selama bridge completely, 3 Cavalry (less one squadron) also withdrew from Terap across the same bridge, which was blown up immediately after, while one squadron was sent to Mahang to relieve 5/2 Punjab. The rest of the unit stayed in the Selama area in the rear of 3/16 Punjab. 5/2 Punjab, on relief at Mahang in the late afternoon, started for Kuala Kangsar.

On the left sector of the Krian river front, the 28th Indian Infantry Brigade relieved the improvised force composed of 3 Mixed Reinforcement Camp, the Bahawalpur State Infantry, one company of 2 Malay and the European elements of the Penang and Province Wellesley Volunteer Forces. 2/1 Gurkha Rifles was on the right covering the Bogah Ferry (at the junction of the S. Bogah and the Krian river) and with detachments at Simpang Lima and Titi Serong. 2/2 Gurkha Rifles was on the left covering the Nibong Tebal road and railway bridges and the ferry at Bandar Bahru. 2/9 Gurkha Rifles was in reserve at Began Serai where also was the Brigade Headquarters. One squadron of 3 Cavalry was at the mouth of S. Chenaham and was made responsible for patrolling the road between the mouth of S. Chenaham and Bandar Bahru. 88 Field Regiment (less one battery) was under the command of the 28th Indian Infantry Brigade.

From Taiping the remnants of the 6th and 15th Indian Infantry Brigades moved back on 18 December to Ipoh, where they were to be re-organised into one combined brigade. The 11th Indian Divisional Headquarters and III Indian Corps Advanced Headquarters also moved from Taiping to Ipoh.

For two days no notable engagements took place and the 11th Indian Division had respite from determined hostile attacks. But on 19 December two events of strategical importance occurred: the 8th Indian Infantry Brigade evacuated Kelantan, the north-eastern state of Malaya, and the Japanese occupied Penang. On 20 December, there was a certain amount of Japanese patrol activity on the Selama sector of the Krian river front and reports were received that they had crossed the river at Mahang and were making for Kampong Redang Panjang area, from which place there was a road to Ulu Sapetang, which was on the main road north of Taiping. In view of this threat to the line of communication, it was decided to withdraw from Selama, and in the evening 3/16 Punjab withdrew through 3 Cavalry positions.

In the 28th Indian Infantry Brigade sector of the Krian front there was increasing Japanese activity on the north bank of the river. In the evening, the commander of the brigade was notified of the intended withdrawal of Krohcol to Ulu Sapetang. About 2100 hours, Krohcol came actually under his command. The withdrawal of Krohcol from the Selama sector necessitated corresponding moves by the other units of the 28th Indian Infantry Brigade. 2/9 Gurkha Rifles and 351 Field Battery were moved to Ulu Sapetang. 2/1 and 2/2 Gurkha Rifles with 352 Field Battery and troop of the 2 Anti-Tank Battery were moved to the Bagan Serai position. The withdrawal from the S. Krian commenced at about 2230 hours, and the two forward battalions withdrew through the squadron of 3 Cavalry which had been brought in from the left flank. The withdrawal was completed during the night without Japanese interference, and by the morning of 21 December, the 28th Indian Infantry Brigade with Krohcol under command was in a new position.

Owing to heavy hostile pressure down the Grik road, a further and immediate withdrawal became necessary. The Divisional Commander was informed that the 12th Indian Infantry Brigade would come under his command at midnight of 21/22 December. On considering the situation, he decided to withdraw the division that night from Ulu Sapetang and Bagan Serai and to post the units in the following areas:—

3 Cavalry with one troop of 215 Anti-Tank Battery to Ct. Jering (five miles south-west of Taiping) to impose the maximum delay on any Japanese advance down the coastal road towards Blanja and Ipoh.

3/16 Punjab to Padang Rengas (nine miles west of Kuala Kangsar).

2/9 Gurkha Rifles to Lawin at the junction of the Grik and main roads.

2/2 Gurkha Rifles to Salak North, four miles east of the Iskandar bridge, where it would be in divisional reserve.

2/1 Gurkha Rifles with 10 Mountain Battery, one troop of 2 Anti-Tank Battery and 17 Field Company (Sappers and Miners) to the road junction six miles west of the Blanja bridge which crossed the Perak river.

2 Anti-Tank Battery (less one troop with 2/1 Gurkha Rifles) and one troop of 273 Anti-Tank Battery between Lawin and Kuala Kangsar.

137 Field Regiment at S. Siput.

By the dawn of 22 December, the 11th Indian Division was disposed as ordered. During that day all fronts were quiet except that of the 12th Indian Infantry Brigade which was heavily engaged by the Japanese troops moving via the river Perak and by road, and all forward troops were fighting north of Kati which was only eight miles north of Lawin. There was every indication of a Japanese outflanking movement to cut the trunk road in the rear of the division on to the far side of the river Perak.

At 1800 hours on that day the Divisional Commander issued further orders. His object was to commence withdrawing at 2100 hours behind the river Perak. The 12th Indian Infantry Brigade was to clear the Lawin corner by midnight and move to the Salak North and S. Siput area, where it could rest on the following day preparatory to the occupation of a position which had been selected on the main road twelve miles north of Ipoh. 2/9 Gurkha Rifles and 3/16 Punjab were to hold the Lawin corner until the 12th Indian Infantry Brigade was clear. 2/9 Gurkha

PLATE V

(Courtesy – *Lt.-Gen. H. Gordon Bennett*)
Lieut.-Gen. A. E. Percival, G.O.C., Malaya, and Major-General H. Gordon Bennett, G.O.C., A.I.F., Malaya

PLATE VI

(Courtesy – *Australian War Memorial*)
Smoke rising from stocks of rubber burned to prevent them from falling into Japanese hands

Rifles was then to be withdrawn to S. Siput, where it could rest the following day prior to being moved to the Siputeh area (between Ipoh and the Blanja bridge). 3/16 Punjab was then to move direct to Siputeh. 3 Cavalry was first to hold Kuala Kangsar and Ct. Jering and then to withdraw at dawn on 23 December by the river route (from Kuala Kangsar to Blanja) and by the coastal road, imposing the maximum delay on any Japanese advance and demolishing the culverts. On reaching the road junction six miles west of Blanja, this regiment was to come under the command of 2/1 Gurkha Rifles, which was then to return to the 28th Indian Infantry Brigade when the latter had reached the Siputeh area. 2/2 Gurkha Rifles was to occupy a bridgehead covering the Iskandar bridge which it would cross and demolish after 2/9 Gurkha Rifles, the last unit, was clear; it was then to go to Ipoh and thereafter come under Corps control.

All these withdrawals were completed before daylight on 23 December, though there were numerous hitches. The 12th Indian Infantry Brigade passed through 2/9 Gurkha Rifles guarding the junction of the Grik and main roads between 2330 hours and midnight. When the Brigade was well on the safe side, 2/9 Gurkha Rifles withdrew across the Iskandar bridge which was then blown by 2/2 Gurkha Rifles.

The role of the 11th Indian Division was now to delay the Japanese advance whilst the reconstituted composite 6/15th Indian Infantry Brigade (the remnants of the 6th and 15th Indian Brigades) constructed a strong defensive position about Kampar, twenty-three miles south of Ipoh. The 28th Indian Infantry Brigade (exclusive of 2/2 Gurkha Rifles but inclusive of 3/16 Punjab) was to hold the Blanja bridge sector of the Perak river whilst the 12th Indian Infantry Brigade held a series of delaying positions in the S. Siput, Kanthan Halt and Chemor areas, north of Ipoh. The commander of the 11th Indian Division was informed that the new 15th Indian Infantry Brigade would come under his command at 0600 hours on 24 December and that the Kampar position was a defensive position which must be held at any cost and not treated merely as a position for a delaying action. The orders which he had received from the Corps Commander on 20 December remained unchanged: he was to hold the Japanese north of Ipoh until at least 26 December.

The division had been thus extricated from General Yamashita's trap. It had escaped; but of its three original brigades two had been completely shattered and one badly mauled, and the stamina of the 12th Indian Infantry Brigade was near the breaking-point.

The Grik Road Contingent

In the Grik road positions, early in the morning of 13 December, 5/14 Punjab was attacked, and by 0900 hours the Japanese were threatening to turn its flanks. Fearing that the road behind this battalion might be cut, withdrawal was effected. It embussed at Betong and moved back to a position just west of Kroh on the Kroh-Baling road. Meanwhile, during the day, 3/16 Punjab had destroyed the balance of the stores, ammunition etc. which could not be evacuated from Kroh and moved to join 5/14 Punjab west of Kroh, leaving behind one company forward of Kroh to delay the Japanese advance and also to cover the blowing up of some demolitions on the road.

With the withdrawal of Krohcol from Kroh, the Kroh—Grik road was left open to the Japanese. This road ran from Kroh to Lawin and covered a distance of ninety-three miles. For the first seven miles between Kroh and Klian Intan it was a second class metalled road. From Klian Intan to Grik it was little more than a track though negotiable in fair weather by 15-hundredweight trucks. This track ran through rubber plantations and jungle for twenty-one miles southwards. Afterwards, a second class metalled road ran up to Lawin[45] for twenty-three miles between Grik and Kg. Kenering; it was bordered by jungle as dense as any in Malaya. Between Kg. Kenering and Lawin, to the south of it on the main road at a distance of forty-two miles, jungle and rubber plantations alternated, with jungle not far beyond on either side. Between Klian Intan and the Chenderoh lake where the Perak hydro-electric company's headworks and power stations were situated, the Grik road was closely flanked by the swift running upper reaches of the Perak river. South of Klian Intan, the Grik road lay in the line of communication area, which was under Brigadier Moir, who had only one section of the Federated Malay States Volunteer Force Armoured Car Company and two platoons of the Perak Battalion available to hold it.

On 12 December, the 12th Indian Infantry Brigade had been ordered to move north to reinforce Krohcol and prevent Japanese interference from the east on the line of communication of the 11th Indian Division. Two of its battalions were with the 9th Indian Division, and of these, this division was unable to release 4/19 Hyderabad Regiment which was with the 8th Indian Infantry Brigade in Kelantan. However, 2 A and SH from Jerantut with

---

[45] There are two Lawins in this paragraph. The first is situated on the river Lawin and to the north of Kg. Kenering. The second is at the junction of Grik and the Grand Trunk road and to the west of Kuala Kangsar. This has a railway station with its own name.

5/2 Punjab and the rest of the brigade troops at Singapore, together with 278 Field Battery of the 122nd Field Regiment, moved up to the 11th Indian Division area. On 13 December at Ipoh, 2A and SH was ordered to detach one company and a section of armoured cars which were sent to Grik.

Apart from this insignificant detachment of volunteers this easy approach to the sole line of communication of the 11th Indian Division was guarded by one company of 2 A and SH which had been sent to Grik on 13 December by the Corps Commander. It was, however, hoped that even with a force as small as one company, considerable delay might be imposed on the Japanese in the reputedly impenetrable jungle between Grik and Kg. Kenering.

2 A and SH (less one company) moved to Baling where it arrived on the evening of 14 December and went into position covering the road junction. 5/2 Punjab, 278 battery of the 122nd Field Regiment and the rest of the brigade troops were still *en route* from Singapore.

On 14 December there was a certain amount of patrol activity in front of the Kroh position. In the late afternoon a strong patrol attacked the left flank of 3/16 Punjab, but was repulsed. Shortly after this, Brigadier Paris, commander of the 12th Indian Infantry Brigade (Malaya Command Reserve) arrived at Krohcol headquarters with orders for the withdrawal of Krohcol during the ensuing night. Brigadier Paris had been given the task of preventing the Japanese Patani Force, which had then occupied Kroh, from reaching Patani (fifty miles west from Kroh). During the night of 14/15 December, the withdrawal of Krohcol from the position west of Kroh was effected without interference.

On 15 December 2 A and SH had a quiet day in the Baling area. The Japanese did not press down the road from Kroh; instead of doing so they moved forward on the Kroh—Klian Intan road and their forward patrols were encountered on the track from Klian Intan to Grik, some five miles north of Grik, by the patrols from the detached company of 2 A and SH at Grik.

The company of 2 A and SH remained in contact with the Japanese at Grik throughout 16 December. There had as yet been no indication that the Japanese were in great strength, but it was evident from their failure to advance west of Kroh that the force which had landed at Patani was destined to exploit the attractions of this road. Nevertheless, the detached company of 2 A and SH was forced to give ground. On 17 December, the company was hard pressed and had to fall back to Sumpitan. It was evident that the Japanese were bringing a strong force to the

Grik area and that British reinforcements would have to be despatched there. As an immediate reinforcement, one company of the Perak Battalion Federated Malay States Volunteer Force, and one section of the Federated Malay States Volunteer Force Armoured Car Company, were ordered to move there from Ipoh. When the news of this Japanese thrust reached the Commander III Indian Corps, he immediately ordered the withdrawal of the 12th Indian Infantry Brigade to Kuala Kangsar, where it was to come under his own command for operations up the Grik road. But on the Grik road the company of 2 A and SH had been forced back to a position covering Langgong which was held by the most war-worthy Independent Company.

Brigadier Paris had been ordered to impose the maximum delay on the Japanese and to prevent them from cutting the line of communication until the 11th Indian Division had withdrawn clear of Lawin. The orders were that Lawin should be denied for at least four days. He decided to reinforce the two companies at Lenggong with the remainder of 2 A and SH and one company of 5/2 Punjab. This whole force was ordered to deny Kotah Tampan (twenty-three miles north of Lawin) to the Japanese. After various vacillations in which advances and withdrawals were made, the position was stabilised two miles north of Lenggong. 278 Field Battery of 122 Field Regiment had meanwhile arrived in the Lenggong area and had carried out some effective firing during the withdrawal.

On the morning of 20 December, 2 A and SH was in contact near Lenggong. A Japanese party which had come down the S. Perak on rafts, by-passing the right flank of 2 A and SH, landed near Kotah Tampan. Here they were engaged by a detached platoon of 5/2 Punjab and by a company of 2 A and SH which had been sent back from Lenggong where news of the Japanese movement down the river had been obtained from a Chinese. The Japanese were then threatening the road four miles to the rear of 2 A and SH, whose immediate withdrawal was therefore imperative. By 2200 hours the whole battalion was across the small causeway, a mile north of Kotah Tampan, which was blown by 15 Field Company.

During the night of 20/21 December the commander of the 12th Indian Infantry Brigade had sent forward the whole of 5/2 Punjab, and at dawn on 21 December the brigade was disposed as follows:—

    2 A and SH held Kotah Tampan,

    5/2 Punjab held the Durian Causeway (MS 18/19), Kg. Sauk (M.S. 13) and the Chenderoh dam,

278 Field Battery was in support of the battalions on the Grik road;

5/14 Punjab was guarding the bridges over the S. Perak, Brigade Headquarters was at Kati (M.S. 8).

Shortly after dawn some Japanese rafts were successfully shot up. 2 A and SH was in contact throughout the day and inflicted heavy casualties upon the Japanese. But ultimately it was withdrawn through 5/2 Punjab to Kati in the evening. During the day 4/19 Hyderabad Regiment also arrived and moved into the position covering Sungei Siput.

On 22 December, 5/2 Punjab with 278 Field Battery in support was in contact with the Japanese, north of the Sauk road junction. During the afternoon the latter put in a fairly heavy attack down the Grik road, but this was checked by 5/2 Punjab who inflicted considerable casualties on them. Meanwhile, orders had been issued for the withdrawal of the 12th Indian Infantry Brigade across the Iskandar bridge. The brigade had passed from the command of III Indian Corps to that of the 11th Indian Division on the previous evening after the decision to withdraw behind the Perak river had been made. 5/2 Punjab disengaged about 1800 hours and moved back from Sauk to Kati. From there 2 A and SH moved off at about 1930 hours and went to Salak North. 5/2 Punjab, when the troop carrying transport had returned, left Kati about 2230 hours and also went to Salak North.

It is difficult to decide whether the retreat east of the Perak river was justified on the day it was ordered. The situation was not too bad on any day before the night of 22/23 December when the last unit had crossed the Iskandar bridge and the bridge itself was blown up. On 20 December the Japanese had not attacked in the Krian area and had been active about Lenggong on the Grik road. They were perhaps more anxious about the crossing of Chenderoh Lake, because the road had been destroyed. On 21 December, the British troops were still not badly pressed in the western sector, although Kuala Lumpur had a pounding from the air and the Grik road recorded a sanguinary fight somewhere to the north of the lake. On 22 December, it was recorded that there was " practically no news of 11 Division to-day. Consider situation satisfactory. 12 Brigade is lying about south end of Chenderoh Lake".[46] But it was supplemented by the news that the Japanese were moving to Siput by rafts on the Perak river during the nights and thereby entering eastern Perak by a process of by-passing. This would appear to have prompted the General Officer Commanding

---

[46] War Diary, General Headquarter Far-East, Appendix No. 299, para 1.

to order the 12th Indian Infantry Brigade to cross the Perak river in the ensuing night.

The strategic policy relating to the withdrawal also appears questionable. According to General Percival, the Chiefs of Staff repeated about this time that the aim of warfare in Malaya was still the security of Singapore Naval Base and no other consideration ought to compete with this.[47] Again, at an inter-Allied conference at Singapore on 18 December, it was decided to hold the Japanese in north Malaya and not let them occupy a strip of land from which they could threaten British aerodromes or reinforcements. On the same day the General Officer Commanding and the Commander of III Indian Corps met at Ipoh to discuss further plans. But the former had already agreed to the principle of withdrawal to the east of the Perak river and the latter had issued orders to that effect.[48] Consequently the General Officer Commanding was beaten by his own instructions and regretted that 'it seemed a pity not to take advantage of the good ground west of the river Perak'.[49] The Japanese accounts too have recorded considerable surprise at the retreat of the Indian-British army in feverish haste on the night of 22/23 December. Of course, the Japanese declared that no movement had taken place on 18 December itself when III Indian Corps had issued the order of withdrawal behind the Perak river; but the situation reports and war diaries of formations throw much doubt on this statement.

[47] *The War in Malaya, op. cit.* p. 153.
[48] *Idem,* page 154. See also War Diary, General Headquarters, Far East, Appendix No. 223.
[49] *The War in Malaya, op. cit.* p. 154.

CHAPTER VIII

The Struggle for Central Malaya

THE GENERAL STRATEGIC SITUATION

Central Malaya consisted of the states of Perak, Selangor and Negri Sembilan in the west, and of Pahang in the east. It may be regarded as the heart of Malaya, whose loss would be fatal to the British hold over that country. It was also the key to the security of Singapore. Central Malaya had important characteristics, firstly, it could be controlled better by sea, especially from the island of Penang, than by land; secondly, it was more difficult to defend on account of the greater area of open land; and thirdly, Kuala Kubu was the key to the possession of Pahang.

Central Malaya, also offered numerous obstacles to an invader, who had to cross many rivers, to penetrate jungles and negotiate swamps. There were few places from where supplies could be drawn, and there were difficult communications between the coast and the main road to Singapore. The rivers Perak, Bernam and Selangor offered natural obstacles to the invader as there were few bridges worth mentioning across them. The sole bridge across the Perak river was at Blanja, but that too was made up of pontoons. Other rivers which were crossed by the main trunk road had also many bridges which, if demolished, once again offered impediments to the invader. As a matter of fact the Perak river was a problem to the British as well as to the Japanese. It ran south from Kuala Kangsar right between the main road and the west coast.

There were only three important positions where the invader and the defender could come into contact with each other, viz., Kuala Kangsar, Ipoh via Blanja Bridge and Telok Anson, and each of these positions was of considerable strategic importance. If an invader crossed the river Perak at Kuala Kangsar he was bound to proceed along the railway and the high-road in a linear direction parallel to the river for over one hundred miles until he could arrive at Kuala Kubu.

Regarding the bridge at Blanja General Percival observed: "This bridge, which was constructed of pontoons, was likely to become a vital point when our withdrawal started. Between it and Kuala Kangsar on the main road a good secondary road ran parallel to the river on the west side, but there was no road on the east side. This we thought would be a weakness as far as defence was concerned because it would give the enemy easy access to the river while at the same time making it very difficult for us to watch it ".[1]

Brigadier Paris emphasised the importance of holding the roads, and remarked: " I loathe this talk of position and holding lines. In this country there is one and only one tactical feature that matters—the roads. I am sure the answer is to hold the roads in real depths ".[2] Another mode of defence was the construction of field fortifications at Ipoh, Telok Anson and Slim river, the blowing up of the bridges, the delaying of the Japanese progress, and the greater use of patrols and fire-power. As against these principles of defence the Japanese evolved the method of ' stabbing the enemy in the side ',[3] destroying the British lines of communication (such as railways, roads, telegraph, telephone etc.), demoralising the spirit of the soldiers, increasing fifth-column activities, and dropping leaflets from the planes for publicity and propaganda of their own political ideas. Movements were made by both the British and the Japanese usually at night and in small numbers, if in advanced posts; or in large columns, if in the rear ones. Terror was attempted by the Japanese by bombing and machine-gunning from the air. When the Japanese landed at Telok Anson and Kuala Selangor, they used only small craft, which no submarine could touch nor any aeroplane could hit except at low level. Whenever the Japanese attempted a critical movement by land, air or sea, their fighters gave full protection to the moving forces.

The objective of the struggle between the British and the Japanese in this large area was the possession of the road to Singapore. The British Cabinet made this point clear on 22 December 1941. The message said, "vital issue is to ensure security of Naval Base. They emphasised that no other consideration must compete with this ".[4] It was added that the Malaya Command must employ delaying tactics and also continue " opposition on mainland to cover arrival of our reinforcements and the execution of maximum demolitions. It is for you to judge when and to what line you are forced to fall back, having regard to the danger of expending your forces unduly before the arrival of reinforcements ".[5] The Japanese were equally determined to get possession of Singapore. In fact, " the capture of Singapore was vital to the success

[1] *The War in Malaya*, pp. 154-5.
[2] War Diary of Headquarters 12th Indian Infantry Brigade (W.D. 372), 24 December 1941.
[3] Enemy Publication No. 278, p. 73, para 2.
[4] War Diary, General Headquarters Far East, Appendix No. 304, para 1.
[5] *Idem*, para 2.

of the Japanese campaign in the south-western Pacific. Not only was the British fortress and naval base a material obstacle to operations against the Netherlands East Indies and India, but it had come to have tremendous psychological value in determining the attitudes of the peoples of all south-eastern Asia. Rightly or wrongly, these peoples felt that if Singapore were to fall, their fate was sealed; and similarly, the Japanese felt that as long as the fortress held out, complete success could never be achieved. Singapore was thus a symbol to both sides in this war—a symbol of the will to victory ".[6]

The Japanese Commander-in-Chief, General Yamashita, knew the condition of the British army too well. It had fought for more than two weeks without rest or adequate equipment, and reinforcements were yet not forthcoming. He decided to strengthen his own army by adding one more division to it and employing two complete divisions simultaneously in the west-coast campaign. Air raids were also to be increased in order that the communications of the British army might be completely destroyed and in consequence the withdrawal of that army might be compelled before the arrival of reinforcements.

Having lost heavily in the first round of the war the British Cabinet was anxious to win at least in the next one. They drew the attention of their Commander-in-Chief, Far East, to a few problems like the evacuation of unwanted civilians in the military areas,[7] scorched earth policy,[8] co-operation between the army and the air force etc.,[9] emphasising thereby the supreme importance of increasing the efficiency of the British army and trying to decrease that of their enemy. At the same time they approved of a series of reforms in the army in Malaya with a view, perhaps, to increasing its usefulness. It is very difficult to say how far these were helpful in waging the war with greater zest. One opinion was that such centralised control from London was detrimental to the British interests in distant Malaya.

The most urgent need of the army in Malaya was reinforcement. The existing battalions required rest and relief for at least a few days. But the British Cabinet could do little to provide these immediately. However, some reinforcements were sent on board *Mount Vernon* in the last week of December 1941,[10] and some quantity of ammunition also was released to the Malaya Command[11]

---

[6] Japanese Land Operations, Section IV. The Malaya Campaign, p. 21, para 1.
[7] War Diary, General Headquarters Far-East. Appendix. Nos. 304 and 318.
[8] *Idem*, Appendices Nos. 287 and 304.
[9] *Idem*, Appendix No. 472.
[10] *Idem*, Appendix No. 362.
[11] *Idem*, Appendix No. 428.

besides one squadron of seventeen light tanks and four hundred men to be in charge of those tanks.[12]

More or less simultaneously the British Government ordered certain changes in the higher command. On 27 December Air Chief Marshal Sir Robert Brooke-Popham was replaced by General Sir Henry Pownall as Commander-in-Chief, Far East, but Sir Henry was instructed to deal with 'major military policy and strategy' jointly with the Commander-in-Chief, Eastern Fleet, and to keep off from 'operational control'. This change gave General Percival more freedom to regulate the fighting in Malaya. At the same time Sir Geoffrey Layton who was in charge of the Eastern Fleet was shifted from Singapore to Colombo; early in January 1942 Mr. Duff Cooper, the Cabinet representative in the Far East, had to leave Singapore on the termination of his appointment and Sir Shenton Thomas, who was the Governor and High Commissioner of Malaya, succeeded him as Chairman of the Far East War Council; and, above all, General Sir Archibald Wavell who was the Commander-in-Chief of the Indian Army was appointed as the Supreme Commander of the American-British-Dutch-Australian (ABDA) area on 3 January 1942,[13] absorbing the Commander-in-Chief, Far East, as his Chief of Staff.

General Percival's sense of responsibility at his level compelled him to make a few changes in the organisation of the army. He had combined the 6th and 15th Indian Brigades into one brigade, known as the new 15th Indian Infantry Brigade; the two battalions of 16 Punjab Regiment (2/16 and 3/16) were formed into one, and the two British battalions (2 East Surrey and 1 Leicester) were combined under the name of 'British Battalion'. The command of this new 15th Indian Infantry Brigade was given to Lieutenant-Colonel Moorhead who had distinguished himself at the head of the contingent on the Kroh Road. General Percival's second act was the retirement of Major-General Murray-Lyon and the appointment of Brigadier Paris as commander of the 11th Indian Division. The vacancy caused by the promotion of Brigadier Paris was filled up by Lieutenant-Colonel I. McA. Stewart.

Slight improvements were made in Army Headquarters also in this period. On 1 January 1942, the smaller Fighter Control Headquarters in Singapore was expanded. It became known as No. 224(F) Group. Group Captain Rice remained in command.[14] On 4 January 1942, Air Vice-Marshal Maltby arrived

[12] *Idem*, Appendix No. 337.
[13] *Idem*, Appendices Nos. 443 and 510.
[14] Sir Paul Maltby's *Despatch*, p. 1373, para 270.

in Singapore as Chief of Staff-designate to the Commander-in-Chief, Far East.[15]

On the side of the Japanese also there were a few significant changes at the beginning of this period. General Yamashita introduced an amphibious striking force to co-operate with the army, proceeding along the main west-coast road. He cancelled operations by parachute troops as the British had fixed sharp bamboo poles all over the open ground and formed an efficient defence in all cleared-up areas. However, he put in three divisions for attack on the British—the *Yamashita Group*, the *Matsui Group*, and *X Group*.[16] In the battles of North Malaya, the Japanese had fought with practically only one division. So far as equipment was concerned their army was fortunate not only in having what it wanted from Japan but also in acquiring what the British army had lost during its withdrawal: ammunition, guns, small sea-craft, petrol and stores of military importance.

Turning to the dispositions of units in the campaign for central Malaya, one may notice generally a crippling scarcity of troops and lack of reserves. The Perak river area demanded one more division for its defence, but this could not be had. The 9th Indian Division could not be transferred to the western zone as it had still a vital task to perform in the eastern part of Malaya, the 18th East African Division could not be expedited in its journey to Malaya, and no extra help was received from Australia. The forces attached to the Singapore Fortress could not be touched in view of the highest value placed on the defence of the island in the whole Malayan defence scheme.

From the strategic point of view the key to central Malaya was the high road to Kuala Lumpur. This could be captured by crossing the Perak river at the Iskandar Bridge or at Blanja Bridge, or by landing troops at the mouths of the Perak and Bernam rivers. The struggle for Central Malaya was decided by the operations at these four vital points, as described below.

THE FALL OF IPOH

The struggle for central Malaya began on 24 December 1941. Its first phase was directed against Ipoh, which fell to the Japanese on 29 December. We may begin the account of the campaign in central Malaya with this episode.

Geographically, the area involved was enclosed by the Perak river and the road from Kuala Kangsar to Blanja in the west,

---

[15] *Idem*, para 271.
[16] Enemy Publication No. 278, Malaya Campaign 1941-42, p. 75, para 3.

by the main road and railway from Salak North to Gopeng and Batu Gajah in the east, and by small strips of roads between Enggor and Salak North in the north and between Blanja and Batu Gajah in the south. Inside this area was a hill running from north to south and covered with forest and swamp. The entrance into this position was either from Salak North southwards or from Blanja pontoon bridge eastwards. So long as these two entrances were guarded, Ipoh was safe.

The defenders organised their defence accordingly at Salak North and Blanja and in their suburban lands. They placed the 12th Indian Infantry Brigade to hold the main road and railway and the adjacent lands up to the mountains from S. Siput to Kantang Halt, while the 28th Indian Infantry Brigade was placed on the Blanja front. A reserve consisting of 5/14 Punjab and three armoured car sections (the Ipoh section of the Federated Malaya States Volunteer Force and two Kedah sections lately formed) was kept as divisional reserve at Ipoh while 3 Field Company, 46 Army Troops Company and 43 Field Park Company were responsible for the demolitions on all roads roundabout Ipoh. The Independent Company was kept at Telok Anson. Very little, however, was done to afford protection against attacks from the air or by sea. Air forces were also not adequate for interrupting the Japanese line of communication along the western coast. This weakness detracted from the effectiveness of the defence.

The Japanese realised that Kuala Kangsar, Ipoh and Telok Anson were well defended and that the best way of attacking them was by directing against each of these an independent division supported by air force and artillery. All the three divisions were to act simultaneously according to plan, and General Yamashita took personal charge of the campaign.

On 23 December 1941, the situation in Perak area was fairly stable. There was contact with the Japanese at Iskandar and near the railway bridges about Kuala Kangsar. While the 12th Indian Infantry Brigade was on the eastern side of the Perak river, the two railway bridges were demolished and the brigade began to move to Chemor, ten miles north of Ipoh. On the Blanja front, 3 Cavalry and a battalion of the 28th Indian Infantry Brigade were still west of the pontoon bridge with the supporting artillery in Parit area and another battalion of the 28th Indian Infantry Brigade in the area west of Batu Gajah. On 23 December the Japanese air force bombed and machine-gunned Ipoh and the Blanja bridge, damaged the railway at Chemor, and attacked the transport vehicles of a battalion of the 12th Indian Infantry Brigade near Salak North, causing some casualties. Of these, the attack on Ipoh was the worst, because an ammunition train which had arrived lately and the signal box at the railway station were hit, and the petrol pump also was destroyed. This produced a shock which rocked the whole of central Malaya for some time to come, especially after the terrible air battle over Kuala Lumpur on the previous day and the consequent withdrawal of all British fighters to Singapore.[17]

When the day dawned on 24 December, there was every hope that the British Commonwealth troops would keep the Japanese on the western side of the Perak river, whatever might happen in the air or on the west coast. The high command had ordered the 12th Indian Infantry Brigade to employ delaying tactics and the 28th Indian Infantry Brigade to prevent the crossing of the river. Both appeared to be comparatively easy tasks.

24 December was a day of comparative calm. The Malaya Command ordered the III Indian Corps to use eight light anti-aircraft guns to protect troops and transport on roads ' only on scale air attack'.[18] The 6/15 or new 15th Indian Infantry Brigade reported that ' CID considers Perak river and Kampar centres of fifth column activity, particular danger from Red Flag Society,'[19] and other units confirmed this with facts which had come to their notice. 5/14 Punjab blew up the two bridges near S. Siput with the idea of delaying the Japanese progress, and 5/2 Punjab was made responsible for this. The road from S. Siput to Kg. Talong was patrolled by armoured cars. There was no contact with the Japanese on the ground anywhere. But the Japanese air force attacked all forward areas with heavy bombs, with the result that all troops were withdrawn to the east of the Perak river and all bridges across were demolished. At the same time, the III Indian Corps withdrew some extra units from forward areas and ordered No. 46 Army Troops Company, Queen Victoria's Own Madras Sappers and Miners, to be in readiness for the ' wholesale destruction of civil installations and services in Ipoh '.[20]

On the Christmas Day, the Japanese allowed the British to enjoy ' generally a quiet day ', but spent their own time in sticking posters in S. Siput, in dropping ' pamphlets in Chinese, Malay and English with scurrilous accusations against the white race '[21] in Singapore Island, and in spreading a wild rumour in Ipoh that

[17] War Diary, General Headquarters Far East, Appendices Nos. 317 and 327.
[18] War Diary, Headquarters, Malaya Command, 1127 hours 24 December 1941.
[19] War Diary, 15 Indian Infantry Brigade, 24 December 1941.
[20] War Diary of No. 46 A Troops Company Queen Victoria's Own, Madras Sappers and Miners, 24 December 1941.
[21] War Diary, Headquarters Malaya Command, 2350 hours, 25 December 1941.

'British officers have been shot owing to fact of refusing to fire on Japs'.[22] They were sending some of the prisoners back to the British side, who were telling their friends that 'our men were not treated badly during capture.... Their mortars are sited well forward. Their casualties have been few. Although our casualties have been much, theirs are not. Consequently their morale is high'.[23] The whole population in S. Siput and Jalong rubber estate areas became unfriendly to the British, and consequently no information about the movement of the Japanese troops could be available. The operations that day were limited to patrol actions between 5/2 Punjab and the Japanese, and Japanese air attacks on the 28th Indian Infantry Brigade near Blanja.[24]

26 December was another quiet day for the front line troops, though the 28th Indian Infantry Brigade area and railway communications at Tapah, Tanjong Malim, Kuala Lumpur, Seremban Tampin and Segamat were attacked by the Japanese aircraft, and the local civil population in Ipoh and Kampar looted all stores even in the presence of local police. It was said that the first consignment of NAAFI stores sent by the III Indian Corps under Royal Army Service Corps supervision to the forward area was lost only by being looted without let or hindrance. The Japanese propaganda was so strong among the civil population that 'the British Resident, Perak, at Tanjong Malim was ordered to keep civil police at duty and not to allow them to withdraw without permission of military commander on the spot.'[25] As against these discouraging symptoms, 5/2 Punjab recorded highly successful skirmishes during the day. The following entries are noticed in the war diary of the battalion on this date:—(i) 'was a successful day for the Bn. quite a lot of fighting and pretty severe losses inflicted on the enemy with comparatively few to the Bn... It was estimated that the Bn. had inflicted at least from 200 to 300 casualties on the enemy, while it had only suffered a total of 15 itself. The men's morale was high, they had fought well during the day without fuss or bother and in a business-like way. It seemed that they could now be trusted to take their fair share in battle'.[26] (ii) 'Sepoy Shiv Ram who had volunteered to go up to ISKANDAR Bridge (a distance of 9 miles in enemy country) on bicycle, brought back information that half a Bn. of enemy had already crossed the bridge while the other half were about to

---

[22] War Diary, 15 Indian Infantry Brigade, 25 December 1941.
[23] War Diary, 5/2 Punjab, 25 December 1941, Appendix I.
[24] War Diary, 3/16 Punjab, 25 December 1941.
[25] War Diary, III Indian Corps, Part II, 2030 hours, 26 December 1941.
[26] War Diary, 5/2 Punjab, 26 December 1941.

do so'.²⁷ (iii) 'A Pl. of enemy on bicycles approached demolished bridge at S. Siput. 'D' Coy. on a prearranged signal from Sep. Shiv Ram opened heavy fire on the forward pl. of the enemy and killed all but about three who managed to escape'.²⁸ It has been recorded that 'the enemy attack generally was not so well-planned as normally. He came in frontally to start and got some heavy casualties. He then tried the left against B. Coy. but did not go wide enough—the ground being open..... The enemy then tried the right flank (A Coy.) but with no more success than on the left—the ground and observation situation being similar'.²⁹ At dusk this battalion withdrew to Milestone 14 position in order that the brigade plan of counter-attack might be carried out successfully.

The new plan required 5/2 Punjab to move to Milestone 14, while 2 Argyll and Sutherland Highlanders attacked the Japanese with the support of two batteries of 137 Field Regiment. 4/19 Hyderabad was to put in a flank attack simultaneously in the area 'east of the limestone cliffs'. The main intention of these attacks was to delay the Japanese without the brigade being heavily committed. The method was a limited attack, and the day and time were 0930 hours on 27 December 1941.

The next day was consequently a day of severe fighting and subsequent withdrawal from the north during the night. The Japanese launched a very heavy attack astride the road at 0615 hours on 27 December which was repulsed but it prevented the brigade plan from being carried out. A fresh attack developed against the right flank at about 0815 hours. The fighting had thickened and hand-to-hand fighting went on along the whole front in which A, B and C Companies of 5/2 Punjab were involved. D Company was ordered to counter-attack and restore the situation on the right flank. This company made a gallant effort but having lost its leader and coming under heavy machine-gun fire failed to restore the position. At 0900 hours the Japanese pressure became heavy and the battalion was compelled to withdraw without being pursued owing to the severe losses suffered by the attacking troops.³⁰ At the same time one company of 4/19 Hyderabad which came in on too narrow a front was wiped out by the Japanese.³¹ In their turn the Japanese also suffered heavy casualties mainly due to the British artillery getting a few splendid targets in the early part of the day. The fighting practically stopped in

[27] *Idem.*
[28] *Idem.*
[29] *Idem.*
[30] *Idem*, Appendix II.
[31] *Idem*, 27 December 1941.

the afternoon, although the Japanese continued to follow up the Indian troops by wide turning movements on their right flank and attacked the area from the air.

The Japanese succeeded more or less equally on Blanja front in pushing back the units of the 28th Indian Infantry Brigade. From 22 to 26 December 1941, they had used three regiments of engineers to improve the road from Taiping to Blanja, brought their artillery and infantry there and kept themselves ready to cross the river in rubber assault-boats. The actual date fixed for the assault was the 27th morning. Just after daylight their bombers spread terror over the brigade area for nearly half an hour, and as the last plane disappeared the assault teams started paddling across the river. But the British machine-guns and batteries opened such an intense fire that the assault was given up and no attempt was made to renew it. Nevertheless, the Japanese succeeded in getting across the river. The 12th Indian Infantry Brigade has recorded 'increasing enemy pressure all day against both Brigades. Both were isolated and there was no Division reserve. So withdrawal was an obvious precaution'.[32] During the night the withdrawal of both the 12th and 28th Indian Infantry Brigades was successfully carried out, and, by the afternoon of 27 December 1941, General Yamashita had put in two divisions to march to Ipoh, one from the north and the other from west. At the end of that day the British dispositions were as follows: 3 Cavalry near Blanja, 12th Indian Infantry Briagde area south of Chemor, 15th Indian Infantry Brigade north of Kampar and 28th Indian Infantry Brigade on Chenderiang Road to the right.[33] The Independent Company continued at Telok Anson, and the naval patrol which had sunk three small craft in the vicinity of Pangkor Island on 26 December maintained a vigil on the coast. General Percival remarks with sorrow rather than a sense of relief that the withdrawals 'proceeded...without a hitch. And so Ipoh went to the enemy.'[34]

The loss of Ipoh appears to have been a consequence of the decisive Japanese advantage in numbers and tactics. The Japanese moved in small detachments at night, moving rapidly and at irregular intervals and incurring only a few casualties when they did so. Further, they put in one whole division in the west coast compaign, which fact was not known to the British. They had brought two specially organised assault battalions and a number of knocked-down motor-boats for their landing at Telok

[32] War Diary, 12 Indian Infantry Brigade, 27 December 1941.
[33] War Diary, General Headquarters Far East, Appendix No. 364.
[34] *The War in Malaya*, p. 162.

Anson. This too was unknown to the British. As stated before, the British 'intelligence' system left much to be desired in this extensive area where the civil population denied all co-operation. Moreover, the British resources were extremely limited. Equipment, transport and personnel had to be used most sparingly. There was no reserve battalion in the 11th Indian Division, and the III Indian Corps, while imposing maximum delay on Japanese progress, had also to remain in being as a fighting formation.[35]

THE STAND AT KAMPAR

The scene then shifted to Kampar where the Indian formations had withdrawn. A glance at the map of north-western Malaya will show, what General Percival has stated, that the Kampar position was probably the strongest position occupied by the Commonwealth forces in Malaya.[36] There were three good reasons for holding this view: firstly, it was more open and better suited to artillery action in which the British enjoyed definite superiority; secondly, the towering hill known as Gunong Bujang Melaka, 4,070 feet high, dominated the roads, railway and the surrounding country through which the Japanese had to pass; and thirdly, the compactness of the whole area to be defended permitted reserves and reserve positions to be maintained further back at Tapah, Bidor, Slim river and Tanjong Malim. If the British could control the sea and the air, the stand at Kampar would have continued until the middle of January 1942 and their objective of 'holding the enemy for as long as we could at arms length from Singapore to enable reinforcements to be brought in', would have been realised.

The Kampar position extended from Gopeng to Bidor and from Telok Anson to Sahum. The main road ran from Gopeng to Bidor through Kampar, Temoh and Tapah, and minor roads connected Telok Anson with Kampar and Bidor through Changkat Jong in the south-west and Gopeng with Bidor through Dipang, Sahum, Chenderiang and Tapah.

The main railway lay more or less outside the perimeter of Kampar position. There were many swamps and water-courses in the whole position, those between the main road in the Kampar region and the minor road between Batu Gajah and Tanjong Tualang being the most important. The Kinta river had ferries at Malim Nawar and Penawat, but no bridges anywhere. The

---

[35] War Diary, General Headquarters Far East, Appendices Nos. 310 and 371.
[36] *The War in Malaya*, p. 194.

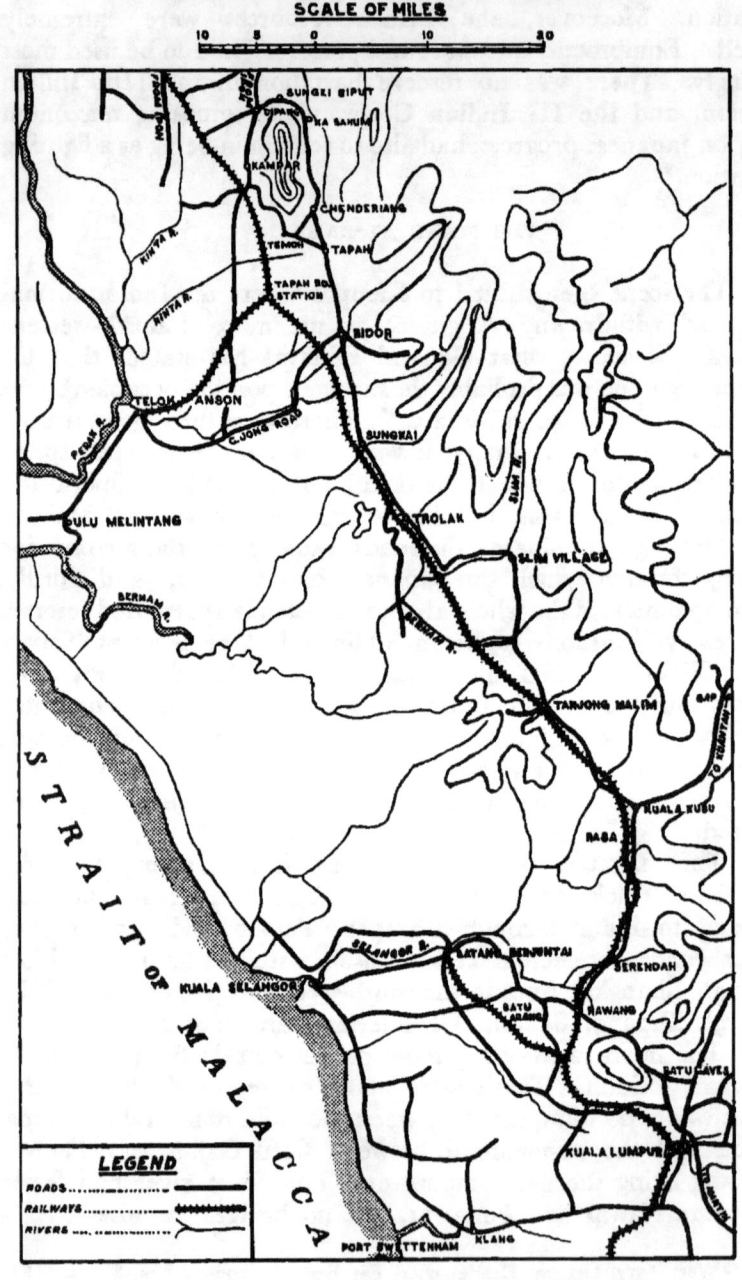

Kampar river had an important bridge at village Kuala Dipong, while the Dipang river, running parallel to Kampar hill in the north, had two bridges, and the Chikus, Pahlawan Besar and Bidor rivers on Ct. Jong and Kampar road had each one important bridge. These bridges would certainly affect the course of war both in point of time and in matter of tactics.

The defensive arrangements were generally as follows: 'The main position was semi-circular covering the township of Kampar from the north, west and south-west on a frontage of about four miles'.[37] Its eastern flank rested against the steep Kampar hill, and its western side was marked by the main road bordered by narrow belts of rubber plantation and by open stretches of tin-tailings beyond it, which afforded field of fire up to twelve hundred yards. To the south-west lay a big rubber plantation, the Cicely Estate. Tin-tailings filled the area between this estate and the trunk road. 'The main approaches to the position were the trunk road, the railway, and the road from Batu Gajah via Tg. Tualang to the Penawat and Cicely Estate ferries, both of which had been destroyed. The latter ferry was guarded by two platoons of 2/16 Punjabis'.[38] If the Japanese came by the main road from Gopeng, they could attack Kampar directly or by-pass it by taking the road to Sahum and Chenderiang. The latter was easier than the former, because it was not so well-prepared for defence. As a result of this the 28th Indian Infantry Brigade was placed to guard this route. If the Japanese entered the Kampar area by railway, it was necessary to place detachments at Kota Bharu and Malim Nawar railway stations with responsibility for actual defence being delegated to the brigades immediately behind them. If, however, the Japanese tried to enter the Kampar positions by the routes provided by ferries, further detachments would be required in the west and south-west.

The details of the defence arrangements deserve some mention. (i) The main Kampar position was held by the 6/15 Indian Infantry Brigade Group. From north to south the western face of the perimeter was held by 1/14 Punjab, 3/16 Punjab (with 351 Field Battery) and 2/16 Punjab, with a detachment at the Malim Newar ferry; the southern face was held by the Jat/Punjab Battalion (with 278 Field Battery); and 273 Anti-Tank Battery was in depth north of Kampar with one troop on the Cicely Estate road. The Brigade Headquarters was in Kampar village. (ii) The Sahum position was given to the 28th Indian Infantry Brigade and 2/2 Gurkha Regiment was made responsible for its defence.

[37] *Ibid.*
[38] History of 11th Indian Division in Malaya, Vol. 1 (original), Chap. XI, p. 191.

2/9 Gurkha Regiment was two miles ahead with an outpost role and in contact with the forward D Company of 1 Leicester, and 2/1 Gurkha was placed about four and a half miles down the road to counter any wide out-flanking move. The Brigade Headquarters was at Sahum. 155 Field Regiment was attached to this brigade. The 2-pounders of one troop of 215 Anti-Tank Battery and two anti-tank rifles were available for stopping tanks, while the bridge on the Sungei Dipang in front of 2/2 Gurkha had been destroyed. It was a standing instruction to this brigade that it should never allow itself to be cut-off. (iii) In Telok Anson area, the defence was assigned to the Independent Company, 5/14 Punjab and 7 Mountain Battery and one troop of 215 Anti-Tank Battery. The Independent Company was so disposed that there was one platoon each at Bagan Datoh and Utan Melingtang and two companies at Telok Anson. 5/14 Punjab was stationed at a distance of four miles on the road from Telok Anson to Ct. Jong. (iv) The 12th Indian Infantry Brigade was originally assigned to Gopeng area to fight a delaying action. It was disposed as follows: 4/19 Hyderabad held an outpost position at Milestone 12, the Argylls and Sutherland Highlanders south of Gopeng, and 5/2 Punjab in depth between Milestone 16 and Milestone 18. The Brigade Headquarters was at Dipang. At Kota Bharu railway station, which was a responsibility of this brigade, the Kedah Armoured Car Company had placed two sections in ambush for the Japanese, with a warning that they should retire to Tapah after the ambushing had been completed. After this brigade had stayed in this area for two days and fulfilled its task, it had permission to retire to Bidor for rest after handing over the bridgehead at Dipang to the 28th Indian Infantry Brigade. (v) The 11th Indian Division had its headquarters at Tapah, and consequently a few units were kept in divisional reserve between Temoh and Tapah. 5/14 Punjab and 7 Mountain Battery were recalled from Telok Anson area to Temoh on 30 December 1941, 22 Mountain Regiment was left at Temoh, 2 Anti-Tank Battery was put in depth between Temoh and Tapah, the Ipoh section and one section of the Kedah Armoured Car Company were asked to remain at Tapah and 3 Cavalry and the ' Gurkha Gang ' were asked to hold positions at Milestones 3 and 25, respectively, on the road to Cameron Highlands. The 16th Light Anti-Aircraft Battery had A troop at Kampar and B troop at Tapah. C troop had of course left on 27 December to join the 9th Indian Division.

These dispositions had been made to strengthen the defences of Kampar, and precautions were also taken to get the help of the

Sakai tribes for service as guides and to drive out the local inhabitants, especially the Chinese and the Sikhs, who, ' although driven out during the day,...... returned at night, and there were doubtless fifth columnists among them '.[39] Nonetheless the available force was not adequate for effective resistance. Kampar position required a full and fresh division to hold it, with a new brigade in III Indian Corps reserve on coastal duty. A few tanks were also required if air and sea forces were not available. The weakness of the whole defence lay at two points, the first in the Sahum position, where the Japanese could infiltrate through jungles, hills and tracks in the mountainous area, and the other in Telok Anson area, where the Japanese with the command of sea and air could land almost anywhere on the coast.

28 December was a busy day for the 15th Indian Infantry Brigade. A report arrived that approximately 2,000 Japanese had been moving towards Pusing and Batu Gajah on that day,[40] and that the ambush arranged with two sections of Kedah Armoured Car Company at Simpang Pulai and Sentu had failed miserably at 1000 hours. 'Japanese artillery which seemed a good bit heavier than infantry guns, had already started to shell Gopeng ',[41] while their aeroplanes were bombing the battalion position. Before noon the position of 4/19 Hyderabad, which was evidently known to the Japanese, came under mortar fire, and by 1400 hours their patrols had come into contact with the forward companies of the Hyderabad Regiment, and one of their patrols had approached also the detachment of the Argylls at Kota Bharu railway station. However, the 501 Field Battery forced the Japanese to stop before they could make a regular attack, and the armoured car patrol of the Argylls wiped out the Japanese mortar detachment near Kota Bharu railway station. Notwithstanding this energetic defensive action, the Japanese continued on both the flanks of the Indian brigade and compelled 4/19 Hyderabad to withdraw to a position about MS 14/16 between the Argylls and 5/2 Punjab, leaving one company as an outpost about four hundred yards ahead of the Argylls.

It has been stated that the object of this withdrawal from Gopeng was to let the Japanese occupy it that night and ' to make a frontal attack with artillery support early the next morning directed to a depth of two thousand yards through Gopeng. The details of the attack and the artillery barrage were all worked

[39] Major E.F.D. Hyde: Account of the Malaya Campaign, vol. I, part III, chap. 2, p. 138.
[40] War Diary, 15 Indian Infantry Brigade, 28 December 1941.
[41] War Diary, 5/2 Punjab, 28 December 1941.

out'.[42] This scheme however failed as the Japanese forestalled it by themselves attacking frontally with tank support. In fact the night of 28/29 December was spent by the Japanese in patrolling and assembling tanks and motor-cycles, which they had probably brought by railway from Batu Gajah to Kota Bharu.[43]

29 December was consequently a day of heavy fighting and confusion for the Commonwealth troops. The high command reported that 'there has been increased enemy artillery activity in Perak area. The guns are not infantry guns and are reported as being of about five-inch calibre.[44] There was also widespread air activity in Kampar area, and eighteen aircraft bombed and machine-gunned Kluang aerodrome, causing no damage, whatsoever. But the situation in front had deteriorated and the 12th Indian Infantry Brigade had to fall back. The Anti-Aircraft Battery was also ordered to withdraw south of Tapah owing to the fact that hostile aircraft were attempting to cut the line of communication.[45] There was very low morale in the entire 12th Indian Infantry Brigade[46] and although it held up the Japanese advance for 48 hours, no alternative was found to withdrawal to Bidor. Major-General Paris visited the brigade to see how the men had fared and also to study the latest situation. He gave permission for its withdrawal from Dipang at 1900 hours, and ordered the 28th Indian Infantry Brigade to cover this withdrawal with two companies at bridge-head. The withdrawal commenced before noon and ended at 1815 hours in the midst of a terrible confusion. The bridge at Kuala Dipang was also blown up soon after; the two companies of 2/2 Gurkha which had given cover for withdrawal returned to their battalion after completing their duty at the bridge-head.

There is no doubt that 29 December was a trying day for the men of the 12th Indian Infantry Brigade. "The (Japanese) tanks, medium and light, moved at 3-6 miles per hour and at 10-20 yards interval. Their machine-gun and cannon fire was intense and intimidating but ineffective except against targets actually on the road".[47] But the night was comparatively easy as the Japanese had also suffered casualties from rearguard action of the 12th Indian Infantry Brigade and the artillery during the night.[48] On 30 December, the Japanese probed into the Kampar defences

---

[42] Anguse Rose: *Who Dies Fighting*, p. 81.
[43] War Diary, 5/2 Punjab, 1445 hours, 29 December 1941.
[44] War Diary, General Headquarters Far East, Appendix No. 377.
[45] War Diary, 15 Indian Infantry Brigade, 29 December 1941.
[46] War Diary, 5/2 Punjab, 29 December 1941,
[47] History of 11th Indian Division in Malaya, vol. I (Original), chap. X, p. 185.
[48] War Diary, General Headquarters Far East, Appendix No.385.

at various points from Sahum to Telok Anson, and attacked the area from the air. As Kampar had a four-battalion front, each battalion was in slight contact on this day. On the 6/15 Indian Infantry Brigade front forward troops on the left flank had a brush with a small number of Japanese troops during early hours.[49] At the same time Japanese forward elements were moving in front of the position and a certain amount of mortar-artillery fire fell in front of the forward company.[50] There was a report that the Japanese were advancing down the Batu Gajah road probably to the Cicely Estate, but a patrol of 2/16 Punjab found no confirmation. None-the-less, a detachment of 1/14 Punjab at Malim Nawar station withdrew after slight contact with the Japanese, and another combined detachment of 2 Jat and 1/8 Punjab at Malim Nawar ferry did the same in view of its dangerously isolated position. The detachment at Tanjong Tualang ferry, however, remained, because it was strategically posted at the Cicely Estate point and it was well supported by a section of Federated Malay States Volunteer Force Armoured Car Company which was patrolling there.

In Sahum area, during the night of 29/30 December 1941, while 352 Field Battery harassed the trunk road north of Dipang and the railway, 155 Field Regiment and the machine-guns of 2/9 Gurkha were involved in a similar action on their front. At dawn of 30 December, the Field Observation Officer ordered eight rounds of gun-fire on four Japanese staff cars and destroyed both men and vehicles. In the morning an ambush was successful in the central track area. Shortly after this a patrol which included a German was destroyed. In the afternoon successful attacks were also made to capture the Manager's House Hill inflicting heavy casualties on the Japanese. Finally when the forward detachment of the 6/15 Indian Infantry Brigade was withdrawn, 2/9 Punjab was also withdrawn to Sahum area.

Meanwhile, the 12th Indian Infantry Brigade was resting at Bidor and reconnoitring positions to the south of it. The divisional commander formed an immediate reserve at Timoh by moving 5/14 Punjab and 7 Mountain Battery from Ct. Jong to that place and by bringing B Squadron of 3 Cavalry from Tapah-Cameron Highlands road to Ct. Jong area; at the same time representatives of the press were permitted to go round and talk to the men, in order to counter false rumours and improve morale.

Before the new year dawned, General Percival, in consultation with the Commander III Indian Corps, had come to the

[49] War Diary, 15th Indian Infantry Brigade, 30 December 1941.
[50] War Diary, 3/16 Punjab, 30 December 1941.

decision " to hold on to the Kampar position for as long as possible and in any case not to fall back behind the Kuala Kubu road junction before 14 January without permissions ". It was essential to hold the Japanese as far away as possible from Singapore to enable the much needed reinforcements, then on their way, to arrive. With the loss of Ipoh, Kampar positions must be held to prevent a rapid Japanese dash southwards. Their pressure on Sahum position continued undiminished, but the Kampar position had not yet cracked.

So the new year 1942 dawned with the Kampar position still intact. But on the morning of 31 December ' air reconnaissance had reported some small steamers with barges in tow moving down the Perak coast ',[51] which was most alarming. Nothing worse could happen to shatter the seeming impregnability of the position. The Japanese landed at 1500 hours at Telok Anson; and they had the choice of three routes viz. to Bidor direct, via the Bernam river to Slim town, and down the coast to Kuala Selangor.

In Sahum area, held by the 28th Indian Infantry Brigade, the new year dawned with comparative peace. But before the day was out, the battalion had to be withdrawn. On 2 January 1942, 2/2 Gurkha (less one company) went to Lima Blas Estate in Slim area, the remaining company going to Temoh to reinforce 2/1 Gurkha, and 2/9 Gurkha with B Battery of 155 Field Regiment remained at Sahum, with permission to fall back on Jabus Mine area if considered necessary.[52] 155 Field Regiment less B Battery moved to Tapah to cover any withdrawal from Kampar to a position in the south. The 28th Indian Infantry Brigade Headquarters was moved to Temoh, and Brigadier Selby assumed command of 5/14 Punjab and 2/1 Gurkha. In the 6/15 Indian Infantry Brigade area a most destructive but successful fight was waged against the Japanese on Thompson Ridge, in which 2/16 Punjab and Leicester-Surrey troops were involved on 1 January.[53]

But these petty successes did not remove the danger, which on the contrary became accentuated owing to the threat of Japanese infiltration into the Perak and Bernam rivers, which exposed the flank of the Central Malaya defence. Endeavours were then made to discover the details of the Japanese forces on the sea, but the air force was unable to make any headway and suffered losses. All that the Malaya Command could then do was to move the 12th Indian Infantry Brigade to reinforce the 3 Cavalry

---

[51] *The War in Malaya*, p. 192.
[52] According to the " History of the 11th Indian Division in Malaya " prepared by Colonel A.M.L. Harrison, 2/9 Gurkha was supported by C Battery of 155 Field Regiment and one troop of 215 Anti Tank Battery—p. 215, File No. 7351/H, Part II.
[53] War Diary, 3/16 Punjab, 1 January 1942.

squadron in Ct. Jong area.⁵⁴ That brigade took up its position at night. A shortwhile before this, the platoon of the Independent Company stationed at Bagan Datoh had withdrawn to Telok Anson after a brush with the Japanese at Simpang Ampat.

In view of the possibility of a Japanese landing further south at Kuala Selangor, 3 Cavalry (less B squadron in Telok Anson area) was moved to Batu Caves area. As the detachment was weak in strength, the 9th Indian Division was ordered to send 3/17 Dogra of the 8th Indian Infantry Brigade to Kuala Lumpur to come under the command of 3 Cavalry. Navy and air force were also at the same time asked to do what they could to deal with this threat '.⁵⁵ This possibility of attack from Kuala Selangor side was not at all an imaginary threat because there were several air raids on Port Swettenham on this day damaging rubber godowns, and on Klang, hitting marshalling yards.

In Kampar position and on Telok Anson road also hard fighting continued on 2 January 1942, but, as the Japanese had appeared in Kuala Selangor area, withdrawal from the Kampar position became necessary and the forces were moved south to reinforce the Kuala Selangor area. However there was no improvement in the situation.

The seaborne threat against the left rear of the 11th Indian Division had further developed, and nearly two battalions had landed in the Perak and Bernam areas near Telok Anson. Though this force was engaged, yet some of the Japanese troops succeeded in breaking off contact and threatened the communications of the 11th Indian Division. Another force attempted a landing at Kuala Selangor where it was engaged by the British artillery, and, though it suffered casualties moved off to the north. This greatly enhanced the danger to the line of communication of the 11th Indian Division, which was ordered to thin out in front in preparation for a general withdrawal to a selected position in the rear.

At that moment Major-General Paris ordered the withdrawal of all brigades in the north during the night, to the Slim position. The zero hour was fixed at 2100 hours for the 6/15 Indian Infantry Brigade, while the 12th Indian Infantry Brigade was directed to deny the road junction at Kg. Ayer Kunin until the 28th Indian Infantry Brigade had cleared Bidor about midnight of 3/4 January, and then to pass through the 6/15 Indian Infantry Brigade at Bidor and occupy the Trolak section of the new Slim

---

[54] War Diary, General Headquarters Far East, Appendix No. 414.
[55] *The War in Malaya*, p. 192.

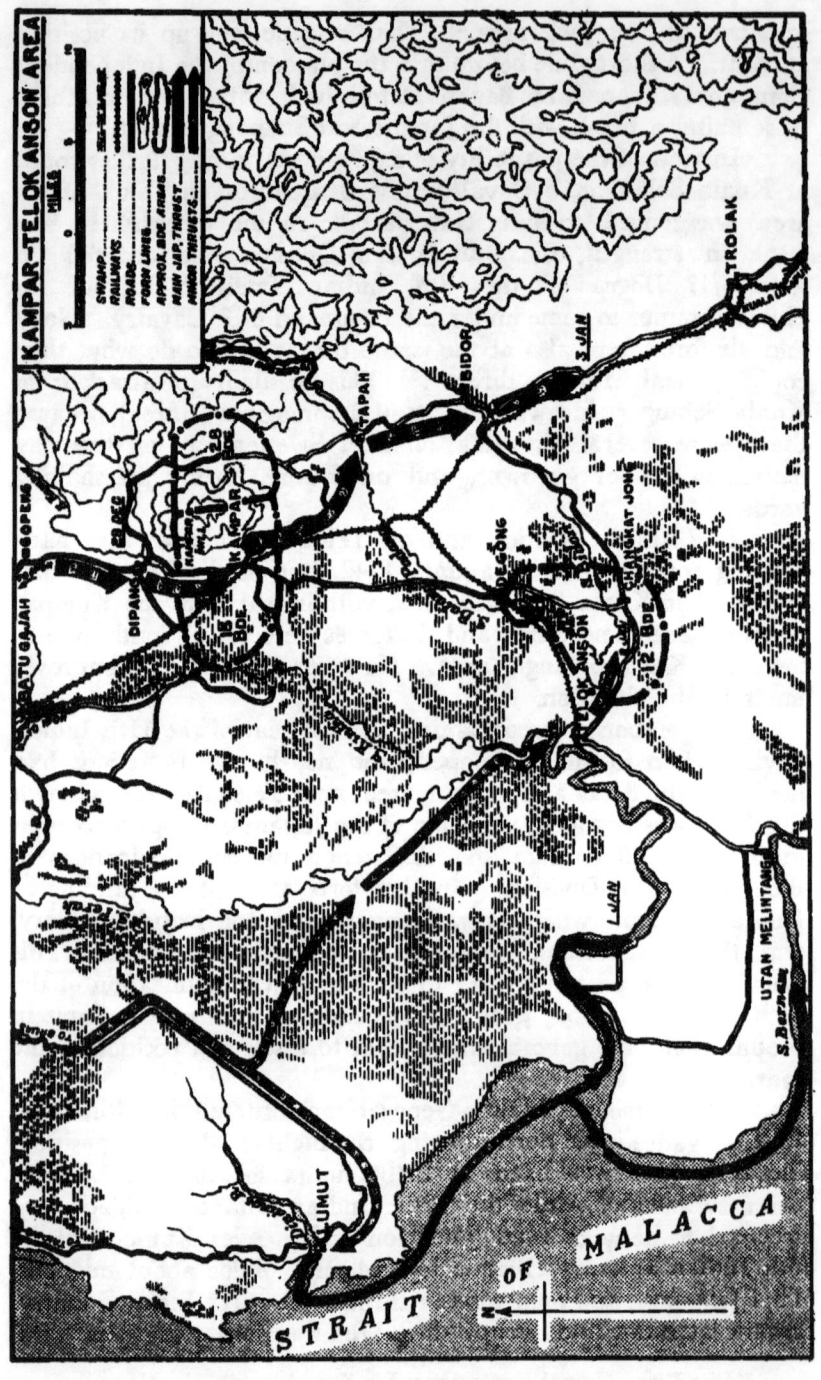

position. B Squadron of 3 Cavalry was to leave the 12th Indian Infantry Brigade and join 2/2 Gurkha Regiment in Slim River area. The divisional headquarters was to be Sungkai.

Consequently, the 6/15 Indian Infantry Brigade moved first, but the withdrawal could commence only at 2130 hours. The forward companies had some difficulty in extricating themselves and suffered casualties. Meanwhile 1/14 and 3/16 Punjab had withdrawn without incident. But 2/16 Punjab starting to withdraw at 2230 hours was attacked by a Japanese company coming from the north. An enfilade fire was opened upon the invaders and the Japanese fell back with some loss. Afterwards the battalion withdrew peacefully. But the Japanese lost no time in returning to their task of following up the withdrawal of the 6/15 Indian Infantry Brigade until 0500 hours on the next day.

In broad outline the dispositions of the 11th Indian Division on the morning of 3 January 1942 were as follows: the 28th Indian Infantry Brigade in Tapah area, the 6/15 Indian Infantry Brigade in Bidor area, and the 12th Indian Infantry Brigade in Ct. Jong area. But this comparatively incidentless withdrawal did not represent the true position, for the Japanese had inflicted considerable damage all over Central Malaya and thereby appreciably weakened the strategic position of the Malaya Command. They had acquired air supremacy and bombed Tanjong Malim,[56] Tengah,[57] Tapah bridge,[58] the Sungkai area,[59] Rasa[60] and Kerling.[61] The British Air Force had suffered further losses; while the land force was none too strong. The Japanese were active not only against the communications of the 11th Indian Division in Selangor and Perak but also were paralysing and destroying the British organisation for effective defence, especially when their resources were at the lowest. The Japanese at this moment had two objectives, the landing at Kuala Selangor at any cost and clearing the Telok Anson area, which they achieved before the end of 3 January 1942. The 12th Indian Infantry Brigade was withdrawn to Trolak area before the dawn of 4 January 1942, and the 6/15 and 28th Indian Infantry Brigades had moved to Sungkai and Slim river areas. 58 Field Regiment (less 464 Field Battery) had moved to Kuala Lumpur in the line of communication area.

[56] War Diary, Malaya Command, 3 January 1942.
[57] War Diary, General Headquarters Far East, Appendix No. 444.
[58] War Diary, 155 Field Regiment, 3 January 1942.
[59] War Diary, 17 Field Company, Royal Bengal Sappers and Miners, 3 January 1942.
[60] War Diary No. 6 Bridging Section (Queen Victoria's Own, Madras Sappers and Miners), Indian Engineers, 2 January 1942.
[61] War Diary, General Headquarters Far East, Appendix No. 431.

Thus ended the stand at Kampar. General Percival's remark that the responsibility for the loss of this battle lay much higher than on the local commanders would appear to be justified.

THE ROUT AT TROLAK AND SLIM RIVER

The next sector provided strong natural defences. The route between Sungkai and Rawang was a narrow corridor running in a north-easterly direction, which if properly held would not allow even a bullock-cart to proceed from the north to the south. The total length of this corridor was about twenty to thirty miles, and road and railway ran very near each other, except between the Slim river and Tanjong Malim. On the eastern side of this long corridor was a thick forest overlooked by high mountains, and on the western side of it was another thick forest behind which was a dangerous swamp almost up to the sea coast. Hence from the point of defence it was an excellent position. Brigadier Stewart of the 12th Indian Infantry Brigade said that " the position to be occupied by 12 Brigade had been selected by me 4 days previously. It was designed in the case of forward battalions to force the enemy into defiles of the road and railway, thus allowing economy of troops on our part, and concentration of targets for our powerful artillery; in the case of the rear battalion, to take advantage of the good lateral communication to meet any wide encircling move through the Jungle as soon as it should emerge ".[62] In the entire area south of the Slim river, terrain was favourable for defence, but it was only at the Slim river that it was exploited. Even the Japanese admitted that ' the terrain at this place is somewhat similar to that encountered by the Japanese in the pass through the Larut Hills, and they were forced to employ the same tactics in their attempts to overcome British resistance at this point'.[63] One may go to the length of saying that the Slim river position was stronger than the Kampar position and that the object with which this position was held, viz., delaying the Japanese progress, to the maximum extent possible without getting deeply committed, appeared to be easier to achieve here than in the previous position.

However, before the natural strength of the Slim river position was exploited, General Percival perceived the danger to the rear of the 11th Indian Division by possible Japanese landings on the coast between Kuala Selangor and Port Swettenham. This would outflank the Indian positions and cut their line of retreat. Hence on 4 January 1942, he told Lieut.-General Heath

---

[62] Brigadier I.M. Stewart: Report on Battle of Slim River, on 7 January 1942. Also, War Diary 12 Indian Infantry Brigade, Appendix A.
[63] Japanese Land Operations, p. 32.

that " you will appreciate great strategical importance of preventing enemy getting control of Kuala Lumpur and Port Swettenham aerodromes for as long as possible ".[64] Lieut.-General Heath was not merely to hold up the Japanese advance down the trunk road but also to guard against Japanese landings from the sea near Kuala Selangor and Port Swettenham. It was obvious that the defensive positions would be outflanked by such landings, and they would be forced to withdraw south to Kuala Lumpur.

This necessitated a further rearrangement of the troops; the 6/15 Indian Infantry Brigade was ordered to withdraw to Tonjong Malim while the 12th Indian Infantry Brigade remained in the Trolak area.

On 4 January 1942, the Japanese bombed and machine-gunned Tanjong Malim intermittently and destroyed several vehicles on convoy duty. They appeared in front of 3/16 Punjab positions in the Sungkai area, but as the 6/15 Indian Infantry Brigade had withdrawn at dusk, no contact was made. The next day, they adopted a new method of air attack by which two or three aircraft at a time bombed the railway or targets on the road, and then circled round looking for targets which they might machine-gun.[65]

In the 4/19 Hyderabad sector there was contact in the afternoon. A large party of Japanese advanced down the railway. The Ahir Company of this battalion held its fire and did considerable damage at short range. Reliable estimates put Japanese casualties at 150.[66] Unfortunately its left forward company grew nervous, necessitating an order for the withdrawal of the whole battalion by the Brigade Major in the absence of the Brigade Commander, which was however later countermanded.

On the main road immediately behind and under the command of the 12th Indian Infantry Brigade, 5/14 Punjab was to hold a position astride the road, about three miles south of Trolak. And behind this battalion was the 28th Indian Infantry Brigade in charge of Slim river position. It was planned that 2/9 Gurkha was to cover the junction of the main road with the loop road near the Slim river railway station; 2/1 Gurkha was to hold a position between the Slim river and Slim; and 2/2 Gurkha was to be responsible broadly for the south-western sector of the whole area. But all the three battalions—2/1 Gurkha, 2/9 Gurkha and 5/14 Punjab were still in harbour, resting in the vicinity of Slim river railway station, and 2/2 Gurkha had its companies

[64] War Diary, Malaya Command, 4 January 1942.
[65] War Diary, Malaya Command, 5 January 1942.
[66] Lieut.-Colonel E. L. Wilson Haffenden: Operations in Malaya F. 601/707A/H.

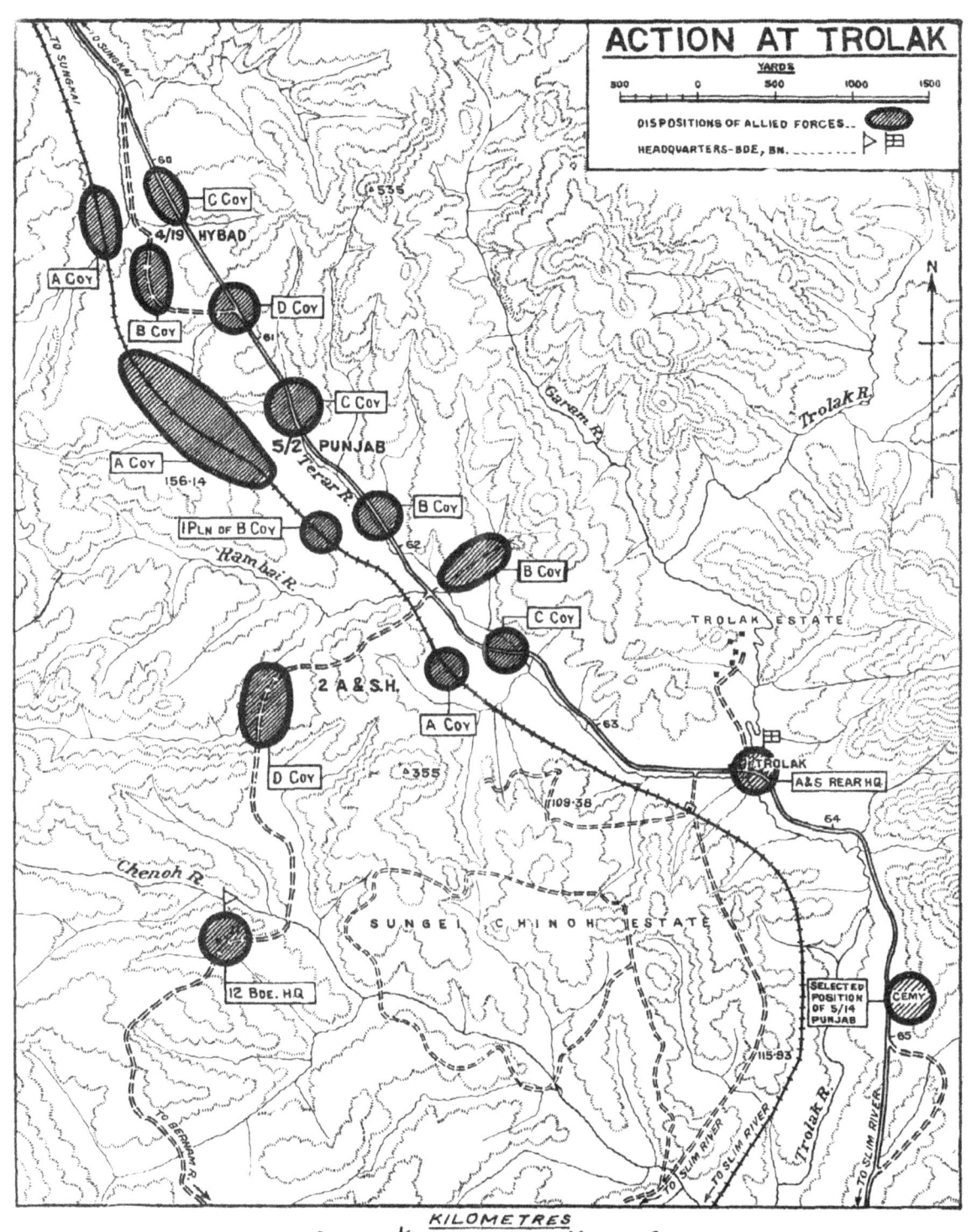

scattered from the bridge over the Bernam river to the Slim river railway station, with responsibility for the roads in that south-western area. The 155 Field Regiment was at the same time allotted to the 28th Indian Infantry Brigade.

The Tank Thrust by the Japanese

This position the Japanese had been preparing most energetically and secretly to storm. Their force ' was timed so as to arrive at the defile early on the morning of 4 January. The division commander had preceded his troops and had his plans all ready when the first of his units arrived at the scene of battle. As in the Larut Hills fight, the only way to advance was for the troops to force their way through the pass by sheer superiority of fire power. All of the division's artillery was brought to bear on the narrow British front, and while the bulk of the Infantry remained well behind in assembly areas, one battalion at a time, aided by a few flame-throwing tanks and specially trained engineer teams, attacked the strong-points in succession and fought desperately against the Indian counter-attacks until the next assault battalion passed through it to assail the strong-points in the rear '.[67] Their preparation was almost perfect, because the Japanese were in possession of full and correct information about ' proximity and nature '[68] of the Indian troops in Perak area, and they had also come to know the time-table of movements and withdrawals of the units from day to day and from hour to hour. In contrast to the meticulous preparations of the Japanese command, the defenders were confused and working in the dark. 'The Brigade Commander ascribed the inactivity (of the Japanese on 6 January) to the knock which the enemy had received on the railway during the previous afternoon, but the Divisional Commander.... suspected that the enemy had initiated an outflanking move through the dense jungle '.[69] Late in the afternoon a Tamil refugee informed the commander of the 12th Indian Infantry Brigade that the Japanese were ready to attack his position with eighty tanks, and the bridge at Sungkai had been repaired. This story was discounted by the brigade commander. At the same time a suggestion was made to him that ' all wheels forward ' should be withdrawn and first-class anti-tank obstacles, such as road-cratering combined with a minefield of some size, might be created. But he refused to accept this idea, because 4/19 Hyderabad had an adequate tank stop in front.[70] But he permitted laying of mines in

[67] Japanese Land Operations, p. 32.
[68] War Diary, General Headquarters Far East, Appendix No. 476.
[69] History of 11th Indian Division in Malaya, *op. cit.* Vol. II, chap. XIII, p. 267.
[70] War Diary, 5/2 Punjab, 6 January 1942.

the two cuttings, leaving the old switchroads clear for wheel movements. The rear minefield was covered by a detachment of two anti-tank guns. The delay in taking adequate measures heightened the weakness of the position and paved the way for the disaster which followed in the course of the day.

According to 4/19 Hyderabad, the Japanese made their attack with a detachment of 30 tanks at 0300 hours on 7 January 1942, in moonlight.[71] At that time both forward companies became engaged, by infantry on the railway and by artillery and mortars on the road. The anti-tank gunners were overrun, and the tanks penetrated the wired barriers, all within twenty minutes of the first contact. Ten minutes later the battalion was found to be breaking up, and permission was given to withdraw. The Japanese attack appeared irresistible. 'The leading tanks were medium ones of the 20-ton variety, each armed with a 4-pdr Anti-tank cannon and two ·303 MGs. In addition, many of them had a light mortar mounted on them which was fixed to fire indiscriminately on one side of the road only, both sides of the road however being covered by having them on different sides on alternative tanks. Behind medium tanks came some light tanks of the whippet variety, each armed with one ·303 MG.[72] Besides, the Japanese made use of noise as an instrument of war. One moment the night was still, with the inky darkness brooding over the jungle; the next moment all hell broke loose, with men yelling, automatics firing, engines roaring, and tins clattering. It was a nerve shattering experience. 4/19 Hyderabad had only three companies, and, in the confusion of the fight, many of them were cut off and were not seen again. The Quartermaster and his drivers threw hand-grenades to stop the tanks, but in vain.

By 0430 hours, the Japanese had entered 5/2 Punjab area. By 0630 hours, they had passed on to the next area, the one held by the Argylls. Their progress was obstructed by the two minefields, artillery fire of the two-pounders of 215 Anti-Tank Battery, and a few anti-tank rifles in action. But the most important factor was the determination of the Punjabis to fight on until the end of their moral and material resources. D Company in forward position was the first to meet the Japanese, but against superior force it failed to maintain its position. By 0450 hours this company had dispersed and was seen no more. Thereafter the Japanese were able to enter the second minefield more easily, and their losses were less than in the first minefield. Only four tanks

---

[71] *Operation in Malaya*, p. 4.
[72] Major E. F. D. Hyde: Account of the Malaya Campaign, p. 183.

were blown up or disabled. Of the other companies, C disintegrated, A was out of touch, and B was still fighting on the rear of the cutting and throwing grenades and ' Molotov cocktails'. At 0630 hours the tanks discovered the disused loop road and passed on to it. This put an end to the organised resistance of 5/2 Punjab and the battalion decided to withdraw. Then it was found that the Japanese had brought their infantry round the east flank by way of the jungle track, to encircle the Indian force. However, 5/2 Punjab managed to make its way through the encircling Japanese infantry.[73]

After the discomfiture of 5/2 Punjab the Japanese arrived in the area held by Argylls at 0630 hours. This battalion was not quite prepared to meet this sudden intrusion, because they ' had hastily gone into position on news of the enemy attack...... no anti-tank obstacle had been prepared to block the road and the battalion......had not had time to put down anything effective.[74]' The tanks passed the Pioneers of the Argylls as they started their work of blocking the road. They went through C Company of the battalion, which was holding the road, and past the headquarters. This compelled the battalion commander to order its withdrawal, and he himself left at 0800 hours and the companies moved on as they liked. A Company reached 2/2 Gurkha near Slim river along the railway, B and C went into the wilderness to the east and west, D turned west to be virtually annihilated, and the two headquarters companies followed their leaders into oblivion.

The Loss of Slim River Area

After Trolak was occupied, the Japanese moved on directly to the Slim river area, which was defended by the 28th Indian Infantry Brigade. The brigade had no warning of the impending attack and consequently suffered disaster. The Japanese mastered the whole position and occupied the main road up to Milestone 79 within a few hours. In this sector the Japanese army had strong air support, which rendered its task easy.

They overran 5/14 Punjab when it was marching to the cemetry at 0715 hours. The Japanese met this force at a point about a mile from the Slim river and by concentrating their fire on the men inflicted very severe casualties. All but a hundred and thirty-five men were dead or ineffective; and the survivors reached Tanjong Malim on the next day.

[73] War Diary, 5/2 Punjab, 7 January, 1942.
[74] Major E. F. D. Hyde: Account of the Malaya Campaign, p. 184.

The next victim of the Japanese tanks was the troop of 215 Anti-Tank Battery which had been moving up towards the north. After this it was the turn of the units of the 28th Indian Infantry Brigade to come into contact with the Japanese. The first among them was 2/9 Gurkha. Being warned in good time of the coming event, the battalion had deployed, although hastily, to the previously reconnoitred points before the Japanese arrived. The invaders were more anxious to go to the road bridge at Slim than to reduce the defences in the Slim river area. They had taken the defeat of even Gurkha units almost for granted. Consequently they just blasted A Company and battalion headquarters of 2/9 Gurkha, ignoring all others, and tore 2/1 Gurkha to pieces at 293804 and left 2/2 Gurkha almost stranded.[75] All that Brigadier Selby could do was to collect all stragglers and let them go to Tanjong Malim across the railway bridge on the Slim, under cover of the Argylls and some Gurkhas of 2/2 Rifles. All vehicles, carriers, medium machine-guns, mortars etc. were ordered to be destroyed. The only party to suffer severe casualties was the group made up of A and C Companies of 2/2 Gurkha, because it tried to cross the river further down and most men were drowned. Many more would have suffered the same fate, had it not been for the heroic efforts of one masalchi, Piraj, who, stripped to the waist and regardless of danger, continually plunged into the fast flowing river and dragged many men to safety.[76]

The Japanese tanks had got through two brigades and could find no serious opposition for ten miles more. The bridge over the Slim river was intact, and the road to Tanjong Malim was practically open. 36 Field Ambulance, 137 Field Regiment and wandering individuals put up some spirited but futile resistance before the Japanese arrived at the bridge. 16 Light Anti-Aircraft Battery fired a few rounds at the bridge, but was overrun and destroyed. When the Japanese were moving by the narrow defile south of the bridge, they were stopped at Milestone 78 by 155 Field Regiment and even pushed back by it. Even this regiment would have been rendered unfit if its 4·5 howitzer had not been equal to its task. It waited until the tanks were only 25 yards away before opening fire and at the second round set the first tank on fire. The crew tried to escape and the commander was shot by the Adjutant who had armed himself with a rifle. The gun continued to engage the second tank but only succeeded in damaging it. When all the gun ammunition had been used, it came out of action and moved back leaving the road blocked by

[75] War Diary, 2/1 G. R., 7 January 1942.
[76] War Diary, 2/2 G. R., 7 January 1942.

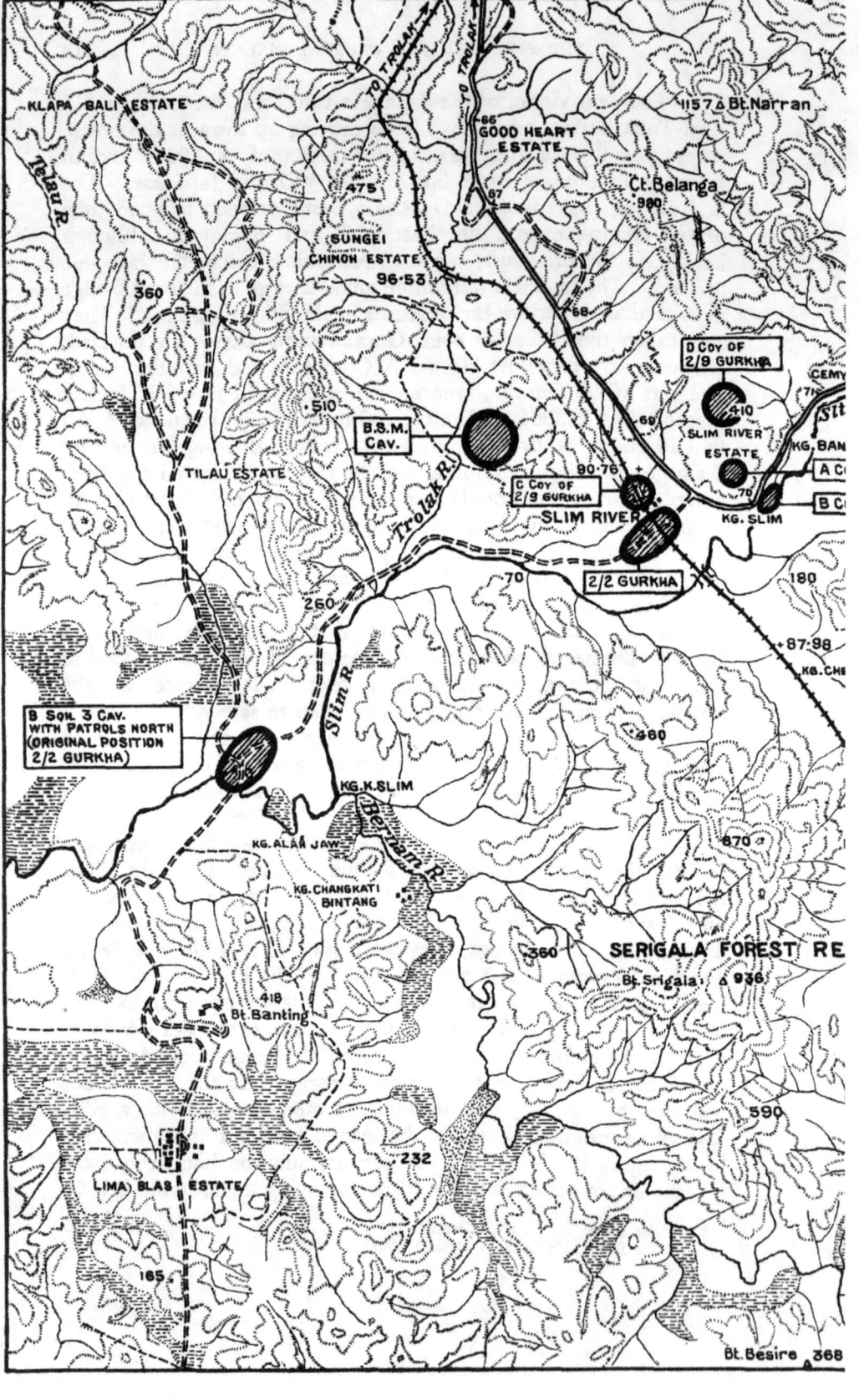

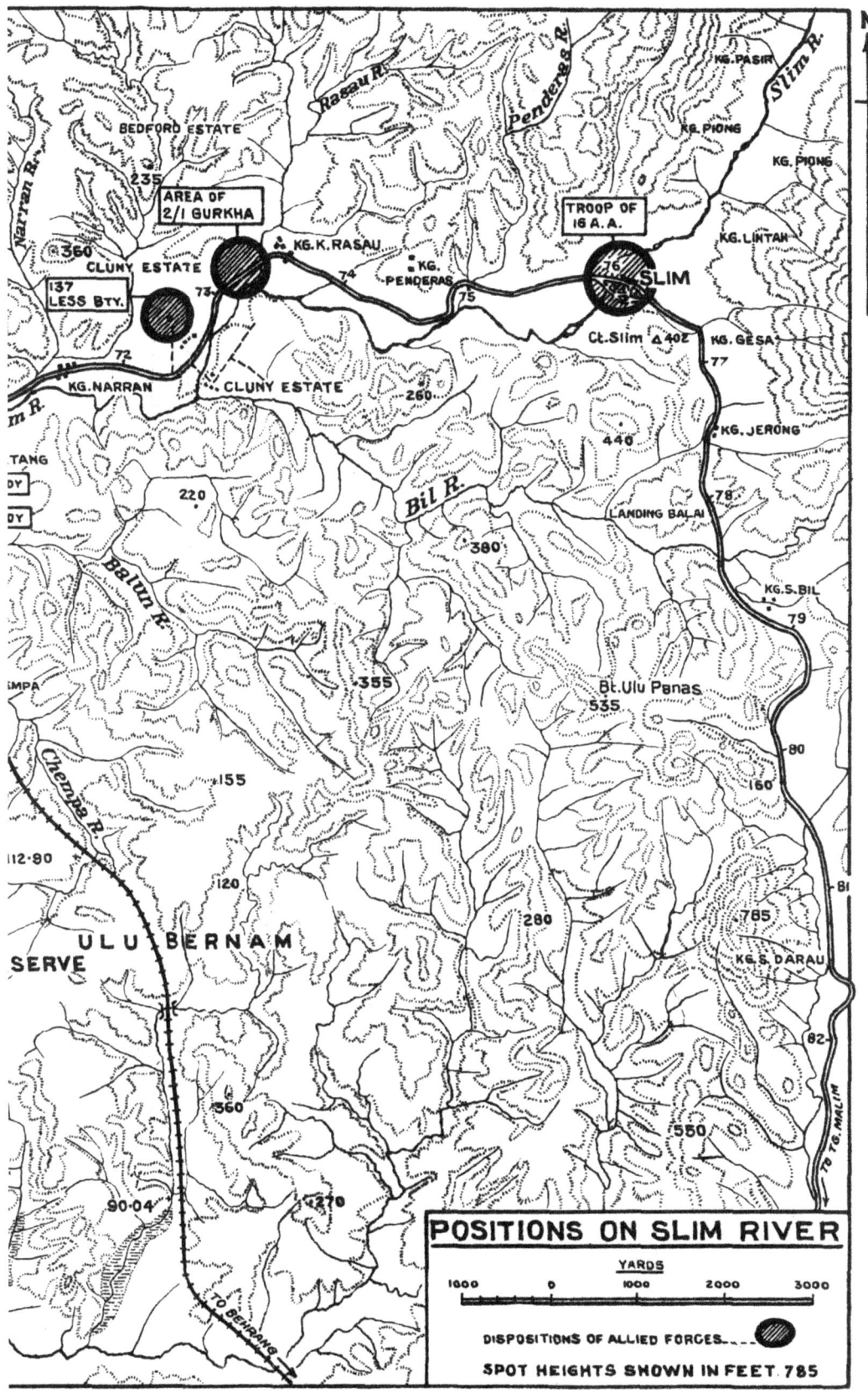

the dead tank.⁷⁷ A few moments later the tanks were reinforced by the lorried infantry, and the regiment was at its worst. But the Japanese tank thrust was halted immediately after, as suddenly as it had begun. The Rear Headquarters and B Battery moved back, while C Battery evacuated all troops and transports. All bridges up to Tanjong Malim were then blown up. The Japanese advance was thereby effectively stopped.

After the battle of the Slim river, the Japanese declared that 'one division of the enemy was almost completely annihilated. The results of the battle were several hundred dead abandoned enemy bodies, 1,500 Prisoners of War, and the seizure of 68 weapons including 12 cm howitzers, anti-tank guns, etc., 50 armoured cars and 500 various types of vehicles'.⁷⁸ On 9 January 1942, the British Command admitted that 'details of fighting by III Indian Corps (are) still not received but it is known that 11 Division has suffered (in Perak and Selangor) heavy casualties in men and equipment'.⁷⁹ It is obvious that tanks caused the disaster, that communications broke down, that bridges were not blown up, and that the troops (both officers and men) were too exhausted to fight the Japanese, who had put in first-class, fresh troops into the field. Although the Japanese used tanks, infantry and aeroplanes, their loss of men was not small. Their respect for the British and Indian resistance was undoubtedly great and sincere, and they took their task very seriously. They were prepared to sacrifice their men and material for quick success.

On the other hand, the defenders had been fighting with tired troops and had little time to adjust the defences to the exigencies of the terrain. After the set-back at Kampar, the hasty manning of the Slim river position did not afford adequate protection against armoured attack. The British and Indian troops stuck to the roads, to the estates and to the one route to the south. The Japanese exploited their advantages by area-bombing, firing into jungles and plantations on both sides of the main road and by occupying cross-roads and road-junctions.

It should also be remembered that Major-General Paris, General Officer Commanding the 11th Indian Division, and Brigadier Stewart, Commander of the 12th Indian Infantry Brigade, had no experience of Japanese tank attacks as demonstrated at Asun and Jitra and perhaps underrated armour potentialities in the thickly wooded Malayan terrain. Apart from the lack of

---

⁷⁷ War Diary, 155 (Lancashire Yeomanry) Field Regiment, Royal Artillery, 8 January 1942.
⁷⁸ Enemy Publication No. 278, p. 66.
⁷⁹ War Diary, General Headquarters, Far East, Appendix No. 509.

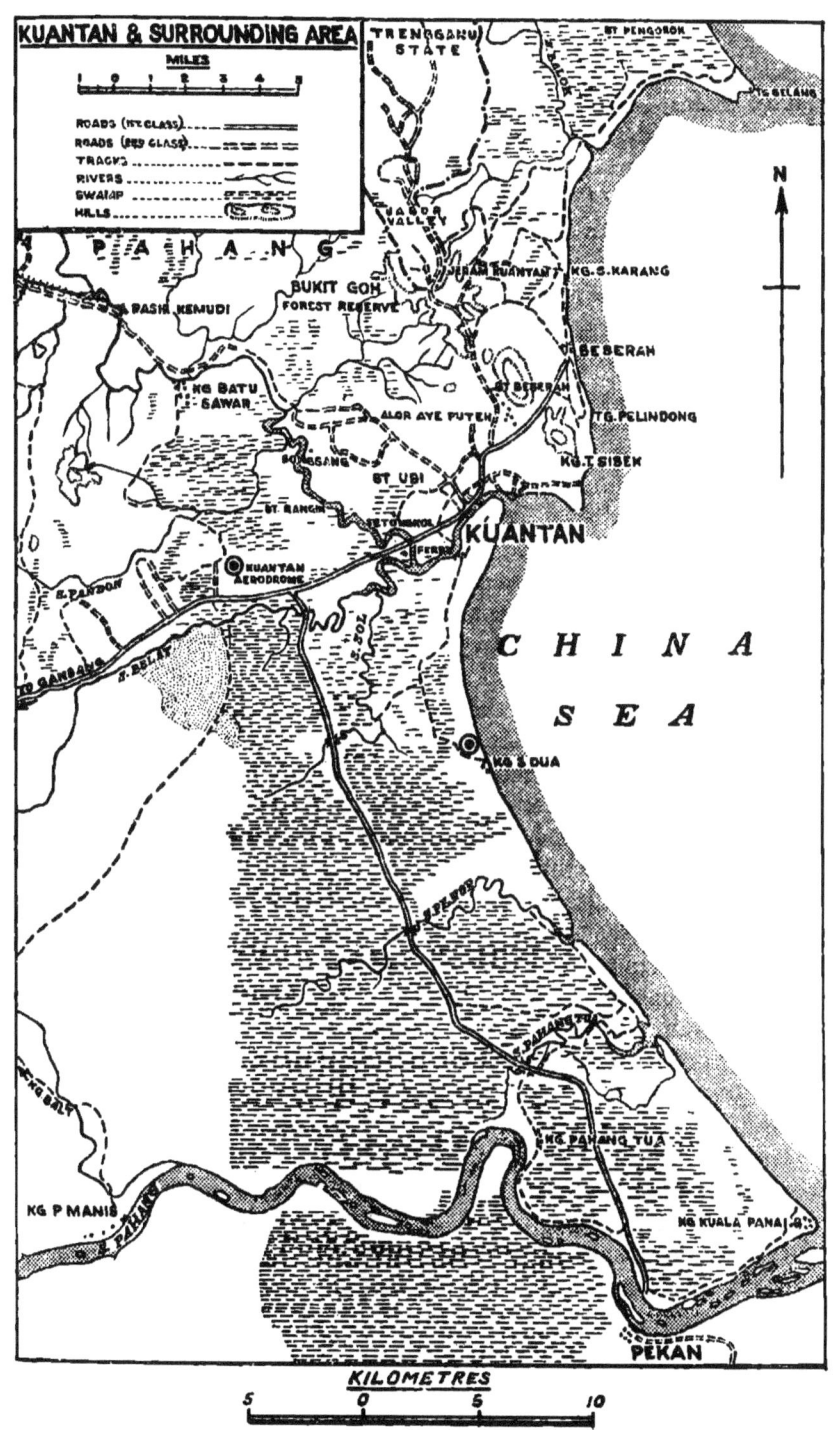

planes, reinforcements, and experienced leaders, there was not enough of planning on the British side. Whatever the causes may have been, it is universally accepted that the disaster on the Slim river jeopardised the defence of the entire Central Malaya, and robbed the Malaya Command of time to prepare adequately the vital defences of Johore and Singapore with the help of the reinforcements which were coming. The onerous task of delaying Japanese advance in Central Malaya to enable reinforcements to arrive was not being achieved.

THE FALL OF KUANTAN

The next phase in the battle of Central Malaya, was the fall of Kuantan. This was a small isolated town on the eastern sea-board of Malaya, and in the same latitude as the Slim river. It was about half-way between Kota Bharu and Singapore, nearly two hundred miles from either of these two places. It became important, with the development of aerial warfare, as a major air base from which a large area of Central Malaya was dominated. Consequently, in the war with Japan, its military importance lay almost solely in the Royal Air Force aerodrome, which was nine miles from Kuantan on the hundred-mile road to Jerantut.

Kuantan was connected with the rest of the country by three possible modes of communication. The first and foremost was by roads towards the north, west and south; the second was by the Pahang river from the sea to a far-off town in the interior, Jerantut Ferry; and the third was by sea to any point on the east coast of Malaya. But these lines of communication could be exploited or blocked, as necessary, by a strong air force. It was also possible to bring an airborne unit and drop it on a rubber plantation or on one of the paddy fields on the western or southern side of Kuantan. The sea-coast was wide and extensive, with long stretches of sandy beach wide open to amphibious attacks. There were two ferries, one at Kuantan and the other at Jerantut, which had to be successfully negotiated by an invader. The points of vantage for the defenders were the clear-cut tracks and lanes branching off to the north and to the south from the main road from Kuantan to Maran. If the defender could plug the entrances to these side-tracks and lateral roads, it was practically impossible for any invader to get into the Kuantan area. The river Kuantan was, however, an uncertain element. If low, it provided the invader an easy crossing, especially in the upper regions. Conversely, if the river was running high, the mouth of the river would offer difficulties which might not be easily overcome. The boom which was specially constructed at the mouth of the Kuantan river could not be easily operated owing to timber and foliage coming down with the current and snapping the wires and bolts in the middle of the river. The Pahang brought sand and deposited it right at the mouth, and prevented anyone from sailing up to any place on its banks in the interior.

In a country like Kuantan, and in the circumstances in which the British were placed, the defence could be organised only along the coast from Tg. Gelang to Pekan and in the north between Trengganu and Pahang states. There was also the task of watching the river-fronts in the Kuantan and the Pahang basins, the preparations of demolitions on the roads and bridges, and the placing of guns at strategic points. For these tasks, one brigade, consisting of two good battalions with some fire support, was considered adequate. The 22nd Indian Infantry Brigade was sent to this area and it comprised 2/18 Royal Garhwal Rifles and 5th Duke of Connaughts Own Battalion, the 11th Sikh Regiment, with one detached section of two 3·7" howitzers of 21 Mountain Battery, Headquarters 5 Field Regiment and 63/81 Battery to support them. Other troops were 22 Field Company Sappers and Miners, 27 Field Ambulance and 47 Mobile Workshops.

The two battalions were disposed as follows:—2/18 Garhwal held the forward line of the defence on the coast from the S. Balok to the mouth of S. Kuantan, to stop any hostile landing on this portion of the coast-line which was divided into three sectors, each sector being allotted to one company. B, A, and D Companies held the southern, central and northern sectors respectively, and C Company was in reserve at the Beserah-Ayar Puteh road junction to cover withdrawal from the northern and central sectors, if that should become necessary. There were four observation posts, one each at Bukit Pengorok, S. Karang, Bukit Beserah and Tanjong Tembeling, to report all ship movements by day and night. With the northern and central sectors were associated a section of carriers in mobile reserve and two 3" mortar detachments.

5/11 Sikh was committed to river line defence from the bend near Bukit Rangin to the first bend west of the bridge on the Pekan road. This however included ferry crossing, anti-aircraft defence of the aerodrome, prevention of Japanese incursion from Pekan and the Pahang in the rear and of hostile penetration from the tracks coming from the north to the Kuantan-Maran road, counter-attacks in the Kuantan forward area and defence against parachute troops in the areas west and south of the river line.

'Certainly a tall order for one battalion'[80]

Besides the pill-boxes there were stockades on the river fronts. A Company was in charge of the aerodrome with one section of carriers, two medium machine-guns and one 18-pounder field-gun. B Company was in charge of what was known as the southern theatre of operations from Milestone 21 to Pekan. C Company stood behind the long river front, from a point about 500 yards to the north-west of Setong Kol via the junction of two rivers and the bridge across the Sungei Belat to the first bend in the river to the west of this bridge. If the Japanese broke through the forward area, this river front would be further extended to two miles up to the river bend, north of Bukit Rangin. D Company was in reserve, located with the battalion headquarters and the headquarters company in the rubber plantations at about Milestone 6 with a number of emergency duties. In all these sections pill-boxes and stockades had been constructed and a plan for demolitions had been made.

The artillery which arrived on 6 December 1941, viz., Headquarters 5 Field Regiment and 63/81 Battery, was distributed widely in the whole area at Beserah, in the rubber plantation near Sungei Balok, at Milestone 5, in Town Camp and at Victory Camp at Milestone 10.[81] The Sappers and Miners and 27 Field Ambulance were stationed at Valentia Camp at Milestone 11. Advanced Brigade Headquarters equipped with Wireless Telegraphy sets, was established at Milestone 1 on the road to Sungei Lembing tin mines. Rear Brigade Headquarters with 8 Supply Issue Section and 7 Field Post Office remained at Volunteer Camp at Milestone 9.

On 8 December, there were in Kuantan aerodorme 21 aircraft, viz., 10 new Hudsons, 8 old Blenheims, 2 Swordfish and 1 Vildebeeste. The aerodrome was well equipped with every type of bomb, including the 500-lb armour piercing bomb, incendiaries and 21 torpedoes. All buildings had been completed, and the aerodrome was under the administrative command of a Wing Commander of the Royal Air Force. There was an emergency landing ground at Kampong Sungei Pahang Tua. Petrol had been stocked in plenty.

There was a plan for the construction of a pontoon bridge several hundred yards to the north of the ferry to supplement the normal ferry crossing. But the necessary material was made available so slowly that it was not completed before the war

---

[80] Captain D. G. Russell-Roberts: The Kuantan Operations, p. 5.
[81] These milestones are on Kuantan-Jerantut road.

broke out. The roads on either side of the projected bridge were however fully laid out by that time.

The history of the Kuantan operations from 8 December 1941 to 8 January 1942 was made up of three phases. First of all came the withdrawal of the Royal Air Force personnel from the Kuantan aerodrome. Then there was lull in the operations from 10 December 1941 to 29 December 1941. Lastly, came the attack which ended in the occupation of Kuantan by the Japanese army.

At noon on 9 December 1941 'Kuantan was subjected to its first experience of high bombing, followed up by the bombers flying low and shooting up at will'.[82] The airfield had no anti-aircraft protection, and there was a dangerous congestion of aircraft. The buildings had been shattered, more than half of the craft had been lost, the armament and two bomb stores had received direct hits, and the Japanese air raids had been continuous.[83] Hence Royal Air Force ordered withdrawal of air force as it was almost useless to risk staying on for no purpose. This withdrawal of the Royal Air Force greatly disheartened the ground troops and reduced the chances of a successful and prolonged defence of the area.

In the evening of 9 December 1941, all demolitions on the Pekan road beyond the bridge at Milestone 21 were blown up, the Pekan Polo-ground being the first. During the night of the same day two ships—one empty and the other with ground staff of Kuantan aerodrome—slipped away to Singapore in spite of the existence of mines in the estuary and also of the scare of Japanese landing in the northern part of the coast. At 1900 hours the first report of the appearance of small ships out at sea arrived from the observation post Bukit Pelingdong. At 2200 hours, a further report of firing on a boat in D Company area was received. Afterwards the whole coast was full of reports of the landing of the Japanese troops at different places. Fire continued until 0200 hours of 10 December 1941. Even the southern front fired, because it wanted to bluff the Japanese that even in that area defence was organised. But when dawn broke there was no sign of the Japanese troops anywhere on the coast. This was due to the fact that the Japanese force had retreated after the first repulse and their object was to probe the British defences and discover the weak spots in it.

During the subsequent three weeks, there were no Japanese troops whatever in the theatre of operations in Kuantan. But

[82] Sir Paul Maltby's *Despatch*, p. 1368, paras 203 and 204.
[83] The Kuantan Operations, p. 19.

there were preparations for war on both sides. The Japanese
planes flew over the area every day and bombed important places
and machine-gunned the town. On 13 December, twenty-seven
planes concentrated their attack on the aerodrome, but did little
damage to it. The British patrols were active all over the country.
Meanwhile, up in the north, the British influence in Trengganu
was gradually giving way to that of the Japanese. As early as
the afternoon of 10 December, all officers were ordered to leave
that state, and the Medical Officer, who was asked to stay on, ran
away the next day. For two or three days there was chaos in
the districts of Kuala Trengganu and Dungun, because the police
had disappeared, there was an air raid by the Japanese planes, and
the administration had broken down. Roads, bridges, ferries and
telephones were intact, and the local Japanese inhabitants in the
mining areas got the upper hand in the affairs of the state. The
Japanese army however did not come to Trengganu until about
20 December 1941.

On that day a subaltern of 2/18 Royal Garhwal Rifles met
a car containing some Japanese about ten miles north of Chukai.
Next day a body of two hundred and fifty to three hundred
Japanese troops was reported to have arrived in Kuala Trengganu,
and in fact the Garhwal patrol did have contact with them near
Kerteh. On 22 December again the Garhwal patrol operating
to the north of the Kemaman river ran into Japanese forces coming south;[84] and the news of the arrival of a large Japanese force
in the area south of Marang and Dungun by motor transport reached Kuantan on 23 December 1941.[85] On this date it was realised
that the Japanese would enter Kuantan by land and not by sea
and therefore certain readjustments became necessary in the general
defence plan. C Company of 2/18 Royal Garhwal Rifles was taken
out of the battalion reserve to occupy the road junction of Jeram-
Kuantan and Jabor Valley roads, and its place as a reserve was
filled up by A Company of 2/12 Frontier Force Regiment. On
24 December, the rest of the regiment and 21 Mountain Battery
(less a detached section already at the aerodrome) arrived from
Kelantan and halted at Milestone 10 and Milestone 9, respectively,
on Kuantan-Maran road. The detached section was shifted to
a position near Milestone 10 to cover the open ground suitable for parachute landings just north of Milestone 10. On
25 December, the Japanese were in civil control of Trengganu and
had arrived north of Kemaman. While the brigade reported

---

[84] War Diaries, General Headquarters, Far East, and 2/18 R. Garh. Rif., 24 December 1941.
[85] War Diary, 22 Indian Infantry Brigade, 24 and 25 December 1941.

150 as the strength of the Japanese to the north of Chukai, 2/18 Royal Garhwal Rifles thought that they were in good strength at Kg. Cherating.[86] On 26 December, 2/12 Frontier Force Regiment and all the six guns of 21 Mountain Battery moved to a hide-out in the rubber plantation which was two furlongs east of Gambang,[87] the guns being fixed on the perimeter of the camp with observation posts on the tracks, and the regiment patrolling and protecting the line of communication from Japanese penetration along the tracks from the north and the south. The Japanese had arrived at Kg. S. War, 150 strong in motor transport. But 2/18 Royal Garhwal Rifles reported as follows: ' 1000 hours, 5 Trucks reported coming down coast towards S. Balok. Enemy troops debussed and dispersed under cover. 1100 hours, enemy were spotted by G. 7 who fired on them. Artillery also fired. 1625 hours, more trucks arrived North of S. Balok, enemy debussed, artillery fired on them '. This Japanese contingent was loaded in five lorries, out of which two were destroyed.[88] As a result of this danger, the artillery was strengthened by transferring the left section of A Troop of 63/81 Battery from northern sector of 2/18 Royal Garhwal Rifles to the Telok Sisek area and by moving F Troop of 464 Battery of 88 Field Regiment Royal Artillery (which had arrived with an establishment of eight 25-pounders on 15 December 1941) from Milestone 5 to a position four miles along the Ayer Puteh Road, with two observation posts, one each in Sungei Balok and Sungei Karang.

On 27 December, the 22nd Indian Infantry Brigade contacted the Japanese troops on the north bank of the Balok river, and its artillery and 2" mortars kept them at a respectable distance. Meanwhile, the Japanese planes flew over Beserah and bombed it, though without inflicting any casualties.[89] On 28 December, a river block was formed at Lubok Paku with suitable combinations of the infantry and the artillery available at Gambang. This was perhaps the last of the preliminary arrangements made to prevent the Japanese from coming into and occupying the Kuantan area. Meanwhile, the Japanese had consolidated their hold on S. Balok position and tried mortaring their opponents. But their mortars were silenced by the superior artillery fire of the defenders. Five Japanese planes bombed forward areas and the

---

[86] War Diaries, Headquarters Malaya Command, 22 Indian Infantry Brigade, 2/18 R. Garh. Rif., 25 and 26 December 1941. Also of General Headquarters, Far East, Appendix No. 339.

[87] War Diary, 21 Mountain Battery, 26 December 1941.

[88] War Diaries, General Headquarters, Far East, Appendix 360, 22 Indian Infantry Brigade, and 2/18 R. Garh. Rif., 26 December 1941.

[89] War Diaries, 22 Indian Infantry Brigade, and 2/18 R. Garh. Rif., 27 December 1941.

beaches, while the Japanese infantry received reinforcements and collected at the S. Balok position.[90] On 29 December also air raids were continuous and severe. Kuantan town was bombed and machine-gunned, and the northern sector was raided by five Army-97 heavy bombers.[91] On 30 December, Gambang was heavily bombed,[92] and very few buildings remained standing after the raid. The hospital was damaged, but there were no military casualties. About the same time one troop of armoured cars of the FMSVF Armoured Car Squadron was made available to patrol the motorable portion of the track north of Jabor Tengah moving well into Trengganu. This addition to his strength was very welcome, because the Brigade Commander considered it likely that the Japanese would advance down the Jabor Valley.

The real attack on Kuantan, however, began early in the morning of 30 December 1941. The Japanese who had full information about the dispositions of the 22nd Indian Infantry Brigade, adopted two lines of advance: one between 5/11 Sikh and 2/18 Royal Garhwal Rifles and the other on the aerodrome. They penetrated into Jabor valley from the north evading patrols, and fighting developed in the area Kg. Jabor Ulu to Semambu Estate.[93] There was, besides continuous activity by groups of three or four reconnaissance bombers, bombing and machine-gunning, but without material damage to property.[94] At 0945 hours fifty Japanese troops were reported at 584902 and 2/18 Royal Garhwal Rifles sent out fighting patrols against them; at 1305 hours the Japanese in considerable numbers were collecting south of Bukit Tinggi cross-roads 610856; at 1515 hours the ferry was heavily bombed and all telephone wires to Kuantan were cut. In the confusion of the fighting, many companies temporarily lost touch with their parent units. Sungei Lembing was evacuated and Kuantan civil officials were sent to Gambang. Considerable air activity of the Japanese was reported throughout the day. The day's fighting showed that the Japanese tactics on the ground were similar to those of the highly trained guerillas. By evening the forward companies of 2/18 Royal Garhwal Rifles had been withdrawn from the coast, and a line was formed from Beserah to Songsang to block the roads from the north. Both the reserve companies had been committed, and the company in the central

---

[90] War Diaries, General Headquarters, Far East, Appendix No. 363, 22 Indian Infantry Brigade, and 2/18 R. Garh. Rif., 28th December 1941.
[91] *Ibid.*
[92] War Diary, 21 Mountain Battery, 30 December 1941.
[93] War Diary, General Staff Branch, Headquarters, 9 Indian Division, 30 December 1941.
[94] *Ibid.*

sector was pulled into reserve. Orders were issued for newly defined outpost line to be taken up by 2/18 Royal Garhwal Rifles, and for all guns and remaining vehicles to be withdrawn across the river during the night.[95] The guns were withdrawn simultaneously. During the night all civil installations in the town, including the wireless station, the wharf and the pier and the APC and 'Socony' oil tanks were demolished, and everything on wheels was taken over to the south bank of the Kuantan. The second ferry was ready at 2000 hours on this date, the first one which had been bombed was fully repaired by 1630 hours,[96] and the two ferries helped to evacuate transport, guns and heavy stores across the river by 0510 hours on 31 December 1941. This was indeed very lucky.

So far as 5/11 Sikh was concerned, C Company worked throughout the night to move ferries forwards and backwards. D Company, which was in reserve, occupied the Bukit Rangin position to counter the Japanese occupation of the Jabor Valley Estate. B Company left the Taj Line (the position at the 21 Milestone on Pekan road, prepared by Captain Khanzada Taj Mohammed Khan M.C.), blew up the Belat bridge and came into reserve near Milestone 6 on the main road. The detachment at Pekan, however, remained there alone. 2/12 Frontier Force Regiment carried out reconnaissance about one mile west of Gambang to select a defensive position.

The Japanese also were busy during the night of 30/31 December 1941. One group was quietly moving in a north-westerly direction to cross the Kuantan river in the upper regions and far beyond the Indian brigade's river line positions, with a view to attacking the aerodrome from the west. Another group, stronger than the first, entered Kuantan town on 31 December 1941, and actually attacked the post at the north bank of the ferry at 0540 hours, only half an hour after the last vehicle had been shipped across the river with the strong current.

In the morning of 31 December, it was discovered that the Japanese had reached the Setongkol area by infiltration. The 2/18 Royal Garhwal Rifles was dispersed over a wide area, with its Headquarters and A Company at Tanah Puteh ferry, its D Company at Beserah Gap covering Beserah-Semambu area, its C Company missing, its D Company reported to be in Bukit Ubi area but cut off from all communications, and its E Company occupying the cross-roads on Kuantan-Beserah road. Because the ground was so thinly held, the Japanese were able to infiltrate

[95] Brigadier G.W.A. Painter: Personal Account, p. 12.
[96] '1830 hours' is another version.

deeply, to cut off communications and to attack the rear areas as far as the Victory Camp. At noon telephone communications broke down, leaving all companies out of touch and beyond reach of any warning. The Brigade Commander and the Battalion Commander maintained touch across the river only by visual signalling and shouting; and therefore the Brigade Commander decided to withdraw 2/18 Royal Garhwal Rifles across the river with artillery and mortar support, either in the course of the day or after sunset. This was duly communicated to the battalion commander by signals. Afterwards, the 9th Indian Division was asked by the Brigade Commander whether 2/18 Royal Garhwal Rifles, likely to be cut off by infiltration, might be withdrawn to Maran. But the reply was against any such move and the Brigade Commander confirmed the abandonment of the proposal, but with the observation that the Japanese ' infiltration round left flank against aerodrome (was) only a matter of time. Fight to deny aerodrome will only result in losses. (He will be) denying aerodrome to-night, withdrawing Garhwal Rifles across river '.

The evening was spent in transporting as many as 300 men of 2/18 Royal Garhwal Rifles across the river, in destroying the ferry and in sending B Echelon transport back to Marar. At night, stragglers were helped to come across the river, the remainder of the battalion was withdrawn near Milestone 9 on the main road, i.e. to the area of the aerodrome, 464 (25-pounder) Field Battery was sent to Jerantut, and petrol dumps on aerodrome and Pekan road junction were destroyed and all engineering and Public Works Department material of value of the Japanese were also denied.

A further withdrawal became necessary immediately afterwards. The flanks of 2/18 Royal Garhwal Rifles were being turned by the Japanese moving through the jungle, and all attempts to extend the arc of defence failed. Forward companies were still in action in the Jabor Valley, Semambu and Jeram Kuantan estate areas, but without communications with the headquarters of their battalion. In these circumstances there was no alternative but to withdraw the whole battalion to the aerodrome area immediately, and the Brigade Commander issued the order accordingly. He also ordered 2/12 Frontier Force Regiment to concentrate near the aerodrome area, leaving one company to find detachments at Pulau Manis and Lubok Paku, where guns of 21 Mountain Battery had now been placed for action against possible movement of hostile craft up the Pahang river.

The new year opened with an order of the day to deny the Japanese the use of the aerodrome up to 5 January 1942 so that British convoys, almost in sight, could reach Singapore. The situation reports on this date referred to several dangerous developments. Confused skirmishes were going on all over the front. The Japanese were continuing their infiltration.

The night of 1/2 January 1942 passed likewise without incident. The situation on 2 January 1942 was practically the same as on the previous day. Then two reports hastened the division to leave Kuantan. The first was the receipt of news from Kuala Lumpur about Japanese landings on the west coast, and the resultant threat to the rear and flank of the 9th Indian Division. At the same time, Singapore reported the arrival of the convoy with reinforcements and supplies. This led the higher authorities to order the withdrawal of the 22nd Indian Infantry Brigade to take effect on the night of 3/4 January 1942. This decision was further justified by the deteriorating local situation, betokening an encirclement of the brigade. The Japanese had infiltrated on to the Batu Sawar track. Fire was exchanged resulting in some loss to the Japanese. Later in the evening, two or three of their scouts peered into the Victory Camp from a point to the north of the track. They were driven out by the British gunners. But it became certain that the Japanese troops were in considerable strength in the north. The night of 2/3 January 1942 was peaceful. But the day of 3 January was fateful for the 22nd Indian Infantry Brigade. Not being at all happy about the lack of information regarding the Japanese to the north of the main road, the Brigade Commander posted four platoon piquets to watch the tracks at approximately Milestones 7, 8, 10 and 11, and also to prevent ambushes on the main road. With these preparations withdrawal began. The first batch to withdraw consisted of 5/11 Sikh, the bulk of 22 Field Company, a portion of the artillery, followers, mess and all others who might prove impediments. A detachment of the pioneers was retained with the brigade for blowing road demolitions which had been prepared. By 1800 hours[97] all units except the Brigade Headquarters, 2/12 Frontier Force Regiment (less two companies), one section FMSVF armoured car company and one section of 63/81 Battery had gone beyond Milestone 11 at great speed, and not an ounce of store or equipment was left behind. But there was little luck after that. The camp perimeter was a long one, and the number of men to guard vital points in it was diminishing gradually on account of withdrawals. This enabled the Japanese to infiltrate at will. Meanwhile darkness was increasing, and visibility had diminished. Firing increased

---

[97] '1830 hours' is another version.

by about 1930 hours, and the Japanese created confusion by using ordinary fireworks such as crackers on all sides. They came in mass from the western boundary of the Volunteer Camp and started hand-to-hand fighting with bayonets, pistols and tommy guns.[98] Very soon the attack came also from the north and at close quarters.

Lucky was the Brigade Headquarters staff which was able to depart in the midst of this noise and firing. Then followed a section of guns at the water tower, the last batch of heavy lorries and two armoured cars. But the fighting on the aerodrome continued to rage fiercely. B Company of 2/12 Frontier Force Regiment had by this time become engaged, though not at close quarters. It was originally at the northern extremity some five hundred yards from the camp, but, as the fighting developed, it had come nearer. 'In this action Lieut-Colonel Cumming, 2 Frontier Force Regiment behaved with the greatest gallantry, for which he was subsequently awarded the Victoria Cross'.[99] Meanwhile, the Japanese climbed up trees and plastered the tracks and pathways with fire and they also occupied all vacant buildings and trenches in the area, although grenades and other weapons caused heavy casualties to them. The slaughter was terrible. But as night advanced the fighting became less intense, and the Japanese occupied the aerodrome at midnight.

The course of the brigade after the midnight of 3 January 1942 was comparatively peaceful. The Japanese did not disturb it either by land or from air. After crossing the Pahang by the Jerantut ferry, the brigade scattered; 2/18 Royal Garhwal Rifles proceeding to Raub, 2/12 Frontier Force Regiment to the Gap and 5/11 Sikh to Betong, and this crossing of the last man and the last vehicle in the early hours of 7 January 1942 brought the Kuantan operations to an end.

It has been said that the Japanese made two serious mistakes in these operations: one was that they underestimated the British artillery and lost one or two thousand men on the whole, and the other was that the British line of communications was not cut off before 3 January 1942.[100] This is true. But the British too made a few serious mistakes: the Brigade Commander, the man on the spot, was overruled in tactical matters; the British High Command was mistaken in expecting the Japanese to attack by sea; the Royal Air Force did not lift one finger to encourage the

---

[98] War Diary, General Staff Headquarters, 9 Indian Division, 10.30 hours, 4 January 1942.
[99] Brigadier G.W.A. Painter; Personal Account. p. 17.
[100] Captain D.G. Russell-Roberts: The Kuntan Operations, pp. 36 and 41.

land force, and the local civil population was ignored. The Japanese created a few surprises: they moved almost crawling and unseen at night, they produced a small arms bullet of ·256 calibre made of hard steel and enclosed in brass against which the British armoured cars were not impervious.

THE BREAKDOWN OF THE LINE OF COMMUNICATION AREA

The next phase in the struggle for Central Malaya related to the breakdown of the lines of communication and the fall of Kuala Lumpur into Japanese hands. This area was of immense strategic importance and the hub of the main communications of Malaya. But the vastness of the area and inadequacy of its defences led General Wavell to the decision to withdraw from this region. When he saw the nature of the country and the condition of British troops on 8 January 1942, he decided to give up its defence. He has recorded his reasons as follows:—' I visited the Malayan front on January 8, the forward troops being then 35 miles north of Kuala Lumpur. The Japanese had broken through their position on the Slim River on the previous day, and the two forward brigades were reduced to a handful of very tired men. After seeing the troops and their commanders down to Brigade Commanders, I came to the conclusion that the 3rd Indian Corps, which had now been fighting and retreating continuously for a month, was of little further fighting value without a rest; and that it would soon disappear altogether if the present policy of gradual withdrawal was followed, especially since the country south of Kuala Lumpur was not suitable for delaying action. I at once issued orders to General Heath....to cover Kuala Lumpur for as long as possible without awaiting full-scale enemy attack, and to impose the maximum delay on the enemy by extensive demolitions. I informed him that I proposed to withdraw the Indian Corps to Johore to rest and refit '.[101]

He continues: ' After discussion with Lieut.-General Percival, General Officer Commanding, Malaya, and with Major-General Gordon Bennett,....I laid down on January 9th, the following general plan for the defence of Malaya:—(a) 3rd Indian Corps, after delaying the enemy north of Kuala Lumpur for as long as possible (I did not think this was likely to be longer than January 11th), to be withdrawn by rail and road into Johore, leaving sufficient mobile rearguards to cover the demolition scheme. (b) 8th Australian Division, less one brigade group in Mersing area

[101] Despatch Operations in South-West Pacific. January 15th—February 25th, 1942 by General Sir Archibald Wavell, G. C. B., C.M.G., M.C., A.=D.=C. para 6 p. 1.

on Eastern coast, to move forthwith to north western frontier of Johore and to prepare to fight a decisive battle on the general line Segamat—Mount Ophir—mouth of Muar river. The brigade group in Mersing area to join the remainder of 8th Australian Division as soon as it could be relieved by troops from Singapore Island. (c) The 9th Indian Division, to be made up from the freshest troops of 3rd Indian Corps and 45th Indian Infantry Brigade (which had lately arrived in Malaya from India, and was now in Malacca), to be placed under General Gordon Bennett for use in the southern portion of the position indicated in (b) above. (d) 8th Australian Division as soon as possible to send forward mobile detachments to relieve the rearguards of 3rd Indian Corps and to harass the enemy and delay him by demolitions. (e) 3rd Indian Corps on withdrawal to take over responsibility for east and west coasts of Johore south of the road Mersing—Kluang—Batu Pahat, leaving General Gordon Bennett free to fight the battle in north-west Johore. 3rd Indian Corps was to rest and to refit 11th Indian Division and to organise a general reserve from reinforcements as they arrived'.[102]

This plan allowed the Japanese to come to the northern boundary of Johore without opposition, and certain risks were taken on the east coast by substituting the Australian brigade group by troops less familar with the ground. But the merits outweighed these defects. The new plan strengthened the western side of Johore which was immediately threatened, limited the Japanese lines of advance to the Segamat-Muar river line on the left, to impenetrable jungle on the right and the sea on the extreme left, and placed full responsibility on General Gordon Bennett's shoulders for the success of defence in this area. General Wavell hoped that the Royal Air Force and the Royal Navy would play their parts as fully as possible in giving close support.

The idea before General Wavell was appointed as head of American, British, Dutch and Australian Command was to hold this area at least for a week or ten days, until the reinforcements arrived and were distributed in different fields of action. The first reinforcement convoy reached Singapore on 3 January 1942, and it brought the 45th Indian Infantry Brigade commanded by Brigadier Duncan, and along with it a pioneer battalion which was a non-combatant labour unit. This brigade was sent at once to the Malacca—Jasin area to get familiar with local conditions and

---

[102] *Ibid.* Para 7. See also War Diary, General Headquarters Far East Appendices Nos. 405 and 504, and *"ABDACOM" An Official Account of Events in the South-West Pacific Command. January-February* 1942, p. 30. According to General Percival the line mentioned in (e) was Endau-Kluang-Batu Pahat, vide, *The War in Malaya, op. cit.*, p. 209.

the Malayan jungle. On 5 January 1942, an important conference was held at Segamat, which was attended also by the representatives of the Australian army. At that meeting, a gradual withdrawal to and the defence of Johore were decided upon. General Percival has said that ' the plan in outline was that the 3rd Indian Corps was to fall back slowly by the west coast roads and take up a position on the general line Segamat-Muar, while the Australian Imperial Force remained responsible for the defence of the east coast '.[103] The river line from Segamat to Muar was tactically excellent, because the Muar river was crossed only by one railway and two road bridges, all of them near Segamat. Between that place and the sea, the river was crossed only by a vehicle ferry at Muar where it was several hundred yards wide. It was " decided to site the defences on the south bank of the river so as to make the best use of the water obstacle"[104] and the swampy valleys on its tortuous course. The conference discussed also the danger of Japanese invasion of Singapore Island from the western side and decided to ask the commander of the Singapore Fortress to strengthen his defences on that side. It settled a few minor questions like sending the 45th Indian Infantry Brigade to Muar, continuing the role of the III Indian Corps to defend the west coast and creating a line of communication area for Johore.

But these earlier decisions were nullified by the disaster at Slim river and General Wavell's new plan. General Percival has observed that ' the main difference between this plan and the original one was that the State of Johore, instead of being divided longitudinally so that each force would be in depth and fall back on its own communications, was now divided laterally. The new plan also involved the temporary splitting up of the Australian Imperial Force which I had been doing my utmost to avoid. All the same, I do not see how any better plan could have been evolved in the circumstances as they existed at the time '.[105] The principal merit of the plan, however, was that the person on whom the heavy burden of defence lay, viz. Major-General Gordon Bennett, had approved of it and he could be depended upon to discharge his duty efficiently and enthusiastically. Another merit of General Wavell's plan was that it involved the necessity of strengthening the defence on the north side of Singapore Island while the Japanese were held up in Johore area. These defences were ordered to be put in hand at once.[106]

[103] *The War in Malaya*, p. 208.
[104] *Idem.*
[105] *Ibid.* p. 210.
[106] Wavell's *Despatch*. Para 9, p. 2.

A slight modification, probably to suit General Gordon Bennett's personal wishes,[107] was made in the plan on 10 January 1942, at another conference at Segamat. It was then decided that the main line of resistance should be on the general line Batu Anam-Muar, as the large open area astride the road near Batu Anam offered excellent field for the artillery and there was also much scope for ambushes. Further, two infantry battalions from the garrison of the Singapore Fortress were ordered to the mainland, 2/17 Dogra attached to the 2nd Malaya Infantry Brigade to the east coast and 2 Garhwal attached to the 1st Malaya Infantry Brigade, less one company, to the Segamat area.

There was to be no withdrawal beyond the line Segamat-Muar without the personal permission of Lieutenant-General Percival, who felt that as the area of fighting was restricted he could exercise a more direct personal control over all operations than had hitherto been possible. This line, connected with the other one along the Endau river, was the last defence line the Commonwealth forces might hold to save Singapore, and no risks were to be taken to preserve this line from being broken by the Japanese.

But in war nothing is more difficult than withdrawal while in contact. In Central Malaya the 11th Indian Division and Line of Communication Brigade were too deeply involved in the struggle with the Japanese to be able to disconnect themselves without some loss.

Meanwhile Selangor was also affected. There the first hint of the coming Japanese attack was received when, on 1 January 1942, Port Swettenham was attacked severely from the air and Klang marshalling yard was also bombed by Japanese planes. On 2 January 1942, a Japanese force attempted a landing at Kuala Selangor; but the British artillery set a small steamer on fire, sank four barges and drove off the rest towards the north. It was now clear that this part of Malaya, from Kuala Selangor to Malacca, known as the Line of Communication Area, and under Brigadier Moir's command, was open to attack by sea and land, and also by air. A complete reorganisation of the defence was an immediate necessity, therefore. At the commencement of hostilities the Line of Communication Area was responsible for the coastal defence of Selangor and Negri Sembilan, and the troops to whom the job was assigned were those of FMSVF Brigade—1 Perak, 2 Selangor, 3 Negri Sembilan and 4 Pahang Battalions, and Kedah and Kelantan Voluntary Forces with

---

[107] *Why Singapore Fell*, p. 81.

auxiliary units. Actually the second and the third of these units were the only two in service within this area. The points guarded were Kuala Lumpur and its aerodrome, Port Swettenham, Port Dickson, Kuala Selangor, and Kapar. By 2 January 1942, 73 Field Battery, 272 Anti-tank Battery and 3 Cavalry (less B Squadron) had come into this area, and 3/17 Dogra Regiment had also been brought into it. This last battalion was sent to Puchong area, while 3 Cavalry was placed in Morib-Sepang and Dingkil section. When the Japanese attempted a landing, as stated already, at Kuala Selangor, there was a minimum of force yet at that point, and it was FMSVF Battery and a troop of 73 Field Battery which drove off the Japanese ships on that day. On 3 January 1942, the Japanese vessels were still near Kuala Selangor while their fighter patrols machine-gunned from the air all British movements throughout the day. The attack by Blenheims on numerous small boats off Port Swettenham was ineffective.[108] On 4 January 1942, the situation at Kuala Selangor became really serious, as many hundreds of Japanese troops landed in the area and infiltration was suspected into the area north east of Batang Berjuntai.[109]

This threat had to be met by a redisposition of the Commonwealth troops.[110] 2/9 Jat was spread over a wide area with battalion headquarters at Kuala Selangor, and its companies respectively at Kuala Selangor, Klang, Jeram, and Batang Berjuntai. The machine-gun company was at Jeram beach, 3 Cavalry was at Kapar but one of its squadrons was at Kuala Selangor with a volunteer 18-pounder Field Battery.[111] In the evening, however, 3 Cavalry was moved to Batang Berjuntai and Bukit Robinson road junction, and 464 Field Battery, which arrived from Kuantan, was sent to Port Dickson, except one troop sent to Morib. There were a few other unit movements, the Independent Company going to Port Swettenham and 2 Selangor Battalion to Dingkil area. In the night of 4/5 January 1942,[112] a Japanese cyclist force of nearly 800 men engaged the defenders at a place eight miles north of Kuala Selangor along the coast and this necessitated the movement of the 15th Indian Infantry Brigade on 5 January 1942 into the Line of Communication Area.[113] The 15th Indian Infantry Brigade had under its command 2/9 Jat, 1/8 Punjab, 3/17 Dogra,

---

[108] Sir Paul Maltby's *Despatch*, p. 1374, para 284.
[109] War Diary, General Headquarters Far East, Appendix No. 447.
[110] *Ibid.*, Appendix No. 462A.
[111] War Diary, 2/9 Jat, 4 January 1942.
[112] Another version is 'During the afternoon of 4 January': War Diary, Headquarters Malaya Command, 7 January 1942.
[113] War Diary, Headquarters 12 Indian Infantry Brigade, 5 January 1942.

3 Cavalry (less B Squadron), 352 Field Battery and FMSVF Light Battery.

The situation continued to remain confused with Japanese pressure being exerted on the 15th Indian Infantry Brigade position. In consequence some troop redispositions were essential, particularly owing to the prime necessity of defending Kuala Lumpur. Thus, on the day that General Wavell visited this area, the troop dispositions in the sector were as follows:[114]

1. *The trunk road*—occupied by the remnants of 28th and 12th Indian Infantry Brigades.

   At Tanjong Malim, 2/16 Punjab, B Battery of 155 Field Regiment and two troops of 2 Anti-Tank Battery.

   At Rasa, The 28th Indian Infantry Brigade with the strength of only one battalion, the rest of 155 Field Regiment, one troop of 2 Anti-Tank Battery, one troop of 215 Anti-Tank Battery, and 23 Field Company.

   In reserve, 425 shattered men of the 12th Indian Infantry Brigade, and B Squadron of 3 Cavalry.

2. *Selangor area*—occupied by the 15th Indian Infantry Brigade.

   In the Socfin Estate, 1/14 Punjab holding the south bank of S. Selangor.

   At Batang Berjuntai, the British Battalion (two miles west of the above).

   At Bt. Robinson, 3/16 Punjab.

   At Rawang, 3/17 Dogra.

   Artillery for these regiments—7 and 10 Mountain Batteries and 273 Anti-Tank Battery, 15 Field Company.

   Coastal road—At Kuala Selangor, Headquarters A and B Companies of 2/9 Jat, 4 Mountain Battery and Volunteer Light Battery.

   At Jeram, C company of the above regiment.

   At Kapar, B company of the same regiment, and headquarters and C company of 3 Cavalry.

3. *The Line of Communication Area*—occupied by FMSVF and others.

   At Klang and Port Swettenham—3 Negri Sembilan Battalion (the latter for Klang Aerodrome).

   At Kuala Lumpur—the rest of 3 Selangor Battalion (one company for aerodrome) a detachment of 14 Anti-Aircraft Battery. Armoured Car Company, FMSVF in reserve.

[114] History of 11th Indian Division in Malaya, Vol. II (Original), p. 319.

> South of the Port Swettenham—Kuala Lumpur Road-Puchong-Dingkil-Seremban-Morib. One company of 3/17 Dogra, the Independent Company of Roseforce, one squadron of 3 Cavalry, 88 Field Regiment, 272 Anti-Tank Battery.
>
> At Port Dickson and Sepang—Two companies of 2 Malaya Battalion, two platoons of 1 Perak Battalion, 278 Field Battery (122 Field Regiment).
>
> At Kajang—In reserve, 5/18 Royal Garhwal Rifles; one troop 16 Light Anti-Aircraft Battery.
>
> East Flank of the 11th Indian Division—22nd Indian Infantry Brigade in the area from the Gap to Raub, 8th Indian Infantry Brigade at the crossings over the Pahang at Jerantut and Temerloh.

The Headquarters of the 11th Indian Division was on that day at Batu Caves.

It will be clear from the above dispositions that the defence was well organised. All the roads to Kuala Lumpur were properly blocked, and if only the Royal Air Force and the Royal Navy could support and if the reinforcements also were had in time, the Japanese army might have been rolled back on the roads by which it had come so far. But this was not to be.

The adoption of General Wavell's plan eliminated confusion and half-hearted moves. Each division and brigade had its own programme of withdrawal, but in co-ordination with the others. The 11th Indian Division was to withdraw only after midnight of 10/11 January 1942. Its first bound was to Mantin, which was thirty-five miles south of Kuala Lumpur, and the number of demolitions on its route was to be as many as possible. 'It was hoped that the combination of big bounds and comprehensive demolitions would enable the division to shake off the pursuit after passing through Kuala Lumpur'.[115] The 9th Indian Division had to withdraw in conformity with the other division to Gemas by railway and by road via. Bentong, Kuala Pilah and Tampin. Withdrawal is never an easy operation and on each of the three fronts—north, north-west and west—the Commonwealth army suffered further losses in the course of it.

9 January 1942 passed off without any serious attack by the Japanese, but every hour was one of anxiety and watchfulness. Kuala Lumpur was about to fall into Japanese hands. The aerodrome was demolished at 1745 hours, and the wireless station closed down. Citizens were evacuating the town and streets

---

[115] *Ibid.*, p. 327.

presented a deserted appearance. Demolitions, strategic and tactical, were being carried out on all roads leading to the city, and scorched earth policy was being applied ruthlessly. At the same time backloading of stores was going on to the maximum working capacity of the railways. This had started even as early as 29 December 1941,[116] but "there were still vast quantities of military and civil stores there and in other parts of the area to be evacuated, which it was quite impossible to move. Pillars of smoke and flame rose into the sky as rubber factories, mine machinery, petrol, and oil stocks, were denied".[117] But the time at the disposal of the Malaya Command was only thirty-six hours, because the 11th Indian Division had been ordered to hold the Japanese away from Kuala Lumpur until midnight of 10/11 January 1942, and the Divisional Commander had fixed 1600 hours as the zero hour up to which all roads should be denied to the Japanese. Further, the 15th and 28th Indian Infantry Brigades and the Line of Communication Area battalions were to withdraw simultaneously using Rawang, S. Buloh and Klang as their respective key-points. These two brigades were to withdraw through Kuala Lumpur while the Line of Communication troops had to deny Batu Tiga while Kuala Lumpur was held; and each brigade was to withdraw only by the routes which had been prescribed for it. Their destinations for the first stage were: Mantin for the 12th Indian Infantry Brigade, Labu for the 15th Indian Infantry Brigade, and Sepang and Port Dickson for the Line of Communication troops. At the second stage the destinations were Tampin for the 28th Indian Infantry Brigade, Alor Gajah for the 15th Indian Infantry Brigade and Malacca for the Line of Communication troops.

Prior to the withdrawal, on 9 January 1942, the 28th Indian Infantry Brigade had been ordered to take up a front line position. Consequently 2/16 Punjab was at a point slightly north of Serendah (one thousand yards ahead of 2/2 Gurkha Rifles' bridgehead), 2/2 Gurkha Rifles (with which 2/1 Gurkha Rifles had been amalgamated) occupied a reserve position to the south of the same village, and 2/9 Gurkha Rifles held the right sector, while 3/17 Dogra Regiment occupied the left sector of the main position, which was approximately one mile behind Serendah village. 5/11 Sikh, which ought to have joined this brigade, was ordered to go to the 15th Indian Infantry Brigade which was reported to be hard-pressed by the Japanese. There was good artillery support for the brigade, 4·5-inch howitzers at Serendah and 25-pounder guns at

---

[116] War Diary, III Indian Corps, 29 December 1941.
[117] *The War in Malaya*, p. 210.

Rawang. But throughout the day there was little contact with the Japanese. Only during the afternoon there was a slight patrol skirmish between 2/16 Punjab and the forward elements of the Japanese, resulting in mortar fire on the former and their slight withdrawal up to almost the north bank of the Serendah river.

In the area occupied by the 15th Indian Infantry Brigade, 1/14 Punjab suffered disaster. It was attacked very early in the morning, and the situation remained obscure during the rest of the day. But the tired and weakened battalion was in fact overrun and practically ceased to be an operational battalion. But for this tragedy, all battalions in this large area enjoyed an uneventful day—the British battalion at Milestone 27 on the S. Buloh road, 3/16 Punjab at Kuang, and 5/11 Sikh and 4 Mountain Battery at the road junction six miles west of Rawang and east of Batu Arang. In the Line of Communication Area also there were no serious developments although the Japanese were active and growing strong in numbers. In the evening a patrol belonging to C Squadron of 3 Cavalry was ambushed north of Kapar and an armoured car was destroyed. Later, 2/9 Jat (except B and D Companies) was withdrawn slightly to the north of Klang due to Japanese fire. It must also be mentioned that, during the afternoon of this day, the Brigadier moved to Morib the following units to defend the area against Japanese landings: A Squadron of 3 Cavalry (C Squadron being still with B and D Companies of 2/9 Jat), the detached company of 3/17 Dogra Regiment, the Independent Company, Roseforce and 464 Field Battery (in addition to 351 Field Battery). There were also slight moves of other local units. These appeared to be rather ominous, because a large portion of the Line of Communication Area troops had been removed from Klang area and Klang was in danger of being occupied by the Japanese. But it was made clear to 2/9 Jat that Klang bridge must be held at all costs until 10 January 1942, the next day.

It was also decided on 9 January 1942, that in view of the threat to the west coast and the possibility of the Japanese pressing eastward towards Kuala Lumpur by one of the roads from west, the 11th Indian Division must clear through Kuala Lumpur during the night of 10/11 January 1942.

During the night of 9/10 January 1942, the 12th Indian Infantry Brigade and 5/14 Punjab moved to the Mantin Pass; the British Battalion and 3/16 Punjab occupied S. Buloh cross-roads and Kuang road junction respectively; and 2/16 Punjab crossed the bridge across the Serendah river under pressure from the Japanese.

10 January was fixed for withdrawal, which, in spite of heavy opposition, started well. On the trunk road the Japanese attacked D Company of 2/2 Gurkha Rifles and the remainder of 2/16 Punjab, but these two retired across the bridge and blew it up. 2/16 Punjab moved back through the brigade position to Milestone 22, just north of S. Choh village. But D Company stayed on, with the Japanese pressing on and outflanking it on the ground and dive-bombing from the air, and at 0900 hours Brigadier Selby reported contact in Serendah position. 2/2 Gurkha Rifles had to withdraw after close fighting amongst houses and gardens, but owing to continuous low flying and dive-bombing attacks it could not start moving until 1000 hours. The battalion arrived at S. Choh and took up its position at 1030 hours to the south of the river. The withdrawal of this battalion, however, helped the Japanese to attack 2/9 Gurkha Rifles and 3/17 Dogra Regiment in the main Serendah position at 0800 hours. The fighting continued for two hours. The 155th Field Regiment gave good support to 2/9 Gurkha Rifles. As the fixation of time for withdrawal was important these battalions were asked to withdraw after 1200 hours. They disengaged at 1220 hours with little trouble and arrived at Milestone 22 where 2/16 Punjab was in position. But S. Choh was then in the possession of the Japanese, and 2/2 Gurkha Rifles (in the south) and all other battalions of the 28th Indian Infantry Brigade (in the north) lost touch with each other owing to the infiltration of the Japanese between them. C Battery of the 155th Field Regiment withdrew in time, while the others were left behind. At about 1300 hours the Japanese attacked 2/2 Gurkha Rifles from the west and on D Company's front heavy fighting took place for a short time.

The other battalions arrived and opened attacks upon the Japanese, but had to fall back when faced with the danger of getting trapped themselves. 2/9 Gurkha Rifles 'moved north-westwards' and escaped destruction, but 3/17 Dogra Regiment was badly caught in the Japanese net. Its D Company entered the heart of the village which was full of the Japanese. 'From houses, from behind walls and hedges, from the trees and from the drains, they opened up a fusillade'[118] and decimated this company. Even B Company was gone and the rest of the battalion took shelter in the wilderness. Unfortunately, Brigadier Selby could get no news of this tragedy which was being staged in the north. The one attempt of Major North of 3/17 Dogra Regiment to make a dash through the Japanese lines in 2/2 Gurkha Rifles carrier failed miser-

---

[118] History of 11th Indian Division in Malaya, Vol. II (Original), p. 349.

ably, and there was therefore no news of the forward units. He, therefore, decided to withdraw, partly to conform with the general plan and partly to escape Japanese enveloping movements on his own flanks. The Japanese were still active overhead with dive-bombing in front and rear of the brigade position, and they were dropping pamphlets too from their planes. At 1500 hours some 3/17 Dogra and 2/16 Punjab carriers made a rush through and managed to arrive at 2/2 Gurkha position. But at about 1530 hours this last battalion withdrew under orders as far as Rawang, taking advantage of cover provided by the rubber trees. Here, the position allotted to it was about two miles further to the south. During this time it was noticed that 2/9 Gurkha Rifles, 2/16 Punjab and 3/17 Dogra had passed through this position on their way to the Kanchin Pass. 2/2 Gurkha Rifles was the last to leave Rawang position, acting as rearguard to the brigade which was in turn the rearmost force on the road. Motor transport arrived after dark and carried the men off at about 2130 hours. Two officers and ten Gurkha other ranks remained behind with the Sapper demolition party and two platoons of B Company, while the rest of the battalion proceeded via Kuala Lumpur to Tampin. The demolitions took some time, and in all some ten or twelve road blocks or blowing of hill-sides on to the road were accomplished, but before the first bridge was blown at Rawang a number of stragglers and some wounded came in. The major party arrived in Tampin area in the early morning of 11 January 1942, and the demolition party reached later in the day. The 155th Field Regiment proceeded to Alor Gajah which was its harbour area.

The 15th Indian Brigade was moving on the central roads, and during the night of 9/10 January Brigadier Moorhead had adjusted his dispositions by withdrawing 5/11 Sikh to the road junction on the Socfin road, five miles west of Rawang, and concentrating the whole of the British battalion at the Batu Arang road junction on the Batang Berjuntai road. He moved his own headquarters and B Company of 1/14 Punjab nearer Rawang.[119] The route of withdrawal of this brigade was Kundang-Kuang-S. Buloh-Kuala Lumpur-Labu. Its troops commenced withdrawal at about 1400 hours on 10 January and moved towards Kundang road junction held by 5/11 Sikh. The Japanese were then harassing this battalion from Bt. Rantau but the unit was well supported by 4 Mountain Battery. They withdrew through Kuang road junction held by 3/16 Punjab and embussed for Labu. 3/16 Punjab passed through the British Battalion at S. Buloh cross-roads

[119] *Ibid.*

and thence to Labu. The British Battalion with 10 Mountain Battery withdrew at about 2100 hours and reached Kuala Lumpur at about 2300 hours. There it waited for its rearguard until 0430 hours. Afterwards, the battalion blew up the main road bridge in the capital town and went to Labu with one company less which acted as rearguard covering demolitions on the way and reaching Labu in the afternoon of the next day. This brigade had provided the rearguard for the withdrawal of the 11th Indian Division through Kuala Lumpur, which was completed in the early hours of 11 January 1942.

Being very near the sea coast and having several roads running to it, Klang was naturally an important objective for the Japanese. The British too placed great store on the defence of Klang bridge, and ordered it 'to be held at all costs until 11 January'. 2/9 Jat, 3 Negri Sembilan Battalion and 73 Field Battery and one company of 2 Selangor were assigned this task. The plan of defence was that A and C Companies of 2/9 Jat were to be in the north (on the right bank of the river) and B and D Companies with C Squadron of 3 Cavalry held the two roads from the north at points two miles each from the town and at the junctions with the lateral road, 3 Negri Sembilan was in the south of the town. B Company of 2 Selangor remained within the town, initially to protect it against loot and later to guard the Estate road three miles on the way to Batu Tiga, and 73 Field Battery was to the south of the river to support the bridge-head troops. This force might have achieved the purpose of defending Klang until the prescribed hour; but the troops were all weary after a move and a counter-move throughout a wet night, and the Japanese were closely pressing on their heels. Fighting began almost as day dawned. At about 1000 hours there was contact with the Japanese on both the roads in the north. By noon, they had infiltrated and outflanked B and C Companies. C Company counter-attacked, but was surrounded by the Japanese and compelled to lay down its arms. However, the defence remained strong in spite of this loss of men and arms. 73 Field Battery worked hard to maintain the position intact. Surprisingly enough, the Japanese appeared hesitant and lacking in their usual *elan*. A war-diarist has recorded as follows: 'This was a minor success for the enemy which he made no effort to exploit, but shortly afterwards about 120 enemy were seen advancing down the road from Kapar on bicycles 5 abreast. They were engaged by the artillery (and) automatics and suffered at least 75 % casualties. Later a similar advance was made down the other road with equally successful results for our forces. After these set-backs the enemy did not show signs of advancing further on the battalion front, but a strong party had now appeared in front of the company of 2 Selangor Battalion which had not the advantage of artillery support'.[120] The Klang bridge was thus saved, and Klang could be held until dusk according to plan.

Sometime in the afternoon Line of Communication Area Brigade issued the Operation Order No. 16, dated 10 January 1942. It laid down that the Japanese advance must be contested all the way, Testerforce was to join up with Jamesforce at Batu Tiga, which must be held at all costs until the 11th Division had cleared Kuala Lumpur at midnight. Four phases of withdrawal were marked out: (A) Richforce to withdraw by Telok Datok, Morib, Batu Laut and Sepang; (B) Jamesforce to hold Batu Tiga; (C) Testerforce to withdraw by Puchong, Kg. Dingkil, Telok Datok, Morib and Sepang; (D) Roseforce to withdraw to Tanah Merah. All non-fighting troops and B Echelon transport were to go to Port Dickson, and all troops other than Roseforce were to harbour at Port Dickson. 3 Negri Sembilan was made responsible for blowing up the Klang bridge.

Klang was cleared successfully by 1830 hours. The withdrawal of the main force towards Batu Tiga proceeded satisfactorily with one flank exposed to the Japanese, and it was on foot lest the noise of motor engines might lead to detection and attack. 2/9 Jat was badly in need of some rest, but "There now began a third night in which the battalion was forced to move, and this after being in contact with enemy all day. The evening meal had not been issued as it was hoped to be able to get it on arrival at Batu Tiga. The men were tired, wet and hungry".[121] But worse was in store for them. At about 2000 hours, 3 Cavalry (less A and B Squadrons) and 2/9 Jat were successively caught in an ambush near Milestone 20. Firing was going on intermittently and terror was heightened by the pitch-dark, rain-lashed jungle and by the yells of the invisible Japanese. Sounds of crashing and rushing threw the troops into panic and the units disintegrated. Some parties reached the railway and the Klang river and arrived at Batu Tiga at about 0200 hours, and among them were the commanders of both the units. Their object was to send lorries or armoured cars to the spot of ambush or thereabout and bring the men to Batu Tiga. But the bridge west of Batu Tiga had been blown, and Jamesforce was in no shape to counter-attack on the Klang road. Further, in the early hours of the 11th morning, news arrived at Batu Tiga that the 15th Indian

[120] War Diary, 2/9 Jat, 10 January 1942.
[121] Ibid.

Infantry Brigade would withdraw through Kuala Lumpur and 2 Selangor Battalion withdrew at once from Batu Tiga. The withdrawal of the remainder of the Line of Communication troops was uneventful. 3 Negri Sembilan withdrew from Klang, after blowing up the bridge at 1930 hours. 2 Selangor withdrew from Batu Tiga Sepang through Kg. Dingkil and Salak to avoid the Japanese at Morib. And the rest of 3 Cavalry (less A and B Squadrons) went to Labu.

"So ended the stand north of Kuala Lumpur. The Division had fulfilled its appointed task and it had not been trapped. But the cost had been heavy".[122]

The rest of the withdrawal was dull and monotonous. The next stage was Tampin-Alor Gajah-Malacca, to be reached during the night of 12/13 January 1942, and after one day on that line the 11th Indian Division was to pass through the Westforce to Johore area. General Percival remarked that "by the fourteenth all troops of the 3rd Indian Corps had passed through the forward troops of Westforce and the command of the forward area passed to Gordon Bennett. Heath assumed responsibility for south and east Johore at 8 P.M. on the same day. During the withdrawal, demolitions were carried out on all roads. In particular gaps were blown in all bridges over what might constitute an anti-tank obstacle, but as usual they did not seem to impose any great delay on the enemy".[123]

On 11 January 1942, the army was disposed as follows: The 12th Indian Infantry Brigade, with which 5/14 Punjab was attached, was at Mantin Pass,[124] supported by 352 Field Battery and 7 Mountain Battery. The 15th Indian Infantry Brigade was in Labu area supported by 22 Mountain Regiment (less 7 Mountain Battery). To the west of this brigade stood the Line of Communication Area brigade covering the coast road, and 5/18 Royal Garhwal Rifles and the Independent Company held the line of the Sepang river. The artillery with the Line of Communication troops consisted of the Federated Malaya States Volunteer Force Light Battery, 88 Field Regiment (less 352 Field Battery) and 73 Field Battery (5 Field Regiment). The 28th Indian Infantry Brigade moved to Tampin, and the 45th Indian Infantry Brigade was in Malacca area with 7/6 Rajputana Rifles at Muar. The Malays in Federated Malaya States Volunteer Force units

---

[122] History of 11th Indian Division in Malaya, Vol. II (Original). Also Wavell's *Despatch*, p. 4, para 14.
[123] *The War in Malaya*, p. 213.
[124] Another version is Setul: War Diary, 12th Indian Infantry Brigade, 11 January 1942.

were permitted to lay down arms,[125] resign and go home if they felt they should do so in their own interest, and many of them took advantage of this permission. On the east flank, the 9th Indian Division was moving back from Bentong to Kuala Pilah in conformity with the 11th Indian Division's withdrawal so as not to expose the right flank of this division. Conversely, the withdrawal of the latter had to be so arranged as to enable the former to withdraw most carefully and through well defined routes.[126] The formation of Westforce was notified on this date.

12 January 1942 was another uneventful day, although the Japanese had come as far as Kajang with three tanks and twelve lorries. The day was however spent in pulling back the units to the next stage viz. Tampin-Alor Gajah-Malacca.[127] The 12th Indian Infantry Brigade alone had to go to Singapore early on the morning of 13 January from Gemas. The 15th Indian Infantry Brigade was to move to Alor Gajah, with 5/11 Sikh going to Jasin. The Line of Communication Area troops were to move back to Malacca area, the 45th Indian Infantry Brigade proceeding back to Muar. The units of the 28th Indian Infantry Brigade spread themselves in the Tampin area; 2/2 Gurkha Rifles north of Tampin, 2/9 Gurkha Regiment with the carrier platoon of 3/17 Dogra Regiment at Kendong Gate road junction further north of Tampin, 3/16 Punjab at the level crossing on Kendong Gate-Alor Gajah road, and 1/14 Punjab a few miles west of Tampin on Tampin-Alor Gajah road. The artillery was distributed conveniently; 23 Mountain Regiment at Tangkak, 38 Field Regiment (less 352 Field Battery) at Tampia, 73 Field Battery (5 Field Regiment) at Tangkak and Federated Malay States Volunteer Force Light Battery at Malacca. 88 Field Regiment (less 352 Field Battery) was allotted for the support of the 28th Indian Infantry Brigade. All withdrawals were made between the evening and the early morning of 12 and 13 January respectively, mostly between the hours of darkness.

General Percival gave some particulars of other aspects of this great withdrawal to Major-General Paris, the commander of the 11th Indian Division. They were: the final position Segamat-Muar to be held at the latest in the evening of 14 January 1942; 15 Field Company to go to Johore and come under Corps control; Line of Communication Headquarters and all volunteer units to get back to Singapore; the Independent Company and 3

[125] War Diary, General Staff Branch of Headquarters 9th Indian Division, 12 January 1942.
[126] *Ibid.*, 9 January 1942.
[127] The details of disposition vary. Those that are given here are according to Major E. F. D. Hyde.

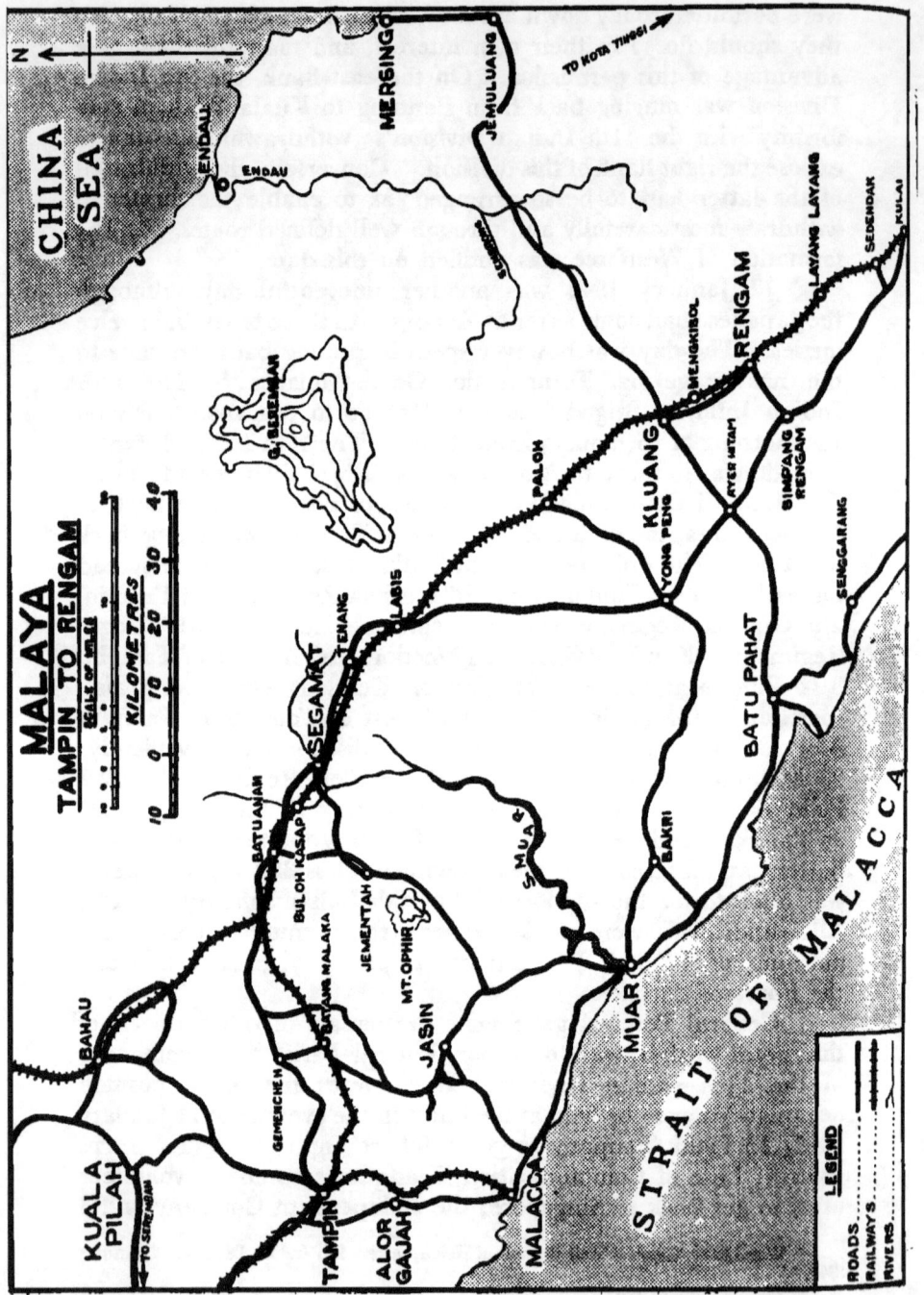

Cavalry to go to Batu Pahat at once with Batu Pahat-Pontian Kechil area under Corps control; D Company of 2 Malaya Regiment to Koris aerodrome (eight miles south of Batu Pahat) and the 28th Indian Infantry Brigade (less 2/16 Punjab) to Pontian Kechil; and the remainder of the 11th Indian Division to Rengam-Kluang area. The Kluang aerodrome was to be guarded by 2/9 Jat which would come under the command of the 22nd Australian Brigade.

The withdrawal of the 11th Indian Division and its companion, the 9th Indian Division, continued without serious interference in the next few days so that the III Indian Corps retired to the Johore area as defined by General Wavell.

By the evening of 14 January 1942, it had completed its withdrawal. The 28th Indian Infantry Brigade moved to harbour in the Socfin Estate at Chaah near Labis. The 15th Indian Infantry Brigade went to Kluang area. The Line of Communication Area troops went to different places: Federated Malay States Volunteer Force units to Singapore, the armoured car company and light battery to Pontian Kechil and 5/18 Royal Garhwal Rifles to Muar. The artillery distributed itself as follows: 88 Field Regiment (less 352 Field Battery) to Segamat area, 352 Field Battery to Buloh Kasap area, 22 Mountain Regiment to Kluang area, 155 Field Regiment also to Kluang area and 73 Field Battery (5 Field Regiment) to Segamat area. Those which remained in Segamat area came under Westforce which was then formed.

General Wavell came to Segamat to meet Lieutenant-General Heath and Major-General Gordon Bennett on 13 January. He noticed that his plan of withdrawal and renewed defence was being put into execution but that the 9th and 11th Indian Divisions had suffered further losses in fighting north of Kuala Lumpur and 'the enemy's advance had been more rapid than I had hoped'.[128] At the same time he was hopeful that the Australians would stabilise the situation and smash the Japanese attacks, although he considered and cabled to the Chiefs of Staff that the battle for Singapore would be a " close run thing ".[129]

But his plan for the defence of Johore was otherwise ready, and the units had been deployed accordingly: 2/30 Australian Battalion ahead of Gemas (with one company some four miles ahead at a bridge over the Gemencheh river) to ambush the Japanese; a brigade of the 9th Indian Division with 2/26 Australian Battalion a little in advance and guarding the flanks between Batu Anam and Gemas; the other brigade of the 9th Indian Division

[128] Wavell's *Despatch*, p. 4, para 14.
[129] *Idem.*

to guard Segamat-Muar road near Jementah; and the 45th Indian Infantry Brigade to prevent the Japanese from crossing the river at Muar, with outposts across the river.

On 14 January 1942, Major-General Paris the commander of the 11th Indian Division was replaced by Major-General Key, because, as General Percival said, "at this stage Heath represented to me that an Indian Army Officer was required to pull together and re-establish confidence in what remained of the 11th Indian Division".[130] Major-General Paris rejoined the 12th Indian Infantry Brigade at Singapore, and Brigadier Lay was leading the 8th Indian Infantry Brigade.

On 15 January 1942, Major-General Key took over the command of the 11th Indian Division, while Colonel Challen—took charge of the 15th Indian Infantry Brigade and Brigadier Moorhead resumed command of 3/16 Punjab. The new divisional commander held a conference of commanding officers at Kahang and decided on rest and close order drill followed by intensive training for a period of eleven days. 2/9 Jat relieved the Australian Imperial Force company at Kahang in the afternoon of this day,[131] and 5/14 Punjab and 1 Bahawalpur State Infantry were allotted to Kluang for aerodrome duty. The 15th Indian Infantry Brigade was warned that it should be ready for operations at Kluang, Ayer Hitam or Yong Peng.

The war in central Malaya was over by 15 January. The formations of the III Indian Corps were then disposed as under:—

Headquarters III Indian Corps	Johore Bahru
Headquarters 11th Indian Division	Rengam
6/15 Indian Infantry Brigade and 11th Divisional Artillery	Kluang
28th Indian Infantry Brigade	Pontian Kechil
3 Cavalry, Independent Company and one Company Malay Regiments	Batu Pahat

While this chapter was closing, reinforcements arrived at Singapore. On 13 January 1942, 53rd Infantry Brigade Group arrived at the Naval Base, and the 35th Light and the 6th Heavy Anti-Aircraft Regiments at Keppel Harbour,[132] and fifty Hurricane fighters with their crew also reached at the same time. It is said that 'on arrival the troops were healthy but soft'.[133] Their equipment was not old and familiar. They had no guns or transport. Above all they were ignorant of Jungle warfare in

---

[130] *The War in Malaya*, pp. 213-214.
[131] War Diary, 2/9 Jat, 15 January 1942.
[132] War Diary, Headquarters Malaya Command, 13 January 1942.
[133] Percival's *Despatch* para 332.

the Malayan style. On 14 and 15 January 1942, the detachment of Dutch Marechaussees reached Singapore by air from the Netherlands East Indies. Its strength was eighty all told with European officers, trained for jungle and guerilla warfare, and it was stationed in Labis area. With these new reinforcements and with rest for the tired veterans of the 11th Indian Division, the prospects for the next round in Malaya appeared distinctly better.

CHAPTER IX

The Stand in South Malaya

THE GENERAL SITUATION

The region lying between Singapore and the line Kempas-Tampin-Gemas-Endau was known as South Malaya. It consisted of Malacca, the state of Johore, and Singapore Island. Malacca and Singapore were directly administered by the British, while Johore, the largest of the three, was under its own Sultan.

The terrain in this area was generally flat, with the inevitable jungle and rubber plantations intervening between fields and swamps. The rivers, particularly the Muar, were long and winding and were navigable for small boats for many miles from their mouths. There were no big towns and only four minor seaports, namely, Bandar Maharani (Muar) and Batu Pahat (Bandar Penggaram) on the west coast, and Endau and Mersing on the east coast. Strategically, the most important line of communication was the road and railway running southwards from Gemas to Kluang and on to Singapore. The importance of this route was enhanced by there being no bridge on the Muar river near Bandar Maharani—the ferry that crossed the wide Muar at that place imposed considerable delays even on normal peace-time traffic. The subsidiary road from Tampin to Bandar Maharani and Batu Pahat joined the main road at Ayer Hitam, which was the hub of road communications in the area. From Ayer Hitam a road went north to Segamat and Gemas; another went east to Kluang on the railway and onwards to Mersing and Endau on the coast; and a third road joined Ayer Hitam to Johore Bahru on the mainland opposite Singapore Island, apart from the road, mentioned already, linking Ayer Hitam with Batu Pahat. Of rail tracks there was only one in the region going from Gemas to Johore Bahru via Segamat, Labis and Kluang. Apart from these strategically important lines of communication, there were two positions of considerable defensive strength. One was known as the Defile and lay on the road Yong Peng to Parit Sulong. For its first six miles the road ran through a belt of rubber trees flanked by a marsh; it then crossed a quarter-mile causeway, and continued along an embankment dead straight for $1\frac{1}{4}$ miles before climbing a forested slope to a small pass. On either side of the pass rose two steep hills, and both overlooked the straight stretch of road. Beyond this Defile, the road was flanked by jungle and ridges and rose steadily, finally over Pt. Payong Saddle, three miles to the north-west. The second strong defensive position was the road running from Endau to Mersing. This stretch was flanked on either side by swamp that was considered impassable.

The geographical features described above were very advantageous to the Malaya Command whose object was to impose the maximum delay on the Japanese in order to give time to the reinforcements which were coming to reach Singapore. On 24 January 1942, General Wavell reported to the Combined Chiefs of Staff that his intention was to hold a line in Johore as long as possible. If the reinforcements due in Singapore in the next two days arrived safely, the situation should be improved.[1] The Allied troops in the forward areas had strict orders not to withdraw without clear permission from the High Command. According to Air Vice-Marshal Sir Paul Maltby, the directive to the air forces in Malaya in this period of the war laid down that " protection of convoys at present takes precedence over action against other Japanese forces. If, however, new expeditions are located threatening the east coast of Malaya or endeavouring to pass south of Singapore, all available air effort should be directed to destroying such targets ". The directive also stressed the importance of " slowing up the Japanese advance on land by attacking Singora, intervening in the land battle and of reducing the scale of Japanese air attack "[2]. On the other hand, the Japanese were intent on capturing Singapore on the earliest date possible. " The moral effect of an early fall of this so-called impregnable fortress upon both their own people and their enemies was one important point, as was also the desire of the Navy to secure possession of the naval base thus obtaining free passage of their ships through the Straits of Singapore....Moreover, the troops engaged in the siege of Singapore were badly needed for the campaign against the Netherlands East Indies which was now well under way, and for the campaign in the Philippines which was not progressing according to plan ". To achieve their objective the Japanese stepped up even further the strength and tenacity of their attacks. Exceptionally courageous by nature well trained and flushed with a series of brilliant successes, the Japanese troops hurled themselves in attacks after attacks irrespective of their own casualties or of the strength of their enemy. In the final stages of the war in Malaya, the deeds of heroism were many, particularly at Bakri and Mengkibol. At Bakri, a Japanese tank company was said to have refused all offers of help and gone

---

[1] Wavell's *Despatch*, Appendix A, p. 13.
[2] Sir Paul Maltby's *Despatch*, p. 1376 para 308.

forth into battle saying, "No. We will go by ourselves". At Mengkibol a Japanese unit commander asked his men to "give me your lives. From now, we are all going to die to the last man in the line of duty".[3] He was as good as his word, and the whole unit sacrificed itself in fanatical attacks soon after. The Japanese also received reinforcements regularly and three divisions were reported advancing along the front from Muar eastwards. Their engineers and armoured units had already distinguished themselves in the fighting in north and central Malaya, and in the south the Japanese bicycle units proved themselves equally formidable. On one occasion in particular these troops made their way through waist-high swamps under constant fire, holding aloft their bicycles. The Japanese also had the advantage of excellent information from the large numbers of their compatriots working in the plantations and towns in the area before the war and from a fairly active fifth column.

The Japanese plan was to attack the Muar-Gemas-Endau line with approximately three divisions. The *55th Infantry Regiment* (with two battalions only) was to advance from Kuantan to Endau and Mersing on the east coast. In the centre was the *5th Division*, strengthened by the *21st Infantry Regiment*, with orders to advance down the Gemas-Labis road. The *Imperial Guards Division* was placed at Malacca on the west coast, and was given the task of capturing Muar and advancing against Yong Peng and Batu Pahat.

Dispositions of the Units

By midday on 14 January 1942, dispositions of the Malaya Command were complete on the Muar-Gemas line. The force was organised in three groups, the Westforce, Eastforce and the 11th Indian Division. These were formed as follows:

Westforce
(1) The 27th Australian Imperial Force Brigade. 2/30 Battalion astride the main road at Milestone 62 (three miles west of Gemas) with one company four miles further forward at the S. Gemencheh to ambush the Japanese. 2/26 Battalion (less one company) in the Paya Lang Estate about four miles east of Gemas, one company covering the road and railway bridges over the Gemas.

[3] Enemy publication No. 278, pp. 133 and 146.

2/29 Battalion was intended to hold the Fort Rose Estate area south of the main road and about four miles east of Gemas, but actually it remained at Buloh Kasep in reserve.

(2) The 9th Indian Division.
   (a) The 8th Indian Infantry Brigade. 1/13 Frontier Force Rifles covered the road and the railway at Milestone 128 west of Batu Anam, with one company patrolling Batu Anam-Jementah road.
   3/17 Dogra Regiment guarded the road and railway at the bridges on the S. Muar near Buloh Kasap.
   (b) The 22nd Indian Infantry Brigade. 2/18 Royal Garhwal Rifles covered the Segamat-Jementah road about ten miles forward of Segamat. 5/11 Sikh stood at the junction of Batu Anam-Jementah-Segamat roads.
   2/12 Frontier Force Regiment guarded the bridge across the S. Muar about 6 miles from Segamat.
   (c) The 45th Indian Infantry Brigade. 4/9 Jat covered the line of the S. Muar from Lenga to Jorak village with two companies (A and C) on the northern side of the river on patrol.
   7/6 Rajputana Rifles were responsible for the line of the S. Muar from Jorak village to the coast at Muar. This battalion also had two companies (B and D) to patrol the northern parts of the river, B for the area north of Tanjong Olak and D for the Kesang area.
   5/18 Royal Garhwal Rifles acted as reserve on the Parit Jawa-Bakri road, with one company watching the coast between Muar and Batu Pahat.

The 11th Indian Division.
   (a) The 28th Indian Infantry Brigade. This comprised 2/9 Gurkha Rifles, the amalgamated 2/2 and 2/1 Gurkha Rifles and the remnants of 1/14 Punjab Regiment besides Federated Malaya States Volunteer Force Armoured Car Company and Federated Malaya States Volunteer Force Light Battery. It was responsible for Pontian Kechil area as far as Benut up the west coast.
   (b) The 15th Indian Infantry Brigade. This consisted of 1 Leicester/2 East Surrey, combined 3/16 and 2/16 Punjab, and combined 2/9 Jat and 1/8 Punjab.

It remained in Kluang as reserve but ready to operate in Batu Pahat, if necessary. At Batu Pahat there were 3 Cavalry, a company of 2 Malaya Regiment and one detachment of the Independent Company.

(c) Aerodrome defence troops. At Kluang, Bahawalpur State Infantry. At Koris, a detachment of Johore Military Force.

(d) 11th Indian Division Headquarters and administration troops in the Rengam Area.

Eastforce

(a) In the Endau area. One company each of 2/19 and 2/20 Battalions, the latter on the southern side of the mouth of the S. Endau and the former partly on the coast up to the S. Pontian and partly in Endau itself. There were a number of boats for movement on the river and two gun-boats at Endau.

(b) In the Mersing area. 2/18 Battalion, 2/20 Battalion (less one company in Endau area), and 2/10 Field Regiment (less one battery).

(c) In the Jemuluang area. 2/19 Battalion (less one company) and one battery of 2/10 Field Regiment.

(d) In the Mawai area. 2/17 Dogra Regiment (less one company) to guard the boom at the mouth of the S. Sedili and the detached one company to patrol the east coast road between Dohol and Jemaluang.

(e) At the Kahang aerodrome. One detachment of Johore Military Forces.

The headquarters of III Indian Corps was Johore Bahru.

The air situation was rather depressing. On the afternoon of 18 January 1942, when an appreciation was made, the state of serviceability of the Air Force in Malaya showed 74 bomber and general reconnaissance aircraft and 28 fighters, all based on Singapore with the exception of a small detachment at Kahang. Moreover, many of these aircraft were obsolete or obsolescent. Against these it was estimated that the Japanese were maintaining in Malaya at this time a force of 150 fighters and 250 bombers.[4] If the situation had to be saved the Royal Air Force needed, in

---

[4] Sir Paul Maltby's *Despatch* p. 1377, para 309. According to Royal Air Force sources the figures were 27 fighters and 55 bombers and ground attack planes, a total of 82 aircraft.

addition to the existing aircraft, four long range bomber squadrons and four long range fighter squadrons, each squadron with 12 aircraft, initial equipment.[5]

As regards sea-power, General Percival remarked "sea-power, supported by air power, had become..........one of the dominating factors in the situation—only this time it was the enemy and not we who held the trump cards".[6]

A word is necessary about the reinforcements. In Westforce, the only new elements were the Australian units and the 45th Indian Infantry Brigade. Of the former General Gordon Bennett said that they moved "forward into battle, happy and confident, giving the "thumbs-up" sign to any of their comrades they passed on the road",[7] and of the latter, General Percival has remarked that they "were very young, unseasoned and under-trained—unfit for service overseas".[8] Of the British soldiers included in the 53rd Infantry Brigade, the opinion was that they looked like square pegs in round holes, and "time was....required for the troops to become acclimatized".[9] All the troops, contained in the 9th and 11th Indian Divisions, were thin, weary and worn-out. There were but three thousand in the latter division with very defective and deficient weapons, and the 9th Indian Division was perhaps just sixty per cent of its total strength. On the other hand, the Japanese forces were well-trained, fresh and enthused with success. They had numerical superiority and new tanks; equipment was adequate; and air co-operation was ready and full. They had captured a lot of British arms and material already, which they were using to the greatest advantage.

THE MUAR SECTOR

The Japanese Attack

As already mentioned, Muar had been given as its objective to the *Imperial Guards Division*. Its commander, General Nishimura, began his drive southwards from Malacca with two regiments. *The 5th Guards Regiment* was on the left, with orders to cross the Muar river well to the east of Muar, and then wheel right and advance towards Bakri and Yong Peng, thus outflanking the garrison of Muar. *The 4th Guards Regiment* advanced directly on Muar, to pin down its defenders and give them no chance to withdraw before their line of communication was cut behind

---

[5] "*ABDACOM*", op. cit., p. 31.
[6] *The War in Malaya*, p. 220.
[7] *Why Singapore Fell*, p. 37.
[8] *The War in Malaya*, p. 207
[9] *Ibid.*, p. 217.

them by *5th Guards Regiment*.[10] After capturing Muar and annihilating the 45th Indian Infantry Brigade there, *5th Guards Regiment* was to advance on Yong Peng, while *4th Guards Regiment* continued its advance down the coastal road and attacked Batu Pahat. General Nishimura was so confident of the success of these moves that he sent a solitary battalion (*1/4th Guards Battalion*) by sea to land far down the coast, to the south of Batu Pahat, so that Batu Pahat also might be cut off from Pontian Kechil.

In accordance with these plans, the Japanese attack began on 15 January, although their bombers had been raiding Muar regularly for the past many days. Troops of *4th Guards Regiment* evaded and cut off the two companies of 7/6 Rajputana Rifles patrolling the north bank of the Muar river. They reached the ferry opposite Muar town, and opened medium machine-gun fire on the town across the river. They also succeeded in quickly obtaining a toe-hold on the south bank between the Advanced Headquarters and Rear Headquarters of the 45th Indian Infantry Brigade. Another attempt to cross the river at its mouth was detected in time, and artillery fire was opened against the boats 'sheltering in the lee of an island'. Under the direction of Major-General Bennett, Brigadier Duncan (45th Brigade) had spread out 7/6 Rajputana Rifles to guard some nine miles of the river front from the sea to Jorak; but some of its platoons were hastily collected to counter-attack the Japanese near the ferry. The situation before Muar town appeared well in hand on 15 January.

But, in the meanwhile, *5th Guards Regiment* had quietly crossed over the Muar river further east near S. Mati. Guarding that sector was 4/9 Jat, which also had been spread out on a front of about 15 miles. The Japanese, therefore, only encountered some weak patrols of the Jats, which were brushed aside. They marched rapidly south and, on 16 January, captured Simpang Jeram and cut the road between Muar and Bakri. The road between Bakri and Parit Jawa was also cut by cyclist and lorry-borne troops. On the same day, Japanese troops landed from boats far to the south, between Batu Pahat and Senggarang.

The Withdrawal from Muar

In the confused fighting that resulted from these moves, all the three battalions of the 45th Indian Infantry Brigade suffered heavy losses. The first to suffer loss was 5/18 Royal Garhwal Rifles. The commanding officer went at 0630 hours on 16 January to the Advanced Brigade Headquarters at Muar, and while he

---

[10] Draft of the Official British History, Vol. I, Part II, p. 452.

THE STAND IN SOUTH MALAYA

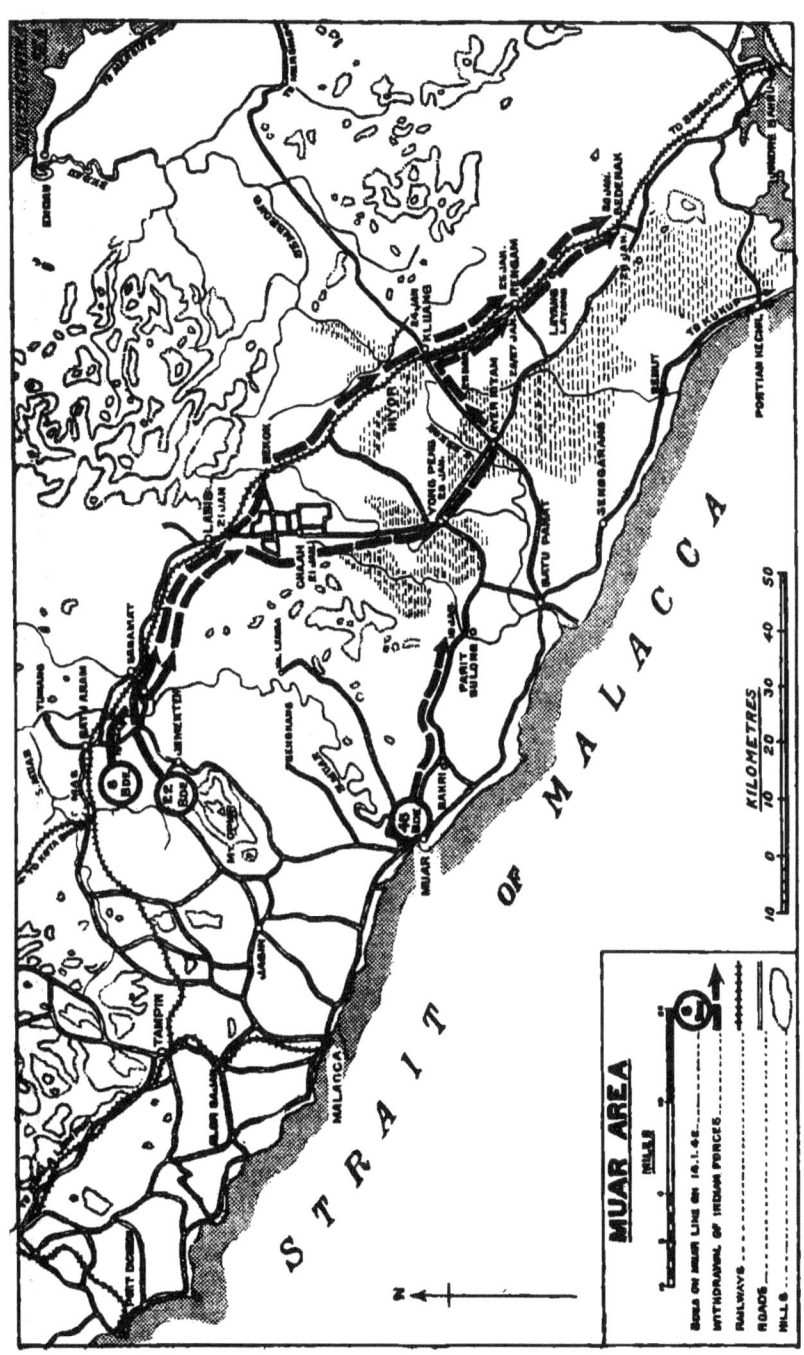

was returning from that place to his advanced battalion headquarters at Simpang Jeram road junction, he ran into a Japanese position and was killed at 1045 hours. By 1245 hours, 5/18 Royal Garhwal Rifles suffered many casualties due to lack of cover and heavy sniping at Simpang Jeram. A counter-attack at 1300 hours failed, and the battalion withdrew. The second force to suffer similarly was 7/6 Rajputana Rifles. At about 0800 hours, A company was sent to reinforce C company on the right, the water-front and the coast line being left to be guarded by miscellaneous headquarter details, supported by A Company of 5/18 Royal Garhwal Rifles. At about 1200 hours, five Japanese motor barges attempted to enter it from the mouth of the river. Each barge could hold 150 men. But they were driven off by a 25-pounder gun belonging to a troop of 65 Field Battery. It was reported at 1350 hours that a small party of the Japanese with machine-guns had been located in the rubber plantation near Dumpar Tringgi School, and one or two battalion carriers had been ambushed about 200 yards south of it. The commanding officer entered this position with thirty men but was shot dead along with many others. At 1745 hours it was reported that A company was practically decimated. At 2000 hours, the Brigade Headquarters ordered the withdrawal of the battalion from Muar to Bakri by the inner one of the two coast roads via Parit Jawa. The third unit, 4/9 Jat in the upper and eastern regions of the Muar river also suffered heavily. At 1800 hours a fighting patrol of D Company attacked the Japanese positions at Milestone 3, but was repulsed with a loss of 27 men killed or wounded.

By the evening of 16 January, therefore, the 45th Indian Infantry Brigade had suffered grievous losses and the Muar sector was beginning to collapse. Such a collapse would have thrown open to the Japanese the vital road to Yong Peng and thus endangered the line of communication of Westforce then fighting near Gemas. The Japanese landing south of Batu Pahat was a further danger, since it threatened both Yong Peng and Ayer Hitam. Major-General Bennett, therefore, held urgent consultations with Major-General Barstow and Brigadier Maxwell, and, later in the evening of 16 January, decided to reinforce the Bakri and Batu Pahat areas. 2/29 Australian Imperial Force Battalion (less one company) was sent to reinforce the 45th Indian Infantry Brigade, which shows that the Japanese strength at Muar was still under-estimated. New arrangements were also made by General Percival for the defence of Batu Pahat. The order said, "Batu Pahat will come under command 11 Indian Division forthwith. 6 Norfolk and Battery 135 Field Regiment join division today and remainder of 53 Brigade tomorrow. Commander

53 Brigade reports Ayer Hitam 0930 hours. One Battalion 11 Indian Division will be prepared to relieve 2/19 Battalion at Jemaluang ".[11] At the same time, the 15th Indian Infantry Brigade was asked to place the British Battalion, a battery of 155 Field Regiment, a troop of 2 Anti-Tank Battery and one section of 3 Field Company at one hour's notice to move to Ayer Hitam, where they were to report at 0930 hours. 3/16 Punjab was ordered to reconnoitre Jemaluang.

In accordance with these decisions, 2/29 Australian Imperial Force left Bakri on 17 January in the morning, 7/6 Rajputana Rifles was located between Parit Jawa and Bukit Muar, and mustered only two companies of about 90 rifles each. 4/9 Jat remained at its camp near Milestone 10, on Craigielea Estate; but, due to the telephone lines being cut, its location was not known to Brigade Headquarters. The third battalion of the 45th Indian Infantry Brigade, 5/18 Royal Garhwal Rifles, was near Bakri and was stronger than these two, having suffered less casualties the previous day. So, when a plan was adopted for a counter-attack on Muar, the Garhwalis were given a prominent role. The plan was for 2/29 Australian Imperial Force to advance from Bakri and 4/18 Royal Garhwal Rifles from Parit Jawa, to converge on Muar. The advance was to begin at 0200 hours on 18 January in order to give time to the Australians to reach Bakri and to enable 5/18 Royal Garhwal Rifles to move out from Bakri to their starting point at Parit Jawa.

But the rapidity of Japanese advance foiled this counter-attack before it began. The 2/29 Australian Imperial Force reached Bakri at 2000 hours on 17 January, and was attacked by the Japanese immediately afterwards. The Australians threw back the attack, and with the help of their anti-tank guns and armoured cars, pushed on to within a few miles of Muar town. But further progress was found impossible. The 5/18 Royal Garhwal Rifles left Bakri for Parit Jawa about 1800 hours, in two columns, one on lorries and the other on foot. The lorried columns, reached near Parit Jawa at 1930. As the men started getting down from their lorries, fire was opened on them suddenly from both sides of the road. Light machine-guns, medium machine-guns and mortars opened up on them from close range, and inflicted heavy casualties before the Garhwalis could disperse and take cover in the bushes flanking the road. Sounds of heavy firing towards Bakri showed that the marching column also had been

---

[11] History of 11th Indian Division in Malaya, Vol. II, (Original), chap. XVIII, p. 387.

ambushed by the Japanese. The Garhwalis, therefore, were attacked and dispersed with heavy losses before they even reached the starting point for their attack on Muar.

Muar Force Cut-off

After the failure of this projected counter-attack on Muar, no important developments took place in the sector for some time. Major-General Gordon Bennett sent another Australian battalion to reinforce the Muar sector. This battalion, 2/19 Australian Imperial Force, moved up from Jemaluang and reached Bakri about 1000 hours on 18 January. The tired and badly battered units of the 45th Indian Infantry Brigade rested that day. The troops of 5/18 Royal Garhwal Rifles and 7/6 Rajputana Rifles were holding a position about 2 miles from Bakri on the Parit Jawa road. The 4/9 Jat was still out of touch with Brigade Headquarters, but was reported to be about 7 miles north of Bakri and withdrawing slowly. Headquarters 45th Indian Infantry Brigade, with four armoured cars, was situated near Milestone 99. Of the Australians, the newly arrived 2/19 Australian Imperial Force was sent forward from Bakri towards Muar to keep the road clear of the Japanese and maintain contact with 2/29 Australian Imperial Force further down the road. The Japanese on 18 January confined themselves largely to an effort to cut off the road behind 2/29 Australian Imperial Force but were frustrated by the active patrolling of 2/19 Australian Imperial Force.

The next day, 19 January, the Japanese renewed their attacks in force. The first attack began about 0800 hours that morning, and, under cover of heavy artillery and mortar fire, the Japanese tried to establish themselves on the Bakri-Muar road behind 2/29 Australian Imperial Force. This attack was beaten back, and the attackers retired, leaving behind many casualties and some light machine-guns. But heavy shelling continued, and at 1000 hours an unlucky hit destroyed the Brigade Headquarters with most of its staff. The Brigade Commander suffered severe shell-shock, and so his Brigade Major temporarily took over the command[11a]. Attacking from the south-west the Japanese then captured the positions held by the Rajputs and Garhwalis south of Bakri, but were thrown back again by a spirited counter-attack. Soon after this, about half of the 4/9 Jat battalion arrived at Bakri, and reported that the remainder was following behind them. But the remainder never arrived. The Japanese soon succeeded in finally cutting the Bakri-Muar road, thus cutting off the

---

[11a]. This is not certain, for according to the Australian account, Col. Anderson of 2/19 Australian Battalion took over. See *Japanese Thrust*, p. 233

retreat of 2/29 Australian Imperial Force and the companies of 4/9 Jat whom it had been vainly trying to save. Ultimately, only a few hundred men of 2/29 Australian Imperial Force and a few dozen of 4/9 Jat succeeded in rejoining their units after evading the Japanese.

During the evening of 19 January, orders arrived for the 45th Indian Infantry Brigade to withdraw from Bakri to Yong Peng. The exhausted remnants of the brigade were obviously unable to hold the Japanese attacks much longer. Moreover, the Japanese landed near Batu Pahat had consolidated their hold, as described later, and were threatening to cut off the 45th Indian Infantry Brigade from Yong Peng. So there was no option before the Malaya Command but to order the force to fall back from Bakri to Yong Peng.

End of Muar Force

But it was already too late. The Muar force began its retreat early in the morning of 20 January. It was a column over a mile long, with the Australians as advance guard and rearguard, the Indians on both the flanks and the guns, armoured cars and ambulances on the road in the middle. At 0800 hours, a road-block was encountered, made up of felled trees and covered by medium machine-gun fire. While men were being moved up to assault and clear the road-block, the rear of the column was also heavily attacked. The Japanese rained bullets, mortar bombs and artillery shells on the packed column, which fought back gallantly. Fighting was fierce, and Brigadier Duncan was killed while personally leading a counter-attack to the rear with troops of 4/9 Jat and some other units. But the Japanese were repulsed and the road block was also cleared by a desperate counter-attack. Darkness had fallen by then, but the exhausted column pushed on and reached Milestone 91 about 2230 hours. After a brief halt, the column began its retreat again and neared Parit Sulong in the grey dawn of 21 January.

Parit Sulong had also been occupied by the Japanese. The advance guard of the column forced its way into the outskirts of the village although the Japanese kept firing steadily into it and the casualties were mounting. The tired and dispirited troops soon grew panicky and could be controlled with difficulty. At 0830 hours (on 21 January) a strong Japanese attack from the rear overran some of the anti-tank guns, but was then halted again. They, however, kept up their incessant attacks throughout the day, and Japanese planes also bombed and strafed the column frequently. In spite of it all, a vigorous counter-attack was launched to force a way to the river. Some troops managed to reach the river bank, but the opposite shore was also firmly held by the Japanese.

The situation was now desperate. The battered and worn-out column was completely surrounded by the Japanese and could neither advance nor retreat. Sniped, mortared, shelled and bombed from the air, the troops could only endure the pounding and fight on as long as possible. Their spirits revived when a message was received saying that a relieving force was on its way, but no one came. When darkness fell, the remnants formed a perimeter and fought off more attacks by Japanese tanks.[12] But, by the morning of 22 January, the Muar force was almost disintegrating. Although some supplies and medicines were dropped to it by the Royal Air Force that morning, its situation was obviously hopeless. Most of its officers were killed and the survivors could hardly remain on their feet after so many days and nights of incessant fighting. It was cruel to leave behind the wounded, but there was no alternative. At 0900 hours on 22 January, Lieutenant-Colonel Anderson, the commander of the force, called his gallant men to pull out by companies and try to reach Yong Peng as best they could across country. The carriers and the guns were destroyed, and the wounded left behind. Surprisingly enough, most of the troops managed to slip through the Japanese positions, and by the evening of 23 January, some 550 Australians and 400 Indians out of the total of 4000 in the Muar force, had rejoined their units at Yong Peng. Thus ended the sad but heroic story of the force defending Muar.

THE JAPANESE CAPTURE THE DEFILE

It is clear from the above account that the Muar force was destroyed primarily because of the Japanese capture of Parit Sulong and the vital Defile section of the road from Muar to Yong Peng. If its line of retreat had not been thus blocked, the 45th Indian Infantry Brigade would have safely withdrawn to Yong Peng. The operations leading to the Japanese capture of the Defile may now be described.

From later information, it seems clear that the Japanese who attacked Bakri on 18 and 19 January belonged to the *5th Guards Regiment*.[13] The *4th Guards Regiment* meanwhile had occupied Parit Jawa and pushed on down the coast road. It crossed the Batu Pahat river north of the town and, turning left, cut the stretch of road between Bukit Pelandok and Parit Sulong. They were the

---

[12] War Diary, 5/18 R. Garh. Rif.,
[13] Draft of the British History, Vol. I, Part II, p. 458.

troops of the *4th Guards Regiment*, who blocked the retreat of the 45th Indian Infantry Brigade at Parit Sulong and ensured its destruction.

General Percival was, of course not aware of these details, but on 18 January he learnt that the Muar sector was being attacked by a fresh and formidable *Imperial Guards Division*. That fact, and the deteriorating situation, convinced him of the grave danger to the 45th Indian Infantry Brigade. Therefore, at 2145 hours on 18 January he ordered the Muar sector to be transferred from the command of General Bennett to General Heath, the commander of III Indian Corps, so that the former could be relieved of responsibility for those distant and critical operations. The next day, orders were issued to the 15th Indian Infantry Brigade to reinforce the British Battalion near Batu Pahat, and to 3/16 Punjab to reinforce 6 Norfolk of the 53rd (British) Brigade at Bukit Pelandok on the road between Bakri and Yong Peng. No Japanese troops were till then in evidence in this area. But it was vitally necessary to ensure the safety of this road, which was the only escape route for the 45th Indian Infantry Brigade which, as already mentioned, was ordered at the same time (19 January) to begin withdrawal along this road from Bakri to Yong Peng.

But the Japanese struck even while these orders were being issued. At 1330 hours on 19 January, the company of 6 Norfolk holding Bukit Pelandok was suddenly attacked and thrown out from its positions. The Japanese quickly established themselves on the slopes of Bukit Baloh also, thus firmly holding the Defile. In the afternoon, 2 Loyals came up and tried to recapture Bukit Baloh, but the attack failed. Brigadier Duke of the 53rd (British) Brigade planned another attack for the morning of 20 January, and ordered 3/16 Punjab to capture Bukit Baloh and 6 Norfolk to reoccupy Bukit Pelandok. The Punjabis attacked first, but, in the gloom before dawn, ran into a party of 6 Norfolk who, unknown to them, were still on the top of the hill. Mistaking each other for the Japanese, 3/16 Punjab and 6 Norfolk exchanged murderous fire, and the Japanese, who appear to have been hiding nearby, attacked both before the confusion was over. Consequently the attack failed with heavy losses. 6 Norfolk also failed to reach Bukit Pelandok, and the vital Defile remained in Japanese hands.

In the afternoon of 20 January, Major-General Key (the 11th Indian Division) ordered Brigadier Duke (53rd Brigade) to make another effort to recapture the Defile, but the latter pointed out that ' its occupation was beyond the power of the troops at his disposal and would not help the withdrawal of the 45th Indian Infantry Brigade.' The General thereupon ordered the 53rd Brigade to attack at dawn next day, and reoccupy the two hills

Bt. Baloh and Bt. Pelandok, but Brigadier Duke again showed, by an analysis of the force on hand, that it was in no strength to carry out this task. Consequently, the whole plan was deferred. Partly as a result of this inaction and partly due to isolation and lack of food, the two platoons of 6 Norfolk detached for duty at Parit Sulong withdrew from that place and reached Batu Pahat on the following day.

Some more plans were made for recapturing the Defile and extricating the 45th Indian Infantry Brigade. General Key ordered the 53rd Brigade to attack the Defile positions at 1400 hours on 21 January, with the Loyals as the spearhead. But the order was wrongly transmitted, which made it impossible to amount the attack at the stipulated time. At 1200 hours on 21 January, the 53rd Brigade and the 45th Indian Infantry Brigade were again placed under the command of Westforce, leading to some more uncertainty about the projected attack. The Loyals could not be concentrated quickly for the attack, so it had to be postponed by a few hours; then the artillery failed to register accurately, so it had to be postponed once more. Finally, on the morning of 22 January, the Japanese planes bombed and strafed the troops deploying for the attack and scattered them. The plan of recapturing the Defile was then given up completely, and the 45th Indian Infantry Brigade was left to extricate itself as best it could, with the result already described.

WITHDRAWAL FORM SEGAMAT

First Contact

While the 45th Indian Infantry Brigade and the 53rd (British) Brigade were fighting hard on the Bakri-Yong Peng road, the Japanese were not inactive in the other sectors. On the main road from Gemas to Yong Peng, the Japanese *5th Division* opened its attack on 14 January. It made an inauspicious start that afternoon when a whole Japanese battalion on cycles was ambushed about 7 miles west of Gemas and lost about 450 men killed. After the ambush, however, the company of 2/30 Australian Imperial Force withdrew to the main positions covering Gemas, leaving behind a damaged bridge to delay the Japanese advance. By the next day, 15 January, the Japanese had repaired the bridge and attacked Gemas with the support of some tanks. In the day-long fighting, 2/30 Australian Imperial Force again inflicted considerable casualties on the Japanese and destroyed six tanks, but withdrew behind Gemas in the evening. On 15 January, the Royal Air Force also attacked the Japanese lorries on the Tampin-Gemas road and destroyed several of them.

By then, the situation at Muar appeared threatening and the Japanese were also reported to have landed near Batu Pahat. To stabilise the situation at Muar, General Gordon Bennett considered it sufficient to send only 2/29 Australian Imperial Force there, as has been already described. But General Percival considered the situation of graver import and on 16 January, he placed Batu Pahat-Yong Peng area under the III Indian Corps, and also felt compelled to send there the newly arrived 53rd (British) Brigade or the 18th (British)Brigade.

Withdrawal Begins

From 16 January to 18 January, the Gemas sector remained quiet, and all attention was focussed on the developments in Muar. By the evening of 18 January, the situation in Muar sector showed no signs of improving, more Japanese troops were reported from Batu Pahat and General Percival had at last learnt that one whole Japanese division was attacking Muar sector and another was operating along the Gemas-Segamat trunk route. It appeared necessary, therefore, to withdraw Westforce from its exposed positions. It was to enable General Gordon Bennett to devote his entire attention to this withdrawal so that the Muar sector was also temporarily transferred from his command to General Heath that evening, as mentioned above.

As ordered, Westforce fell back to Buloh Kasap during the night of 18-19 January. The road and rail bridges before Buloh Kasap were blown up. The 1/13 Frontier Force Rifles and 2/10 Baluch had minor skirmishes with the Japanese during the withdrawal, but no serious Japanese pressure developed.

New Plans

At 1420 hours on 19 January, there was a conference at Yong Peng in which Generals Percival, Heath, Gordon Bennett, Key and Brigadier Duke took part. Situation reports were heard, and a discussion took place on what should be done next. General Percival issued orders in accordance with the resolution at the conference, as follows:—

"1. The 53rd Brigade Group should hold a position from the bridge at Parit Sulong to the high ground west of the causeway.
2. The 45th Brigade Group should withdraw at once through the above to a position west of Yong Peng.
3. The Segamat force should continue its withdrawal at once.
4. The 22nd Indian Infantry Brigade, on its arrival at Yong Peng on the night of 20/21 January 1942 from

the Segamat front, should be at the disposal of the 11th Indian Division ".

As soon as the Generals returned to their respective headquarters they hastened to give effect to these orders. The Australian troops withdrew to Yong Peng; the 8th Indian Infantry Brigade proceeded to Campong Chasah; and the 22nd Indian Infantry Brigade got back to Labis. 5/11 Sikh Regiment was temporarily detached to hold the main river crossing. After having been in contact with, and inflicting casualties on, the Japanese forward elements, this battalion also rejoined the brigade in the Labis area.

At this stage General Sir Archibald Wavell made a general survey of the situation in Malaya. He came to Singapore on 20 January 1942 and discussed the situation with Generals Percival, Heath and Keith Simmons. Afterwards, he reported to the Combined Chiefs of Staff in Washington that the situation had greatly deteriorated, and added: ' My hope of holding the enemy on the Segamat—River Muar line until the whole of the 18th Division could be landed to reinforce the forward troops and until the 11th Division was rested and re-fitted, had been disappointed. The raw and partly trained 45th Indian Infantry Brigade had been unable to stop the enemy from crossing the Muar river and had been cut off east of the river together with two Australian battalions. The 53rd Brigade, the leading brigade of the 18th Division had had to be committed to the battle without waiting for the arrival of the remainder of the division and was already heavily engaged. It was obvious that the force would have to fall back to the approximate line Mersing-Kluang-Batu Pahat and that there was every prospect of the force being driven from Johore into Singapore Island. I found that very little had been done in the preparation of the defences in the northern part of Singapore Island;..... I instructed General Percival to continue the fight in Johore and to endeavour to hold the enemy on the mainland until further reinforcements arrived; but to make every preparation for the defence of Singapore Island.'[14] On 21 January, he received a cable from the Chiefs of Staff, London, drawing his attention to certain important points in case the Malaya force should be compelled to withdraw into Singapore Island. These points included:—

(i) use of fortress guns against landward attack,
(ii) obstructing land approaches to the Straits and landing places,

[14] Wavell's *Despatch*, p. 6, para 21.

(iii) diversion of some of the beach defences and machine guns from South to the North of the island.
(iv) control of boats and small craft,
(v) creation of self-contained defensive localities and switch lines,
(vi) measures against surprise night landings,
(vii) defence of aerodromes against airborne troops,
(viii) dispersal and control of the civil population and suppression of Fifth Column activity,
(ix) use of personnel in fixed defences for tasks in local defence schemes, and
(x) development of a good signals communication system within the fortress and to aerodromes in use in South Sumatra'.[15]

As a result of the withdrawals ordered, by the morning of 21 January the 27th Australian Imperial Force Brigade had reached Yong Peng cross-roads and was holding the road open to enable the 53rd Brigade and 45th Indian Infantry Brigade to withdraw from the Defile area towards Ayer Hitam. The 22nd Indian Infantry Brigade was then near Labis, with 2/12 Frontier Force Regiment at Milestone 101, 2/18 Royal Garhwal Rifles at Milestone 100, 5/11 Sikh near Milestone 99 and the Brigade Headquarters just behind it.[16] Behind the 22nd Indian Infantry Brigade was the 8th Indian Infantry Brigade, with 3/17 Dogra and 1/13 Frontier Force Rifles on either side of the road, and 2/10 Baluch backing them up.

At this stage, the utmost care was required to coordinate the withdrawals of these three brigades and the 22nd Indian Infantry Brigade through Yong Peng, so that confusion and blocking of the single road might be avoided. To ensure this coordination, the command of the 45th and 53rd Brigades in the Defile area was handed back to General Gordon Bennett with effect from 1200 hours on 21 January.

In a conference at Yong Peng that day, General Percival announced that his intention was to hold the Japanese at the line running from Jemaluang on the east coast to Batu Pahat on the west coast, passing through Kluang and Ayer Hitam. When the withdrawal to this line was completed, the available brigades were to be reorganised into three forces, each with a separate line of communication to Singapore. These forces were designated Eastforce in the Jemaluang-Mersing area based on Kota Tinggi road, the Westforce (which was to receive back 2 Loyals) in Yong

[15] "ABDACOM", op. cit. p. 31, Para 23 (f).
[16] A Diary of 5th Battalion (D.C.O.). The Sikh in the Malaya Campaign, p. 13.

Peng—Ayer Hitam–Kluang area covering the trunk road, and the 11th Indian Division in Batu Pahat area, covering the coastal road to Pontian Kechil and onwards to Skudai. Operations on the following days were based on this plan.

The Withdrawal Completed

The 22nd Indian Infantry Brigade started to withdraw on 21 January, from Labis through the positions of the 8th Indian Infantry Brigade. Since the Japanese were pressing hard on its heels, an ambush was laid for them near Milestone 101, and 2/12 Frontier Force Regiment was posted on either side of the road. The Japanese came rushing in, and suffered about 600 casualties within five or six minutes, although the coughing of a 'Jawan' gave away the stratagem before all the Japanese were truly in the bag. The 22nd Indian Infantry Brigade then withdrew without interference and reached Kluang, 2/18 Royal Garhwal Rifles suffering some losses in Japanese attacks near Paloh. The 8th Indian Infantry Brigade then remained the rearguard of Westforce, holding back the Japanese near Kampong Bahru. By 24 January, the 8th Indian Infantry Brigade also withdrew to Kluang.

On 22 January, the 8th Indian Infantry Brigade was attacked by the Japanese, who succeeded in infiltrating behind the Indian troops through the numerous routes in the Socfin Oil Palm Estate. This resulted in a withdrawal of about six miles that evening, and the front was stabilised behind the river Bakok.

According to the plan of withdrawal, the 53rd Brigade started to evacuate its positions west of Yong Peng on 23 January. While thus engaged, it was heavily attacked by the Japanese infantry and tanks. In the confusion, some bridges were blown up before all the troops had crossed over, and all units of the brigade, particularly 3/16 Punjab, suffered heavy casualties. However, they somehow got away and reached Ayer Hitam the next morning, leaving behind 2 Loyals which joined Westforce. The other two battalions of the Brigade, viz., 3/16 Punjab and 6 Norfolk, were put in lorries and immediately rushed off via Skudai to the Batu Pahat sector, which in the meantime had started crumbling.

THE BATU PAHAT SECTOR

The arrival of the Japanese in the Batu Pahat area has already been mentioned. As the operations developed in the Muar sector, General Nishimura, the Commander of the *Imperial Guards*

Division, decided to encircle and destroy the British troops in Batu Pahat area. He had already sent *1/4 Guards Battalion* to land on the coast south of Batu Pahat. He now ordered another battalion to attack the town frontally, while *4th Guards Regiment* went round to encircle the garrison and link up with its isolated battalion on the coast. The *5th Guards Regiment* was ordered to cross the Batu Pahat—Ayer Hitam road further east, then wheel west and cut the coastal road also at Bengit. A double ring of steel would thus be thrown around the doomed garrison of Batu Pahat. The operations that resulted from these plans are described below.

From 16 January onwards, there were rumours of strong Japanese forces landing on the coast and quietly infiltrating inland. On 17 January, the 11th Indian Division had established its headquarters at Ayer Hitam and the 15th Indian Infantry Brigade was made responsible for the defence of Batu Pahat area. Some units of the 15th Indian Infantry Brigade had frequent skirmishes with small parties of Japanese troops on 19 January, and the next day a weak Japanese attempt to cross the river near Batu Pahat was beaten back.

These incidents left Brigadier Challen (15th Indian Infantry Brigade) definitely uneasy about the situation that was developing, and he feared that both the Ayer Hitam and Pontian Kechil roads might be cut behind him. He represented this to Generals Heath and Key when they visited Batu Pahat on 21 January, but was ordered to hold fast in his sector, and, with 5 Norfolk to assist his brigade, to maintain active patrolling. It was also arranged to stock ten days provisions and supplies at Batu Pahat, in the hope that, even if cut off the town might serve as another Tobruk.

The same evening (21 January) the Japanese reached the Ayer Hitam road and established a road-block near Milestone 71. This was smashed on 22 January by 5 Norfolk advancing from Ayer Hitam and the British Battalion from Batu Pahat. But the Japanese attacked a field battery on the coastal road also on the same day, and again cut the Ayer Hitam road near Milestone 72. On 23 January, 5 Norfolk and the British Battalion attacked this road block, but were repulsed, and retired to Ayer Hitam and Batu Pahat respectively. 5 Norfolk was then sent round by bus to Pontian Kechil to try to reach Batu Pahat by the coastal road.

Brigadier Challen was alarmed by the growing threat to his force in Batu Pahat. Since his wireless was temporarily out of order, and he could not get in touch with the 11th Indian Division, he ordered a retreat from Batu Pahat on his own initiative. Later the same day, (23 January) the wireless link was restored, and he

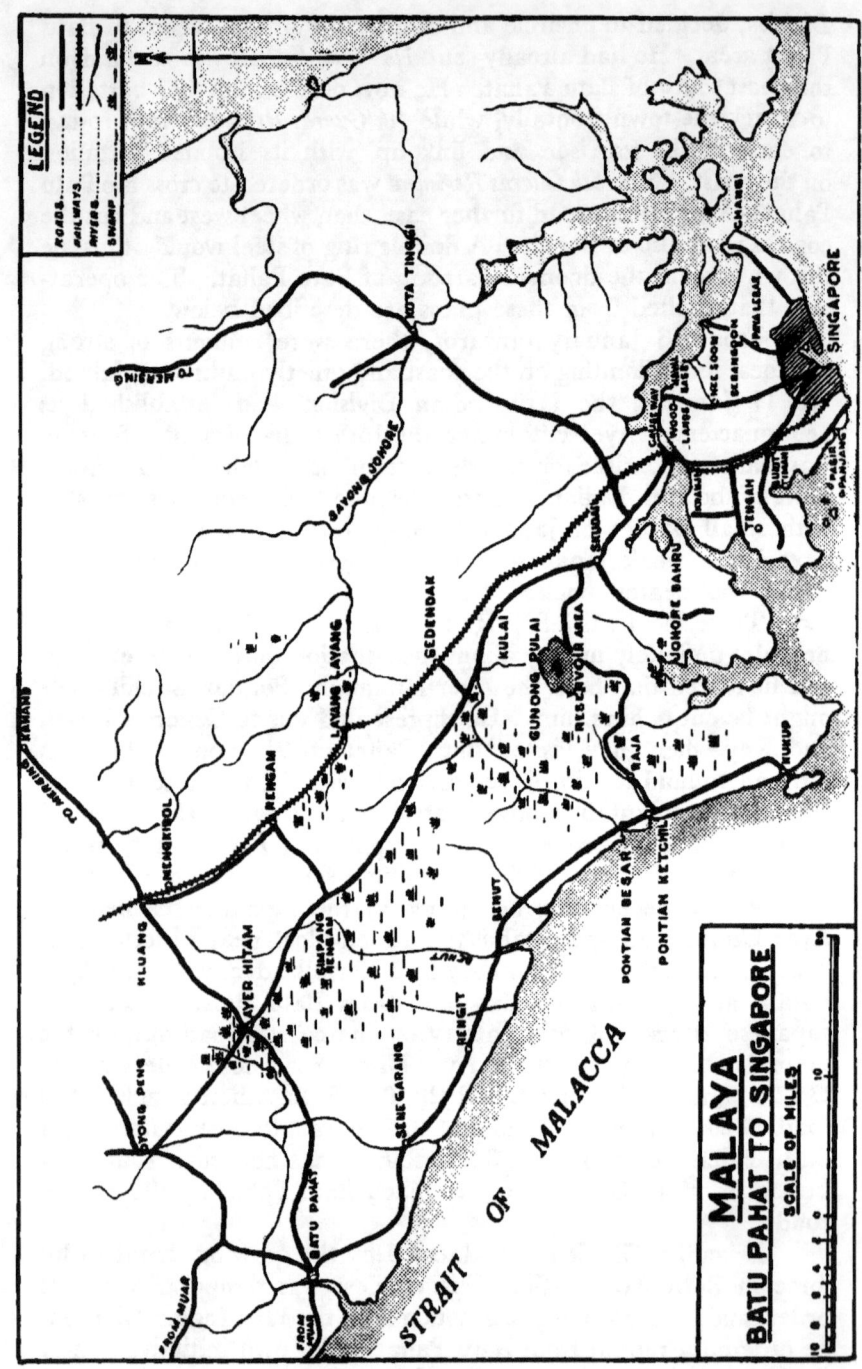

reported his decision to General Key, who had clear orders to hold on to Batu Pahat. He knew that General Percival's whole plan of defence was anchored on that town. Hence he counter-manded the order to retreat, reporting the matter to the III Indian Corps also in view of the real threat to the 15th Indian Infantry Brigade in the area. General Heath confirmed General Key's order, and the 15th Indian Infantry Brigade retraced its steps and reoccupied Batu Pahat during the night of 23-24 January.

CONCLUSION

In the Endau—Mersing area, at the other end of the defence line, the third week of January was relatively quiet. Japanese patrols were in contact with the defenders from 14 January onwards, and their planes frequently bombed Endau and Mersing. By 17 January, Japanese pressure had grown considerably in the sector. Brigadier Taylor, commanding the 22nd Australian Imperial Force Brigade in that area, had only two battalions, since 2/19 Australian Imperial Force had been sent to Bakri, as already mentioned. Brigadier Taylor, therefore, decided not to risk a major operation. During the night of 17-18 January, 22nd Australian Imperial Force pulled back to Mersing after systematically and thoroughly destroying all bridges, culverts, hamlets, crops etc, and blocking the road at several places. This scorched earth policy hampered the Japanese advance. By the evening of 18th the Japanese pushed on to Mersing, but they had to wade through swamps and clear the road block, and so could not attack Mersing in strength for many days. At Mersing, Brigadier Taylor was told that his new role was to protect the Jemaluang—Kota Tinggi road and his force would be known as Eastforce from 19 January.

As a result of the operations described above, the defence line in south Malaya up to 24 January ran from Batu Pahat to Ayer Hitam and thence to Kluang and Mersing. In accordance with General Percival's plan of 21 January, the whole force was divided into three separate formations, Eastforce, Westforce and the 11th Indian Division. Each had its own line of communications to Singapore and III Indian Corps was placed in overall command of the three forces. The stage was thus set for the next round in the Malayan campaign.

A few points concerning these operations may be noticed before describing the subsequent course of the fighting in Johore.

The original intention was to delay the Japanese advance until the reinforcements would arrive and as long as possible. The army was to fight within the Segamat-Muar line and not to withdraw behind it without the personal authority of General Percival, and navy and air force were to cooperate in the realisation of this object. This was a severe though necessary limitation on the liberty usually enjoyed by old and experienced battalion and brigade commanders, especially in a wild and undeveloped country like Malaya where communications were extremely difficult and undependable. But the special circumstances of the case justified General Percival in taking exceptional measures in an attempt to halt the retreat.

The method adopted to slow down the Japanese advance was to block the roads and to hit them hard if and when they tried to move round the flanks. Consequently brigades and battalions were placed at cross-roads like Segamat and Muar. River banks, bridges, tracks and the sea coast were watched and patrolled, and hill-tops, valleys and ridges were occupied with platoons and artillery parties. The net result of all these measures was to stem the tide of Japanese advance in this part of Malaya for at least one week, from 15 to 22 January 1942. But it was achieved at a tremendous cost, and the loss of men and material in Segamat front would be difficult to compute. But it is certain that there was practical annihilation of the army in the Muar front and reduction of battalions to a few companies in Segamat area. The loss of equipment was no less shattering.

With such losses, some deterioration in morale was inevitable. Some units were jumpy; some withdrew either before time or to a more distant place than prescribed for them; a few men ran away, either never to return or to rejoin their units much later, and almost all were sick of war in the existing circumstances. But General Gordon Bennett has testified to the high spirit of the men in his remark that, "On questioning several men, I found that the fatigue and resultant depression is more evident among senior officers than among the men, whose spirits are exceptionally high".[17] Also, this deterioration did not go so far as to induce them to quit; and it was this determination to fight and keep on fighting until the last man and last round or until it was wise to stop and retreat, that enabled the whole army to gain ten days time for the Supreme Commander to reorganise his forces for a better defence of Malaya and Singapore Island.

[17] *Why Singapore Fell*, p. 127.

CHAPTER X

The Last Week in South Malaya

THE FIGHT FOR JOHORE

General Wavell reported the situation on 24 January 1942 to the Combined Chiefs of Staff: 'Japanese obviously making intense efforts on whole front with object obtaining quick successes. We can only use our limited resources to check enemy as far forward as possible by hard fighting taking offensive action whenever possible. We shall incur heavy losses on sea, land and air during this period and further efforts will depend on their being made good rapidly....Troops in Johore are being very hard pressed by fresh Japanese divisions and have had heavy losses but Japanese losses also undoubtedly very heavy. We shall hold line Mersing-Kluang-Ayer Hitam-Batu Pahat as long as possible but may be forced back into Singapore island itself. Enemy numerical superiority in air and our lack of suitable small craft make it difficult to stop enemy infiltration along coast. Reinforcements of Australian machine-gun battalion and Indian brigade due in Singapore today and tomorrow, two brigade groups 18th Division due three days later. If all these arrive safely situation should be much easier. Enemy's air offensive has been intense and air losses on both sides considerable, unconfirmed report that Hurricanes shot down twenty enemy bombers yesterday without loss. Enemy has been reconnoitring and bombing aerodromes in Sumatra to increasing extent....Generally we will keep on holding and hitting enemy as hard as our resources allow till time comes to strike back. With adequate air we should be able to take considerable toll of his shipping. Enemy should not be able to replace his air losses as we can and we should be able to build up gradually air superiority and drive back his bases and re-establish those we have lost. Next few months will be anxious and difficult but have every hope of getting through them successfully'.[1]

The 44th Indian Infantry Brigade arrived at Singapore on 25 January 1942, and the 18th Division (less 53rd Brigade) came to Singapore four days later, on 29 January 1942. Australian machine-gun battalion and reinforcements for the 18th Australian Division reached Singapore on 23 January 1942, while drafts for the III Indian Corps and No. 100 Indian Light Tank Squadron were at Singapore on 29 January 1942. But according to General

[1] Wavell's *Despatch*, Appendix "A" p. 13.

Percival, those which arrived on 23 and 25 January 1942 were unfit or untrained for war. ' I dared not send it (44th Indian Infantry Brigade) into action at once on the mainland....The reinforcements also included 7,000 Indian troops. They also were extremely raw and untrained. To make matters worse there were very few non-commissioned officers among them and that was what we most needed now in the Indian units....From Australia came a machine-gun battalion and 2,000 reinforcements....Excellent material they were but not soldiers as yet '.[a]

As stated by General Wavell in his situation report, the intention of Malaya Command was to save Singapore as long as possible from Japanese invasion and to deploy the 18th Division accordingly. A secondary purpose was to keep the string of aerodromes and landing grounds at Kahang, Kluang and Koris intact with the purpose of preventing the Japanese from doubling the scale of their air attacks on the Singapore area and on the reinforcement convoys as they came in. The one lateral road connecting these three places was an important factor in the war in this large area.

As mentioned earlier, the defence of the lateral road and south Malaya was organised in three sectors, each held respectively by the Westforce, Eastforce and the 11th Indian Division with an overall control by the III Indian Corps. The principal function of these three forces was to hold the Japanese army to the north of Batu Pahat—Mersing line and prevent any large-scale infiltrations by the attackers to the south for such time as the defences of the island of Singapore had been effectively organised. The task was difficult, as the area of observation was large and the defending troops were both weak in numbers and exhausted after a long and continuous fighting retreat. The situation at no stage was any better than critical, but in spite of heavy odds the Indian, British and Australian troops were able to impose a delay of seven days in the attack on Singapore Island, as also to save a part of the force which could retreat into it and participate in its defence. The story of these crucial seven days is one of many disasters and losses, but it has its bright spots also in the frequent display of heroism, counter-attacks and the orderly withdrawal of the various units. However, the narrative of the period from 24 January to 31 January is confused owing to lack of unity in the operations of the three forces and occasional over-stepping of the main directions by some battalions owing to the unexpected developments in the situation at any place. The operations have therefore to be discussed chronologically in the three separate sectors.

[a] *The War in Malaya*, op. cit., p. 235.

On 24 January, very little activity was in evidence on the front but for a Japanese air attack on Ayer Hitam and a counter-raid by the Royal Air Force on the Japanese troops holding the bridge at Labis and the oil tanks at Muar. The 11th Indian Division was straining every nerve to provide relief to the 15th Indian Infantry Brigade and prevent Japanese landings at Pontian Besar and Pontian Kechil. At the same time planning for the defence of Rengit and Benut was being pushed ahead. The 9th Indian Division was giving attention to the reoccupation of Paloh which had been lost by 2/18 Royal Garhwal Rifles on the previous day. Major-General Gordon Bennett ordered the whole of the 22nd Indian Infantry Brigade to re-establish position at Paloh.

COUNTER-ATTACK AT NIYOR

24 January 1942 was an absolutely colourless day for the British army, the only exception being the heroic fight on 5/11 Sikh at Niyor. When 2/30 Australian Battalion was attacked at 1335 and 1505 hours by fifteen Japanese bombers at Ayer Hitam and up and down the road to Simpang Rengam, the Royal Air Force sent twenty-one fighters to defend, but, by then, the Japanese aircraft had gone off and the weather also was unsuitable'.[3] Eleven Vildebeestes and three Albacores, however, attacked the Japanese troops on the bridge at Labis on the Segamat-Singapore road whilst three others bombed oil tanks left standing at Muar.

There was not much activity on the 11th Indian Division front. The entire attention of its commander was directed to the relief of the 15th Indian Infantry Brigade and to prevent the Japanese from landing at Pontian Besar and Pontian Kechil, and cutting off the line of cummunications of the central and eastern forces at Skudai. Rengit and Benut received the greatest attention in the planning of the defence of this coastal area. The Japanese were in the meantime getting stronger on the east flank of the Malaya army and making its withdrawal rapidly to the south inevitable.

It is said that fighting continued in the town of Batu Pahat throughout this day (24 January), resulting in fatigue of the men who had been on the move for several days without sleep. Their morale was, however, undiminished, because they were told that 53rd British Brigade would come to their support within twenty-four hours and further secure their line of communication with

---

[3] War Diary, Headquarters Malaya Command, 24 January 1942.

Senggerang and Benut. The 53rd British Brigade consisted now of two weak battalions, namely 6 Norfolk and 3/16 Punjab Regiment, and it is surprising that great hopes were built on the reinforcement promised by it to the desperately situated 15th Indian Infantry Brigade at Batu Pahat. At 0800 hours the order of battle was issued, and at 1030 hours the 8th Indian Infantry Brigade (with 88 Field Regiment less one battery and one troop of Anti-tank regiment) was ordered to defend the Kluang area and the 22nd Indian Infantry Brigade (with 5 Field Regiment and a troop of Anti-tank regiment) was sent to defend Sungei-Sembrong at railway Milestone 411.[4] The idea behind this order was that the 8th Indian Infantry Brigade which had just come out of action should give place to the 22nd Indian Infantry Brigade for the counter-attack. By afternoon, the former was in its position in the Kluang area: 2/10 Baluch on the westerly entrances to Kluang extending on a very broad front to the limits of the aerodrome (which was defended by the Bahawalpur State Forces), 3/17 Dogra covering the northern approaches astride the railway, and 1/13 Frontier Force Rifles staying on about two miles south of Kluang. The preliminary movements of the 22nd Indian Infantry Brigade for the counter-attack had also in the meantime commenced. The plan of counter-attack was as follows:—5/11 Sikh with battery under command to move in main advance by a route west of the railway as far as Niyor and the 'remainder of the Brigade' (now consisting of weak and denuded 2/18 Royal Garhwal Rifles and one-company-strong 2/12 Frontier Force Regiment combined) was to move simultaneously to the same place along the railway. No information was given as to the whereabouts of the Japanese, and no maps were available for the greater part of the route prescribed for the Sikh battalion. The march commenced at 1400 hours.[5] The Bahawalpur infantry could scarcely defend the aerodrome and thus the burden of defence of the whole position fell on the combined unit. Consequently the move of this unit along the railway in conformity with that of the Sikh battalion had to be abandoned. Fortunately, 1/13 Frontier Force Rifles of the 8th Indian Infantry Brigade saved the combined unit from disaster and the Japanese too did not press their attack any further. Meanwhile the Sikhs had gone on advancing towards Niyor. At 1600 hours they had cleared the network of roads in the rubber estate and got on a clear-cut road to Niyor. At 1730 hours when the battalion was only about three miles from Niyor " an incomplete message was received by W.T.

[4] War Diary, General Staff Headquarters 9 Indian Division, 24 January 1942.
[5] *Ibid.*

from Brigade ordering us to abandon the original objective and make for MS 416 on the railway ".[6] The intention was to bring it on to the flank of the Japanese and thus relieve the other unit from the strain of fighting. Unfortunately, this plan could not be carried out in action. Owing to jungle and swamp, the advent of night in an unknown place, the presence of guns and transport and the absence of maps, the commanding officer decided to continue his advance to Niyor and thence to strike south to point MS 416 on the railway. In doing so his men came immediately into contact with the Japanese and a grim fight ensued until the morning of the next day.

FURTHER WITHDRAWALS DECIDED

25 January 1942 was a day of a few important decisions for the opposing sides—the British and the Japanese. The former decided to withdraw behind Mersing-Kluang-Ayer Hitam-Batu Pahat line and as a corollary to it to demolish the airfields at Kahang, Kluang and Batu Pahat; while the latter resolved on a determined action by continuing the fight even during the night, delivering the hardest blow at dawn.

The Japanese point of view was that the line which the British army was defending was indeed the last stronghold of the Singapore defence......'a lifeline......"[7]. The best method of driving that army behind that line was to give it to rest and to cut the line of communication in Johore.

The Malaya Command too was keenly watching the developments on the west coast, and the utmost that they could hope for was to transfer the force at Batu Pahat to Pontian Kechil and to let the 15th and 28th Indian Infantry Brigades, reinforced by the 53rd British Infantry Brigade, hold the Pontian Kechil-Skudai—Johore Bahru road against the Japanese penetration into south Johore, as long as possible. At the conference of commanders presided over by General Percival at 1515 hours at Westforce Headquarters (near Rengam) on this date, important decisions were taken. Major-General Key reported that the force at Batu Pahat had been heavily engaged all the morning and that the coast road had been blocked near Senggarang. General Gordon Bennett added that the situation at Kluang was confused but that the 9th Indian Division was holding the Kluang road junction and he believed the counter-attack carried out by the Sikhs had been successful. The only matter therefore for consideration

[6] War Diary, 5th Battalion (D.C.O.) The Sikh, p. 15.
[7] Enemy Publication No. 278, p. 143.

at the conference was the immediate policy for the conduct of operations. All agreed on the necessity of the following four immediate steps:—

(1) The Batu Pahat garrison must withdraw at once and link up with the 53rd British Brigade in the Senggarang area.
(2) Westforce should withdraw at night to the general line S. Sayong Halt—S. Benut.
This position was to be held until the night of 27/28 January 1942 at least. Subsequent withdrawals might take place to positions, to be laid down in advance, which would in turn be held for a minimum fixed period or longer if possible.
(3) Movement of Eastforce and the 11th Indian Division must conform to that of Westforce under orders to be issued by III Indian Corps.
(4) In view of a threat in Pontian Kechil area, the commander of Westforce ought to hold a battalion in reserve and make it available at that flank as rapidly as possible.[8]

The III Indian Corps was asked to issue orders accordingly and to coordinate the action of various columns, and as the agency responsible for all these operations, it was expected to work out the details of these resolutions and make them available for the Malaya Command.[9]

The course of other events on 25 January 1942, may be rapidly recorded. As the west was key to the whole front, the incidents at Batu Pahat and to the south of it have a priority about them. By all accounts the situation was bad enough, but by 1630 hours it grew worse and the Malaya Command ordered at 2230 hours that an aircraft should drop medical supplies to the force in that area at first light on the following day.[10] The brigade in Batu Pahat area moved to Senggarang during the night of 25/26 January 1942 and reached it at dawn. General Percival adds the following: "I had hoped that this brigade would have been able to brush aside opposition and continue its fight down the coast. But it was not to be. Finding its passage blocked south of Senggarang it deployed its leading battalion and attacked but

---

[8] Percival's *Despatch*, Appendix "G".
[9] While the minutes of the meeting do not contain any record of the discussion or resolution relating to withdrawal on the night of 31 January/1 February 1942 from the mainland to Singapore Island the writings of Generals Percival and Gordon Bennett affirm that that withdrawal was discussed and decided on at that meeting. History of 11 Indian Division, Colonel A.M.L. Harrison, p. 446.
[10] War Diary, Headquarters Malaya Command, 25 January 1942.

made no headway ".[11] The 53rd British Infantry Brigade occupied Benut and Rengit without opposition, and its forward unit, 6 Norfolk, reached Senggarang without any incident. But "the eventful move to Senggarang......was not shared by its tail, which was ambushed eight hundred yards south of the village".[12] The Japanese had come between Senggarang and Rengit from a point on Batu Pahat—Ayer Hitam road, and had pinned down the Batu Pahat force to the north of Senggarang until the arrangements to cut the Pontian Kechil road were complete. It is recorded that the 15th Indian Infantry Brigade could have been successfully withdrawn on 25 January 1942 but Major-General Key was not permitted to do so until the evening of the next day, with the result that the brigade was encircled and practically written off.

In central Johore the Japanese launched an attack on 2/30 Australian Imperial Force Battalion under cover of mortars and infantry guns. This attack was however defeated. The point of defence was the bridge over the Sungei Sembrong to the north of Ayer Hitam. At 2000 hours the withdrawal commenced. 2/26 Australian Imperial Force Battalion went to Milestone 46 and 2/30 Australian Imperial Force Battalion halted near Milestone 40. 2 Gordon which had taken the place of 2 Loyal (sent to Singapore) had moved to Milestone 49. With one company of 2/30 Australian Imperial Force Battalion 2 Gordon remained as the forward detachment of the Australian force. The 9th Indian Division was again ordered to retreat along the railway, which caused serious difficulties for the wheeled transport of the division. Once again 5/11 Sikh made history on this day with its bayonets. It fought gloriously until noon, captured machine-guns, motor-cycles, and more machine-guns before it withdrew to Kluang. According to the war diary of the unit, " since 1400 hours on the 24th of January the Battalion had marched over 33 miles and had been in action for 18 hours. Our casualties were 40 including 3 gunners; enemy casualties were conservatively estimated at 150...This was a very heartening action. It gave the men confidence and relieved all pressure on 22 Brigade and later on 8 Brigade for a full 24 hours. On the 25th not a shot was fired on their fronts ".[13] Orders had meanwhile been issued for a withdrawal to Rengam, and the divisional commander, who only a few hours before had been stressing the necessity of re-establishing

---

[11] *The War in Malaya*, p. 242.
[12] History of 11th Indian Division, Vol. II (Original), p. 441.
[13] A Diary of 5th Battalion (D.C.O.) The Sikh, pp. 17-18.

the situation at Paloh, issued orders for bringing the 5/11 Sikh back to its brigade at the earliest moment. The battalion returned by the same route as it had used in its advance, and rejoined the brigade in the evening (about 1700 hours) with sufficient time only for a meal and brief rest before joining in further withdrawals. The whole brigade arrived at 0200 hours to a harbour area north of Rengam. It was fortunate that as this withdrawal began 2/18 Royal Garhwal Rifles Battalion Headquarters and Headquarters Company rejoined the Brigade.

The 8th Indian Infantry Brigade had a fairly quiet day. Only C Company of 2/10 Baluch had some contact with the Japanese near the aerodrome. During the afternoon the artillery and transport thinned out, and at 1730 hours orders were given for a general withdrawal of the brigade. 1/13 Frontier Force Rifles held a position through which 3/17 Dogra and 2/10 Baluch passed. After a night march of some twelve miles the brigade (less 1/13 Frontier Force Rifles) spent the night in a rubber estate at Sayong Halt and 1/13 Frontier Force Rifles which was in Mengkibol area served as the outpost battalion covering the position of the whole brigade to the south of it.[14]

In the eastern part of Johore which 'about this time...... came at last into the limelight' (in Lieutenant-General Percival's words), this day too passed off without any serious incident. The Japanese continued their pressure against the Australian troops in the area, compelling them gradually to fall back near Milestone 74 and Jemaluang.[15] Previous to this retreat the bridge across the Mersing was blown up. Connected with these actions was the withdrawal of 2/9 Jat from Kahang aerodrome, which even as early as 20 January 1942 had been advised to be demolished,[16] to Milestone 42 on the Jemaluang-Kota Tinggi road. The role of this battalion was to watch for the Japanese approach by tracks from the east and to prepare ambushes in Wang Tengah-Lubok Pusang area. These movements were ordered on account of the change in the general policy of defending the eastern sector. According to General Percival " The new defence centred round Jemaluang with Mersing held only as an outpost. Moreover, we had had to withdraw our advanced troops from Endau, a likely landing place twenty miles north of Mersing ".[17] As a matter of fact, the Japanese did land an airfield battalion on the night of 25/26 January 1942.

[14] *Why Singapore Fell*, p. 126.
[15] War Diary, 2/9 Jat, 24 January 1942.
[16] *Ibid.*, 20 January 1942.
[17] *The War in Malaya*, p. 244.

15TH INDIAN INFANTRY BRIGADE CUT OFF

26 January 1942 was another day of misfortunes for the Allies. Once again, the west coast area demanded the first attention of the Malaya Command. The problem there was to withdraw the Batu Pahat force, now consisting of the British Battalion, 6 and 5 Norfolk, 2 Cambridgeshire, B Battery of 155 Field Regiment, carriers, and much transport including ambulance, successfully to Rengit before the morning of 27 January 1942. Unfortunately nothing could be done to accomplish this great purpose. The Japanese placed road blocks in at least six places between Senggarang and Rengit, posted detachments to the left and the right of the coast road without being seen by any one moving on the road and made reconnaissance of the whole area from the air. Their idea was to lock up the 15th Indian Infantry Brigade at Senggarang and to destroy all communications with it from outside.

In the difficult task of withdrawal, the 15th Indian Infantry Brigade was assisted by the 53rd British Brigade. The only matter of ill-luck was that after 0600 hours the wireless communication on which alone the coordinated movements depended, ceased to function, and the substitute for it was by sending special columns and aeroplanes through the Japanese occupied bits of territory. The best example of the former method was 'Bancol'. This column, consisting of a troop of armoured cars, four carriers (two of which were from 3/16 Punjab), a section of field battery, a detachment of a field company and a number of ambulances and led by Major Benham of 336 Field Battery of 135 Field Regiment, proceeded under the special orders of Major-General Key to perform two distinct tasks, viz. to open the road to Senggarang and to inform Brigadier Challen that he should reach Rengit on 27 January 1942. But unfortunately this special column was destroyed within two minutes.'[18] However, by the gallant efforts of the commander, and driver of the carrier, (which belonged to 3/16 Punjab) the commanding officer was able to pass through all the Japanese road-blocks and reach Brigadier Challen some time after 1400 hours. A second method of contacting the 15th Indian Infantry Brigade devised by Major-General Key was by means of aircraft. The Royal Air Force had no aeroplane to spare for this urgent task, but the Volunteer Air Force sent one. This was a little Moth capable of eighty miles per hour and hedge-hopping at low level, both of which proved to be most annoying to the Japanese dive-bombers. The pilot was not only able to reach

[18] History of 11 Indian Division, Vol. II (Original), p. 449.

Senggarang and drop medical supplies to the brigade in good time but also to come back safely to the Divisional Headquarters and report " that he had found Senggarang congested with transport and British troops who had waved at him as he flew at a hundred feet above the town ".[19] But all the efforts of Major-General Key were ultimately of no avail. Brigadier Challen tried his utmost to destroy and penetrate through the barriers of the Japanese but not one of his several attempts succeeded. By afternoon, therefore Brigadier Challen was faced with a serious problem: if he moved to fight his way through and save guns and vehicles, men would be killed as at Muar, but if he avoided battle and saved his men he would lose his arms and vehicles. If he did not decide at once, the Japanese, who were strong between Senggarang and Rengit and who had begun occupying the road within a mile south of Rengit, would attack the British force both in front and in the rear. Secondly, he had been ordered to reach Rengit on the following day. Rengit was eight miles away, and too far for Brigadier Challen's force to reach by a night march, and a night march would invite repetition of the disaster which had overtaken 2/9 Jat during its withdrawal through Kluang. Finally, Brigadier Challen decided on the latter course; he decided to destroy and abandon seven 25-pounders, eight anti-tank guns, six armoured cars and all vehicles, to leave the wounded with the Red Cross and to rejoin the division by a detour west of the road. His brigade started its trek at 1815 hours. At 0100 hours on 27 January 1942 Rengit was also evacuated by the detachment which had originally consisted of A Company of 6 Norfolk, a section of 336 Field Battery and D Company of 3/16 Punjab, but now contained only a handful of men belonging to 6 Norfolk and Selangor Battalion, and the whole of the west coast road became open up to Benut for the Japanese.

Consequently, the situation facing the 11th Indian Division on the night of 26/27 January 1942 was once more a black one. The 15th Indian Infantry Brigade was apparently written off and the 53rd British Infantry Brigade reduced to 3/16 Punjab (less one company in wilderness) and 3 Cavalry (less a squadron with the 15th Infantry Brigade also in wilderness). The danger to the western sector had correspondingly increased, because it was not only exposed as before on the coast but also at strategic points like Milestone 22 on the Pontian Kechil-Skudai road.

The fate of Westforce on 27 January was no better than on the day before. Lieutenant-General Gordon Bennett appeared, however, much less confident; "Realizing the danger that would

[19] *Ibid.*, p. 459.

result should the enemy land at Pontian Kechil or should they break through from Batu Pahat via the coastal road, thus opening the way for an uninterrupted approach to Singapore, I ordered the 2/19 and the 2/29 Battalions which were reorganising and refitting after their heavy losses at Bakri, to be prepared to occupy a position on Pontian Kechil-Skudai road at short notice ". Later the commander of the 27th Australian Brigade requested authority to withdraw 2 Gordons from a forward position to the area held by 2/26 Australian Imperial Force Battalion, and this was granted without question. According to Major Hyde ' this withdrawal from the MS 49 position (to MS 42) was a day ahead of schedule. Moreover a demolition that should have been blown at MS 49, had not been effected '.[20] The Japanese, however, did not seize their advantage immediately.

WITHDRAWAL OF THE 9TH INDIAN DIVISION

In the 9th Indian Division also, both the 8th and the 22nd Indian Infantry Brigades were ordered to withdraw by successive bounds along the railway, the former leading the way. The arrangement was that the 22nd would deny the line astride the railway at Milestone 437 up to 28/29 January, the 8th hold Sedenak up to 30/31 January and the former Kulai up to 31 January/1 February. According to this time-table, 8th Indian Infantry Brigade was astride the road and railway about four miles north of Rengam railway station; 1/13 Frontier Force Rifles was in the outpost positions at Mengkibol; 3/17 Dogra and the Bahawalpur State Forces were in the Rengam railway station area. At about 1100 hours, 1/13 Frontier force Rifles passed to a position about $1\frac{1}{2}$ miles to the rear of 2/10 Baluch; but before withdrawing fought " a successful action with the enemy, killing thirty, destroying four motor cycles and capturing a mortar and two light machine-guns ".[21] However, by 1600 hours the Japanese had come in contact with 2/10 Baluch; D Company was guarding the railway bridge and all others were around the area. It was therefore quite easy to disperse the Japanese with artillery fire. But they penetrated the battalion area in darkness and fired on A Company— the rearmost of the companies—during the night. The Commander 22nd Indian Infantry Brigade was not happy at the instructions which he had received, because he realised the weakness of the plan owing to the fact that the entire line of movement was exposed to flank attack by the Japanese who were familiar with the tracks

---

[20] Major E.F.D. Hyde: Account of the Malayan Campaign, p. 287.
[21] *Why Singapore Fell*, p. 126.

and roads of the plantations. According to him, a position south of Layang Layang was the only tenable position, but he was not permitted to depart from the prescribed route. He realised that " the position was tactically bad but that orders permitted of no alternative as Brigade had to keep north of a line East and West through railway MS 435 until 1600 hours on 28 January." 5/11 Sikh occupied the position by 1630 hours. Japanese air activity made the situation quite uncomfortable in the night. Meanwhile, in the words of the diarist of the battalion, " Late in the evening a message was received that everything on wheels had to be clear of MS 435 by 1700 hours next day, and that 8th Brigade would pass through us about that time. 22nd Brigade itself having got rid of all transport would withdraw down the railway having held their present positions until 1630 hours on 28 January. This meant that we were to fight for 24 hours in a position which was agreed to be tactically unsound, without any support, without carriers, without mortars, with no reserve ammunition other than dumps, and without any means of even eventual hope of evacuating wounded. Further, no sapper assistance was available for blocking roads which in any case had to be left open until 1630 hours on 27 January to let through transport and carriers of 8th Brigade. After this we were to withdraw 10 or 15 miles (the position which 8th Brigade was going to occupy was not then nor was it ever known to us) still without any supporting arms or means of evacuation of wounded.......Throughout the afternoon and all the next day until 1600 hours when they had to be sent back in accordance with orders, the carriers patrolled wide to both flanks and reported even more roads and link roads than those shown on the map".[22] These orders of General Gordon Bennett were intended to guard against a possible flanking threat of the Japanese to the trunk road so vital to the withdrawal to Singapore. Unfortunately, however, they produced an erroneous impression in the minds of the Indian troops, particularly in view of the earlier warning to deny the lateral tracks to the Japanese until a stated hour[23].

THE FRONT BEGINS TO CRUMBLE

In the eastern sector, at the same time, it had been decided to withdraw the 22nd Australian Imperial Force Brigade from Mersing. When this was done, 2/18 Australian Imperial Force Battalion was in possession of the area between Milestone 76 and Milestone 74 on Mersing-Jemaluang road. As this area was most

[22] Diary of 5th Battalion (D.C.O.) The Sikh, 26 January 1942.
[23] Brigadier G.W.A. Painter: Personal account, p. 24.

suitable for ambush, one was prepared therein, with elaborate artillery and mortar support. It is mentioned that the Japanese did make contact with British patrols at about 1800 hours near Milestone 76 and moved into the rubber estate to the west of the road. They could have come into contact with a company of 2/18 Australian Imperial Force Battalion in that estate, but it was a part of the ambush plan not to be discovered therein and so nothing happened. The hostilities commenced at 0115 hours on 27 January 1942 when another company, the one at Milestone 74, contacted the Japanese. One hour later a third company, the one at mile 74½, was also in touch with the Japanese. These movements of the Japanese proved to be extremely valuable for the Australian force. They had entered the trap. At 0330 hours 2/10 Field Regiment and mortars opened their fire on the Japanese more or less concentrated on the ridge, east of the road near Milestone 75. All the companies of 2/18 Australian Imperial Force Battalion took part in the stormy attack and continued their fight for nearly five hours, until 0800 hours. As a result, the Japanese advance was checked, and the Australian withdrawal was accelerated and carried out according to plan.

On 27 January 1942, the situation in the words of the Supreme Commander was as follows: " The fighting in Johore continued to go badly, and I realised that there was danger that the troops on the mainland would be destroyed before the reinforcements (44th Indian Infantry Brigade and remainder of 18th Division) could disembark at Singapore and reach Johore. The Japanese had made a fresh landing on the east coast at Endau. I judged that it would be better to withdraw the force from the mainland into the island and continue the fight there rather than that it should be overwhelmed before the reinforcements landed. On 27 January I cabled to General Percival giving him discretion to withdraw into the island if he considered advisable".[24] The following was the actual cable: " Primary objects are to gain time and cause maximum loss to enemy. You must judge when withdrawal to island is necessary to avoid disorganisation and unnecessary losses of men and material which may prejudice defence of island, which you must be prepared to hold for many months. You can only judge time by keeping very close watch on battle. Good luck, am sure can trust your judgement. Keep me frequently informed ".[25] General Percival had been assessing the whole situation quite independently of the Supreme Commander. To him the decisive factor was the disappearance of the

---

[24] Wavell's *Despatch*, pp. 6-7 Para 21.
[25] *Ibid.* Appendix " B ". p. 13.

15th Indian Infantry Brigade as a fighting force and the opening of the west coast road to the Japanese. The collapse of that sector had jeopardised the defence all along the line in south Johore.

In the western sector of the three brigades, 15th and 28th Indian Infantry Brigades and 53rd British Infantry Brigade, the first had been disorganised, as mentioned earlier, and the problem on 27 January was one of the survival of individuals. Of those who went towards the coast, as many as two thousand[26] crowded at Ponggor and went to Singapore by quiet nightly evacuations by sea. There were minor evacuations from the mouths of the Senggarang and Bata rivers and from other scattered spots on the seashore. At the same time those who went into the interior of the country to the east of the road, reached Benut, where 3/16 Punjab (less one company) and a battery of 135 Field Regiment awaited the arrival of these unfortunate men. These included a party of 6 Norfolk and the missing company of 3/16 Punjab and some of 2 Cambridgeshire and 5 Norfolk from Senggarang. It is interesting to note that the Japanese did not in the least interfere with the naval evacuations and only threw grenades across the river in the Senggarang area. So far as the 53rd British Infantry Brigade was concerned, its main task was to withdraw behind the 28th Indian Infantry Brigade. Brigadier Duke was given discretion to destroy the bridge at Benut but he must hold the village until the dawn of 28 January 1942, awaiting the arrival of the men of the 15th Indian Infantry Brigade.

In Westforce area withdrawals continued during the 27th. The Japanese contacted 2/26 Australian Imperial Force Battalion and infiltrated round its left flank. Determined counter-attacks were launched at them, but at about 1800 hours the battalion withdrew from Milestone 46 to Milestone $41\frac{1}{2}$, to come on the right of 2 Gordons. This "uncovered the junction of the main and Layang Layang roads before all 9th Division transport had completed its move to the main road from Layang Layang, but the enemy did not follow up 2/26th Battalion sufficiently quickly as to interfere".[27] The Japanese continued their aerial bombings on the 27th Australian Brigade Group, paying particular attention to the field artillery positions, but the Australians changed the position of guns as often as possible. The 8th Indian Infantry Brigade was in contact with the Japanese at dawn, but there was no particular pressure on it. At approximately 1000 hours, 2/10 Baluch withdrew through 1/13 Frontier Force Rifles and took up positions

---

[26] War Diary, Headquarters Malaya Command, 27 January 1942, 2140 hours.
[27] Major E.F.D. Hyde: Account of the Malaya Campaign, pp. 292-3. The Australian account says that the withdrawal took place after the 9th Divisions guns and transport had come through. See *The Japanese Thrust*, pp. 270-71.

astride the railway just north of Rengam railway station. The Bahawalpur State Force remained astride the main road on the left. Then at about 1200 hours 1/13 Frontier Force Rifles passed through 2/10 Baluch and went back to a position which was two miles away, astride the railway line. 3/17 Dogra stood on the left covering the Rengam—Simpang Rengam road. At about 1300 hours the Japanese ground forces made contact simultaneously with this brigade, especially 2/10 Baluch. There were some casualties, some of whom had to be left behind. The Japanese worked rapidly round the left, and consequently the Bahawalpur battalion and 2/10 Baluch were ordered out and a road bridge was blown by the sappers and miners before leaving. The brigade axis of withdrawal was the railway, because by 1630 hours all guns and 'wheels' had been withdrawn and sent off by a roundabout route to a place thirty miles behind. Everything essential for forty-eight hours had to be carried 'on the man'. Men were supplied with one hundred and eighty rounds each, and all automatic magazines were filled and carried by hand. The intention of the divisional commander was to send rations up by rail on subsequent days, casualties being evacuated in the same manner.

By 1900 hours the 8th Indian Infantry Brigade concentrated in a rubber estate close to Layang Layang railway station, prepared for a short rest before moving back again on the following morning to positions through which the 22nd Indian Infantry Brigade was to come. But at 2030 hours the Japanese artillery opened long-range fire and the bivouac area was being shelled by mortars transported by rail. Brigadier Lay decided to move back another two or more miles to the position which he was due to occupy only the next morning. He informed the commander of the 22nd Indian Infantry Brigade by telephone that he was doing so forthwith. It was a moonlit night and the brigade moved back conveniently. But in the words of Brigadier G.W.A. Painter, " this action sealed the fate of 22nd Brigade. During the night the enemy moved in strength in MT round the right flank where numerous roads existed far clear of the position and occupied Layang Layang unopposed, thus cutting the railway behind the brigade "[28] When the 8th Indian Infantry Brigade withdrew through the 22nd Indian Infantry Brigade the Japanese followed up closely, and 5/11 Sikh which was covering the withdrawal of 1/13 Frontier Force Rifles became engaged. But soon the situation was stabilised although all carriers had gone and only two 3"

[28] Brigadier G.W.A. Painter: Personal account, pp. 24-25.

mortars had remained behind. At nightfall they closed in towards the railway and asked for permission to withdraw gradually down the road to Layang Layang. This was not given as the divisional commander wanted them to withdraw slowly down the railway on to the brigade during the next day. It was then decided that they might withdraw to a position half a mile south, and permission was sought to send a company to hold Layang Layang. The latter also was not agreed to. At 1950 hours the Japanese opened mortar and machine-gun fire and finding none at Layang Layang, as time went on, they moved from both flanks and occupied it, missing the rear party of the 8th Indian Infantry Brigade by less than one hundred yards. 5/11 Sikh had the worst position in all these changes in which it settled before midnight but had the greatest difficulty in establishing communication with the brigade, which was eventually possible by hooking in on the railway telephone wires.

In the eastern sector 2/18 Australian Imperial Force Battalion withdrew to positions in depth on the east coast road between Ulu Sedili and Dohol. One company was left in the rear of 2/20 Australian Imperial Force Battalion to cover its withdrawal. As the Japanese were still recovering from the shock of the previous day 2/20 Australian Imperial Force Battalion enjoyed a quiet day at Jemaluang and withdrew in the evening to Milestone 29 area, about four miles north of Kota Tinggi. 2/18 Australian Imperial Force Battalion also withdrew then.

THE 9TH INDIAN DIVISION DECIMATED

28 January 1942 was remarkable for two incidents, one the final decision to withdraw the whole British army from the mainland to the Island of Singapore and the other the disaster to the 22nd Indian Infantry Brigade. General Wavell had left the decision about the timing of withdrawal to the Malaya Command which came to the conclusion on 28 January that withdrawal without any further delay was necessary to save the situation. General Wavell agreed to it and despatched the following cable to the British Chiefs of Staff. " Percival telegraphed last night (28 January 1942) that after consulting commanders in Johore he had decided to withdraw to Singapore Island by night January 30/January 31. I have approved decision. In view Japanese superiority on ground and in air and landing fresh troops Endau early withdrawal inevitable and desirable to do so with as little loss and disorganisation as possible ".[29]

[29] Wavell's *Despatch*, Appendix "C" p. 13.

The plan of withdrawal, which had been drawn up in detail by the III Indian Corps "envisaged a coordinated withdrawal by night on all four routes with a final withdrawal to the island on the night 30-31 January.....this was to be carried out rapidly in MT. For the immediate ground defence of the Causeway an outer and inner bridgehead were organised......Careful plans were made for the anti-aircraft defence of the Causeway and for the conveyance of troops, but not vehicles, by water craft as an alternative to the Causeway". Three battalions with supporting arms were allotted for the defence of the outer bridgehead, and one battalion (2 Argyll and Sutherland Highlanders), for the defence of the inner bridgehead.

The second important development was the disaster which overtook the 9th Indian Division on the railway front. First of all Major-General Barstow disappeared, whose body was later found by the Japanese and then the whole of the 22nd Indian Inantry Brigade went into liquidation leaving only a few survivors to relate its fate.

All was quiet in the camp of the 8th Indian Infantry Brigade on the morning of 28 January and the 22nd Indian Infantry Brigade was expected to pass through during the night of 28/29 January 1942. Unfortunately the railway bridge between milestone 439 and milestone 440[30] in the south of Layang Layang, had been blown up before time the previous night, and this was a severe handicap to the withdrawal of the 22nd Indian Infantry Brigade, besides snapping the wire which served as the only communication between the two brigades at this time. At 0900 hours Major-General Barstow, the commander of the 9th Indian Division, passed up the railway line on a trolley to make contact with the 22nd Indian Infantry Brigade, as it was now out of touch with the other brigade. He ordered 2/10 Baluch to occupy the commanding ridge position which had not been done earlier and then proceeded on the trolley up to the deomlished bridge and then walked across it. At about half a mile further on and on the railway embankment, they were ambushed at close range. Soon after their departure shots were heard; and, later, the two staff officers arrived at 2/10 Baluch Regiment headquarters. They reported that they had escaped, and they could say nothing of Major-General Barstow who had jumped on the opposite side. It was presumed that he was shot dead.

The fate of the 22nd Indian Infantry Brigade was, equally tragic. Its ordeal began on 28 January 1942 and ended on 2

---

[30] A diary of 5th Battalion (D.C.O.) The Sikh, p. 21, para 15.

February 1942, thus lasting five days. Brigadier Painter had to get back to Layang Layang according to the understanding with Brigadier Lay. He put forth his best efforts in reaching it, from morning till evening, through the swamp and jungle on the western side of the railway. He failed. Meanwhile he learnt that the 8th Indian Infantry Brigade had gone back to Sedenak. He decided to abandon Layang Layang as his objective and to go to Sedenak through the jungle west of the railway. Unfortunately he lost his way and wandered in the forests for three days without food and shelter. His responsibility was great. Not only was he to lead the whole brigade, but he was also to carry the many wounded on stretchers up the hills, over fallen trees, through thorny bushes and across ravines and swamps. In the absence of compasses and maps the brigade reached a belt of open country and was lucky in coming across some Chinese guides. With the help of one of these the brigade crossed to the east of the railway. On 31 January it was able to find a hospital to leave the wounded with a doctor and a few attendants. On 1 February, the brigade broke up but some of the men were fortunate enough to cross into Singapore Island during the night from points facing the Naval Base.

FURTHER WITHDRAWALS

Elsewhere withdrawal proceeded without any remarkable incident. On the west coast road, 3/16 Punjab waited for the blowing up of the bridge at Benut and, when it was done, withdrew through 3 Cavalry positions to an area behind, the S. Sanglang, about eight miles south of Benut. 3 Cavalry then passed through to a position about one mile in the rear. About midday the bridge over the S. Sanglang was blown and 3/16 Punjab withdrew through the 28th Indian Infantry Brigade to the Boulder position near Milestone 22 on Pontian Kechil-Skudai road, where it was to cover the Gunong Pulai reservoir. 3 Cavalry rejoined the 28th Indian Infantry Brigade. 2/2 Gurkha Rifles saw approximately one thousand men of the 15th Indian Infantry Brigade, about two hundred Garhwalis (all that then remained of the 45th Indian Infantry Brigade), and men of the 53rd British Infantry Brigade, pass through them. The night was quiet; and a party of twenty men moved off to the water-works which were four miles from the main road with the dual role of linking up with 1/14 Punjab and delaying the Japanese if they should come down along one of the tracks leading from the north and the water-works to a point at Milestone 27 on the Pontian Kechil-

Skudai road. 2/9 Gurkha Rifles remained about a mile behind the T junction at Pontian Kechil, with one company forward of the Pontian Besar river. 1/14 Punjab covered the Pontian Kechil—Kukup road with one company to the east of 2/2 Gurkha Rifles near the T junction and another company at the Boulder Position. The Japanese planes kept flying over the track from the Pontian Besar water-works to Milestone 27 on the Pontian Kechil—Skudai road and caused apprehension regarding the security of the brigade's line of withdrawal. To render this line of communication more secure, 2/9 Jat which was at Milestone 8 on Johore Bahru—Kota Tinggi road was shifted to Milestone 29 on Pontian Kechil—Skudai road with its role ' to prevent any parties of the enemy from crossing the road and moving southward between inclusive 33 milestone to inclusive 29 milestone '.[31] However its further orders were to move to Singapore " after 28th Indian Infantry Brigade had passed through to the area of 25 MS "[32] and the battalion moved in motor transport for Singapore,[33] on the following day at 2100 hours.

In the centre, Westforce was none too happy, because ' the enemy is in such close contact ', and men were fatigued.[34] The Japanese attacked 2 Gordons at 0900 hours, 2/26 Australian Imperial Force Battalion at 1400 hours and 2/30 Australian Imperial Force Battalion at 1530 hours, the gap between 2 Gordons then in the forward position at Milestone 41½ and 2/30 Australian Imperial Force Battalion at Milestone 40½ being one mile; their flanks resting on a thick jungle. By 1700 hours the last of these three battalions saved 2 Gordons by a bayonet attack and also took charge of the position involving an area about a mile long. The whole brigade then withdrew by 2200 hours to the area between Milestone 30½ and Milestone 27.

So far as the 8th Indian Infantry Brigade was concerned its losing contact with the 22nd Indian Infantry Brigade compelled the divisional commander to move the troops on to the ground covering the vital railway bridge[35] and to ascertain the situation and clear up the position by capturing the high ground through which the railway had made a cutting, at a mile south of Layang Layang. D Company which was selected as a fighting patrol of 2/10 Baluch moved forward along the railway, but before it could reach the railway cutting it was fired on and took cover. B Company was then sent with instructions to occupy the ground

[31] War Diary, 2/9 Jat, 27 January 1942.
[32] *Ibid.*, 28 January 1942.
[33] *Idem.*
[34] *Why Singapore Fell, op. cit.*, pp. 132-133.
[35] Colonel W.A. Trott: Short account, chiefly from the Q. side. p. 9.

on the left side of the railway, the idea being that this would help the capture of the high ground by this company. B Company started on its route at 1030 hours. But it was soon caught in a swamp. Besides, the jungle was very thick, control of men and movement became difficult, and the Japanese were in stronger numbers than had been reported. It was not long before the wounded and other men began to come back with Bren guns for which they had no ammunition. B Company had consequently to fall back and join A Company. For some time the situation looked serious. But as good luck would have it the Japanese did not immediately follow up and when they did, they did not press round the flanks as usual. Probably the 'going' was as bad for them as it was for the Baluch Regiment. In the afternoon, six boxes of ·303 ammunition arrived, and later, a further consignment was received. But these were practically useless, because in the late evening, orders for the usual withdrawal came, and the brigade reached Sedenak in the early hours of 29 January 1942, 464 Field Battery covering the brigade withdrawal. During the afternoon the Bahawalpur State Infantry had gone in advance to Sedenak to protect the artillery and transport. When the whole brigade and 464 Field Battery troop reached Sedenak this Indian State Infantry was sent back to Kulai area. The troop attached to 464 Field Battery also moved back to this area soon after.

In the east 2/18 Australian Imperial Force Battalion was disposed, by morning of 28 January 1942, in depth on the road between Dohol and Mawai, less one company at Lombong lying at the end of a side road running off to the west. Immediately behind this battalion was 2/17 Dogra in the neighbourhood of Mawai crossroads with one company watching the mouth of the Sedili river. There was no contact with Japanese ground troops but their aeroplanes were fairly active, bombing the vacant Jemaluang area. In the evening 2/18 Australian Imperial Force Battalion withdrew through 2/17 Dogra and then, passing through 2/20 Australian Imperial Force Battalion moved to Milestone 23 about three miles south of Kota Tinggi.

29 January 1942 was not conspicuous for any major event. It was a day of coordinated withdrawal from all fronts. In the western front the Japanese movements were extremely puzzling. There were any number of entrances into the British zone, and they were making use of most of them. The crowd at Ponggor remained still to be evacuated. On this date one senior officer, eighteen officers and four hundred and fifty other ranks were evacuated, and six hundred still remained there at the end of the

day. The Japanese were reported entering in rubber boats up the Santi river.

2/2 Gurkha Regiment was the forward battalion on the west coast road area. The Japanese came into contact with a platoon of D Company of this battalion at 0930 hours. Two Japanese cyclists drew level with the platoon position, and it was possible to catch them and take them prisoner. But when this was attempted the Japanese opened up machine-gun fire. After half an hour a heavy concentration of the Gurkha's gun-fire was brought down on and around the position occupied by the Japanese. In spite of this, the Japanese, whose strength was about one company, deployed some distance down the road, but were again fired on by two platoons of D Company. There was sporadic Japanese fire on D Company's position during the morning, which, however, caused no further casualties. The Gurkhas had the support of four 4·5-Howitzers with A Company, and these gave continuous help by firing at rapid intervals and plastering the road and the scrub jungle in front of D Company. In the afternoon the Japanese fire ceased entirely in front of D Company, but one of their aeroplanes made a machine-gun attack on the Gurkha position on Pontian Kechil, without causing any damage, however. At 1800 hours, D Company withdrew from its position half a mile north of Pontian Besar and passed through A Company, which also then withdrew, and the bridge at Pontian Besar was blown up. Shortly after dark, this battalion arrived at Milestone 27, which was nine miles from Pontian Kechil, and took up its positions for the night. It may be added that when it passed Pontian Kechil at 1845 hours, 5/14 Punjab covered it and came in reserve afterwards at a point one mile behind milestone 27. 2/9 Gurkha Regiment was in position on the right of 2/2 Gurkha Regiment, and 3 Cavalry and B Company of 1/14 Punjab was in the Reservoir Area.[36]

As had been expected, the Japanese had tried to outflank the main British position by coming down a track leading to the Water-works, and D Company platoon did some useful work in checking the Japanese movement before withdrawing according to plan and in conformity with the battalion's withdrawal. The details of this action will not be irrelevant here.[37] The action opened at 1430 hours, when a platoon of 5/14 Punjab observed some Japanese platoons moving eastwards along a track three hundred yards from the far bank of the river. Thereafter all three platoons of company of 5/14 Punjab were afforded fleeting

[36] Colonel A.M.L. Harrison: History of 11th Indian Division in Malaya.
[37] Ibid.

targets as the Japanese passed eastwards or approached the demolished bridges. Evidently things were piling up for the platoon of 2/2 Gurkha Regiment's D Company, which was holding the pumping station to protect a track which took off via the Gunong Pulai reservoir to the Skudai road. At 1600 hours, two Japanese scouts approached the pumping station, and after them came the main body of those scouts. As soon as these were in sight and at two hundred yards range, the Gurkha platoon opened fire, killed eight and scattered the rest of the Japanese. But at 1630 hours the Japanese returned and attacked this platoon with machine-gun and mortar fire, and by 1730 hours the attackers numbered two companies. Time was now precious, because this platoon, along with C Company of 5/14 Punjab, had been made responsible for the protection of the north flank of the Brigade's withdrawal up to 1830 hours, when the two were to withdraw via the reservoir to Milestone 22. The platoon informed the Punjabi company that it would try strictly to stick to the time-schedule, but might not be able to hold out much longer. At 1745 hours, the Japanese outflanked the platoon astride the track to the Reservoir but were still three miles from the Skudai road. So the platoon sidestepped westwards to join C Company of 5/14 Punjab, which was at Parit Lama, and they withdrew together to 2/9 Jat's position at Milestone 29 along a track.

At 2200 hours a squadron of 3 Cavalry reported that it was being heavily attacked in the Reservoir Area and falling back to the Causeway.

The 53rd British Brigade and 2/9 Jat left for Singapore after dark. On arrival there Brigadier Duke assumed command of the original battalions, namely, 5 and 6 Norfolks and 2 Cambridgeshire. 3/16 Punjab, which contained barely one hundred men, and 2/9 Jat joined the 15th Indian Infantry Brigade.

In the Westforce, during the day the Japanese were particularly active against 2/26 Australian Imperial Force Battalion and 2 Gordons, both on the ground and in the air. During the afternoon the Japanese penetrated the position occupied by 2/30 Australian Imperial Force Battalion. A counter-attack adjusted matters very satisfactorily and the position became quiet again. 2/30 Australian Imperial Force Battalion moved back to 25-mile post during the late afternoon, and 2 Gordons commenced their withdrawal after nightfall. While 2/30 Australian Imperial Force Battalion withdrew two miles more to get nearer 2/26 Australian Imperial Force Battalion which was at 21-mile post, 2 Gordons went as far back as 5 mile to take up its role as a bridge-head force.

So far as the 8th Indian Infantry Brigade was concerned, there was no great activity during the day. At Sedenak, 1/13 Frontier Force Rifles was forward astride the railway, 3/17 Dogra stood on the right side and 2/10 Baluch faced both flanks. Transport had been waiting and supplies were replenished. Part of 464 Battery remained to give support. But at 1700 hours the Japanese struck at A Company of 2/10 Baluch, which suffered several casualties within half an hour, especially among men moving about with reserve ammunition. Immediately afterwards the Japanese moving down the railway engaged 1/13 Frontier Force Rifles, and one of their parties began to work round the left of 2/10 Baluch. But as it was already time to withdraw in accordance with the divisional orders, the brigadier decided to pull out. 3/17 Dogra had a hard job in breaking off the fight, but did so finally without undue casualties. 1/13 Frontier Force Rifles followed suit and withdrew to positions about one and a half miles behind on the railway line. 2/10 Baluch in turn passed through 1/13 Frontier Force Rifles. Unfortunately this battalion did not know that one company of 1/13 Frontier Force Rifles had not come back when the Baluch withdrew. Most of this company was temporarily lost, some rejoining the brigade later. As usual, the Japanese did not follow up as darkness came on.

On arrival at Kulai at about 2200 hours the brigade halted, and defensive positions were taken up during darkness, 2/10 Baluch astride the railway with 1/13 Frontier Force Rifles echeloned back on its right. Once again 464 Battery was in support. The 8th Indian Infantry Brigade rested till daylight of 30 January.

In the eastern sector[38] on 29 January 1942, the forward troops of Eastforce comprised 2/17 Dogra which was covering the Mawai cross-roads area. There was no contact with the Japanese ground forces during the day. In the afternoon the detached company at the Sedili Boom was withdrawn. Meanwhile 2/20 Australian Imperial Force Battalion which was near milestone 29 (about four miles north of Kota Tinggi) moved back through 2/18 Australian Imperial Force Battalion, which was at Milestone 23, to the Tebrau area to be ready to take its place in the Johore Bridge-head force. When it was evening 2/17 Dogra fell back to the line of the Kota Tinggi river and the bridge was blown. As the last troops were withdrawing from Mawai, sounds of firing were heard from the direction of the mouth of the Sekati river, and it was probable that the Japanese landed there after the company of 2/10 Dogra had left.

[38] Major E.F.D. Hyde: Account of the Malaya Campaign. 29 January 1942.

EVACUATION OF THE MAINLAND

30 January 1942 was the last day of the struggle of the British army on the mainland of Malaya. On the Skudai road, there was patrol contact on the fronts of 2/2 Gurkha Rifles at Milestone 27 about 1000 hours, and of 3 Cavalry at the reservoir just before 1430 hours, which was the hour fixed for the start of the withdrawal. From dawn, patrols of A Company, D Company and headquarters company worked wth 2/9 Gurkha Rifles and 3 Cavalry, who were sending patrols on the right flank. All was quiet on this front, although the sounds of fighting heard throughout the night from the direction of the main road were still coming. But, as stated already, a slight disturbance started at about 1000 hours and the British artillery brought down a heavy barrage on the road and neighbouring country. Later on in the morning, additional small parties of Japanese troops were seen once again by B Company of 2/2 Gurkha Rifles but were dispersed as before by the British artillery. Throughout the morning a Japanese reconnaissance plane was circling over the whole of Gurkha position and preventing them from moving about. Shortly after midday, the brigadier announced the orders for the final withdrawal from the mainland to the Island of Singapore. The Malaya Command had spared no attempts to find the 22nd Indian Infantry Brigade but had failed.[39] Meanwhile, General Wavell, who had proposed visiting Singapore with air Marshal Sir Richard Peirse[40] (Air Chief of American British Dutch and Australian command and commander of the Allied Air Force), arrived at Singapore on this date, visited Johore, saw Generals Percival, Heath and Gordon Bennett and discussed plans for the withdrawal.[41] It was decided at this meeting that this withdrawal could not be delayed any longer in the hope of recovering the 22nd Indian Infantry Brigade in time to get on to Singapore Island before the Causeway was blown up. 1430 hours was also fixed as the hour when movements relating to withdrawal would begin in this sector. In consequence of this decision, 2/2 Gurkha Rifles began the first backward move covered by 2/9 Gurkha Rifles and the armoured cars of 3 Cavalry. The withdrawal was divided into four stages, the first stage being Milestone 23 for A company, Milestone $23\frac{1}{2}$ for D and H Companies, Milestone 24 for C Company and Milestone $24\frac{1}{2}$ for B Company. 2/9 Gurkha Rifles was in a similar position on the road in the rear of 2/2 Gurkha Rifles. The withdrawal

---

[39] "*ABDACOM*", op. cit., p. 33, para 23, sub-para (m).
[40] Wavell's *Despatch*, Appendix "C" p. 13.
[41] *Ibid.*, p. 7, para. 21. Also *Wigs: Singapore Fell*, p. 135.

of forward companies was accomplished without incident, although the armoured cars of 3 Cavalry had a successful encounter with a party of the Japanese in the village at Milestone 27. The morale of the brigade was excellent. A Company of 2/2 Gurkha Rifles reached Milestone 23 at 1600 hours, and the second stage of withdrawal began at 1700 hours. This ended at a position between Milestone 19 and Milestone 18 just before dark. At Milestone 22 a position, known as Boulder Position, had been held by the companies of 2/2 Gurkha Rifles and 5/14 Punjab, and here the battalions passed all brigade transport which had been sent back during the previous night. At 1900 hours it started raining. But motor transport arrived to carry every one for all the remaining miles up to Singapore. The third stage was carried out exactly like the second, with companies taking up positions at half mile intervals, so that from Milestone 11 to Milestone 20 there were troops at regular intervals guarding the road. Finally, after thirty minutes halt, the companies embussed once again and started on the fourth stage. This withdrawal started from Skudai T junction and passed through Johore Bahru. There was, fortunately, no interference by the Japanese. There was a standing order that Skudai corner must be denied to the Japanese until midnight of this day, but the Japanese made no attempt to interfere with the withdrawal. The brigade therefore reached Singapore Island about the midnight of 30/31 January 1942, 3 Cavalry acting as rearguard with 344 Field Battery in support.

On the morning of 30 January 1942, Westforce was disposed north of Kulai as mentioned earlier. Owing to the convergence of the main road and railway there, the 27th Australian Imperial Force Brigade and 8th Indian Infantry Brigade were very near each other. The Japanese aeroplanes were extremely active, but most of their bombing and machine-gunning was directed against the artillery with the Indian brigade and the Australians on the left. At 1000 hours, the order of withdrawal to Singapore at the end of the day arrived. At 1330 hours it was discovered that the Australians on the left of the 8th Indian Infantry Brigade had gone back up to Milestone 19 leaving the left flank of the Indian brigade completely exposed. A and C Companies of 2/10 Baluch were therefore slightly withdrawn and adjusted to meet the situation. In the afternoon this battalion fell back through 1/13 Frontier Force Rifles to take up a position on the right of the Australian brigade, just north of Kulai railway station. 1/13 Frontier Force Rifles, Bahawalpur State Infantry and 3/17 Dogra were then ordered to withdraw through 2/10 Baluch. As these units reached the railway station area, the Japanese appeared in Kulai village on top of the brigade headquarters, which was also moving back. It was the usual cyclist force which had made flanking movement from the east. 1/13 Frontier Force Rifles attacked the Japanese with two companies and by dusk cleared the area.

With the 8th Indian Infantry Brigade in this position, volunteers were chosen to remain on the mainland and get into contact with the lost 22nd Indian Infantry Brigade with a view to helping the men to reach the coast. They were given certain secret signals and rendezvous on the coast of Johore, opposite the Singapore Island. But this party had no success in its mission and ultimately rejoined its brigade in Singapore.

As soon as it was dark, the 8th Indian Infantry Brigade and the Australians commenced to withdraw. In the former 1/13 Frontier Force Rifles was followed by 3/17 Dogra and Bahawalpur State Infantry, with 2/10 Baluch bringing up the rear. The Japanese shelled the road and tried to interfere with the withdrawal, but without success. After a short march, the brigade embussed and proceeded to Singapore.

In the eastern sector there was still no contact on 30 January between Eastforce and the Japanese, and 2/17 Dogra had a quiet day in its positions beyond the Kota Tinggi river.

The following account by General Percival describes the end of the withdrawal. "The final withdrawal across the Causeway on the night of 30-31 January was carried out without incident and with little interference from the enemy's air force. By about 6 a.m. on 31 January all troops, except those in the bridgeheads and those still missing, were back on Singapore Island. All were weary. Many had been fighting, and withdrawing to fight again, in an exhausting climate and cruel country for seven weeks on end and in the face of a powerful enemy equipped with every advantage. The most remarkable thing perhaps is that so many of them were still full of fight after such an ordeal.

"By 7 a.m. the 1st battalion of the outer bridgehead, the Gordons, was crossing the Causeway. Behind it came the inner bridgehead, the Argylls, headed by their pipes. By 8 a.m. Lieutenant-Colonel Stewart stepped out of Johore on to the Causeway, the last to do so. The Causeway, which was solidly built, was seventy feet wide at the water line and wider below it. Its demolition presented certain technical difficulties. Nevertheless, a demolition had been successfully inserted in it by the Royal Navy, and at 8·15 a.m. it was exploded. A moment later the water was racing through a seventy-foot gap. The operations on the mainland were at an end and the battle of Singapore had begun".[48]

[48] *The War in Malaya*, p. 249.

CHAPTER XI

The Battle of Singapore

TOPOGRAPHICAL

At the beginning of 1942, Singapore was the gateway to the Far East and the fifth largest port in the world. It ranked with Pearl Harbour, Heligoland and Gibraltar as one of the four modern "impregnable" fortresses. It was also the symbol of the British Empire; with its possession from 1819 and the expenditure incurred in building the Naval Base, including the famous floating dock, the largest in the world, Britain had become the dominant power in East Asia.

The Island of Singapore, oblong in shape, measures twenty-seven miles from east to west and thirteen miles from north to south and has an area of over two hundred and twenty square miles. On the north and west it is separated from the mainland by the straits of Johore which at their narrowest point, namely Putri Narrows in the north-western corner of the Island, are seven hundred yards wide. It was connected to the mainland, however, by a stone Causeway 1,100 yards long and wide enough to take the railway and a broad road. As the straits were sufficiently deep, the foundations of the Causeway were strong, broad-based and much below the surface of the water. On the eastern side of the Causeway, the straits were from 1,100 to about 5,000 yards wide, and could take the biggest vessels afloat as far as the Naval Base.

There were numerous smaller islands which were intimately connected with the development and defence of Singapore Island. Pulau Ubin in the north-eastern part of the Island gave connection to Kota Tinggi through the mouth of the Johore river. Pulau Tekong lay almost covering the mouth of the Johore river, but its importance was due to the existence of Pengerang Hill, a few miles east, at the southern tip of the Johore mainland. Immediately south of Singapore Island lay Pulau Blakang Mati, Pulau Brani and Pulau Bukum, of which the first was a military reserve and the third contained the Asiatic Petroleum Company's main reserves of naval fuel, petrol and lubricating oils. There were several other islands further south, but these were generally of no use to the garrison of Singapore.

At the time of Japanese invasion the population of the Island was about 800,000 made up of 8,000 Europeans, 20,000

Malays, 20,000 Indians and 700,000 Chinese. Singapore's prosperity was due to the export of rubber and tin, and shipping. Communications were generally good. There was a network of good metalled roads and many unmetalled ones in the rubber estates. But the interesting feature about all main roads was that they radiated in all directions only from the city of Singapore. The principal road was the Bukit Timah road which was in its southern half, a double track road with a canal in between. On the whole, this was the only road from the south to the north connecting the Island with the mainland. The main line of the railway crossed the Johore Causeway and ran from north to south in the centre of the Island as far as Singapore city and port.

The surface of the Island is undulating, with a number of small hills varying from seventy to five hundred and eighty-one feet in height. The highest of these, Bukit Timah, lies in the centre of the Island, and with it is a group of hills called Bukit Mendai about three miles north, and Pasir Panjang Ridge about three miles south. The latter is four miles long and runs parallel to the coast about a few furlongs from the sea, from Pasir Panjang village to the western outskirts of Singapore city.

Apart from the built-up areas, Singapore Island, like the rest of Malaya, was thickly covered by rubber and other plantations while on the northern and western coasts there were extensive mangrove swamps. These swamps had, of recent years, owing to extensive works of drainage, lost much of their value as military obstacles. It is worthy of notice that while the western coastline was full of creeks a few of which only were navigable, the eastern and southern coastlines from Changi to Pasir Panjang were less broken and more beautiful, with extensive sandy beaches and very little mangrove. Consequently, the sea edges of the former area, which were not overlooked from any point inland, could not be covered by direct or observed fire, while those of the latter were more or less perfectly defended by planned fire from the interior.

The centre of the Island contained the MacRitchie, Peirce and Seletar reservoirs, and the municipal catchment area, a large jungle area traversed only by a few tracks. To the north, the Naval Base reservation also covered a large tract of country.

ORGANISATION OF DEFENCE

As described earlier, the problem of defending Singapore had received every careful thought and examination. The pre-war British appreciation was that the best locality for a defensive position was that portion of land which lay between the Sungei Kranji and the Sungei Turong. The view then held was that the most vulnerable beaches of the Island were those facing south and east towards the open sea. The general lay-out of the defensive plan was, therefore, formulated on these assumptions, and fixed defences were constructed generally to meet this contingency. But when the Japanese came from the north, it became evident that the British preparations and plans would require readjustment. These fixed defences had taken years to build, involving much highly skilled labour and planning. It was therefore no easy task to modify them to meet the unforeseen northern attack, but the work was put in hand and was still in progress on the eve of the Japanese invasion. Furthermore, the Japanese indifference to swamps, however deep and thorny, gave an unpleasant shock to the British commanders and Chiefs of Staff. New dispositions had therefore to be selected, obstacles built, and the troops put in new positions as quickly as possible.

It was for this reason that General Wavell was constantly reminding General Percival of the strengthening of the north side of the island and of allied tasks. The Chiefs of Staff in London had, as already stated, given a list of particular measures to be taken for the better defence of Singapore Island, and General Wavell had reported that all those measures were being taken.[1] The general outlook in the whole of the south-west Pacific at the end of January 1942 was pessimistic and, although Mr. Churchill had enjoined that the war must be fought up to the last bit of land in the Island, and General Wavell in his turn had ordered Malaya Command that it must fight for every foot of the Island, the opinion of the High Command on the spot was that they " could do no more than try to defend Singapore Island..... and that the arrival of the air reinforcements promised might yet turn the scale ".[2]

General Wavell made an estimate of the resources at his command for the defence of the Island. He wrote, "much depended on the ability of the garrison of Singapore Island to make a prolonged resistance. General Percival had the 18th British Division practically intact, the 8th Australian Division of two brigades at good strength after arrival of reinforcements, and the equivalent of some four or five brigades of mixed British and Indian Infantry, besides local forces. In view of the size of the island this force was obviously weak in numbers, but the enemy could not employ large forces, and I considered that an active defence should enable the island to be held for some time, for some

---

[1] "*ABDACOM*", *op. cit.*, pp. 34-35, para. 24(d).
[2] Wavell's Despatch, pp. 7-8, para 23. See also para 25.

months I hoped. I had instructed General Percival to place the fresh 18th Division on the front most likely to be attacked and the 8th Australian Division in the next most dangerous sector, keeping the Indian troops as far as possible in reserve for reinforcement and counter-attack. He estimated that the Japanese were most likely to attack in the north-east of the island and placed the 18th Division there. He put the Australians in the north-west".[3] It may be convenient here to analyse other preparatory measures for the defence of the Island which had been taken in accordance with the instructions from above.[4]

To begin with the fixed artillery positions, the fortress guns of the heaviest calibre had all-round traverse, and many of the other fixed defence guns had arcs of fire over the mainland. The 15-inch guns, however, had no landward firing ammunition, and the 9·2-inch had only 25 rounds per gun, though high explosive ammunition for the 6-inch guns was adequate. But the flat trajectory of these guns made them unsuitable for counter-battery work. Also observation of fire was difficult owing to topographical features of the land, while air observation was not available. Nevertheless, according to General Percival, ' an improvised but workable counter-bombardment organisation was built up and fields of fire were cleared '.[5]

Food supplies for the whole garrison of the Island, which included those saved from the mainland and the new arrivals, amounted to three months' meat, four months' flour and tinned vegetables, and five to six months' stock of other items. Stocks of food for the civil population were sufficient for four months, with six months' flour and nine months' meat which could serve to supplement army stocks. After the loss of Johore water-supply was reduced from 27 to 15 million gallons per day, and this was rationed immediately. Steps were taken to evacuate "useless mouths" as quickly as possible. But, in spite of these measures, when the refugees came from the north, and the air bombardment broke the water mains which were continuously supplied by water from the two pumping stations working at full pressure, water scarcity became acute.

Ammunition stocks were ample. Pistols and Thompson sub-machine-guns had 12 days' stock; ·55 anti-tank rifles 23 days stock; small arms ammunition, grenades and mortars, 45 days' stock; and artillery 90 days or more. General Percival did not consider the administrative situation as critical, except in the matter

---

[3] *Idem.*, para 24.
[4] " *ABDACOM* ", *op. cit.*, pp. 34-36, para 24.
[5] *The War in Malaya*, pp. 251 and 253.

of "field-gun and light anti-aircraft ammunition". The main difficulty, however, was that the "military dumps and depots had been widely dispersed......to avoid excessive loss from air attack. The weakness now was that many of them, and especially the main ones, were in the centre of the island, where they were more exposed to capture by the enemy than if they had been in the town area. For instance, the main military food supply depot was just east of Bukit Timah village while a large dump of food back-loaded from the mainland was on the race-course. This was not an ideal arrangement....... Similarly there were two large petrol depots near the race-course, so that the Bukit Timah area had become of very great tactical importance. On the other hand, most of the civil government's food reserves, both for Europeans and Asiatics, were in the Singapore town area".[6] Clothing was sufficient for two months, and general stores and mechanical transport were also adequate for the same length of time. It was, however, noticed that there would be no reserve stocks of weapons and no spares when units had drawn arms to replace losses.

General Defensive Measures

Obstruction of land approaches to the straits and landing places in the Island with wire, mines, booby traps or other means was in hand; but there was a shortage of technical supervisory personnel and labour. Field guns from the beach defences in the southern sector were moved to the northern and western sectors. Boats and small craft were collected at places of security. Preparation of all-round defensive localities with switch lines was in hand, as were also measures to guard against surprise night-landings. Measures to defend aerodromes included provision of troops, armoured cars and anti-aircraft defences at each aerodrome. Plans for dispersal and control of the civil population and for the suppression of fifth column activities were made, and dispersal camps were in existence. The arming of the personnel of fixed defences had been arranged. Signal communications throughout the Island and to aerodromes in use in Sumatra were provided.

Innumerable pill-boxes had been constructed, with field-fire trenches running in all directions in between; searchlights were kept to detect all river crossing operations; the entrances into harbours and straits were mined; Pulau Ubin, Pulau Tekong, Pengerang, and Changi were blocked and equipped with special types of cannon; the west coast was also strengthened with cannon

[6] *Ibid.*, p. 257.

and layers of barbed wire; and several anti-aircraft emplacements surrounded the central part of the Island. After the blowing-up of the causeway, the reservoirs were strongly defended on all sides. The so-called "fortresses" were built in the west from Ayer Bajau to south coast, in the north in Kranji area, the Naval Base and Seletar area, and in the east around Loyang. Other defended positions with barbed wire entanglements were to the west of Hill 437, to the south of Hill 327, to the east of Hill 105 in semicircle to the north of Bukit Mandai, and from Bukit Timah (Hill 581) to the south eastern end of the MacRitchie Reservoir. Machine-gun positions were constructed at all possible landing places along the south coast from the Jurong to the Changi. At the last moment before the Japanese invasion of the Island the entire coast facing Johore State was fortified, and obstacles were constructed on land and sea, with searchlights in various places.

Naturally, in these hurried preparations, some defects were noticeable. General Percival was not slow to realise these, which he has listed as follows:—(i) land mines were unreliable, because corrosion would set in quickly in the humid climate of the Island and they would explode at any moment; (ii) much dependence was placed on the comparatively narrow neck of land between Sungei Jurong and Sungei Kranji to oppose a landing on the western shores of the Island. But here the ground had been cleared though no actual defences were constructed until after the outbreak of war with Japan; (iii) no defences had been constructed on the north and west coasts in the pre-war days, and only limited defences were put up even after the war had started. The two reasons for this state of things were the high policy governing the protection of the Naval Base and the non-availability of funds for such a work; (iv) the defence of the northern shore of Singapore Island was delayed on one side by a scarcity of labour and complicated on the other by the intersection of creeks and mangrove swamps.

The 'Denial' Policy

The War Office in London had instructed the Malaya Command, sometime in the third week of January 1942, to destroy all valuable stocks to deny their possession to the Japanese. General Wavell sympathised with the Malaya Command in their unenviable position and agreed that ' you cannot fight and destroy simultaneously with 100 per cent efficiency in both'.[7] After a thorough discussion from every point of view the Chiefs of Staff

[7] *Ibid.*, p. 260.

finally replied that 'demolition of the Naval Base should be given first priority and Fortress guns second priority. Other valuable stores, equipment and installations should be destroyed on a priority basis, but their destruction should not be allowed to weaken the defence'.[8] General Percival adds that his plans to carry out this order were such that while actual execution of any denial was to be done by men in administrative charge of it, the ordering was reserved to himself, or, in any crisis, to the commander on the spot. And so far as civil installations were concerned the Director-General of Civil Defence was made responsible for their destruction.

DISPOSITION OF THE ARMY

The disposition of the Commonwealth army in the Island engaged the immediate attention of the Malaya Command. The basis of defence was, according to General Percival, "that the enemy must be prevented from landing, or, if he succeeded in landing, that he must be stopped near the beaches and destroyed or driven out by counter-attack". This required an "offensive spirit", which General Percival invoked in his instructions to all formation commanders on 3 February. He wrote, "All ranks must be imbued with the spirit of attack. It is no good waiting for the Japanese to attack first. The endeavour of every soldier must be to locate the enemy, and having located him, to close with him".[9] This amounted to fighting the Japanese on the coast perimeter wherever they might land, with the aid of mobile forces generally and with reserves in emergency. The general plan therefore was to use strong and fresh units in the north-west and north-east, other units as reserve, and to leave no possible gaps anywhere. According to General Percival the last of these three principles was the most difficult of all to be attained in practice. The length of the coastline on the whole was between seventy-two and eighty miles and there were only 70,000 men on hand, which amounted to less than a thousand for every mile without any men in depth or in reserve. Secondly, speed was the essence of the Japanese plan, and they would not allow the defenders to be reinforced by any means. 'On land no more reinforcements were available for some weeks,'[10] nor new weapons and equipment.

General Wavell considered the removal of fighter aircraft to Sumatra and the reorganisation of Indian formations as an

---
[8] "*ABDACOM*", *op. cit.*, p. 36, para 24 (e), the last sub-para.
[9] *The War in Malaya*, pp. 263-64.
[10] Wavell's *Despatch*, p. 8 para 25.

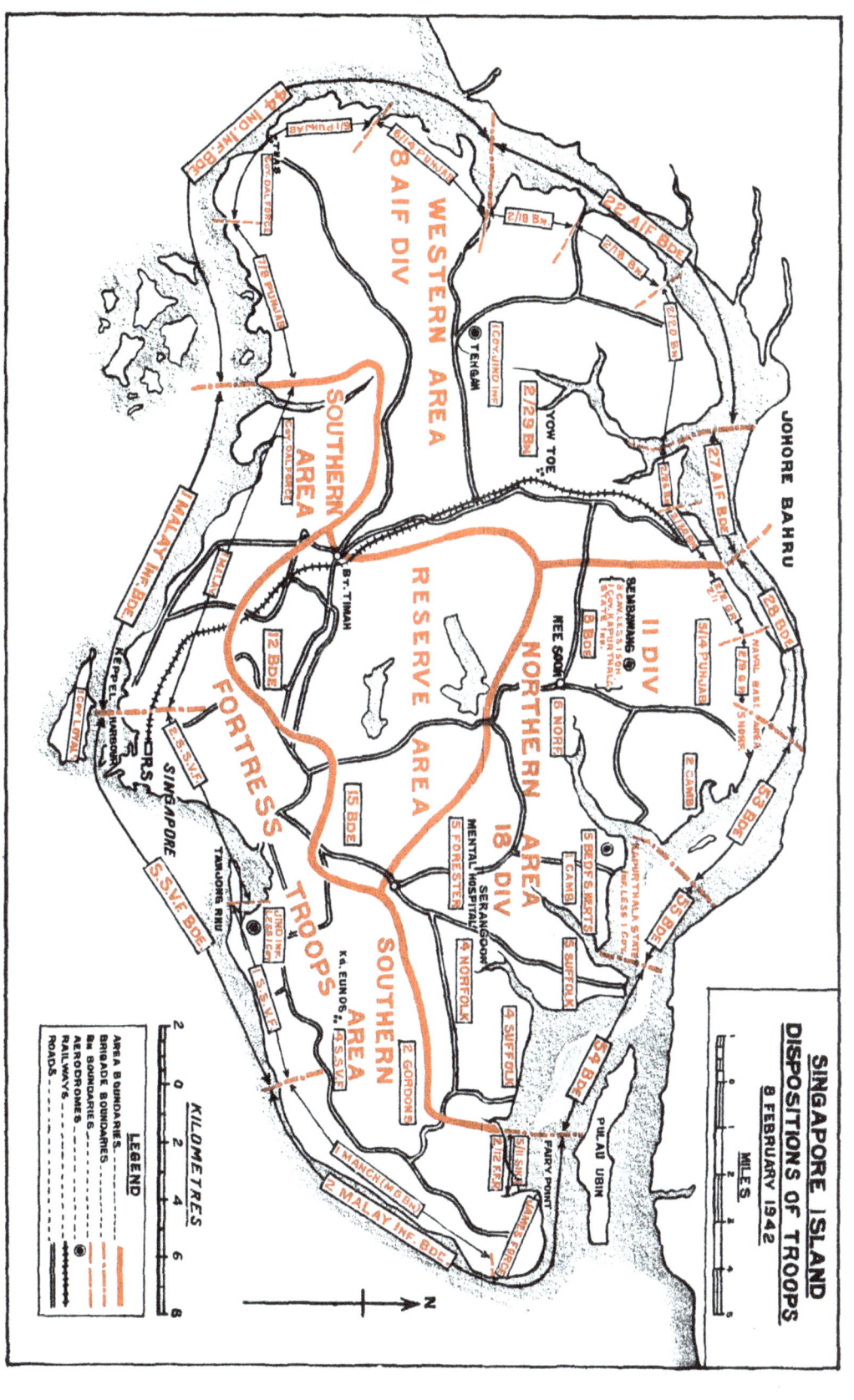

essential preliminary to the organisation of the general defence of the Island. The withdrawal of the troops from the mainland exposed three out of the four aerodromes on the Island to artillery fire. These were Tengah, Sembawang and Seletar. The increased scale of Japanese air attack on aerodromes had already necessitated the removal of the bomber squadrons to more secure bases in Sumatra. To leave fighters on the exposed aerodromes in Singapore was to invite their destruction in a few days. Hence General Wavell ordered the withdrawal of the majority of the fighters to Sumatra to protect the air bases there, which, with the loss of Malaya, became absolutely vital to the defence of the remaining Allied possessions. The equivalent of one fighter squadron was kept in Singapore, to be reinforced, as occasion demanded, by other fighters from Sumatra. This decision was open to criticism as not only depriving the land forces of protection against air attacks but also demoralising the whole fighting force and the civil population; but it was inevitable. The fighter squadron retained on the Island (one flight of eight Hurricanes and another of eight Buffaloes) was based at Kallang (without the advantage of observed artillery fire), and to it were added on 1 February 1942 forty-eight Hurricanes of the latest type, although generally speaking air reinforcements were only sufficient to replace wastage.

So far as Indian formations were concerned, they were reorganised so that a small Corps Headquarters was retained not only to control all Indian divisions and brigades but also to be in operational command of the Northern Area and in charge of the domestic affairs of the 12th and 44th Indian Infantry Brigades. Further, remnants of the 9th Indian Division were incorporated with the 11th Indian Division. The III Corps was made up of the 11th Indian Division and the 18th British Division. Thereafter the defences of Singapore Island were organised in three areas, together covering the entire coastline of the Island. Details of the three areas were as follows:—[11]

(i) *Northern Area*, under III Corps. Troops: 18th British and 11th Indian Divisions. Area: from the Causeway eastwards to Changi, i.e. exclusive Changi village—exclusive Yan Kit village—inclusive Paya Lebar village-exclusive Pierce Reservoir—exclusive Point 135 (7519)—exclusive Woodlands. Dispositions: Right—18th British Division, with 54th Infantry Brigade on the right and 55th Infantry Brigade on the left. Left—11th Indian Division, with 15th Indian Infantry Brigade on the right, 8th Indian

[11] *The War in Malaya.* p 262

Infantry Brigade in the centre and 28th Indian Infantry Brigade on the left. After a few days, the 53rd British Infantry Brigade occupied the right, and 15th Indian Infantry Brigade went into reserve.

(ii) *Western Area*, under 8th Australian Division. Troops: Australian Imperial Forces and 44th Indian Infantry Brigade. Area: from the Causeway round the west coast to Sungei Jurong, i.e. inclusive Woodlands—inclusive Point 135—inclusive Bukit Timah village—inclusive Kampong Sungei Jurong—exclusive Sungei Jurong—inclusive Tanjong Balai. Dispositions: 27th Australian Infantry Brigade (less one battalion) on the right, 22nd Australian Infantry Brigade in the centre, and 44th Indian Infantry Brigade on the left. One battalion of 27th Australian Infantry Brigade with a machine-gun company and detachments from administrative and reinforcement units was in reserve.

(iii) *Southern Area*, under Singapore Fortress. Troops: 1st and 2nd Malaya Infantry Brigades, Straits Settlements Volunteer Force and Fixed Defence Units. Area: the southern coast from Sungei Jurong to Changi, i.e. inclusive Changi village—inclusive Yan Kit village—exclusive Paya Lebar village—inclusive road junction 898143—inclusive Botanical Gardens—inclusive Wai Soon Gardens—exclusive Bukit Timah village—boundary of Western Area. Inclusive also Pengerang, Tekong and Blakang Mati island. Dispositions: 1st Malaya Infantry Brigade on the right, the Straits Settlements Volunteer Force in the centre (the Singapore Town area), and 2nd Malaya Infantry Brigade on the left (including Pengerang area and Tekong Island).

(iv) *Command Reserve:* 12th Indian Infantry Brigade.

To supplement the above forces, General Percival organised the personnel of all combatant administrative units to defend their own establishments, and secondly, he organised a force of Chinese Irregulars, Dalforce, to be placed as detachments under Area Commanders for patrolling swampy areas and other forward tasks. Anti-aircraft defences were reorganised with special reference to the docks area. All artillery was to be co-ordinated under a single brigadier. Pulau Bukum was to have a small garrison from the Independent Company. All inhabitants were to be cleared off the Sembilan Islands, which would then be 'denied' by fire to the Japanese. A belt half a mile deep on the western and northern coasts was to be absolutely devoid of inhabitants. Pengerang area was garrisoned by the personnel of the Fixed Defence Force and the Mysore (Indian) State Force battalion. Pulau Tekong was defended by the personnel of the Fixed Defence Force and 2/17 Dogra Regiment. Orders were issued for officer patrols to be sent across the Straits regularly into South Johore to reconnoitre the Japanese dispositions and ascertain their intentions, while the Royal Navy arranged for its craft to patrol the sea approaches to Singapore Island.

The defence plan had some weaknesses in it. The Island was not uniformly defended on all sides, nor was it a compact and easily manageable unit of territory. Most of the soldiers who fought and died for the Island had not seen it before nor carried a correct idea of its defences. This lack of familiarity with the terrain inevitably reduced the effectiveness of the defence. Moreover, all the three sectors were thinly held, and there were gaps, small and big, between companies, between regiments and between Command Areas, and there were swamps, creeks and jungles.

At this time there was some discussion about the best method of defending the coast. In the beginning it was considered that the beaches should be held lightly with watchers supported by a thin rifle company, and that the rest of the force should be situated well back from the sea to put in a massive counter-attack in the event of a hostile landing. But the final decision was to concentrate the defending forces right along the coast, and to repel the invaders before they could secure a footing on the Island. According to this scheme, the whole coastline was to be held by a series of platoon posts with beach-watchers and patrols, although it involved still further dispersions within each battalion. Moreover, the defensive preparations were far from complete. The coastline had not been fully wired and defended localities had still to be constructed. Owing to the fact that the whole area was overlooked from the mainland and bombed from the air, movements during the day were cut to a minimum. Rations, wire, etc., had to be carried over long distances through mangrove swamps. Motor transport was meagre enough, and it was useless off the roads. Then again, tides interfered with wiring and construction work. These difficulties were, it appears, particularly acute in the sector held by the 44th Indian Infantry Brigade, but the 28th Indian Infantry Brigade also felt likewise.[18]

The position in respect of troops was none too satisfactory either. The Indian brigades had suffered a bad shaking in South Malaya, and initially the intention appears to have been to alllow them time for rest and reorganisation before being called upon to face the brunt of Japanese offensive. The troops were tired and no battalion was up to strength. Nevertheless, from the very

---

[18] War Diary, 2/2 G.R., 31 January 1942.

beginning they had to man the exposed areas of the island coastline. The 44th Indian Infantry Brigade, with its three Punjab battalions was allotted the defence of a stretch of the west coast, approximately 15 miles in length, from exclusive S. Berih to S. Jurong. There were no prepared positions in the area except a small fort at Pasir Laba with two six-inch guns and two 18-pounders. The line was so long that inevitably wide gaps were left between company positions, covered with mangrove and timber allowing easy infiltration to the Japanese. The force was otherwise in good morale and practising counter-offensive tactics. Similar was the story of the other Indian brigade, the 28th Indian Infantry Brigade, with 1/14 Punjab, 2/2 and 2/9 Gurkha as its component units. Its area of allotment was the Naval Base, a large and complicated area with houses, docks, roads and the Sembawang aerodrome.

The situation of the 12th Indian Infantry Brigade and the 15th Indian Infantry Brigade was slightly different. When the 12th reached Tyersall, it was the sole reserve of Malaya Command. Its two battalions, 5/2 Punjab Regiment strengthened with raw recruits from India, and 4/19 Hyderabad Regiment scarcely more fortunate, were hardly in a fit condition to fight. The only battalion in any fighting condition in this brigade was 2 Argyll and Sutherland Highlanders. The 15th Indian Infantry Brigade was deployed in Bidadari. It was the reserve of the III Corps, and comprised three battalions (which had sustained a series of reverses), mixed with a fair percentage of half trained reinforcements. Consequently, this brigade too carried no high offensive value. The 8th Indian Infantry Brigade was the reserve of the 11th Indian Division in Nee Soon—Sembawang area, consisting of 1/13 Frontier Force Rifles, 2/10 Baluch Regiment and 2/18 and 5/18 Royal Garhwal Rifles combined.

A few changes in the organisation and administration of the units became inevitable in view of the probability of the Japanese invasion from the north-east. 2/9 and 4/9 Jat were combined, after the former had separated from 1/8 Punjab, so that the strength of the new Jat battalion was 15 British officers and 680 other ranks. It then joined the 15th Indian Infantry Brigade,[13] and experienced men were distributed among its companies. On 6 February 1942, 5/11 Sikh was amalgamated for tactical purposes with 2/12 Frontier Force Regiment, which, being only 150 strong, was in a miserable plight. On the following day this combined battalion was placed under the 8th Indian Infantry Brigade, but

---

[13] War Diary, 2/9 Jat, 4 February 1942.

this was cancelled on 8 February 1942, and fresh orders were issued for it to join the 2nd Malaya Infantry Brigade in Changi area.[14] 3/17 Dogra Regiment which had lost much of its fighting value on 11 January near Serendah, 7/6 Rajputana Rifles which had lost everything in the Muar battle, and 1/8 Punjab which became separated from 2/9 Jat, were also reorganised individually.

THE JAPANESE PREPARATIONS FOR INVASION

It is needless to observe that the Japanese intention was to conquer the Singapore Fortress. The invasion of Singapore Island was in the logic of events the culmination of the campaign in Malaya, and was carried out as quickly as practicable. One week of preparations was, of course, necessary to cross the straits with men, munitions and equipment.

The assault on Singapore was to be carried out by all the three Japanese divisions in the *25th Army*, namely the *Imperial Guards Division*, the *5th Division* and the *18th Division*. Each division was organised for this attack into two groups or wings, with a third group in reserve. Special engineer troops were also allotted to each division for crossing the straits, apart from the normal complement of transport, medical and signal units.[15]

In the Japanese High Command, some officers thought that the mere presence of the Japanese army would bring about the fall of Singapore.[16] But most of them feared that the British army would literally resist to the last man. The battle of ideas between these two schools started on 13 January in Kuala Lumpur and ended on 31 January 1942. The Chief of Staff decided to accept the latter view and laid down the following directive:—

(a) The entire strength of the Japanese must be used for the invasion.

(b) 1,000 rounds of ammunition must be provided for each gun.

(c) The old troops (now exhausted), fresh crack forces, and 'Very Clever' troops must be exploited, each in its own way, to the utmost.

(d) There must be perfect economy and co-ordination in the utilisation of moral and material resources, while those of the British must be destroyed.

(e) The British must be also deceived about the Japanese plan and the advantage of surprise must be obtained.

[14] A Diary of 5th Battalion (D.C.O.) The Sikh Regiment, *op. cit.* 8 February 1942.
[15] For details see Kirby, S. Woodburn, *The War Against Japan*, Vol. I, Appendix 25; Her Majesty's Stationery Office, London, 1957.
[16] *Japanese Land Operations, op. cit.*, p. 35.

As a preliminary to the execution of this plan, the railroads were quickly repaired, and steps were taken to move down men, artillery, ammunition and other materials. Among these were their landing-craft, which consisted of steel barges, with a capacity of forty men each. General Percival has noted that 'they were brought overland by road from Pontian Kechil on the west coast of Johore.'[17] The plan of attack was decided upon by 31 January 1942, when all the force had assembled at Kluang. One group was stationed in the dense forest east of Johore, another one along the railway, while the third, which consisted of crack troops, was positioned in the rubber plantations to the rear of Johore. The big guns, with 1,000 rounds per gun, were deployed on Johore Bahru line, with manned balloons to observe the effect of their firing. Officer patrols were despatched to reconnoitre the British positions and the terrain and to search the coastal strips. Above all, the inhabitants of Johore beach area were ordered to withdraw into the interior within three days, and none but the Japanese were allowed in the forward sector thereafter.

The Japanese army and naval air forces were made to act in close co-operation with the ground forces, day and night. Their morale was very high, and they had carried out no less than sixty attacks on Singapore from 29 December 1941, the targets being air bases, aerodrome installations, the Naval Base, government offices, etc. The Japanese chronicle mentions that in the night attack on Kallang on 31 January, they had shattered twenty-two searchlights, and in the one on Sembawang airfield, they had destroyed all but four. It adds that in the attack during the day on the same date on Seletar airfield, the Japanese air force shot down thirteen out of the fifteen aircraft there, (thirteen Hurricanes and two Buffaloes); and that on another date the same force bombed an oil tank which blackened the island for several hours.

But the greatest preparation of all on the Japanese side was the deceptive movement of their forces to the eastern side of Johore State in order to make the British believe that they would be attacked on the north-eastern corner of the Island. As a result of this deception, the British disposed a powerful defence force in this part of the Island, while the Japanese kept up the feint by creating heavy motor traffic on the roads leading to south-east Johore. The Japanese deception plan fully succeeded in its object as related later on.

Moreover, the Japanese brought up for the assault on Singapore all the equipment and personnel they considered necessary.

[17] *The War in Malaya*, p. 271.

There were special 240-m.m. howitzers for massive bombardment of the Island's defences. Tanks were secretly concentrated in south Johore, giving the invaders a tremendous advantage over the "death-trap carriers" of the Malaya Command. The troops and the tactics employed against Singapore were equally carefully selected. The men were fresh, highly trained and full of 'elan'. They could work their way rapidly and confidently through swamps and jungle. Their tactics were to approach a defensive position at night, feel their way round and through it without attacking, and establish ambushes and road-blocks behind the position. Then at dawn the defenders found themselves cut off, and were compelled to turn about and attack the road-blocks. But with daylight also came the Japanese planes, bombing and strafing the Allied troops and harassing all movement. These tactics were no longer novel, but the defenders had still to evolve successful counter-measures against them.

THE ASSAULT BEGINS

The first few days of February 1942 were taken up by the last minute preparations on either side. Only the Japanese planes continued their bombing and machine-gunning attacks. But gradually the number and intensity of these attacks had stepped up. Then, at 1800 hours on 5 February, Japanese artillery suddenly opened a heavy barrage. "The bombardment ......is said to have been the heaviest concentration of fire ever put in by the Japanese army. The guns used were of all calibres, but the main punch came from modern 240-m.m. howitzers, which had been specially built for this very purpose".[18] The barrage was specially directed towards the area just south of the Causeway, and was, therefore, considered only a feint, as the Malaya Command was convinced that the real attack would come in further east. However, the British artillery replied to the barrage, but had gradually to slacken the fire as guns got knocked out and ammunition began to run short.

While this artillery duel continued, a few Japanese patrol boats appeared in the channel on 7 February. And the same night the Japanese started a surprise attack on Pulau Lubin. Only about 400 Japanese troops were used in this attack, but it was pressed on with vigour. At first the Malaya Command considered it a feint, as it indeed was. But it revised its opinion by the morning of 8 February. The Japanese were still attacking

[18] *Japanese Land Operations*, p. 36.

furiously and had secured a footing on Pulau Lubin Island. So the defenders of Singapore opened a heavy bombardment of Lubin. Then, when the preparations were complete in every detail and the British attention was distracted towards Lubin, the real Japanese assault went in through the north-west sector of the Singapore defences, held mainly by the Australians.

The story of the Japanese assault at midnight of 8 February is undoubtedly thrilling, and their advance into the defended positions against stiff Australian resistance is equally remarkable. On 8 February, Japanese artillery bombardment and air attacks rapidly mounted in intensity, until by the evening the Japanese guns roared and lit the straits with brilliant flashes and their air force dropped one hundred and ten tons of bombs, so as to hold the British Commonwealth forces in the Island absolutely spellbound. The diary of General Gordon Bennett bears out this statement clearly.[19] During that morning, his headquarters was very severely air-blitzed; throughout the day the western part of the Island was heavily shelled and bombed; and during the evening the bombardment increased in intensity until about 2300 hours when it became almost unendurable and made the General sit up in bed. General Percival also confirms this.[20] But this continuous barrage of bombs and artillery fire stopped abruptly at sixteen minutes past midnight, when a green signal flare flashed in the sky to announce that the first group of the Japanese troops had crossed and landed safely on the Island. Then, at twenty minutes past midnight, a red signal flashed to say that their second group also had landed safely. Of course, the guns supporting these landings continued to fire furiously and filled the sky with dazzling light.

The Australian battalions too had by this time become alert and convinced that the Japanese had attacked the land on their front, and consequently they too started firing upon the crossing-points, raising pillars of water from the straits, sinking many Japanese boats and killing many men. Then the battle began on the Island itself. The Japanese soldiers, with white bands around their bodies and the ashes of their comrades-in-arms in bags hanging from their necks, rushed the Australians, in spite of concentrated fire of machine-guns and mortars, and started a hand-to-hand fight under the moonlit sky. The Japanese chronicler proceeds to describe the vicissitudes of the battle as follows: "The British at once attempted a counter-attack....... But the attack seems to have gone astray in the darkness and

[19] *Why Singapore Fell*, pp. 145-46.
[20] *The War in Malaya*, pp. 268-69.

confusion of the fighting; only one company of Australian troops succeeded in reaching the Japanese position. Here a sharp hand-to-hand fight took place, and for a while it looked as if the Japanese might indeed be driven back to their boats. But another battalion came over in time, and from then on the attackers were never in any danger of losing what they had gained".[21]

BEACH-HEAD ENLARGED

The Japanese had begun well. The 22nd Australian Brigade though still fighting hard was badly mauled; almost a fourth of the Island in the north-west had been occupied and the Japanese had touched Bukit Timah in the heart of the Island. To counter this lightning advance, the 12th and 15th Indian Infantry Brigades were placed under the Australian General's command, and the 44th Indian Infantry Brigade was ordered to fall back on to the left of the Kranji position, because Tengah aerodrome, which had been ably held by Jind Infantry,[22] and the Jurong road which was their only line of communication, were directly threatened. General Wavell reported that "the British forces withdrew under pressure to the general line Sungei Kranji—Bulim—Hong Kak—Sungei Jurong".[23]

6/14 Punjab was on the right flank of the 44th Indian Infantry Brigade and immediately to the left of 2/19 Australian Imperial Force Battalion of the 22nd Australian Imperial Force Brigade. At 2000 hours on 8 February, the Japanese shelling on the sector of the 22nd Australian Imperial Force Brigade hit certain targets in the sector of Punjab battalion, and for half an hour it "stood to" in reserve. An attempted landing between Ayer Bajau and Pasir Laba was then driven off by its A Company. Nine Japanese landing craft attempted to move up by the Sungei Bajau creek, but they were shot up by A Company's post located at the head of that creek. The mortars and machine-guns caught them at short range and hit two Japanese crafts while the remainder made north up the coast. A Company's post at the head of Sungei Telok reported later that they too had driven back six Japanese boats with automatic weapons and, these boats went north across Sungei Berih. At 2300 hours the 44th Indian Infantry Brigade informed 6/14 Punjab that the Japanese had effected a landing on

---

[21] *Japanese Land Operations*, p. 36, column two.
[22] *Why Singapore Fell*, pp. 147-48.
[23] "*ABDACOM*", *op. cit.*, p. 38, para 25 (e). For this phase of the campaign, the war diary of 7/8 Punjab is not available. The war diaries of 6/1 and 6/14 Punjab are probably not those which were sent by the units from day to day, but they appear to be substantially correct so far as they go.

the Australian sector and ordered it to "stand to By 0100 hours of 9 February 1942, however, the battalion " stood down ", the men being too wet and uncomfortable to sleep. The Japanese shelling still continued, but at a reduced rate.

6/1 Punjab, another battalion of the 44th Indian Infantry Brigade, had a different experience on 8 February. In the afternoon of that day, records its historian, " we saw what appeared to be the last British fighter shot down into the sea, and before the close of the day one company of Dalforce arrived to act as beach watchers under the command of B and D Companies. But for these two events, the regiment had a peaceful time ".[24]

On 9 February the situation was ominous. The right flank of the 44th Indian Infantry Brigade was in danger of being completely curled up and the entire brigade being outflanked. Information was coming to the brigade that the invasion was making headway, but that the 12th and 15th Indian Infantry Brigades, which were in reserve, would counter-attack. An official message was received to say that "the 22nd Australian Brigade was still fighting", the authenticity of which was doubtful. At 0630 hours 6/14 Punjab reported that the Japanese were still shelling in the vicinity of Choa Chu Kang village, which was near C Company's area, and also that some Japanese troops had penetrated into the mangrove opposite to A Company's position. At 0900 hours, C Company reported Australian withdrawal on its right as there were stragglers coming into its area, and at the same time they heard sounds of fighting approaching Choa Chu Kang village. Upon this D Company, then in reserve, was asked at fifteen minutes notice to move. At 1000 hours, shelling of the above village and C Company's position was reported, and until 1130 hours, C Company maintained its position satisfactorily. The Japanese who contacted it slipped out, but due to the jungle in that area it was difficult to catch or even observe them. However, D Company was brought into action behind C Company to connect up with 7/8 Punjab. Between 1300 and 1600 hours, the progress of the Japanese was so rapid that they occupied Choa Chu Kang village, pushed the Australians back and commenced their own movement eastward along the main road which would have cut off C and D Companies within a few hours. D Company withdrew from Choa Chu Kang village, but also lost contact with 7/8 Punjab.

At 1640 hours, the Brigade ordered the withdrawal of all battalions eastward along the Jurong road to Milestone 11. While

---

[24] Lieut.-Colonel J. D. Sainter: History of 6/1 Punjab, p. 10.

this withdrawal was to commence as soon as possible after dark, about 1900 hours, thinning-out was to commence at 1830 hours. At the same time the Brigade Reserve was increased to three rifle companies with an adequate number of vehicles, and the fort at Pasir Laba was further strengthened by one platoon. Later in the afternoon, about 1710 hours, when bombing was more intense, the Brigade Headquarters ordered all battalions to abandon their positions forthwith and withdraw east of the Jurong river. 6/1 Punjab left its position at 1815 hours and reached the destination at 2200 hours. It was fortunate in having all its companies concentrated, and also in having good communications for them. The men of 6/14 Punjab, however, were miserable in several ways. The route of withdrawal was south of Bukit Choa Chu Kang, and they had three trucks to carry men and material. At 1830 hours, one hundred and twenty Australians arrived, and they were asked to join the rear party on foot. A company had to collect its water party which was in Ayer Bajau before it could move back. Most men carried their bedding besides their arms, a few among them doing it for eight miles without a proper meal since the night before. At 2200 hours the battalion reched its destination, which was not marked out beforehand and which could not be prepared for a camp until the next morning. It was also too dark to take note of casualties and the missing men. C and D Companies, which withdrew together, had to fight a rear-guard action for the first few miles of their journey. Officers and men of these companies were quite tired when they arrived, and as men of all companies had practically no sleep in the previous night and were tired and hungry, all except sentries and patrols lay down to sleep. The only incident in 6/1 Punjab sector was the destruction of the splendid post at Tanjong Gul, which had been held by A Company. " It was a searchlight and artillery observation post commanded by a gunner Sergeant Major. The searchlights were the most powerful in the world, and the other installations were of an intricate and highly technical nature ",[25] but orders to destroy the post were given at 1800 hours on 9 February 1942.

Meanwhile, the 28th Indian Infantry Brigade had been facing the Japanese forces, with a narrow sea in between. On 1 February, this brigade moved slightly to the left and came within two hundred yards of the Causeway, and additional fire support was provided by twenty-four guns of Hertfordshire Yeomanry and a battery of 22 Mountain Regiment, the eighteen

[25] Ibid.

Vickers machine-guns of A Company Manchester Regiment having been allotted to 2/2 Gurkha on the extreme left. A feeling of tension was ever present in this brigade, affecting its spirit of confidence. That was the strange setting for a front-line position provided by the deserted Naval Base and the enormous magazines with steel doors, bomb-proof corridors and earthen mounds resembling hills. On 2 February the brigade moved two miles inland close to the entrance to the Naval Base at Canberra Gate, because the Japanese had bombed one of the large oil tanks, and the headquarters of the brigade could not be kept anywhere near it or any other oil tank in the area. The Japanese flew over the brigade area several times in the day, disturbing the defensive works which had to be carried out during the hours of daylight. On 3 and 4 February, reinforcements arrived, battalions changed their headquarters for tactical reasons, and 2/9 Gurkha took the place of 1/14 Punjab which went into reserve, making the right flank also pretty strong.[26] In the evening of 4 February, the Japanese artillery started registering on the naval offices and continued to fire shells and mortars intermittently, the next day also. In fact they often fired duds only, on and around the brigade position. Their large bombers proceeded over the head of this brigade to Singapore. On 6 and 7 February, the Japanese, who could see every movement and action in this brigade area, gave cause for anxiety by shelling 2/1 Gurkha's A Company area immediately after Major-General Heath's visit. The brigade was also depressed by the fact that gunners had only a limited supply of ammunition and could not answer fire by fire. At night on 7 February, the Japanese moved motor transports without any camouflage and also 'put up a large smoke screen which drifted down the Johore straits from East to West past our position'.[27] It was not until midday on 9 February, that the news of a Japanese landing in the north-west corner of the Island was fully known. However, reports about the Australian situation were extremely hazy. The 28th Indian Infantry Brigade had no reason to be panicky and rightly assumed that as long as the Australian force withstood its ground, its own position was not in danger. This feeling seems to have persisted, although at about 1400 hours, the Japanese opened a strong, continuous bombardment lasting one and a half hours.

---

[26] From 31 January to 7 February 1942, 1/14 Punjab and 5/14 Punjab were amalgamated into one battalion—File No. 601/639/H.
[27] War Diary, 2/2 G.R., 7 February 1942.

THE LOSS OF BUKIT TIMAH

The 12th Indian Infantry Brigade, in reserve, had been put at one hour's notice from about 0400 hours on 9 February, but no move was ordered till 1030 hours, when 2 Argyll was ordered to move by motor transport to Keat Hong village, and the brigade itself was placed, as already stated, under the command of the 8th Australian Division. Owing to the bombing of transport, harbours and the battalion on the march, all men reached the village rather tired and harried, and although they were only 850 in all, they occupied a defensive position astride the road just west of the village in the right sector Kranji-Jurong line, popularly called the Neck. The line of defence lay actually between Point 156 and Point 65, with armoured cars down the road and two 3" mortars. There were a number of high-level attacks from the air, and ' during the afternoon we were encouraged to see some of our few remaining Hurricanes engaged in successful dog-fights with enemy aircraft....... Our artillery was blazing away and shells were whistling overhead continuously'.[28]

While these movements were taking place, the Japanese had attacked on a front between the Causeway and the Kranji at 1930 hours on 9 February, and the Malaya Command was constrained to carry out a further withdrawal after midnight. This step created a gap between the position held by the 27th Australian Imperial Force Brigade and the newly formed Kranji-Jurong line and exposed some important hill features overlooking the Causeway. The defence line had fallen back to as far south as Bukit Timah village. The new plan of defence was to hold a perimeter which included the Kallang aerodrome, the MacRitchie and Peirce reservoirs and the Bukit Timah area.[29]

Bukit Timah village was situated strategically in the centre of the island. Its capture would give the Japanese not only the command of the north where a number of hillocks were situated but also of the south as far as Pasir Panjang village. Every effort was made to strengthen this point and to hold the Japanese at the Jurong-Kranji line. But their attack from the west could not be checked, and it was found quite impossible even to delay their progress towards Singapore Town. 10 February 1942 was fixed by the Japanese for the attack on Bukit Timah. The order was that ' the forces will attempt a night attack with bayonets on the 10th to secure Bukit Timah Heights by dawn on 11th, Kigensetsu'.[30] In other words, the Japanese army was asked to

[28] *Who Dies Fighting*, p. 129.
[29] *The War in Malaya*, p. 273.
[30] Enemy Publication No. 278, p. 223.

celebrate the anniversary of the coronation of the Emperor Timmu, which fell on 11 February, by conquering Bukit Timah.

The Japanese pressure had apparently caused confusion and panic in some sectors of the defence line, and some of the defending units withdrew owing to the constantly deteriorating tactical situation. The 27th Australian Imperial Force Brigade, holding the left flank of the 28th Indian Infantry Brigade, withdrew to the Mandai Road, while the 22nd Australian Imperial Force Brigade retired to the Bulim area. Similarly 6/1 Punjab and its two companion Punjab battalions (6/14 and 7/8) fell back to Pasir Panjang village thus leaving a serious gap in the 44th Indian Infantry Brigade area. The units were later sent back to their original forward positions and next day, 10 February, General Wavell told all troops in his order of the day that Singapore must be held to the last.[31]

On the morning of 10 February, the general defence situation was as follows:—

(1) In the western sector which was the most important of all, the troops stood in close touch with one another. From north to south they were the 12th Indian Infantry Brigade, a part of 22nd Australian Imperial Force Brigade, the 15th Indian Infantry Brigade and the 44th Indian Infantry Brigade. Behind these were units of the 29th Australian Brigade.

(2) In the northern sector the western area was in a perilous situation. The order in which the troops in this area were stationed was 27th Australian Imperial Force Brigade, 8th Indian Infantry and 28th Indian Infantry Brigade.

(3) The Brigade of the 18th British Division and those placed in the Changi area were taken out, as day wore on, to Bukit Timah area and its eastern suburbs to strengthen the line.

The Japanese weight was first felt by the 12th Indian Infantry Brigade. At first light on 10 February, 4/19 Hyderabad, attached to this brigade, moved back from its position to the left of Choa Chu Kong Road at Milestone 12½, on Hill 145, which was northwest of Bukit Panjang Road junction. 2 Argyll, then near Milestone 13, came under pressure very soon when some troops of the 2/21 Australian Battalion fell back. Japanese dive-bombers had come back to the brigade area at sunrise. At 0745 hours the forward companies were in contact. There was heavy firing by the Japanese, and at 0900 hours the forward troops withdrew. But the Japanese continued to fire from the ridge in front and threatened to turn the Argyll right flank. It then

[31] War diary, 2/2 G. R., 10 February 1942

became necessary to fall back behind the Sungei Peng Siang. Here, this battalion made contact with 2/29 Australian Imperial Force which went into position covering the road bridge and the area to the south in the Keat Hong Estate. A little later a further withdrawal was made to Bukit Panjang village. The battalion headquarters was established at the Public Works Department quarries on the main road; the two Marine companies were kept in reserve and the two Argyll companies were disposed on the reverse slopes of Bukit Gombak. The bombing attacks of the Japanese continued till late in the afternoon when the position eased. Orders were then sent to withdraw the forward companies and await the instructions for a counter-attack on the next day. The detachment of the Jind State Infantry, which had previously been stationed on Tengah aerodrome, moved to positions on Bukit Panjang feature.

The 15th Indian Infantry Brigade began to arrive at its position north of the Jurong road, and near the headwaters of the Jurong river, four miles west of Bukit Timah village, from the midnight of 9/10 February and completed its move by about 0430 hours. This enabled the 44th Indian Infantry Brigade to come into its own position to the left of the 15th Indian Infantry Brigade and south of the Jurong road. On the right flank of the 15th Indian Infantry Brigade was an Australian special reserve battalion, and on their left flank 6/1 Punjab of the 44th Indian Infantry Brigade. At about 1030 hours this Australian unit whose right flank, as a result of the withdrawal of 2/29 Australian Imperial Force Battalion mentioned above, was unprotected, fell back from the Bukit Timah feature. To cover the right flank of the 15th Indian Infantry Brigade, therefore, 3/16 Punjab moved up immediately. But by 1100 hours the forward positions of this brigade came under heavy Japanese mortar fire. 6/1 Punjab, which covered the road and was to the left of the brigade, gave ground a little. As a consequence, by 1300 hours, the Japanese, who were lapping round the left flank of the brigade, infiltrated into the rear of 6/1 Punjab. Consequently, at about 1430 hours, this battalion moved south creating confusion in the other battalions of the 44th Indian Infantry Brigade and compelling the whole brigade to move to Pasir Panjang by 1730 hours, and from thence to Milestone 10 on the Reformatory Road by night. This wholesale move was made through 2 Malaya Regiment, of the 1st Malaya Infantry Brigade, holding the lower parts of Sungei Jurong and Sungei Pandan. A company of Dalforce also was in this area and a small skirmish had taken place between part of the 44th Indian Infantry Brigade and that company owing to each mistaking the other for the Japanese. With the rapid departure, however, of the 44th Indian Infantry Brigade, the 15th Indian Infantry Brigade found both its flanks exposed. Hence it withdrew to positions between Milestone 9 and Milestone 8½ on the Jurong Road by about 1600 hours. The combined Jat Regiment was on the right, north of the road, 3/16 Punjab astride the road and the British battalion was in reserve in the rear. At a position south of the road on a prominent hill feature was a part of the Australian special reserve battalion.

In the northern sector Brigadier Maxwell had withdrawn the Australian troops for good reasons.[32] Taking advantage of this, the Japanese started repairing the Causeway and their patrols established themselves on Hill 95 by the morning of 10 February 1942. The withdrawal of the Australian troops had left the Causeway practically undefended as 2/2 Gurkha with only a company in the vicinity would be unable to resist the Japanese move onwards and artillery in Mandai Road could not be used unless alternative positions were found for the guns. Moreover, the Bukit Timah road was open to the Japanese as the 27th Australian Imperial Force Brigade held a position one mile east of Mandai Road village, and Major-General Key urged that brigade to move to that village and block the road against Japanese advance. To save the situation, the 8th Indian Infantry Brigade, moved northwest to close the gap between the 27th Australian Imperial Force Brigade and the 28th Indian Infantry Brigade, and occupied Han Kow, Bt. Sembawang and Marsiling Estates. But the following plan was decided upon to deal with the immediate situation:—(a) one platoon of B Company of 2/2 Gurkha was to take up position on the Naval Base Road and near the Causeway facing west; (b) a fighting patrol consisting of one platoon of B Company was to proceed to Hill 95 to deal with any Japanese troops in position there and to establish a light machine-gun post on the hill; (c) one company of 1/14 Punjab from the brigade reserve was to take up a position on Wireless Telegraph Hill south of B Company's position; and (d) one officer and thirty men of the Northumberland Fusiliers machine-gun battalion were to form a reserve platoon under command of B Company. The total armament of these volunteers consisted of one tommy gun, and a few pistols apart from the usual rifles.

Unfortunately the platoon suffered casualties soon after and seemed unable to hold up the attacks on its front. Thereupon B Company was strengthened with a rifle platoon of

---

[32] Wigmore : *The Japanese Thrust*, pp. 328-9.

9 Northumberland Fusiliers and two light automatic sections of 5 Searchlight Battalion's detachment, and ordered to hold a track leading from Hill 125 to the headquarters of 2/2 Gurkha. It was now 1000 hours. 5/14 Punjab had sent its C Company to occupy Hill 95. Half an hour earlier, the 8th Indian Infantry Brigade too had started on a similar mission, supported by 135 Field Regiment. 1/8 Punjab was transferred from the 8th Indian Infantry Brigade Command to divisional reserve.

Once again, as in the case of B Company platoon, bad luck attended the company of 5/14 Punjab and the 8th Indian Infantry Brigade. At 1000 hours 2/18 Royal Garhwal Rifles occupied the Bt. Sembawang Estate without opposition, but after that hour not a word was received about the whole brigade to which it belonged. Of 5/14 Punjab also there was no news at all. Thereupon D Company was sent with orders to occupy Hill 95 without delay, and 135 Field Regiment was asked to give support to this company.

Meanwhile two important events took place. The first was that the 11th Indian Division was 'ordered to reconnoitre the Peirce Reservoir area; it looked as though the "fight to the last man" was yet once again to prove an empty slogan'.[33] The second was General Wavell's visit to the front at noon and his encouragement to officers and men of all ranks to keep on fighting in spite of the critical situation.

At 1300 hours the entire situation still seemed to be confused. While 2/18 Royal Garhwal Rifles was evidently still fighting in the Marsiling Estate, 1/13 Frontier Force Rifles in the Han Kow and Bt. Sembawang Estates had met the Japanese and its forward company was being sniped from Hill 95. The former battalion had committed three companies to the attack, of which the forward ones were pinned to the ground and suffered heavily, in close fighting. One company of the battalion was in hand. 2/10 Baluch, like 1/13 Frontier Force Rifles, was dispersed in the dense broken country. 5/14 Punjab Regiment was still nowhere near Hill 95.

Fresh orders were, therefore, issued by the Divisional Commander that the 8th Indian Infantry Brigade should be prepared to attack Hill 95 with 1/13 Frontier Force Rifles if 5/14 Punjab's attack failed, and to attack the Marsiling Estate at dawn with 2/10 Baluch if the Garhwal battalion proved unable to occupy it. Both attacks were to be supported by 135 Field Regiment. Later on this order was made obsolete as 5/14 Punjab reported that it was impossible to attack Hill 95 owing to

---

[33] History of 11th Indian Division in Malaya, pp. 518-19.

the existence of an obstacle consisting of a high iron paling fence interlaced with barbed wire between Hill 125 and Hill 95.

Seeing that 2/18 Royal Garhwal Rifles was losing heavily and remained still in the Han Kow Estate, 1/13 Frontier Force Rifles took up the position and duties of the Garhwal battalion. By about 1300 hours, this unit began moving towards Hill 95 and by about 1700 hours, and after a preliminary artillery bombardment, occupied it with no opposition. During the evening, however, the company which captured the hill vacated it, probably due to lack of ammunition. But luckily it was not taken up by the Japanese during the night and hence 1/13 Frontier Force Rifles was able to reoccupy it at first light on 11 February 1942.

In the position held by 2/2 Gurkha, the Japanese made an infiltration immediately to the south and close to B Company headquarters. There was a little sniping at this headquarters but the Japanese could not be easily located. Minor adjustments were made in the location of the platoons and machine-gun posts of the battalion.

But the most exciting and important news of all during the day was ' the welcome news that a counter-offensive was to take place at dawn to oust the Japanese from the Island.'[34] The chronicler of a Gurkha Regiment has recorded as follows: " Shortly before dark, Colonel Harrison, the General Staff Officer (I) 11th Division, visited the battalion headquarters with the news that severe fighting was in progress along the Bukit Timah road with the enemy penetration as far south as Bukit Timah village thereby delaying the return of the Australians to their original positions on our left. At the same time he said that a big drive was being organised for which all available British, Australian and Indian troops would be employed with the object of sweeping in a north-westerly direction to drive all the enemy back into the sea. This was the first good news that we had heard that day and gave grounds for renewed confidence that the situation would be restored".[35]

General Percival has recorded that on his return to the headquarters along with General Wavell at about 2·30 p.m., he heard of the unsatisfactory situation in front of Bukit Timah village, which was "vital to the defence—partly because it is an important road junction, partly because there is direct observation from the hills north-west of the village as far as Singapore Town itself, and partly because of the important dumps and depots which lay to the east of it". To relieve the situation he asked General Gordon Bennett "to stage a counter-attack to re-establish the

---

[34] *Ibid.*, p. 521.
[35] War Diary, 2/2 G.R., 10 February 1942.

Kranji-Jurong line. Orders for this were issued without delay. The counter-attack was to be made in three stages. The first was to secure by 1800 hours the same evening the Bukit Panjang and Bukit Gombak features. These two hills lie a little west of the main road north of Bukit Timah village and parts of them were already held, so very little advance was necessary. The second and third stages, which were to take place on the morning and afternoon of the following day respectively, aimed at re-establishing the Kranji-Jurong line".[36] This counter-attack was to be carried out by the 12th Indian Infantry Brigade in the north, the 15th Indian Infantry Brigade in the centre and the 22nd Australian Imperial Force Brigade in the south, with the 44th Indian Infantry Brigade in reserve, all of them being under General Gordon Bennett's command. It was understood that if this counter-offensive failed it would probably be necessary to withdraw the 18th British Division and the 11th Indian Division from the coast to a perimeter around Singapore Town.

The situation, however, worsened as evening approached. At about 1600 hours General Percival heard reliably that the Japanese were approaching Bukit Timah village. He ordered at once that the large reserve petrol depot east of the village be destroyed at 1800 hours. This was done, and petrol burnt furiously for two or three days. By dusk, the 12th Indian Infantry Brigade was in position astride the main road south of Bukit Panjang village according to plan for the counter-attack. But by 2015 hours it was attacked from the west of the village by the Japanese, and for the first time their tanks made an appearance on the island.

The 12th Indian Infantry Brigade was then covering the Causeway—Bukit Timah road from the west between Hill 145 (736197) and Bukit Gombak. It was subjected to air attacks during the afternoon and the units to the west of the Bukit Timah road had shell and mortar fire also. In the evening at about 1800 hours, modifications became inevitable in the disposition of troops. 4/19 Hyderabad on Hill 145 was directed to send one company to the Bukit Panjang feature to link up with the Jind Infantry and to the railway and the main road leading to the Causeway. 2 Argyll was withdrawn from the Bukit Gombak area to the two sides of the Bukit Timah road in the vicinity of the level-crossing near Milestone 9. But before 4/19 Hyderabad could take up its new positions, Hill 145 was subjected to a heavy mortar fire, which caused the disintegration of this battalion in

---

[36] *The War in Malaya*, pp. 276-77.

PLATE VII

(Courtesy – *Australian War Memorial*)
Australian soldiers manhandling an anti-tank gun

(Courtesy – *Australian War Memorial*)
A forward Australian patrol

PLATE VIII

(Courtesy – *Australian War Memorial*)

The Parit Sulong bridge towards which survivors of the 45th Indian Brigade and the 2/19th and 2/29th Australian Battalions fought their way in January 1942. (Post-war photograph)

no time. At about 1945 hours, the commanding officer ordered the men remaining with him to repair to the brigade headquarters area, stationed near the junction of the main road with another leading to the Singapore Dairy Farm. The Japanese troops followed up the withdrawal and were engaged by a company of 2/19 Australian Imperial Force Battalion covering the Bukit Panjang village road junction. When success was in sight, the Japanese foiled it by bringing several tanks down the Choa Chu Kang Road at about 2030 hours. No previous preparations had been made to meet this new threat as neither tank obstacles had been created nor was the detachment of 4 Anti-Tank Regiment attached to 4/19 Hydreabad available, having withdrawn earlier to the Reformatory Road area. One company of 2/29 Australian Imperial Force Battalion struggled hard to hold up the tanks and put two of them out of action. As forward troops of the 12th Brigade had already been withdrawn behind the 2/29 Battalion, C and D Companies of this battalion were moved nearer the crossroads, while B Company and the headequarters remained there during the night only to withdraw to the Race Course next morning when they found themselves being pressed by the Japanese forces moving on the main road to Bukit Timah village. Meanwhile, at about 2200 hours, the commander of the 12th Indian Infantry Brigade finding an armoured vehicle halted on the Bukit Timah Road opposite to his headquarters, which he discovered to be a Japanese light tank, moved his headquarters back down the side of the road. The Japanese tanks reached a road block which 2 Argyll had established across the main road. They were held up some time which enabled part of the battalion to withdraw down the road towards Bukit Timah village, the other half positioned east of the road, remaining there for the night being unaware of the withdrawal by the rest of the battalion. During the night and the early hours of the morning of 11 February, the remnants of the ill-starred 12th Indian Infantry Brigade withdrew to the south of Bukit Timah village and were completely disorganised. The Jind State Infantry in Bukit Gombak, successfully encountered a Japanese push for a time, but ultimately withdrew across country to Nomanton Camp. Before the day dawned on 11 February, the Japanese tanks and infantry had reached the Bukit Timah village road junction; a serious situation had now developed for the British forces.

FUTILE COUNTER-ATTACKS

On 11 February, the position was critical. The total number of troops available to the 22nd Australian Brigade, which was to have taken part in the counter-offensive was very small. Of the reserve portions of this brigade also only some 150 men were left who were trying to re-form behind the Reformatory Road. The 44th Indian Infantry Brigade was still holding a position about the Junction of the Reformatory and Ulu Pandan Roads, but its strength had been reduced to two battalions (6/1 and 6/14 Punjab, each with six hundred men), and the headquarters and one company of 7/8 Punjab. There were some men from 3 Mixed Reinforcement Camp also. Utter confusion prevailed in the area, and the suddenness of Japanese attack had upset all the counter-offensive plans. The position of troops on 11 February 1942 on the Reformatory Road between Milestones $9\frac{1}{2}$ and $8\frac{1}{2}$ was as follows: 7/8 Punjab on the ridge west of the road opposite its junction with Ulu Pandan Road, 6/1 Punjab a little lower down the road and 6/14 Punjab near the loop in the road at 759112, linking with 2 Loyals of the 1st Malaya Infantry Brigade.

Of all the brigades which had been ordered to counter-attack at dawn of 11 February 1942, the 15th Indian Infantry Brigade was the only one ready on the Start Line, but it was completely isolated astride the Jurong Road at Milestone 9 with 3/16 Punjab on its right and the British Battalion on the left. The Jat Battalion which had held the right flank of 3/16 Punjab was out of touch with its brigade. The only other force on the forward positions in addition to the 6/15th Indian Brigade was the small Australian Reserve Battalion.

The Jat Regiment, a combination of 2/9 and 4/9 Jat, had encountered the Japanese force the previous day, one of its companies being sent to silence a hostile mortar on Bukit Batok. Hill 220 was the objective of the Jat battalion, which it nearly attained, but finding no sign of the 12th Indian Infantry Brigade, it decided to move to the north of Bukit Timah village before that brigade. Thus it was not available on the morning of 11 February to join the 15th Indian Infantry Brigade to take part in the counter-offensive.

The fortunes of the other two battalions of the 15th Indian Infantry Brigade were no better.[37] The flanks of the brigade were exposed. To cover its left flank, the British battalion was moved to the south of the road. To the left of the British battalion were some 220 men of the Australian Special Reserve Battalion in position. But all communications to the rear of the brigade were severed. At about 0530 hours, the Brigadier, realising the critical situation of his force decided to cancel the counter-attack which was due to begin one hour later. However, at about 0730 hours, the Japanese attacked

[37] This account is based on Major E.F.D. Hyde's Account of the Malayan Campaign, pp. 344-45.

3/16 Punjab on the northern side of the Jurong Road from the northwest, and the British Battalion, on the other side of the road from the south, south-west and west. The brigade commander thereupon decided to withdraw to Bukit Timah village but his headquarters being attacked simultaneously from the direction of the village, he decided at 0930 hours to withdraw across country in the south-easterly direction to the Reformatory Road. The backward movement was carried out in three columns, the British Battalion on the west flank, the Australians in the centre and the Punjabi units on the east flank. The troops faced constant fire from the flanks and the rear, which compelled them to scatter and split up, and when they repaired to the Reformatory Road, 3/16 Punjab had only sixty men, the British Battalion only one hundred and thirty men, and the Australian Reserve Battalion had only eighty men. They were sent further back to refit and reorganise.

Thus had failed the counter-attack which had never been launched as the Japanese did not allow any opening for attack, rather, on the contrary, they had attacked first everywhere and penetrated deep into the Allied positions. The plan of counter-offensive resulted also in the disintegration of two important brigades, the 12th and the 15th Indian Infantry Brigades, without delivering a single blow on the Japanese except in desperate self-defence. General Percival notes with sorrow that " the 12th Brigade, decimated after its gallant efforts, ceased to exist as a formation, though parties of Argylls formed themselves into guerilla bands and went on fighting ".[38] Japanese records convey a better picture of the battle leading to the annihilation of 12th and 15th Indian Infantry Brigades. " The fierce battle that raged in front of the Bukit Timah heights was a do-or-die, hand-to-hand battle ".[39] " The noise of guns, the rumbling of tanks, the bombing of our air force and the explosion of shells made this a veritable hell of blood and death. The strong pill-box positions on Bukit Timah Heights were attacked over and over again in the midst of all this, but they would not yield. A glorious hand-to-hand battle developed in the midst of the abandoned enemy dead bodies and the dead bodies of our comrades-in-arms ".[40]

The fight for aerial supremacy reached its culmination on 10 February, when the few battered planes and their weary pilots of the Royal Air Force were withdrawn finally from Singapore to Sumatra. The men had been fighting against tremendous odds for many weeks. Their will remained indomitable, but

[38] *The War in Malaya*, p. 278.
[39] Enemy Publication No. 278, p. 220.
[40] *Ibid.*, pp. 222-25.

the battle had clearly gone against them. To continue the unequal struggle with the few Hurricanes still remaining serviceable would only have involved the sacrifice of highly trained men and precious planes without affecting materially the outcome of the battle for Singapore.

11 February 1942, as shown already, was another miserable day for the Allied forces in the Island. General Percival has given a picture of the crisis facing his command at the dawn of this day. 'The enemy's successful attack during the previous night had created several danger points. In the first place, a wide gap had developed between the Machitchie Reservoir and the troops on the Bukit Timah road. To fill this I sent up a composite force from the reinforcement camps......secondly, a strong attack was launched shortly after dawn against the rear of the 6th/15th Indian Brigade from the direction of Bukit Timah village......Then, Bukit Timah village itself had fallen into the enemy's hands and a conuter-attack by Tomforce, launched with the object of recapturing the village, was held up on the line of the railway. Later in the morning a strong enemy attack developed against the 22nd Australian Brigade, now reduced to a few hundred men only,...... near the junction of the Reformatory and Pandan roads'.[41]

To this General Gordon Bennett has added the straggler position which had become alarming in Singapore Town. Several thousand soldiers were occupying the lower floors of the stouter buildings, the position being quite beyond the control of the police. Further, he has stated that he considered the situation too bad for any remedy: "I consider that the end is near and that it is only a matter of days before the enemy will break through into the city. I fear the consequences of the street fighting that will ensue, should that come to pass. There is no resistance left on the island and every enemy attack makes progress. His attacks are now concentrated against Tom Force on the east of Bukit Timah road and against the left flank near the coast which is now held by fortress troops under Major-General Keith Simmons ".[42]

The Tom Force had been commissioned on 11 February " to proceed at first light......... to mop up the enemy in the Bukit Timah village and retake the position previously occupied by 12 Brigade".[43] At 0630 hours all the battalions of this force moved forward, but when they reached the railway line the leading troops came under small-arms fire and were held up. On the right side contact was made in the thick country astride the pipe-line, with the result

[41] *The War in Malaya*, p. 279.
[42] *Why Singapore Fell*, pp. 154-55.
[43] Narrative of " Tom Force " Singapore, 10/12 February 1942, p. 2.

that the front stabilised on this general line (770165-763140) for the rest of the morning. An attempt was made in the afternoon to improve the situation but the pipe-line unit ran into the Japanese, the left wing party disappeared into the blue and was heard of only late in the afternoon, and the centre contingent was pushed back east of the light railway. Consequently, towards the evening, this force, which was on a very extended front, was withdrawn to more concentrated positions astride the Bukit Timah Road, with the right battalion in the Race Course area and the left one south of Race Course Village. But Tom Force could not give up the main road, nor could it be given the duty of guarding the area up to the Reservoir. An independent arrangement had to be made for the latter, and consequently 4 Suffolks was ordered to that side, the point of contact being the Swiss Rifle Club. Similarly the point of contact with the Australian Imperial Force on the left was fixed at about point 115 (777133). The whole force, which had come already under the 18th British Division, came under the command of Massy Force from the midnight of 11/12 February 1942, the object being to make Brigadier Massy-Beresford responsible for the entire front from the Thompson Road to the Bukit Timah Road.

THE WORSENING SITUATION

By 0700 hours on 12 February it was clear that a dangerous gap existed between the MacRitchie Reservoir and the Race Course. As a temporary measure a small force, Murray Force, consisting of 5/2 Sikh and 7 British Reinforcement Camp, was sent to cover the approach from the west across the Singapore Golf Course. Later a troop of light tanks pushed further west as far as the Swiss Rifle Club Hill. Also General Gordon Bennett had formed a perimeter of all the Australian Imperial Force units and decided to make his final stand on it. As his right flank was vulnerable he sent 2 Gordon Highlanders to protect it, facing Bukit Timah Road, with the remnants of 2/29 Australian Imperial Force Battalion on the Gordon's right and facing the same way. But the Japanese continued to push in the south-eastern part of Bukit Timah village throughout the day, and the 22nd Australian Imperial Force Brigade 'which had incorporated the 2/4 Machine-Gun Battalion now fighting as infantry held its ground most gallantly in face of infantry attacks supported by aerial bombing, artillery, mortar, and small arms fire'.[44] Further to the south also the Japanese had penetrated as far as Buona Vista where the battery of 15-inch guns was destroyed by the crew itself. The British artillery maintained pressure

---

[44] *The War in Malaya*, p. 279.

on the gap in the Causeway which the Japanese failed to repair. At the same time, a project was formed to recapture Bukit Panjang village, in order to ease the pressure on the Bukit Timah Road, but the 27 Australian Imperial Force Brigade failed to make any impression. The British forces were fighting a losing battle. Their woes were aggravated when at about 0800 hours the main reserve petrol depot, east of the Race Course, was set on fire by Japanese action and destroyed. However, the spirit of the defenders was not yet broken and when the Japanese Commander-in-Chief dropped a letter from the air demanding the surrender of the fortress, it was treated with contemptuous silence. 'They had answered with a counter-attack in place of a messenger'.[45]

During the morning, once again, in order to form a second line on Bukit Timah Road, Malaya Command ordered 4 Straits Settlements Volunteer Force (the reserve battalion of the Straits Settlements Volunteer Force Brigade holding the Singapore Town sector) to prepare and take up positions astride the Bukit Timah and Dunearn Roads on the general line Lornie Road—Adam Road, which was to be the line of the final perimeter in this sector.

The 44th Indian Infantry Brigade was subjected to devastating air, artillery and mortar bombardment. A third of the brigade and half of the survivors of the 22nd Australian Imperial Force Brigade were killed or wounded. In the evening the units were so disposed as to extend their line to Ayer Raja Road in order to connect it with the 1st Malaya Infantry Brigade on the left. 7/8 Punjab faced north along the Ulu Pandan Road with its right astride the Reformatory Road. 6/14 Punjab was in brigade reserve. Its battalion headquarters was established near a track east of Knoll 115. 6/1 Punjab took up a position known as the Bracken, east of 6/14 Punjab. By evening the remnants of the British Battalion of the 15th Indian Infantry Brigade had come under the command of this brigade and were placed in reserve just north of Hill 125. On the left of the 44th Indian Infantry Brigade, 1st Malaya Infantry Brigade was reinforced by 5 Bedfordshire and Hertfordshire of the 55th British Infantry Brigade, and a newly organised Royal Engineers Battalion held the Reformatory Road from the oil tanks to Pasir Panjang and the coast, thence to Jardine Steps.

By midday of 12 February, the front line in the south ran approximately from the hill east of the Bukit Timah Rifle Range on the right, along the line of the railway, then forward to the junction of Ulu Pandan and Reformatory roads and then south

[45] Enemy Publication No. 278, p. 231.

to a point on the coast north of Pasir Panjang village. The position in the northern area was equally difficult. Two attempts to occupy Bukit Panjang village, one by the combined 2/26 and 2/30 Australian Imperial Force Battalions and the other by 2/10 Baluch had failed miserably. In the case of Australian Imperial Force Battalions, not only was artillery support found not feasible, but also the two battalions were out of touch with each other and the brigade headquarters except by liaison officers. And in the case of the Indian regiment, the Japanese had come between this unit at Milestone 13 and D Company of 2/30 Australian Imperial Force Battalion at Milestone 13½, and no effort of the Indian regiment could drive the Japanese away. The Japanese would not be driven out of Hill 95 either, and their infiltration through the rubber estates north of the Mandai Road threatened to cut in behind the rear of the 8th Indian Infantry Brigade in the Woodlands Estate area. This infiltration also threatened the important Nee Soon road junction. At about 1400 hours, therefore, this brigade began to withdraw in order to form a line covering Sembawang aerodrome and the Nee Soon junction. 1/13 Frontier Force Rifles was attacked as it was in the process of thinning out, but it managed to disengage and withdrew through 2/18 Royal Garhwal Rifles. Both these units then fell back without further incident by estate roads to Sembawang Aerodrome area. 2/10 Baluch on the Mandai Road withdrew at about 1700 hours to the west of Nee Soon road junction, which, during the day, had been covered by 1/8 Punjab which had been sent forward from Bidadari when the 8th Indian Infantry Brigade had been ordered up to the Causeway area. By evening, the dispositions of the 8th Indian Infantry Brigade units were: right, 1/13 Frontier Force Rifles west of Sembawang Aerodrome; centre, 1/18 Punjab between excluding the south-western corner of the Aerodrome and excluding Milestone 11 of the Mandai Road; left, 2/10 Baluch including Milestone 11 on the Mandai Road and along the east edge of Seletar Reservoir; in reserve, 2/18 Royal Garhwal Rifles in area Hill 110 near Milestone 11 on the Nee Soon—Naval Base road. On Sembawang Aerodrome was a company of Kapurthala State Infantry, and 3 Cavalry (less one squadron) was also in this area. On the left of 2/10 Baluch and south of Seletar Reservoir facing west was the Bahawalpur State Infantry.

The 28th Indian Infantry Brigade, which was in the Naval Base area and had been instructed to hold on to the last man and to the last round, was quiet enough, in spite of Japanese bombing and shelling on the Base. At about 1400 hours, however, 2/2 Gurkha Rifles heard about the withdrawal of its adjacent brigade from Hill 95 area and decided at once to swing back its left flank in order to face west. Later in the afternoon, this battalion was ordered to withdraw east to positions behind the New Cut. At the same time 2/9 Gurkha Rifles was to swing back its left flank from the coast behind the upper portion of this waterway. Moreover, to extend the west front of this brigade to the south, orders had been issued by the 11th Indian Division for 2 Cambridgeshire Regiment (less one company) of the 53rd British Infantry Brigade to move up to positions south of the Naval Base behind the waterway. However, while these dispositions were in the process of being taken up, fresh orders arrived for the evacuation of the Naval Base to take place during the ensuing night.

So far as the 18th British Division was concerned the only complete infantry battalion was 5 Suffolk of the 54th British Infantry Brigade. The 55th British Infantry Brigade had two companies of 5 Bedfordshire and Hertfordshire Regiment and two companies of 2 Cambridgeshire Regiment. The Kapurthala State Infantry which was on Seletar Aerodrome was moved to the beach defences in front of it. 125 Anti-tank Regiment (less a battery), which was organised for an infantry role, was sent south of Seletar Rifle Range to protect the division's left flank, along with 288 Field Company Royal Engineers.

The Coastal sector from Fairy Point to Sungei Tampines, which had been held by 5/11 Sikh until it went forth to Massy Force, was taken over by 3/17 Dogra.

The principle behind all these moves was that the 11th Indian Division should not become isolated and it should also secure the left flank of the 18th British Division. As a preliminary to this general close-up, the Corps of the Royal Engineers of the 11th Indian Division was ordered to demolish the cranes, docks, pumping machinery, power-house, oil tanks and other installations in the Naval Base.

During the night of 11/12 February 1942, the 11th Indian Division fell back to the line Sungei Simpang—Simpang village-Sembawang Aerodrome—Seletar Reservoir. According to American British Dutch Australian Command, " at the end of these (all fronts) operations the general line was Naval Base—Nee Soon Village—Peirce Reservoir—Race Course—Holland Road—Road Junction 7513—Pasir Village ".[46] Colonel Harrison has remarked that "the zig-zag 'Line' from MacRitchie Reservoir to the Chinese High School, from the Chinese High School to Reformatory School, and thence to Pasir Panjang, was no line of defence but

---

[46] "*ABDACOM*", *op. cit.*, p. 39, (para 25, sub-para j).

a line of gaps—gaps between formations, of gaps within formations of dispersed and in many cases isolated detachments in an area ill-suited to a defensive battle. The troops were there, not by pre-arranged planning, but because they found themselves there owing to the force of events ".[47] It may be due to this fact that General Percival thought that the time had come to shorten and clarify the range of the entire defence of the Island.[48]

During the night of 11/12 February 1942 several important moves took place. At midnight III Indian Corps, in charge of the Northern Area, took over the command of all troops as far left as the Bukit Timah Road inclusive, and the Western Area included the Ulu Pandan Road. The Naval Base was evacuated without interruption by the Japanese. Two companies of 1/8 Punjab simply disappeared, and the Japanese infiltrated into their position. 1 Cambridgeshire Regiment of the 55th British Infantry Brigade replaced 5/11 Sikh Regiment in Massy Force at the junction of Syme and Lornie Roads. There was Japanese activity in the Singapore Golf Course area, in the course of which Murray Force had accidentally fought with 4 Suffolk. 3/17 Dogra was ordered to move to Thompson Road and come under Massy Force. On the Reformatory Road the British artillery carried out considerable harassing and defensive fire. This did not, however, prevent a certain amount of Japanese infiltration. To fill the gap on the right of the 22nd Australian Imperial Force Brigade, 2 Gordon Highlanders moved from Tyersall Park to positions commencing from a forward point near Pandan-Holland Roads junction to Hill 115 (north of Holland Road). In the southernmost area, held by the 1st Malaya Infantry Brigade, there was a certain amount of Japanese patrol activity and a few Japanese troops had also infiltrated into Buona Vista—Ayer Raja Road junction from where they sniped the whole of the next day.

"Thursday, 12 February, opened with a strong Japanese attack", says General Percival, " with tanks down the Bukit Timah road......there was a very real danger that the enemy would break through on that front into Singapore Town, for we had very little behind the front with which to stop him if he once effected penetration ".[49] In other words, the problem of the Malaya Command on this day was ' How shall the Japanese progress be stopped and Singapore Town saved ?' The resources were extremely scanty, scantier than ever. The units would never know what their individual strength was or could be. They reported

[47] History of 11th Indian Division in Malaya, Vol. II, p. 535.
[48] *The War in Malaya*, p. 281.
[49] *Ibid*

as being an odd hundred or two, but a little later, when men detached or considered lost rejoined, full strength. As noticed already, food, petrol, equipment and weapons were getting in short supply.

At the same time Malaya Command's responsibility was growing. The most urgent task before it was to suit defence to the resources available. The first measure in this direction was the shortening of the perimeter of defence and confining it to a five or six miles radius round Singapore Town. In consultation with the Commander of Northern Area the sources of water supply were included in this plan. There were three objects involved in the execution of this plan: (1) The 11th Indian Division and the remainder of the 18th British Infantry Division must cover water-supply points and link up with the Southern Area at the north-eastern point of Kalang aerodrome and hold the front held by Massey Force. (2) Southern Area should withdraw from Changi and the beaches east of Kalang. (3) The vital point to be defended was the Bukit Timah corner in the north-west. The general line of this perimeter was St. Patrick's School on the south coast about six miles from the centre of Singapore Town (935111)—the junction of Macpherson and Paya Lebar Roads (898142)—Bidadari (8815)—MacRitchie Reservoir—Race Course—the Reformatory Road—Pasir Panjang village. The formation boundaries were; between Southern Area and III Indian Corps—Macpherson Road; between III Indian Corps and the Australians—Bukit Timah Road; and between the Australians and Southern Area-Ayer Raja Road. Sometimes these lines were not clearly drawn and thus created confusion, but this could not be helped. All moves were to be completed by 13 February 1942, if they could not be done earlier. 2 Gordon Highlanders of the 2nd Malaya Infantry Brigade came under the Australian Command after moving to Tyersall Park. "It was intended that the Mysore State Infantry on Pengerang and 2nd Dogra on Tekong should be withdrawn under cover of darkness by the Navy on 13 February, but this never eventuated owing to the ships being sent away from Singapore on that night with selected personnel, whom it was suddenly decided to evacuate ".[50]

The second series of measures was to warn the civil government of the danger it was in. General Percival writes that the Governor and Malaya Command had to take several important decisions: "One concerned the Malayan Broadcasting Station which was now less than a mile from the front line. We decided ......to destroy it. Another concerned the stocks of currency

[50] Major E.F.D. Hyde: Account of the Malaya Campaign, p. 357. See also "ABDACOM", op. cit., p.39, para 25, sub-para (j).

notes held by the Treasury......We decided to destroy some of the notes and to keep the rest".[51] Food and water were diminishing in quantity rapidly because the formation of the shorter perimeter and withdrawal of troops near Singapore Town had brought a very large number of individuals to share the limited stock of these two necessities of life. As calculated on this date, food reserves could last only one week and if the reserves with the units and civil authorities were included they might hold on for a few more days. Water was causing greater anxiety. Pearl's Hill reservoir near the General Hospital was empty and dry, and the Fort Canning reservoir was being used up rapidly. In Singapore Town, generally, water was running to waste owing to breaks in the "mains" caused by Japanese bombing and shelling. One consequence of this was the fall in pumping pressures and failure in the rise of water to above ground-floor levels. Lest public morale and health should decline rapidly, water was supplied in carriers by organised parties, and from this date, 12 February 1942, Royal Engineer personnel and military personnel were called in to assist the civil staff.

So far as petrol was concerned there was only one small dump on the island, besides what was available in the vehicles themselves. But fortunately there were the reserves of the Asiatic Petroleum Company on the Pulau Bukum.

But on 12 February, further Japanese landings at Loyang, west of Changi, were reported. This fact, as well as the shortening of the perimeter, made III Indian Corps withdraw its headquarters from Changi. There was no further development there.

The Japanese aim at this stage was the complete encirclement of Singapore Town by a three-way pincer movement as well as by an aerial and naval blockade. There were at least three zones into which they had divided the whole area; the northern, around the water reservoirs; the central, east of the Race Course; and the southern, south-west of Singapore Town. After the evacuation of the Naval Base, the Causeway was repaired and the Japanese brought more men, more material and more tanks with which they could overwhelm the British army and bring the campaign to an early end. The Japanese chronicler writes that they "used the German so-called spearhead method of attack; that is the fighting was done by two columns which penetrated the British line and then fanned out behind it, to the east and west. The result was that before the battle was over, they had broken the British army up into a number of 'islands of resistance', the principal

[51] *The War in Malaya*, pp. 282-83.

ones of which were located at the Royal Air Force Base at Seletar, the fortress of Changi, the high Ground north of the reservoir, and the high ground around Bukit Timah.   This last-named place.... was considerably aided by fire from the guns in the batteries off the south coast...... ".[52] The Japanese command at this stage was completely decentralised, each regiment or column commander changing the direction of his attack as he judged best in the circumstances. This created more confusion in the British army, with the result that it soon collapsed as a fighting force.

In the northern area, 2/10 Baluch, which was at Milestone 11 on the Mandai Road, opened fire at about 0730 hours on a party of the Japanese moving towards Nee Soon and scattered it with great effect. In order to fill up the gap on the right of this Baluch unit, a field company of Sappers and Miners was put into the line, but the Japanese pressed on and threatened Nee Soon road-junction. 2/9 Gurkha Rifles was therefore called and ordered to make a counter-attack and fill the gap in the line of the 8th Indian Infantry Brigade. There was no artillery to support, and at the same time the Gurkhas became accidentally engaged with 3 Field Company and part of 1/13 Frontier Force Rifles. Consequently the intended objective was not reached, but a line sufficiently far advanced to stop temporarily the Japanese penetration, was gained. While this was going on, the 53rd British Infantry Brigade and the 28th Indian Infantry Brigade moved back through Nee Soon, the former to the south of the Sungei Seletar and the latter to the west of the Serangoon Road and north of the Sungei Whampoe. At about 1500 hours, three Japanese tanks came down the Mandai Road to the Nee Soon cross roads and were knocked out by 2/10 Baluch and a detachment of 80 Anti-Tank Regiment. At about 1600 hours, the 8th Indian Infantry Brigade began to withdraw to Bidadari area, and 5 Norfolk and 2/9 Gurkha Rifles returned to their respective brigades.

The 53rd British Infantry Brigade withdrew further south during the ensuing night and occupied a position to the east of Peirce Reservoir by 0400 hours, with 2 Cambridgeshire on the right and 5 Norfolk on the left, astride the Thompson Road. Each of these battalions had one company as outpost. 2/30 Australian Imperial Force Battalion was now in Ang Mo Kio village area, serving as brigade reserve.

In the central zone the situation was getting somewhat stabilised. The British line of defence in this zone was almost a straight line from MacRitchie Reservoir (813155) to the curve

[52] *Japanese Land Operations*, p. 37.

on the Sime Road (808148), from that curve to a point west of Adam Road (812145), and then almost parallel to Adam and Farrer Roads about a few hundred yards to their west. The Japanese attack in this zone was in two places, viz., the Golf Course and the Bukit Timah Road.

At 0800 hours the Japanese tanks attacked down the Bukit Timah Road and forced Tom Force to withdraw from the Race Course village line to the line Adam—Farrer Road. At the same time 5/11 Sikh Regiment moved to a point south of Walton Park where the Japanese aircraft had already appeared. Meanwhile, 3/17 Dogra had been ordered to withdraw from its sector on the north-east coast of the Island and to occupy a position on the Farrer Road. But while these troops were moving to their respective positions it seems that " troops, British and Australian, were coming back in groups along the Bukit Timah Road ".[53] The situation on the flanks was not known. By 0930 hours all troops had passed to the general line Adam—Farrer Road. But all of them were soon subjected to very heavy bombing from the air followed by intensive mortar and artillery fire and suffered a number of casualties. At 1200 hours on 12 February, 1 Cambridgeshire discovered a gap on its left, and similarly 5/11 Sikh complained of a gap on its left. As ill-luck would have it, two Japanese tanks appeared at 1230 hours on the Bukit Timah Road, and half an hour later the Australians started bombarding the position, but in the prevailing confusion as to what constituted the front line, some bombs fell among the forward companies of the British. Nothing could be done to stop this tragedy and so at 1330 hours when these forward companies had reported twenty-four casualties they were withdrawn to an alternative position about one hundred and fifty yards back.

The following was the disposition of the force in the central zone at 1330 hours on 12 February :—[54]

- 5/11 Sikh on the general line of the road leading to Chasserian Estate II.
- 18 Division Recce Battalion along the Adam Road.
- 4 Norfolk to the left of 18 Division Recce Battalion.
- 3/17 Dogra on the left of 4 Norfolk.
- 1/5 Sherwood Foresters in the area of Hill 80.
- 4 Straits Settlements Volunteer Force in line of Mount Pleasant Road.
- 1 Cambridgeshire in Adam Park area.

---

[53] A Diary of 5 Battalion (D.C.O.) The Sikh Regiment, 12 February 1942.
[54] Notes on the Fighting in Singapore Island south of the MacRitchie Reservoir, p. 2.

4 Suffolk on the right of 1 Cambridgeshire, south east of Singapore Golf Course.

Murray Force holding the Singapore Golf House.

During the afternoon, about 1430 hours, 5/11 Sikh withdrew to a position on the Farrer Road to the left of 3/17 Dogra. Actually it was to be placed some hundred yards east of the Adam Road and north of the Bukit Timah Road, but the commander of Tom Force took up positions from excluding road junction south along the Farrer Road, with battalion headquarters and reserve companies on Cluny Hill. There was a gap on the left of this regiment to the extent of about a thousand yards, beyond which its patrols made contact with a company of 2 Gordon Highlanders. This gap was most carefully patrolled day and night. Fortunately, no attack developed against this sector on 12 February. "A little sniping, mortaring and artillery fire and a grenade attack on the carrier patrol, which wounded two men, were all that occurred ".[35]

On the Golf Course, Murray Force was being pressed throughout the day, and it was counter-attacking with equal vigour. At 1700 hours, the Japanese compelled this force to withdraw. It was then assigned the task of protecting the Impounding Reservoir at the east end of MacRitchie Reservoir, thence south on the line Lornie and Sime Roads linking with 1 Cambridgeshire which was in the Adam Park area. At 1800 hours, elements of the 18th British Division began to arrive from the north coast in the area Sungei Kampines—Sungei Seletar. They formed a composite force known as Wells Force consisting of a company of 5 Bedfordshire and Hertfordshire and two companies of reinforcements for the same British regiment and 1/5 Sherwood Foresters. In view of the danger of a Japanese attack across the Golf Course, a reserve defence line was formed on the general line of Mount Pleasant Road. 4 Norfolk went back to Hill 80; 3/17 Dogra side-stepped to the left along the Farrer Road replacing 5/11 Sikh which went into reserve in the Raffles College (8112) and Bukit Brown (8113) areas.

In the southern zone, the Japanese were trying to get control of strategic road positions, and the British withdrew to more formidable points on the neighbouring hills. The withdrawal of Tom Force on the morning of 12 February had opened the Reformatory Road to the Japanese, and at 0930 hours (12 February) the Japanese infantry debussed near the Reformatory-Pandan Road junction and pushed 7/8 Punjab back. Having

---

[35] A Diary of 5th Battalion (D.C.O.) The Sikh Regiment, 12 February 1942.

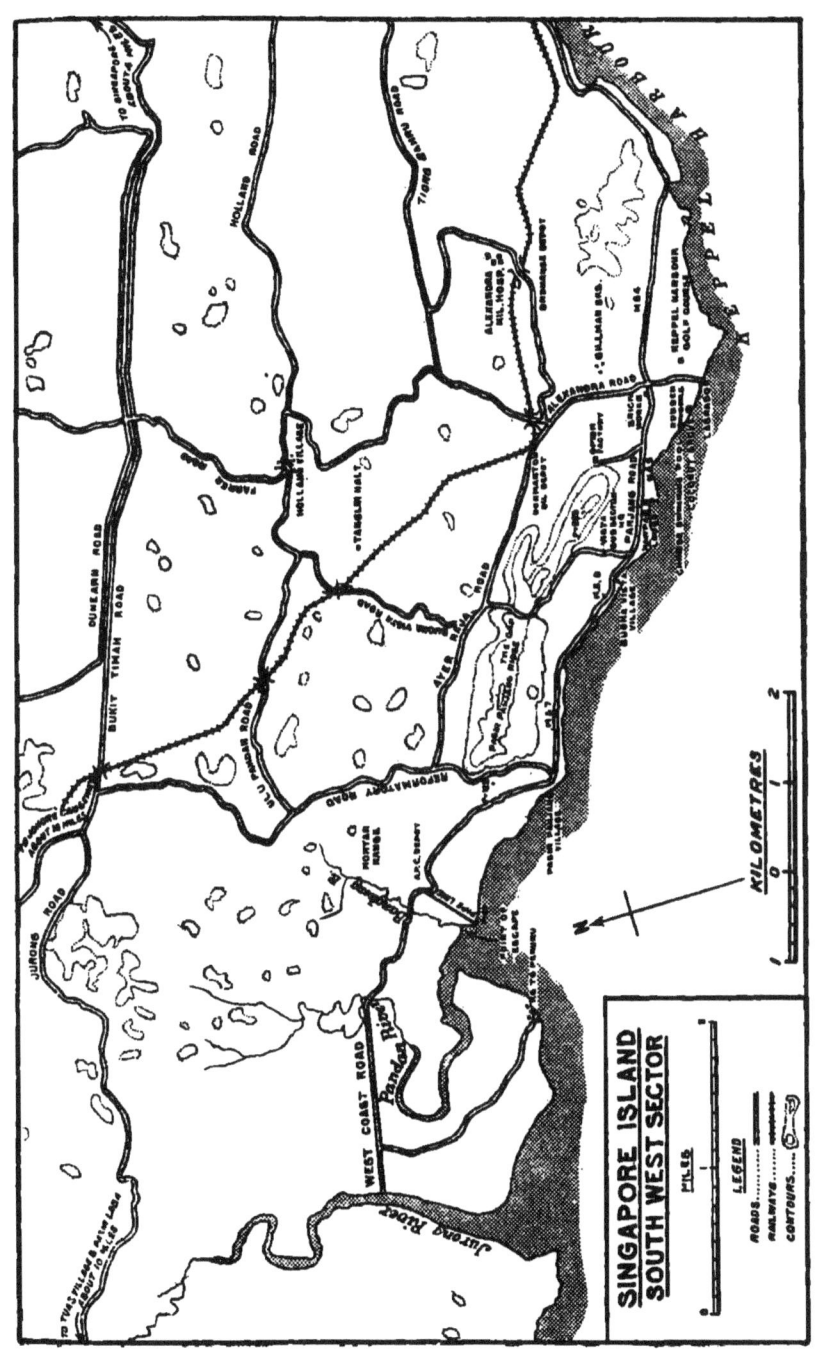

cleared this road junction, the Japanese moved down a water course south of the Ulu Pandan Road and threatened to cut through and separate 22nd Australian Imperial Force and 44th Indian Infantry Brigades. This was however prevented by the British Battalion which was in the low ground between Hill 125 (7611) and Hill 115 (7712). But the Japanese gained strength during the day and attacked the British positions on Pandan IV area at 1915 hours. An hour later, as the Japanese were coming round the left flank of the British units a general withdrawal of these units became necessary. The 22nd Australian Imperial Force Brigade pulled back accordingly, connecting with the 18th British Division on the Farrer Road and 5 Bedfordshire and Hertfordshire west of the Buona Vista Road. But this meant that shortly before midnight the Ulu Pandan—Holland Road junction lay open to the Japanese.

A similar withdrawal was made by the 44th Indian Infantry Brigade at 0100 hours of 13 February 1942. The entire day of 12 February 1942 had been quiet for this brigade, the British Battalion had come back and joined it, and 1/5 Sherwood Foresters had gone away. But the whereabouts of the Australians were not known to this brigade. At 2000 hours the units were situated as follows:—6/1 Punjab in the area of square 765111, 7/8 Punjab along the track running east of the loop of the Reformatory Road with brigade headquarters approximately one thousand yards along the track going east from the Reformatory Road. After 2200 hours there was a brigade conference at which withdrawal was arranged; but at 2400 hours when the Japanese shelled and attacked the brigade headquarters it was ordered that this withdrawal must commence at 0130 hours at the latest. The brigade went due south up to the Ayer Raja Road, where orders were given to move to the Buona Vista Road, where we took up a position facing north-west near where the road cuts the F.M.S. Railway and immediately west of the Tanglin Halt Railway Station.[56]

On the front held by the 1st Malaya Infantry Brigade, there was stir but no activity worth the name. In the morning the Japanese had crossed the Jurong river and pushed 1 Malaya Regiment up to the Asiatic Petroleum Depot. But they did not proceed any further, although they made the Malayan battalion nervous about infiltration from its rear. 1 Malaya Battalion was, therefore, strengthened by the addition of a detachment each of 3 Heavy Anti-Aircraft Battery, 2/4 Machine-Gun Battalion, and 2 Loyals Carrier Section, all on Pasir Panjang village and Ridge

[56] Lieutenant Colonel J. D. Sainter: History of the 6/1 Punjab, p. 16.

areas. But to make the line more secure, 2 Loyals was ordered to link up with the left of 5 Bedfordshire and Hertfordshire, which was slightly forward of the 44th Indian Brigade between Hills 125 and 120 on the Buona Vista Road, and then it was to carry the line across the Ayer Raja Road at Milestone 6½ towards the Pasir Panjang Ridge. 2 Malaya Battalion would then continue the line along the northern slopes of that Ridge to link up with 1 Malaya Battalion which still overlooked the coast, west of the Reformatory Road. These withdrawals were eventually completed by about 0300 hours on 13 February 1942, the exception being 2 Loyals which did not move at all. The gap between this unit and 5 Bedfordshire and Hertfordshire was however filled by 31 Battery of 7 Coast Defence Regiment.

THE LAST DAYS IN SINGAPORE

The official account of Abdacom narrates the incidents of Friday, 13 February 1942, as follows:—" On the 13th enemy pressure from the north compelled a withdrawal to the MacRitchie Reservoir area. Further attacks developed in the Paya Lebar area and in the west. The whole of Singapore town was by now within range of the enemy's field battery. Whilst reiterating that he must fight it out, as he was doing, it was suggested to General Officer Commanding Malaya that, after everything humanly possible had been done, some bold and determined personnel might be given the opportunity to escape by small craft to Sumatra.

"General Officer Commanding Malaya reported on 13th February that in addition to the whole town being within field artillery range of the enemy, the troops were in danger of being driven off their water and food supplies. His subordinate commanders considered that the troops already committed were too exhausted either to withstand a strong attack or to launch a counter-attack. In these conditions it was unlikely that resistance could last more than a day or two. His subordinate commanders were unanimously of the opinion that the gain in time from prolonging resistance would not compensate for the extensive damage and heavy casualties which would occur in Singapore town. The General Officer Commanding represented that a stage must come when in the interests of the troops and the civil population further bloodshed, which could serve no useful purpose, should be averted. He was carrying out the strict injunctions issued on the 10th to fight to the last, but in view of the circumstances now represented he requested that giving him wider discretionary powers should be considered. In reply, the General Officer Commanding was ordered to continue to inflict maximum damage on the enemy for as along as possible, by house to house fighting if necessary".[57]

The dawn of 13 February found the 11th Indian Division intact. During its fight on Singapore Island, it had, it is true, been practically left unmolested. No attack had been launched on its front except down the Mandai road on the previous day, and even this attack, which had involved only 3 Field Company, 1/8 Punjab, 2/9 Gurkha Rifles and 2/10 Baluch, had not been pressed home. But during the night of 12/13 February 1942, the 28th Indian Infantry Brigade had been heavily bombed for two hours in its position at the Wireless Station and had suffered a number of casualties. It was therefore moved to a position south of Braddell Road in Toa Payoh area north of the river Whampoe. Only two battalions constituted the brigade after the transfer of 5/14 Punjab to the 8th Indian Infantry Brigade; 2/9 Gurkha Rifles was on the right and 2/2 Gurkha Rifles was on the left of the front. In the rear of this brigade and north of Ballestier Road, 3 Cavalry had been positioned.

The 8th Indian Infantry Brigade occupied its sector of the new perimeter by noon. Its position was in an area from MacPherson Road to about one thousand yards west of Serangoon Road, facing north-north-west. On the right was 5/14 Punjab on the line of small hill features along Paya Lebar Road. In the centre and in the Bidadari Cemetery area, up to and including Serangoon Road, was 2/10 Baluch. Forward and to the left of Braddell Road and on the Biscuit Factory ridge was 1/13 Frontier Force Rifles. In reserve and behind 2/10 Baluch was 2/18 Royal Garhwal Rifles, in the southern portion of Bidadari Cemetery. At about 1245 hours on 13 February, the Japanese patrols appeared on the brigade front and considerable motor transport traffic was observed moving towards Paya Lebar village. They had come from the direction of Serangoon village and were probably tired. They stopped at that village and, apart from some mortaring, they kept quiet and allowed the Gurkhas also some rest for the remainder of the day.

So far as the 44th Indian Infantry Brigade was concerned, it had arrived in its positions at about 0400 hours and bivouacked. By first light the battalions had understood their situation clearly. They had their positions on the right of 5 Bedfordshire and Hertfordshire holding Buona Vista Hill 50 and also a composite battalion of the Australians, and on the left of a Royal Engineer battalion. 6/14 Punjab was left forward, 6/1 Punjab right forward

---

[57] "*ABDACOM*", op. cit., pp. 39-40, para 25; sub-paras (j) and (k).

and 7/8 Punjab in reserve. The day passed quietly. The Japanese aircrafts were however very active and flying low, but there was not much shelling. At about 1600 hours the Japanese attacked the forward company of 5 Bedfordshire and Hertfordshire and drove it from Hill 50. The British battalion prepared a counterattack, but abandoned it; instead it withdrew from its general position. This was apparently necessary to conform with the withdrawal of the Malaya Brigade on its left. But the Indian brigade was not informed of this until after 5 Bedfordshire and Hertfordshire had actually vacated its position and left the former's left flank absolutely open to the Japanese. It was lucky that, although the Japanese engaged this brigade with mortar fire, they did not press their attack. Meanwhile, the brigade commander, being totally unaware of this danger, was at this moment planning the routine night patrolling with the adjacent Australian battalion headquarters, and co-ordinating the general defence arrangements of his brigade position. But when he saw the danger of the new situation he immediately issued preliminary orders for withdrawal. Forward positions were to be vacated by 2100 hours, and withdrawal to commence at 2230 hours. The route was the railway line for 6/1 Punjab and the pipe-line for 6/14 and 7/8 Punjab; the British battalion of the 15th Indian Infantry Brigade was to cover the withdrawal. The rallying point was 486th mile on the railway line and the Nock Sen Brick Works on the Alexandra Road, where guides would lead all to the final destination. All battalions met together at 0130 hours on 14 February 1942, and every regiment was told that their final destination was Mount Echo near the Japanese Golf Links. They reached this place at about 0400 hours and came under the command of Southern Area. All accounts show that this was a nice place promising food and rest. The dispositions were as follows: on the right and south slopes of the Japanese Golf Course and Mount Echo, 6/1 Punjab; on the south-eastern slopes of Mount Echo, 7/8 Punjab; and on the north slopes, 6/14 Punjab. The British battalion was centrally placed on Mount Echo.

On 13 February, the 18th British Division was disposed from (exclusive) Woodleigh cross-roads to (inclusive) Double Road. The Chinese High School was the limit in the latter area. It had a five-mile front, and there had been much mixing of units as a result of the piecemeal withdrawal from beach defences. The only event worth noting on this long front was the withdrawal of the 53rd British Infantry Brigade from south of Nee Soon to its position in the main perimeter on the Braddell Road in consequence of Japanese attacks from 0400 hours to 1100 hours on this day. Another incident was the rejoining of 2/30 Australian Imperial Force Battalion with its parent unit, the 8th Australian Imperial Force Division in Tyersall Park area. Otherwise, apart from the Japanese shelling and mortaring and low-level aircraft attacks, the 18th British Division enjoyed a quiet day. There were three Indian units also in this division, viz. 5/11 Sikh, 3/17 Dogra and the Kapurthala State Infantry. The Sikhs were subjected to considerable Japanese mortar and artillery fire, besides bombing from the air. But the worst of all their experiences was the shell fire from the British artillery in error which practically wiped out one platoon. At 1700 hours the battalion was relieved by Suffolks and 3/17 Dogra and thereafter moved into brigade reserve on Raffles Hill.[58] 3/17 Dogra side-stepped to the left on the Farrer Road and Kapurthala State Infantry moved further behind the 54th British Brigade Headquarters. Between the left flank of 3/17 Dogra and the right flank of the 8th Australian Imperial Force Division there was a gap of about 1000 yards, which was to some extent neutralised by the fact that the right of the Australian line ran forward from the Farrer Road in a westerly direction forming thereby a salient with the line held by the 18th British Division.

The main Japanese offensive on 13 February 1942 developed, however, along the Pasir Panjang Ridge on the left of the general Island defence. Here the Japanese *18th Division*, which had fought in the Mersing area and later taken part in the initial attack against Singapore Island, came into action. After two hours of heavy shelling and mortaring, it attacked the Malaya Regiment which was holding this feature. The latter fought magnificently in spite of suffering very heavy losses. By the afternoon the Japanese had reached the Gap which was an important position where the Buona Vista Road crossed the Ridge. Further north the Japanese gained another local success. After dark all British forward troops fell back, under orders, to positions covering the important Alexandra area, in which were situated the Main Ordnance Depot, the Alexandra Ammunition Magazine, the Military Hospital and other installations.

As the stranglehold on Singapore Town increased, the agony became intolerable. There was obviously no use further fighting. "The Governor stressed the dangers which would result if Singapore with its large population was suddenly deprived of its water supply ".[59] Major-General Key, who was consulted by Malaya Command on capitulation or " a simultaneous advance

[58] A Diary of the 5th Battalion (D.C.O.) The Sikh, 13 February 1942.
[59] Percival's *Despatch*, p. 1324, para 568.

on all fronts as a dying gesture" told his commander that "if early capitulation was inevitable......it should take place while the Japanese soldiery could be controlled by their Commander".[60] General Gordon Bennett writes: "During the day I sent a cable to the Australian Prime Minister advising of the seriousness of the position and telling him that the Australian Imperial Force had formed a perimeter on which it would stand to the last. In the event of other formations falling back and allowing the enemy to enter the city behind us, I advised that it was my intention to surrender to avoid any further needless loss of life".[61] The situation was bad enough to deserve being reported to the Government of Australia, but it is regrettable that this cable should have been sent without the knowledge of Malaya Command. General Percival considered this "a most extraordinary procedure". He writes "No doubt he (Gordon Bennett) was perfectly entitled to communicate with his own Prime Minister but surely not to inform him of an intention to surrender in certain circumstances when he had not even communicated that intention to his own superior officer".[61a]

By 14 February, the position in Singapore was desperate. It had been encircled by sea, land and air, and no reinforcements could come in. Due to infiltration, units were cut off and held up in isolated pockets and ammunition was diminishing. Above all, water supply was causing anxiety. At the most, it would last for forty-eight hours, but it might be available only for twenty-four hours. What would happen to the people after the water supply ceased? Every one could give his own answer. Encirclement and infiltration and fifth column activities had worsened the situation. The responsibility of the British army and government for the lives of the innocent and helpless mass of humanity that had taken shelter in Singapore city was weighing heavily on General Percival. So he began to press his superior authorities to allow him to take the obvious step to avoid further bloodshed. Here is a summary of the efforts of the Malaya Command: "Later on the 14th the General Officer Commanding Malaya reported that owing to extensive damage to the mains the water supply was limited to a maximum of 48, or possibly only 24 hours. If the enemy captured the pumping station, which he was then attacking, the period would be further reduced. That had now become the governing factor, because the prospect of coping with a million civilians without water had produced an entirely new situation. He stated that he

---

[60] *History of 11th Indian Division in Malaya*, p. 553.
[61] *Why Singapore Fell*, p. 160.
[61a] Percival: *The War in Malaya*, p. 284.

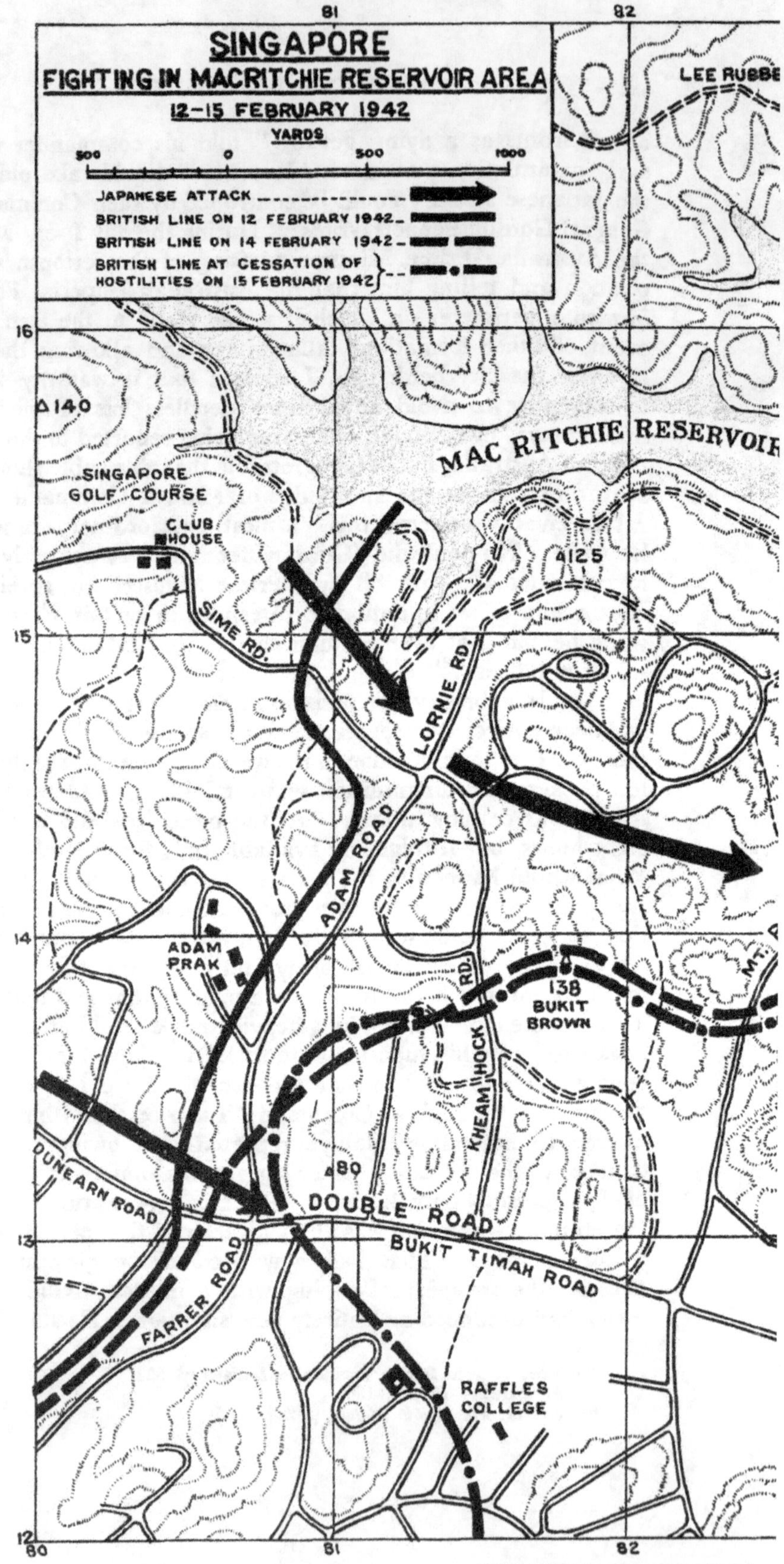
SINGAPORE
FIGHTING IN MACRITCHIE RESERVOIR AREA
12–15 FEBRUARY 1942
YARDS
500 0 500 1000
JAPANESE ATTACK
BRITISH LINE ON 12 FEBRUARY 1942
BRITISH LINE ON 14 FEBRUARY 1942
BRITISH LINE AT CESSATION OF HOSTILITIES ON 15 FEBRUARY 1942
LEE RUBBE
MAC RITCHIE RESERVOIR
SINGAPORE GOLF COURSE
CLUB HOUSE
Δ140
SIME RD.
LORNIE RD.
125
ADAM ROAD
ADAM PRAK
138 BUKIT BROWN
KHEAM HOCK RD.
MT.
DUNEARN ROAD
80
DOUBLE ROAD
BUKIT TIMAH ROAD
FARRER ROAD
RAFFLES COLLEGE
81
82
16
15
14
13
12
80
SPOT HEIGHTS SHOWN IN FEET THU

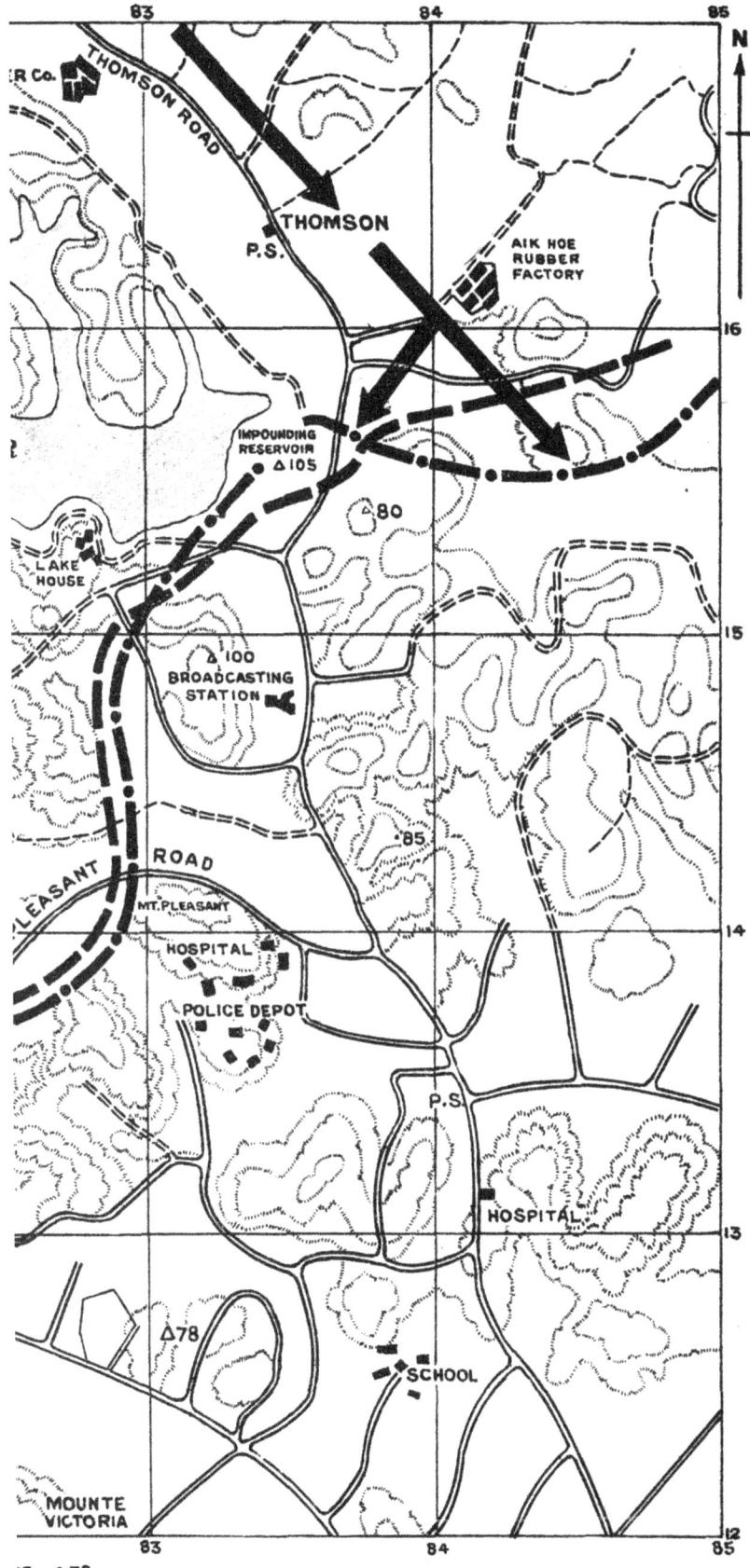

was watching developments and fighting on, but he might find it necessary to take an immediate decision. In reply to this message orders were issued to the General Officer Commanding that in all places where a sufficiency of water existed for the troops they must go on fighting. The Governor of the Straits Settlements informed the Colonial Office that he had represented to the General Officer Commanding the danger of pestilence resulting from deprivation of water for a million people concentrated within a radius of three miles. The General Officer Commanding made a further representation on the above lines and in reply was told that his gallant stand was serving a purpose and it must be continued to the limit of endurance ".[62]

The progress of war on 14 February, was inconsiderable, but significant. The Japanese attack developed at the east end of MacRitchie Reservoir, but the situation was restored by a counter-attack by the 28th Indian Infantry Brigade. By the evening, however, the pressure was so great that the forward troops were pushed back to the line Mount Pleasant—Hill 130—south west of Bukit Brown—Crossroads at Bukit Timah—Adam Road, on which the situation was for the moment stabilised. Also various areas in Singapore Town were bombed and shelled throughout the day, which led to some large fires and considerable damage to the water supply line which the engineers were making frantic efforts to repair.[63] Early in the morning, Wellsforce was driven from Hill 105 at the east end of MacRitchie Reservoir, and the left flank of 2 Cambridgeshire of the 53rd British Infantry Brigade was also driven in. These left a big gap between Hill 90 and Hill 80 into which the Japanese penetrated in the morning and pressed the rear of the British brigade. To restore the situation and fill the gap, 2/2 Gurkha Rifles, which was behind this brigade, was ordered to move up on the left of the brigade and occupy Hill 75 north of Grave Hill. At the same time the gap between the left of 2 Cambridgeshire and the right of 6 Norfolk was filled by moving the reserve company of 5 Norfolk into a position south of the Braddell Road, facing north-west. 2/2 Gurkha Rifles failed to reach Hill 75 because they were unable to identify the hill in the absence of a map or a guide. But the Gurkhas occupied a feature slightly behind Hill 75, from where they were able to fulfil the task of blocking the 1200-yard gap between Hill 90 and Hill 80.[64] 2/9 Gurkha Rifles, the remaining battalion of the 28th Indian Infantry Brigade, also moved from the area of the Wireless Station (some way to the west of the

---

[62] "*ABDACOM*", *op. cit.*, pp. 41-42, para 25, sub-para (O).
[63] *Ibid.*, p. 40, para 25, sub-para (N).
[64] War Diary, 2/2 G.R., 14 February 1942.

Serangoon Road) to the Pineapple Factory (on the east side of the road). Later it was shifted further south to Bondamoer to protect the headquarters of the 11th Indian Division.

At dawn on this date the forward battalions of the 8th Indian Infantry Brigade were dug in behind wire after hours of arduous labour. The morning passed quietly in the 11th Indian Division area, apart from continuous shelling. Occasional bombing also took place, in the course of which 2/9 Gurkha Rifles brought down one aeroplane in flames. The effect of this stray incident has been described as one of delight which was almost pathetic. During the previous night, the Japanese had been active on the front of 2/10 Baluch from the side of Paya Lebar, and in the early morning it was found that the three forward companies had disappeared, probably by being surrounded and captured. 2/18 Royal Garhwal Rifles which was in reserve was sent forward to fill the gap, which it occupied without opposition. In view of the reports that the Japanese were moving south on the Paya Lebar Road and east of it, and also in order to form a more satisfactory link with the Jamesforce, 3 Cavalry was sent in the afternoon to the area of Macpherson and Paya Lebar road junction on the right of 5/14 Punjab. The remnants of 3/16 Punjab, about fifty in all, were also placed under the 8th Indian Infantry Brigade, and they arrived in their position in the evening, where they were in reserve in the Alkaff Garden area under the command of 5/14 Punjab. In the meantime reports had been arriving that since noon the Japanese were pressing forward at the junction of 5/14 Punjab and the 2nd Malaya Infantry Brigade. The Division Commander ordered 3 Cavalry and Kapurthala State Infantry to form a defensive flank along the southern boundary of the Paya Lebar airfield. This combined unit got the impression initially that there was needless alarm about the security of the forward localities of the 2nd Malaya Infantry Brigade and only minor infiltrations had taken place. But two hours later the Japanese renewed their attack in this area, and the right forward locality of 5/14 Punjab was captured. This was however re-occupied by an immediate counter-attack. Unfortunately, the Japanese infiltrated at the same time through 1 Manchester Regiment of the 2nd Malaya Infantry Brigade and rendered it almost helpless. An S.O.S. arrived from this battalion at 3 Cavalry headquarters which sent two squadrons and restored the situation somehow. These squadrons returned at midnight only after being relieved by a company of a Malayan battalion. They had sustained ten casualties. Meanwhile, a Japanese tank approached the road-block at the junction of the Paya Lebar and Macpherson Roads.

85 Anti-Tank Regiment stationed at that point was unable to face the situation and 5/14 Punjab defended it successfully until a troop of 272 Anti-tank Battery came and forced the tank to withdraw. But it was now evident that the Japanese efforts were being directed at or about the Paya Lebar Airfield which should be checked before they assumed a formidable aspect. The Commander of III Indian Corps therefore ordered four carriers of 3 Cavalry to carry out a raid on the Japanese in the huge area covered by Geylang Serai, Malaya Settlement, Teck Hock village, Paya Lebar village and Woodleigh. When the commander of the 11th Indian Division protested, he was over-ruled. The result of this adventure in Japanese-infested country was the loss of all but one carrier. In the evening the Divisional Commander visited the 8th Indian Infantry Brigade. All troops were at their respective posts, and the pressure on 5/14 Punjab had died down to minor sniping. During the night, however, B Company of this regiment repulsed a strong attack after a grenade battle of half an hour's duration. About midnight, 1 Manchester Regiment began machine-gunning the 8th Indian Infantry Brigade, but realised the mistake soon after. The 2nd Malaya Infantry Brigade withdrew during this awful night to the 'Kalang Switch' and left the right flank of the 11th Indian Division to be guarded by the precarious strength of the combined 3 Cavalry and Kapurthala State Infantry formation and the covering fire of the machine-guns of 1 Manchester Regiment.

On all other fronts 14 February 1942 was marked by the usual fighting. The Japanese main thrust was once again against the western front of the Southern area. Here very heavy fighting at close quarters went on throughout the day in which the Loyal Regiment and the Malaya Regiment distinguished themselves. At the end of the day the British troops had been driven back by the weight of the attack to the line Alexandra—Gillman Barracks—Keppel Golf Course. Further north, the Japanese reached the Alexandra Hospital area as stated earlier, but were prevented from making further progress by 5 Bedfordshire and Hertfordshire and a composite Royal Engineers unit.

On the front held by the 18th British Division, 1 Cambridgeshire continued to hold its position west of the Adam Road where it had shown great determination in resisting the Japanese attacks during the last three days. To the right of this battalion the Japanese developed a strong attack, supported by artillery and tanks at about 1800 hours, and succeeded in advancing nearly a mile until they were held up by defences along the line of the Mount Pleasant Road. A deep dent in the British line was thus created. Wellsforce recaptured Hill 105 east of MacRitchie Reservoir, and 4 Suffolk which had been attacked by tanks on the Sime and Lornie Roads withdrew to the Mount Pleasant area for reorganisation. But parties of the Japanese also penetrated as far as the Mount Pleasant Road during the day, occupying a number of houses which, despite several counter-attacks by 4 Suffolk, were never properly cleared of the Japanese.

The part played by 5/11 Sikh in the British Division zone may be described here. At 0930 hours, on receipt of orders from the brigade headquarters, this battalion moved north of the Bukit Timah Road to deal with a supposed break-through by the Japanese. This report proved to be incorrect. The battalion was then ordered to hold a line from the Mount Pleasant Road and along south of Bukit Brown to the Kheam Hock Road with two companies, the remainder of the battalion being in the brigade reserve about half-way between the Bukit Timah Road and Bukit Brown. A portion of 6 Norfolk was to the west of the battalion headquarters and on the left of the forward companies facing north, and a little beyond were the Foresters, while details of the Recce Battalion and machine-gunners were along the Mount Pleasant Road. The position here was, and continued to be, nebulous. Patrols were sent out to obtain a clear picture of the situation but they suffered casualties and brought no information of value. Further, a few more casualties occurred from the Japanese artillery and mortar fire. About 1730 hours this double fire started again, continued for twenty minutes, stopped for three minutes and commenced again. Suspecting some sinister purpose in this sort of firing, the reserve companies were ordered to stand to, and as they were moving into position fire was opened on the battalion headquarters by three light machine-gun groups at close range. Thereupon the battalion cleared the ridge with a few casualties. The Japanese withdrew in haste, but the Sikhs came under very heavy small-arms fire from their own troops in the rear. This was of course due to confusion in this part of the front on account of the withdrawal of a number of troops and of the formation of a new line of defence along the Mount Pleasant Road by the brigade. The brigadier was told that the Sikhs had been cut up and was not informed of their ignorance of the new line formation. When he learnt this, he ordered the delivery of news at once to the forward companies south of Bukit Brown, and they withdrew to their allotted place in the new line. At 2100 hours, finding no trace of Japanese troops in the vicinity, the troops were ordered back, and the line was re-formed by dawn.

On the eastern front of the Southern Area there were some local engagements between 1 Manchester and Japanese detachments.

Throughout the day there was fairly heavy shelling of the selected areas, directed from the Bukit Timah hills. The British replied smartly. There were also attacks from the air, to which the British could make no effective reply. General Percival writes that "our light anti-aircraft guns had some wonderful targets on this day as the Japanese aircraft, with no fighters to oppose them, were flying at low altitudes. Several were brought down, but our reserves of Bofors ammunition were now getting short".[65]

Before dawn on 15 February 1942, it was reported that one company of 2/10 Baluch had gone over and surrendered to the Japanese, as the result of a clever trick; three 'European' officers in Australian uniforms, it seems, approached the troops and declared that surrender of Singapore had been agreed to, and so they should go across to the Japanese lines and capitulate. The Baluch company fell for the trap. These men were seen seated on a hill south of Paya Lebar, and 135 Field Regiment bombarded the hill during the day. The Japanese attacked the remainder of 2/10 Baluch with mortar fire in the morning, but without much effect. 'Petrol Hill' in 5/14 Punjab sector was captured by the Japanese, but 3/16 Punjab re-occupied it before noon. In the afternoon, the mortars of 1/13 Frontier Force Rifles dispersed a Japanese battalion massing in front of it, and at 1500 hours Japanese tanks and lorries approaching the Paya Lebar airfield were halted by a troop of 272 Anti-Tank Battery. During the day, 3 Cavalry was in contact with the Japanese in the vicinity of the Paya Lebar—Macpherson Roads junction.

The 44th Indian Infantry Brigade suffered heavy losses on 15 February. The Japanese attacked incessantly on this day 1 Malaya Infantry Brigade which was to the left of 44th Indian Infantry Brigade, and inflicted heavy casualties on all its units, especially 2 Loyal Regiment. The line of defence fell back to the east end of Alexandra Depots area—Mount Washington—east end of Keppel Golf Links. In the strenuous fighting, the 44th Indian Infantry Brigade could not escape punishment. Japanese shelling and mortaring on the high ground to the left and rear of the brigade caused heavy losses of men. The huts, constructed of dried palm fronds, caught fire and men inside them were burnt to ashes. There were small calibre shells, about 3·7-inch and with high velocity, popularly described as 'whiz 3-bangs', which caused more confusion among men of the units. There was an occasion

---

[65] *The War in Malaya*, p. 290.

PLATE IX

Smoke from the naval base overshadows Singapore, February 1942.

(Courtesy – *Australian War Memorial*)

PLATE X

(Courtesy – *Australian War Memorial*)

After withdrawal of the defending air forces from Malaya to Sumatra, the Singapore Island was subjected to increasingly heavy air attacks. Bombs are seen falling in the background of this picture, taken in February 1942.

(Courtesy – *Australian War Memorial*)

The causeway to Singapore Island was blown after the withdrawal of Indian and other Allied forces from the Mainland. The 70-foot gap in the Causeway can be seen below the Johore Administration building.

when the Japanese, with machine-guns and mortars in position, were eight hundred yards from this brigade. "We were able to turn our 3-inch mortars on to this target", writes the war-diarist, "but could get no artillery fire, as apparently, there was none available. It was becoming obvious that as the day went on our situation would become worse rather than better".[66] But by 1730 hours the Japanese shelling decreased considerably; by 1800 hours orders to cease offensive action except on being attacked and to maintain the present position were received by the 44th Indian Infantry Brigade; and at about 2000 hours an order proclaimed that terms of capitulation were being negotiated and all arms and ammunition were to be stacked and counted.

3/17 Dogra and 5/11 Sikh Regiments remained in their positions on the Farrer Road and in Bukit Brown area respectively. The latter's war-diarist has recorded that 'at about 1200 hours a car with a white flag passed through along the Bukit Timah Road and we learnt that terms were being sought'.[67]

During the night of 14/15 February 1942, the Japanese infantry infiltrated in all sectors of the 18th British Division front and also succeeded in getting a footing on the Mount Pleasant Ridge. The lack of an organised reserve made it difficult to deal with these pockets of penetration. Nevertheless, local counter-attacks were staged, and some of the lost positions on Mount Pleasant Ridge were regained.

In this connection the activities of 2/2 Gurkha Rifles deserve some notice. Briefly, this battalion did not at once occupy Hill 75 which had been assigned to it on the previous day. It was asked early in the morning to remain where it was, pending the arrival of the Brigade Commander. Later when he came, owing to deterioration in the situation of the 53rd British Infantry Brigade on the right, the battalion was asked either to occupy Hill 75 or to go the right side of the brigade to help. While preparations were made for reconnoitring a position on the right flank, the commander ordered the unit verbally to move to Hill 75. A little later low-flying Japanese planes began to come over the area again. But on this occasion they were engaged by small arms fire, and one company opened heavy Light Machine-Gun and rifle fire at a ground target which was suspected to be a fifth-column group. "A curious phenomenon seen on several occasions during these last few days was a silent stream of red lights, similar to red tracer, shooting into the air from within our positions. Presumably they were fired by fifth columnists and were an indication

[66] History of the 6th Battalion 1st Punjab, p. 18.
[67] A Diary of 5th Battalion (D.C.O.) The Sikh Regiment, 15 February 1942.

to enemy air or artillery. The weapon, or whatever it was that discharged them, was soundless ".[68]

On the afternoon of 15 February, the Gurkhas were moving up to occupy Hill 75. But in the middle of this move, a message arrived from the 53rd British Infantry Brigade. It ran as follows:—
" An emissary proceeded to Japanese Headquarters at 1130 hours. At 1600 hours all troops under command will cease fire but remain in present positions. If attacked by the enemy after 1600 hours the officer or N.C.O. in command of the party concerned will raise the white flag. There will be no destruction of arms or equipment but all secret papers, codes and ciphers will be destroyed. Water and rations must be conserved. All money will be burnt ". The commanding officer was satisfied with the genuineness of the message, which bewildered everyone in the unit. But at 1600 hours fire did not cease as expected, and both sides continued hostilities. Firing did not cease entirely until 2100 hours. At about 1700 hours the battalion commander issued an order for collecting all arms and ammunition in a central dump and for the closing in of all companies close to Battalion Headquarters. Arrangements were made for sentries and also for raising white flags at battalion headquarters and by companies when the Japanese arrived. But no developments took place, so all went to sleep and rose only on the next day.

There was little Japanese activity against the 8th Australian Imperial Force Division also on this day, except for some shelling and air action. During the morning there was some pressure on the front of 2/26 Australian Imperial Force Battalion on the Farrer Road. During the afternoon there were signs of the Japanese preparing to make a thrust in a northerly direction from the Alexandra end of the Ayer Raja Road against the south-western face of the Australian perimeter. But by evening no attack had been launched.

On the eastern side of the Southern Area, the Japanese arrived in Kampong Eunos early on the morning of this day. This led to the reorganisation of defence with a view to stabilising it from the Reclamation ground in the airport area up to the Kalang switch line on the west bank of the Sungei Kalang. The situation, however, remained basically the same.

The Capitulation

The story of the capitulation has been narrated in more or less identical words by all historians of the war in Malaya. There

---

[68] War Diary, 2/2 G.R., 15 February 1942.

was a conference of commanders at Fort Canning at 0930 hours on 15 February. The Director-General of Civil Defence, the Inspector-General of Police and a Staff Officer of Northern Area had been invited and were present at the meeting. Each gave his own account of the situation, and Malaya Command gave a summary of the whole, and permitted a discussion on the general situation. Lieutenant-General Heath stressed water-shortage for the Indian troops in his corps. The plight of the civil population was fully analysed and noted. The question was put: 'Shall we counter-attack? Or, shall we capitulate?' The formation commanders were unanimously of the opinion that, in the existing circumstances, a counter-attack was impracticable. Some of them also doubted the British ability to resist another determined attack of the Japanese and pointed out its consequences on the crowded population in the town. Capitulation was, therefore, silently and sadly, decided on.

The Supreme Commander of South-West Pacific, General Wavell, had telegraphed to Malaya Command, that...... 'When you are fully satisfied that this (defence) is no longer possible I give you discretion to cease resistance'. In reply and as a result of the commanders' conference, General Percival notified General Wavell of the decision to cease hostilities.

General Yamashita wanted General Percival to come personally and offer the surrender unconditionally. The latter, accompanied by Brigadier-Generals Torrance and Newbigging and Major Wilde, the interpreter, went to the Ford Automobile Factory at 1840 hours (late by an hour and ten minutes). The Japanese General entered the room five minutes later and shook hands with the British General, whose 'face was swollen red and ......eyes were bloodshot'. The following questions and answers were then noted:

General Yamashita (pointing to the written terms)—I will stop fighting if these unconditional terms are accepted. I want some simple questions answered. Just answer Yes or No.
General Percival—Yes.

Y Have you any Japanese Prisoners-of-War?
P None.
Y Any Japanese?
P They were all sent to India. Their safety is in the hands of the Indian Government.
Y Have you any intention of surrendering unconditionally? Yes or No?
P I would like to defer any answer until tomorrow morning.

Y   Tomorrow morning? What do you mean? The Japanese forces will make an attack tonight. Is that all right?
P   In that case, I would like to have until 2330 hours Japan time.
Y   2330 hours? In that case the Japanese forces will continue attacking until then.
P   (No answer).
Y   Is that all right? Yes or No?
P   Yes.
Y   In that case I will stop fighting at 2200 hours Japan time. I will send 1,000 guards into Singapore City to police the city tonight. It that all right?
P   Yes.
Y   If these terms are broken, I will launch a general attack upon the city tonight.
P   I would like to have the safety of British and Australian troops remaining in Singapore guaranteed.
Y   Be at complete ease about that point.

The unconditional surrender was signed at 1950 hours.

The terms of this surrender are not known from any official record. General Percival has given them from memory. They were as under:—

(a) There must be unconditional surrender of all military forces (Army, Navy and Air Force) in the Singapore Area.

(b) Hostilities must cease at 2030 hours local time or 2200 hours Japanese time.

(c) All troops must remain in position occupied at the cessation of hostilities pending further orders.

(d) All weapons, military equipment, ships, aeroplanes and secret documents must be handed over to the Japanese Army intact.

(e) In order to prevent looting and other disorders in Singapore Town during the temporary withdrawal of all armed forces, a force of 100 British armed men to be left temporarily in the Town area until relieved by the Japanese.

Of all the terms the fourth was the one which was most disappointing to the Japanese. They got none of the stores, weapons and documents of value, as they had been destroyed already under orders. General Yamashita acquiesced in the result of British action. The war ceased at 2030 hours local time punctually.

CONCLUSION

General Yamashita did not permit his force to enter Singapore Town. On the contrary he sent it out of Singapore Island on the next day. He treated all prisoners with consideration and permitted them to be at ease and to enjoy freedom in eating and drinking. Records are full of expressions of surprise at the Japanese clemency after capitulation. But, those who tried to escape from the clutches of the Japanese were severely punished.

Thus ended the campaign in Malaya, thirty days earlier than even the Japanese had dared to hope. There can be no minimising the disaster. The casualties in Malaya ran to: British 38,496, Indian 67,340, Australian 18,490, and local Volunteer troops 14,382, " giving a grand total of 138,708, of which more than 130,000 were prisoners of war ".[69] The loss in prestige and morale was even greater. In fact the fall of the " impregnable fortress " exploded the myth of white supremacy in the east, and it only remained for the resultant myth of Japanese invincibility to be exposed before the colonial peoples of south-east Asia could arise' and claim their own. But these developments lay still in future. For the moment, the Japanese were triumphant. Apart from Hong Kong and Malaya, Indian troops were fighting in defence of British interests in Borneo also, and their story may be briefly told before winding up this account of disasters in succession.

---

[69] Kirby : *The War Against Japan*, p. 473

Sarawak and Borneo

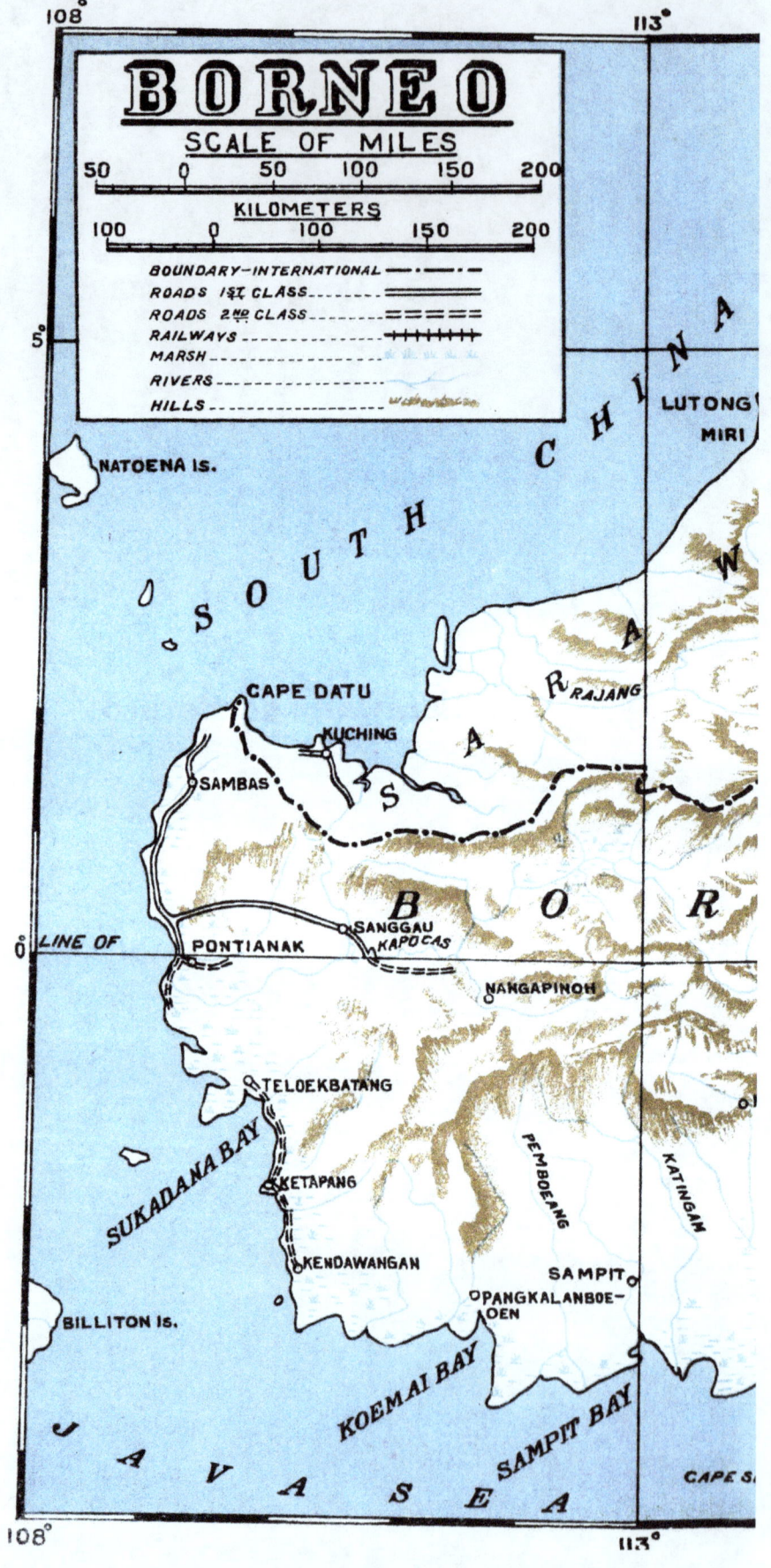

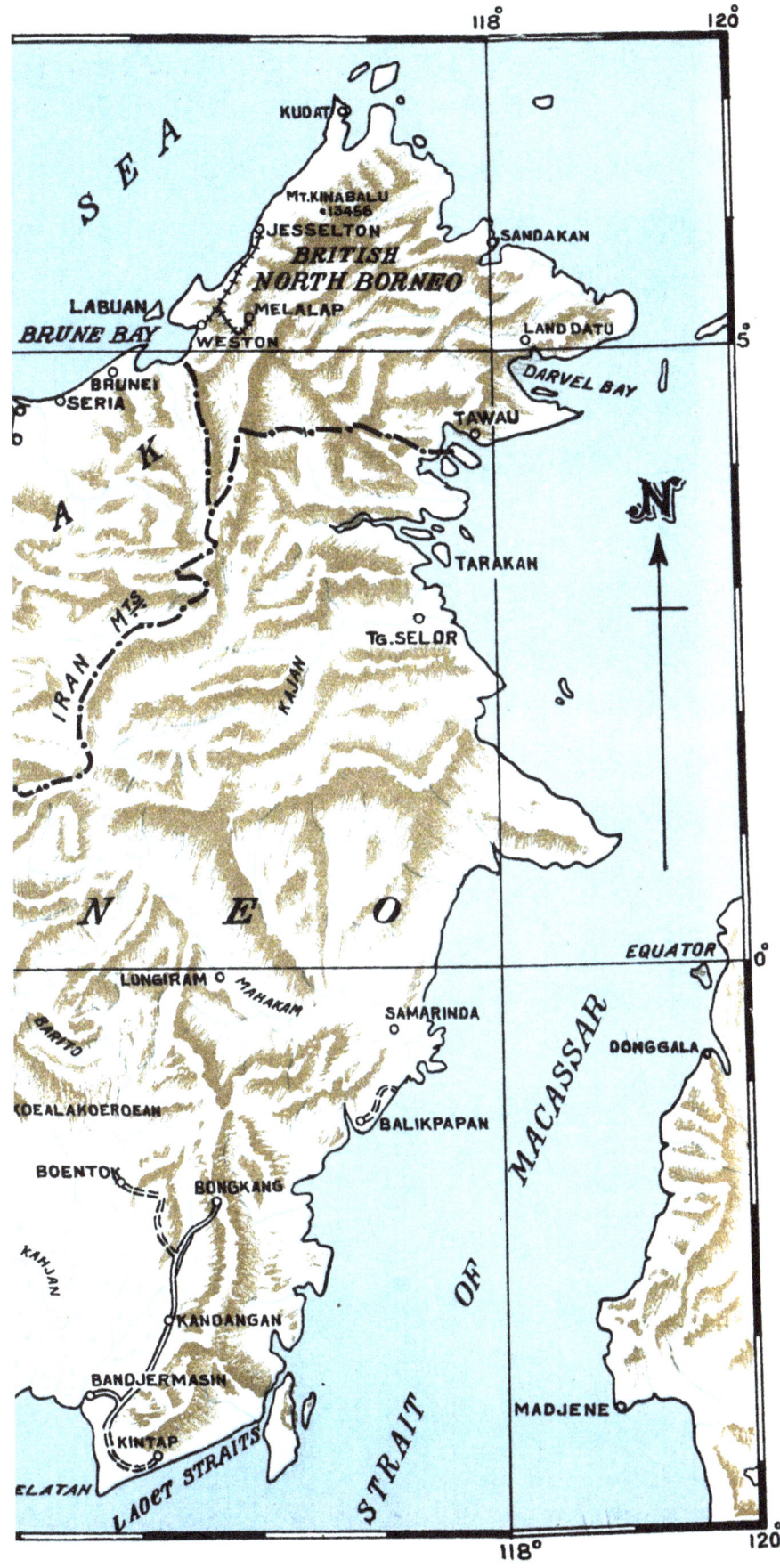

CHAPTER XII

Japanese Attack on Sarawak

Apart from the invasions of Hong Kong and Malaya described in the preceding chapters, the Japanese attacked the Philippines, Borneo, Java and Sumatra also within a few weeks of the outbreak of hostilities in South-East Asia. In all that vast region, desperate fighting was in progress from December 1941 onwards. The defenders were the Americans, the Filipinos, the Dutch and the Indonesians, but a lone battalion of the Indian army also fought the Japanese on the island of Borneo in this region. It is necessary to relate its story before concluding this study of the initial campaigns against the Japanese in South-East Asia.

SARAWAK, THE LAND AND ITS PEOPLE

Lying just north of the Equator, the whole of British and Dutch Borneo covered an area of nearly 289,000 square miles, of which the state of Sarawak occupied roughly 50,000 square miles along the north-west coast. The state had a well defined boundary to the east, determined by the watershed of the Iran mountains, but a less obvious frontier in the south where the ground was broken up by a number of irregular hill ranges. The coastline between Kuching and Miri was mostly low and flat, allowing a certain amount of cultivation. Much of the coastal area, however, in Sarawak and the rest of Borneo was swampy and malarious.

Inland, the jungle was dense and prolific. There were no railways, and only a few roads existed in the immediate neighbourhood of small towns. The main roads radiating from Kuching ran east to Pending, four miles away, north-west to Matang and south to Serian, which was situated at a distance of forty miles. A road led to the west also which passed through Bau and terminated at Krokong. Hence, with the exception of difficult tracks, the only means of communication in most parts of the island was by the streams and rivers which flowed in all directions from the central mountain ranges. The largest river was the Rejang while the Baram ranked second. The Rejang was navigable for vessels up to 800 tons as far inland as 160 miles approximately, and the Baram for about 100 miles, but there was a formidable bar at the mouth of the river. Some of the other rivers had rapids in their upper reaches, and even the lightest of craft required skilful handling while approaching them. The wider rivers also provided first-class seaplane anchorages and, in the course of operations, Royal Air Force planes made several landings at Sintang[1] on the Kapoeas river nearly 200 miles inland.

In spite of the equatorial position of Sarawak the climate in many parts of the hills and interior regions might almost be described as temperate. Around the coast, however, and in the low-lying marshy districts extending about 200 miles inland, the atmosphere was dense, humid and inclined to be oppressive. Temperatures remained fairly constant throughout the year, about 84° by day and 72° by night. Rainfall, too, varied little from one month to another, and the annual rainfall ranged from 140 to 170 inches. The north-east monsoon blowing from October to March brought heavy rainfall and bad weather down the coast, but in some areas the wettest months were between April and October, as in India. The coastline was not subject to the typhoons, so frequent off the China coast, but the after-effects of these were usually felt in the form of a heavy ground swell and bad visibility lasting several days.[2] Low morning mists extended over coastal areas causing great inconvenience to shipping and aircraft.

The population was estimated at about 500,000,[3] mainly Malays and such indigenous peoples as Dyaks, Kenyahs, Kayans and Muruts. But there was a large immigrant Chinese community which was mainly settled in the Rejang delta. The Malays were found mainly in the coastal regions and their language was the lingua franca of the State. There was a clearly marked division of trades and professions among the different nationalities as in other parts of the East. The merchant and artisan (especially carpentry) classes were mainly composed of the Chinese, who also made first-class agriculturists, water-carriers and cooks. The Malays were fishermen and woodsmen, and they supplied the bulk of the domestic servants. The small Indian shopkeeper and 'dhobi' or washerman were to be found throughout the State. The various important nationalities, in the main, preserved their national dress.

Agriculture, Industries and Trade

The coastal area is suitable for cultivation, and wherever possible sago and pepper, the chief agricultural products, were grown. Rubber plantation had steadily grown in importance

---

[1] See Map facing p. 361.
[2] Lane's Operations in Sarawak and Dutch Borneo, p. 7.
[3] A. M. Hyamson gives the population as 6,00,000 in 1939 (*A Dictionary of International Affairs*, p. 277).

during recent years and fishing was an important industry. The interior of the country was devoid of organised agriculture and the natives resorted to "shifting cultivation".

The vast mineral resources of Sarawak were not fully tapped. Prior to the outbreak of war, the Sarawak Oilfields Ltd. had successfully worked the important oilfields at Miri and Bakong in the Baram District. From Miri, the oil was pumped to the Lutong refinery on the coast, "from which loading-lines ran out to sea as there were no deep-water wharves at Lutong and no ocean-going vessels could come alongside".[4] Gold had been successfully worked out from the quartz reefs at Bau on the Sarawak river and antimony had been discovered in the same area. Sapphires of good quality were found in abundance in the mountain streams in the interior but they were too small to have much commercial value. Coal had also been found in several places especially near Selantik along the Kelingkang range.

Prior to the war, Sarawak carried on a substantial export trade mainly through Singapore. According to Dudley Stamp, the total value of exports came to £3,000,000 in 1936[5] out of which half was yielded by rubber. Other items of export were kerosene and crude oil, benzene, sago flour, pepper and fish.

History

Prior to 1839, Sarawak formed part of the State of Brunei ruled by the Raja Muda Hasaim. A rebellion broke out in 1839 against the tyranny of the ruler and the rapacity of his officials. The ruler, unable to subdue the rebels with his limited forces, asked a retired British Officer of the Indian Army, James Brooke, for assistance. Brooke has been aptly called "a counter-buccaneer". He was professionally engaged in suppressing piracy with his own boats and crew. As a reward for his help in subduing the rebels, the Raja of Brunei gave him Sarawak on 24 September 1841. James Brooke thus became the first white Raja of the territories. Two years later Brooke with the help of Captain (afterwards Admiral Sir Henry) Keppel expelled the Dyak and Malay pirates from the Saribas and Batang Lupar rivers, and crushed the naval forces of the notorious Lanun pirates, who had long been "the scourge of the seas".

In 1857 the Chinese rebelled against the authority of Raja Brooke. They sacked Kuching and temporarily succeeded in establishing their authority over Sarawak; Raja Brooke narrowly escaping with his life. His nephew Charles quickly organised a

[4] *The War in Malaya*, p. 165.
[5] *Asia, A Regional and Economic Geography* (Seventh Edition), p. 437.

force of Malays and Dyaks and with its help suppressed the insurrection. The first Raja died in 1868 and was succeeded by his nephew. Under an agreement of 1888, Sarawak was recognised as an independent State under Great Britain's protectorate, and Sir Charles Johnson Brooke was formally recognised as Raja of Sarawak by King Edward VII in 1904. He was succeeded by his eldest son, Charles Vyner Brooke, in 1917, who continued to control the destinies of the State till the outbreak of war against Japan in 1941.

Government and Administration

Until September 1941 when the centenary of the rule of Brooke was celebrated, Sarawak was ruled as an absolute monarchy. The people had no voice in their own governance. The Raja was assisted by a Supreme Council of seven which consisted of the three most important European officials and four nominated Malay magistrates. In addition to this, there was a General Council (Council of Negri) consisting of about a hundred members drawn largely from the principal tribes of the State. This council met once every three years and therefore could not exercise any control over the day to day administration of the country. The civil service carried on the entire administration, the senior members of which were Englishmen while the natives could only aspire to junior posts.

At the time of the centenary celebrations (19-24 September 1941) the ruler, Raja Sir Charles Vyner Brooke, promulgated the first constitution of the State, under which the Supreme Council became the executive council and the Council of Negri the sole legislative authority. Soon after, the Raja left for a holiday in Australia and did not return till war broke out. His absence was keenly felt by the population because Sarawak needed strong leadership, which he alone could provide. "His influence", according to Lieut.-General Percival, "based on a hundred years of family tradition, would have been far greater than that of a newly appointed council ".[6]

Strategic Importance

Even a cursory glance at a map of the Far East would show the commanding position of Borneo within the East Indies archipelago. It covered the approaches to Singapore and Malaya by the South China Sea, and control of its coastline was essential for any drive towards Java, Australia and New Guinea. Occupy-

---

6 *The War in Malaya*, p. 94.

ing as they did the whole north-west coastline of Borneo, the states of Sarawak and Brunei and British North Borneo were clearly positioned to receive the first blow from the Japanese. Nor could the potential value of these countries as bases for further aggression on the part of the Japanese be ignored. Besides the three reasonably good harbours of Kuching, Victoria (Labuan Island) and Sandakan (British North Borneo), first class seaplane and submarine anchorages could be found in the many rivers and inlets which intersected the coastline. Several aerodromes and landing grounds, too, though incapable at that time of taking heavy bombers, could be used with effect as fighter bases and could undoubtedly be enlarged to accommodate heavier planes if required.

Borneo might for strategic reasons be aptly called " part of the outer defences of Malaya ". Its western part was within easy striking distance of bomber aircraft from Malaya and vice versa. It could therefore have been of immense use to the Allies if it could be retained by them, but neither the British nor the Dutch had then sufficient resources to hold it.

APPRECIATIONS AND PLANS

The Pre-war Consultations

The outbreak of World War II in September 1939, as has been discussed earlier, found the Allied powers without a definite plan for the defence of their possessions in the Far East. Between September 1939 and the entry of Japan into the war in December 1941, the Allies had enough time to prepare to meet the expected threat from Japan. A number of conferences were held during this period but when Japan actually struck, the Allies were not in a position to offer either a determined or a prolonged resistance. The main reason for their inadequate preparations is to be found in the fact that, as already mentioned, Britain did not have sufficient resources in money and material to defend properly all the far-flung parts of her vast empire.

The establishment of General Headquarters, Far East, in November 1940, and the conferences between the British, the Dutch and the American representatives for defending their possessions in the Far East, have already been mentioned. In the Singapore Conference of October 1940, the possibilities of the Japanese attempting to seize bases in British Borneo were also discussed and it was felt that without command of the seas, it would be extremely difficult to defend these strategic points. The Conference thought that a cover of not more than 200 planes should be provided for the protection of Dutch and British Borneo, although with the existing resources the Royal Air Force was not in a position to undertake any commitment in British Borneo or elsewhere outside Malaya. The Dutch were assigned the important task of providing local defences throughout the Netherlands East Indies. This decision was arrived at on the recommendation of the Chiefs of Staff contained in their *Far Eastern Appreciation* (also known as *Tactical Appreciation*) dated 16 October 1940, in which they wrote: " The Dutch authorities should be pressed to provide additional troops and anti-aircraft defences used in the NEI and in particular, to station some units in Borneo ".

The Conference also gave earnest consideration to the maintenance of essential supplies of aviation spirit from Borneo and the Dutch East Indies to Australia and New Zealand. In case, however, it was not possible for the Allies to protect the oilfields by adequate force, because of the requirements of war in other important theatres, they had an oil denial scheme for putting the oil installations at Miri and Seria out of action before the Japanese troops could land there. The Dutch also had a similar oil denial scheme for Balikpapan and Tarakan if their capture became inevitable, but details of the Dutch scheme were not available when the Conference met.

In their *Tactical Appreciation* the Chiefs of Staff laid down the minimum requirements for the defence of British Borneo, Brunei and Sarawak against Japanese attack. It was estimated that a force of one brigade of three battalions with one battery in addition to the existing local forces would be sufficient to repel any attack. It was also assumed by the Chiefs of Staff that units participating in Borneo would be of a high standard, organised and equipped in accordance with British War Establishments. The term " brigade " was specifically defined and it was used to indicate a formation consisting of :—

(1) Infantry Brigade Headquarters,
(2) Infantry Brigade Signal Section,
(3) Brigade Anti-tank Company of nine Anti-tank Guns,
(4) One Field Regiment Royal Artillery (25-Pounder Gun Howitzers),
(5) One Anti-tank Battery, Royal Artillery,
(6) One Field Company Royal Fusiliers, and
(7) The necessary administrative units.

Appendix B of the Singapore Defence Conference Report contained observations on the defence of air bases in British Borneo and the Miri and Seria oilfields. Out of the two aerodromes at Kuching and Jesselton, it was recognised that the latter might not be held against a determined attack. It was therefore decided to hold Kuching only, where "the natural difficulties make a sea-borne landing in force improbable". The defence of this area was confined to the protection of the aerodrome and guarding the river approach. It was estimated that this would require defence by one company and one machine-gun platoon.

The Miri-Seria area, extending for about 40 miles in length, presented greater difficulties, since the nature of the terrain made it possible for an invader to land anywhere along the coast. At the time the appreciation was written there were no local forces in Brunei and Sarawak except the Sarawak police which could act only against saboteurs. It was understood, however, that if detachments of Imperial troops were stationed in Sarawak, the police could assist them in repelling any external attack. For the proper defence of the area a large force was necessary which was not likely to be available. It was therefore recommended that the role of the garrison there would be to gain sufficient time for the oil denial scheme to be carried out should that become necessary. The strength of the garrison to be stationed in this area was estimated at two companies.

Four months after the Singapore Conference, Anglo-Dutch-Australian conversations were held in Singapore during February 1941. This conference emphasised the necessity of collective action against Japanese aggression and agreed to the principle of mutual reinforcement, the Dutch undertaking to provide submarines for operation in the South China Sea. "The principles on which sea communications would be defended were outlined, and emphasis was laid on the importance of making the passage of the Northern line of the Dutch possessions as difficult as possible for the Japanese". In the event of an attack on West and East Borneo, all available Dutch naval forces were to be concentrated for action in the Strait of Macassar and Allied air forces were to attack the Japanese from the aerodromes in Borneo. The possibility of the United States intervening actively on the Allied side was considered, and it was estimated that, if the United States of America intervened, Japan would be forced "to adopt a defensive strategy and abandon her major expeditions to the south". The Allied conferences and agreements after February 1941 also kept under constant review the problem of defending Borneo.

2/15 Punjab to Sarawak

In November 1940, shortly after its arrival in Singapore, 2/15 Punjab had been ordered to send detachments amounting to one company to Miri and Kuching in Sarawak. C Company was detailed for the task and, after a preliminary reconnaissance by the Company Commander, the party sailed in HMS *Kedah* on 21 December 1940.

The Miri detachment (2 officers and 98 Indian Other Ranks) disembarked on 23 December and was given the task of covering, in the event of war, the destruction of the oil refinery and other installations in the Miri-Lutong-Seria area. They were also to cover the withdrawal of skilled technicians and essential machine parts to Singapore. The force was later entrusted with the organisation and training of local state forces at Miri and Seria (Brunei State) and 'co-ordinating the combined force into a defence scheme'.[7] The detachment worked on the construction of log and sand pill-boxes for a close static defence of the Lutong Oil Refinery.

The other detachment for Kuching, consisting of one officer and 52 Indian other ranks, landed there on 24 December and was made responsible for the protection of civil demolition parties, should the latter be called upon to destroy the aerodrome about 5 miles south of Kuching. Possessing, apart from rifles, only four light machine-guns, one anti-tank rifle and a truck, this detachment could have little tactical value beyond stiffening the morale of the people. As Lane puts it, "Tactically, the detachment had no value, but its bluff and propaganda value might, it was thought, slow up an attack and stiffen the morale of the civil demolition parties".[8] The detachment, however, proved useful as an advance party for the remainder of the battalion by becoming well-acquainted with the country and its mixed population of Malays, Dyaks and Chinese.

As war approached nearer, efforts were made to complete the defensive preparations. Towards the end of March 1941 a strategic and tactical reconnaissance of the Kuching area was carried out by two staff officers from Headquarters Singapore with the object of making recommendations regarding the employment of a regular Indian infantry battalion (less a company) for its defence. After a week's reconnaissance, a report was prepared which dealt with the topography and strategic position of the area, its security and measures to be taken against fifth column activities. The report, in addition to being topographically inaccurate, was later considered to have taken into account few considerations of strategic or tactical importance. Due to the failure to realise many essential points, the report gave a highly optimistic view of the defence scheme as manned by one battalion

[7] Lane's Report, p. 4.
[8] *Ibid.*

less one company. It suggested that with the control of the Pending area, Matang bottleneck and Samariang by the defenders, the Kuching aerodrome might be successfully held against enormous odds. The untrue picture painted in the report was unfortunate, since its effects could not be erased from the minds of Headquarters Singapore until too late. Colonel Lane states, "HQ Malaya Command took a greater cognizance of the findings of the staff report than they did of the later reports made by those having a considerably greater experience of this type of country".[9]

On the receipt of this report at Singapore, the whole battalion (2/15 Punjab) was put on move at short notice. Early in May 1941 both the Commanding Officer and his Second in Command left for staff appointments in India. Lieut.-Colonel C.M. Lane, M.C., took over command and on 9/10 May, the battalion sailed for Kuching, arriving there three days later. The battalion (less D Company) moved into tented accommodation at Batu Lintang while more permanent quarters were being prepared for them. D Company was sent to Lutong area to relieve the detachment of C Company there, which then rejoined the battalion on 22 May.

2/15 Punjab was the first British Indian unit to be stationed permanently in Sarawak and it is gratifying to note that the men got on extremely well with the local population. There was close liaison between the officers of the battalion and State officials and this went a long way towards making a success of the planned role of the troops, which included the task of raising and training local levies. Many difficulties in raising local troops and training them suitably were easily overcome by officers of the Battalion.

To suit local requirements, the battalion was reorganised as follows:—

A, B, C, D, E Companies	(1-15 Platoons)
Battalion Headquarters	(16 Platoon)
Signals	(17 Platoon)
18-Pounder Field Guns	(18 Platoon)
3" Mortars	(19 Platoon)
Armoured Fighting Vehicle	(20 Platoon)
Outboard Gunboat	(21 Platoon)
Sub-Machine-Gun	(22 Platoon)
Mechanical Transport	(23 Platoon)
Administration	(24 Platoon)

In addition to the above, the unit possessed first and second line reinforcements and a platoon of Jats from 4/15 Punjab giving

[9] *Ibid.*

a total battalion strength of 1,075 all ranks. Together with the four State forces, " Sarfor " (all Indian and local State forces in Sarawak and Brunei) in May 1941 numbered 2,565 officers and other ranks.

On the arrival of 2/15 Punjab at Kuching in May 1941, Lieut.-Colonel Lane, Officer Commanding " Sarfor " immediately ordered an extensive reconnaissance of both the Kuching and Miri areas. The role of the troops in the Kuching area had been to provide cover for destruction parties and if possible to retain the aerodrome for the use of Allied aircraft, failing which, to deny its use to the Japanese as a last resort. But such a static defence was wholly inconsistent with the topography of the country round Kuching with its many river approaches and poor communications. Lieut.-Colonel Lane therefore decided to prepare plans for mobile defence.

Plan " A "

A plan of action (known as Plan " A ") was consequently prepared with a view to providing mobile defence in conjunction with the four Sarawak State forces—the Sarawak Coastal Marine Service (S.C.M.S.), Sarawak Rangers (S.R.), Sarawak Armed Police (S.A.P.) and Sarawak Volunteer Force (S.V.F.). The object of the plan was to ensure the holding of the landing ground at Kuching, for as long as possible, and to hold off the Japanese till the denial schemes could be carried out and all important facilities destroyed.

The plan divided the whole of the Kuching area into eight sectors for purposes of defence, but since the plan was not ultimately given effect to, details may not be of much use here. The role of the State forces was definitely defined. The Sarawak Coastal Marine Service was to maintain a close watch from the coast on shipping and aircraft movements and to give information to the garrison commander. It was provided with river launches which were to patrol the coast to prevent secret infiltration and give early information of hostile landings or advance. To the Sarawak Rangers was assigned the role of providing observation and harassment platoons in the Mangrove—Nita belt north of the Matang Road and east of Rock and Simmangan Roads. The Sarawak Armed Police was to provide local protection to civilian demolition parties. On completion of this role they were to come into reserve for line of communication protection along the Bau Road. Miscellaneous duties were assigned to the Sarawak Volunteer Force. Its Engineer Company was " to aid in the carrying out of demolition roles, road and bridge maintenance or destruction", and Mobile Workshop Company was to operate in two portions east and west of the Sarawak river. The Motor Transport Company was asked to assist in the movement of mobile companies of the 2/15 Punjab.

2/15 Punjab was also given definite roles along with the Sarawak State forces. Its rifle companies were to operate in specifically assigned sub-areas of the main Pending-Kuching area while the "specialist" platoons in Headquarters Company were all to be used to the fullest advantage. A gun-boat platoon was to operate in conjunction with Sarawak Coastal Marine Service. Moreover, the 18-pounder platoon was to cover the Moeratabas in front of Pending with two guns mounted at Biawak. Another two guns at Bintawa were to cover the area of the Sarawak river about Lintang. The 3" mortar platoon (consisting of six mortars) was to support the gun positions with two mortars to each gun area and the balance of two mortars was to be held in reserve at the Race Course.

Such in brief was Plan "A". Its object was to strike " the enemy as early as possible on the rivers, forcing him if possible into the swamps, engaging him by Mobile Forces in his advance to the aerodrome ".[10] Later, if the Japanese advance could not be halted by these means, the aerodrome could be demolished and the whole force withdrawn in small parties into the hills and jungles from where by guerilla action the Japanese in the Kuching area could be harassed and prevented from using the landing ground.[11]

On 27 May 1941, before the Plan had been completed, a change of battalion commander took place. Lieut.-Colonel Peppers (2/15 Punjab) took over from Lieut.-Colonel Lane as Officer Commanding Troops.

Liaison Visits

On 28 June 1941, Air Chief-Marshal Sir Robert Brooke-Popham, Commander-in-Chief Far East, visited Kuching and gave his approval to the operational Plan "A". As no liaison with the Netherlands East Indies troops had so far been possible, he flew to Singkawang II aerodrome and met the Dutch Air Commander who was to provide air support for operations in the Kuching area.[12] Apart from this visit no staff officer from Headquarters Singapore came to Kuching from November 1940 to September 1941. Headquarters was therefore out of touch with the local situation

---

[10] Lane's Report, p. 18.
[11] *Ibid.*
[12] Singkawang II aerodrome was evacuated shortly after the beginning of operations, and with the exception of a small air attack on Japanese shipping off Kuching, no air support whatsoever was available for "SARFOR".

in Sarawak and owing to the fact that much delay had occurred in the settlement of some urgent problems between Sarawak and Singapore, it was agreed to send Lieut.-Colonel Lane to Singapore to clarify the situation.

Lieut.-Colonel Lane visited Singapore towards the end of August with a view to eradicate some of the "erroneous ideas" that were prevalent at the Headquarters. His visit originally scheduled to last only three days continued for a period of ten days by which time most of the urgent problems were disposed of. The visit was a success and a staff officer who accompanied Lieut.-Colonel Lane back to Kuching was able to get a first hand knowledge of the defence problems in Sarawak. He was fully put into the picture as to the force's limitations and requirements before his return to Singapore.

The value of close liaison with the Dutch does not appear to have been realised by Headquarters Singapore and whenever broached by Officer Commanding Troops Sarawak, it was put off as long as possible. When it eventually took place in September 1941, it led to exchange of much valuable information, although the strategic situation in Sarawak appeared somewhat gloomy to the Dutch. In any case the Dutch knew for the first time what the actual situation in Sarawak was. Unfortunately a return visit planned by Lieut.-Colonel Peppers never materialised with the result that neither he nor Lieut.-Colonel Lane (who had again taken over as Officer Commanding Troops) fully realised "the true nature of the situation in Dutch North-West Borneo"[13] until after the battalion had actually withdrawn from Sarawak.

Change in Defence Plan

At the Conference between British and Dutch military officers in Kuching in September 1941, the British Intelligence Officer, who had been described as "a man of vast military experience and with a knowledge of the Japanese, their strategy and tactics probably equalled by few other Europeans in the Far East ",[14] expressed the belief that Kuching could not be held by the forces available to "Sarfor" if the Japanese landed between 3,000 and 4,000 troops supported from the air and sea. In view of the clear strategic importance of Kuching and the facilities offered by it as a base for operations against Singapore and the Netherlands East Indies, he anticipated that the Japanese force was likely to be far larger. Due to the paucity of troops available for defence and uncertainty of air and naval support, it was felt

[13] Lane's Report on Operations in Sarawak and Dutch Borneo, p. 25.
[14] *Ibid.*, p. 28.

that "to expect success for even a matter of hours was wishful thinking".[15] This opinion confirmed the fears previously entertained by the Secretary for Defence, Sarawak. The Sarawak State Government was now convinced that a successful defence of either Kuching town or of the aerodrome was out of the question without substantial reinforcements. Unless the available troops were reinforced, the production of elaborate defence plans might be a matter of "mere defences on paper". A copy of the minutes of the Conference was sent to Headquarters Singapore where, Lieut.-Colonel Lane claimed, they were suppressed and certain remarks were changed so as to give "an unwarranted tenor of optimism". The State Government, on the contrary, had urged that either reinforcements be sent by Headquarters Singapore or all British Empire troops be withdrawn from the State forthwith.

Fully realising that the former of these alternatives was not likely to be accepted by Headquarters Singapore, in view of heavy military commitments in other theatres of war, and fearing that the State forces might be ordered to non-co-operate should the inhabitants of Kuching be compromised by an attempt to defend the town (as in Plan "A"), the Officer-in-Charge of troops in Sarawak was forced much against his will to consider a complete change of plan. A fresh plan (Plan B) as a result was drawn up and, though it offered little hope of success, it had finally to be adopted.

Plan "B"

The new plan, contrary to Plan A, was based on static defence. Troops and stores were to be concentrated within the $3\frac{1}{2}$ mile perimeter of the aerodrome to ensure its demolition, but no serious effort was to be made to halt the Japanese advance north of Kuching. As Sir Robert Brooke-Popham put it, "The only place which it was decided to hold was Kuching, the reason for this being not only that there was an aerodrome at that place, but that its occupation by the enemy might give access to the aerodromes in Dutch Borneo at the north-western end of the island, these aerodromes being only some 350 miles from Singapore, i.e. much nearer than any in South Indo-China".[16] Although Labuan was an important cable and wireless station, no attempt was made to defend it against the Japanese.

The new plan was inherently defective and pregnant with dangers which were obvious to the local commander. Static defence in a limited area exposed the troops to the danger of being

---

[15] *Ibid.*, p. 27.
[16] Brooke Popham's *Despatch*, p. 538, para 16.

surrounded and cut off from outside help and being "systematically bombed out of existence with no A. A. defences to defend them, shelled with no batteries to give answer and starved by the enemy at will".[17] Moreover, in the new plan the State forces could not be fully employed since the Rangers were trained only as guerilla troops and it was difficult to see what the Coastal Marines and Armed Police could do under the plan. Lieut.-General Percival, General Officer Commanding Malaya, visited the garrison on 28 November 1941, and signified his approval to Plan B though he was fully informed of the very meagre chances of its success. He also seems to have had some misgivings about it. He writes, "I left the country with a sense of great sympathy for the people but with an uneasy feeling that all was not well and with a feeling of frustration that one could do so little to put things right".[18]

Thus, only ten days before the outbreak of war with Japan, and after six months spent in fruitless planning, a scheme of defence was prepared which was wholly out of harmony with the lessons of warfare in the past two years. A static defence, without depth, of a limited area, imperfectly prepared, could hardly withstand the attacks of a hostile force supreme in the air and numerically superior in all other respects. Such a defence could not last more than a few days.

According to this plan, all stores of food, ammunition and petrol were brought within the perimeter of the aerodrome. But at the outbreak of war on 8 December, despite the extremely hard work put in by Empire and State troops, little progress had been made with the defences. When the Japanese eventually attacked just over a fortnight later, there were still no concrete pill-boxes or dug-outs, no anti-tank or shrapnel mines and but a few slit trenches surrounded by a double-apron barbed wire fence. In the circumstances it is not surprising that within four days a quarter of 2/15 Punjab had been killed or captured, while the rest of the battalion had to be withdrawn wearily to Dutch North-West Borneo.

OPERATIONS AT SERIA AND MIRI

The two defence plans, discussed earlier, had reference to the protection of Kuching and its aerodrome only. They did not envisage the defence of the oilfields in Seria-Miri, which were of great strategic value, since their acquisition by the Japanese

---
[17] Lane's Report, p. 28.
[18] *The War in Malaya*, p. 94.

would have appreciably enhanced their oil resources. The large oilfield at Seria in the State of Brunei along with the Miri oilfield in Sarawak, fed the refinery at Lutong. The Seria oilfields were comparatively new and were in the process of development before the outbreak of war with Japan.

The defence of the Seria-Miri area was greatly complicated by the distance intervening between the two oilfields and the paucity of troops. The road connecting the two oilfields, 32 miles apart, was incapable of being used by mechanical transport owing to obstacles provided by rivers and its closeness to the beach which afforded good landing grounds for the invader. The oilfields, therefore, were almost impossible to defend against a determined attack with the resources available. Consequently, it was decided to destroy the oilfields before they were captured by the Japanese. Under instructions received from the British Government in August 1941, a denial scheme was prepared " with the object of making it impossible for the enemy to obtain oil from the fields at least for an extended period ".[19] The responsibility for successfully carrying out the demolition scheme devolved upon the army. It was no mean responsibility considering the " exposed situation " of the oilfields.

Before the outbreak of war, a partial denial scheme was brought into effect by reducing the output of the oilfields by about seventy per cent. Steps were also taken to remove the surplus machinery to Singapore. The Miri oilfields were closed down in September and all the flowing wells at Seria were completely blocked. Early on the morning of 8 December 1941, orders were received for the further destruction of all oilfields and installations and by the evening of the same day the demolition work had almost been completed. The breakage of engines, furnaces and pumping machinery was followed by the blowing up of the sea loading lines and the destruction of subsidiary plants. The entire work was carried out in a most expeditious manner. According to General Percival, " The damage done to the Sarawak oilfields was certainly among the most successful of those organised under the scorched earth policy ".[20] The next day the Miri landing ground was rendered unusable for hostile aircraft. In Seria all necessary demolitions were carried out by the evening of 9 December and all military personnel there moved to Lutong where they arrived at about 2300 hours on the 10th. From Lutong they left for

[19] *The War in Malaya*, p. 166. According to Japanese accounts it appears that they hoped to obtain about 500 tons of oil from British Borneo during the first year of their occupation and the target figures for the second and subsequent years were to depend upon developing conditions.

[20] *The War in Malaya*, p. 166.

Miri to await evacuation by sea to Kuching. During the week there was some air activity over Miri. Japanese reconnaissance planes flew over the area on several occasions but they made no attempt to interfere with the work of the demolition parties.

On 13 December all military personnel were assembled at Miri and during the night of 13/14 December, the whole party sailed for Kuching in H.M.S. *Lipis*, H.M.S. *Maimuna* and S.S. *Shinai*. A Japanese bomber, which bombed and strafed the *Lipis* on her journey south, was successfully driven off by small-arms fire. Little damage was caused to the ship, but Major A.W.D. Slatter (Officer Commanding Troops, Miri and Seria) and three Indian other ranks were killed in the engagement. Major Slatter set a magnificent example to his men by climbing to the exposed bridge of the ship and personally firing an anti-tank Bren gun (whose crew were wounded) until he was killed. The three ships after this engagement reached Kuching safely. The company of the 2/15 Punjab from Miri thus rejoined the rest of the battalion at Kuching.

The destruction of the oilfields had been completed just in time to save them from falling intact into Japanese hands, for at 0330 hours on 16 December, the Japanese landed at Seria and immediately took possession of the demolished oil installations in the locality. At the same time Japanese naval forces appeared in strength before Miri. Ten warships and a tanker were sighted off Miri and Lutong on 16 December, and were the object of an immediate attack by Allied bombers. The first attack launched on 17 December by 6 Glenn Martins and 5 Buffaloes of the Netherlands East Indies Air Force from Singkawang was a failure, but another attack the same day from Samiuwkoa was partially successful. One of the bombers scored a direct hit on a Japanese destroyer.

AIR RAID ON KUCHING

The Japanese air force reacted vigorously to the Allied attacks against their shipping. On 19 December, about 15 Japanese bombers attacked Kuching town and aerodrome. Flying at an altitude of about 15,000 feet, well out of the reach of small-arms fire, the Japanese planes launched an attack on the landing ground but only succeeded in producing a few small craters on the runway. A seaplane which followed the bombers caused some damage to the Royal Air Force barracks by dive bombing attacks. In the town of Kuching, a petrol dump was set on fire by the bombers. Civilians suffered approximately 100 casualties.

The raid was probably carried out with the object of ascertaining whether there were any anti-aircraft defences and to find out how quickly, if at all, Allied fighters could provide cover to the defenders of Kuching. Although little material damage was caused, the propaganda value of the raid was immense, demonstrate as it did the complete Japanese mastery of the air and the inability of Headquarters Singapore to provide even a single plane for the defence of Kuching and Sarawak. It also emphasised the futility of concentrating all troops and stores within the aerodrome perimeter; but it was too late in the day to consider any change in the defence plan.

The raid led to wide scale evacuation of the civilian population from the town. Labour, difficult to obtain otherwise, was now impossible to procure. All sorts of rumours were current and it was widely believed that the Japanese were about to attack the town in force. The government met the situation calmly and courageously, but all its efforts to sustain morale were ineffective. There were some desertions from the local State forces and the morale of the Malaya troop was specially low.

Meanwhile a strong note was sent to Headquarters Singapore on the failure of the Allied air force to come to the rescue of the defenders, but their reply was to the effect that many towns in England had to face air-raids without any air support and Kuching might also have to face a similar ordeal. But Headquarters failed to appreciate " the vast difference between a town in England and the capital of the State of Sarawak, especially in relation to a native population and the native forces wavering between support for the government or possibly the enemy ".[81] It was now clear to the officers commanding the troops in Kuching that the promise of air support was an empty one and could not be implemented.

THE SITUATION ON 22 DECEMBER 1941

On 22 December 1941, " Sarfor " was disposed as follows:—

2/15 *Punjab*
Battalion Headquarters—Batu Lintang Camp
A Company—(less one platoon at Bukit Siol) Pending, with orders to withdraw to the western perimeter of the aerodrome when attacked.
B Company—along the north-east perimeter of the aerodrome.

---
[81] Lane's Report, p. 34.

C Company—(less one platoon north of the Matang Road)—
    along the north perimeter of the aerodrome.
D Company—along the south perimeter of the aerodrome.
E Company—in the south-west perimeter arc of the aerodrome.

Headquarters Company
(1) *Gunboat platoon*, in conjunctions with Sarawak Coastal Marine Service and Sarawak Rangers, was to supply information of Japanese movements and to harass them within the network of rivers north of Kuching.
(2) *Carrier platoon* had one section at Pending, one section at the landing ground near Batu Kitang junction, one section between Kitang and Penrisan junctions, and another section in Batu Lintang Camp.
(3) 18-*pounder and 3" mortar detachments* at Bintawa and Biawak. Two 3" mortars were at Pending, while another two were kept in reserve.
(4) *Sub-Machine-gun platoon*, one section at Bukit Siol; two sections at Pending; the remainder at the aerodrome.

Force Headquarters
This was located at about 700 yards north-west of Batu Lintang Camp.

Sarawak Coastal Marine Service and Sarawak Rangers
They were working in close conjunction with the Punjab gunboat platoon north of Kuching, the main role assigned to them being that of coastal patrol work and observation.

Sarawak Volunteer Force and Sarawak Armed Police
The Sarawak Volunteer Force had been mobilised as far as possible, but " lack of uniforms, equipment, ammunition and stores made a full-scale mobilisation impossible ". The Sarawak Armed Police were also mobilised and were ready to move to battle stations within the aerodrome defences.

In spite of every effort made to complete the defences at Kuching aerodrome, when the Japanese attacked, there were no concrete pill-boxes or dug-outs and the number of slit trenches was not large.[22] Preparations for road and bridge demolitions, however, had been for the most part completed.

[22] *Ibid.*, p. 36.

JAPANESE LAND AT KUCHING

At about 1800 hours on the evening of 23 December 1941, a Japanese convoy was sighted off G. Santubong, news of which was reported to Headquarters Singapore immediately. Two hours later, contrary to all defence plans and previous instructions, orders came through for the immediate destruction of the aerodrome. Another message from Singapore received shortly afterwards conveyed the somewhat tardy news that an Allied reconnaissance plane had sighted the convoy nearly 100 miles north-west of Kuching at 0500 hours of the same day.[23] Why Kuching was not informed of this for nearly 16 hours is by no means clear. It is probable that the delay was due to some communication difficulties. Before arrival in Santubong, however, the Japanese convoy was attacked by Dutch submarines, which reported having sunk or disabled one tanker and three transport ships. But " there is no evidence to show whether this was before or after the sighting by our reconnaissance aircraft referred to above ".[24] Immediately upon receipt of the order to destroy the landing ground, Officer Commanding the troops in Sarawak was convinced that it could not under any circumstances be used by the Allies as an advanced operational base. He also felt that even after destruction, the use of the aerodrome could not be denied to the Japanese for any length of time, as was originally contemplated under Plan " B " mentioned earlier.

Taking into full consideration all the relevant factors of the critical situation with which Lieut.-Colonel Lane was confronted, he sent an urgent message to Singapore pointing out that since all troops and stores were concentrated within the perimeter of the aerodrome, it was too late to change back to mobile defence. He also felt that it was useless to sacrifice his men for defending the airfield, and proposed, therefore, at 2080 hours (23 December), that he should be given permission to withdraw as soon as possible via Bau into Dutch North-West Borneo. General Percival, on receipt of this signal at 1305 hours on 24 December, immediately replied to the effect that Lieut.-Colonel Lane should fight as long as possible near Kuching and then act in the best interests of Dutch West Borneo as a whole.

In the meantime, during the night of 23/24 December, the demolition of aerodrome landing strips and the Royal Air Force Direction Finder had been completed without interruption from

---

[23] According to Percival (*War in Malaya*, p. 169) the convoy consisted of nine Japanese warships and transports.

[24] *War in Malaya*, p. 169.

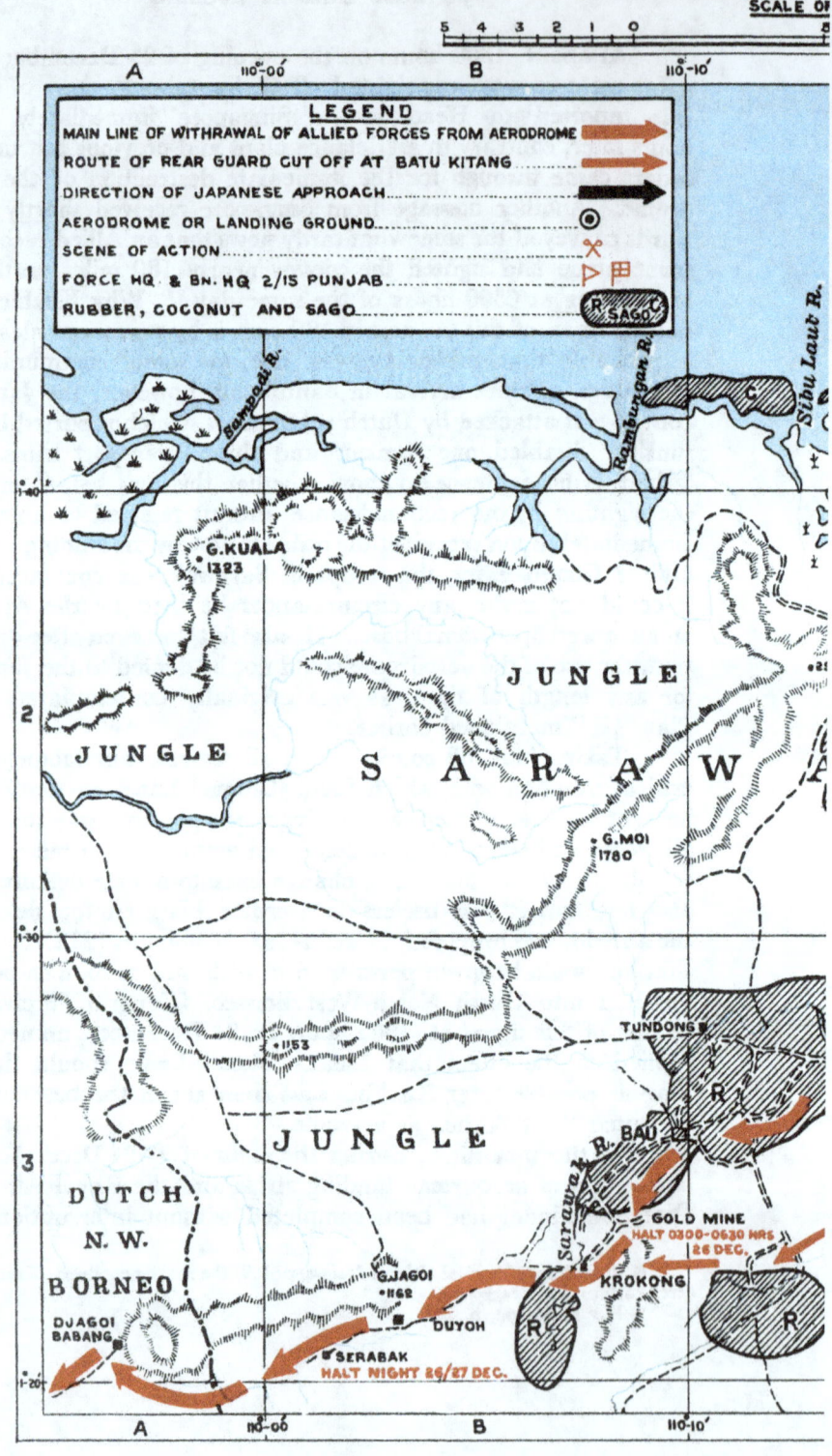

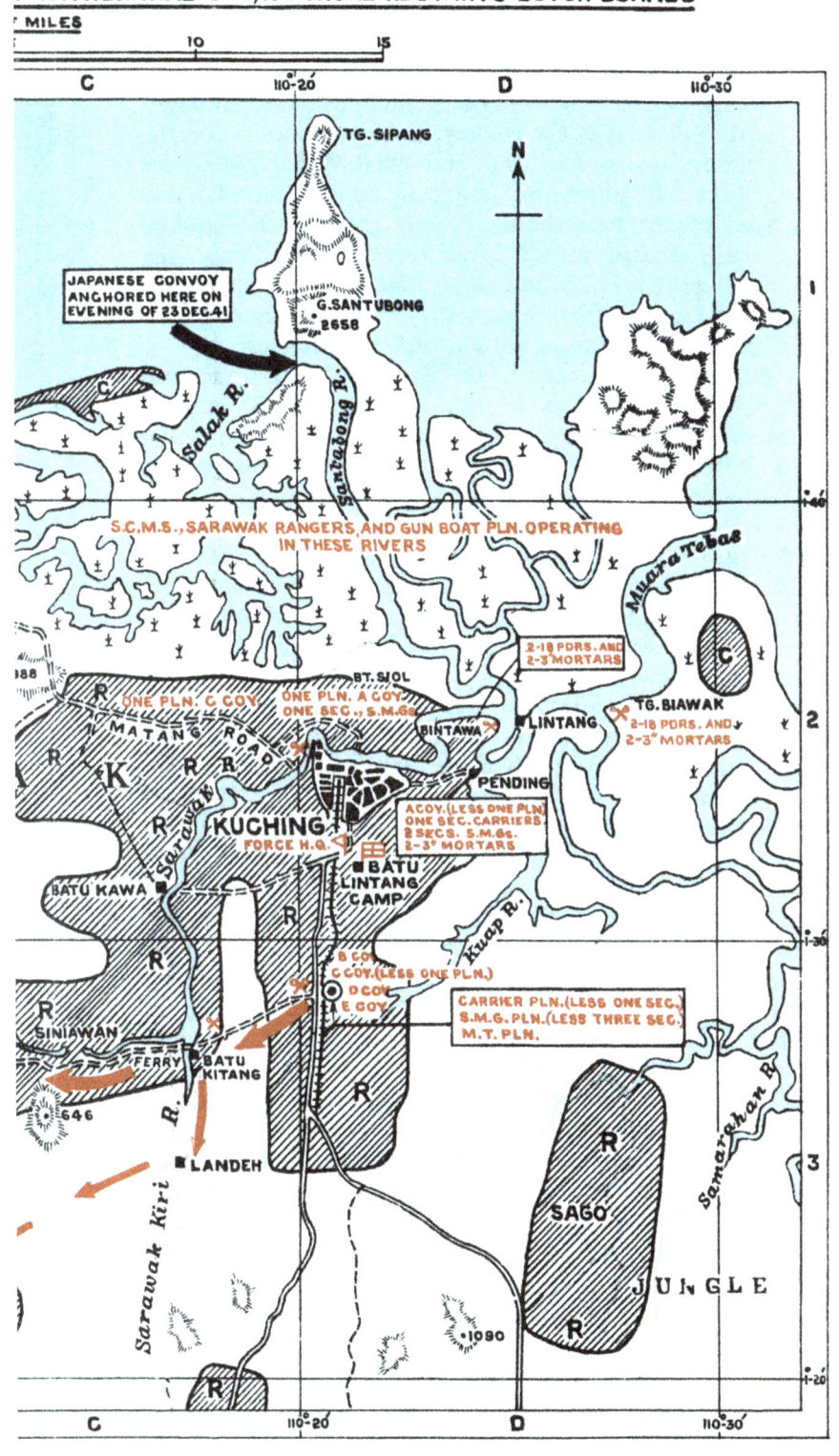

the Japanese. Active patrolling took place during the whole night but no contact on land was made with the Japanese.

At first light of 24 December, eight Japanese ships were observed at anchor between the Sibu Laut and Santubong estuaries. From the number of ships in the convoy, it was estimated that the Japanese strength was between 3,000 and 4,000.[25] Till 0900 hours they did not take any action, but then twenty Japanese landing craft were seen approaching the Santubong river. After landing the troops, the Japanese assault boats went up the Santubong river. The small gunboat platoon of 2/15 Punjab fought a withdrawal action near Lintang from where they retreated by stages up the Kuap river to the aerodrome without suffering any loss.

By 1100 hours the Japanese gunboats reached Lintang and shortly afterwards the Bintawa 18-pounder guns and 3" mortars opened fire, sinking four Japanese craft outright before being surrounded and completely destroyed by Japanese landing parties. At about the same time the reserve section of carriers was rushed from the aerodrome to reinforce Pending.[26]

By the morning of 24 December, it was clear that the Japanese occupation of Sarawak was only a matter of days. As already mentioned, General Percival also gave implied permission that morning for a withdrawal. Events moved quickly thereafter, as related below.

The Japanese started landing troops on the north flank of the Sarawak river about midday after advancing through the jungle, and, during the afternoon more Japanese troops landed on the north and south banks of the Sarawak river. Kuching town was captured at 1630 hours and the Japanese flag was hoisted on the Astana, the residence of His Highness the Raja. From the Pending area A Company of the Punjab Regiment was withdrawn to the aerodrome according to a pre-arranged plan and was in position there by 2400 hours. The Company's platoon at Bukit Siol, after being severely divebombed earlier in the day, was heavily ambushed[27] at the Kuching suspension bridge west of the town and all but three of the platoon were either killed or captured by the Japanese.

At Biawak, three more Japanese landing craft were sunk by 18-pounder and 3" mortar fire before the Punjabis were withdrawn from the area; but Japanese landings continued and at about 1700 hours they made first contact with the aerodrome defences.

[25] Lane's Report, p. 37.
[26] *Ibid*, p. 38.
[27] The Japanese troops who ambushed this platoon were wearing Sarawak Constabulary uniforms as a disguise (See Lane's Report, p. 39).

Dutch bombers operating from Singkawang II aerodrome, attacked Japanese ships at anchor in the Santubong estuary in the course of the evening. As a result one ship, which probably carried munitions, was reported blown up. Throughout the night of 24/25 December, intermittent firing took place in the area of the aerodrome as the Japanese carefully felt their way around the eastern and western sides of the perimeter without launching any major attack. It was becoming more and more apparent that they intended first to cut off all escape routes and then destroy the besieged force at leisure.

KUCHING EVACUATED

With the dawn of Christmas day, there was a lull in the firing, but Japanese troops continued their encircling movement. Since the danger of being totally cut off was growing every hour, the remaining personnel of A Company with their guns were sent to hold the vital ferry crossing of the Sarawak-Kiri river at Batu Kitang. Aerial reconnaissance kept the Japanese fully informed of all these moves but the morning passed quietly with little interference from them.

At 1300 hours on 25 December a conference of officers took place at battalion headquarters where the whole position was discussed again. It was decided to withdraw to Dutch West Borneo, the withdrawal commencing at 1800 hours. The withdrawal plan in brief was :—

Headquarters Company and E Company to withdraw to Batu Kitang at 1800 hours ; B and D Companies to commence retreat along the same route half an hour later, while C Company, which was assigned the role of fighting a rearguard action, was to take an easterly short cut through the jungle on to the Batu Kitang road. The destination of all the companies was Bau.

In the early afternoon, shortly after Lieut.-Colonel Lane had issued orders for the withdrawal of " Sarfor ", heavy firing was heard from the direction of the ferry at Batu Kitang and the force commander, fearing that Japanese troops were already astride his escape route, ordered the withdrawal to commence immediately. Headquarters Company covered by carriers led the withdrawal at 1530 hours, and met with no opposition from the Japanese. D Company was fired upon just before reaching Batu Kitang road. B and C Companies had to face the full brunt of the Japanese attack and were cut off from the rest of the troops while still in the aerodrome area. Of these two companies, only one platoon of B Company succeeded in rejoining the main body of the battalion by 1700 hours. The remainder, totalling 4 officers, 6 Viceroy's Commissioned Officers and some 230 Indian Other Ranks, were either killed or taken prisoner.

At the Batu Kitang ferry, trouble developed after firing had broken out in the vicinity. The result of this was that all local inhabitants fled into the jungle, leaving the ferry on 'the far side of the swift-flowing stream'. Subsequently, ferrying had to be carried out in small native *prahus*, a slow and tedious task, but by 1900 hours all except the covering troops had crossed the river and were on their way to Bau. All vehicles left on the east bank of the river were rendered useless and similarly all heavy weapons were denied to the Japanese. D Company was put into position on hillocks that covered the immediate approaches to the ferry and the carrier platoon was asked to render the company all possible aid in its alloted task. At this juncture the Japanese launched a second attack which cut off temporarily the rearguard of the battalion consisting of the officer-in-charge and about 180 personnel. But the party managed to escape south towards Landeh on the Sarawak river and, after a forced march of nearly 60 miles through dense jungle with little food and water, the party eventually rejoined the battalion at Singkawang II aerodrome on 31 December.

Meanwhile, the main body of the battalion had to march over the Batu Kitang—Bau Road which was, according to Lieut.-Colonel Lane, in "an extremely poor condition".[28] After a short halt at Siniawan, the troops proceeded to Bau where they intended to pass the night. The village, however, proved to be unsuitable as a halting place and the withdrawal was continued as far as a gold-mine just short of Krokong where the whole party was assembled by 0300 hours on 26 December. There were several false alarms during this rapid withdrawal, but no Japanese troops were actually encountered.

[28] Lane's Report, p. 41.

CHAPTER XIII

Operations in Dutch North-West Borneo

2/15 PUNJAB ENTER DUTCH BORNEO

Sarawak thus passed into Japanese hands, but its defenders continued the fight in Dutch Borneo. At daybreak on 26 December 1941, after a brief rest at the gold-mine, the column of Indian and State troops moved on to Krokong, just beyond the gold-mine. The covering force at Bau was withdrawn, and the sick and wounded were moved ahead of the marching troops. At Krokong the track came to an end and a foot-wide foot-bridge across the Sarawak river rendered impossible the carrying of mechanical transport and heavy equipment. These were therefore effectively destroyed before the column proceeded further.

From Krokong most of the Sarawak Rangers returned to their homes " in view of their agreement to serve in Sarawak only, and in the best interests of their property and families." Only two members of the force chose to remain with the Punjabi battalion through Dutch West Borneo and in the later moves to South Borneo. English officers with the State forces, however, chose to serve with the battalion and were sent on ahead from Krokong to trace a route and make arrangements with Dyak villagers for food and accommodation. Henceforth "Sarfor" ceased to exist as a combined Indian/Sarawak State force and 2/15 Punjab, now less than 800 men strong, carried on alone.

A narrow but fairly good foot-path ran from Krokong to Serabak via Duyoh, which afforded a well-covered line of withdrawal through rough cultivation and jungle. By nightfall on 26 December, the troops reached Serabak without incident. The following day they crossed into Dutch North-West Borneo and passed through thickly wooded country as far as Djagoi Babang. When the Allied troops crossed this village they were safe from the Japanese threat of cutting off their withdrawal route, from the north-east, but danger still lurked for them from the south-east. The track from Risau to Silooas was wide enough to allow troops to move in file, but heavy rain had made the passage muddy and difficult. After crossing the river Koemba, about 80 yards wide, in growing darkness, the party halted for the night at Silooas where they were met by a Dutch patrol from Bengkajang. The latter were fully informed about the situation in Sarawak which had resulted in the withdrawal of the battalion, and the strength of the Japanese forces. It was also explained to the Dutch that due to bad tracks, the Japanese were most unlikely to closely follow the retreating Allied troops.

On the morning of Sunday, 28 December, the battalion resumed its journey towards Sanggau roadhead which was about twenty miles away. They reached Satatok at 1330 hours where they originally intended to pass the night on information from the Dutch that the place afforded sufficient accommodation. Contrary to the expectations, the battalion, finding only " Coolie lines " at the village, decided to continue the journey in an impending rainstorm, which soon rendered the road muddy. This delayed the march of the troops and they could not reach the banks of the Tanggi river opposite Sanggau until the early hours of the morning of the 29th. Due to some misunderstanding with the Dutch outpost commander, the troops had to wait many hours before they were eventually allowed to cross over, and by midday all were comfortably installed in the evacuated Royal Air Force barracks of Singkawang II aerodrome.

At daybreak on 29 December a code message was sent to Headquarters Singapore regarding the action in Kuching and withdrawal to Sanggau. It was suggested that the unit be withdrawn from Dutch Borneo.

During the afternoon, all European women and children (who appear to have accompanied the column during its withdrawal), remaining State force personnel and surplus regular personnel (with the exception of three Sarawak Volunteer Force officers and one Sarawak Rangers' Officer) were sent to Pontianak for evacuation to Java. After a long delay, the party[1] was finally evacuated on 25 January 1942—only two days before the capture of the town by the Japanese.

On the morning of 30 December, Lieut.-Colonel Lane, officer-in-charge of the troops, paid a visit to the Dutch territorial commander (Lt.-Col. Mars) at Sampau and fully acquainted him with the situation, but the latter did not volunteer any information regarding the location and number of his troops. It was decided that Allied troops should remain at Sanggau until 4 January 1942, by which time it was hoped that the troops would be thoroughly rested and reorganised.

REORGANISATION OF THE BATTALION

The following day, Captain Chapman and the remainder of the rearguard which had been cut off at Batu Kitang ferry

---

[1] " The attitude of the Dutch officials, civil and military, and civilians towards this party, not excluding the women, was one of open hostility and discourtesy ". (Lane's Report, p. 44).

rejoined the battalion in an exhausted condition. On the same day, an order was received from Headquarters Singapore placing 2/15 Punjab under Dutch command. The next day, a Dutch Lieut.-Colonel, Gertmans, arrived from Java to assume with Lieut.-Colonel Mars the joint command of British and Dutch forces in West Borneo. Lieut.-Colonel Gertmans was assigned the task of training the forces for guerilla warfare while Lieut.-Colonel Mars was to prepare for a static defence of Singkawang II aerodrome and the Sanggau roadhead. The joint command arrangements worked most unsatisfactorily for, as Lieut.-Colonel Lane remarks in his account of operations, the force was " placed at the disposal of both of them and as a result was receiving separate orders for separate plans from both—sometimes involving sending the same body of troops to two places simultaneously ".[2]

Meanwhile the reorganisation of the battalion was going ahead. Nearly 300 casualties had been suffered in the action at Kuching; B and C Companies (less one platoon), one platoon A Company (less three men), two sections of E Company, one 18-pounder section and one 3". mortar detachment had proved a total loss. The remainder of the battalion, numbering 783, was divided into four " Mono-class " companies: A (Sikh), B (Punjabi Muslims), C (Khattak) and D (Jat)—armed only with rifles, Bren guns and sub-machine-guns since all mechanical transport and heavy equipment had to be abandoned earlier at Krokong during the course of withdrawal from Kuching. Weapons and ammunition manhandled from Kuching to Sanggau consisted of 603 rifles, 21 Bren guns, 21 sub-machine-guns, 2 Lewis guns, 2 Browning machine-guns taken from a crashed Dutch plane, 31 revolvers, 54 hand-grenades and about 53,000 rounds of small-arms ammunition.

OPERATIONS NORTH-EAST OF SANGGAU

By 4 January 1942, the reorganisation of the 2/15 Punjab Battalion was complete, D Company less one platoon, with one sub-machine-gun section and a few Dutch troops in support, was sent to Silooas to patrol the area as far north as Djagoi Babang and generally to delay the Japanese advance as long as possible.[3] B Company took up static positions at the Sanggau roadhead while A Company assumed responsibility for the defence of Singkawang II aerodrome where the remainder of the battalion was held in reserve.

[2] Lane's Report, p. 46.
[3] According to Lane, the Dutch intention was to make Silooas a base for guerilla action along the Krokong track towards the frontier (p. 45).

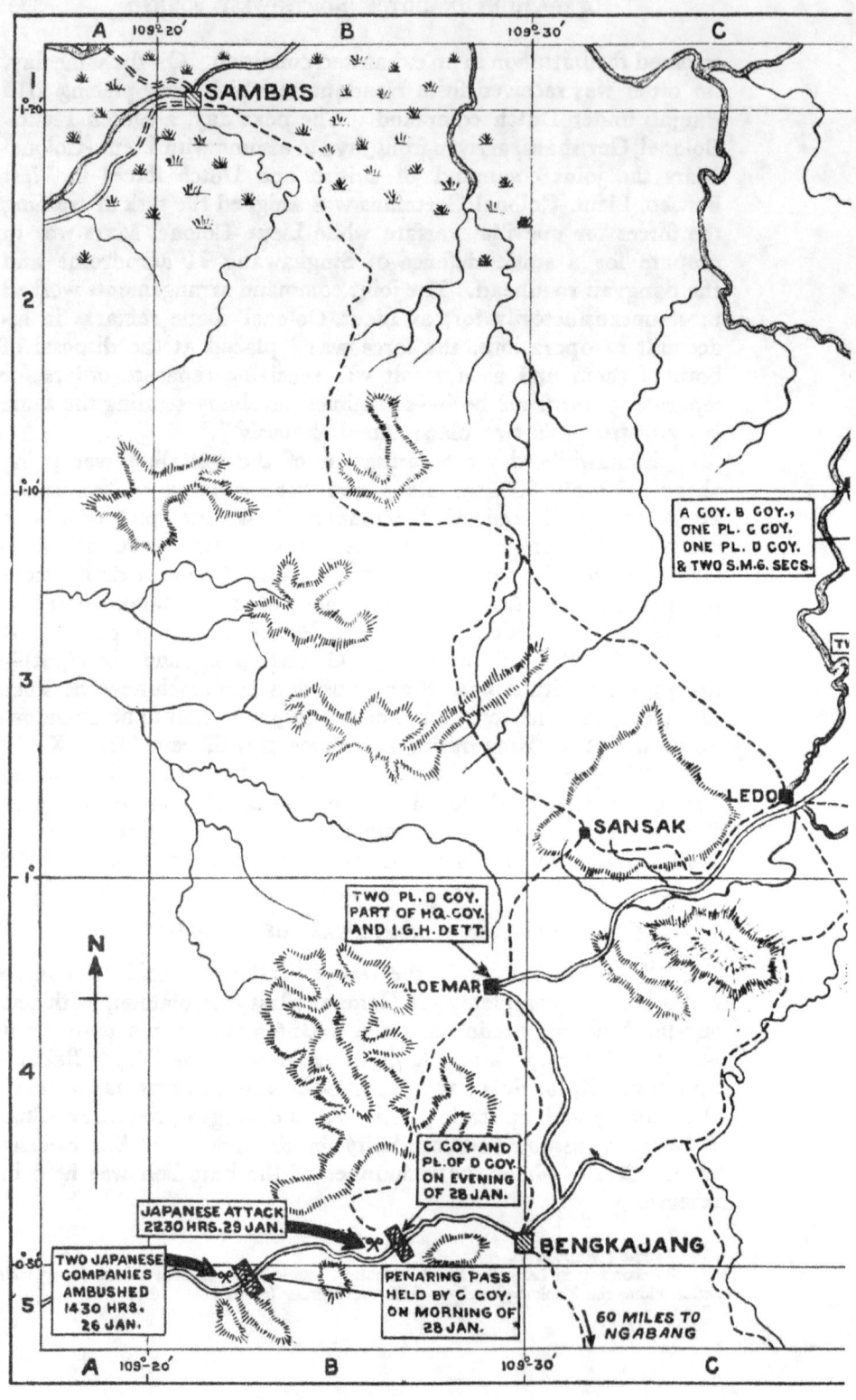

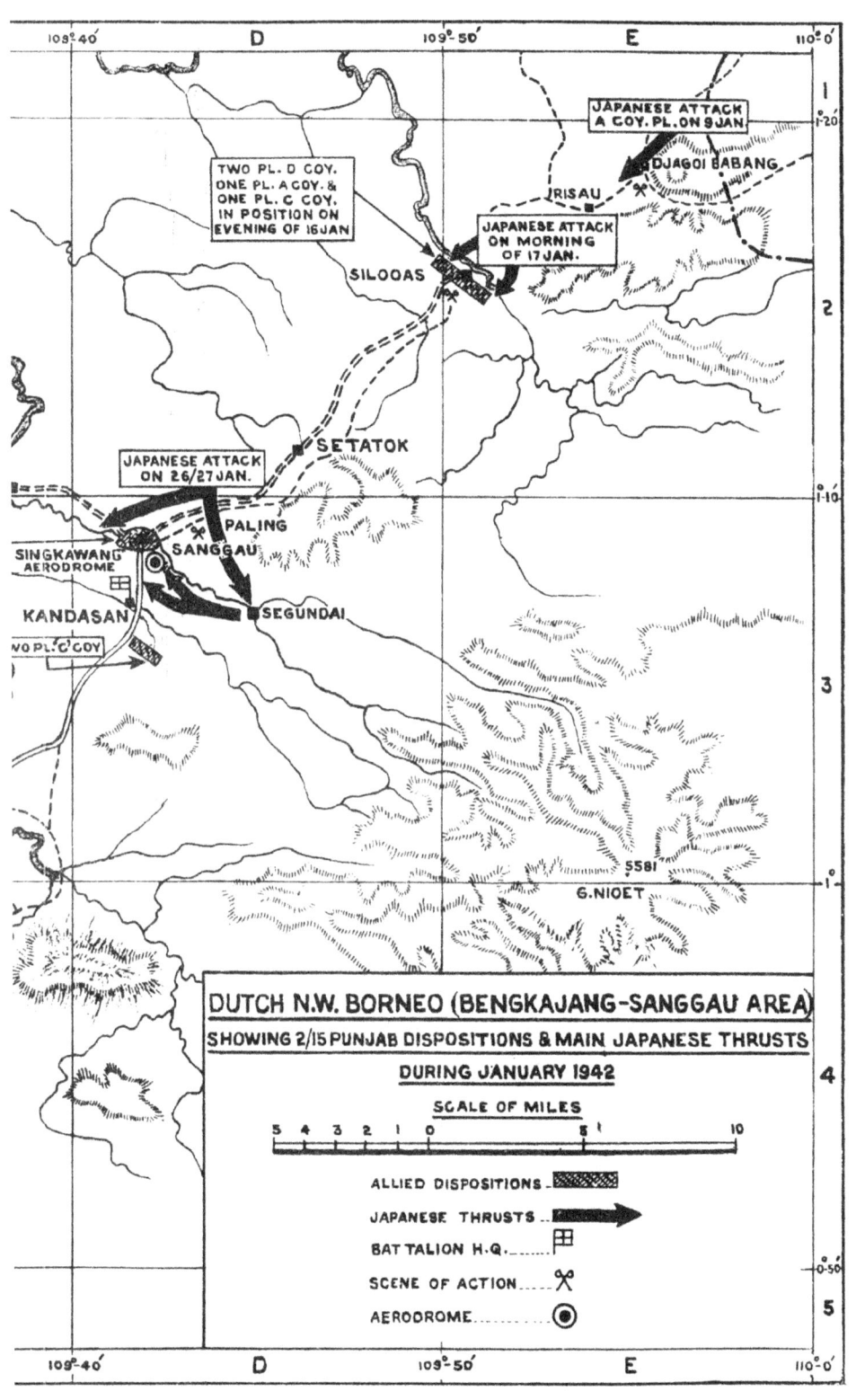

On 6 January, a Japanese party, some 50 strong —the first Japanese troops to cross the Sarawak—Dutch North-West Borneo Frontier—was reported to be in Saratok, about 6 miles northeast of Djagoi Babang. The next day one platoon A Company was sent to Babang under orders to patrol from there towards the Sarawak border. Two days later at about 1830 hours a strong Japanese attack forced the Punjabi platoon to withdraw three miles south of Babang. Reinforcements, consisting of one platoon D Company, were immediately rushed to stabilise the position south of Babang. In a surprise counter-attack, the Punjabi platoons succeeded in inflicting some casualties on the Japanese on 10 January. But it was only later during the course of the day when the other platoon and a section of sub-machine-guns arrived from Silooas that the position was evantually stabilised about $2\frac{1}{2}$ miles south of Djagoi Babang.

During the next week the Japanese were content to hold their position at Djagoi Babang while their troops were being reinforced steadily. At the same time Indian troops patrolled vigorously between Risau and Babang, maintaining contact with the Japanese. On 12 January, a frontal attack was launched by these troops with the object of regaining Babang but they failed to achieve their object due to the failure of the Dutch troops to deliver the previously planned flanking attack simultaneously. When contact was made by the Indian troops with the Dutch three days later, the latter were " 10 miles behind the British outpost line ".[4] Captain Crosland was of the opinion that Babang could have been retaken up to 11 January, but not after that date since the village had been heavily reinforced by the Japanese.

In the meantime, the Japanese announced on 11 January 1942 that a state of war existed between them and the Netherlands East Indies, " because of the hostile attitude of the Netherlands Government in aiding the enemies of Japan since the outbreak of the war of Greater East Asia ". The Japanese obviously hoped to prevent any concerted Allied action by delaying the declaration of war but they were disappointed because the Dutch struck at once. Tarakan, an island off the east coast of Borneo and an oil centre, was the first important Dutch possession to fall to the Japanese on 12 January after the oil-denial scheme had been carried out.

With Babang as their base of operations, the Japanese felt that they could safely outflank the defenders to the south of it and carry on their thrust towards Silooas. The Indian troops found

[4] Lane's Report, p. 46.

themselves in danger of being cut off by the Japanese, and their commander, therefore, obtained permission from Lieut.-Colonel Gertmans on 16 January to withdraw his three platoons from their vulnerable position south-west of Djagoi Babang to the secondary roadhead of Silooas. A platoon of C Company had been sent to reinforce Silooas on 14 January and on the evening of the 16th the whole party took up defensive positions along the line of the Koemba river. On 17 January, the Dutch troops were withdrawn under orders from Lieut.-Colonel Gertmans from Silooas to Setatok and the Indian troops were left behind to hold the village. At about 0900 hours the same day, the Japanese, having successfully crossed the river, launched an attack on both the flanks of the hastily prepared defence line. The attack on the right flank was repulsed, the Japanese suffering heavy casualties, but on the left they broke through in strength. This necessitated an immediate withdrawal of Indian troops. By the following day all the four platoons had reached Sanggau, 10 miles south of Silooas via Setatok. From Sanggau, in view of their exhausted condition, these troops were sent to Bengkajang for a short rest ".[5]

During the period 4-18 January, Captain Crosland had twice pressed for reinforcements to be sent to Silooas if it was intended to hold the Japanese north of Sanggau, but these requests were turned down in view of the inability of the commander to spare troops which were urgently required for other tasks. As large parties of men from the battalion had been employed in repairing the motor-road between Sampau and Singkawang II, it had only been possible to send two platoons from A and C Companies and these had proved altogether insufficient for the task of repelling the Japanese attack.

There was a lamentable lack of co-operation between the Dutch commander and the officer-in-charge of 2/15 Punjab. Dispositions of Dutch troops were never disclosed to the latter. The declared policy of the Dutch was to fight to the last man, but in reality they appeared to be always planning to withdraw into the interior without making any determined attempt to check the invaders.[6] The Dutch even refused, it is alleged, to supply 2/15 Punjab with arms, ammunition and clothing.

Meanwhile at Singkawang II aerodrome the demolition of landing strips, stores and barracks had commenced immediately after the news of the evacuation of Silooas was received. These demolitions were completed by 20 January.

[5] Lieut.-Colonel Lane (OC troops) was taken sick on 19 January and Lieut.-Colonel Ross-Thompson temporarily assumed command of the Punjab Regiment.
[6] Lane's Report, p. 46.

THE SANGGAU ACTION

At this juncture, Lieut.-Colonel Lane took into consideration the possibility of the Japanese making a landing on the west coast in view of their naval and air superiority while simultaneously pressing Sanggau from the north. Therefore, in order to avoid encirclement, he drew up a secret plan for the evacuation of Indian troops to Java or Malaya from Dutch Borneo. In the event of the Japanese capturing the coastal areas, it was proposed to move the battalion to Pankalanboon and Sampit in South Borneo. These two ports were selected because they were farthest away from the Japanese threat. But with the arrival of a Dutch liaison officer from Java, this plan was abandoned and fresh plans were discussed and drawn up for the defence of the Sanggau roadhead. In accordance with these new plans, dispositions of troops were as follows:—

A Company	Singkawang II aerodrome
B Company (plus two sub-machine-gun sections)	Sanggau roadhead and astride the Sanggau-Momong road.
C Company	One platoon at Sanggau. Two platoons in a lay-back position one mile south of Kandasan.
D Company	One platoon at Sanggau. Two platoons at Loemar, where was also stationed the Headquarters Company.
Battalion Headquarters	Kandasan with a liaison officer at Sanggau.

Supporting Dutch troops consisted of one platoon Vickers machine-guns and two light tanks at Sanggau; 80 men at Kandasan; 80 men at Ledo; and Force Headquarters at Loemar.

In response to telegrams from the commander of the battalion, a British liaison officer from the General Headquarters Far East in Java visited the Indian and Dutch headquarters on 24 and 25 January. He stressed the futility of further resistance in Dutch Borneo and, at the same time, urged that the battalion should be withdrawn to an operational theatre where its services would be more useful.

Reports of increasing Japanese activity in the Silooas-Setatok area were at this time being received from patrols of the Indian battalion. On 25 January, Paling, $2\frac{1}{2}$ miles north-east of Sanggau, was occupied in force by the Japanese. It was therefore decided to dislodge them from the village the next day by means of a counter-attack. A Company attacked the Japanese positions, but could not achieve much success. The first line of the Japanese trenches was captured after a vigorous assault, but the initial advantage could not be pressed home because of the inability of the Dutch troops to carry out a simultaneous flanking attack. The Dutch troops, whose task was to cut off the Japanese rear, unfortunately ran into an ambush and their commander was killed. The remnants of the troops appear to have withdrawn into the jungle but they were never seen afterwards. So after inflicting some casualties on the Japanese troops, the Indian troops were also forced to withdraw.

The same evening, following up this withdrawal, about 200 Japanese troops attacked and drove out the Indian platoon defending Segundai, on the right flank of the Sanggau position. The Japanese were not slow to take advantage of this success, and at 0700 hours on 27 January, they launched a very strong attack on the Sanggau position from Segundai. At the same time a Japanese party was sent southwards with the object of outflanking the aerodrome.

By 0900 hours the position of the Indian troops became critical, and an immediate withdrawal was ordered by force headquarters to Ledo, 10 miles south-west on the Sambas river. A Company and the C Company platoons which were disposed around the aerodrome, successfully disengaged themselves, from the Japanese and the former safely reached Ledo. C Company successfully held the ridge known as Dyak Farm, covering the road until all troops had passed through, and then withdrew across the Sambas river to Ledo. One platoon of B Company and the D Company platoon also managed to escape, though the latter suffered heavily while withdrawing with B Company Headquarters through the jungle to the west of the road. The remaining two platoons of B Company were cut off from the rest of the battalion by the Japanese and found escape impossible. With the Japanese attacking from both east and west of Sanggau, Subedar Faramurz Khan, Commander of the platoons and second-in-command of B Company, exhorted his men to fight to the last. He himself set a fine example to his troops by his exemplary bravery, and the gallant party continued to fight till late in the afternoon against tremendous odds. It was only when its ammunition was exhausted that the party agreed to surrender. Japanese reports later gave their own casualties as amounting to between 400 and 500 men killed or wounded. Of the Indian troops (approximately 100), only three managed to escape. The remainder were never seen again.[7]

[7] There is a report that the Indian prisoners were cruelly done to death by the infuriated Japanese troops, but it has not been corroborated.

By the evening of 27 January, the Indian battalion less two platoons of B Company had managed to reach Ledo. Bridges between Sanggau and Ledo were blown up by Dutch engineers under cover of Indian troops, and positions for the night were occupied on the high ground west and south-west of Ledo with battalion headquarters at Sansak. The Dutch troops at Ledo had in the meanwhile withdrawn to Bengkajang.

JAPANESE LANDINGS ON THE WEST COAST

Meanwhile on 24 January, a reconnaissance plane over the Kuching area had reported a large concentration of small craft in the waterways around the town. This led to the inference that the Japanese contemplated an attack on Permangkat and the aerodromes in the Singkawang I area.[8] Steps were at once taken to block the Sambas river at Permangkat and previously prepared demolitions were carried out. The extreme shortage of troops, however, prevented active defence measures being brought into effect.

The threatened Japanese landing at Permangkat took place in strength on the night of 27/28 January. Advancing north-east and south from Permangkat, the Japanese quickly captured Sambas, Singkawang I, Mampawah and Pontianak, meeting little resistance from the few Dutch troops in the area. On the morning of 28 January, the Indian troops were ordered by Lieut.-Colonel Mars to clear the Japanese from the coastal area. Since no mechanical transport was available to execute this "amazing manoeuvre",[9] the distance to the coast alone being 100 miles, Lieut.-Colonel Ross-Thompson was unable to comply with this order. He pointed out that since the Japanese troops were already advancing from Singkawang I towards Bengkajang, it was in the interest of the remnants of the Dutch and Indian troops to stop them on the road so that the line of withdrawal might not be cut off. It was decided in pursuance of this plan to send a company to reinforce the Dutch troops holding Penaring Pass, 10 miles west of Bengkajang.[10]

C Company was despatched to Penaring, while two platoons of D Company were sent to reinforce the Dutch troops holding the Medjalin road, south-west of Bengkajang. One platoon of B Company was sent ahead to hold the Mandor-Sidas Ridge and to cover any Japanese advance from Pontianak

[8] See Map facing p. 393.
[9] Lane's Report, p. 49.
[10] See Map facing p. 385.

along the Pontianak-Ngabang Road until A Company arrived to reinforce it. Battalion headquarters was moved temporarily to Bengkajang.

The Dutch company at Penaring withdrew immediately on the arrival of C Company at 1400 hours. On 28 January the Dutch commander told the company commander that he had orders from Lieut.-Colonel Mars to withdraw forthwith. The withdrawal of the Dutch troops was a great setback and in their absence the role allotted to C Company proved to be beyond its strength.

The Penaring position was admirably suited for defence. To the west the road, running through an exposed cutting with open ground on either side, made anything in the nature of a frontal attack well-nigh impossible. But, with only a single company for defence, the flank of the position could not be sufficiently protected. Under the circumstances, the utmost that was expected of this small force was to delay the advance of the Japanese for a few hours.

At about 1430 hours on 28 January the advance guard of the Japanese, estimated at approximately two companies, was seen approaching on bicycles. Waiting until the foremost Japanese troops were less than 150 yards away, C Company opened fire inflicting considerable casualties on them. Throughout the afternoon and early evening the company held the position. But the Japanese, bringing up strong reinforcements for their flanking parties, threatened to encircle the Penaring position and made it untenable by 1930 hours. The action was therefore broken off to enable Dutch engineers to destroy bridges along the road. The company withdrew in order about 2030 hours to a second position five miles nearer Bengkajang.

Here the company was joined by a platoon of D Company and a platoon of Dutch troops who arrived in front of the position at about 2230 hours, and the combined force using sub-machine-guns and hand grenades inflicted heavy casualties on the Japanese. Attempts by the latter to move off the road resulted in their being bogged down in rice-fields covered by light machine-guns. Unfortunately at this stage the Dutch platoon withdrew without sufficient cause, leaving a weak spot in one of the defence sectors. The Japanese were not slow to exploit this point of vantage and after bringing down heavy and accurate mortar fire, broke through the resulting gap at 2345 hours. This necessitated a further withdrawal by Indian and Dutch troops, and during the early hours on 29 January the last troops passed through Bengkajang on their way south towards Ngabang. By 1300 hours the whole battalion less A Company, had reached Ngabang. A Company continued to hold until 1900 hours a position one mile west of Sidas on the Mandor road, in order to cover the withdrawal of possible stragglers.

During the evening of 29 January, the officer commanding the Indian troops went to see the Dutch commander at Sosok, who informed him that Indian troops should hold Ngabang while the Dutch would hold the line Tajan-Sosok. The British commander felt that it was easy to bypass the Ngabang position by a track leading south-south-east from Singkawang II aerodrome to the Dutch position at Sosok. It was finally agreed that Ngabang should be lightly held until the Indian troops could occupy Sanggau on the Kapoeas river in strength. Therefore A Company left immediately for Sanggau which it reached by dawn of the 30th and took up positions, covering the approach to the river. B and D Companies continued to hold Ngabang, while C Company took up covering positions on the Ngabang-Sanggau Road.

Later, on the morning of the 30th, the battalion's stores and equipment arrived at Sanggau. At the same time a certain amount of transport, food etc., were obtained from the Dutch, whose native troops in the area, it is alleged, deserted in large numbers due to intermittent aerial reconnaissance by the Japanese, and whose discipline under threat from the air was almost negligible.

Ammunition for the troops was now down to "an average of 60 rounds per rifle and one filled magazine per LMG with no reserves". The men were thoroughly exhausted by continuous marching and fighting since 25 December, while their clothing and boots were worn out.

Thus, at the end of January 1942, two companies of the Indian battalion held Ngabang; one company was positioned between Ngabang and Sanggau, and the fourth company, together with battalion headquarters and all supplies, was in the Sanggau area. The battalion was not destined to fight another major action with the Japanese, but further hardships in the shape of a long and gruelling march through the almost unchartered hinterland of South Borneo had still to come.

WITHDRAWAL TO SOUTH BORNEO

Secret Plan of Withdrawal
On 31 January 1942, Lieut.-Colonel Ross-Thompson paid a visit to Lieut.-Colonel Mars at the Dutch headquarters and expressed his intention of withdrawing his battalion to South

Borneo. The Dutch commander produced a counter-plan which envisaged the withdrawal of battalion headquarters and one company to Sintang, one company to Semitau, and two companies to Sekadau, but this plan was not approved by Lieut.-Colonel Ross-Thompson. He felt that the Dutch plan was a "clever move to draw the enemy after British troops and facilitate a clear get-away of Dutch troops to Ketapang", a harbour on the west coast, since Dutch supplies existed on the general line Sanggau-Ketapang, and not on the line Sanggau-Sekadau-Sintang. He therefore decided to break away from the Dutch and follow a secret plan prepared by Lieut.-Colonel Lane, earlier in the month. This plan was to have been executed in the event of a possible collapse in North-West Borneo and a successful Japanese landing on the west coast.

According to the plan now adopted by the British commander, the Indian battalion was divided into two columns which were to make their way south across country to Sampit and Pangkalanboon. In case the Japanese had already occupied these two ports before the two columns reached their respective destinations, the battalion had instructions to divide itself into groups of 50 men each and disperse into the interior of the island. General Headquarters Far East was informed of this plan as early as 14 January and five Sarawak Volunteer Force Officers were recalled from Pontianak to reconnoitre routes and possible food dumps between Bengkajang and Nangapinoh.

After his return to Sanggau from the Dutch headquarters, the officer commanding Indian troops proceeded by car to Sekadau. Here a meeting of officers took place and final details of the jungle march were worked out. From Sekadau, Lieut.-Colonel Ross-Thompson accompanied by some officers proceeded further to Sintang to meet the Dutch Resident. The latter gave much useful information for the proposed march.

Orders were issued to Indian troops to start thinning out on 31 January and to withdraw by daylight of 1 February. All the sick considered incapable of undertaking the proposed march were sent by lorry to Sintang at first from where they were later moved by boat to Poertisibau up the Kapoeas river. C Company marched out of Ngabang and took up positions covering the Kapoeas river between Sanggau and the ferry, while headquarters company safeguarded the south bank of the ferry. B and D Companies passed through about midday to Sekadau and at about 1800 hours C Company followed them and proceeded straight to Nangapinoh. Almost the entire battalion with A Company as rearguard reached Blimbing

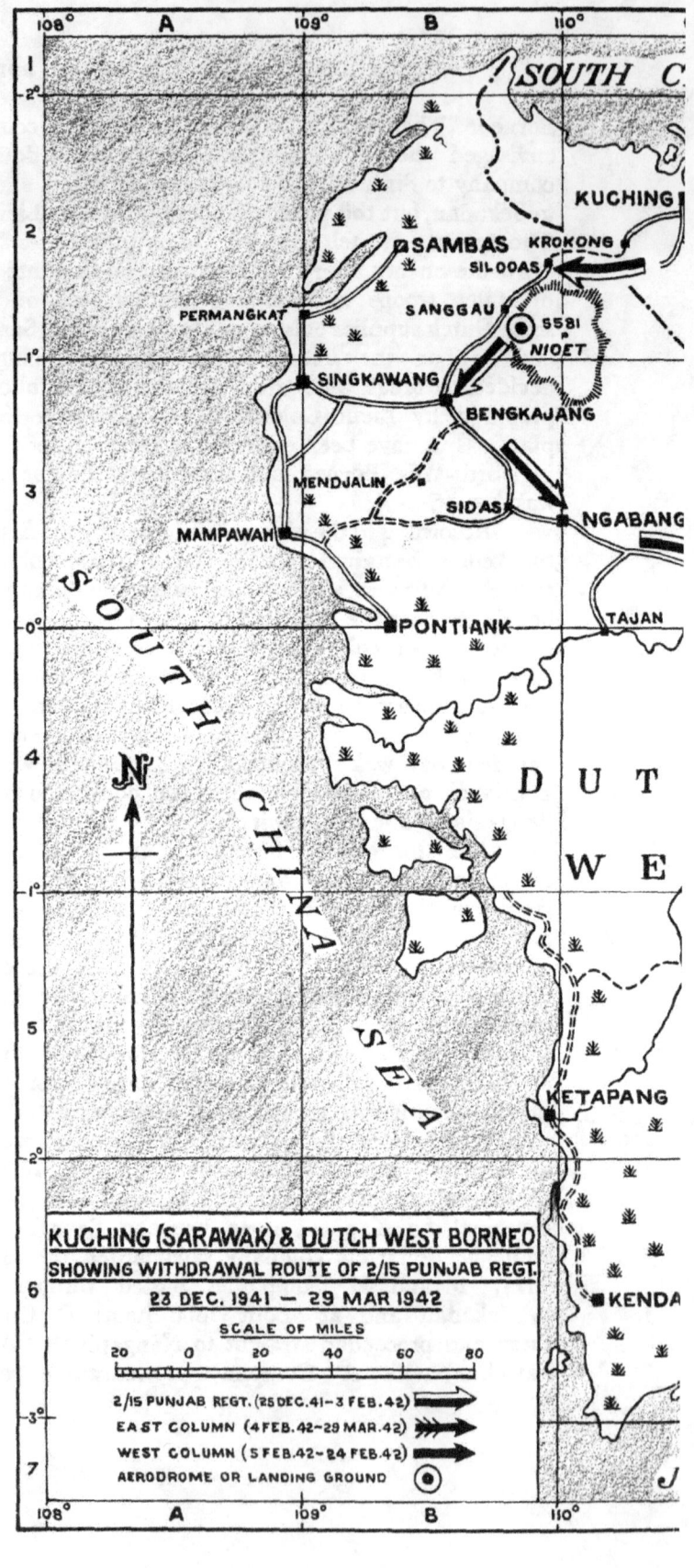

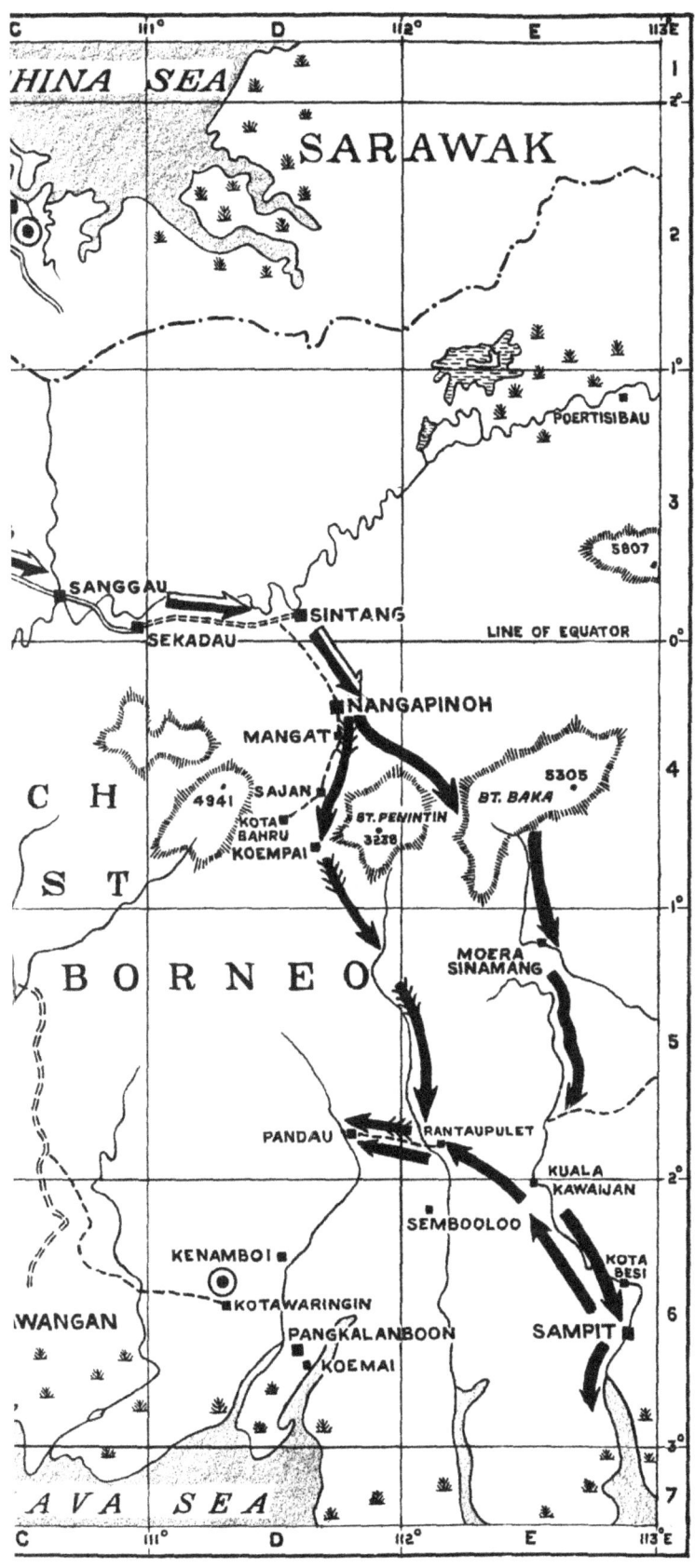

ferry on the night of 2/3 February. The road as far as this ferry was in an extremely poor condition and the troops had to cross several weak bridges every two or three miles.

The battalion reached Nangapinoh on 3 February where it spent the whole day completing all necessary preparations for the march.[11] At Nangapinoh it was divided into two columns of about equal strength, each consisting of three parties as under:—

West Column

This had 9 officers, 8 Viceroy's Commissioned Officers and 344 other ranks with Major Milligan in command and comprising,

A Company
B Company
Part of Headquarters Company.

East Column

10 officers, 5 Viceroy's Commissioned Officers and 349 other ranks with Lieut.-Colonel Ross-Thompson in command, comprising of

C Company
D Company
Remainder of Headquarters Company.

The 'Blitz' Party

In addition to the West and East columns, a 'blitz' party consisting of two officers and four other ranks was formed to make for Sampit with all speed to contact General Headquarters Java by wireless or any other means available. Should it not be possible to make contact at Sampit, the party was given instructions to cross over to Pangkalanboon wireless station, and if that method also failed, to requisition a boat and sail to Java with news of the battalion's whereabouts.

This party left on the evening of 3 February and after travelling most of the way in river craft down the Mendawi and Mentaja rivers, arrived at a place about four miles north of Sampit on 14 February. A Chinese trader at this place told the party that the Controleur at Sampit had left by boat on the 12th, two days earlier, after destroying the wireless station and other public works. They were also told that the native officer had gone to the mouth of the river to meet the Japanese to arrange for terms of truce. This statement was corroborated by three other traders who had just returned from Sampit while the conversation was taking place.[12] It was then decided to make for Pangkalanboon

---

[11] On the same day two seaplanes from Java landed at Sintang and Lieut.-Colonel Lane was sent by boat there for evacuation. Unfortunately he arrived at 0600 hours on 5 February—just 30 minutes after the planes had left and, despite repeated requests to Java Headquarters for another plane, none arrived.

[12] Lane's Report, p. 55.

via Sembooloo where the party had further proof of the confusion in the Dutch civil administration caused by Japanese landing.

The party reached Pangkalanboon on 19 February after an arduous march of over 100 miles in five days, and from there they were able, through the wireless set of the Dutch military commander, to contact British Headquarters Java. The news of the whereabouts of the battalion had already reached Java a fortnight earlier from the seaplanes that had landed at Sintang. The "blitz" party was ignorant of this.

East Column

On 3 February, Lieut.-Colonel Ross-Thompson explained to his men the necessity of withdrawal to South Borneo and the dangers inherent in a march over unchartered and unfamiliar terrain. They were told that there was no means of carrying all those who fell sick, who would have to remain behind in the nearest village. The other dangers of the trip were also mentioned: short rations, unfriendly natives, and the possibility, even probability, of the Japanese reaching the destination before them.[13] Men were offered the choice of marching south or remaining behind, but with one voice they all volunteered to go.

At dawn on 4 February, East Column left Nangapinoh with C Company in the lead, following nearly the same route as that already taken by the "blitz" party. The column reached the headwaters of the Sereojan river on 8 February after a very difficult march "mostly through very heavy sandy mud and thick jungle".[14] Here the column was told that it was difficult to go down the river in boats because there were too many bad rapids. It was therefore decided to cross to the Mendawi river. The leading party reached the river on 13 February where it halted for three days to build rafts. During the journey, food was scarce and only a little rice could be purchased from any village which they met *en route*. All the three parties were at this stage within a few miles of one another, although marching separately. With the rafts completed, the column took to the water and for three days drifted and paddled its way down this "very difficult river full of ledges, fallen trees and rocky rapids".[15] Though no one was drowned during this period, a total of 51 rifles and 2 Bren guns was lost by the column.

A short distance above Moera Sinamang village on the Mendawi river, on 19 February, a number of boats were obtained,

[13] *Ibid.*, p. 53.
[14] *Ibid.*
[15] *Ibid.*

and in these the journey was continued to a point some 12 miles east of the village. From here the column crossed to the Mentaja river, C Company dragging one boat along with it, and on large rafts proceeded without incident as far as Kuala Kawaijan. Lieut.-Colonel Ross-Thompson who, with his headquarters party, was the first to reach Kuala Kawaijan, carried straight on to Sampit, which he reached on 1 March. On arrival there, he immediately sent up two motor launches to meet the remainder of the column. D Company was ordered to halt at Kota Besi between Kuala Kawaijan and Sampit to help the local authorities to maintain law and order while C Company and the headquarters party continued to the junction of Mentaja and Sampit rivers, some 18 miles south of Sampit village.

The Headquarters party and C Company assembled in the junction area on 6 March, and had been in their new position only one day when Japanese troops were reported to have landed some nine miles downstream from a large ship. A platoon of C Company which was sent to investigate the report soon contacted the Japanese and was pushed back by them under heavy small-arms and 2" mortar fire. As the column had insufficient ammunition to carry on the action, Lieut.-Colonel Ross-Thompson decided to withdraw to Sampit. For a large number of troops " the 18-mile march to Sampit along a clay path made extremely slippery by continuous rain, on top of the month's march through the jungle on reduced rice diet, proved too much "[16] and, out of a total of five officers, 3 Viceroy's Commissioned Officers and 183 Indian Other Ranks, 2 Viceroy's Commissioned Officers and 102 Indian Other Ranks failed to reach Sampit, for the most part falling out into native houses on the way.

The same night (7/8 March), the remnants of C Company and Headquarters party set off upstream in motor launches, collecting D Company at Kota Besi *en route*. The column reached Kuala Kawaijan on 10 March where 30 other men were reported missing and search parties failed to find them. The party then marched through the jungle on a compass bearing for five days and came out near Rantaupoulet on the Seroejan river. At this place the first news from West Column was received in the form of a brief message stating that the Netherlands East Indies had surrendered to the Japanese.

The column marched to Pandau on the right bank of the Aroet river and Lieut.-Colonel Ross-Thompson went ahead by fast boat to Pangkalanboon. Boats were sent up and the whole

---

[16] *Ibid.*, p. 54.

battalion was assembled in Kenamboi on 29 March pending the arrival of Japanese troops prepared to accept their surrender.

West Column

The difficulties encountered by Major Milligan and his column in their march from Nangapinoh to Kenamboi were nearly in all respects the same as those experienced by the East Column. With little more than half the distance of the latter to cover, however, Major Milligan was able to reach his destination much earlier.

Leaving Nangapinoh in separate parties on 5/6 February, the complete column marched overland via Mangat and Koempai to the Seroejan river. The route via Mangat was fairly clear of vegetation at first but later changed to jungle paths. The officer commanding the column cycled to Kota Bahru ahead of his men to get information regarding the best route over the hills. From the source of the Seroejan river, the column rafted as far as Rantaupoulet over fifty miles of river through many rapids. In one of these a boat crashed on the rock which resulted in the drowning of four Sikhs of A Company. From Rantaupoulet the column crossed overland to Pandau where it met a Dutch patrol from Pangkalanboon. A and B Companies marched overland to Krabau where they boarded motor boats, and on 24 February the last of the column reached Kenamboi where food was available.

The marches of both East and West Columns were almost wholly non-operational, yet each was in itself a tribute to the training, discipline and high morale of 2/15 Punjab. Through the thick jungle and almost uncharted territory of South Borneo, in a wet and humid climate, on short rations and with but a meagre hope of escape at the other end, the men had kept going with a large number of arms and much ammunition, thereby showing great courage and exemplary devotion to duty. As Lieut.-Colonel Lane remarks in his summing up of the Column's achievements, "The endurance and determination of the men of both Columns ......especially those who were suffering from malaria and dysentery......was worthy of the highest praise".[17] General Percival described the withdrawal as "a feat of endurance which assuredly will rank high in the annals of warfare".[18]

Just before the arrival of the West Column in Pangkalanboon, an officer from General Headquarters paid a visit to Kotawaringin to the south-west of Kenamboi and gave orders for its defence by Indian troops. He emphasised that Indian troops could not be

[17] Lane's Report, p. 55.
[18] *The War in Malaya*, p. 173.

evacuated from South Borneo and their future role was to hold the aerodrome lightly and form themselves into guerilla bands to harass the Japanese in the Kotawaringin-Pangkalanboon area. The entire force was to live upon supplies procured on the spot. The Indian troops were to be assisted in their task by a Dutch force consisting of 250 men armed with rifles and light machine guns. On the day the column reached Kenamboi a small ship arrived from Java with a fair amount of food, clothing and ammunition. The food was sufficient for about a month's ration.

OPERATIONS ELSEWHERE IN DUTCH BORNEO

While Japanese forces were striking at Indian and Dutch forces in West Borneo, Dutch garrisons along the eastern coast were being similarly engaged by strong Japanese landing parties.

We have already noted elsewhere the capture of Tarakan by the Japanese on 12 January 1942. By-passing the important Samarinda aerodrome the Japanese sailed south towards Balikpapan. On 23 January, a large Japanese invasion fleet was sighted off North-East Borneo heading south through the Macassar Strait. The convoy was successfully attacked by Dutch medium bombers based on Samarinda and hits on six ships were claimed. American and Dutch submarines and a surface force consisting of two American cruisers and four destroyers also inflicted severe losses on the Japanese. It is estimated that their losses came to five or six ships sunk and many others damaged.[19] Yet " The Battle of Macassor Strait did not prevent the Japanese from taking Balikpapan, but they were stalled there for some time ".[20]

The town was set on fire by the Dutch defenders and when the Japanese occupied it they found only a mass of smoking ruins, so thorough had been the " scorched earth " tactics. The Dutch garrison slowly withdrew westwards in the direction of Samarinda and the Japanese made little attempt to follow up the Dutch withdrawal.

From Balikpapan, the Japanese began a long and determined overland advance to the south-west which eventually enabled them to occupy Bandjermasin on 10 February, and to land south of Sampit less than a month later. As has already been related, East Column which had arrived in the area only a day previously was forced to retire, leaving the Japanese in undisputed possession of every main town on the east coast from Sandakan to Sampit.

[19] On 24 January, a Dutch submarine sank a Japanese cruiser and on the following day American bombers sank two transports anchored at Balikpapan.
[20] *The War with Japan*, Part I (7 December 1941 to August 1942), New York, 1945.

CAPITULATION

The first intimation of a general surrender in the Netherlands East Indies was received at Pangkalanboon on 8 March in the form of a broadcast message from the Dutch Commander-in-Chief, Java, stating that all organised resistance in the Netherlands East Indies had ceased. On the morning of the next day, a proclamation came over the radio from Nerom (Batavia) calling upon all Allied forces in the Netherlands East Indies to lay down their arms and surrender unconditionally.

Confronted with this order and the threat of renewed fighting if his troops continued their resistance to the Japanese, and after a conference with the Dutch Commander and Controleur of Pangkalanboon, Major Milligan decided to comply. Receipt of instructions was acknowledged through the Dutch radio station to Headquarters Java at 0930 hours on 9 March. It was realised by all officers that even if the Nerom broadcast was a bluff—the terms stipulating that all denial and destruction was to cease appeared suspicious in view of the declared "scorched earth" policy of the Dutch—there was no alternative left but to surrender. The threat of reprisals, especially upon prisoners of war at Kuching aerodrome and on the native population of Borneo, was considered too great to warrant further resistance.

The possibility of retiring into the jungle individually or in small parties was considered at length, but Major Milligan decided that the chances of more than a handful surviving such conditions as would have to be faced in the jungles of Borneo were too small to make such a step worthwhile. Arms and ammunition were already in short supply and little food could be obtained in the interior regions. These factors pointed to the unwisdom of such a course being followed.

The decision to lay down arms was made known to all ranks on parade in the late afternoon on 9 March. Lieut.-Colonel Lane arrived at Pangkalanboon the same evening to resume command of the battalion. After waiting at Sintang for another plane to arrive[81] until 18 February, by which time the Japanese were reported to be only a six hours' journey away, Lieut.-Colonel Lane had left for Nangapinoh. From there, he, in company with two Dutch officials and six Indian soldiers, had made his way south via Kota Bahru to Pangkalanboon.

Between 2 March and 3 April there was a lot of discussion among British and Dutch officers as regards the surrender decision.

---

[81] Lane's Report, p. 56.

Several conferences were held at which the position was reconsidered from every possible angle, but the decision was not changed. On 13 March a message was sent by Lieut.-Colonel Lane to the officer commanding East Column informing him of the decision to capitulate to the Japanese and on 31 March, by which time the Indian battalion was assembled at Kenamboi, a Japanese naval vessel arrived at Koemai to accept the surrender of all Indian and Dutch troops.

Arms and ammunition were handed over on 1 April. West Column embarked at Koemai two days later, arriving at Tanjong Priok Prisoner of War Camp (Batavia) on the 5th. The last troops of the East Column left Koemai on the 7th, reaching Cycle Camp (Batavia) the following day. The Japanese naval staff in Borneo treated the troops very well and the embarrassing task of handing over was carried out to the satisfaction of all concerned.

The operations in Sarawak and Dutch Borneo described above were only of subsidiary importance compared to the other events in South-East Asia during those disastrous months of 1942. Tactically they must be considered a failure, since they ended in the Japanese occupation of the entire area. But strategically they might be considered successful, because they served to delay the Japanese thrust southwards, and denied the use of the Miri and Seria oilfields to the enemy. Grievous losses and great privations were suffered by the defending Indian troops, but they added another story of heroism and dogged resistance against overwhelming odds, to the annals of the Indian Army.

APPENDIX A

Garrison in Hong Kong

ORDER OF BATTLE—EXCLUDING ANCILLARY UNITS

(A) *7th December* 1941
   CHINA COMMAND   G.O.C.–Major-General C.M. Maltby, M.C.
   MAINLAND BDE   Brigadier C. Wallis
     5 Rajput   Lieut.-Colonel Cadogan-Rawlinson
     2/14 Punjab   Lieut.-Colonel Kidd
     2 Royal Scots .. Lieut.-Colonel White

   ISLAND BDE   Brigadier J.K. Lawson
     1 Middlesex   Lieut.-Colonel Stewart, M.C.
     Winnipeg Grenadiers ... .. Lieut.-Colonel J.L.R. Sutcliffe
     Royal Rifles of Canada   Lieut.-Colonel W. J. Home, M.C.

FORTRESS TROOPS

Attd. Mainland Brigade
  No. 1 Coy, HKVDC
  Chinese (Nucleus) Coy
  1 and 2 Mtn Btys, 1 HK Regt HKSRA
  22 Field Coy, RE

Hong Kong Island
  Nos. 2, 4, 6 and 7 Coys HKVDC–Colonel Rose
  8 and 12 Coast Regiments, RA
  5 AA Regiment, RA
  3 and 4 Med Btys, 1 HK Regt HKSRA
  965 Def Bty, RA
  40 Field Coy, RE

Stonecutters Isle
  No. 3 Coy, HKVDC

(B) *15th December* 1941

   CHINA COMMAND   Major-General Maltby

EAST INF BDE   Brigadier Wallis
  5 Rajput
  Royal Rifles of Canada
  "B" and "D" Coys 1 Middx
WEST INF BDE   Brigadier Lawson
  2/14 Punjab
  Winnipeg Grenadiers
  2 Royal Scots

FORTRESS TROOPS
Of the units listed in "(A) FORTRESS TROOPS" above:—

1 HK Regt HKSRA was divided into East and West Groups, RA, each Group working in close conjunction with its respective Bde HQ.

Nos. 1 and 2 Coys HKVDC, in the Eastern Sector, were commanded partly by Brigadier Wallis and partly by Ft. HQ.

Remaining Units, together with "A", "C" and "Z" Coys 1 Middx, all came directly under command of Ft. HQ.

APPENDIX B

Copy of Propaganda Leaflets dropped by the Japanese over Hong Kong

You British Nationals!

Be awakened immediately to the actual situation of the world!

Millions of Imperial Troops are already advanced to India, and the Rising Sun Flags are already flying in such major cities of the Far East as Manila, Batavia, Bangkok, Singapore, Rangoon, etc. The cry for co-prosperity is raised all over the whole of those areas. In Europe the German army has occupied Moscow the Red capital, its violent attacks threatening to extend to the Ural regions. London, the British capital, is in a most perilous situation. The American Pacific Fleet, which has been leading the camp of democracies, has been heavily damaged by the Japanese Navy and is now solely devoted to the defence of its own country. You British officers and men who are encamped in Hong Kong and Kowloon! Stop continuing to offer futile resistance within the narrowly limited areas without the knowledge of the changed international situation. Your strategic establishments are sure to collapse before the serious attacks by the Imperial Army. You panic-stricken citizens on the solitary island in helpless isolation!

In order to save Kowloon and Hong Kong from the scene of mutual slaughter of human lives and also to avoid the loss of your fathers, husbands and children as well as your properties, bring pressure upon the government authorities to deliver Hong Kong and Kowloon without bloodshed and resistance. We firmly believe you will choose this wise measure without fail.

SHOULD YOU DESTROY THE IMPORTANT ESTABLISHMENTS AND MATERIALS IN HONG KONG AND KOWLOON IN ORDER TO PREVENT THEIR UTILIZATION BY THE IMPERIAL ARMY, AFTER THEIR OCCUPATION THE JAPANESE ARMY WILL SURELY ANNIHILATE ALL BRITISH NATIONALS IN RETALIATION.

To all Chinese emigrants in Hong Kong.
Commander of the Japanese Army.

Now the Japanese army tightly sieged Hong Kong where you live and where you accumulate your wealth, and the occupation of Hong Kong by the Japanese Army close at hand. But what the Japanese Army long for is not the destruction of your lives and properties or of Hong Kong but the destruction of the influence of the English.

But if you let the English to resist in vain being used as their tool and run away giving up your houses and property, all your properties will be robbed by the mob and the white, and still more the Japanese Army also will be forced to destroy your lives with the Hong Kong Island. You should trust to the faith of the Japanese Army and let the British surrender to the Japanese Army giving up their resistances, and wait for the Japanese Army protecting your properties by your own hands. When reached, the Japanese Army would assure you of your lives and properties; moreover, would assert to help your prosperities in future.

APPENDIX C

Malaya Command
ORDER OF BATTLE — 8 DECEMBER 1941
H.Q. Malaya Command

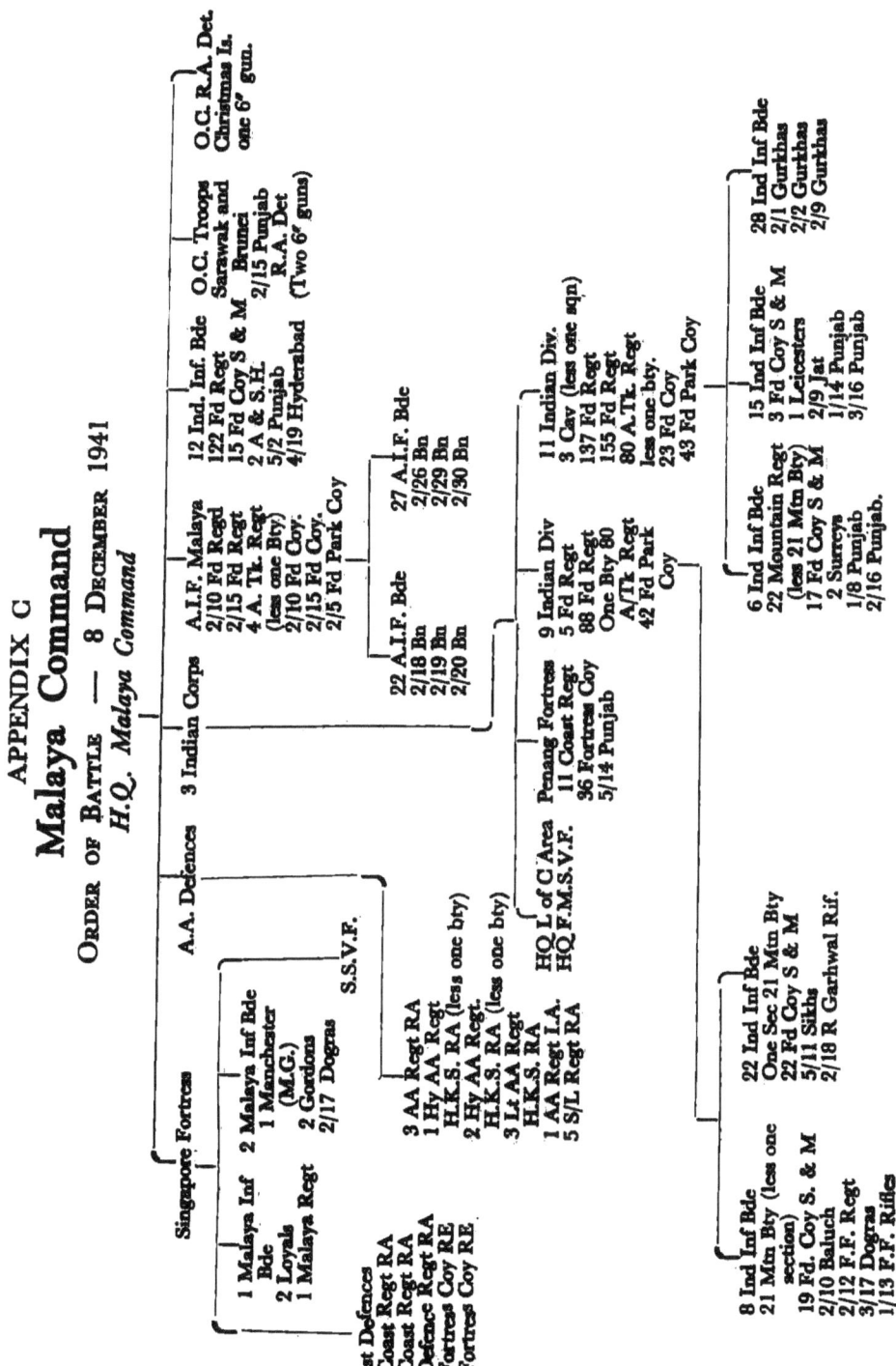

APPENDIX D

The Japanese 25th Army

BRIEF ORDER OF BATTLE—8 DECEMBER 1941

Lieut.-General T. Yamashita, the C.-in-C. of the 25*th Army*, had under his command the *Imperial Guards Division* (Lieut.-General T. Nishimura), the 5*th Division* (Lieut.-General T. Matsui), and the 18*th Division* (Lieut.-General R. Mutaguchi,) as the principal formations. The 56*th Division* was also assigned to the 25*th Army* originally, but was not actually included in Lieut.-General Yamashita's force. He also had a Tank Group of four tank regiments, an Independent Anti-Tank Battalion and eight independent anti-tank companies, an independent Mountain Artillery Regiment, two Heavy Field Artillery Regiments and a Heavy Field Artillery Battalion, three Mortar Battalions, and proportion of Engineer, Signal units, etc. The Transportation and other Line of Communication units alone numbered over 36,000 men, and the total of Japanese troops earmarked for Malaya was 1,25,408 men with 7,320 vehicles and 11,516 horses, though the members actually landed in Malaya fell far short of these figures.[1]

A Japanese Tank Regiment, the *1st* for example, consisted of 37 medium tanks and 20 light tanks organised into a regimental headquarters, three medium tank companies and one light tank company, with a regimental munition train. A medium tank company had ten medium and two light tanks, the light tank company had ten light tanks, and the regimental munition train had five medium and three light tanks. The regimental headquarters had two medium and one light tank. The medium tanks (16 tons) were armed with one 57 mm gun and two 7·7 mm light machine guns each: a light tank (8 tons) contained one 37 mm gun and one 7·7 mm machine gun.

A Japanese Division contained three or four regiments plus a reconnaissance regiment or cavalry battalion, with the usual complement of artillery, engineer, signal, transportation, ordnance and medical units. An Infantry regiment consisted of three battalions.

[1] For detail see Kirby, S. Woodburn : *The War Against Japan*, Vol. I Appendix 15; Her Majesty's Stationery Office, London 1957.

APPENDIX E

Order of Battle—8 Ind. Inf. Bde.

7 December 1941.

Bde. H.Q. and Sig. Sec.
Employment Pl.
73 Fd. Bty. R.A. (5 Fd. Regt. R.A.)
272 A/Tk. Bty. R.A.
21 Mtn. Bty. (less one Sec.)
Det. Hong Kong and Singapore Regt. R.A.
19 Fd. Coy. R Bombay S. and M.
2/10th Baluch Regt.
2/12th F.F. Regt.
1/13th F.F. Rifles
3/17th Dogra Regt.
One Coy. Malaya Regt.
1st Hyderabad Inf. I.S.F.
Mysore Inf. I.S.F.
Two M.G. Pls. Pahang Bn. (Volunteers)
One Coy. Kelantam Vols.
Fd. Amb.
8 Ind. Inf. Bde. Tpt. Coy.
43 Reserve M.T. Coy. (Malaya)
One Labour Pl.

APPENDIX F

Order of the Day Issued on the 8th December 1941

Japan's action today gives the signal for the Empire Naval, Army and Air Forces and those of their Allies, to go into action with a common aim and common ideals.

We are ready. We have had plenty of warning and our preparations are made and tested. We do not forget at this moment the years of patience and forbearance in which we have borne, with dignity and discipline, the petty insults and insolences inflicted on us by the Japanese in the Far East. We know that those things were only done because Japan thought she could take advantage of our supposed weakness. Now, when Japan herself has decided to put the matter to a sterner test, she will find out that she has made a grievous mistake.

We are confident. Our defences are strong and our weapons efficient. Whatever our race, and whether we are now in our native land or have come thousands of miles, we have one aim and one only. It is to defend these shores, to destroy such of our enemies as may set foot on our soil, and then, finally, to cripple the power of the enemy to endanger our ideals, our possessions and our peace.

What of the enemy? We see before us a Japan drained for years by the exhausting claims of her wanton onslaught on China. We see a Japan whose trade and industry have been dislocated by these years of reckless adventure that, in a mood of desperation, her Government has flung her into war under the delusion that, by stabbing a friendly nation in the back, she can gain her end. Let her look at Italy and what has happened since that nation tried a similar base action.

Let us all remember that we here in the Far East form part of the great campaign for the preservation in the world of truth and justice and freedom; confidence, resolution, enterprise and devotion to the cause must and will inspire every one of us in the fighting services, while from the civilian population, Malay, Chinese, Indian, or Burmese, we expect that patience, endurance and serenity which is the great virtue of the East and which will go far to assist the fighting men to gain final and complete victory.

R. BROOKE-POPHAM,
  Air Chief Marshal,
  Commander-in-Chief, Far East.

G. LAYTON,
  Vice-Admiral,
  Commander-in-Chief, China.

APPENDIX G

Malaya Command Operation Instruction No. 40

Ref. Map JOHORE and SINGAPORE 1/25,000.

1. Enemy attacked Western Area in strength 9 February and succeeded in penetrating to the EAST of TENGAH aerodrome. A party of the enemy is reported to have blocked the rd HONG KAH VILLAGE 6917—rd Junc 6313 in rear of 44 Ind. Inf. Bde.

2. A.I.F. MALAYA have been ordered to withdraw to and hold the line S. KRANJI-BULEM VILLAGE 6919—S. JURONG. 6/15 Bde has been placed under comd. of A.I.F. MALAYA.

3. Should it be impossible to hold the enemy on the line mentioned in para 2 above, G.O.C. Malaya intends to withdraw to an inner posn on which the final battle for SINGAPORE will be fought.

4. General line of this inner posn will be:—
West Bank of KALLANG river in 8711—thence WEST of the inundated area in 8611, 8612 and 8712 to MT. VERNON 8814—NORTH of PIERCE RESERVOIR 8118—Hill 581 in 7616—WEST OF BUKIT TIMAH VILLAGE 7515—pt. 105 in 7412—PASIR PANJANG VILLAGE 7409—thence along the SOUTH coast of SINGAPORE ISLAND to WEST Bank of ROCHORE RIVER in 8710. PULAU BLAKANG MATI, PULAU BRANI, PULAU TEKONG and the defended perimeter of Pengerang will also be held.

5. This posn will be divided into three areas:—

NORTHERN AREA	Comd ..	Comd 3 Ind. Corps
	Tps ..	3 Ind Corps of 11 Ind. Div and 18 Div.
SOUTHERN AREA	Comd ..	Comd Southern Area (Major General KEITH SIMMONS)
	Tps ..	existing garrison of Southern Area.
WESTERN AREA ..	Comd ..	Comd A.I.F. MALAYA

NOTE—Allocation of 12 Ind. Inf. Bde and 44 Ind. Inf. Bde will be decided later. At least one of these formations will be in Comd Reserve.

6. BOUNDARIES
The defended area defined in para 4 above will be divided into sectors by boundaries as follows:—

Between 3 Ind. Corps and A.I.F. Incl. A.I.F. Electric Transmission Line 7716—incl SWISS RIFLE CLUB 7715—incl rd junc 780143—incl BUKIT TIMAH RD—rd junc 838117.

Between 3 Ind. Corps and Southern Area. Incl 3 Ind. Corps MACPHERSON RD—SERANGOON Rd—excl FARRER PARK—rd junc 838117.

Between A.I.F. and Southern Area. Incl Southern Area track 750107—AYER RAJA RD—ALEXANDRA Rd—rd junc 809092-incl rd junc 812102—GRANGE Rd—incl rd junc 827102—excl rd junc 829108—excl rd junc 838117.

Comd Southern Area will be responsible for defence of PULAU BLAKANG MATI, PULAU BRANI, PULAU TEKONG and PENGERANG.

7. Reconnaissances of Areas will be carried out at once and the plans for the movement of formations into the areas allotted to them will be prepared. Formations will arrange to move back and locate in their new areas units located in their present areas which are under command of H.Q. Malaya Command.

8. C.A.A.D. will remain responsible to G.O.C. Malaya for A.A. Defences.

9. H.Q. of G.O.C. Malaya will be located at Fort Canning (Battle H.Q.) together with H.Q. Southern Area.

10. Administrative adjustments which can be made now to fit in with the above organization will be put in hand immediately.

11. ACK.

Lieut.-Colonel
for Brigadier,
General Staff, Malaya Command.

Adv. H.Q.M.C.
10th February, 1942.

APPENDIX H
Japanese Units and their Commanders in South-East Asia.

(This list is supplied by Historical Division, Defence Agency, Tokyo, Japan)

HONG KONG

Units and their commanders engaged in the Hong Kong Operations:-

23rd Army
(Lt.-gen. Takashi Sakai)

38 Division   228i (Col. Sadashichi Doi)
(Lt.-gen. Tadayoshi Sano)   229i (Col. Ryozaburo Tanaka)
     230i (Col. Toshishige Shoji)

MALAYA

Principal units and their commanders engaged in the Malaya Operations:—

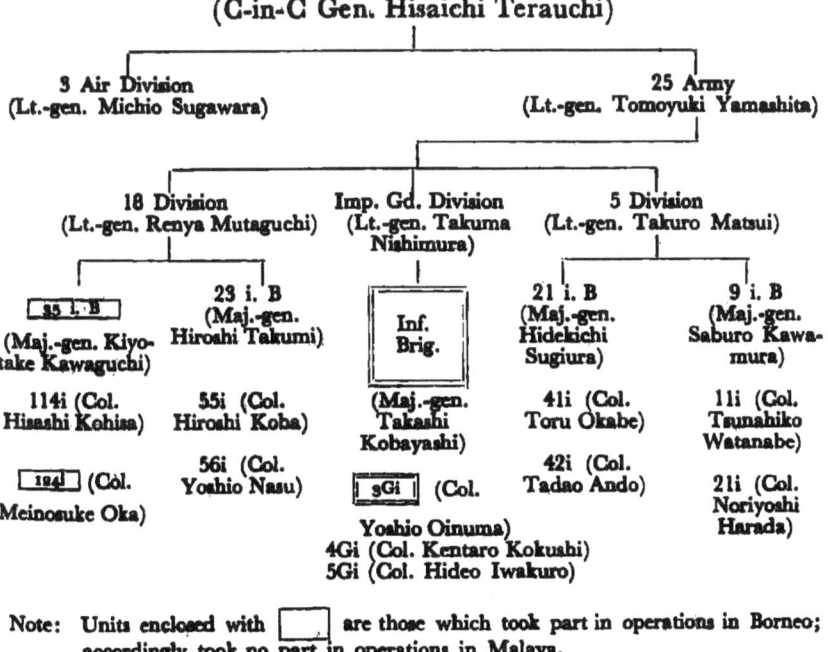

Note: Units enclosed with ▢ are those which took part in operations in Borneo; accordingly took no part in operations in Malaya.
Units enclosed with ▭ are those which were engaged in guard duty in F.I.C., and had not taken part in operations in Malaya.

Areas of operations of Japanese Units in Malaya:—
(i) Unit which landed at Patani and thence operated towards K. Kangsar through Grik:—
Ando Detachment (Cdr. Col, Tadao Ando, 42 Inf. Regt.)
- 42i
- TK Co.   1
- Recon Co.   1
- At btry.   1
- FA „   1
- Eng Co.   1
- Others

(ii) Unit which landed at Kota Bharu and occupied Kuantan after advancing south along the east coast:—
Takumi Detachment (Cdr. Maj-gen. Hiroshi Takumi, Cdr. 23i.B)
- 23iB Hqs
- 56i
- MA btry.   1
- Eng. Co.   1
- Others

(iii) Units embarked at Lumut (1 Jan. 1942) and landed at Telok Anson:—
Watanabe Detachment (Cdr. Col Tsunahiko Watanabe, Cdr. 11i)
- 11i (Main body)
- FA btry.   1
- Eng. Co.   1
- Marine Eng. Co   1
- Others

(iv) Undermentioned unit was expected to occupy the Kuantan Airfield after landing there at the end of January 1942. But it suspended landing at Kuantan as Takumi Detachment came just then from Kota Bharu in the north.

(Koba Detachment landed at Kota Bharu and reached Kuantan by land, thence it advanced to Endau and Mersing.)

Koba Detachment (Cdr. Col. Hiroshi Koba, Cdr. 55i)
- 55i (less 1 bn)
- MA btry. 1

BRITISH BORNEO

Kawaguchi Detachment
    Maj.-gen. Kiyotake Kawaguchi
        35 Inf. Brig. Hqs. 124 Inf. Regt. and others

Note: This unit was under the command of the 18th Division but it separately engaged in the operations in British Borneo.

DUTCH BORNEO

Sakaguchi Detachment
    Maj.-gen. Shizuo Sakaguchi.
        Inf. Brig. Hqs., 146 Inf. Regt., a Field Artillery battalion and others.

Note: This unit was under the command of the 56th Division but it separately took part in the operations in Dutch Borneo.

BIBLIOGRAPHY

The present volume of the Official History of the Indian Armed Forces in the Second World War is mainly based on the official documents collected in the C.I.S. Historical Section, Ministry of Defence, India. Among these the first place goes to the 'War Diaries' of the various Indian Units which took part in the campaigns against Japan in Hong Kong, Malaya, Sarawak and Duth West Borneo. The 'Despatches' written by the different military commanders soon after the completion of the operations entrusted to them are our next important source of information. They reveal not only the details of the operational activities but also the lines of high policy and facts of administrative organisation. In addition, a number of 'Appreciations' and 'Reports' completed either during the course of war or after the completion of various plans and operations have also received due attention. The class of the sources designated as 'Personal Accounts and Narratives' and the 'Unit Histories' have also been found useful in presenting an overall account of the respective campaigns.

Since these original sources were amply available, the secondary published sources have been depended upon to a minimum. A selected list of all these sources, both original as well as published, is given below:—

WAR DIARIES

War Diaries of the units that took part in the campaigns against Japan in Hong Kong, Malaya, Sarawak and Dutch West Borneo, and particularly of the following:—

General HQ Far East, HQ Malaya Command, III Indian Corps; 9th Indian Division; 12th, 15th, 22nd and 28th Indian Infantry Brigades; 137th and 155th Field Regiments. Also War Diaries of the smaller units comprised in the above.

DESPATCHES

1. Despatch by Air Chief Marshal Sir Robert Brooke-Popham, GCVO, KCB, CMG, DSO, AFC, Commander-in-Chief in the Far East, on *Operations in the Far East from 17 October 1940 to 27 December 1941*. (Published in the Supplement to the London Gazette of Tuesday, the 20th January, 1948).
2. Despatch by Major-General C. M. Maltby, MC, late GOC, British Troops in China, on *Operations in Hong Kong from 8 to*

25 December 1941. (Published in the Supplement to the London Gazette of Tuesday, the 27th January, 1948).
3. Despatch by Lieut-General A.E. Percival, CB, DSO, OBE, MC, formerly GOC Malaya on *Operations of Malaya Command, from 8 December 1941 to 15 February 1942.* (Published in the Second Supplement to the London Gazette of Thursday, the 26th February 1948).
4. Despatch by General Sir Archibald Wavell GCB, CMG, MC, on *Operations in South-West Pacific from 15 January to 25 February, 1942.*

APPRECIATIONS AND REPORTS.

1. Singapore Defence Conference Report, 1940.
2. ABDACOM—An Official Account of events in the South-West Pacific Command, Jan.-Feb. 1942.
3. ADB Conversations: Report Office of the Commander-in-Chief, China Station, 27th April 1941.
4. Chiefs of Staff Appreciation of the Situation in the Far East, 16 August 1940.
5. The Kuantan Operations—By Captain D.G. Russell-Roberts.
6. Preliminary Report on Canadian Participation in the Hong Kong Operations.
7. A Report on Operations in Sarawak and Dutch Borneo by Colonel C.M. Lane.
8. Report by Sir Paul Maltby, Air Vice-Marshal (Published in Supplement to the London Gazette, the 26th February 1948).

PERSONAL ACCOUNTS AND NARRATIVES

1. Narrative of Thom Force, Singapore, 10/12 February 1942.
2. War Record of the 6th Bn. 1st Punjab Regt. by Lt. Col. J.D. Sainter.
3. Narrative on Operations in Malaya, 1939-1942, by Lt. Col. J.G. Frith.
4. Operations in Malaya, 1941-42—An account by Lt. Col. E.L. Wilson Haffenden.
5. Account of the Malaya Campaign, by Major E.F.D. Hyde.
6. The Malayan Campaign—(Nov. 1941 to Feb. 1942)—Precis of a lecture given by Lieut.-General Sir Lewis Heath KBE, CB, CIE, DSO.

UNIT HISTORIES

1. History of 11 Ind. Division in Malaya, by Colonel A. M. L. Harrison.

2. The War in Hong Kong—2/14 Punjab Regiment, 8 to 25 December, 1941
3. War Diary and Narrative of East Infantry Brigade and Attached Troops by Brig. C. Wallis.
4. War Diary and Narrative—Mainland Infantry Brigade and attached Troops by Brig. C. Wallis.

PUBLISHED WORKS

1. Angus Rose: *Who Dies Fighting*
2. Bennett H.G.: *Why Singapore Fell*
3. Churchill : *The Second World War Vol. II*
4. *Japanese Land Operations* (From Japanese Sources) from December 8, 1941 to June 8, 1942, Military Intellegence Service, War Department, Washington 1942.
5. Kirby, S. Woodburn: *The War Against Japan*, Vol. I
6. Percival: *The War in Malaya*.
7. *The War with Japan*, Pt. I. New York, 1945. (U.S.M.A. Printing Office).
8. Wigmore: *The Japanese Thrust*.

INDEX

Aberdeen: heavy bombing at, 42; under shellfire from sea, 44
ABDACOM: 343
ADA Conference: 99, 101
Alor Star: Japanese air raid at, 122; Royal Air Force evacuated from, 148; Allied withdrawal from, 169; Japanese tanks at, 170
Asun: 2/1 Gurkha Rifles in, 148; Japanese Infantry infiltrates to, 151
Australian Army (Australian Imperial Force):
    8th Australian Division: 2/30 Australian Battalion rejoins, 346; see also 105, 117, 233, 234, 303-4, 309, 320, 354
    18th Division: 275-6
    22nd Brigade: 249, 273, 286, 309, 316-17, 321, 326-7, 330-1, 335, 342
    27th Brigade: 118, 254, 269, 285, 288, 299, 309, 320-21, 323, 332
    29th Brigade: 321
    2/18 Battalion: 286-7, 290, 294, 297
    2/19 Battalion: 262, 273, 285, 316, 327
    2/20 Battalion: 290, 294, 297
    2/21 Battalion: 321
    2/26 Battalion: 249, 254, 281, 285, 288, 293, 296, 333, 354
    2/29 Battalion: 255, 260, 261-3, 267, 285, 322, 327, 331
    2/30 Battalion: 249, 254, 266, 277, 281, 293, 296, 333, 338, 346
Ayer Hitam: Japanese air-raid at, 277

'Bancol' (a column): destroyed in action, 283
Barstow, Major-General, A. E. (Commander 9th Indian Division): 134, 260; death of, 291
Batu Pahat Sector: 270; operations at, 271-3; fighting throughout the day at, 277
Benham, Major (Commander, Bancol): tasks allotted to, 283
Bennett, Lieut.-General H. Gordon: in Malaya, 117; 45th Indian Infantry Brigade comes under, 234; decides to reinforce Bakri and Batu Pahat areas, 260; reinforces Muar Sector, 262; orders 22nd Indian Infantry Brigade to re-establish position at Paloh, 277; counter-offensive at Bukit Timah by, 325-6; forms a perimeter of all Australian forces, 331; cables to Australian Prime Minister and informs his intention to surrender, 347; see also 233, 235-6, 246, 257-8, 267, 279, 284, 286, 325, 330
Blanja front: 28th Indian Infantry Brigade at, 198; Japanese success at, 202
Bond, Lieut.-General Sir Lionel (GOC Malaya): appreciation for the defence of Malaya by, 94
British Army:
    18th Division: 268, 275, 287; 303-4, 308, 321, 326, 331, 334, 336, 339, 342, 345-6, 350, 353

53rd Brigade: comes under Westforce, 266; Japanese Infantry and tanks attack on, 270; assists 15th Indian Infantry Brigade in the withdrawal, 283, proceeds to Singapore, 296; see also 267-9, 277-81, 283-4, 288, 292, 309, 332, 334, 338, 348, 353-4
54th Infantry Brigade: 334
55th Infantry Brigade: 334-5
2 Argyll and Sutherland Highlanders: Japanese attack the forward company of 182; at Baling, 189; see also 181, 184, 188-9, 191, 201, 206, 218, 311, 320-21, 326
5 Bedfordshire and Hertfordshire: 332, 334, 340, 342-5, 350
1 Cambridgeshire: 339-40, 350
2 Cambridgeshire: 283, 288, 296, 334, 338, 348
5th Duke Of Connaughts Own Battalion: 223
2 Gordons: 116, 281, 285, 288, 293, 296, 331, 335-6, 340
1 Leicester: 140, 142, 159, 160-2, 164-5, 166-9, 172, 174-5, 196, 206, 255
2 Loyals: 116, 265, 270, 281, 328, 343
1 Manchester: 116, 350, 352
1 Middlesex: 38, 51, 54, 56, 65
3 Negri Sembilan: 244, 246
4 Norfolk: 339
5 Norfolk: 271, 283, 288, 296, 338, 348
6 Norfolk: 260, 265-6, 270, 278, 281, 283-4, 288, 296, 348, 351
9 Northumberland Fusiliers: 324
2 Royal Scots: 23, 26-31, 34, 36, 38, 53-6, 58, 61, 65
2 Selangor: 244-6
4 Suffolks: 331, 335, 340, 351
5 Suffolks: 334
2 Surreys: 116, 143, 160, 164-5, 168-9, 172, 174, 176-9, 196, 255
Brooke-Popham, Air Chief Marshal Sir Robert (Commander-in-Chief Far East): decides not to order operation Matador, 120; replaced by General Sir Henry Pownall as Commander-in-Chief Far East, 196; visits Kuching and gives his approval to the Operational Plan 'A', 371; see also 103, 105
Buffalo Hill: 27, 29
Bukit Timah: the loss of, 320-7; severe fighting at, 325; Allied counter offensive at, 325-6; Japanese tanks and Infantry at, 327; Allied futile counter-attack at, 327-31; Japanese account of the battle at, 329

Canadian Army:
    Winnipeg Grenadiers: 28-9, 34, 38, 55, 58, 61, 65

Carpendale, Brigadier (Commander 28th Indian Infantry Brigade): placed in command of 15th Indian Infantry Brigade also, 159; asks for reinforcements from 6th Indian Infantry Brigade, 159; *see also* 148, 162, 164, 168, 175-7

Castle Peak Road: operations along, 26

Challen, Brigadier: takes charge of 15th Indian Infantry Brigade, 250; alarmed by the growing threat to his forces at Batu Pahat Sector, 271; faced with serious problem, 284

Cicala (gun-boat): 60

Cumming, Lieut.-Colonel: award of Victoria Cross to, 232

Dalforce: 322

Defence Plans: Allied Defence Plans in South-East Asia, 5-7; for Hong Kong, 12; for Malaya, 93-118; for Singapore, 308-10; for Sarawak, 365-8; Plan 'A', 370; Plan 'B', 373

Devil's Peak: fighting in, 34-6; Japanese dive-bombing at, 35; Allied withdrawal from, 35-6

Dobbie, General (GOC-in-C, Malaya): Appreciation of 1938 by, 93-4; *see also* 116

Don Jose (Canadian Ship): 15

Duke, Brigadier (Commander 53rd British Brigade): assumes command of 5 and 6 Norfolks and 2 Cambridgeshire, 296; *see also* 265, 288

Duncan, Brigadier (Commander 45th Indian Infantry Brigade): arrives at Singapore, 234; killed in Murar action, 263; *see also* 258

Dutch North-West Borneo: 2/15 Punjab in, 388; Japanese land in the west coast of, 390-2; operations elsewhere in, 398; capitulation of, 399-400

East African Division 18th: 197

East Column: comprising of, 394; Lieut.-Colonel Ross-Thompson explains the necessity for the withdrawal of, 395; leaves Nangapinoh, 995; crosses Mendawi river, 395; difficulties faced by during withdrawal, 395-6; assembles at Kenamboi and prepares to surrender, 397

Eastforce: 254, 256, 273, 297

Electra (destroyer): 115

Encounter (destroyer): 115

Express (destroyer): 115

Faramurz Khan, Subedar: sets fine example to his troops by his bravery, 389

Feraplant, S. S. (Canadian Ship): 15

FMSVF (Federated Malaya States Volunteer Force): 153, 231, 238, 246, 249

Garrett, Brigadier (Commander 15th Indian Infantry Brigade): 148, 151, 159

Gertmans, Colonel (Dutch): assigned the task of training the forces for guerilla warfare, 385

Gin Drinkers' Line: 14, 26

Gray, Major G. E.: 23, 25

Grik road: Japanese attack on, 181; the contingent of, 188-92; *see also* 184

Gurun: the battle at, 170-9

Harrison, Colonel: 325

Heath, Lieut.-General Sir Lewis (Commander III Indian Corps): assumes responsibility for south and east Johore, 246; Muar Sector command comes under, 265; visits 2/1 Gurkha company area, 319; stresses water shortages for Indian troops in his corps, 355; *see also* 214

Heather Hill: 27

HKVDC: 34, 48, 50-3, 60, 63, 65

Holmes Force: comprised of, 179; under command of 28th Indian Infantry Brigade, 182

Hong Kong: topography, area and population, 8-10; administration, 10; early history, 11-12; defence schemes for, 12-14; forces in, 14-15; air power in, 15-16; Naval defence of, 16; difficulties in the defence of, 17; British troop dispositions in, 18-20; Japanese attack and the forces in, 22; initial attack on, 23-4; repeated Japanese bombing of, 31; end of the first phase of the campaign for, 37; peace offer and refusal by the Governor of, 37; disposition of Allied troops in, 38; Japanese bombardment and fifth column activities in, 40-42; Japanese landing in, 45-6; fighting in the eastern half of, 56-8; fighting in the Western sector, 58-60; surrender of, 67-9

Indian Army:
III Corps: establishes in Kuala Lumpur, 118; withdraws from Kuala Lumpur, 233; retires to Johore area, 249; disposition of the formations of, 250; plan for the withdrawal of Allied forces from Malaya to Singapore by, 291; withdraws Headquarters to Changi, 337; *see also* 105, 161, 165, 181, 185, 190, 192, 199, 203, 207, 209, 220, 233-6, 249, 256, 273, 275, 280, 308, 311, 335, 350

9th Division: in Malaya, 117; disposition of, 255; withdrawal of 285-6; disasters and liquidation of, 290-2; *see also* 105, 188, 197, 211, 230, 234, 239, 247, 249, 257, 277, 279, 281, 288, 308

11th Division: ready for operation Matador, 139; ordered to occupy Jitra position, 139; not fit for further operation, 180; takes Krohcol under command, 180; immediate role of, 184; 15th Indian Infantry under the command of, 187; Japanese threaten the communication of, 211; disposition of, 219; heavy casualties to, 220; Major-General Key takes the command of,

250; disposition of, 255; Batu Pahat under the command of, 260; provides relief to 15th Indian Infantry Brigade, 277; reconnoitres Peirce Reservoir area, 324; *see also* 105, 116-18, 139, 153, 158-9, 170, 178-9, 181-2, 185-90, 203, 206, 214, 234, 236, 239-41, 244-7, 249, 254, 256-7, 268, 271, 273, 277, 280, 284, 308, 311, 326, 334, 336, 344, 349-50

6th Infantry Brigade: 139-40, 143-4, 160-1, 165, 172, 174-80, 182, 185, 196; combined with 15th Indian Infantry Brigade, 196

8th Infantry Brigade: moves to Kelantan, 123; primary task of, 123; dispositions of, 125-30; precarious situation of, 135; evacuates Kelantan, 185; as rearguard to Westforce, 270; withdraws to Kluang, 270; defence of Kluang area by, 278; withdrawal from Malaya, 297; as reserve to 11th Indian Division, 311; bad luck to, 324; disposition of the units of, 333; withdrawal to Bidadari area, 338; divisional commanders' visit to, 350; *see also* 188, 211, 239, 255, 268-9, 282, 285, 288-93, 296, 299-300, 308, 321, 323, 333, 344, 349

12th Infantry Brigade: disposition of, 190-1, under the command of 11th Indian Division, 191; disposition of, 206; low morale in, 208; trying day for, 208; withdraws to Trolak area, 213; Japanese dive-bombers in the area of, 321; Japanese air attacks on, 326; ceases to exist as a formation, 329; *see also* 137, 176, 178-82, 186-90, 192, 198-9, 202, 206, 208-11, 214-15, 238, 240, 246-7, 308-09, 311, 316-17, 320, 327-9

15th Infantry Brigade: arrives in Malaya, 117: 6th Indian Infantry Brigade come under, 178; 6th Indian Infantry combined with, and called the new 15th Indian Infantry Brigade, 196; Colonel Challen takes the command of, 250; encircled by Japanese and practically written off, 281; cut off from other Allied forces, 283-4; as reserve to III Corps, 311; *see also* 139-40, 143-4, 148, 160-1, 165, 172, 174-5, 177, 179-80, 182, 185, 199, 205, 207, 209-11, 213, 215, 237-8, 240-1, 243, 245-7, 249, 255, 260, 265, 271, 273, 277-9, 281, 288, 292, 308-9, 311, 316-7, 321-3, 326, 328-9, 332, 345

22nd Infantry Brigade: arrives at Malaya, 117; at Kuantan, 223; at Kluang, 270; disasters to, 290; liquidation of, 291; *see also* 118, 227-8, 231, 239, 255, 267-9, 277-8, 281, 285, 289, 298, 300

28th Infantry Brigade: Krohcol under the command of, 185; 155 Field Regiment allotted to, 215; disaster to, 218; comprised of, 255; heavy bombing attack by Japanese on, 344; *see also* 143, 147, 165, 172, 174-5, 176-80, 182-3, 185, 187, 198-200, 202, 205-6, 208, 210-11, 213, 215, 219, 238, 240, 242, 246-7, 249-50, 255, 279, 288, 292-3, 309, 311, 318-9, 321, 323, 333, 338, 348

44th Infantry Brigade: arrives at Singapore, 275; Japanese air, artillery and motor bombardment on, 332; withdrawal by, 342; suffers heavy losses, 352; *see also* 276, 287, 308-9, 316-17, 321-3, 326, 328, 342-4, 353

45th Infantry Brigade: arrives at Singapore, 234; sent to Malacca, 234; heavy losses to, 258; under the command of Westforce, 266; *see also* 235, 246-7, 250, 255, 257-8, 260-3, 265, 267-9, 292

1 Bahawalpur State Infantry: 184, 250, 278, 285, 289, 300

2/10 Baluch: 134, 136-7, 267, 269, 278, 282, 285, 288-9, 291, 293, 297, 299-300, 311, 324, 333, 338, 344, 349, 352

2/10 Dogra: 297

2/17 Dogra: 116, 236, 256, 294, 297, 300, 309,

3/17 Dogra: 116, 131, 134-8, 211, 237-9, 241-3, 247, 255, 269, 278, 282, 285, 289, 297, 299-300, 312, 334-5, 339-40, 346, 353; caught in Japanese net, 242; comes under Massey Force, 335

2/12 F. F. Regiment: 118, 131, 133-8, 226-7, 229-32 255, 269-70, 278, 311

1/13 F.F. Rifles: 118, 131-8, 255, 267, 269, 278, 282, 285, 288-9, 297, 299-300, 311, 324-5, 333, 338, 344, 352

2/1 G.R.: 143, 147-49, 151, 161, 167-8, 175-7, 180, 184, 186-7, 206, 210, 215, 219, 240, 255, 319

2/2 G.R.: 143, 147, 160, 164-5, 168, 175, 177-8, 180, 184-7, 205-6, 208, 210, 213, 215, 218-9, 240, 242-3, 247, 255, 292-3, 295-6, 298-9, 311, 319, 323-5, 333, 344, 348, 353

2/9 G.R.: 143, 147, 159, 164-5, 167-9, 176-8, 180, 184-7, 206, 209, 215, 219, 240, 242-3, 247, 255, 293, 295, 298, 311, 319, 334, 338, 344, 348-9

4/19 Hyderabad: 116, 137, 188, 191, 201, 206-7, 215-17, 311, 321, 326-7

2/9 Jat: 117, 140, 142, 162-4, 166-9, 209, 237-8, 241, 244-45, 249-50, 255, 282, 284, 293, 296, 311-2, 328

4/9 Jat: 255, 258, 260-3, 311, 328

1/8 Punjab: 143, 145, 160, 162, 164, 168-9, 172-4, 176, 179, 182, 209,

237, 255, 311-12, 324, 333, 335, 344
1/14 Punjab: 117, 142, 144-5, 148-9, 151-2, 159, 182, 205, 209, 213, 238, 241, 243, 247, 255, 292-3, 295, 311, 319, 323
2/9 Punjab: 209
2/14 Punjab: 15, 18-19, 23, 25-32, 34-6, 38-9, 42, 53-4, 56, 58, 61, 68
2/15 Punjab: proceeds to Sarawak, 367-8; task for, 368; to Kuching, 369; re-organisation of, 369; disposition of, 377; in North-West Borneo, 383; under Dutch Command, 385; re-organisation of, 385; *see also* 371, 374, 376, 380, 387, 397
2/16 Punjab: 143, 146, 148, 152, 159-60, 163-4, 166, 168, 172, 176-9, 205, 209-10, 213, 238, 240, 241-3, 249, 255
3/16 Punjab: 117, 148, 153-7, 161, 184-9, 196, 205, 213, 215, 238, 241, 243, 247, 255, 260, 265, 270, 278, 284, 288, 292, 296, 322-3, 328, 352; joins 15th Indian Infantry Brigade, 296; Japanese attack on, 329; placed under 8th Indian Infantry Brigade, 349
4/15 Punjab: 369
5/2 Punjab: 179-82, 184, 188-91, 199-201, 206-07, 217-18, 311, 331
5/14 Punjab: 116, 152, 154, 156-7, 161, 180, 188, 191, 198-9, 206, 209, 215, 218, 241, 246, 250, 295-6, 299, 324, 344, 349-50, 352
6/1 Punjab: 317-18, 321-2, 328, 332, 342, 344-5
6/14 Punjab: 316-18, 321, 328, 332, 344-5
7/8 Punjab: 317, 321, 328, 332, 340, 342, 345
5/7 Rajput: short of food and ammunition and reduced in number, 64; hand-to-hand fighting with the Japanese, 67; *see also* 15, 19, 24, 27, 29-30, 31, 35-6, 38-9, 42, 46-50, 54-5
7/6 Rajputana Rifles: at Muar, 246; suffers casualties, 260; *see also* 255, 258, 261-2, 312
2/18 Royal Garhwal Rifles: 116, 223, 226-30, 232, 236, 255, 269-70, 277-8, 282, 311, 324-5, 333, 344, 349
4/18 Royal Garhwal Rifles: 261
5/18 Royal Garhwal Rifles: 239, 246, 249, 255, 258, 260-62, 311
5/11 Sikh: dispositon of, 223; heroic fight at Niyor by, 277; part played by in the British zone, 351; *see also* 118, 228-9, 231-2, 240-1, 243, 247, 255, 268-9, 278, 281-2, 286, 289-90, 311, 334-5, 339-40, 346, 353

2 Anti-tank Battery: 185, 206, 238, 261
4 Mountain Battery: 144-5, 160, 241, 243
7 Mountain Battery: 144-6, 206, 209, 238, 246
10 Mountain Battery: 144, 153, 238, 244
21 Mountain Battery: 131, 223, 226-7, 230
73 Field Battery: 244, 246-7, 249
16 Light Anti-aircraft Battery: 219
215 Anti-tank Battery: 162, 172, 186, 206, 217, 219, 238
272 Anti-tank Battery: 239, 350, 352
273 Anti-tank Battery: 172, 175, 186, 205
278 Field Battery: 189-91, 205, 239
352 Field Battery: 175, 185, 209, 238, 246-7, 249
464 Field Battery: 241
501 Field Battery: 207
3 Cavalry: 184-7, 206, 209-11, 213, 237-9, 241, 244-7, 250, 256, 284, 292, 295-6, 298-9, 333, 344, 349-50, 352
88 Field Regiment: 172, 185, 239, 246-7, 249, 278
122 Field Regiment: 188, 190
137 Field Regiment: 160, 178-9, 182, 186, 219
155 Field Regiment: 144, 160, 167, 172, 206, 209, 219, 238, 242-3, 249, 261, 283
22 Mountain Regiment: 116, 144, 206, 246, 249, 318
23 Mountain Regiment: 247
80 Anti-tank Regiment: 144, 175, 177-8
Indo-China: Japan occupies the northern portion of, 97
Ipoh: the fall of, 197-202; Japanese air-raid at, 198

Jamesforce: 245, 349
Japan: becomes an industrial power, 1-2; her expansionism, 2; her relations with U.K. and U.S.A. after the outbreak of war in 1939, 3-5; goes out of League of Nations, 7
Japanese Army:
  25th Army: 312
  5th Division: 254, 266, 312
  18th Division: 312, 346
  The Imperial Guards Division: 254, 257, 270, 312
  4th Guards Regiment: 257-8, 264-5, 271
  5th Guards Regiment: 257-8, 264
  21st Infantry Regiment: 254
  55th Infantry Regiment: 254
Jind State Infantry: 322, 326-7
Jitra position: defence of, 140-5; Japanese tanks at, 151; Allied retreat from, 159-70; difficulties faced by the

Indian Division during the retreat from, 169
Johore: 76; relation with British Crown, 80; the fight for, 275-7; Japanese attack on, 281; General Wavell at, 298
Jupiter(destroyer):115

Kai Tak aerodrome: Japanese bombers attack on, 23-4; Royal Air Force evacuates from, 29
Kapurthala State Infantry: 334
Kampar: Allied stand at, 203-14; defensive positions at, 205; air activity at, 208; Allied withdrawal from 213-14
Kedah: Japanese attack on, 149; Allied disasters at, 150-2; situation at, 178-9
Kedah, H.M.S.: 368
Keith Simmons, Major-General: 330
Kelantan: situation in, 123; war starts in, 123-38; 8th Indian Infantry Brigade in, 123; attack on the aerodromes at, 132; Allied withdrawal from, 138; 8th Indian Infantry Brigade evacuates from, 185; *see also* 75, 78
Key, Major-General: takes command of the 11th Indian Division, 250; orders 53rd Brigade to reoccupy Bt. Baloh and Bt. Pelandok, 265-6; consults Malaya command on capitulation, 346; *see also* 131, 133-4, 136, 279, 284, 323
Kidd, Lieut.-Colonel: 33
Kota Bharu: Japanese attack on, 121; Allied withdrawal from, 136; Japanese Battleship, cruisers and Destroyers at, 147
Kowloon: fifth columnists in, 31; Allied withdrawal from, 34; Japanese restoring order in, 39
Krian river: Allied withdrawal south of, 179; 11th Indian Division withdraws to the south of, 181; 11th Indian Division to hold the line of, 184; Japanese patrol activity at, 185
Krohcol: operations of, 152-8; role of, 153; ceases to be under the command of 11th Indian Division, 157; again comes under the command of 11th Indian Division, 180; disbandment of, 183; under the command of 28th Indian Infantry Brigade, 185; withdraws from Kroh, 188; *see also* 170, 189
Kuala Lumpur: troop dispositions for the defence of, 238; end of the stand in the north of, 246
Kuala Selangor: serious situation at, 237
Kuantan: the fall of, 222-32; 22nd Indian Infantry Brigade at, 223; Japanese bombing of, 225; Royal Air Force withdraws from, 225; Japanese bombing and Machine-gunning of, 228; attack on, 228; Japanese enter in, 229; end of the operations at, 232
Kuching: 2/15 Punjab at, 369; role of the troops at, 370; Plan 'A' for the defence of, 370; Air Chief Marshal Sir Robert Brooke-Popham at, 371; conference of British and Dutch Military officers at, 372; Plan 'B' for the defence of, 373; Japanese air-raid on, 376-7; Japanese land at, 379-81; fall of to Japanese, 380; Allied evacuation of, 381-2

Lamma Island: Japanese land at, 31
Lane, Lieut.-Colonel: takes command of 2/15 Punjab, 369; as commander Sarfor, 370; mobile defence of Sarawak by, 370; visits Singapore, 372; orders Sarfor to withdraw from Kuching, 381; secret plan to evacuate Indian troops to Java or Malaya from Dutch Borneo by, 388; arrives at Pangkalanboon 399; sends message to East Column to surrender, 400; *see also* 384-5
Lawson, Brigadier: 38, 53
Lay, Brigadier: counter-attack under the personal command of, 173; escapes from death, 174; commands 8th Indian Infantry Brigade, 250; *see also* 162, 176, 289, 292
Layang Layand: Japanese occupation of, 290
Layton, Admiral Sir Goeffrey: 119, 196
Ledge: action at, 153-4
Leighton Hill: Japanese infiltrate in, 64; Japanese dive-bombing, artillery and mortar bombardment at, 65; Japanese occupation of, 65
Lipis, H.M.S.: Japanese bombing on, 376

Malaya: geography of, 73-6; climatic conditions in, 77-8; political system and economic resources of, 78; the straits settlements of, 78; Federated States of, 79-80; unfederated States of, 80; general status of, 81-2; population in, 82-4; economic resources of, 84-6; railways in, 86-8; roads in, 88-9; waterways of, 90; signals, 90-1; electricity supply for, 92; protected water supply for, 92; Appreciation of 1940 by the Chiefs of Staff for the defence of, 94-98; air and land forces for the defence of, 96; Singapore Defence Conference for the defence of, 97-8; discussion with U.K., U.S.A. and Dutch in 1941 for the defence of, 99-107; Operation Matador for the defence of, 107-8; Operation Sandwich for, 108; defence plans for, 108-11; defence plans for the Northern frontier of, 109-10; defence plans for the east coast of, 110; Air force, Navy and Army in and reinforcements required for, 111-18; Japanese invasion begins at, 121-3; air raids on the aerodromes of, 122; war in the North-east of,

123-38; war in the North-west of, 139-52; the general startegic situation in Central Malaya, 193-7; campaign in the central part of, 197-202; break down of the line of communication area in, 233-51; end of the war in the central part of, 250; general situation in the south of, 252-4; dispositions of troops in, 254; evacuation of troops from, 298-300; end of the campaign at, 357; total casualties in the campaign of, 357

Malaya Infantry Brigade 1st: 236, 328, 332, 335, 352

Malaya Infantry Brigade 2nd: 236, 309, 311, 322, 349-50

Malaya Regiment 2nd: 249, 256

MacRitchie Reservoir: Japanese attack develops at the east end of, 348

Maimuna, H.M.S.: 376

Mainland: withdrawal of troops from, 31-4; evacuation of, 298-300

Maltby, Air Vice-Marshal Sir Paul: 197, 253

Maltby, Major-General: decides to withdraw from the Mainland, 30; decides to withdraw all troops from the island, 36; dispersal of forces under, 39; reinforces Wanchai gap, 61; orders cease fire and surrenders to the Japanese commander, 68

Mars, Lieut.-Colonel: 392

Masaichi Niimi, Vice-Admiral (Japanese): 43

Massy-Beresford, Brigadier: 331

Massy force: 331

Matador (operation): object of, 107; cancellation of, 122; 11th Indian Division kept ready for the operation of, 139; disposition of troops for the operation of, 139; cancellation of, 139; *see also* 119-20

Maxwell, Brigadier: 260, 323

Milligan, Major: as commander West column, 394; difficulties experienced by during withdrawal, 397

Miri: operations at, 374; denial scheme at, 375; air activity at, 376; evacuation of, 376; Japanese naval forces appear in strength at, 376

Monastery ridge: 29

Moorhead, Brigadier: as commander of new 15th Indian Infantry Brigade, 196; resumes command of 3/16 Punjab, 250

Mount Cameron: Japanese dive-bombing at, 62; Japanese capture of, 63

Mount Vernon, H. M. S.: 195

Muar Sector: Japanese attack at, 257-8; Allied withdrawal from, 258-62; plan for the counter attack at, 261; Japanese renew their attack at, 262; Allied forces cut off at, 262; end of the Allied forces at, 263-4

Murray force: 331, 335, 340

Murray-Lyon, Major-General D. M.: takes charge of 11th Indian Division, 116; retirement of, 196

Needle Hill: 28

Negri Sembilan: 76

Nishimura, General (Japanese): decides to encircle and destroy British troops in Batu Pahat sector, 271; *see also* 257-8

Niyor; allied counter-attack at, 277; heroic fight of 5/11 Sikh at, 277; plan of counter-attack at, 278

North, Major: 242

Painter, Brigadier G. W. A.: 289, 292

Pahang: 75

Palliser, Admiral: 119

Parit Sulong: Japanese occupation of, 263

Paris, Major-General: emphasises the importance of holding the roads, 194; as commander of 11th Indian Division, 196; visits 12th Indian Infantry Brigade, 208; replaced by Major-General Key as commander 11th Indian Division, 250; rejoins 12th Indian Infantry Brigade at Singapore, 250; *see also* 116, 189, 211, 220

Penang: evacuation of by Allied forces, 183

Pearl Harbour: Japanese attack on, 23; *see also* 115, 301

Penaring: Dutch company withdraws from, 391; Japanese threaten to encircle Allied troops at, 391; Allied withdrawal from, 391

Pepper, Lieut.-Colonel: 371

Percival, General: appreciation for the defence of Singapore by, 93; assumes command of Malaya, 117; changes in the organisation of the army by, 196; decides to hold Kampar position, 210; perceives danger to the rear of 11th Indian Division, 214; new arrangements for the defence of Batu Pahat by, 260; transfers Muar Sector command from General Bennett to General Heath, 265; conference at Yong Peng and orders regarding further plans, 267; exceptional measures to hold the retreat of Allied forces in Malaya by, 274; conference at Westforce Headquarters and decisions taken by, 279-80; description of the withdrawal from Mainland by, 300; invokes offensive spirit in the defence of Singapore, 307; orders General Bennett to stage a counter-attack at Bukit Timah, 325; details of crisis facing his command, 330; notifies General Wavell of the decision to cease hostilities at Singapore, 355; approves plan 'B', 374; *see also* 103, 119, 138, 158, 193, 233, 235-6, 246-7, 257, 287, 309, 336, 347

Perak river: Allied withdrawal east of, 184; creates a problem to the British

and the Japanese, 198; fifth column activities at, 199; demolition of bridges across, 199
Perlis: bitter fighting at, 138
Permangkat: Japanese landing at, 390
Phillips, Admiral Sir Tom: 115, 119
Plan 'A': object of, 370-1
Plan 'B': General Percival's approval to, 374; *see also* 373
Pownall, General Sir Henry: 196
Prince of Wales, H.M.S.: 115, 149
Punjab Hill: 27

Rawlinson, Lieut.-Colonel C: 33, 46
Repulse, Battle Cruiser: sunk by the Japanese aircraft, 149; *see also* 115
Rice, Group Captain: 196
Richforce: 245
Rose, Colonel H. B.: becomes commander of West Brigade: 58
Roseforce: 245
Ross-Thompson, Lieut.-Colonel (Commander East Column): visits Lieut-. Colonel Mars, 392; explains the necessity for the withdrawal of East Column, 395; decides to withdraw to Sampit, 396; *see also* 393-4

Sanggau: operations north-east of, 385-7; the action at, 388-90; disposition of troops at, 388; Japanese attack on and occupation of, 389
Sarawak: the land and its people, 361-2; climate and population of, 362; agriculture, industries and trade in, 362-3; early history of, 363-4; Government and administration in, 364; strategic importance of, 364-5; Appreciations and plans for the defence of, 365-8; 2/15 Punjab proceeds to, 367-9; Plan 'A' for the defence of, 370-1; liasion visits in, 371-2; Plan 'B' for the defence of, 373
Sandwich (operation): object of, 108
Sarfor: disposition of, 377-8; withdraws from Kuching, 381-2; ceases to exist as a combined Indian/Sarawak State force, 383
Segamat: important Allied conference at, 235; General Wavell at, 249; Allied withdrawal from, 266-70
Selby, Brigadier: 170, 219, 242
Seria: operations at, 374-5; denial scheme in, 375; Japanese landing at, 376
Shingmun Redoubt: 27-8
Shatin Pass: 33
Singapore: Appreciation by General Percival for the defence of, 93; General Dobbie's Appreciation of 1938 for the defence of, 93; *Prince of Wales* and *Repulse* at, 115; Japanese air-raids in, 121; War Council at, 158; Inter Allied conference at, 192; as a symbol of the will to victory, 195; Air Vice Marshal Maltby at, 196; reinforcement convoy arrive at, 234, 250; 44th Indian Infantry Brigade at, 275; topography of, 301; organisation of defence at, 302-5; general defensive measures at, 305-6; denial policy in, 306-7; disposition of the Commonwealth army in, 307-12; defence organised in three areas for, 308-9; weakness in the defence plan of, 310; Japanese preparation for the invasion of, 312-14; Japanese assault begins at, 314-16; Japanese landing at, 315; general defence situation on 10 February in, 321-7; Japanese aim to encircle the town of, 337; Allied last days in, 343-54; Allied desperate position at, 347; capitulation of Allied forces in, 354-6
Shinai, S. Ship: 376
Singapore Defence Conference, October 1940: reviews the entire situation in the Far East, 97-8; possibilities of Japanese attempt to seize bases at British Borneo, and discussion arrived at, 365-6
Singkawang II aerodrome: 385, 387-8, 392
Slatter, Major, A.W.D.: 376
Slim River: Allied rout at, 214-15; the loss of the area at, 218-20
Stanley area: Japanese cut the water supply in, 62; Japanese offensive at and caputre of, 66
Stewart, Brigadier I. McA: 196, 214, 220
Stonecutters Island: 31
Swettenham Port: 77, 211, 214-15, 236

Tactical Appreciation by the Chiefs of Staff: 366
Taikoo: operations east and west of, 47-50
Taipo Road: 24-6
Takaishi Sakai, Lieut.-General (Japanese): 43
Tanjong Malim: Japanese bombing and machine-gunning at, 215
Taylor, Brigadier: new role of, 273
Telok Anson: Japanese land in, 210; Allied rout at, 214; *see also*, 198, 202
Testerforce: 245
Thailand: attack on and Japanese land in Singora and Patani, 121
Thomas, Sir Shenton (Governor and High Commissioner of Malaya): becomes Chairman of the Far East Council, 196
Tomforce: commissioned for, 330; withdrawal of, 340; *see also* 339
Tojo, General (Japanese): New Japanese Cabinet under, 3
Trengganu: Allied withdrawal from, 226; Japanese in civil control of, 226; *see also* 75, 78
Tytam Gap: withdrawal of Allied troops from, 50-2

Wanchai Gap: adverse position for the defence of, 63; Japanese occupation of, 66; see also 62, 68

Wallis, Brigadier: appreciation of the situation at Tytam Gap by, 50-1; new plan of attack by, 57; attacks Japanese positions and captures Bridge Hill, 59-60; independent command of Stanley area by, 62; counter-attack near Stanley prison, 66; orders ceasefire for Stanley force, 67; see also, 27, 30, 36, 38, 47

Washington Conversations: 99

Wavell, General Sir Archibald P: as Supreme Commander of the American-British-Dutch-Australian area, 196; proposal to withdraw III Indian Corps to Johore, 233; new plan by, 235; visits Kuala Lumpur, 238; confusion and half hearted move of troops eliminated by the plan of, 239; meets Lieut.-General Heath and Major-General Gordon Bennett at Segamat, 249; general survey of the situation in Malaya by, 268; meets Generals Percival, Heath and Keith Simmons, 268; reports south Malaya situation to Combined Chiefs of Staff, 275; agrees to the withdrawal of Allied forces from Malaya to Singapore, 298; estimates the resources for the defence of Singapore, 303; sympathises with Malaya Command, 306; removes fighter aircraft to Sumatra and reorganises Indian formations, 307-8; orders all the troops to hold Singapore to the last, 321; visits battle front at Singapore, 324; gives Malaya Command discretion to cease resistance, 355

West Brigade: role of, 58; dispositions of, 65

West Column: comprising of, 394; difficulties experienced by during withdrawal, 397; arrives at Kenamboi, 397; Lieut.-Colonel Lane's remarks about the achievements of, 397

Westforce: disposition of, 254; 45th Indian Infantry Brigade and 53rd British Brigade come under the command of, 266; withdrawal of, 288; enemy in close contact of, 293; see also 246-7, 249, 254, 273, 279-80

Wells force: 340, 348, 351

Wong Nei Chong Gap: engagements at and Japanese occupation of, 52-6; attack by Winnipeg Grenadiers on, 61; Japanese Local Headquarters and organising centre at, 64

Yamashita, General (Japanese Commander-in-Chief): introduces an amphibious striking force, 197; arranges two divisions to march to Ipoh, 202; wants General Percival to come personally and offer surrender unconditionally, 355; questions by, 355

Yong Peng: 267

Young, Sir Mark (Governor, Hong Kong): 37

Zempei Masu Shima, Lieut. (Japanese): 46

INDIAN DIVISIONS WON A FINE REPUTATION IN WORLD WAR TWO

Field Marshal Auchinleck, Commander-in-Chief of the British Indian Army from 1942, asserted that the British *"couldn't have come through both wars (World War I and II) if they hadn't had the British Indian Army"*.
British Prime Minister Winston Churchill also paid tribute to
"the unsurpassed bravery of Indian soldiers and officers".

Between 1945 and 1947, the Director of Public Relations, War Department, Government of India, published a series of short publications covering the individual histories of the WWII Indian Divisions. They followed a consistent format, having between 44 and 48 pages within illustrated soft card covers. They have an average of 50 monochrome photographic illustrations, and each has a full colour centrespread depicting a scene from the Division's wartime operations (drawn by official war artists). They were printed at various presses in Bombay and New Delhi, and each contains at least one map.

As condensed histories they are useful – particularly those which relate to Divisions for which no other record was ever produced.

The British Indian Army during World War II began the war, in 1939, numbering just under 200,000 men. By the end of the war, it had become the largest volunteer army in history, rising to over 2.5 million men in August 1945. Serving in divisions of infantry, armour and a fledgling airborne force, they fought on three continents: in Africa, Europe and Asia.

This Army fought in Ethiopia against the Italian Army, in Egypt, Libya, Tunisia and Algeria against both the Italian and German Army and, after the Italian surrender, against the German Army in Italy. However, the bulk of the British Indian Army was committed to fighting the Japanese Army, first during the British defeats in Malaya and the retreat from Burma to the Indian border; later, after resting and refitting for the victorious advance back into Burma, as part of the largest British Empire army ever formed. These campaigns cost the lives of over 87,000 Indian service-men, while another 34,354 were wounded, and 67,340 became prisoners of war. Their valour was recognised with the award of some 4,000 decorations, and 18 members of the British Indian Army were awarded the Victoria Cross or the George Cross.

RED EAGLES
The Story of the 4th Indian Division
9781474537520

During the Second World War, the 4th Indian Division was in the vanguard of nine campaigns in the Mediterranean theatre, Egypt, Eritrea, Syria, Tunisia, Italy and Greece. The 4th Division captured 150,000 prisoners and suffered 25,000 casualties, more than the strength of a whole division. It won over 1,000 honours and awards, which included four Victoria Crosses and three George Crosses. Field Marshal Lord Wavell wrote: "The fame of this Division will surely go down as one of the greatest fighting formations in military history."

THE FIGHTING FIFTH
History of the 5th Indian Division
9781474537513

As described in much greater detail in Anthony Brett James's book 'The Ball of Fire', the division saw active service in East Africa, North Africa and Burma.

GOLDEN ARROW
The Story of the 7th Indian Division
9781474537506

The role of this division is also duplicated by a much larger work: the book by Brig. M. R. Roberts. However, this booklet gives a good account of Kohima and Imphal and the crossing of the Irrawaddy. In 1945, the division was flown into Siam, so becoming the first Allied formation to re-enter South East Asia.

BLACK CAT DIVISION
17th Indian Division
9781474537483

This formation was committed to Burma from the early days when the British were in full flight from the invading Japanese. It remained in Burma right through to the end, when the starving remnants of the Japanese Army were making their own desperate retreat.

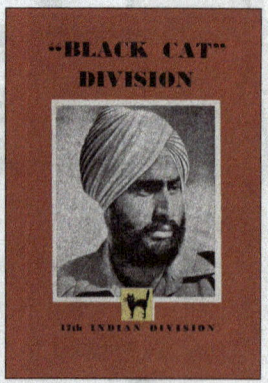

ONE MORE RIVER
The Story of the 8th Indian Division
Biferno, Trigno, Sangro, Moro, Rapido, Arno, Senio, Santerno, Po, Adige

9781474537490

The 8th Indian Division started its overseas service in the Middle East in the garrisoning of Iraq and then the invasion of Persia to secure the oil fields of the area for the Allies, before moving to Italy in 1943. Landing at Taranto, it pushed up the length of the peninsula in a series of major battles: breaking the Sangro Line, forcing the Rapido and turning the defences at Cassino, breaking the stubborn German resistance at Monte Grande and, finally, forcing the Po River. It won four VCs, 26 DSOs and 149 MCs along the way. During the war the 8th Indian Division sustained casualties totalling 2,012 dead, 8,189 wounded and 749 missing.

TIGER HEAD
The Story of the 26th Indian Division
Arakan, Ragoon

9781474537452

This is a history of the division said later by the Japanese to have been the opponent which they most feared. The 26th held the Allied monsoon line in the Arakan during two such seasons, repulsing every attack launched against it. Later it made a series of leap-frog landings down the coast to clinch the issue in the Arakan. It was the first division to enter Ragoon, invading the city from the sea.

THE TWENTY THIRD INDIAN DIVISION
"The Fighting Cock Division"
Burma, Malaya, Java

9781474537469

The Fighting Cock Division is well recorded in the book by Doulton. This book gives coverage of the heavy fighting at the Kohima Battle, the capture of Tamu, the reoccupation of Malaya in August 1945, and then its strange role on the island of Java – concurrently disarming the Japanese garrison, fighting the insurgent Indonesian nationalists, and caring for 65,000 former internees pending the arrival of a new Dutch administration.

A HAPPY FAMILY
The Story of the Twentieth Indian Division,
9781474537476

One of the few Indian divisions in the 14th Army trained specifically for the war in Burma. Raised in Bangalore in 1942, it commenced active operations in late 1943 and served from Imphal through to the end. It established the 14th Army's first brigade-head across the Chindwin and its second such brigade-head across the Irrawaddy. Its final task was to round up the Japanese in French Indochina.

TEHERAN TO TRIESTE
The Story of the Tenth Indian Division
9781783317028

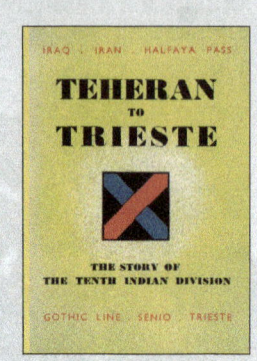

This History deals with the 10th Indian Div's exploits in Iraq (under Maj Gen "Bill" Slim) its role in the Libyan battles leading up to El Alamein, the following two years of garrison duties in Cyprus and Syria, and finally, its fighting services in the Italian campaign (from Ortona onwards).

THE STORY OF THE 25th INDIAN DIVSION
The Arakan Campaign
9781783317585

Formed in Southern India in August 1942 for defence of that area in case of Japanese invasion, the "Ace of Spades" Division had its baptism of fire in Arakan in February 1944. It served throughout the remainder of that campaign the climax being the battle of Tamandu. Its victorious fight for the Kangaw roadblock was considered by many to have been the fiercest battle of the entire Burma war, while its liberation of Akyab was the first convincing proof to the rest of the world that the tide had turned against the Japanese.

DAGGER DIVISION
The Story of the 19th Indian Division
9781783317035

Raised in the late 1941, the 19th was the first "standard" Indian Division. Its troops were the first to breach the Japanese defence line in Burma and to raise the flag at Fort Dufferin. It crossed the Chindwin in November 1944, driving on to Mandalay and Ragoon during seven months of continuous fighting. The 19th's exploits are graphically described also in John Masters' personal memoir, *The Road Past Mandalay*.

www.ingramcontent.com/pod-product-compliance
Lightning Source LLC
Chambersburg PA
CBHW060416300426
44111CB00018B/2868